Donatello, Michelangelo, Cellini

SCULPTORS' DRAWINGS FROM RENAISSANCE ITALY

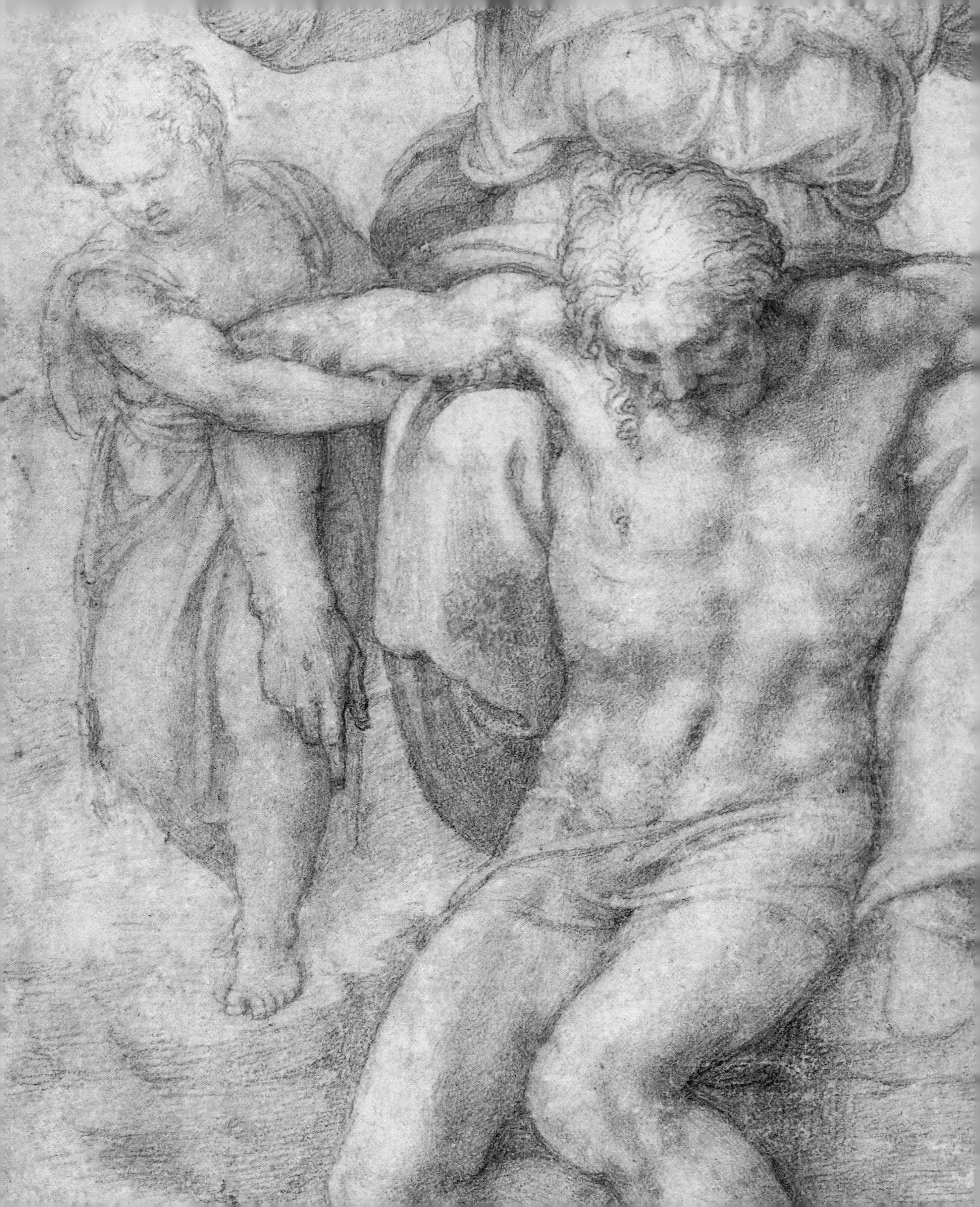

Donatello, Michelangelo, Cellini

SCULPTORS' DRAWINGS FROM RENAISSANCE ITALY

Edited by

MICHAEL W. COLE

with essays by

MICHAEL W. COLE • DAVIDE GASPAROTTO • ALINA PAYNE

OLIVER TOSTMANN • LINDA WOLK-SIMON

Isabella Stewart Gardner Museum, Boston

Paul Holberton publishing, London

2014

Accompanies the exhibition

Donatello, Michelangelo, Cellini

SCULPTORS' DRAWINGS
FROM RENAISSANCE ITALY

Curated by Oliver Tostmann and Michael W. Cole
at the Isabella Stewart Gardner Museum, Boston
23 October 2014 – 23 January 2015

This exhibition was generously sponsored by Bank of America. Additional support was provided by The Andrew W. Mellon Foundation, the Samuel H. Kress Foundation, and the National Endowment for the Humanities. The Museum receives operating support from the Massachusetts Cultural Council.

MCC
massculturalcouncil.org

NATIONAL ENDOWMENT FOR THE
Humanities

Bank of America

A catalogue record for this book is available from the British Library

ISBN 978 1 907372 70 4

Produced by Paul Holberton publishing,
89 Borough High Street, London SE1 1NL
www.paul-holberton.net

Designed by Laura Parker
www.parkerinc.co.uk

Printed by E-Graphic, Verona

COVER: Baccio Bandinelli, *Self-Portrait*, c. 1545 (cat. 28), detail
BACK COVER: Andrea del Verrocchio, *Measured drawing of a horse facing left*, 1481–88 (cat. 7), detail
FRONTISPIECE: Michelangelo Buonarotti, *The Pietà*, 1540 (cat. 23), detail
PAGE 6 Maso Finiguerra, *Young draftsman*, 1450s (cat. 4), detail
PAGE 11 Baccio Bandinelli, *The Deposition*, 1625–30 (cat. 21), detail

Contents

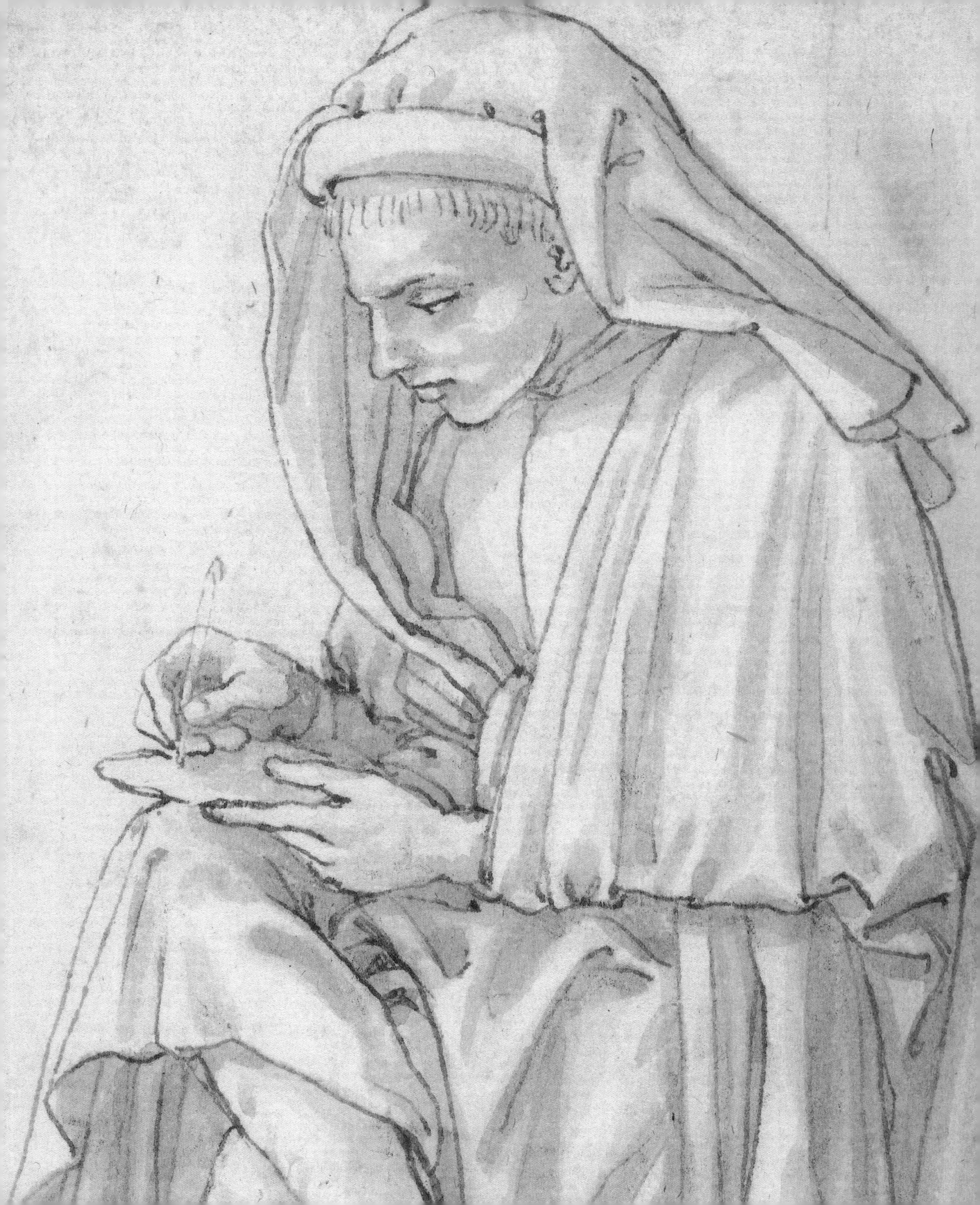

Director's Foreword

WE ARE PLEASED TO PRESENT this exhibition of drawings by Italian sculptors spanning the 200 years between Donatello and Bernini. Collected throughout the centuries, drawings by the Renaissance masters Michelangelo, Baccio Bandinelli, and Benvenuto Cellini have been widely praised and admired. They are celebrated for their beauty and elegance, technical mastery and ingenuity. Despite their popularity, exploring the drawing practices of sculptors is still an understudied field. This is the first show that focuses exclusively on this topic and considers these drawings in the context of the working practices of a sculptor's studio. What, how and why did Renaissance sculptors draw?

Sculpting is a complex and time-consuming process. No matter how a sculpture is formed, either carved out of stone or cast in bronze, it usually starts with a model or a drawing. With pen and paper, the artist could quickly hatch out the subject, explore intricate details of its construction or create a means to convey his idea to others. Comparing sculpture and related drawings in this exhibition allows us better to understand the close connection between the two media. Drawings also played an important role in the representations of sculptors. As shown in two painted portraits, skilled draftsmanship helped to shape a sculptor's professional image.

By bringing together drawings, sculptures, and paintings, the multimedia approach of this exhibition engages the viewer's eye on many levels. Sculptures invite movement. Drawings invite an intimate, still examination. Paintings project form and color. Throughout her collection, Isabella Stewart Gardner carefully arranged paintings with sculptures, drawings, and decorative arts, merging media in an original fashion. She was one of the greatest collectors of Italian Renaissance art, and, indeed, her juxtaposition of, say, Titian's *Europa* with a bronze putto by Ducquesnoy and a drawing by Van Dyck invites a different and perhaps more complete way of looking at art. Our collection of drawings is arguably one of the least studied parts of the collection, and I am particularly glad to see one of our most famous drawings, Michelangelo's *Pietà,* highlighted in this show. Inspired by a self-portrait by Baccio Bandinelli in the Gardner's collection, this innovative exhibition asks new questions about the relationship between drawing and sculpture in Renaissance Florence, while at the same time inviting conversation about the role of two- and three-dimensional artworks at other times, including our own. In this regard, the exhibition serves several major goals of programming here at the Museum. In addition to advancing scholarship about a rich historical time period, it illuminates larger questions about artistic processes and about the role of the creative individual in society. We are profoundly grateful to Oliver Tostmann, Susan Morse Hilles Curator of European Art at the Wadsworth Atheneum, and Michael Cole, Professor of Italian Renaissance and Baroque Art at Columbia University, as well as the excellent team of scholars whose work is recorded here, for so vividly bringing Bandinelli and his colleagues—Michelangelo, Donatello, and Cellini—to life.

This exhibition was generously sponsored by Bank of America. Additional support was provided by The Andrew W. Mellon Foundation, the Samuel H. Kress Foundation, and the National Endowment for the Humanities. The Museum receives operating support from the Massachusetts Cultural Council.

ANNE HAWLEY
Norma Jean Calderwood Director of
the Isabella Stewart Gardner Museum

Curator's Foreword

BACCIO BANDINELLI made his living as a sculptor, yet in the Isabella Stewart Gardner painting that portrays him, he is shown not with a marble or a small bronze or even a model, but with a drawing. The artist was particularly proud of his skills as a draftsman. Contemporaries admired his works on paper far more than his statues. And in the Renaissance as today, that set Bandinelli apart.[1]

Still, Bandinelli was not the only sculptor who left drawings of real quality and historical importance. And—in part because the study of drawing and the study of sculpture have become two highly specialized and compartmentalized fields—these often get little attention. The goal of this exhibition is to look comparatively at the graphic practices of Italian Renaissance sculptors.

Its survey begins with Jacopo della Quercia, one of the earliest Renaissance sculptors to whom drawings have been attributed. It concludes with a group of artists active around 1600, adding a pair of drawings by Gian Lorenzo Bernini and Alessandro Algardi as a sort of epilogue. The exhibition focuses attention on the portrayal of sculptors as draftsmen in sixteenth-century paintings, and, where possible, includes three-dimensional objects related to the drawings it features: notably, it shows a *bozzetto* by Michelangelo for the first time in the United States, alongside a group of related drawings, and it assembles more objects by Benvenuto Cellini than have ever previously been exhibited together outside Italy. Through the example of Bandinelli, in particular, the exhibition seeks to pose questions both about the sequences of drawings that lay behind individual sculptural inventions and about the teaching of drawing in the Renaissance sculptor's workshop.

Practical constraints required the curators to make some difficult choices and to omit some fascinating, controversial objects, including the drawings that have been attributed to Lorenzo Ghiberti, Nanni di Banco, Tullio Lombardo, Jacopo Sansovino, and Alessandro Vittoria. As the catalogue entries make clear, questions of authorship also bear on a number of works the show features. The curators had to decide how to distribute attention between exceptional artists like Michelangelo and Bandinelli, who left hundreds of drawings, and those like Donatello and Leone Leoni, who left very few. We also had to consider that the surviving drawings we have from any given sculptor may not fully represent that artist's actual practice. Benvenuto Cellini, for example, wrote repeatedly and with pride about his skills as a draftsman; a record in his account books documents that he sold 300 drawings to Benedetto Accolti in 1540, and his *Treatise on Goldsmithery* reports that he left many of the studies from his Roman years behind when he returned from France to Italy five years after that.[2] Today, however, there is consensus around perhaps a dozen attributions, and these differ dramatically in style, function, and quality.

Ultimately the exhibition's two curators decided that we should include multiple works by important and prolific draftsmen, ideally works done for different purposes or in different media. From Michelangelo, we show studies after the antique, a project drawing, and a gift drawing (the Gardner's own important Colonna *Pietà*); from Bandinelli, we selected figure studies and compositions, in ink and in chalk; from Cellini, we have works from the middle and end of his career. One consequence of these choices is that the exhibition, like the surviving Renaissance material as a whole, reveals more about Florence and Rome than about other regional traditions. Drawings by Central Italian sculptors exponentially outnumber those who worked in other places. And that fact itself merits reflection: throughout the Renaissance, Florence was associated with the idea of *disegno* (drawing, design), and the fact that sculptors there drew more, or that collectors preserved more, may point to concerns that fall outside sculptural practice as such. It is difficult to imagine a North Italian sculptor being portrayed like Bandinelli.

Every exhibition allows multiple paths through it, and in fact the Gardner installation and this catalogue take two different approaches to organizing the material. One story the book tells, across the essays as well as the entries, is that of a professional transformation. Many of the early Renaissance artists who made drawings seem to have done so because they were trained as goldsmiths; at least through the fifteenth century, such apprenticeships required extensive practice at drawing, leaving the artists with skills and habits that they continued to rely upon even as they moved into other areas. Many of the later Renaissance artists who made drawings did so as they moved into the field of architecture. Some of these artists seem to have taught themselves to draw because it was necessary for the professional course they sought to follow. One could say that the trajectory of Renaissance sculpture between 1400 and 1600 was from goldsmithery to architecture, and drawings help document this.

This exhibition and catalogue benefited from the generosity of many colleagues who shared their time and expertise with me and with our team. Luke Syson offered guidance and advice from the moment of the exhibition's inception to the last stages of writing. Daria Foner provided bibliographical materials for several of our authors, and Rachel Boyd devoted great time and effort to helping me prepare the manuscript for submission to the press. Fronia Simpson's perceptive proofreading saved us from many errors; Paul Holberton and Laura Parker took exceptional care with every detail of the book they produced. I would like to extend particular thanks to to Oliver Tostmann, who invited me to co-curate the exhibition with him, Elizabeth Reluga, who managed much of the production both of the exhibition and of this book with extraordinary patience and skill; to Christina Nielsen, who inherited the project but threw her full support behind it; and to Anne Hawley, who has now overseen a series of collaborative projects that have made the Gardner a truly distinctive and intellectually adventuresome institution. It has been an honor and a pleasure to work with all of them.

MICHAEL W. COLE

Notes

1 Consider, for example, the remark of Detlef Heikamp, one of the most important modern historians of Renaissance sculptors' drawings: *Cellini, come molti altri scultori del XVI secolo, non era un buon disegnatore* ("Cellini, like many other sculptors of the sixteenth century, was not a good draftsman"): Heikamp 1966, p. 53.

2 Milanesi 1857, pp. 87 and 248. See the discussion in Plon 1883, pp. 368–69.

Acknowledgments

The Isabella Stewart Gardner Museum appreciates the contribution made toward the preparation of this exhibition and catalogue by: Katie Anderson, Stephen Astley, Joost Vander Auwera, Carmen C. Bambach, Caroline Baumann, Lisa Bevilaqua, Lorraine Bigrigg, Rachel Boyd, Babette Buller, Peggy Burchenal, Thomas P. Campbell, Raymond Carlson, Pieranna Cavalchini, Hugo Chapman, Jess Chloros, Michael Clarke, Ryan Clee, Caitlin Condell, Benoît Constensoux, Dominique Cordellier, Anne Dary, Gail Davidson, Matthew Derosier, Anne-Lise Desmas, Damian Dombrowski, Helen Dorey, Alexandra Eliopoulos, Peter Ertl, Mark Evans, Anne-Marie Eze, Marzia Faietti, Marta Fodor, Daria Foner, Kerry Gaertner, Holger Gehremann, Rossella Giovannetti, Margaret Grasselli, William M. Griswold, Paul Holberton, Peter Huestis, Tomomi Itakura, Joachim Jacoby, Isle Jung, David Kalan, Ingrid Kastel, Guillaume Kazerouni, Hannah Kendall, Yugon Kim, Wenda Kochanowsky, Christopher Lewis, Elena Lombardi, T.K. McClintock, Neil MacGregor, Miranda McLaughlan, Jackie Maman, Giorgio Marini, Marcella Marongiu, Katherine Marshall, Jean-Luc Martinez, David Mathews, Peta Motture, Alessandra Nardi, Diane Naylor, Diane Nixon, Malgorzata Pajkert, Beatrice Paolozzi Strozzi, Laura Parker, Susi Piovanelli, Gianfranco Pocobene, Timothy Potts, Earl A. Powell III, Pina Ragionieri, Cornelia Reiter, Elizabeth Reluga, Christopher Richards, Furio Rinaldi, Andrew Robinson, Malcolm Rogers, Martin Roth, Per Rumberg, Agata Rutkowskam, Holly Salmon, Eike Schmidt, Christian Tico Seifert, Marjorie N. Shelley, Fronia W. Simpson, Ann Walt Stallings, Kimberly Stella, Stephanie Stepanek, Alexander Sturgis, Luke Syson, Naoko Takahatake, Valentine Talland, Jacqueline Thalmann, Christine Thompson, Amanda Venezia, Louis Waldman, Patricia Wengraf, Catherine Whistler, David Wilson, and Dimitrios Zikos.

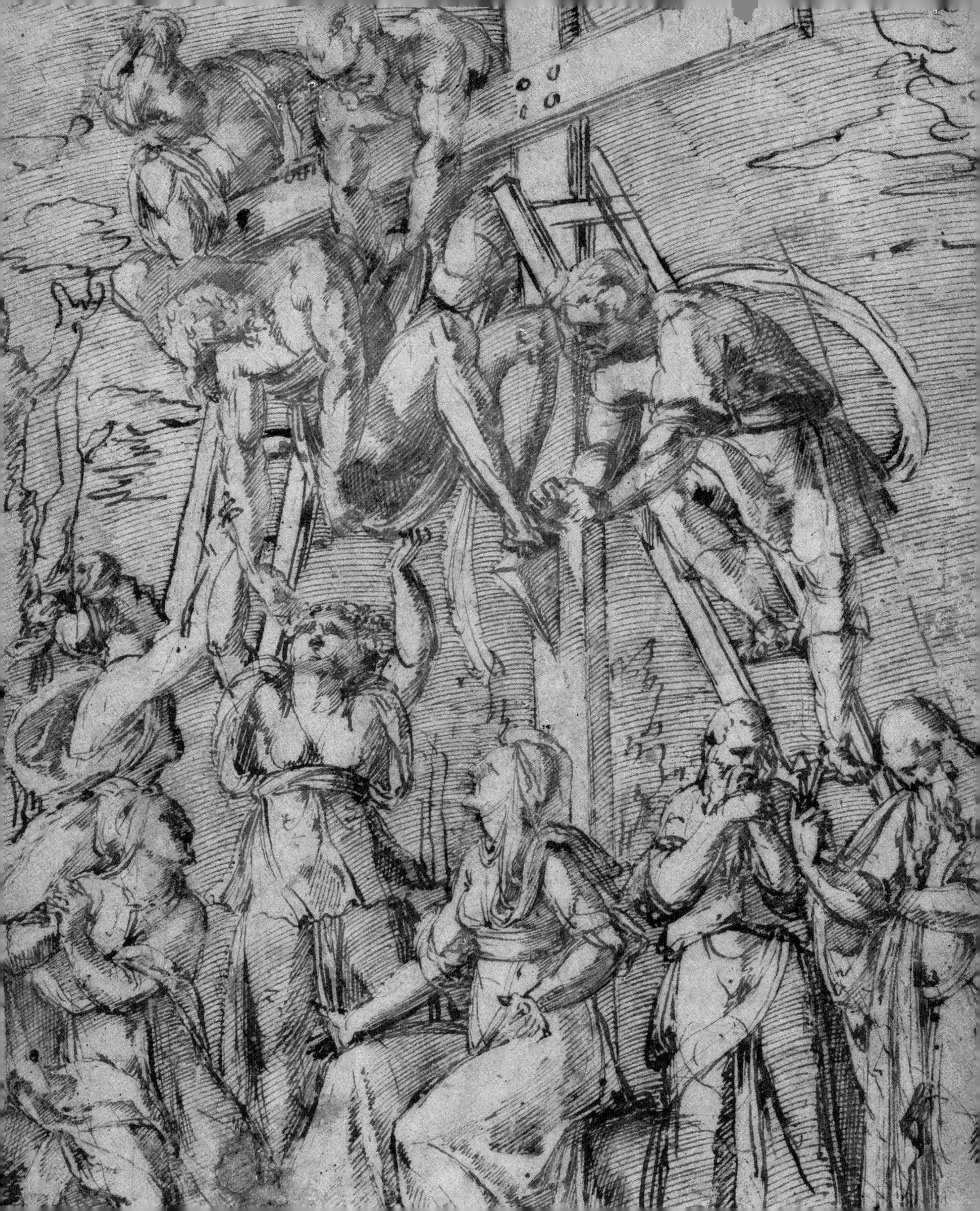

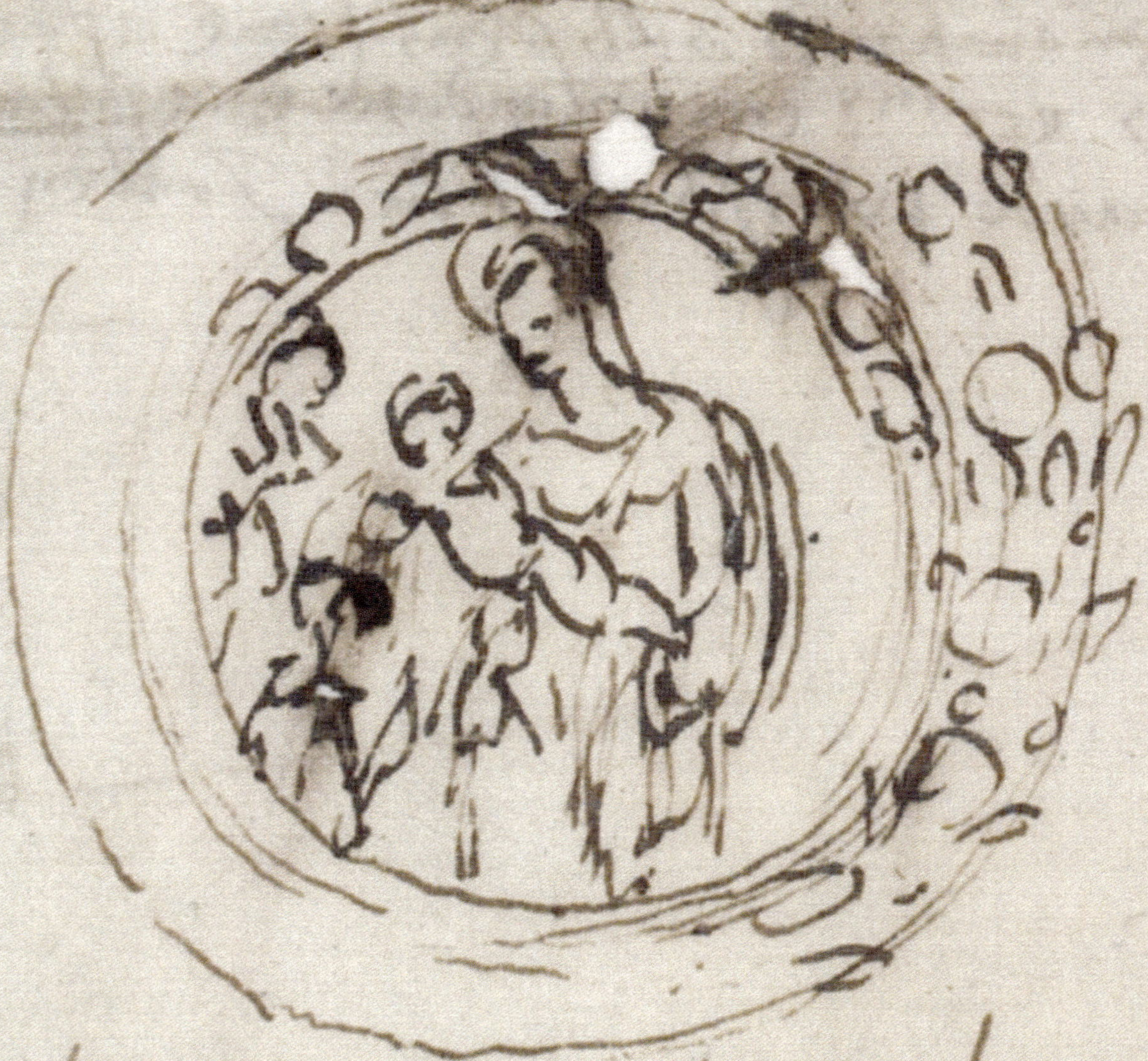

palmi di cann.° tre largo e lungo
tondo el vano senza el feston

La madonna, lo figlio, san giovanni
una monacha di sancto spirito con
un breve sch mano dira.
Sit mens sana in corpore sano

Di bone e belle figure, con belli colori

Why Did Sculptors Draw?

MICHAEL W. COLE

IN THE PREFACES ON TECHNIQUE that he added to the 1568 edition of his *Lives of the Artists,* Giorgio Vasari described a fundamental difference between the characteristic design practices of painters and sculptors:

> For when the intellect puts forth refined and judicious conceptions, the hand that has practiced drawing for many years exhibits the perfection and excellence of the arts together with the knowledge of the artist. But because sculptors sometimes do not much practice in lines and contours, and consequently cannot draw on paper, they make men, animals, and other three-dimension things in clay or wax, and in this way they do the same thing as those who draw perfectly on paper or another surface.[1]

As Vasari would have it, drawing was a standard exercise for painters but not for sculptors, whose process of design often began in three dimensions. Is this true? Sculpture, of course, was the one *arte del disegno* that Vasari had not himself mastered, so the report has to be taken with a grain of salt. And the surviving corpus of Renaissance sculptors' drawings remains to be fully defined.[2] Vasari himself eventually decided that the recto and verso of a sheet now in Chatsworth (fig. 1) was by the stonecarver Nanni di Banco, after earlier thinking that it was by Donatello; without his inscription, it would have been difficult for later viewers to associate it with either sculptor, as we have so little graphic work to form the basis of a comparative corpus.[3] It is possible that Desiderio da Settignano made two small sketches of the Madonna and Child now in the Uffizi (fig. 2), though that attribution has met with still more doubt: the Madonna and Child was the single most common subject for *all* artists of the period.[4] Sheets like these typify a broader situation: in nearly every case where we *seem* to have a sculptor who made drawings, major questions of authorship surround that artist's graphic oeuvre.

CAT. 17 Fra Mattia della Robbia
Design and contract for a tondo (detail)

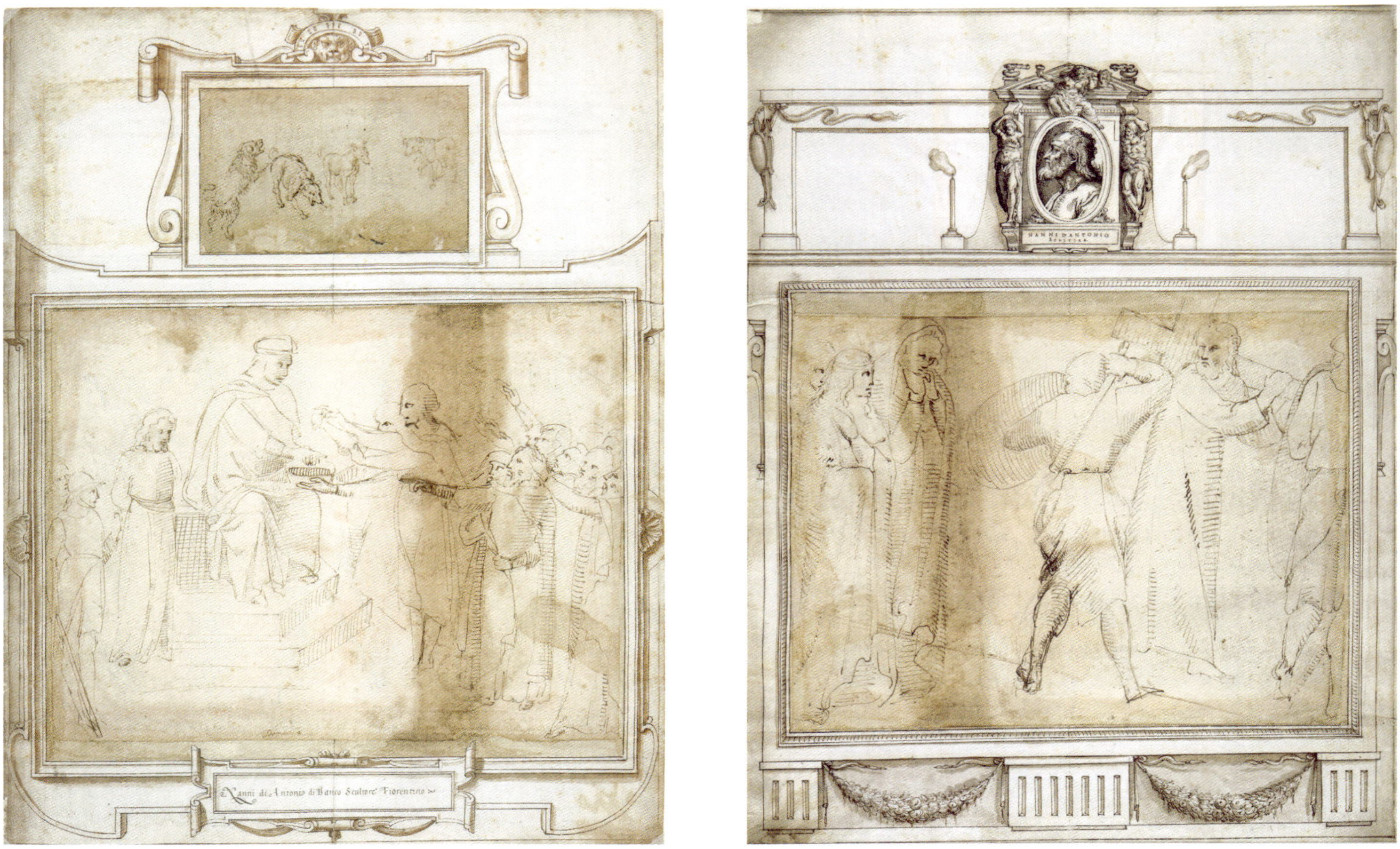

FIG. 1
Nanni di Banco, attributed to
Pilate Washing His Hands (recto),
Christ Carrying the Cross (verso)
Pen and brown ink, on paper, with Giorgio Vasari's late 16th-century mount,
292 × 376 mm (recto); 288 × 378 mm (verso)
Devonshire Collection, Chatsworth

Most Renaissance sculptors had to deliver occasional drawings; contracts refer to these, and other records indicate that artists entered drawings into competitions for sculptural commissions.[5] Such drawings, however, represent only a qualified exception to Vasari's real point, that sculptors did not rely on drawing as part of the creative process. Against the thin evidence suggesting that some sculptors did sketch ideas in two dimensions, moreover, we have to weigh the indications that many lacked the skills for this. It seems telling, for example, that Alfonso of Aragon turned to the painter Pisanello (or a member of his workshop) rather than to a sculptor when seeking a design for the marble entrance arch that sculptors would execute for the Castel Nuovo in Naples.[6] Piero di Giovanni Tedesco, when working on the sculptures for the façade of Florence Cathedral, received drawings from painters, as did Niccolò Lamberti, when making the tomb of Marco Datini.[7] Painters provided drawings for sculptors in Raphael's workshop.[8] Giambologna relied on drawings by Tommaso Laureti when working on the fountain of Nepture in Bologna.[9] Cesare Nebbia appears to have designed one of the reliefs on the fountain of Moses in Rome, the Cavaliere d'Arpino a statue subsequently sculpted by Valsoldo.[10] To my knowledge, no drawings have been confidently attributed to Michelozzo, Luca or Andrea della Robbia, Bernardo Rossellino, Mino da Fiesole, Nicolò

FIG. 2
Desiderio da Settignano, attributed to
The Madonna and Child
Pen and brown ink with wash, on paper,
267 × 192 mm
Gabinetto Disegni e Stampe degli Uffizi,
Florence

dell'Arca, Bertoldo di Giovanni, or Benedetto da Maiano, to name just a few of the more eminent sculptors active in the later fifteenth century. Slightly more survive from the sixteenth century, when drawings began to be collected and thus better preserved. From Andrea Sansovino, Raffaello da Montelupo, Giovanni Angiolo Montorsoli, Tribolo, and Giambologna, for example, we have a handful each.[11] Still, Andrea Bregno, Tullio and Antonio Lombardo, Willem van Tetrode, Leone Leoni, Alessandro Vittoria, and Vincenzo Danti, among others, have left no more than a single sheet or two.[12] Several of these drawings are doubtful, and many reinforce Vasari's impression that sculptors "had not much practice in lines and contours."

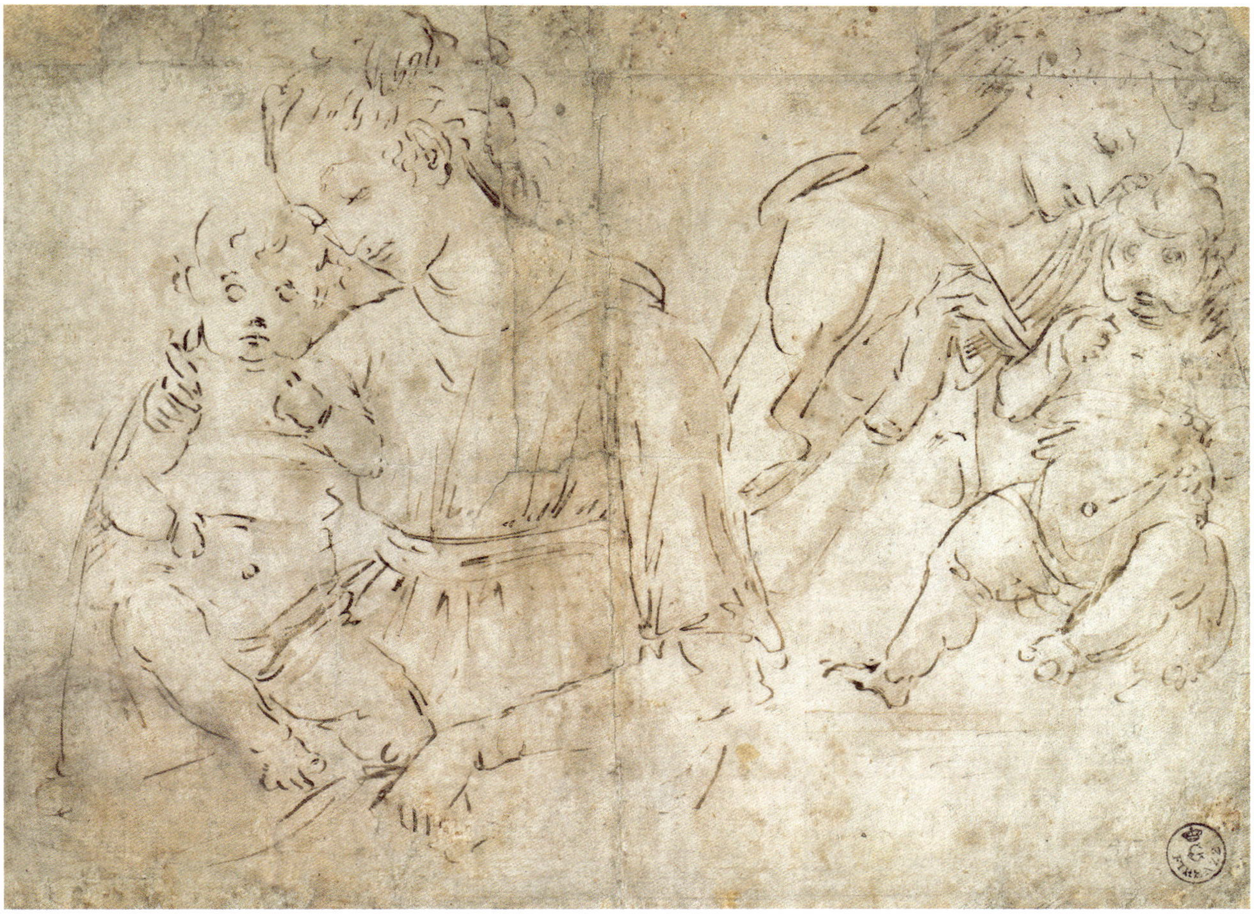

FIG. 3
Andrea del Verrocchio
Head of a woman, late 1460s or early 1470s
Black chalk or charcoal, partly reworked with brown ink and grey wash, on paper, 411 × 327 mm
Christ Church, Oxford

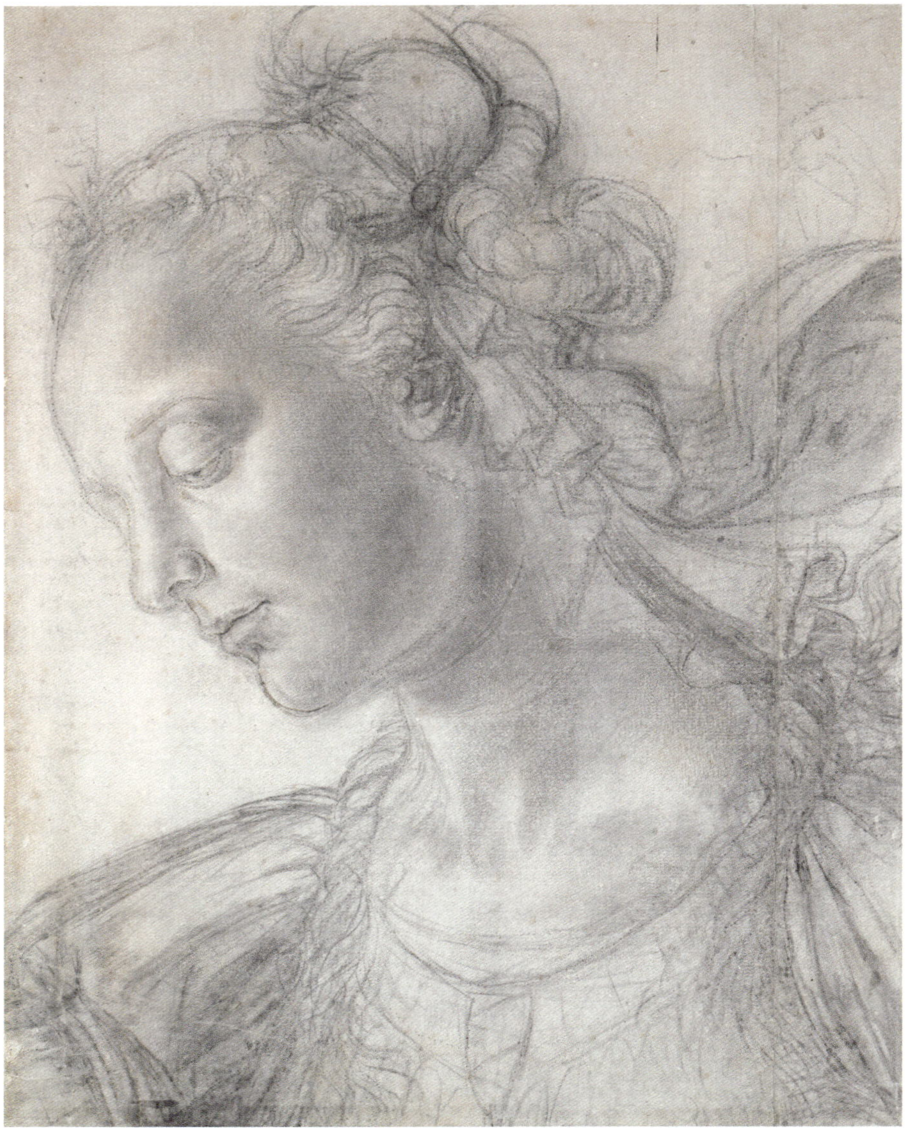

So if Renaissance sculptors' drawings are the exception rather than the rule, what are the circumstances surrounding those we do have? Answering this question faces an array of difficulties. To begin, the "sculptor" was not a clear professional category. Vecchietta, Antonio del Pollaiuolo, Francesco di Giorgio, Andrea del Verrocchio, and Michelangelo were accomplished draftsmen, but they—like Baccio Bandinelli, the most prolific sculptor-draftsman of the Renaissance—were also trained painters, who would have been expected to master two-dimensional media as youths.[13] The few drawings that seem to come from the workshop of Vecchietta were done with a brush.[14] The largest group of drawings now attributed to Verrocchio consists of head studies done in chalk or silverpoint that are more closely connected to paintings than to sculptures (for example, fig. 3).[15] Michelangelo's earliest secure drawings are studies of paintings, and the drawings he made in the course of designing paintings far outnumber those for sculptures.

We can also make distinctions within the profession of the "sculptor." In Florence, the city from which we have more relevant material than any other, those artists who worked primarily in stone belonged to a different guild than those who worked in metal; those who apprenticed in goldsmith shops cultivated different skills and habits—drawings among them—than those who learned their crafts under masons.[16] An artist like Leonardo da Vinci, whom we think of today as a draftsman before all else, occasionally occupied himself with sculpture, but for most of his life it was not from sculpture that he made his living.

When true sculptors did produce drawings, those sheets often have no direct connection to surviving works in three dimensions. And when there is an evident relationship between a drawing and a surviving or documented sculpture, it can be difficult to tell which was based on the other. Occasionally, it seems possible to hypothesize on the basis of style or subject matter that a given drawing was made by a sculptor rather than by an artist in a different professional field. Nevertheless, surviving drawings by sculptors can vary quite dramatically in manner, medium, and format. For this reason, it seems prudent to approach the history of sculptors' drawings as one not just of style but of circumstances. What motivated sculptors to make drawings? What factors lay behind the decision to produce a design on parchment or paper rather than in wax or clay?

Installation

If, with Vasari, we think of drawings as an alternative to models, we might also notice that nearly all the works in wax and clay we have from before 1700 are for bodies, draperies, and the occasional animal. Even allowing for the disappearance of many other objects, it seems possible to infer that the first function of these three-dimensional forms was to allow sculptors to think through *pose*, usually the pose of the human figure. Many of the sculptors' drawings that have come down to us, by contrast, are not what we would call figure studies: they show functional or decorative objects, ground plans for buildings, ideas for fountains, tombs, and coats of arms. Can we say, then, that sculptors were most likely to draw when devoting their efforts to particular kinds of subject matter?

Michelangelo used drawings as he moved away from figuration while working at San Lorenzo in Florence.[17] And we might be able to see that episode as part of a longer history that starts well before Michelangelo's birth and has as much to do with the history of a profession as with the path of one individual. Among the few candidates for inclusion on the list of surviving sculptors' drawings made before 1450, for example, are two sheets showing Jacopo della Quercia's Fonte Gaia. The long history of the fountain's production involved at least two documented drawings, one from 1408 and a second in Jacopo's own hand from about 1416, at a moment when the design was being significantly revised and expanded; others may have been made in between. The drawings on parchment in New York (cat. 1) and London (cat. 2) are today generally regarded as fragments of what was once a single folio. They give their personifications wings that were dropped in the fountain that was built and show animals that were never executed; the figures also occupy niches with Gothic arches, unlike the modern round arches that were built. All of this, together with differences in the drawn and sculpted figures' respective poses and arrangement, suggests that the sheets belong to an early stage of the project. The drawings may be by Jacopo himself, or he may have relied on someone else to pitch his idea: the figures in the drawings are slimmer and less articulated than Jacopo's sculptures.[18] What seems more certain is that the New York and London drawings represent the end of one phase of the design process, not the process itself. These sheets, which have no pentimenti or underdrawing, seem meant to be shown to a patron. They are not studies that would guide the handling of individual blocks but proposals for the composition of a larger ensemble.

Jacopo was hardly alone in relying on drawing when confronting the problem of conceiving an architectural setting that would include sculpted figures. We see something comparable in a tempera drawing from the circle of Lorenzo Ghiberti that envisions a new sculpture in a renovated niche for the exterior of Orsanmichele (see fig. 17). The figure in the drawing is close though not identical to the bronze *St. Stephen* that Ghiberti modeled in 1427: the general pose and costume are similar, and the saint holds the same attributes, a palm of martyrdom in his right hand and a book in his left, allowing the possibility that the figure already existed in some form—perhaps a preliminary model—at the time the drawing was made.[19] What most sharply differentiates the drawing and the final

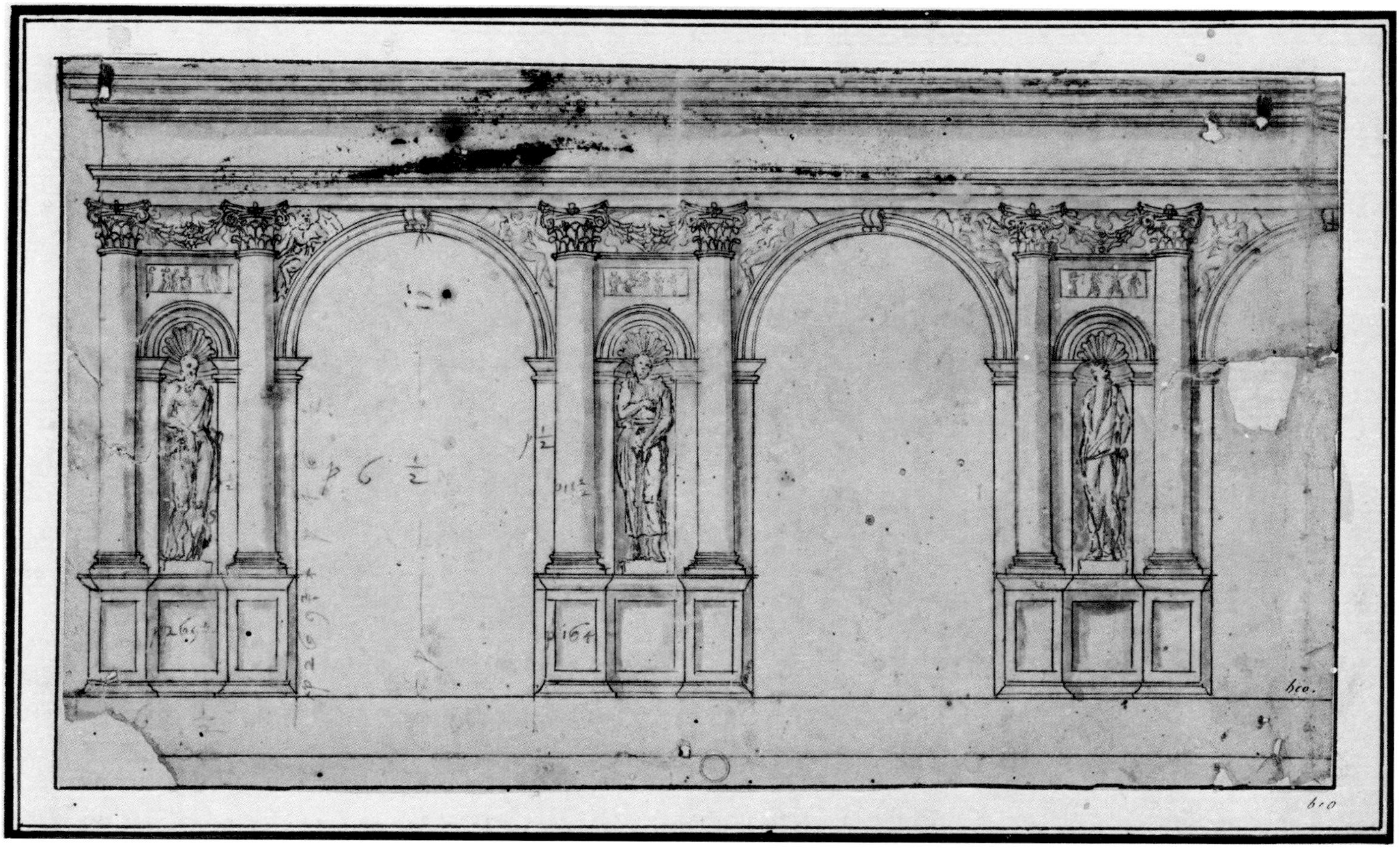

work is not the figure but the niche. Particularly after Donatello's *St. Louis of Toulouse* had demonstrated that a statue and its tabernacle might be conceived as a single cohesive unit, patrons at Orsanmichele would have been concerned as much with the frame as with the figure, and Ghiberti's contract stipulated that he was not just to make a new statue but also to beautify and reornament the pilaster where it would be displayed.[20] In the end, no niche was fashioned in the way this drawing shows, but the draftsman's concern with the architecture is a strong clue to dating the drawing before the statue's installation in late 1428 or early 1429. It appears to have been made not to propose a figural invention but to envision an architectural setting.

When sculptors became practicing architects, the procedure of coordinating sculpture and framework probably became more flexible. A drawing by Tullio Lombardo for a tomb of Dante that his family's workshop was executing shows the architecture in something like its final arrangement but includes only an initial idea for the central relief, which took its definitive form only sometime later.[21] We know from documents that when Jacopo Sansovino oversaw the creation of the Loggetta in Piazza San Marco, Venice, the construction of the architecture preceded the casting of the statues.[22] That may help explain why, in the drawing attributed to Sansovino in the Victoria and Albert Museum (fig. 4), the

FIG. 4
Jacopo Sansovino
Project for the Loggetta in Piazza San Marco, 1537
Pen and ink with brown wash, on paper, 279 × 156 mm
Victoria and Albert Museum, London

FIG. 5
Niccolò Tribolo
Study for a fountain with Aesclepius in a niche, 1548–49
Pen and brown ink, on paper, 301 × 227 mm
Musée du Louvre, Paris

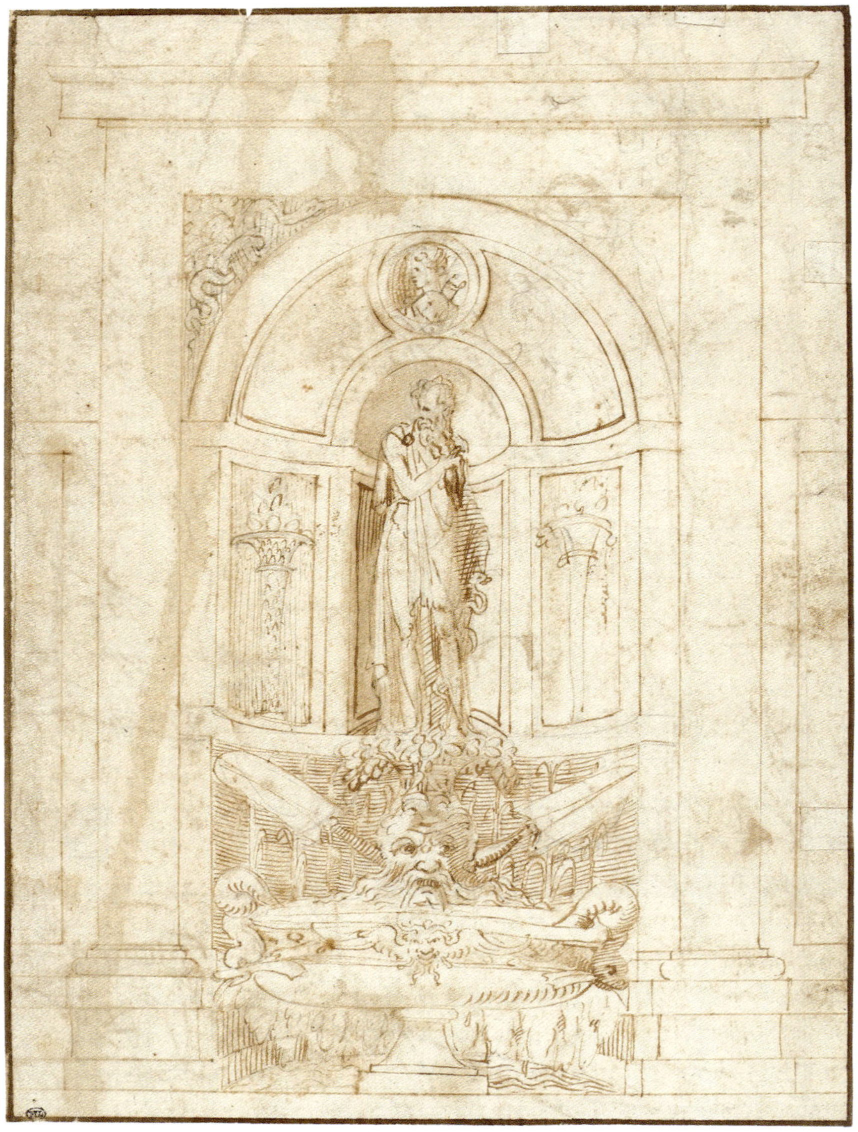

architectural elements already seem close to those that were ultimately executed but the characters in the niches do not: perhaps his patrons wanted to see ideas for the elevation before they decided what the statues should represent, or perhaps they changed their mind about the sequence. Either way, it appears that Sansovino devoted real attention to the figures only after the architectural elements had been worked out.[23] Cellini writes in his autobiography that he redesigned the entrance to the French palace at Fontainebleau, correcting the proportions of the passageway and placing a properly rounded lunette above it.[24] The description makes it sound as if he were working on paper, probably with a compass. Only after this, he writes, did he design the *Satyr* meant to ornament the door. A surviving drawing of the satyr (cat. 26) includes a shaded square at the top and a cast shadow behind, indicating its architectural function as a kind of caryatid.[25] More difficult to judge is the *Aesclepius* that is now broadly accepted as a drawing by Niccolò Tribolo (fig. 5). This seems to date to 1548–49, and both the central figure and the basin below correspond closely to the finished carvings. Yet documents establish that Tribolo died in 1550 and that both objects were completed only after this by the sculptor Antonio Lorenzi. Could Tribolo not have used drawing in this instance to work out an idea for the niche into which a figure that he had modeled but not yet carved could be installed?[26] A later fountain design by Giambologna (cat. 41) was almost certainly made at a moment when the sculptor already knew not only the form of his figure but also the form and dimensions of the antique basin over which it would stand.[27] The drawing concerns the coordination of these two elements, elaborating a framework for them.

In the early Renaissance, the sculptors most likely to have been skilled draftsmen were those trained as goldsmiths. Later, however, we find more drawings from stone carvers, most of them made when the artist was confronted with a task that went beyond the production of figures and reliefs: Montorsoli, Ammanati, Giambologna, and Vittoria are all examples of sculptors whose surviving drawings are primarily for architectural projects. In part, this may be because drawing allowed more linear precision than modeling, though a tomb like Tullio's or a fountain like Giambologna's also required collaboration with teams of builders and clear communication with the workers at the site.

Comparison

In addition to the canvas in the Louvre, one other drawing has frequently been attributed to Ghiberti, and it is entirely different in form and conception. Now in the Albertina, it shows variations on the Roman soldiers of Christ's Flagellation (fig. 6), and the central figure in the top row appears to be either a study for or a derivation from the left-hand figure on Ghiberti's first set of doors for the Florence Baptistery. If this drawing were by Ghiberti, it would have to date well before 1424, when the doors were complete, a surprisingly early moment for any artist to be sketching on paper, the support in this case.[28] This kind of study, moreover, which shows the artist moving limbs in search of a satisfactory pose, is precisely the sort of experimentation one might sooner expect an artist to pursue with a model of clay or wax—especially since he would eventually have to make the wax for casting anyway.

FIG. 6
Lorenzo Ghiberti
Five figure studies for The Flagellation of Christ, late 1410s
Pen and ink, on paper, 216 × 166 mm
Albertina, Vienna

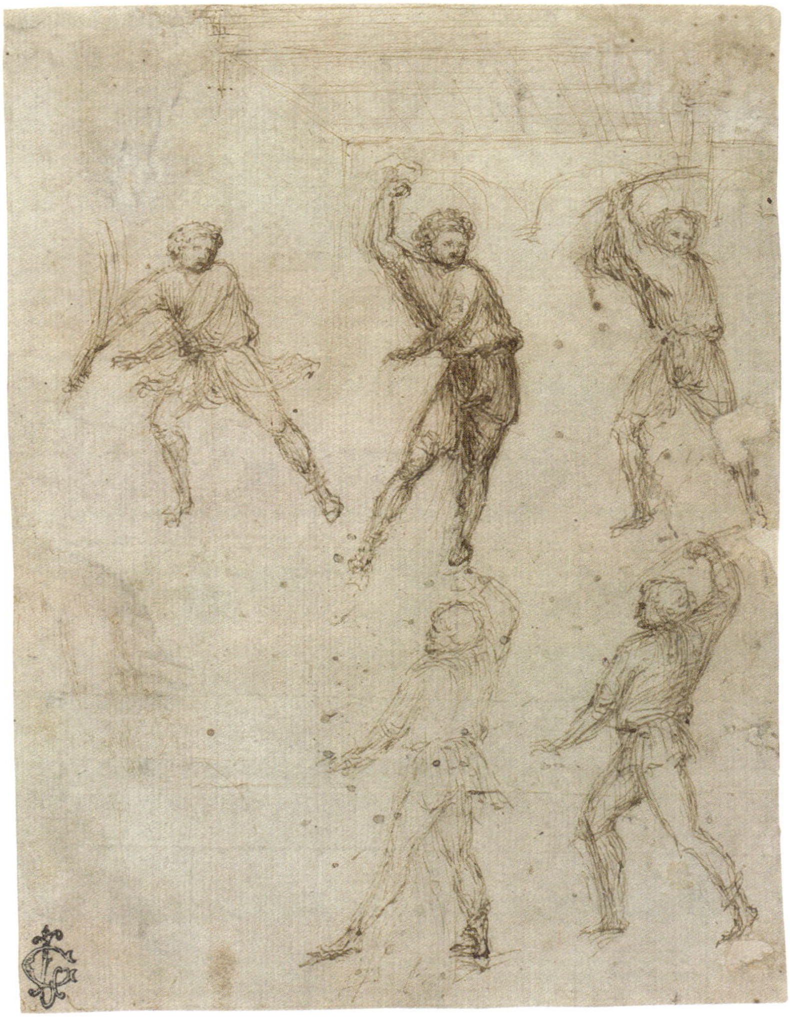

Yet, the figures on the sheet embody the sinuous curve we celebrate in Ghiberti's early sculpture, and above them are the indications of a ceiling, cornice, arch, and column comparable to the loggia in the background of Ghiberti's panel. Ghiberti was certainly a wide-ranging draftsman; he is documented to have produced designs for stained glass and stone carving no less than for metalwork. Early works on paper seem to have survived poorly; if Ghiberti was sketching on this support as early as the 1410s, it would help explain why so few of his drawings have come down to us. The drawing also illustrates what an artist could not easily do with models—compare multiple versions of a figure to see which one worked best. When Benvenuto Cellini wrote about using wax and clay, he described how, "beginning with the front view, and before it is completely resolved, [the sculptor] raises and lowers the limbs of the figure, pulling them forward and pushing them back, bending and straightening them." After that the artist rotates the figure, determines which parts of his invention do not work from the new point of view, and continues the process.[29] Cellini's description implies that each new design idea erased the previous one. Once the artist had moved the model's arm, only the memory of an earlier pose remained. Drawing preserved more, as we are reminded by the pentimenti in Ghiberti's individual figures, no less than in the group of *pensieri* his page collects.

A drawing in Rennes that most drawings specialists attribute to Donatello (cat. 3) shows a figure drawing on the verso and, beside that, a second design in the same hand for the same figure's head. The second head is finished as a bust and lacks the cape that the draftsman added to the first figure. The artist has sketched it more quickly, omitting both the underdrawing and the wash of the figure beside it, and barely bothering to align the bridge of the nose with the nostrils. This very quickness shows the advantages of the pen: in seconds, the draftsman has imagined a different hairstyle, which would have taken time and care to consider in the form of a three-dimensional model. Though contemporary documents do not connect Donatello to drawings as they do Ghiberti, we know that Donatello worked for a period as Ghiberti's assistant, when he presumably could have learned from the older artist's example.

Donatello's practices, in turn, may have provided a model for later fifteenth-century sculptors. The present exhibition includes a design by Antonio del Pollaiuolo for an equestrian monument, now in the Metropolitan Museum of Art (cat. 6). This is related to another drawing, now in Munich (fig. 60), which shows a variation on the figure underneath the horse and modifies the face of the rider above. It would seem that Pollaiuolo either made two similar proposals for different monuments or envisioned variations in the course of designing a single one.[30] Either way, people around Pollaiuolo would have been able to examine and reflect on the differences in the two inventions, just as we do now.

As paper became more readily available, drawings of this type also became more common. A group of drawings that are generally attributed to the late fifteenth-century sculptor Francesco di Simone Ferrucci (fig. 7) shows the artist taking up an idea from Donatello and more immediately from Verrocchio, considering slight variations on a design for a young boy.[31] A sheet by Michelangelo now in the Uffizi contains five sketches representing ideas for the Bruges *Madonna*; another in the Ashmolean (fig. 8) has six pen studies for his marble *Slaves*.[32] In the work of Baccio Bandinelli and Guglielmo della Porta, two sixteenth-century sculptors from whom we have an exceptionally large body of surviving drawings, we frequently find groups of ideas for single objects. When Della Porta took up paper to experiment

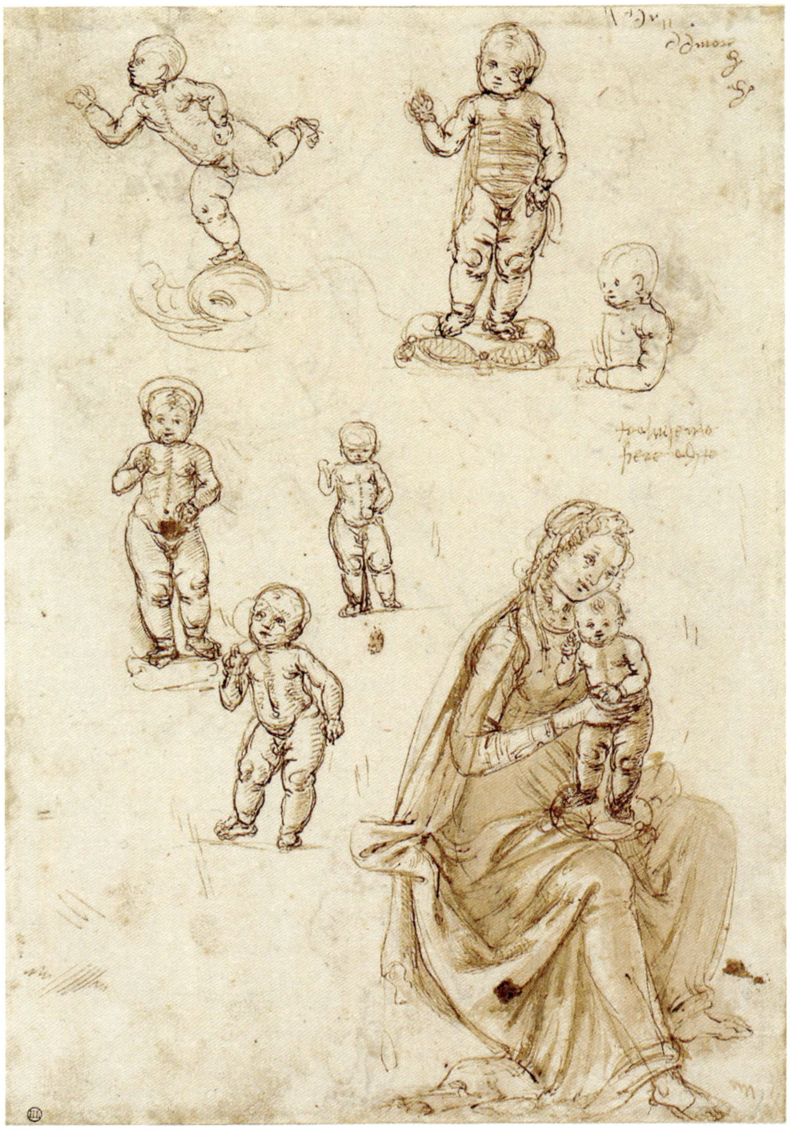

FIG. 7
Francesco di Simone Ferrucci
Sheet of studies with a putto on a dolphin and the blessing Christ Child, c. 1487
Pen and brown ink with wash, on paper, 270 × 190 mm
Musée du Louvre, Paris

with Ghiberti's old theme of Christ's Flagellation, he used the medium the same way that the draftsman of the Albertina sheet did, sequentially adjusting poses.[33]

Sometimes comparisons like this were not just for the artist. Multiples could be useful for distributing ideas to different places, or for getting ahead in a market like Florence's, organized around competition and comparison. As we have seen, a number of the earlier surviving sculptors' drawings were made for eyes outside the workshop. They pitch an idea to a prospective patron, or they bind artist and patron to an agreement. But artists also discovered that it could be strategic to give patrons choices, and that it was more efficient to offer different options on paper than in clay. Bandinelli refers to this practice: a 1551 letter to Jacopo Guidi, for example, promises that "[Bandinelli] will do several more drawings for the fountain in the piazza, as the most illustrious duke commands, so that [the duke] can deliberate on them at his pleasure."[34]

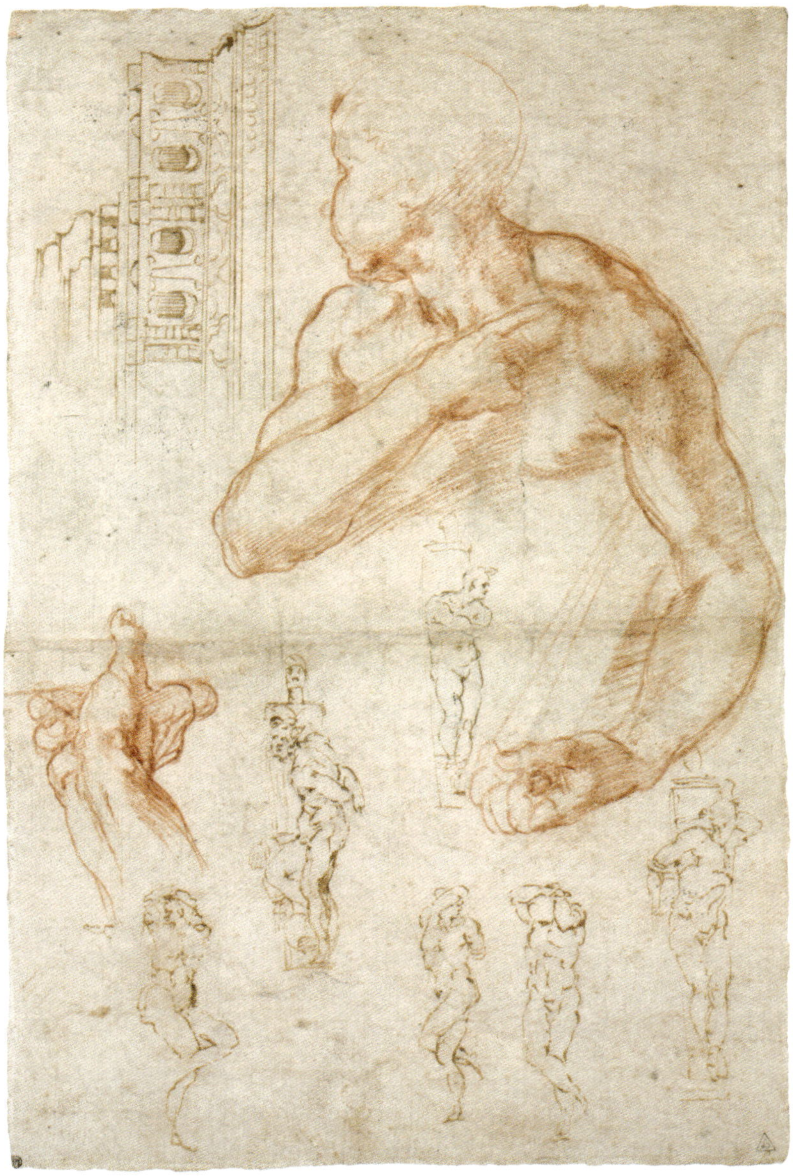

FIG. 8
Michelangelo Buonarroti
Studies for the Sistine Ceiling and for Slaves for the tomb of Pope Julius II, 1512–13
Red chalk and pen and ink, on paper, 286 × 194 mm
Ashmolean Museum, Oxford

Composition

The recto of the sheet in Rennes (cat. 3) depicts a fragment of a Massacre of the Innocents, with mothers clutching children and soldiers with raised swords in the background.[35] This is a subject Donatello never carried out in sculpture, though the crush of overlapping figures making dramatic gestures, including veiled women with large expressive zones around the eyes, bears comparison with numerous late Donatello reliefs (the *Lamentation* in the Victoria and Albert Museum of about 1460, for example). Works like this, which must once have been more numerous, seem to have made a great impression on associates and followers, the strong contours, simplified hatching, and the sense for weight and balance providing a powerful model for Antonio Rossellino, Antonio del Pollaiuolo, and even Bandinelli. Still, this approach may represent a local practice more than

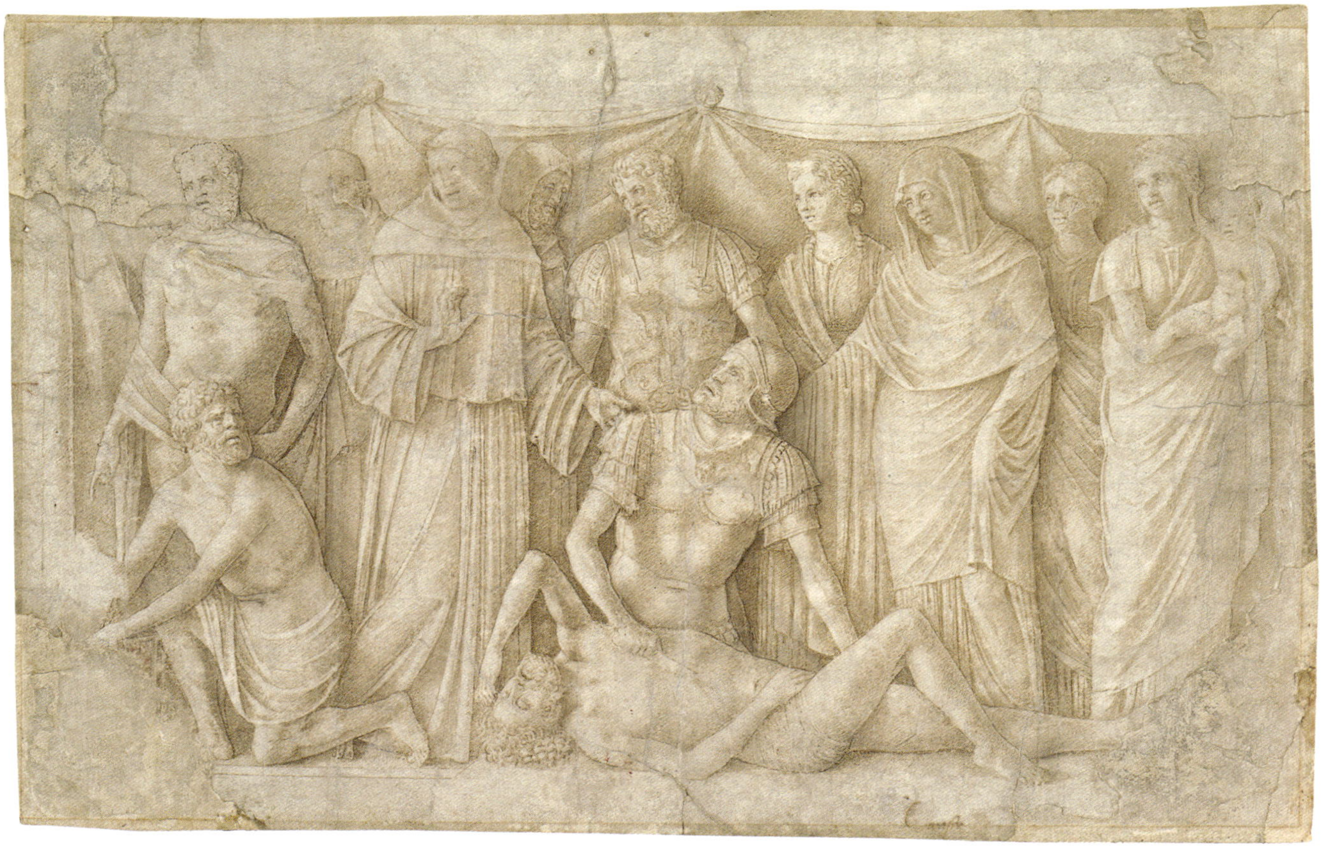

FIG. 9
Antonio Lombardo, attributed to
St. Anthony of Padua and the Miracle of the Miser's Heart, 1501 (?)
Pen and brown ink, brush and brown wash, on paper, 248 × 393 mm
The Metropolitan Museum of Art, New York

a paradigm for sculptors' drawings generally. Among the most beautiful early sixteenth-century drawings sometimes said to be by a sculptor is one ascribed to Antonio Lombardo in the Metropolitan Museum (fig. 9). It seems to have served as a proposal for the marble relief of St. Anthony of Padua and the Miracle of the Miser's Heart that Antonio's brother Tullio completed between 1520 and 1525, following Antonio's death, though the series of reliefs had been under way since the beginning of the century. The change in composition between the drawing and the finished work may indicate that the patron was unhappy with Antonio's original idea or it may reflect Tullio's decision not to use Antonio's design following the transfer of the assignment. Yet the distance between this drawing and the practice of Donatello is striking, especially given that Pomponius Gauricus was celebrating Donatello's draftsmanship in Padua in these very years and that the sculpture was for a church that held some of Donatello's greatest reliefs. Produced with delicate short hatchings and subtly graded tones of wash, the drawing helps the viewer imagine the modeling of smooth marble forms. Were this a Florentine work, we might conclude that it came from an artist trained in painting, and it may well represent an instance of a sculptor collaborating with someone outside the workshop.[36] At the same time, the brushed hatching within the ink contours is comparable to what we find in other drawings that appear to have come from the Lombardi.[37] Perhaps Venetian sculptors took a more painterly approach to the page.

More cautiously, we might set aside style and consider genre. Most of the drawings that show the strongest debt to Donatello seek to arrange multiple figures, or occasionally figures and elements of a setting, across a surface. Stylistically distant as the Metropolitan *Miracle* is from this tradition, Antonio Lombardo was, like Donatello, an especially fine designer of sculptural relief, a specialization that often led sculptors to draw. A number of Michelangelo's compositional drawings seem to have been for sculptures.[38] And when we speak of sculptors using drawing as a path into architecture, the pages in question are frequently architectural compositions (tombs, fountains) rather than studies of individual elements (capitals, entablatures). This is true of the "architectural" drawings of Ghiberti, Bregno, Giambologna, and Alessandro Vittoria, different as they are otherwise.

One sixteenth-century artist who unquestionably relied very heavily on paper was Guglielmo della Porta; as a sculptor he predominantly made reliefs. Drawings for his equestrian monument to Charles V show plans for a base with prisoners but also devote extensive space to what he labeled *storie*: in contrast to earlier artists like Donatello and Verrocchio, the horse and rider here seem the least important part of the monument.[39] Della Porta wrote proudly of the fourteen bronze reliefs he composed to elaborate the history of Christ's Passion.[40] And years ago, Leopold Ettlinger identified the woman at the lower left of Della Porta's *Allegory of Sculpture* as the personification of Historia.[41] It is from that that the personification of Fame rises.

Yet if Della Porta considered himself first and foremost a narrative artist, he nevertheless maintained a decorative sensibility. *The Banquet of the Gods* in the Metropolitan Museum, a variant of which was executed as a plaquette (cat. 34, 35), shows Della Porta's characteristically odd figures, with limbs that are not foreshortened but instead extend across the picture plane. (Note the two reaching arms of the couple at the upper right or the leg of the figure on this side of the table below them.) The effect is to flatten everything, to convert all forms into profiles. A comparison with Bandinelli's roughly contemporary designs for reliefs and prints shows what is distinctive in Della Porta: Bandinelli gives a sense of space to be occupied, Della Porta of a surface to be covered.

A concern with surface was another factor that could make paper attractive as a design medium, especially when the artist was already thinking

FIG. 10
Guglielmo della Porta
Prudence, c. 1545
Pen and ink, on paper, 284 × 211 mm
Sammlung der Kunstakademie, Düsseldorf

about the limit imposed by an anticipated frame. Though the *Banquet* drawing is damaged at the edges, enough remains to demonstrate that Della Porta's figures respect a notional curve at right, conforming to the oval shape he presumably imagined for his plaquette. We see adjustments of this kind across his drawings: the banner in a *Resurrection* plaquette curves to follow the edge of the metal, the characters in a projected altarpiece conform to the lobes of a panel, a design for a tomb starts with the curve of the niche that was to contain it.[42]

Vantage

Cellini's description of modeling emphasizes the challenge of designing a figure to be seen in the round. An attraction of wax and clay was that they allowed the artist to rotate the figure he was working before completely resolving any single view. Conversely, sculptors sometimes turned to drawing when conceiving figures that were *not* meant to be seen in the round, figures on which the point of view was to be controlled. This was famously a concern of Donatello, who approached many of his sculptures with an awareness of where the viewer would be positioned.[43] It may help explain why the David depicted on the verso of the Rennes drawing resolves itself so well into a view that is not frontal—indeed, it is remarkably close to the view Michelangelo selected when drawing a David. In the case of a marble sculptor like Michelangelo, drawings sometimes corresponded to the face of the block into which the sculptor would carve.[44] Vasari described Michelangelo carving into the stone block from one side only, so that the figure seemed to emerge from a receding surface.[45] And while this should not be taken as an accurate account of the way Michelangelo consistently worked, drawing the composition that the carver would then follow into the stone did, as a practical matter, determine a principal view onto the eventual figure.[46]

The drawings Bandinelli made when designing his *Hercules and Cacus* (cat. 18–20) seem to have taken account not only of the faces of the block into which he would carve but also the viewpoint of a pedestrian entering the square where the statue was to stand.[47] When we see Della Porta drawing an allegory of Prudence (fig. 10), we cannot be sure just what it was for: it has been cautiously connected to the tomb of Pietro de Solis, though Della Porta frequently imitated Michelangelo by incorporating pairs of recumbent

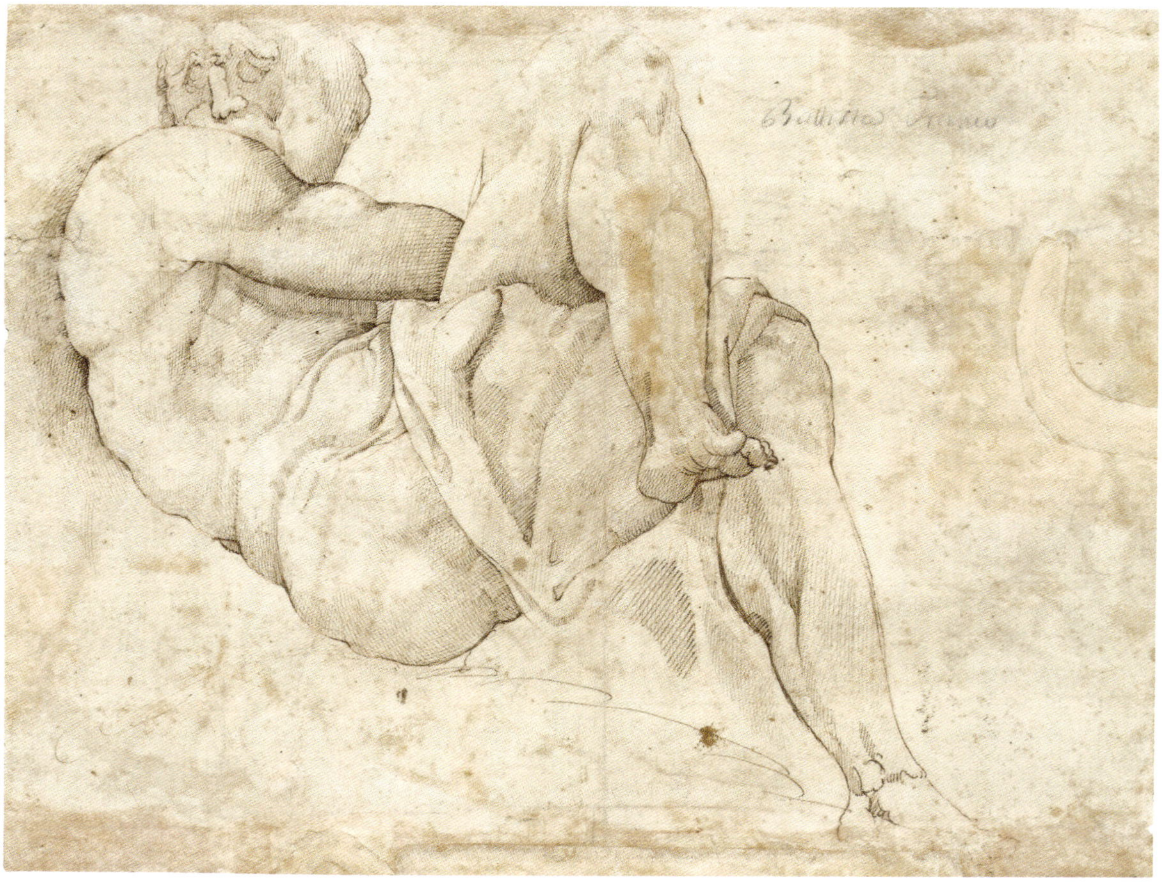

FIG. 11
Battista Franco
Il Giorno (after Michelangelo's tomb of Giulano de' Medici), c. 1536
Pen and ink, on paper, 265 × 340 mm
Musée du Louvre, Paris

figures into tombs and façades.[48] What we can say is that the figure, if executed, would almost certainly have been one that a viewer could see from a single side only. While Della Porta made many drawings for this sort of figure, none considers angles like those that interested the painters who drew after Michelangelo's New Sacristy (fig. 11). Nor, for that matter, do we see Della Porta following anything like Michelangelo's procedure in designing such figures, which involved studying the limbs of a live model from various angles.[49] Comparing the *Prudence* to drawings that use similar motifs to crown the field for an inscription raises doubts about whether such figures would even have been executed in the round.[50]

A pair of drawings from Willem van Tetrode (fig. 12), who may have worked for a time in the Della Porta shop, show a putto carrying a vase, done after an ancient marble then at the Villa Farnese at Caprarola.[51] The two renderings, though similar in scale and finish, differ in the aspect of the sculpture that they show. Evidently the artist made one of them, then moved twenty or thirty degrees before making the second. This is a small change; it seems less likely that Tetrode thought the sculpture was intended to work from multiple angles and more likely that he was searching for the position from which the contour was most pleasing, as though a view from the correct angle would resolve the figure back into a plane.

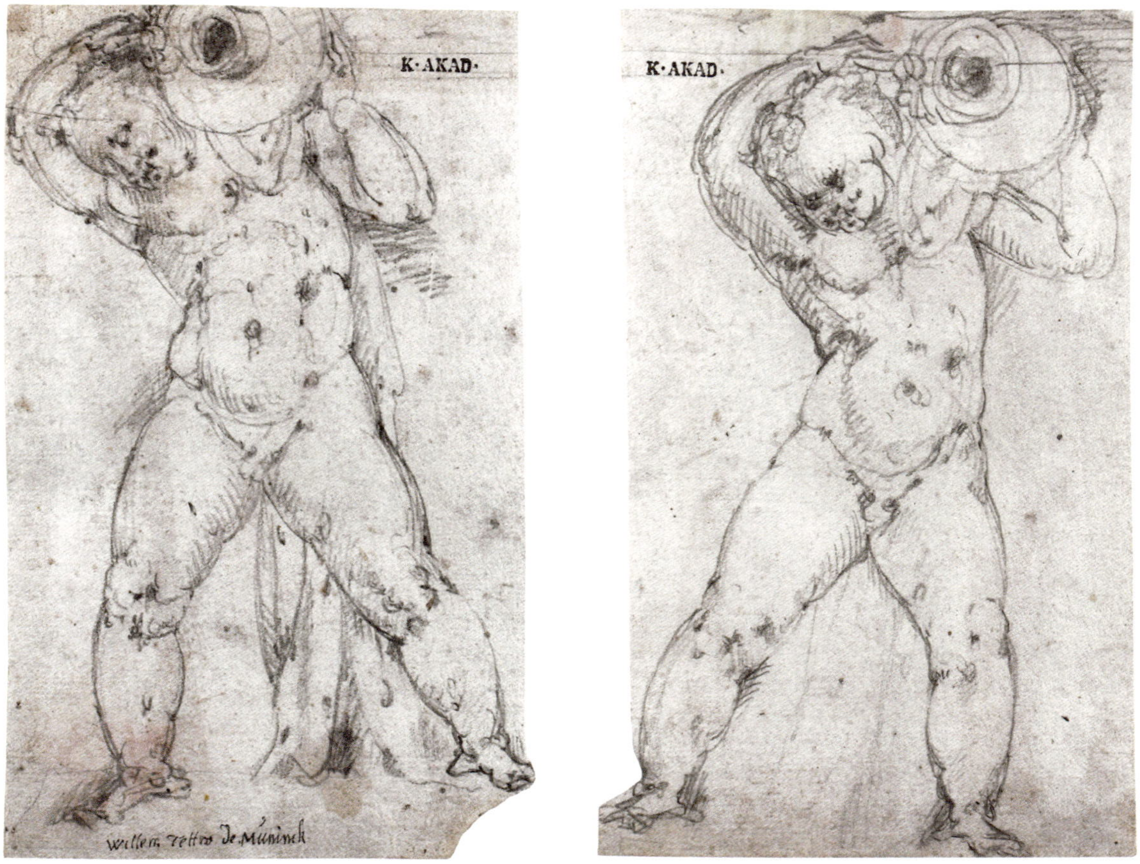

FIG. 12
Willem van Tetrode
Puttos bearing a vase, c. 1560
Black chalk, on paper, 180 × 113 mm and 180 × 116 mm
Akademie der bildenden Künste, Vienna

Mobility

Another consideration that might have led sculptors to work on paper was its portability. After the death of Goro di Naroccio, Ghiberti asked for the return of some drawings that the sculptor had borrowed and taken to Siena.[52] Pollaiuolo's equestrian drawings were made in Florence but probably sent to other cities. Michelangelo, working in the New Sacristy, used drawings to communicate with a patron in Rome.[53] Sculptors or their agents made sketches of marble blocks which could be sent to men in the quarries to guide excavations.[54] And if drawings traveled easily, so did they allow artists to work outside the studio.[55] Among the few drawings that have persuasively been linked to Jacopo Sansovino are a group of studies made after antiquities.[56] The representations of Venus by Michelangelo in the present exhibition show the artist using drawing to make sense of an ancient marble fragment (cat. 12–15).[57] Most sheets of this sort would have to have been made on-site.

The same can be said of the drawings sculptors made after works by their Renaissance predecessors.[58] Raffaello da Montelupo, for example, drew after venerable Roman sculptures but also after Michelangelo's Sistine Ceiling.[59] Della Porta drew antiquities but also façades by Polidoro da Caravaggio. Such renderings—like Michelangelo's drawings after Giotto and Masaccio—would have required sculptors to move from place to place,

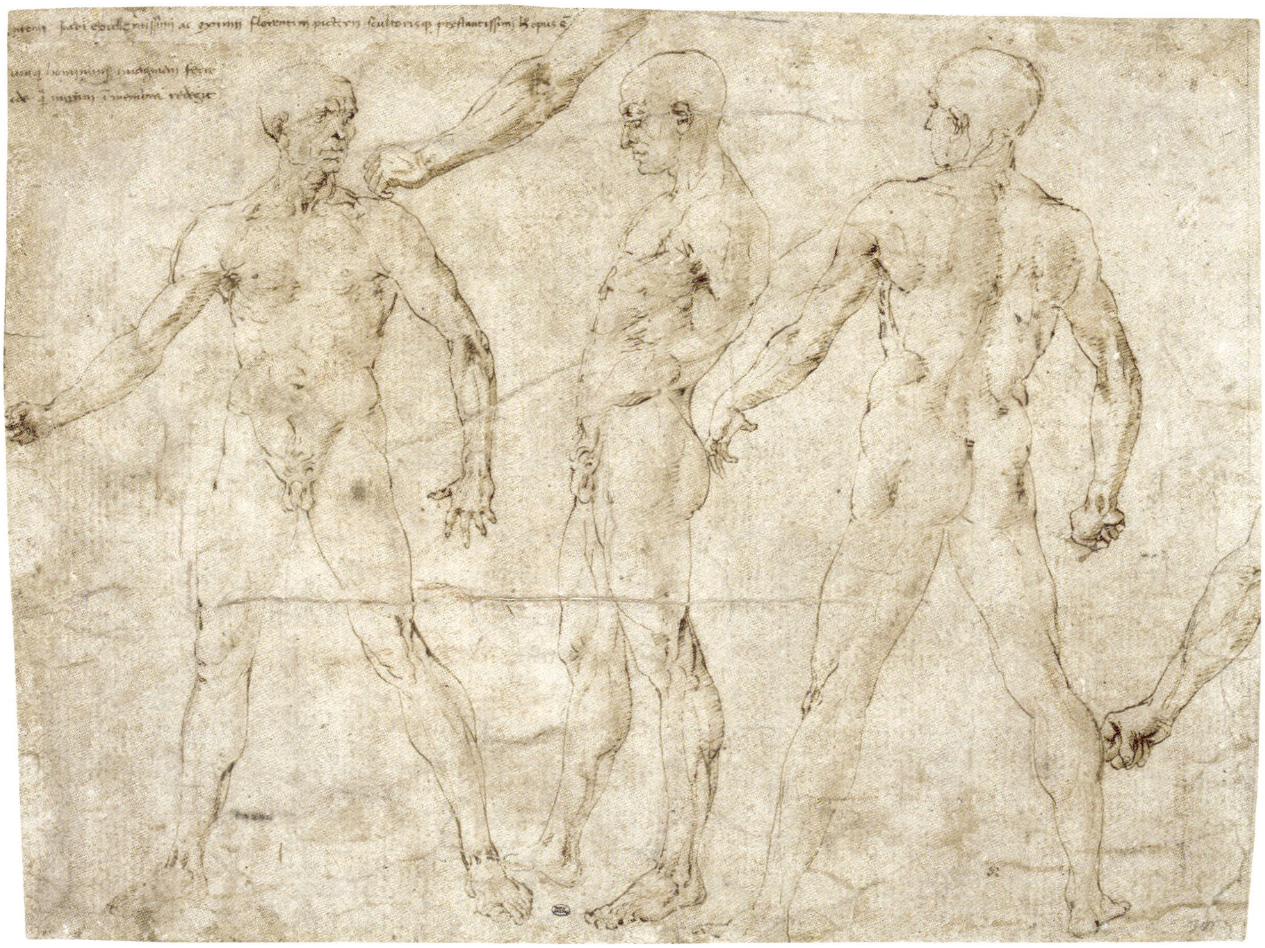

and Della Porta's technique of ink over leadpoint may be revealing: might he have made a preliminary sketch on-site that he redrew on his return to the studio? The drawing by Leone Leoni in this exhibition (cat. 25) includes what appears to be a drawing after an ancient sarcophagus. At least one of the head studies on the page, moreover, appears to have been done from life. If this is correct, he, too, probably reworked the drawing back in the studio, in his case drawing a circle around one head to see how the framing would work and adjusting the features of the face. While it was not impossible to make models outside the workshop—Tetrode and Giambologna both did, and paintings depict the practice—one could carry around only so much wax or clay.

FIG. 13
Antonio del Pollaiuolo
Study of three male nudes and two arms, early 1470s
Stylus, pen and dark brown ink with light wash, on paper, 265 × 357 mm
Musée du Louvre, Paris

Documentation

Drawings allowed sculptors, like painters, to assemble repertories of motifs from various places. Sometimes, however, the works that sculptors reproduced in drawings were their own. Among Pollaiuolo's best-known drawings is one in the Louvre, generally thought to represent views of a model (fig. 13).[60] Its circumstances of production could have been very much like those we see in sixteenth-century engravings of Bandinelli's academy in Rome, which show artists, presumably sculptors, drawing after models (cat. 38).[61]

Studies like these were done in the first place to train the eye and hand, but they could also preserve designs that originated in models that would not themselves survive or to which the draftsman knew he would not later have access. The sculptor Antico is documented to have made drawings after his own models, presumably with this intent.[62] A better example, though, is Cellini. Both the Washington drawing (cat. 26) and his drawing of Juno now in the Louvre seem to have been made after versions of figures that had not yet been carried out in metal. To each of these, Cellini added an inscription, identifying the subject as one he made in France. He may not, as scholars once thought, have produced these two drawings as *ricordi,* but the texts demonstrate that the drawings came to serve as documents of what Cellini was leaving behind on his rash departure.[63]

The present exhibition also includes a group of drawings after Giambologna's models by Pietro Francavilla (cat. 43, 44). These differ from the other drawings just mentioned in that they were made not by the model's inventor but by a member of his studio. Perhaps their production was again related to what we see in the engravings of Bandinelli's academy (cat. 38). There, too, the draftsmen are presumably members of a larger workshop, and the models are those of the workshop master. Giambologna himself seems to have made few drawings, but that was not true of those around him. Like Francavilla, for example, Adriaen de Vries, another northerner who worked for a period with Giambologna, produced a number of sheets. The single drawing by de Vries that has been linked to a specific sculpture is the *Apollo* now in Gdansk (fig. 15). This has been taken to be a preparatory study for a bronze statuette of the same subject now in the Metropolitan Museum (fig. 14).[64] But the drawing shows the sculptural composition in something very close to its final form, and from a low angle. It is not the aspect one would expect a sculptor to find most useful if his intention was to translate the design into three dimensions, but it *is* the kind of drawing a sculptor might generate when examining an existing model from different perspectives. The drawing indicates a view onto the figure from which the profile was particularly attractive.

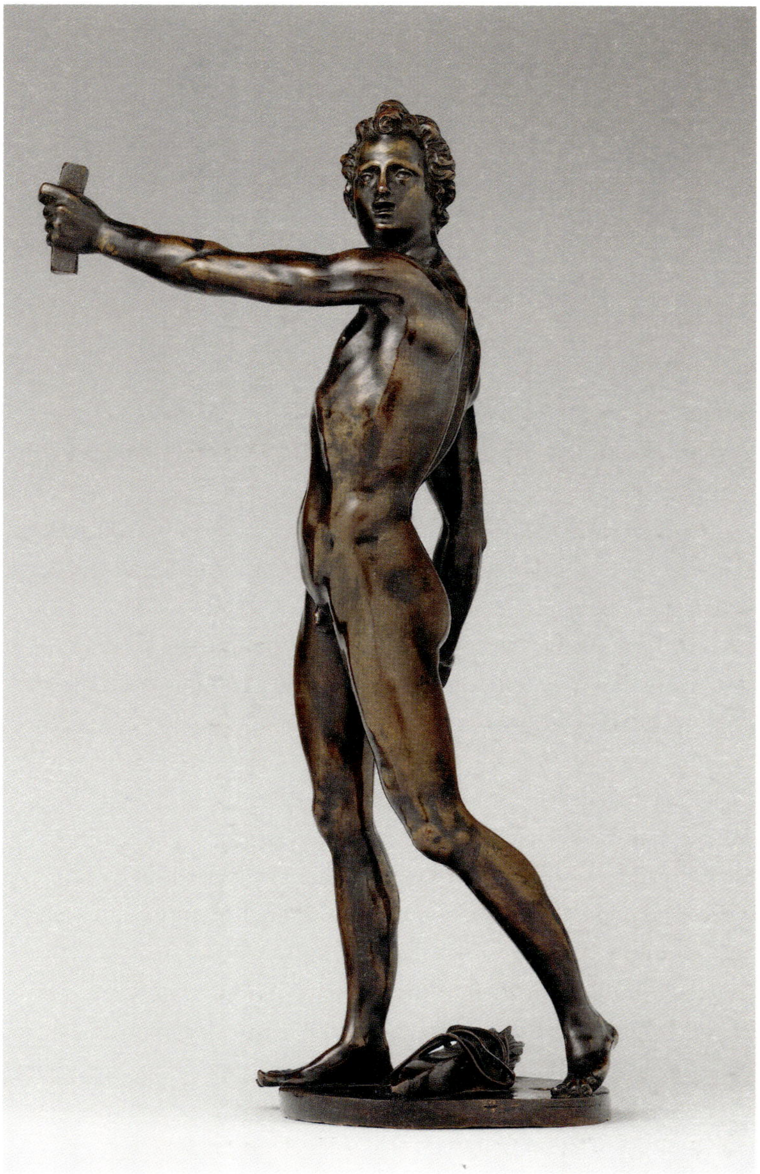

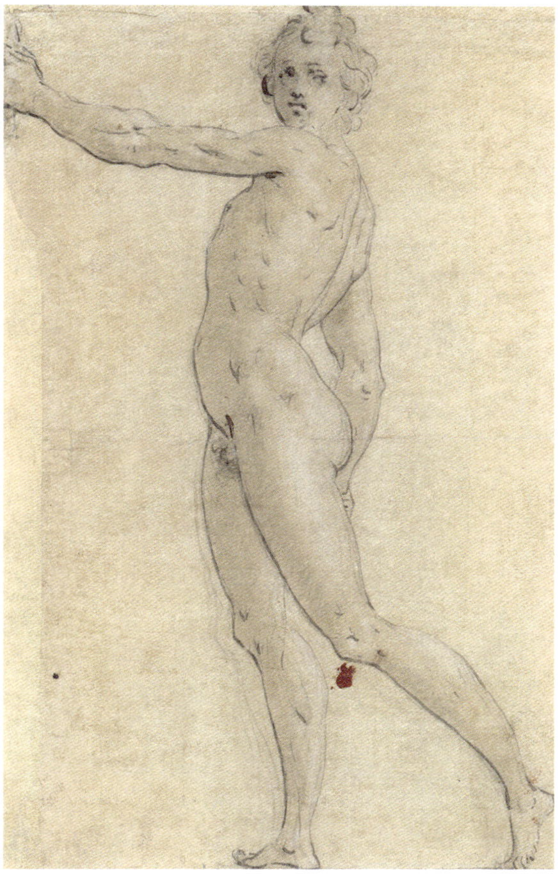

FIG. 14
Adriaen de Vries
Apollo, c. 1594–98
Bronze, 47.6 × 27 × 19.1 cm
The Metropolitan Museum of Art, New York

FIG. 15
Adriaen de Vries
Apollo, c. 1595
Pen and brown ink with wash and white heightening, over black chalk, 294 × 174 mm
Museum Narodowe, Gdansk

Annotation

It has frequently been observed that Renaissance sculptor-draftsmen tended to employ pen and ink as their medium; ink suited the linear virtuosity that all goldsmiths had to cultivate, and it could convey the edges of metal or stone forms.[65] The point should not be pressed too hard. Ink was a common medium, one that painters favored as well. And sculptors from Verrocchio to Bandinelli to Perino da Vinci to Vincenzo de' Rossi also made drawings in chalk, many of them exquisite.

Nevertheless, the ink medium becomes more significant if we step back from the question of style to look at other possibilities it offered. The Pollaiuolo drawing in the Louvre (see fig. 13) bears an inscription in the upper left: "This is the work of the excellent and famous Florentine painter and outstanding sculptor Antonio di Jacopo. When he depicts a man look how marvelously he renders the limbs."[66] The epigram—penned, like the figures themselves, with brown ink—must have been added soon after the drawing was made, since parts of it reappear in early copies, and the copyists could be said to be doing just what the words enjoined, looking at how marvelously Pollaiuolo renders the limbs. Few other media allowed such a direct exchange between artists and writers.

An even more remarkable sheet (fig. 16), also in the Louvre, shows a group of infants drawn by Verrocchio, together with a roughly contemporary Latin encomium to the sculptor:

> They have seen the horse, finished with marvelous art,
> [the horse] that the Venetian nobles entrusted to you.
> Believe me, practical Verrocchio, you ornament of Florence:
> Their eyes will make them love you more and care for you
> and honor you.
> And if Jupiter infuses spirits into [this horse],
> Even Lord Salmonicus would ask you to do the same for him.
> Fare you well who read this.[67]

The final lines employ the same conceit that poets would direct to Benvenuto Cellini's *Perseus* more than half a century later, comparing the pouring of bronze to the divine infusion of spirits into the body.[68] And while the inscription refers to a work not depicted on the sheet—the Colleoni monument Verrocchio designed for the Venetian Republic shortly before his death in 1488—the link between word and image here may be more than incidental. Verrocchio's interest in putto figures would certainly have derived from Donatello, for whom they were a major motif across numerous works. And Donatello and his contemporaries understood the figures to represent what they called "*spiritelli*," little spirits, personifications of the life forces that inhered in wine, blood, water, or liquid bronze.[69] The drawings on this sheet lend the infants an energy that could well be the primary thing Verrocchio was trying to depict.[70] In this case, by contrast to the Pollaiuolo, the lines are directed to Verrocchio himself, though that address may be a poetic conceit intended for other eyes. The point is that, by the later fifteenth century, the images on a page could change the way we read its words, and vice versa.

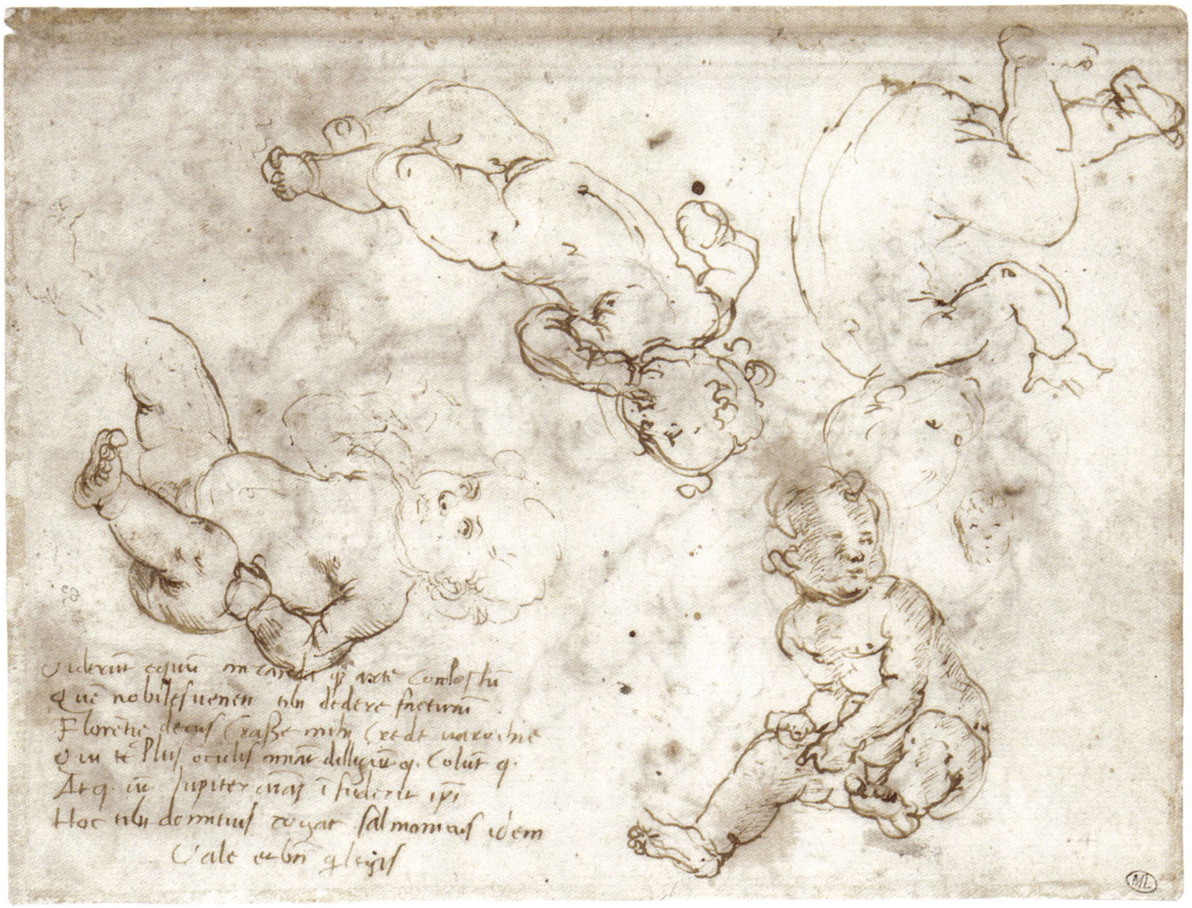

FIG. 16
Andrea del Verrocchio
Four nude infants, late 1460s or 1470s
Pen and brown ink over traces of leadpoint or black chalk, on paper, 158 × 210 mm
Musée du Louvre, Paris

Of course, artists and writers might use the same page for more mundane reasons as well. Drawings were commonly used in the course of establishing contracts between artists and clients. Though the drawings were sometimes done on separate sheets that subsequently became detached from the text portion of the agreement, making even those that survive difficult to recognize, a few have been identified. The only drawing known to have been produced by the Paduan sculptor Giovanni Minelli was formerly attached to the contract commissioning the tomb of Cristoforo Recanati.[71] The only drawing to come down to us from any member of the Della Robbia family is one now in the Ashmolean that served as a contract between sculptor and patron (cat. 17). The sculptor indicated in visual form what he intended to make, and then words pinned down his obligations.[72] Such practices were once more common than these rare surviving examples indicate.[73]

Many of the texts we see on Renaissance sculptors' drawings, moreover, come from the artists themselves. Some of these cases imply nothing more than frugality, the artist using what was at hand.[74] In other cases, however, an inscription offers insight into why the artist chose to draw in the first place. One drawing by Verrocchio that might seem to conform more closely to the expectations set by the Pollaiuolo circle is a pen-and-ink drawing of a horse (cat. 7). It is largely a contour study, lacking even the washes that Pollaiuolo tended to use to model forms. In this case, the contours allowed Verrocchio to record measurements, using the head as the basic modular unit. Measurement would be a basic practice when sculptors studied surviving antiquities; later sculptors from Guglielmo della Porta to Gianfrancesco Susini would write at length about the importance of measure to sculpture, and encomiastic portraits would show sculptors with measuring devices (cat. 45).[75] Drawing and writing in these cases were interdependent forms of learning.

All of this, finally, reminds us of one other reason sculptors turned to drawing: sometimes they needed to record not only forms but also written information. Drawing in pen, more readily than any other medium, allowed sculptors to make notes while they worked. In a letter describing the equestrian monument he was planning for Charles V, Della Porta wrote of "a small drawing of statues and heads modeled after the appropriate antiquities and cast in metal, and on this drawing are written the sizes and names so that it might adorn the study of some prince."[76] Della Porta's architectural drawings commonly use the page not only to imagine spaces but also to specify the functions and dimensions of rooms. Sometimes he explains the rationale behind a design decision.[77] Other times, he uses text to record ideas that the drawing itself could not convey: on one sheet, he wrote, "the eight prisoners on the base will be of metal and the four others on the corners of marble."[78] Della Porta could not draw the difference between bronze and marble; he needed writing for that.

Michelangelo famously used the same page for drawings, poetry, and other texts.[79] In this, he is characteristic rather than exceptional. Nearly all of Benvenuto Cellini's surviving drawings, for example, also contain writings in the artist's hand. One series depicts and explains his proposals for the seal of the Accademia del Disegno in Florence, and one example included in this exhibition (cat. 40) shows an alphabet of tools. This neatly emblematizes the connection between drawing and literacy, the fact that the sculptors who favored the medium were often those accustomed to using pen and paper for other purposes.

For Giorgio Vasari, the concept of *disegno* brought together a medium (drawing) with a notion that art amounted to ideas (design). To say that sculptors "*non possono disegnare in carta*" was not just to describe a difference in practice, it was to intimate something about the relative status of sculptors in the new academic regime. In fact, many—probably most—Renaissance sculptors could draw, and they did so for many reasons. But one thing we see across the categories this essay has sketched is a sense that sculptors often turned to drawing for reasons that Vasari would have understood perfectly, reasons that transcended workaday functions of the *bottega*. When painted portraits of Bandinelli or Giambologna show them as draftsmen, when Della Porta drew an emblem that had Fame arising from something very much like what Della Porta himself made, drawing became a matter of status. It was the medium through which the sculptor could *pursue* fame, presenting his abilities beyond his home city. It was the medium through which he could declare himself an architect, distancing himself from labor and manual craft. Not least, it was the medium that let his art seem most bookish, theoretical, accessible, and appealing even to those who were not artists themselves. Drawing, for sculptors, was a form of ambition.

Notes

I owe thanks to Victoria Avery, Carmen Bambach, Cammy Brothers, Francesco Caglioti, Hugo Chapman, Claudia La Malfa, Fernando Loffredo, Alison Luchs, Francesca Marzullo, Steven Ostrow, Johannes Röll, and Patrizia Tosini for advice, opinions, and references in the course of writing this essay. Luke Syson and Linda Wolk-Simon generously read a complete draft and offered much helpful advice and criticism.

1 Vasari-Milanesi 1906, vol. 1, p. 169: *perchè, quando l'intelletto manda fuori i concetti purgati e con giudizio, fanno quelle mani che hanno molti anni esercitato il disegno, conoscere la perfezione ed eccellenza dell'arti, ed il sapere dell'artefice insieme. E perchè alcuni scultori talvolta non hanno molta pratica nelle linee e ne' dintorni, onde non possono disegnare in carta: eglino, in quel cambio, con bella proporzione e misura facendo con terra o cera uomini, animali ed altre cose di rilievo, fanno il medesimo che fa colui, il quale perfettamente disegna in carta o in su altri piani.*

2 Alessandra Bigi Iotti, for example, notes that there are some 190 drawings related to funerary monuments in the Uffizi, most of them still catalogued as anonymous works. See Bigi Iotti 2008, pp. 757–59.

3 For Vasari's reflections on the drawing, see esp. Degenhart and Schmitt 1968, vol. 1, pp. 342–43. Kenneth Clark did not believe the drawings to be fifteenth-century works at all, but rather sixteenth-century copies of earlier works; see Clark 1970, pp. 262–63.

4 Martin Weinberger, Ulrich Middeldorf, and Bernhard Degenhart and Annegrit Schmitt believed the drawing to be by Antonio Rossellino; Giacomo de Nicola, Leo Planiscig, and Luigi Grassi by Desiderio; Harold Stanley Ede by Donatello. For the fullest discussion and a review of the literature to 1968, see esp. Degenhart and Schmitt 1968, vol. 1. George Goldner accepts the Rossellino proposal and attributes a new drawing to Desiderio in Goldner 1989, pp. 469–73. Joachim Poeschke, by contrast, revives the Desiderio attribution in Poeschke 1993, p. 424.

5 See the discussion in Krautheimer 1952, esp. p. 273.

6 Dominique Cordellier in Cordellier and Marini 1996, pp. 418–19; Syson and Gordon 2001, p. 233.

7 Eisler 1981, n.p.

8 See, for example, the entries by Jaochim Jacoby in Jacoby and Sonnabend 2012, pp. 219–28. See also Davide Gasparotto's essay in this volume, which draws attention to the drawings Giulio Romano, Perino del Vaga, and Francesco Salviati provided for three-dimensional objects.

9 See Tuttle, forthcoming.
10 See Giovanni Morello's entries in Madonna 1993, esp. pp. 350–52, where Morello also attributes a drawing to Prospero Bresciano.
11 For Andrea Sansovino, see Middeldorf 1932, Middeldorf 1933, Middeldorf 1934a, Höfler 1992, and Bigi Iotti 2008. The foundational study of Raffaello da Montelupo was Berenson 1935, revised in Berenson 1938, vol. 1, pp. 255–63. For Montorsoli, see Laschke 1993; for Tribolo, Waldman 2008 and Davis 2013, with earlier bibliography. Giambologna's drawings have not been systematically studied, but see the checklist and notes in Avery 1987, pp. 273–74, and the comments in Cole 2011, pp. 186–91.
12 For Bregno, see Caglioti 1997 and Caglioti 2005, pp. 403–7; for proposals about Danti as a draftsman, Davis 2008; a surviving drawing by Alessandro Vittoria was published and discussed in detail by Reinle 1994, pp. 313–34; it is also discussed in Laschke 1998 and Camerlingi 1999, pp. 47–57. Riccardo Gatteschi attributes five drawings to Baccio da Montelupo with very little discussion in Gatteschi 1993, p. 86.
13 For Bandinelli's debts to painters, see Linda Wolk-Simon's essay in this volume.
14 The drawings seem to be studies or copies after studies for paintings rather than sculptures. See Popham and Pouncey 1952, pp. 61–63.
15 Butterfield 1997, pp. 184–92.
16 Most of the early sculptors who devoted themselves to drawing started as goldsmiths: this is true of fairly prolific draftsmen like Pollaiuolo, Verrocchio, and Raffaello da Montelupo, as well as of the exceptionally prolific Bandinelli. Luke Syson has remarked to me that while Michelangelo's beginnings as a sculptor are usually framed in relation to his connection to Settignano stone carvers, we should also ask what he learned from the goldsmith Bertoldo in the Medici household.
17 See Brothers 2008.
18 I tentatively favor the inference of Krautheimer 1952, that the drawings represent an early project for the fountain, predating its modification and expansion after 1415. In her entry on the drawings in this volume, Carmen Bambach proposes a different possibility, that the two fragments document the monument as it appeared in 1415–16. This would imply that nearly all the figures for the fountain, or at least full-scale models for them, were complete at the point they were rejected, and that Jacopo was asked to redesign a whole series of finished works. The question of who made the drawings is important when considering other attributions to the artist, on which see Seidel et al. 2010.
19 The most recent discussion of the drawing—or more properly, the small painting, which is done in tempera on canvas—is Dominique Cordellier's entry in Paolozzi Strozzi and Bormand 2013, p. 320, with full review of the earlier literature and attribution debate. Cordellier proposes that the figure in the drawing represents either the trace of the Andrea Pisano sculpture that Ghiberti was replacing or *una prima idea personale del Ghiberti destinata a evolversi in seguito*.
20 For the documents, see Krautheimer and Krautheimer-Hess 1982, p. 114.
21 For the argument that the drawing was made in two phases, see Pincus and Comte 2006; Matteo Ceriana's entry in Beltramini, Gasparotto, and Tura 2013, pp. 101–2, reads the drawing in a different way.
22 Howard 1987, p. 29.
23 The best introduction to Sansovino as a draftsman is Boucher 1991, vol. 2, pp. 377–78. The most substantial discussion of the Victoria and Albert drawing is Davies 1994. A comparable scenario may explain an architectural elevation that Peter Ward-Jackson attributed to Leone Leoni. It shows the tomb he executed for Gian Giacomo de' Medici in Milan Cathedral, without its figures. In this case, however, we may be dealing instead with a drawing made by another artist after the tomb or the model Leoni prepared for it. See Ward-Jackson 1979, pp. 82–84.
24 Cellini 1971, p. 416: *Io detti bellissima proporzione al vano ditto; di poi posi sopra il ditto vano un mezzo tondo giusto.*
25 See Claudia Kryza-Gersch's entry in this volume, and for the statue's architectural function, Cole 2003, pp. 39–58.
26 Two different interpretations of the evidence in Holderbaum 1957 and Keutner 1965.
27 See the entry by Kelley Helmstutler in this catalogue.
28 Degenhart and Schmitt regarded the Albertina drawing as autograph, the Louvre canvas as a workshop production; see Degenhart and Schmitt 1968, vol. 1, pp. 289–93, which includes a review of attribution debates to 1968. The Albertina drawing is likewise accepted in Krautheimer and Krautheimer-Hess 1982, p. 129, and in Goldner 1989. The strongest recent case against that attribution is Bellosi 1980.
29 Cellini, "Sopra l'arte del disegno," in Cellini 1980, p. 810: *Addunque questo modo del disegnare è quello che hanno usato i miglior maestri, con il qual si fa la mirabil pittura: e fra i migliori pittori che noi aviamo mai conosciuti, Michelagnolo Buonaroti, nostro fiorentino, è stato il maggiore. E non per altra cosa è stato quell gran pittore che io dico, solo per essere il maggiore scultore di che noi aviamo avuto notizia; e le maggior lode che si dà a una bella pittura e' se gli dice:—La par propriamente di rilievo.—Addunque il rilievo è il vero padre, che è scultura, e la pittura è un de' sua figliouoli. La pittura è una parte delle otto parti principali a che è ubligata la scultura. E questo interviene che, volendo fare un ignudo di scultura o qualsivoglia altra figura vestita o in altro modo (ma sol voglio ragionare dello ignudo, perché sempre si fanno prima ignudi e poi si vestono) e' piglia un valentuomo terra o cera, e comincia a imporre una sua graziata figura; dico graziata perché, cominciando alle vedute dinanzi, prima che ei si risolva, molte volte alza, abbassa, tira innanzi e indietro, svolge e dirizza tutti e' membri della sua detta figura. E da poi che quella prima veduta dinanzi ei se n'è satisfatto, quando ei volge poi la sua figura per canto (che è una delle quattro vedute principali), il più delle volte si vede tornar l'opera con molto minor grazia, di modo che gli è sforzato a guastar di quella bella veduta che ei si era resoluto, per accordarla con questa nuova veduta.*
30 For competing views, see Bambach 2003, pp. 274–77; Wright 2005, p. 137; and Wright's entry in this catalogue.
31 For good discussions of the illustrated sheet, see Alison Wright's entry in Rubin and Wright 1999, pp. 220–21.
32 See Hirst 1988, pp. 33 and 37, and his chapter "Inventing the Motive" more generally for Michelangelo's early practice of devising *primi pensieri* for sculptures on paper.
33 Gramberg 1964, Zeichnungen, vol. 2, p. 82.
34 Waldman 2004, p. 459: *havendomi a disporre a trovare inventione di fontane, farò anchora qualche disegno della fontana di piazza, come mi commando l'Ill.mo Duca, a ciò che possa deliberare a suo piacimento.*
35 See the entry in this volume by the present author and Ulrich Pfisterer, who disagree on the attribution. Still fundamental on Donatello as a draftsman is Degenhart and Schmitt 1968, vol. 1, pp. 243–73.
36 The most extensive discussion of the relief is Matteo Ceriana's entry in Ceriana 2004, pp. 220–21; Ceriana attributes the work to *Giovanni Bellini e bottega*, but notes that he had not personally seen the drawing, which in 2004 was in a private collection.
37 Compare, in addition to the drawing for the tomb of Dante, mentioned above, the drawing attributed alternatively to Antonio and to Tullio Lombardo in the Fogg Museum, discussed most recently in Luchs 2010, pp. 150–51, with further references.

38 Hirst 1988, esp. pp. 48–49.
39 Gramberg 1964, Zeichnungen, vol. 2, p. 107.
40 Gramberg 1964, Zeichnungen, vol. 1, p. 224.
41 Ettlinger 1950.
42 Gramberg 1964, Zeichnungen, vol. 1, p. 101; vol. 2, pp. 34–36, 113–14.
43 See, for example, the exemplary discussion of Johnson 1995.
44 Hirst writes, with regard to a sketch in the British Museum for the Bruges *Madonna*, that its "economy of contour ... suggests a work to be hewn from a block," adding that in the sketch Michelangelo appears to have been considering "what is one of the main views of the group from the central nave." Similarly, Hirst writes of a pen drawing for Michelangelo's Minerva *Christ* that it both shows the principal view and corresponds to the face of the block. See Hirst 1988, pp. 33–34 and 68.
45 Vasari-Milanesi, vol. 1, p. 154.
46 An early drawing by Michelangelo shows one of the Apostles he was designing for Florence Cathedral from the side. We might infer that he made this drawing with the uncut face of the block before him; in the end, however, he did not carve what he had put down on paper. See Hirst 1988, p. 3. In describing how the sculptor should approach marble carving, Cellini writes: "When you are satisfied with your model you draw the principal views of your statue onto the stone, and mind it be well drawn, for if not you may miscut your block. The best method I ever saw was the one that Michelangelo used; when you have drawn on your principal view you begin to chisel it round as if you wanted to work a half relief, and thus gradually it comes to be cut out": Cellini 1967, p. 136. Note that Cellini, by contrast to Vasari, has the sculptor draw on (and presumably then cut into) multiple sides of the block.
47 See the discussion by Raymond Carlson in this volume.
48 For the drawing, see Gramberg 1964, Textband, pp. 31 and 41.
49 I am referring to the studies of the right arm of *Night* in the Ashmolean Museum, discussed in Hirst 1988, p. 62.
50 Gramberg 1964, Textband, p. 86, made a similar point about another group of figures: *Sie breiten sich in die Fläche aus, die der vollplastischen Rundskulptur des Cinquecento durchaus wesensfremd ist. Es muss sich vielmehr um Entwürfe für Relieffiguren auf flächigem Hintergrund handeln.*
51 Scholten 2003, pp. 19–20.
52 On these *charte degli uccelli*, see Degenhart and Schmitt 1968, vol. 1, p. 290. For Ghiberti's letter, Milanesi 1854–56, vol. 2, p. 120.
53 For the movement of Michelangelo's drawings, see Hirst 1988, pp. 20–21.
54 See, for example, Hirst 1988, pp. 74–75, and Waldman 2004, pp. 281, 482.
55 For this general topic, see Wood 2005.
56 Francesco Caglioti attributes six drawings after the Column of Trajan to Paolo Romano; see Caglioti's essay in Pinelli 2000, vol. 1, pp. 817–18. Michael Jaffé's entry in Jaffé 1994, pp. 160–61, instead took them to be by a "a fifteenth-century Florentine draftsman in Rome."
57 See the thorough discussion in the entries by Carmen Bambach in this volume.
58 Wright 2010, pp. 46–50, no. 13, and Röll 2012, pp. 249–54.
59 Jaffé 1994, nos. 53–56, and Turner 1986, nos. 100–101.
60 See esp. the excellent discussion in Wright 2005, pp. 158–62, with a review of the essential earlier literature.
61 See Denise Allen in Franklin 2005, pp. 282–83, as well as the entry by Linda Wolk-Simon in this volume, which observes that at least some of the models in these engravings are Bandinelli's personal inventions.
62 Eleonora Luciano, "Antico: Pier Jacopo Alari Bonacolsi (c. 1455–1528)," in Luciano 2011, p. 11.
63 See the entry by Claudia Kryza-Gersch in this volume. If Bambach is right that the Jacopo della Quercia drawings in London and New York document the fountain at a moment before its revision, those would provide a much earlier example of the kind of drawing we see also in Cellini. Perhaps the figures in Jacopo's drawings, too, were models rather than stone carvings.
64 See Kaufmann 1984 and the same author's entry in Scholten 1999, p. 248.
65 Wright 2005, p. 155.
66 I take the translation from Alison Wright's entry on the sheet in Rubin and Wright 1999, pp. 244–45. The Latin reads: *Antonij jacobi excellentissimi ac eximij florentinj pictoris scultorisque prestantissimi hoc opus est/ umquam hominum imaginem fecit/ [v]ide quam mirum in membra redegit.*
67 I owe thanks to Ulrich Pfisterer for help with the translation, which differs from that in Seymour 1971, p. 173, and in Bambach 2003, p. 252. The Latin reads: *Viderunt equum mirandaque arte confectum/ Quem nobiles veneti tibi dedere facturum / Florentiae decus crasse mihi crede Varochie/ Qui te plus oculis amant dilliguntque coluntque/ Atque cum Jupiter animas infuderit ipsi/ Hoc tibi dominus rogat Salmonicus idem/ Vale et bene qui legis.*
68 Cole 1999, pp. 215–35.
69 See Dempsey 2001 and Pfisterer 2002.
70 Looking back at Verrocchio from a distance of nearly a century, the sculptor Baccio Bandinelli would single out this kind of subject as Verrocchio's most important legacy: *Ma de' moderni maestri ch'è piaciuto imitare tale maniera è istato Andrea del Verochio; li piacque tanto imitare simile età, che vi fecie una asoluta maniera, ma fu tropo cho' le cicie resegata; nientidimancho fu i' modo acieta a' sua disciepoli, che molto fu imitate. Ma Lionardo da Vinci, chome valente disegniatore, ne chavò quelo che fusi posibile di fare banbini di tale età: chon tanta dolcieza e bela grazie li dipinse tale che è superato tuti. I' tale età e modi di dintorni e muscholi di banbini da late che servono a Nostre Done e storie de' Nocienti o a' virtù di Charità vogliono esere nel modo deto; posto che di più età posino istare, nientedimancho tale ordine e maniera pare più chonveniente.* Bandinelli perceived Leonardo's debt to Verrocchio and also associated it with drawing. See Waldman 2004, p. 906.
71 The drawing was discovered and published in Carpi 1930, but according to Pincus and Comte 2006, p. 742, it is now lost.
72 See Rachel Boyd's catalogue entry in this volume.
73 See O'Malley 2005, with further references.
74 This seems to be the case with a number of Bandinelli's drawings. See Waldman 2004, pp. 545, 642, 680, 692, 727.
75 See, for example, the comments on measure in Della Porta's "Memoriali et discorsi sopra le opera fatiche fatted a Mi[chelangelo] per la sedia App.," in Gramberg 1964, Textband, p. 117. Susini would put the word into the title of his 1618 "Disegni e misure e regole d'attitudine del chorpo umano," which includes a number of ancient and modern sculptures annotated with measurements.
76 Gramberg 1964, Zeichnungen, vol. 1, p. 120: *Anchora si narra uno diesegno piccolo de statue et teste formate sopra le proprie antiche e getate di metallo, et in ditto disegno è scritto la grandezza e li nomj per adornare uno studio a qual si voglia principe.*
77 See, for example, Gramberg 1964, Zeichnungen, vol. 1, p. 56, no. 33.
78 Gramberg 1964, Zeichnungen, vol. 2, p. 127, no. 141: *li otte presoni da baso serano di metallo le 4 di alto sarano di marmo suli canti trofei.*
79 Barkan 2010.

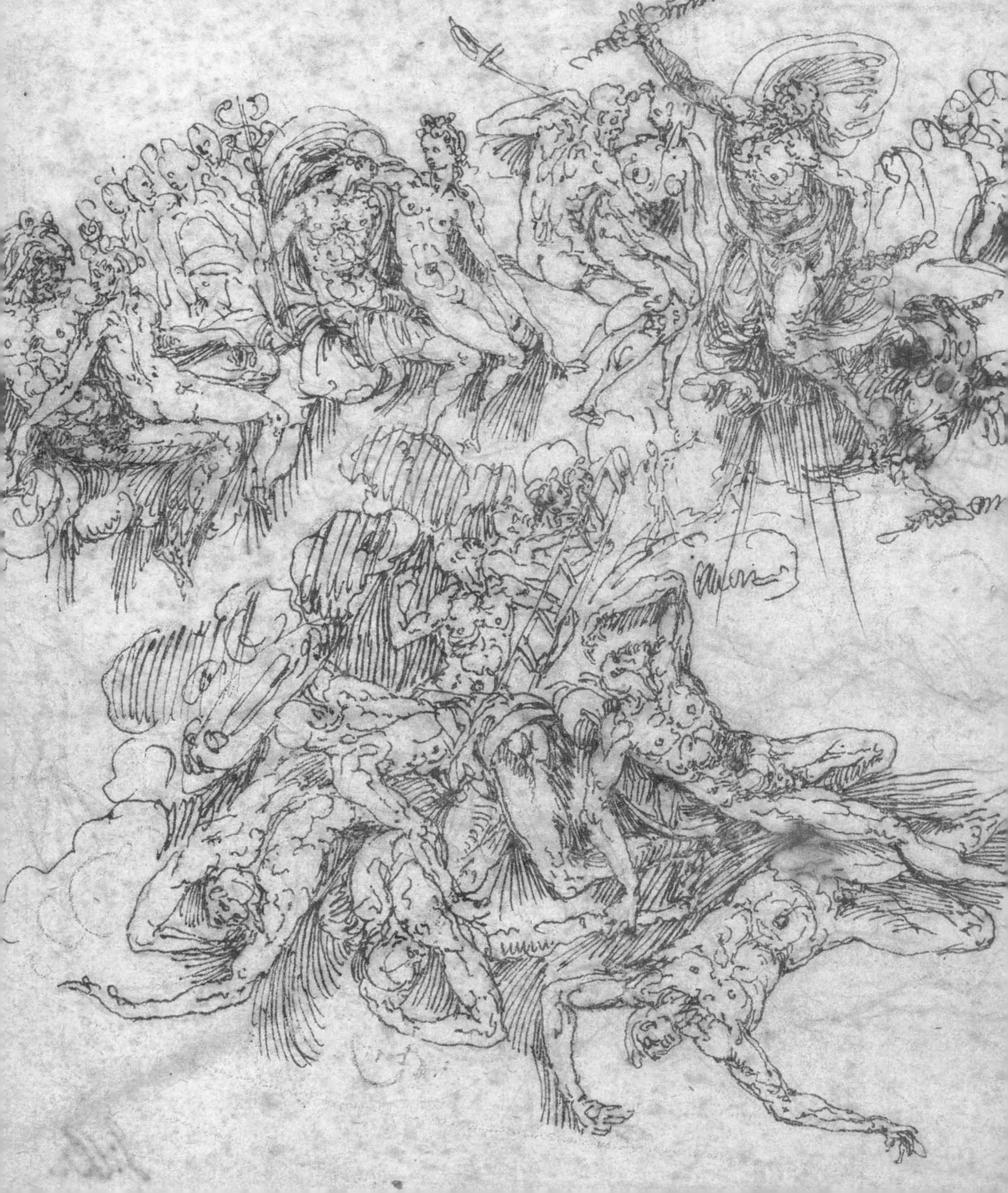

The Power of Invention: Goldsmiths and *Disegno* in the Renaissance

DAVIDE GASPAROTTO

The supremacy of disegno

In the *Commentaries,* written at the apex of his career, Lorenzo Ghiberti offers one of the most extraordinary statements of the ambition and self-awareness of a Renaissance artist. In the autobiography that concludes the second *Commentary,* he recalls with pride that "few things of importance that are made on our Earth have not been drawn and arranged by my hand," giving the assurance that he provided "to many painters and sculptors and statue makers ... very many models of wax and clay ... and for painters [he had] designed many things."[1]

Ghiberti's assertion is entirely confirmed by documentary evidence and surviving artworks. We know, for example, that in 1418 Ghiberti gave the goldsmith Guariento di Giovanni—who had to produce two candlesticks for Orsanmichele—a drawing *in quodam folio magno de papiro*, probably a model of 1:1 scale.[2] A single project drawing of this type, albeit in a reduced scale, survives: it is a study for *St. Stephen within a Tabernacle* in the Louvre (fig. 17), which, despite not being entirely autograph, is of fundamental importance for the visualizing of a graphic project from Ghiberti's workshop, as well as for reconstructing the original idea for the tabernacle that was never built.[3] The statue is inserted into an elegant architectural setting, very similar to that of the nearby *St. Matthew*, with a mixture of elements that are classical (the triangular pediment and the fluted pilasters with Corinthian columns) and Gothic (the pointed arch of the niche and the exquisite urns situated above the cornice)—an idea of unambiguously Ghibertian taste.

Ghiberti's career reached a crucial turning point in 1401, when as a young man he won the celebrated competition to execute one of the doors of the Florentine Baptistery, defeating six other artists, among them his peer Filippo Brunelleschi. Both Brunelleschi and Ghiberti came from a solid training in goldsmithery, an art that, by virtue of the complexity of its technical procedures and of the intrinsic value of the materials involved, was

CAT. 36 Guglielmo della Porta
The Fall of the Giants (detail)

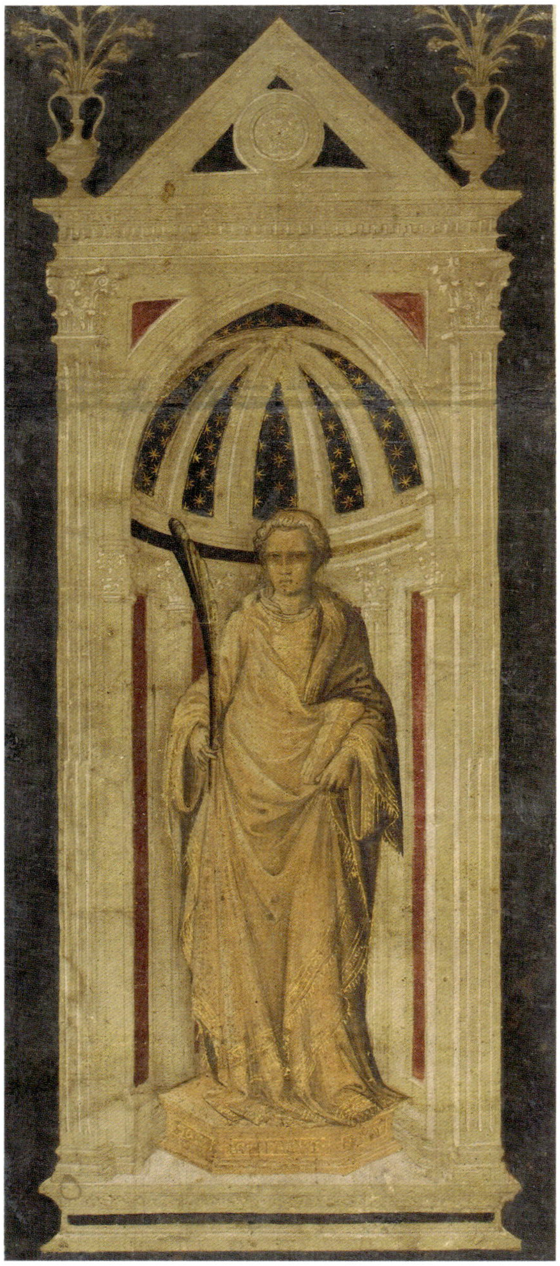

FIG. 17
Lorenzo Ghiberti and workshop
Study for the statue of St. Stephen at Orsanmichele, 1427–29
Tempera with gold highlights, on canvas, 69.8 × 30.5 cm
Musée du Louvre, Paris

considered at the time to be at the heart of all the arts, enjoying far greater prestige than painting or sculpture.[4] The notion of *disegno* occupies a central place in the *Commentaries*: for Ghiberti *disegno* is the "origin and foundation of every art."[5] It is the visible manifestation of *ingegno* (talent) and of the capacity of the artist to conceive works. It is an act of the hand and the mind at the same time. Unlike the limited meaning that we give to it today, *disegno* in the Renaissance possessed a broad spectrum of senses that ranged from the concreteness of the graphic plan to the most theoretical character of "invention," and even to abstract judgment of value ("to have good *disegno*").[6]

In fifteenth-century Florence the goldmith was characterized above all as a designer, and from the practice of goldsmithery emerged artists who pursued prestigious careers not only as goldsmiths but also as architects, painters, and sculptors. Other than Brunelleschi and Ghiberti, we need only recall that Masolino da Panicale, Antonio del Pollaiuolo, Andrea del Verrocchio, Sandro Botticelli, and Domenico Ghirlandaio all trained with goldsmiths. In 1471 the Florentine patrician Giovanni Rucellai, enumerating the artists whose works he possessed, employed the term "master of *disegno*" in relation to Maso Finiguerra and Antonio del Pollaiuolo,[7] who are, in fact, well documented not only as goldsmiths but also as designers for other artisans, in particular for embroiderers and makers of marquetry.[8] Finiguerra specialized in the practice of niello, the incision of a design on a sheet of silver using a burin whose grooves were subsequently filled with *nigellum* (an ink with a base of silver, lead, copper, and sulfur). Using this technique Finiguerra realized sophisticated and ambitious compositions, such as the pax with *The Coronation of the Virgin* in the Bargello, which is identifiable with the niello for the Baptistery of Florence for which he was paid in 1452 (fig. 18).[9] Finiguerra made numerous sulfur casts and prints on paper from nielli. He employed a complex process that was originally developed to control the phases of the work and to preserve a memory of the completed niello but subsequently became a formidable means of diffusing the original "inventions" and the capabilities of the artist as a draftsman.[10]

Goldsmiths were among the first to recognize the enormous potential of the intaglio print as a means to promote their fame, as is well demonstrated by the famous *Battle of the Nudes* by Antonio del Pollaiuolo (fig. 19).[11] The realization of a design demanding such great labour, the unusually large size of the sheet (approx. 410 × 610 mm) and the proud apposition of the

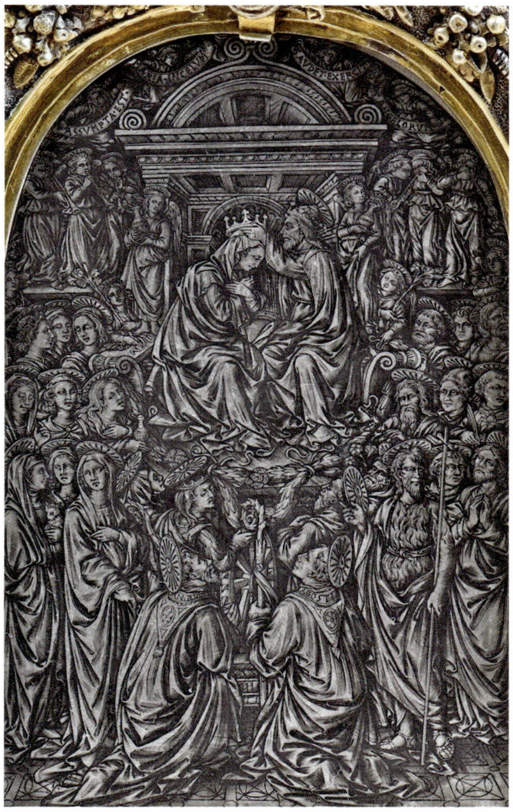

FIG. 18
Maso Finiguerra
Pax with *The Coronation of the Virgin*, 1452–55
Silver with niello inlay, 21.5 × 15.5 cm
Museo Nazionale del Bargello, Florence

FIG. 19
Antonio del Pollaiuolo
The Battle of the Nudes, 1465–70
Engraving, 424 × 609 mm
Cleveland Museum of Art

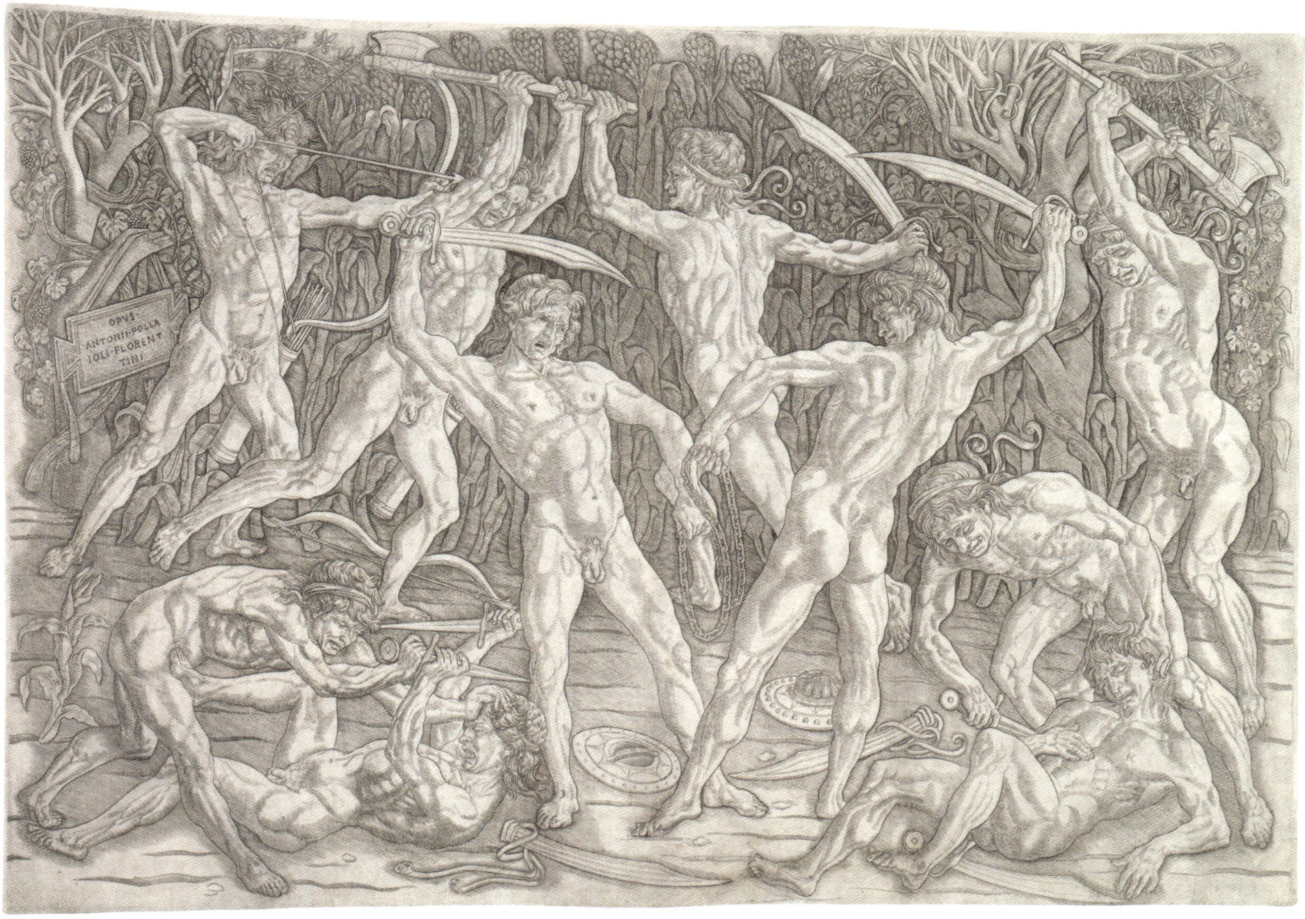

signature are eloquent indices of Pollaiuolo's ambitions. They show his desire to prove his extraordinary capability as a designer able to represent the nude human figure in movement as well as to master perfectly a rather new technique. The close rapport in mid-fifteenth-century Florence between goldsmiths, *disegno*, and engraving on metal plates is exemplified in the print attributed to Baccio Baldini, *The Planet Mercury and His Children* (c. 1460–65):[12] Mercury, protector of merchants, is flying over a goldsmith shop in which the master intently uses a burin to engrave a design on a sheet of metal while an assistant shows products to a potential client.

Roughly a century later, Vasari placed the concept of *disegno* at the center of the theoretical framework supporting his *Lives*: *disegno* is the father, the foundation of the three arts—architecture, painting, and sculpture—while all the other artistic techniques are implicitly downgraded to more distant kin of the greater arts.[13] This extremely influential vision would structure the modern "system of the arts" de facto until at least the eighteenth century.[14] In this new hierarchy goldsmithery plays a subordinate role, and in many pages of the *Lives*, especially in the second edition of 1568, we see an implicit critical judgment against goldsmiths.[15] Although Vasari recalls on multiple occasions that in fifteenth-century Florence goldsmiths were generally good draftsmen, he does not miss the opportunity to emphasize the weaker graphic skills of his goldsmith contemporaries, as well as their dependence on models of other masters. In his eyes the goldsmith was simply an excellent artisan capable of realizing with *pazienza* (patience) and *diligenza* (diligence) the design executed by a painter.

In the case of an artist such as Valerio Belli of Vicenza (whom he much admired), Vasari writes that "in his works [he] makes use either of the drawings of others or of antique intaglios."[16] It is true that Belli availed himself of the help of painters for his own compositions, as is testified by a superb drawing by Polidoro da Caravaggio at Windsor of *The Kiss of Judas*, which was preparatory for a composition that Belli engraved in crystal.[17] And again between 1520 and 1521 Belli repeatedly requested that Michelangelo provide him with a drawing to engrave on a "beautiful, large stone," specifying through an intermediary that "he would not mind having a depiction of an ancient sacrifice or another subject; it matters only that it is by your hand."[18]

Other sources testify to the insufficient talent for *disegno* and invention of the other great maker of crystal intaglios of the first half of the sixteenth

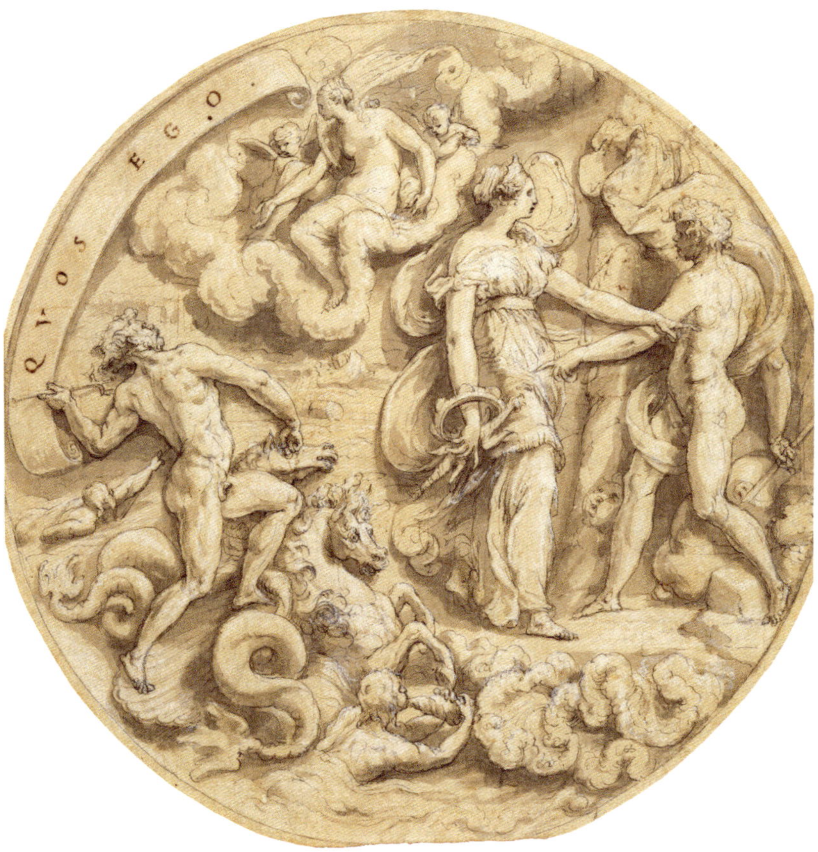

FIG. 20
Perino del Vaga
Juno Visiting Aeolus and Neptune Calming the Tempest, c. 1540
Pen and ink and wash, on paper, 220 × 215 mm
Royal Library, Windsor Castle

century, Giovanni Bernardi da Castel Bolognese. In a February 1540 letter to the medalist Alessandro Cesati, Annibale Caro provided the elaborate program for the reverse of a medal in honor of Giovanni Guidiccioni of Lucca, which was to represent the famous *Quos ego* scene from the *Aeneid* with Neptune placating a tempest. In the letter he records that, having found himself passing through Castel Bolognese, he asked Bernardi to make "a bit of a sketch on the reverse of the medal of the bishop, and it is such that I am ashamed to send it to you: therefore, because I desire to have a drawing that is excellent, I request that as soon as possible you send me one by your hand, or by Perino del Vaga."[19] It is known that a superb drawing by Perino corresponds perfectly with the invention requested by Caro, a sign that at a certain point the artist had to satisfy the wish of the great *letterato* (fig. 20).[20] The medalist Cesati seems to be an exception in an environment where goldsmiths were reduced to mere executors of the inventions of great masters. Vasari, in fact, valued his "universality" in *disegno*, the "grace" and "goodness" of his compositions—a judgment that is above all confirmed by Michelangelo's praise of a medal that Cesati coined for Paul III.[21]

It is precisely within this profoundly transformed context that we find the insistent assertions that pervade Benvenuto Cellini's autobiography and treatises regarding his own skill as an inventor and draftsman. Their near obsessiveness shows a goldsmith who grew up in the Florentine tradition reacting against a world that was already radically changed.[22] In different passages of his autobiography, Cellini recalls that masters of the caliber of Giulio Romano and Michelangelo himself had declared that he had no need "of the drawings of others,"[23] while the sculptor Pietro Torrigiano, observing Cellini's graphic efforts, had told him that his drawings were "more by a sculptor than by a goldsmith."[24] Even Porzia Chigi, astonished by some of Cellini's designs of mounts for jewels, "said that he drew too well for a goldsmith."[25] The sixteenth-century prejudice toward goldsmiths' capacity as inventors and designers further reveals itself in the words that Cellini puts in the mouth of his eternal rival, the sculptor Baccio Bandinelli: "for these goldsmiths, it is necessary to make drawings of these beautiful things."[26]

The son of a goldsmith that Cellini himself describes as a "man of merit,"[27] Baccio Bandinelli realized his immense ambition for success in the competitive Florentine arena precisely through the strenuous exercise of drawing, a practice in which he reached such heights of excellence even to merit the praise of Vasari (who was never favorable toward Bandinelli). Vasari wrote that "[Bandinelli's] drawing—toward which one sees he was more attentive than anything else—was of such excellence that it overcame all of his innate defects, and it makes him known as a rare man of this art."[28] In a letter of 1551 Bandinelli clarifies the essential value that he held drawing to assume in relation to *invenzione*:

> I have finished another drawing to please Your Excellency, whom I beseech, that if you see fit to hear the cause for which at present I have not sent it to you, it is because I find myself very disposed to find very beautiful inventions, and of such things I have just begun another, and I will not be able to continue with finishing them all. But it is necessary, if I want to vary the inventions, that I see in front of my eyes all the drawings that I make, because for me each one sheds light upon the other in understanding the truth of the errors of each, because I see them in comparison, and in this way I will vary and improve them in such a way that they will please Your Excellency, because drawings are not made for another reason than to see them together in comparison.[29]

The trajectory of Bandinelli—from goldsmithery to sculpture—is comparable to that of Leone Leoni, Vincenzo Danti, and Cellini, all goldsmiths who at a certain point in their careers made the leap to monumental sculpture (above all in the form of the large bronze cast), which they perceived as a more noble commitment likely to leave a more durable trace. A propos of this, we should recall that Giambologna—at least according to the historian Scipione Ammirato—was discontented with Duke Francesco I de' Medici, who "had employed him to make little birds, little fish, lizards and other minute animals" instead of to realize "colossal sculptures and large machines" toward which his ambition drove him, and that his talent would finally be recognized only when the new Grand Duke Ferdinando I had entrusted him with the production of the equestrian monument dedicated to his father, Cosimo.[30]

Unlike Bandinelli or Danti, however, Cellini continued to consider himself the heir of the glorious Florentine goldsmith tradition and never repudiated the specific nature of his training. In the polemic that was triggered in Florence when it was necessary to choose an emblem for the seal of the fledgling Accademia del Disegno in 1563, Cellini strenuously defended the right of goldsmithery to be elevated as the fourth alongside the three "arts of *disegno*" (architecture, painting, and sculpture). Shortly thereafter, personifications of the three arts were incorporated into the Florentine tomb of Michelangelo, and Vasari assigned them absolute centrality in the second edition of his *Lives*, letting goldsmithery slide inexorably toward the realm of the "industries."[31]

What happened? When and why did goldsmiths begin to lose ground to painters and sculptors in *disegno* and *invenzione*? Goldsmiths' progressive loss of status can be associated with the growing intellectual ambition of painters and sculptors along a trajectory that—at the theoretical level—can be followed from Leon Battista Alberti's *On Painting* to Leonardo's thoughts on the *paragone*. The new ambition of Renaissance artists to elevate the "mechanical arts" (which they practiced) to the status of the "liberal arts" led to a growing and conscious distinction between "invention" and "production," with an emphasis on the intellectual character of artistic practice. The crucial turning point is represented by the theoretical reflections of Leonardo, for whom painting was above all a mental discourse, an "exertion of the mind."[32]

The primacy of invention (of which the visible manifestation is *disegno*) over execution is particularly evident in the field of the decorative arts, within which the two were increasingly assigned to distinct artistic personalities

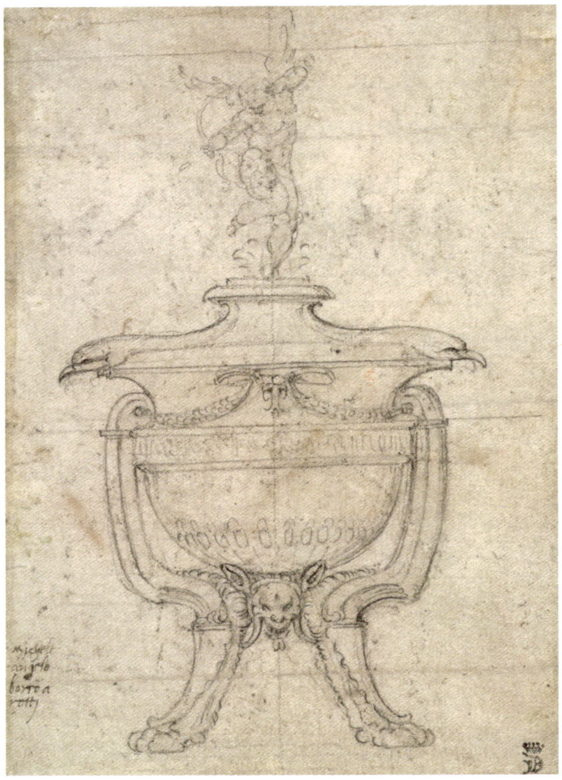

FIG. 21
Michelangelo Buonarroti
Design for a saltcellar, 1534–41
Black chalk, on paper, 214 × 155 mm
British Museum, London

with different skills and competencies. The model of the court artist who might be asked to furnish inventions for tapestries, silver, jewels, and metals, epitomized in the fifteenth century by masters such as Pisanello and Mantegna, became the norm in the sixteenth century, when it was typical for the design of an object—a vase, a saltcellar, a jewel, a medal, an engraved rock crystal, a tapestry—to be the work of a celebrated painter (Raphael, Michelangelo, Giulio Romano, Perino del Vaga, Francesco Salviati), while the manufacture was the work of a specialized artisan, occasionally known and admired for his technical ability but in many cases anonymous.

In the shadow of Michelangelo and Raphael: monumental models and decoration all'antica

In the sixteenth century Michelangelo embodies—through his simultaneous practice of architecture, painting, and sculpture—the concept and the supremacy of *disegno* as the foundation of all the arts. In this sense, the famous presentation drawings for Tommaso de' Cavalieri represent a new status reached by drawing, understood as an autonomous work of art in all its effects, a reflection of Michelangelo's incomparable mastery of invention. Although loath to involve himself in projects for the decorative arts, even Michelangelo at times capitulated to requests of friends (such as the goldsmith Giovanni di Baldassare, "il Piloto") and of insistent clients for *invenzioni* destined to the luxury arts.[33] The most notable instance is none other than the drawing for a saltcellar destined for the duke of Urbino, Francesco Maria della Rovere, a project that is fortunately documented by a beautiful sheet in the British Museum and by a letter from an agent of the duke dated 4 July 1537 (fig. 21):

> In response to one of your [letters] of the 22nd of the past [month], I tell you that the model of the saltcellar in relief was finished months ago, and now under way in silver [are] several animal paws, where it will be necessary to place the body of the saltcellar, and around this vessel there go certain festoons with a few masks, and on the cover a figure in complete relief, with a few other leaves, which I will organize according to Michelangelo and following what appears in the completed model as is said above.[34]

The letter is interesting for several reasons: it speaks of a "model" (which could have been made of terracotta or wood or lead) that represented the intermediate stage—that of a trial—between the sheet and the completed work,[35] and it lingers on the *all'antica* motifs of the decoration. Notwithstanding a few somewhat original details, such as the bird heads of the cover, the overall appearance of the saltcellar—in particular the form of the vessel, with feet made of lion's paws and the satyr mask at the center —recall an antique work of great fame in the sixteenth century, the so-called Tazza Cesi, a marble conch that at that time adorned the Cesi garden in Borgo Vaticano.[36]

The increasing adoption of large-scale models for creations of goldsmithery in small dimensions is a meaningful indication of the will to compete with the monumental arts: Cellini recounts that at a young age he had produced a saltcellar in the form of a "sarcophagus based on that in porphyry that is in front of the door of [Santa Maria della] Rotonda," which is to say copied from the large porphyry sarcophagus that could be found at that time in front of the portico of the Pantheon, greatly admired since the fifteenth century for its elegant form.[37] The same model also served Giulio Romano in a drawing, now in Chatsworth, for another silver saltcellar, intended for Ferrante Gonzaga.[38]

The two most famous objects of goldsmithery of the sixteenth century —Cellini's saltcellar (Kunsthistorisches Museum, Vienna) and the Farnese Casket (Museo di Capodimonte, Naples)—clearly betray the desire to equal the magnificence and grandeur of monumental sculpture and architecture. The mentality used to approach such creations is the same with which Vasari exalts the "*maniera* of little figures" of the miniaturist Giulio Clovio, the "small and new Michelangelo."[39] The Farnese Casket, the production of which took nearly twenty years (1543–61), is truly an epitome of the diverse competencies necessary to realize an especially complex work of goldsmithery: the metal part of the exceptionally precious casket, commissioned by Cardinal Alessandro Farnese, was realized by Manno Sbarri, a Florentine goldsmith apprenticed to Cellini; the oval reliefs in crystal were engraved by Giovanni Bernardi after drawings furnished by Perino del Vaga, perhaps on the basis of an "iconographic program" devised by Fulvio Orsini, the cultured librarian of the cardinal; the statuette of Hercules on top derives from a model prepared by Guglielmo della Porta;

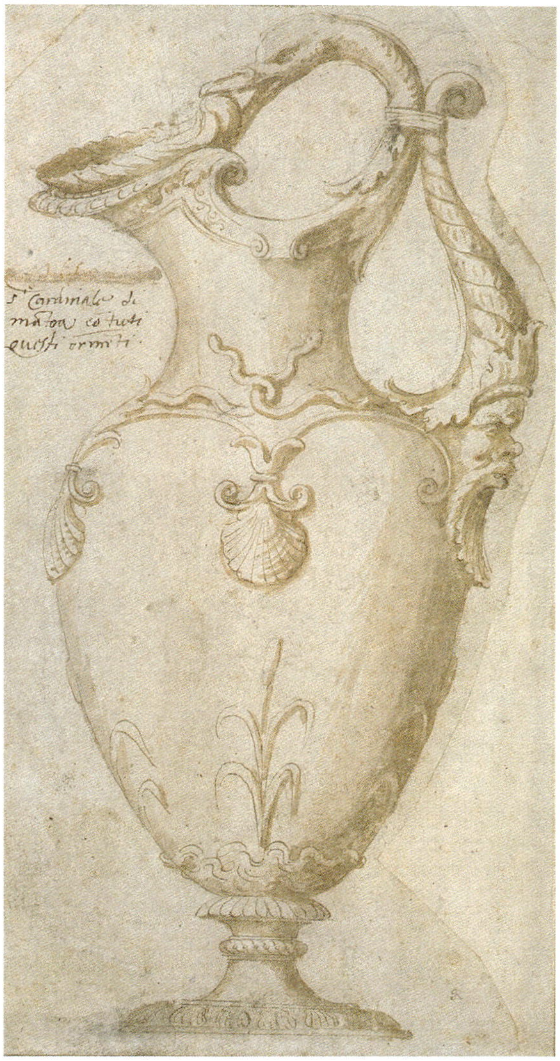

FIG. 22
Giulio Romano
Design for a ewer, c. 1540
Pen and ink and wash, on paper, 281 × 152 mm
Victoria and Albert Museum, London

and the overall design of the object, it has been reasonably argued, was conceived by Francesco Salviati.[40]

If we move from the comprehensive structure of such objects to consider the question of their embellishment, we could liken Michelangelo's drawing for the saltcellar to a page in the first book of *Architecture* by Sebastiano Serlio (Paris, 1545), which contains detailed instructions for the geometrical construction of diverse vases, but entrusts the "beautiful ornaments" to the imagination of the artist.[41]

The greater complexity required of *invenzioni* for increasingly demanding clients who were thirsty for novelty and originality, the necessity to master a new *all'antica* decorative repertoire, the capacity to lay out *istorie* with a degree of complexity unprecedented in the figural tradition (as in the case of those who engraved crystals)—all of these things help to explain the decline of the goldsmith as a designer and inventor and the requirement for famous artists to design "unique" objects.

Above all it is around Raphael and his workshop that there accumulates an important array of evidence in this regard. Certainly Raphael made drawings for plates and vessels: it is worth recalling that in 1516 Isabella d'Este acquired a pair of gilded silver bowls and two bronze carafes "in an antique style, designed by Raphael," perhaps executed by Antonio da San Marino or by Cesarino Rossetti da Perugia, two goldsmiths with whom the Umbrian artist had documented collaborative relationships.[42] Nearly all of Raphael's pupils inherited from their master not only a willingness to collaborate with goldsmiths but also the mastery of an up-to-date decorative register. Giovanni da Udine furnished, with the mediation of Pietro Aretino, drawings for glass vessels to be manufactured in Murano: in a letter of 1531 Aretino records the shipment of several glass vessels to the duke of Mantua, Federico Gonzaga, so that the duke could admire the "appearance of antiquity designed by Giovanni da Udine."[43] Ten years later Aretino again requested from Giovanni da Udine "a full sheet of those designs to be made in glass," insisting again on the artist's "facility with the antique."[44] The most dedicated among Raphael's pupils, Giulio Romano, was also the most extraordinary sixteenth-century designer of decorative arts objects. According to Vasari he was "rich and copious with invention and artifice."[45] A large group of surviving drawings by Giulio are those associated with objects of goldsmithery for the Mantuan court of the Gonzaga (fig. 22).[46] Though unfortunately none of the objects

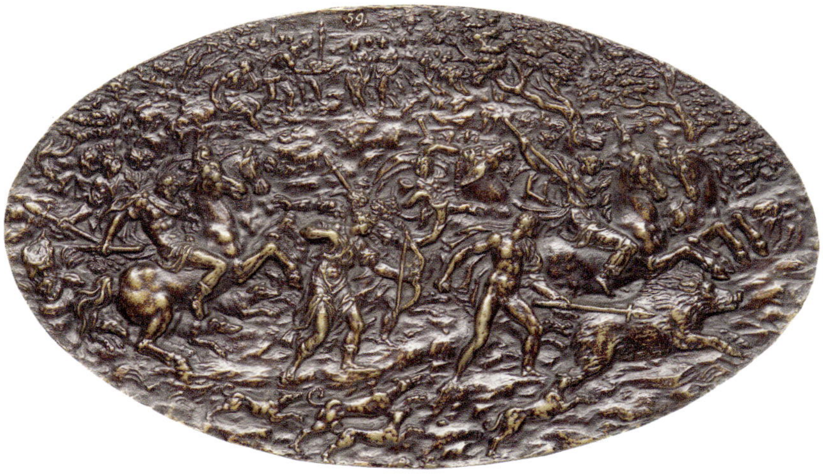

FIG. 23
After Guglielmo della Porta
Meleager Hunting the Calydonian Boar, 1560s
Bronze, 13.2 × 23 cm
Kunsthistorisches Museum, Vienna

designed by him survives, analyzing his drawings together with a remarkable amount of archival documentation makes it possible to follow, sometimes even step by step, the translation by goldsmiths of Giulio's inventions into metal, with all of difficulties of a technical-practical nature that came between the *disegno* and its concrete realization.[47]

In the workshop of Guglielmo della Porta: invention, production, copyright

The case of the workshop of the sculptor Guglielmo della Porta is exemplary for illustrating the role of *disegno* and the notion of *invenzione* in the environment of goldsmithery in the sixteenth century. Guglielmo led one of the largest workshops in Rome during the middle years of the century, and from it emerged some of the most prominent goldsmiths and sculptors of the next generation, so that the biographer Giovanni Baglioni characterized it as the "great school."[48] Guglielmo conceived a series of grandiose sculptural projects; apart from the splendid tomb of Pope Paul III, he did not manage to bring any to completion, but his vivid imagination exerted itself in drawing and in the creation of small models, many of which were intended for the production of luxury objects.

Particularly significant is a series of sixteen reliefs, eight oval and eight octagonal, illustrating episodes from Ovid's *Metamorphoses*. The series is known in different versions with various degrees of quality and finish, the most complete of which is that in bronze in the Kunsthistorisches Museum in Vienna (fig. 23).[49] It is evident, however, that the series was conceived from the outset to be reproduced in precious metal (gold or silver) by specialized artisans. Baglione attributes the invention of the series to the Flemish sculptor Jacob Cobaert (c. 1535–1615), known in Italy as Cope (or Coppe) Fiammingo.[50] On the other hand, various scholars, above all Werner Gramberg, have drawn attention to a group of drawings undoubtedly by Guglielmo's hand that are the original *invenzioni* for the *Metamorphoses* reliefs (cat. 34, 36),[51] and the sculptor declares himself the author of these inventions in his diary, which is now in Düsseldorf together

FIG. 24
Jacob Cobaert (?) after Guglielmo della Porta
Meleager Hunting the Calydonian Boar, c. 1560
Terracotta, 14 × 9.8 cm
Victoria and Albert Museum, London

FIG. 25
Cesare Targone, attributed to, after Guglielmo della Porta
Meleager Hunting the Caledonian Boar, c. 1580–1600
Tooled and chased gold on slate veneered with lapis lazuli and adorned with four carnelian cabochons, 14 × 24.5 cm
Private collection

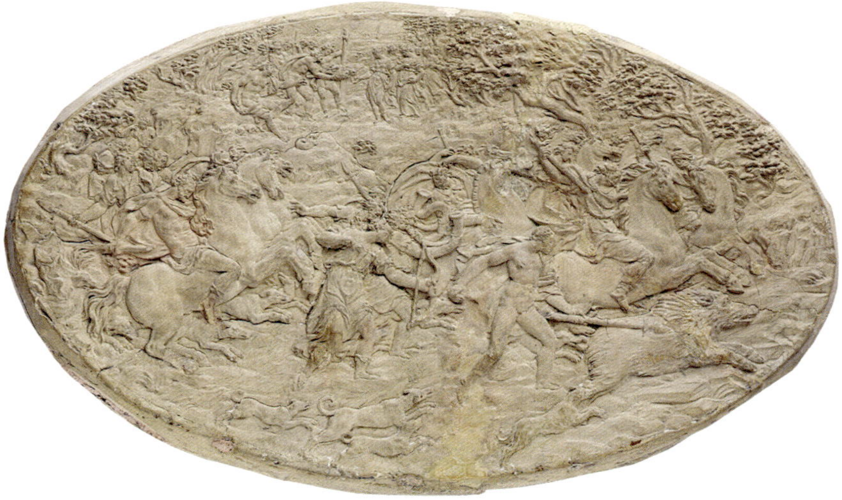

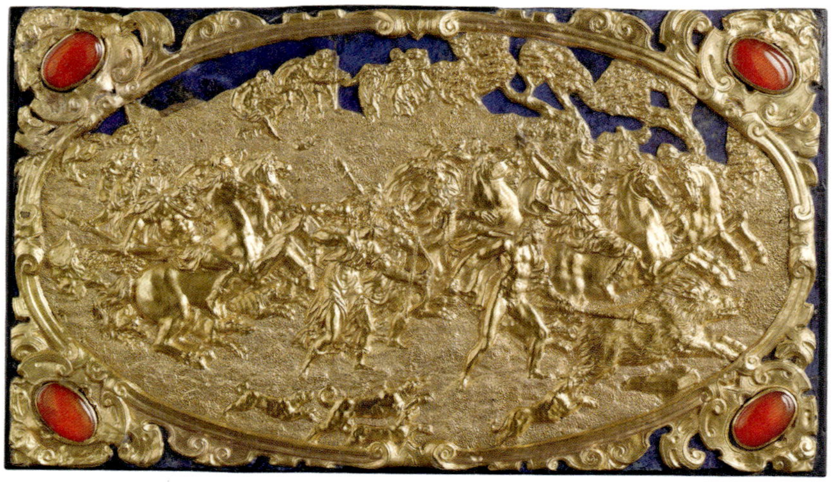

with two books of drawings.[52] In the inventory compiled after his death in 1577, among the workshop models were found "twelve little stories of Ovid to adorn tables made by the hand of Coppo,"[53] which Gramberg enticingly proposed to identify with two surviving terracotta models in the Victoria and Albert Museum in London (see fig. 24).[54] It is therefore possible to imagine that in the workshop Cobaert made the models of the Ovidian myths on the basis of drawings by Guglielmo della Porta, perhaps with the assistance of the master himself.

Another source helps clarify the role of Cobaert and several crucial aspects of the workshop's operation. In 1609 Teodoro della Porta, son and heir of Guglielmo, accused the caster Sebastiano Marchini and the goldsmith Antonio Gentili da Faenza of having stolen from the Ufficio del Piombo several of his father's models made of clay, wax, and plaster, among which were the clay models for the *Metamorphoses* series.[55] Teodoro's principal concern was that these artisans were using the models to produce new casts in precious metal, thereby infringing his right as heir to the property of his father's workshop to the use of the original molds. The various witnesses summoned by the judge provide a fascinating and complex picture of workshop practices in Rome during the late sixteenth century, and they demonstrate how much the production of these artisans depended on the use of drawings and compositions of masters who were endowed with greater creative capacities. They also show how much Guglielmo della Porta's *invenzioni* were still sought after more than thirty years after his death.[56] The documents from this process reveal how quickly the copies of the original models, both in clay and in wax, were produced and sold in the city by various other artisans. It is in this context that we can consider a series of eight reliefs in gold worked with embossing and applied on a ground of lapis lazuli with carnelians inserted in the corners, now divided among the Bode Museum in Berlin, the Metropolitan Museum of Art (see cat. 35), and a private collection (fig. 25).[57] These were clearly made by a goldsmith of great ability, and in my opinion they are the work of the Venetian artist Cesare Targone, based on inventions of Guglielmo della Porta (compare fig. 26 and cat. 35). The important role of "design leader" that Guglielmo had in Rome in the middle decades of the sixteenth century is further demonstrated by his close collaboration with Gentili, one of the greatest goldsmiths of that time. Gentili's most ambitious and best-documented work is the group of liturgical objects (a cross and two candlesticks) donated in 1582 by Cardinal Alessandro Farnese to St. Peter's Basilica.[58] The cross is signed, and a few years later (1587) Antonio even commissioned the painter Bernardino Passerotti to make a print that reproduced it, in which he proudly defines himself as *Aurifex inventor* (*Antonius Gentiles faentinus Aurifex Inventor anno suae aetatis LI*). The truth, however, is much more complex. In the first place the cross was commissioned in 1561 from a different goldsmith, the Florentine Manno Sbarri—perhaps helped by a drawing by the painter Salviati—who left the work incomplete at the time of his death in 1574.[59] In the second place, we can demonstrate that some significant figurative elements were based on Guglielmo della Porta's inventions: the *Crucified Christ* derives from a model that the great sculptor developed and repeatedly replicated, while the powerful Michelangelesque telamons on bases have been identified with two splendid terracotta models that are without doubt to be attributed to Guglielmo as well.[60] It is evident that Gentili's pretenses as "*inventor*" had more to do with self-promotion than with his actual skills as designer and draftsman.[61]

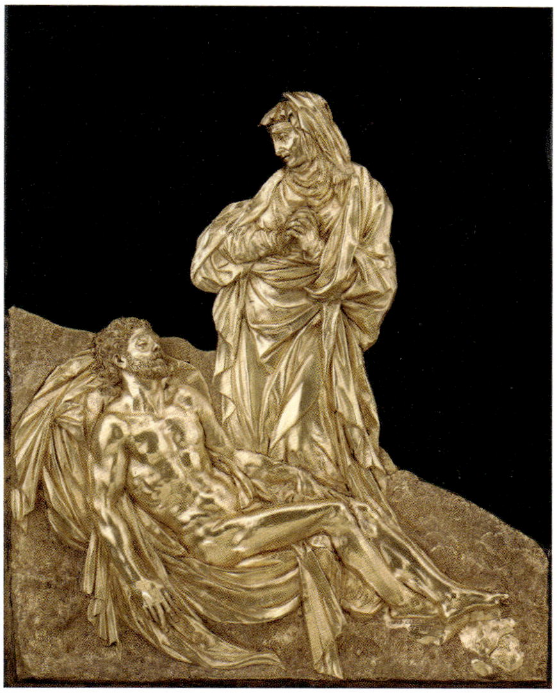

FIG. 26
Cesare Targone after Guglielmo della Porta
The Virgin Mourning the Dead Christ, c. 1580–1600
Chased embossed gold on obsidian, 28.9 × 26 cm
J. Paul Getty Museum, Los Angeles

Translated by Raymond Carlson

Notes

1 Ghiberti 1998, p. 97: *poche cose si sono fatte d'inportanza nella nostra terra non sieno state disegnate et ordinate di mia mano*"; "*a molti pictori e sculptori e statuarii ... moltissimi provedimenti di cera e creta ... et a' pittori disegnato moltissime cose.*

2 Krautheimer and Krautheimer-Hess 1982, pp. 390–91, docs. 118–19.

3 See most recently Dominique Cordellier in Paolozzi Strozzi and Bormand 2013, pp. 320–21, no. III.17; on Ghiberti's workshop, see Galli 1998.

4 On the position of goldsmithery in the system of the arts during the period between the Gothic and the Renaissance, see esp. the important work of Marco Collareta (2008; 2010; 2012; 2013).

5 Ghiberti 1998, p. 47: *Origine e fondamento di ciascuna arte*. On *disegno* as the foundation of goldsmithery, see also what Antonio Manetti writes in the *Life of Brunelleschi*: "And in that profession [goldsmithery] he quickly became very much universal with respect to *disegno*, which quickly appeared in him very marvelous" (*E in quel mestiero [l'oreficeria] diventò presto molto universale rispetto al fondamento del disegno, che subito apparì in lui molto maraviglioso*): Manetti 1992, pp. 50–51.

6 On the significances of *disegno* in the Renaissance, see esp. Holman 1997, pp. 3–14; Syson and Thornton 2001, pp. 135–82.

7 See Rucellai 1960, vol. 1, pp. 23–24.

8 On Finiguerra as a designer of inlay, see Haines 1983, pp. 165–75; on Pollaiuolo as designer for embroiderers, see Wright 2005, pp. 258–85.

9 See Marco Collareta in Collareta and Capitanio 1990, pp. 136–41, no. 39.

10 On Maso Finiguerra and chalcography, see Whitaker 1998, pp. 46–71.

11 See Langdale 2002; Wright 2005, pp. 176–81.

12 See Landau and Parshall 1994, p. 98.

13 Vasari-Bettarini 1966, vol. 1, pp. 26, 111, 172.

14 Kristeller 1951–52.

15 Fundamental to this topic is Collareta 2006.

16 Vasari-Bettarini 1966, vol. 4, p. 625: *si valse sempre o de' disegni d'altrui o degl'intagli antichi nelle sue cose.*

17 See John Shearman in Burns, Collareta, and Gasparotto 2000, p. 287, note 1; for a discussion of the relationship between the drawing by Polidoro da Caravaggio and Belli's translation of it into crystal, see Davide Gasparotto in Burns, Collareta, and Gasparotto 2000, pp. 87–88.

18 See Manuela Barausse in Burns, Collareta, and Gasparotto 2000, p. 398, note 15: *non gli dà noia più sacrifizio che altra materia, e li basta solo che sia di man vostra.*

19 See Caro 1957, vol. 1, pp. 178–81, no. 134: *un poco di schizzo per rovescio de le medaglia del Vescovo, ed è tale che mi vergogno a mandarvelo: pure sarà con questa, perché desidero d'averne un disegno che venga dal buono, e vi priego che quanto prima me ne mandiate uno di vostra mano, o di Perino del Vaga.*

20 See Hirst 1965, pp. 569–71; on the drawing and the medal, see also Elena Parma in Parma 2001, p. 211, nos. 101–2, and Attwood 2003, pp. 38–41.

21 Vasari-Bettarini 1966, vol. 4, p. 628: "and Michelangelo Buonarroti himself, watching him, with Giorgio Vasari present, said that the time for the death of the art had arrived, given that he could not see better" (*e Michelangelo Buonarroti stesso, guardandole, presente Giorgio Vasari, disse che era venuto l'ora della morte dell'arte, perciò che non si poteva veder meglio*). In reality, however, for the reverse of this medal, which represents Alexander the Great kneeling in front of the high priest of Jerusalem, Cesati used an invention of Francesco Salviati, which is known through a beautiful drawing in red chalk and a print by the Master I.R.S. On the drawing, the print, and the medal, see Alessandro Nova in Monbeig Goguel and Hochmann 1998, pp. 280–83, nos. 111–12.

22 On Cellini, Vasari and goldsmithery, see Collareta 2003.

23 Cellini 1971, "Vita," I, XL, XLI: *delli disegni d'altri.*

24 Cellini 1971, "Vita," I, XII: *più da scultore che da orefice.*

25 Cellini 1971, "Vita," I, XIX: *disse lei che troppo ben disegnavo per orefice."*

26 Cellini 1971, "Vita," I, XLV: *a questi orafi, di queste cose belle bisogna lor fare e' disegni.*

27 Cellini 1857, p. 8.

28 *Il suo disegnare, al che si vede che egli più che ad altro attese, fu tale e di tanta bontà, che supera ogni suo difetto di natura, e lo fa conoscere per uomo raro di questa arte*: Vasari-Bettarini 1966, vol. 5, p. 276; on Bandinelli as a draftsman, see most recently Viatte 2011, pp. 19–42, and now Linda Wolk-Simon's essay in this volume.

29 *Io ho finito un altro disegno per farne la voglia di Sua Eccellenza, la quale supplico, che si degni udire la causa perché al presente io non l'ho mandato; si è perché io mi trovo molto disposto a trovar bellissime invenzioni, e di già ne ho cominciato un altro, e non resterò di seguitare a dar fine a tutti. Ma egli è necessario, se io voglio fare variate le invenzioni, che io mi vegga tutti i disegni, che io fo, innanzi a gli occhi, perché l'uno mi fa gran luce all'altro in conoscere la verità degli errori di ciascuno, perché gli veggo al paragone, ed in questo modo varierò e migliorerò in modo che piaceranno a Sua Eccellenza, perché i disegni non si fanno per altro che per vederli insieme a paragone*: Bottari and Ticozzi 1822, vol. 1, pp. 94–95, no. XXXIX; see Barkan 1999, p. 305, for a more extensive comment.

30 Ammirato 1594, p. 107: *lo aveva adoperato in far uccellini, pesciolini, ramarri et altri animali minuti*; *colossi e machine grandi*. See Gasparotto 2006, p. 93; on the ambition of Giambologna to distinguish himself from goldsmiths and to operate on a grand scale, see Cole 2011, pp. 68–70, 78–82.

31 See Cole 2002, pp. 121–27; Collareta 2003; Collareta 2006.

32 Leonardo 1993, p. 144: "*fatica de mente.*"

33 For Michelangelo and the decorative arts, see most recently the important contribution of Clifford 2002.

34 *In resposta de una de V.S. de' vinti due del passato, gli dico che più mesi essere finito il modello della saliera de rilievo, e principato de argento alcune grampe de animali, dove se ha a possare il vaso della saliera, et a torno di esso vaso ci va certi festoni con alcune mascare, et i' nel coperchio una figura de rilievo tutta, con alcuni altri fogliami, secondo Michelangelo ordinò e secondo appare nel modello finito detto di sopra*. For the drawing, see Wilde 1953, p. 105, no. 66; Gaetano Milanesi published the letter of the agent of the duke of Urbino, Girolamo Staccoli, in his commentary to Vasari's *Life* of Michelangelo (Vasari-Milanesi 1906, vol. 7, pp. 383–84).

35 On models for works of goldsmithery, of which only very rare examples are conserved, see Syson and Thornton 2001 (p. 163, fig. 128, shows the model in terracotta for a ewer conserved in the Gilbert Collection, London).

36 See Bober and Rubinstein 1986, pp. 124–25, no. 92.

37 Cellini, "Vita," I, XIV: *cassonetto d'argento ritratto da quello di porfido che è dinanzi alla porta della Retonda.* For the *fortuna* of this sarcophagus, see Gasparotto 2003, p. 145.

38 See J.T. Martineau in Chambers and Martineau 1981, pp. 196–97, no. 189.

39 Vasari-Bettarini 1966, vol. 6, p. 217.

40 On the Farnese Casket, essential are Robertson 1992, pp. 38–49; Riebesell 1995, pp. 58–69; Linda Martino in *Collezione Farnese* 1996, pp. 134–35, no. 4.3.

41 Serlio 1584, p. 22.

42 See Luzio and Renier 1893, pp. 230–34: *de desegno et fogia antiqua, desegnati da Raphael.*

43 Aretino 1957, vol. 1, p. 20, no. 6: *foggia de l'antiquità disegnata da Giovanni da Udine.*

44 See Bottari and Ticozzi 1822, vol. 3, pp. 103–4: *un pien foglio di quei disegni da mettere in vetro ... spiriti della facilitade antica.*
45 Vasari-Bettarini 1966, vol. 4, p. 67: *ricco e copioso d'invenzione e di artifizio.*
46 On Giulio Romano as a designer of silverware, see Jane Martineau in Chambers and Martineau 1981, pp. 195–96; Ugo Bazzotti in Polano 1989, pp. 454–57; Taylor 2007.
47 On this topic, see the excellent studies of Holman 2000 and Rebecchini 2012.
48 Baglione 1649, p. 100: *Gran Scuola*. On the workshop of Guglielmo della Porta, see Dickerson 2008.
49 See Planiscig 1919, pp. 188–92, nos. 395–410, pls. 19–26; see also Cannata 1982, pp. 72–76; Susanna Zanuso in Di Lorenzo and Frangi 2007, p. 124, no. 43.
50 Baglione 1649, p. 152; Gramberg (1968, pp. 89–92) and Riebesell (2003, pp. 50–54) have hypothesized that examples of reliefs in precious metals could constitute the ornament of a table of a type akin to the Farnese Table in the Metropolitan Museum of Art, New York (58.57). Pietro Aldobrandini documents an example of a table put together with silver reliefs (González-Palacios 1988, pp. 45–46).
51 Gramberg 1960; Gramberg 1968.
52 See Gramberg 1964, Textband, p. 100, no. 180, and p. 108, no. 200.
53 Masetti Zannini 1972, p. 305: *dodici storiette d'Ovidio per adornare tavole fatte per mano di Coppo.*
54 Gramberg 1960, pp. 42–43.
55 Bertolotti 1881, pp. 120–61.
56 For the reuse of Guglielmo's models, see Middeldorf 1977 and Walker 1991.
57 See Bange 1922, pp. 2–3, nos. 8–13, pls. 5–6 (with a professed provenance from the Borghese collection in Rome) for the reliefs in Berlin; Phillips 1939 for the Metropolitan relief; Christie's, London, 9 December 2010, lot 285, for the relief in a private collection.
58 On the cross and the Vatican candlesticks in relation to Manno Sbarri and Antonio Gentili, see principally Lotz 1951; Chadour 1982; Dickerson 2008, pp. 37–39.
59 A trace of this first phase of labor could be the splendid sheet by Francesco Salviati in Turin showing the project for the base of a cross and a candlestick (see Cristina Riebesell in Monbeig Goguel and Hochmann 1998, pp. 256–57, no. 99).
60 On the influential model of the crucifix developed by Guglielmo della Porta and replicated multiple times, see Gramberg 1981; the two models in terracotta, now in a private collection, are published by Susanna Zanuso in Di Lorenzo and Frangi 2007, pp. 118–21, no. 40.
61 For a different interpretation of the position of goldsmiths in Rome of the second half of the sixteenth century, see Dickerson 2008.

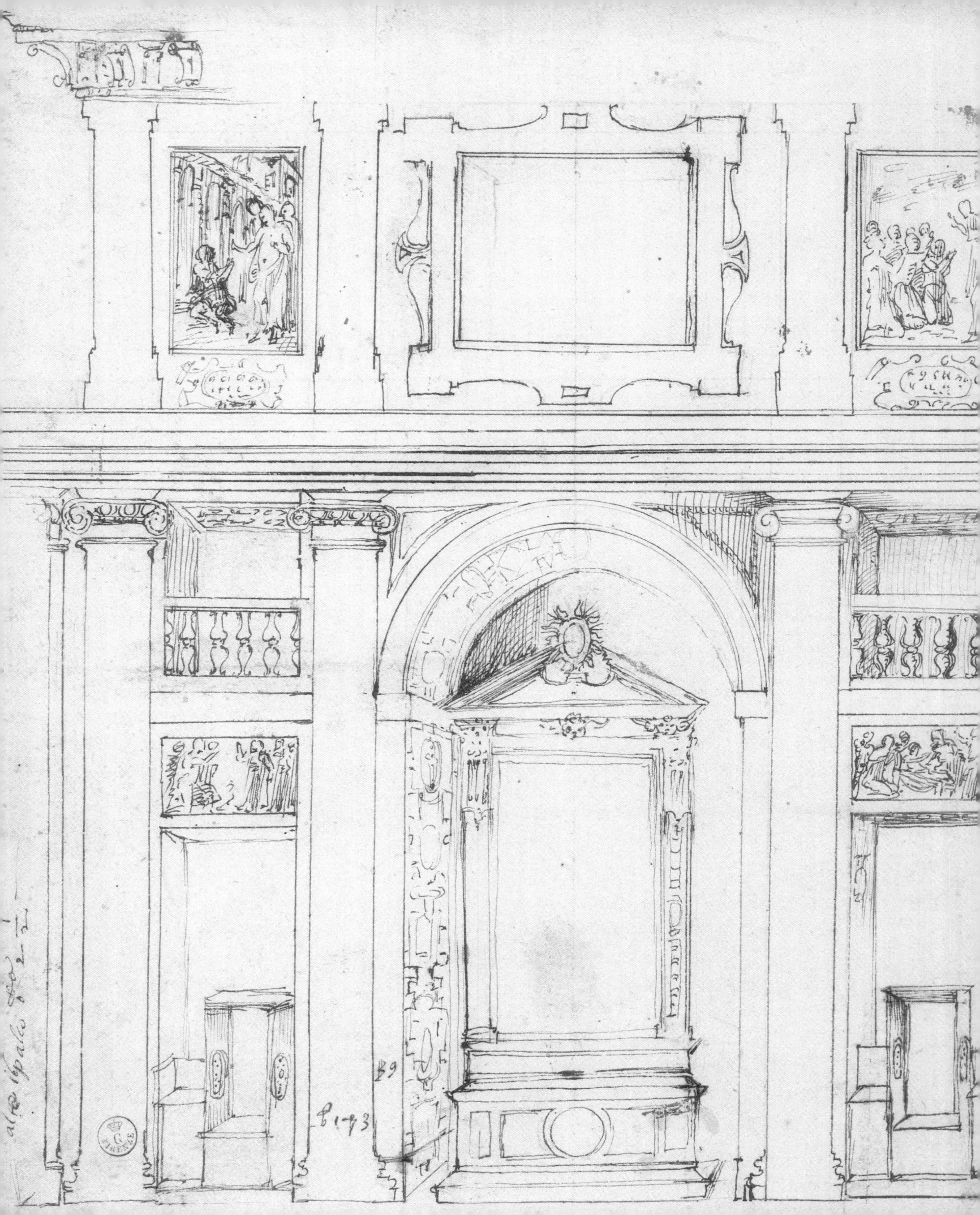

The Sculptor-Architect's Drawing and Exchanges between the Arts

ALINA PAYNE

TO WRITE ABOUT SCULPTORS-ARCHITECTS and their drawings is to strike at the very heart of the relationship between the visual arts—the relationship between two three-dimensional arts and their mutual interaction with the planar dimension of drawing and its medium, paper. That this should be an expected, even unproblematic relationship was forcefully argued in one of the most celebrated testimonies of the Renaissance, Giorgio Vasari's *Lives of the Artists* (1550, second edition 1568), which collected between the covers of one book the lives and artistic achievements of the Italian artists of his day. Yet despite Vasari's insistence that drawing (*disegno*, the Italian term also meaning design) was the meeting point of the arts and justified their coming together into the Accademia del Disegno in Florence (started in 1563), this relationship was always fraught and certainly not to be taken for granted.

Indeed, for all Vasari's assurance of artistic overlap, the few surviving drawings by sculptors seem to belie this since widely accepted commonplace. One reason for such paucity may be that the flatness that drawings inevitably imposed made them impractical tools for designing figures in the round and hence inhibited sculptors' use of them.[1] In the case of sculptors who were also architects, however, the nature of the engagement with drawing may be expected to have been different. After all, architects were increasingly voracious users of pen and paper in the sixteenth century, precisely during the time Vasari raised the issue of *disegno* as a shared practice uniting the arts, and remained so for a long time. How architecture and sculpture met and intersected on the terrain of drawing is what this essay proposes to investigate. Of course, it cannot be but an attempt at sketching some areas that deserve further attention. However, as several episodes analyzed below begin to suggest, one such promising area is the sculptor-architect's engagement with the relief as means of understanding three-dimensional form in close dialogue with drawing. Also a classic site of overlap with painting, the relief then may well emerge as the perhaps unexpected terrain where all the arts productively converged.[2]

CAT. 42 Bartolomeo Ammannati
Project for the interior side elevation of the church of San Giovannino, Florence (detail)

The paragone

Vasari himself was the first to cast doubt on the arts' unity based on *disegno* (a major theme of the 1568 edition of his book) when, after extolling its virtues and deep relevance to all three arts, he proceeded to note how often sculptors dispensed with drawing by carving with their iron tools directly into virgin stone.[3] However, the terminological ambiguity between design and drawing contained in *disegno* helped suggest that all artists drew, an implication that Vasari certainly reinforced in his definition of the accomplishments of *terza età* artists from Leonardo onward who had brought the arts to perfection. The ambiguity was probably deliberate, for in the first edition Vasari used the words *schizzi* (sketches) and *contorni* (contours) to describe the act of drawing in his introduction to the work, whereas in revising these passages later he only used the term *disegno* to make his case for its central role.[4] Yet when he turned to introduce the individual arts—and he focused on painting, sculpture, and architecture, clustering the minor arts under their capacious umbrellas—he made no mention of drawings when attending to sculpture. Indeed, when he explained the sculptor's working process he traced the stages leading up to the finished piece across a series of small- to full-scale models of soft and easily carved materials.[5] In a much more developed statement in the 1568 edition he bracketed out the sculptors altogether, recognizing implicitly that in practice they did not need to turn to drawing.[6] He had already admitted as much in his 1547 (1546 according to the Florentine calendar) response to Benedetto Varchi in which he, alongside seven other artists, including Cellini and Michelangelo, debated the respective nobility of painting and sculpture at the humanist's invitation: "... many sculptors produce excellent work without ever using drawings."[7] What the sculptor took from drawing, in his telling, was the *veduta per veduta*, or sequence of discrete, step-by-step views of a figure in the round so as to identify "the one that will succeed best" and that he would then sketch out in his model. When it came to the architects, however, Vasari was as adamant as he was unambiguous: sketches (drawings) served *massimamente* since the architect's work "is made up of nothing but lines, and thus the drawing is the beginning and end of his art, since the rest of the work is executed by others, stone carvers and masons."[8]

Not everyone agreed. Benvenuto Cellini was violently opposed to this supremacy of the flat medium of drawing (and by extension, painting) over sculpture, though he used drawings himself (cat. 26, 32). In his own

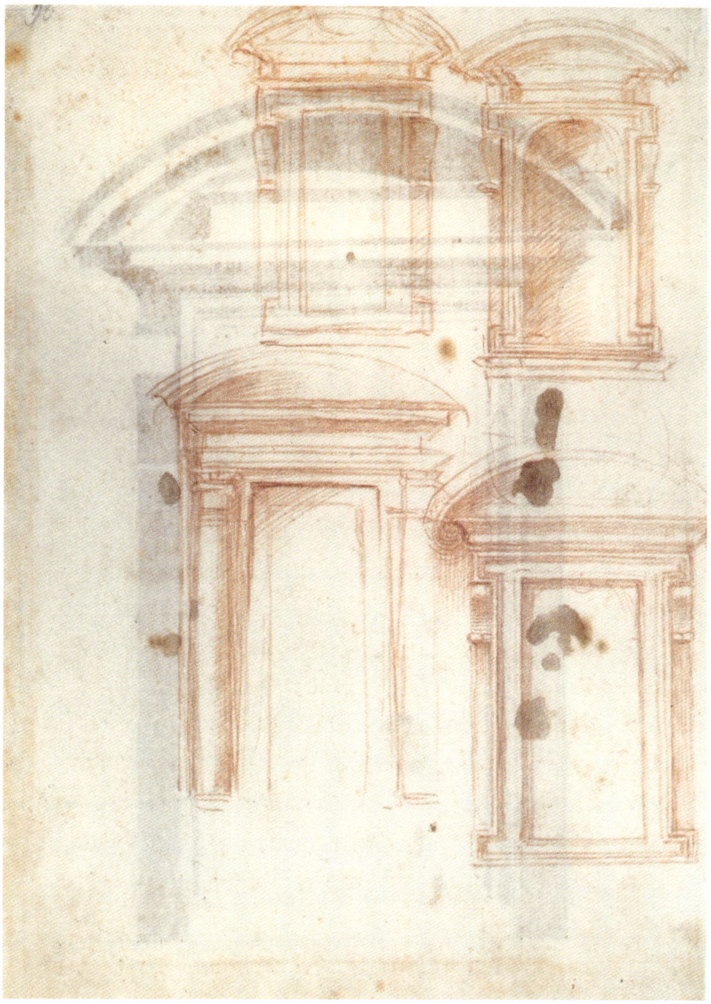

FIG. 27
Michelangelo Buonarroti
Study of windows and tabernacles, 1526
Red chalk, pen and ink, on paper,
332 × 227 mm
Casa Buonarroti, Florence

letter of 1547 to Varchi, he argued for the primacy of the three-dimensional model and acerbically denigrated the value of the drawing.[9] Designs on paper, however beautiful, when turned into three-dimensional objects, he argued, turn out false and foolish (*falso e sciocco*). And he went even further. In his view, Michelangelo's exceptional painting was due to his working from sculpted models, not from drawings. Likewise, for architecture, he continued, Michelangelo's inventions of exquisite windows were conveyed to the stonemasons by way of terracotta models, and only later translated into drawings to explain their exact measurements (fig. 27). This sequence, he admonished, should be followed by all other architects who in their ignorance make a small drawing and from it a model, and as result do not come close to Michelangelo in the beauty of their works.[10] For Cellini then, the drawing was not the essence of the architect's work, quite the contrary. And he concluded that sculpture was the mother of all the arts of design. The choice of term—sculpture as "mother" of the arts—may well be at the root of Vasari's own definition of drawing/*disegno* as the "father of the arts," trumping Cellini through gender and family precedence in a direct rebuttal to the sculptor with whom he did not see eye to eye.[11]

The debate had no winner, despite Michelangelo's ironic yet largely conciliatory contribution praising both figural arts (the debate had not included architecture, though Cellini brought it up), and the fragmented and fraught funeral monument produced for his tomb nearly twenty years later by the warring painters and sculptors became a testament to the disintegration of ties between artists within the academy rather than their productive co-existence under the aegis of *disegno*.[12] But beyond this sometimes petty and sometimes philosophical discord, these two contemporary artists reveal the complex function of drawing for architecture and sculpture, two arts that were fundamentally three-dimensional and shared both tools and materials (indeed, Vasari's catalogue of stones and quarries in his *Lives*, referring interchangeably to their use by both sculptors and architects, clearly indicates this overlap).[13]

Architecture and drawing

At the very origin of Renaissance artistic literature Leon Battista Alberti had acknowledged unease with drawings in his comprehensive treatise *De re aedificatoria* (c. 1450; printed 1486) when he warned the architect to beware of the flat medium: the model was the real guide to a successful building and would reveal many hidden errors that the drawing inevitably hid (II, 1).[14] The association of architecture and sculpture that Alberti implied by way of the model as three-dimensional litmus test for a building design was in fact a common and direct career thread for many Renaissance artists. Starting in the fifteenth century with Michelozzo, Bernardo Rossellino, and Francesco di Giorgio Martini (apprenticed to the sculptor Vecchietta) and continuing in the sixteenth with Jacopo Sansovino and Baccio d'Agnolo (both apprenticed to Andrea Sansovino), Michelangelo and Ammannati (apprenticed to Bandinelli and then Jacopo Sansovino), to name only a few, Vasari's pantheon of most notable architects consisted of artists who started as or apprenticed to sculptors. Even Alberti had been an active participant in resurrecting the art of casting bronze medals and plaquettes in his years in Ferrara.[15] Some became sculptors of note before turning to architecture (such as Sansovino and Ammannati);[16] others moved straight from their sculpture training to architecture, or made the latter their main focus of activity (such as Baccio d'Agnolo). Whichever route they took, the slippage of one art into the other was a common phenomenon.

The sculptor-architect overlap may have been a predominantly Tuscan trait. Already Jacob Burckhardt noted in his *Geschichte der Renaissance in Italien* (1867) that almost all Florentine Quattrocento artists (and that included most architects) started as goldsmiths, Brunelleschi being only the most celebrated among those who followed this path.[17] The observation that working in metal on reliefs and on figures in the round informed the aesthetic sensibility of artists in Florence when they turned to the other arts—and this meant sharpness of contours, edges, detail, and filigree as well as the *factura* of three-dimensional form—deserves more attention than it has received.[18] Bernard Berenson's famous "tactile forms" in Florentine painting (1896) offer another perspective into this phenomenon, though he does not attribute it directly to training in sculpture nor does he reference Burckhardt. Instead, the sculptor Adolf von Hildebrand's *Das Problem der Form in der bildenden Kunst* (1893) was one of his significant sources,[19] a work that likewise drew from a deep knowledge of Florentine art (like Berenson, Hildebrand had settled in Florence). What such observations offer in our context is insight into the significant presence of sculpture-based training and the attending artifactual and tactile sensibility arising from it at the root of much Florentine art.

To be sure, the painter-architect was also a growing phenomenon, perhaps less among Tuscans (Vasari's own passage from painting to architecture is somewhat of an exception) and more in the wake of artists such as Bramante and Raphael and their own formative experience in the Urbino milieu steeped in perspective construction concerns. As Erwin Panofsky noted long ago, numerous artists working in the Raphael's *bottega* or influenced by him (such as Perino del Vaga, Giulio Romano, Domenico Beccafumi, etc.) became noted architects, architectural decorators, and designers of façades in a move that he dubbed "the rebellion of the non-architects."[20] And the Lombard painter Giovanni Paolo Lomazzo certainly reinforced the painting-architecture connection in his *Trattato dell'arte della pittura* of 1584, which contains a short but exhaustive treatise on the orders and in which he insisted on the importance of prior painting experience for architects and in particular on the importance of perspective construction for all the arts.[21]

That said, it is clear that sculptors and architects had much in common, not least of all the complicated relationship to drawing.[22] And where and how

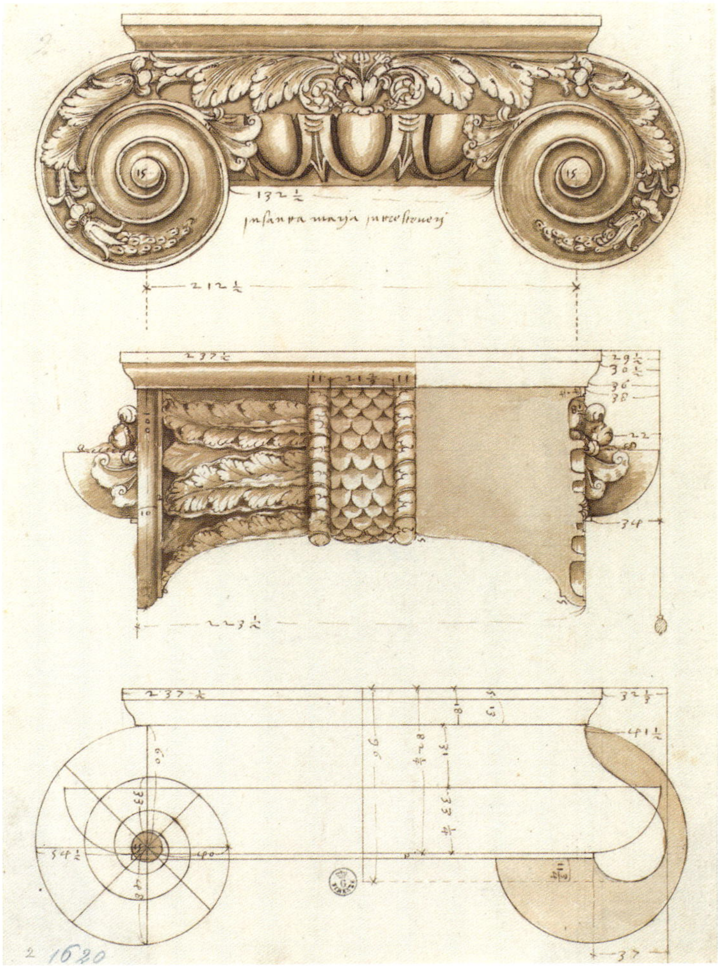

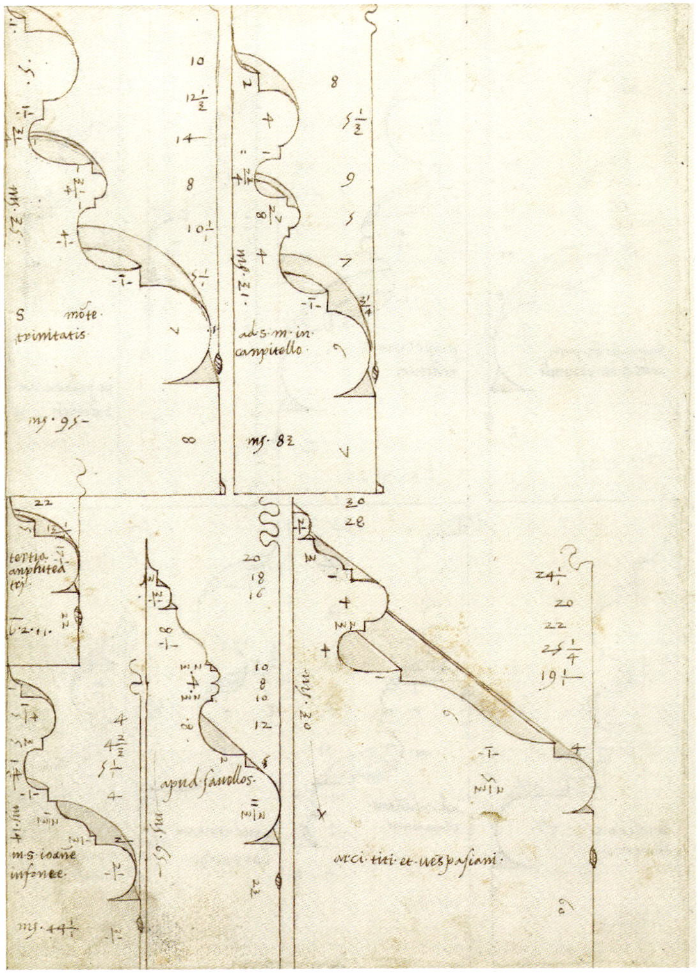

FIG. 28
Circle of Antonio da Sangallo the Younger
Ionic capital found in Santa Maria in Trastevere measured and drawn in three ways, c. 1530–46
Pen and brown ink and wash, on paper, 296 × 219 mm
Gabinetto Disegni e Stampe degli Uffizi, Florence

FIG. 29
Bernardo della Volpaia
The Codex Coner: Studies of bases, c. 1515
Pen and ink, on paper, 225 × 160 mm
Sir John Soane's Museum, London

drawing intersected with the conceptual design and the three-dimensional nature of their art is anything but self-evident. The low survival rate of drawings from some important architects has been attributed to the lack of artistic value their graphic work enjoyed at the time. Thus drawings by Brunelleschi, Alberti, and Francesco di Giorgio (other than small illustrations for his treatise) are among the most egregious absences. Sketchbooks and drawings of architectural details from the Cinquecento are much more plentiful—the Sangallo corpus being among the most notable and vast (fig. 28)—and probably indicate the use and re-use of these copies of ancient fragments by various related workshops.[23] Indeed, Michelangelo's copies of such ornamental details from the Codex Coner show how these sketchbooks functioned as a kind of architectural abacus as well as promoting the fragment as the building block for original ornamental assemblages (figs. 29, 30).[24]

This practice may not seem that different from the painters' drawings of various bodies and body parts, of characteristic gestures and expressions or of drapery details that formed their "inventory of ideas."[25] Yet it was not really a case of slippage from one art to the other but had more to do with a general strategy and the consequences of recording the fragmented remains of

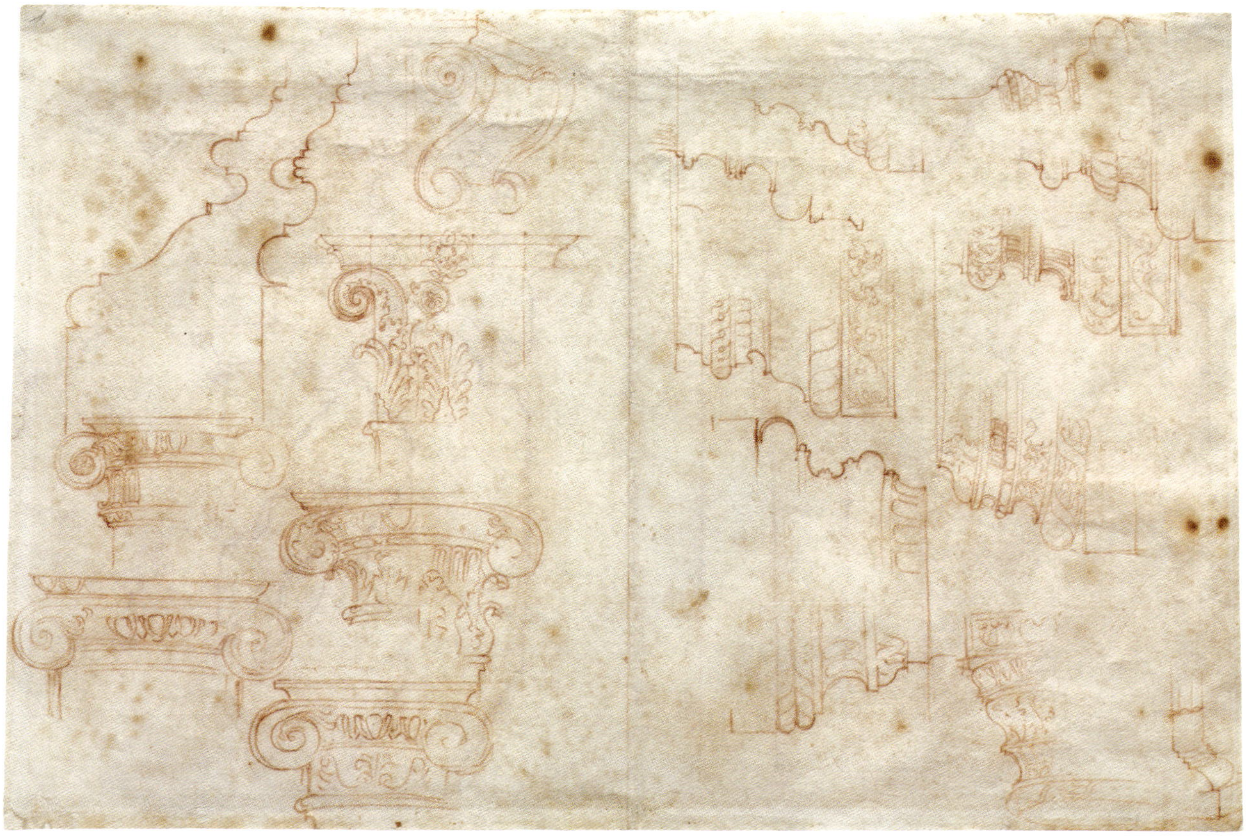

FIG. 30
Michelangelo Buonarroti
Ornamental bases and capitals (copy from the Codex Coner), c. 1516
Red chalk, on paper, 285 × 425 mm
Casa Buonarroti, Florence

antiquity in all its forms.[26] Quite often the drawings of body parts recorded in manuals were taken from ancient sculpture fragments and the details were tied to a desire for a close-up view of volume, texture, and shading effects, which would have been impossible to discern in a whole-body representation (see cat. 12–15). This approach was different from the architects', whose focus on fragments was much more analytical and concerned with developing a corpus of measured ornamental units to be reassembled into ever new assemblages rather than about seeing visual effects in close-up.

What was unique to the architects, however, was that great invention of the early Cinquecento traditionally attributed to Raphael (that is, to a painter-architect), namely the orthographic decomposition of architectural form (although half a century earlier Alberti implies the use of this method, in II, 1).[27] This was a convention or system of notation that allowed a three-dimensional object to be translated into three flat planes intersecting at right angles (plan, section, and elevation). As I have argued elsewhere, recomposing antiquity from scattered remains required a set of coordinates on which to plot them so as to permit the reconstruction of what was lost and difficult to imagine whole, and the orthographic set of drawings was an answer to this very specific problem.[28] Since the departure point was not a complete building but its fragments, these drawings functioned like three interconnected grids that allowed information to be added as it was recovered, hence enabling its reconstitution into one whole. However, using such an approach in the design process (rather than reconstruction) held many pitfalls—and holds many pitfalls to this day, as any architect working in pre-AutoCAD days can amply confirm. Indeed, Alberti signaled the importance of the model, at scale, to test repeatedly from the beginning of design through construction that what the drawings showed would resolve itself into a three-dimensional whole, that the corners actually joined and that there were no awkward intersections of planes and volumes (II, 1; IX, 10).[29]

These types and uses of drawing illustrate quite clearly how problematic, though necessary, drawings were to architects, and the complex strategies they resorted to in order to describe accurately the appearance and dimensions of their work. In some ways the sculptors shared these problems. Imagining a figure in the round required seeing it in three dimensions and decomposing and recomposing it on the various facets of the stone to be carved. For some sculptors the solution was to draw directly on the block (rather than on paper) so as to guide their chisel. As Vasari recounts, Michelangelo so produced his works, "drawing on the stone."[30] Evidently, the sculptor's response was not the orthographic set but may have involved a similar "decompositional" strategy. It is this difficult process that sculptors invoked when positioning their art above painting in the *paragone* debates, and that provided another bridge to architecture.

The relief

When looking at the exchanges between architecture and sculpture across drawings it is also important to recall the types of projects that the two most often shared: alongside monuments, fountains (see cat. 41), and *Kleinarchitektur* (miniature architecture such as ciboria, altars, etc., that was placed indoors and that was carved by the architect-sculptor and his team), the most frequent was the wall-tomb. Though freestanding monuments of various scales also provided cross-pollination (especially as urban devices), the wall-tomb, embedded as it was into the wall and therefore an extension of the architectural fabric, offered the most direct overlap between the two arts.[31] With its architectural frame of niches, arches, pilasters, and entablatures that contained the sarcophagus and the representation of the deceased, quite often the wall-tomb was more architecture than sculpture.

The triumphal arch—with its obvious connotations of triumph over death and oblivion—was a much invoked ancient model that reinforced the genre's hybridity, being itself halfway between architecture and sculpture. It is no surprise therefore that most sculptors started their architectural careers designing such monuments—Michelangelo's unfinished Julius II tomb being one of the most famous examples—aided by the fact that it was also a very frequent commission from patrons eager to commemorate themselves and their dynasties (see cat. 8).

As a result, much of the shared domain between architecture and sculpture lay on the terrain of the tomb monument. Yet as an ensemble it came across as a sculptural high relief since the architectural components could not extend too far into the space of the chapel or church aisle in which it was located, however three-dimensionally the wall-tomb may have been conceived. Thus the wall-tomb became a form of three-dimensional tableau that implied space yet collapsed it into a series of layered planes. In so doing not only did the wall-tomb connect the architect and the sculptor, but through its relief-like quality and relative flatness it brought both closer to two-dimensional representation, that is, to painting and drawing. Significantly, while for Pope Julius's tomb Michelangelo negotiated between architecture and sculpture, thinking it through a relief-like representation, he did so by way of a drawing. This thinking "in relief" is true even of his Medici tombs, despite their arrangement in the round (fig. 31). The chapel walls in white Carrara marble complete with the sarcophagi and figures are independent sculpted units clearly inserted in and separated by the grey *pietra serena* giant order (or grid), and resolve themselves into giant high reliefs.

Likewise, the design of building façades, often as separate projects conceived much later than the bodies of the buildings themselves, was an exercise in monumental relief work and relief drawing for the architect as well. Just like the wall-tomb, the façade involved window recesses and niches, arches and pediments, series of superimposed columns and freestanding sculpture embedded in it. All of these elements were contained within the thickness of the front wall, and their composition also frequently cited the hybrid genre of the triumphal arch. Indeed, second only to ornamental details, it is the most frequently represented drawing in the corpus of Renaissance architects' graphic work.

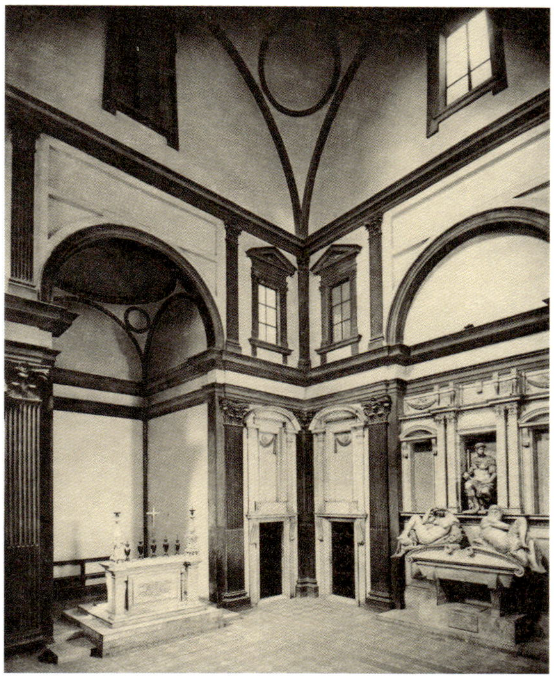

FIG. 31
Michelangelo Buonarroti
The Medici Chapel, San Lorenzo, Florence
(Photograph from Carl von Stegmann and Heinrich von Geymüller, *Die Architektur der Renaissance in Toscana*, vol. 8, 1904)

FIG. 32
Michelangelo Buonarroti
The Madonna and Child, 1522–24
Black and red chalk, pen and brown ink, on paper, 541 × 396 mm
Casa Buonarroti, Florence

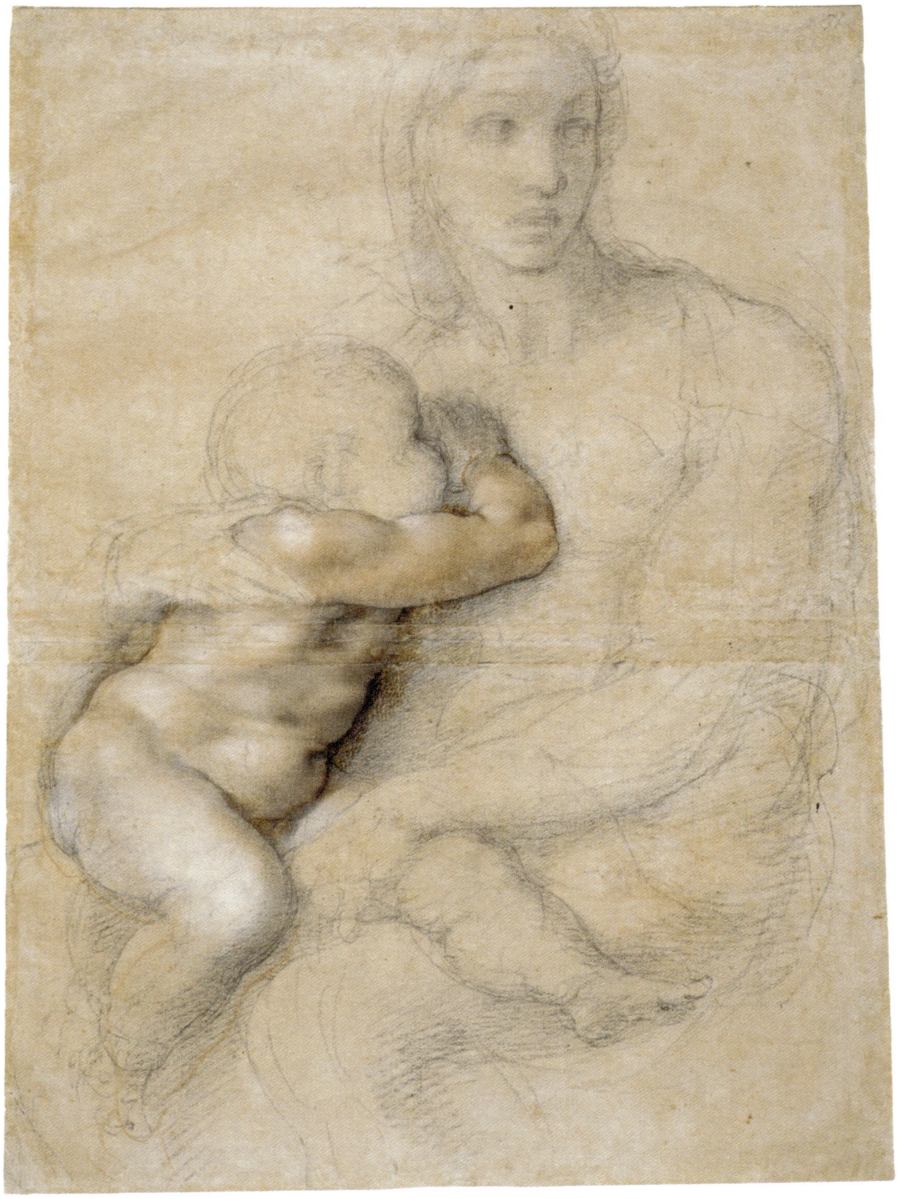

It is then precisely this oscillation between genres at the root of the relief and between flatness and space that can be sensed in Michelangelo's drawings, which offer a classic example for exploring how a sculptor's drawing and architectural sensibility intersected. For example, the *factura* of a drawing such as *The Madonna and Child* (probably for the Medici chapel group; fig. 32) stands in a close relationship to that of the central portal frame for the Porta Pia (fig. 33): both leap from the page, pushing hard, almost layer by layer, into the viewer's space. The child's highly modeled hip, arm, and torso at the center left of the page, gradually melting into the paper background, give the powerful impression of a sculpted relief—which indeed, the intended arrangement approximated.[32] The image seems to break through the flatness of the paper, pushing through the picture plane as if curving outward, building up gradually into the third dimension, as

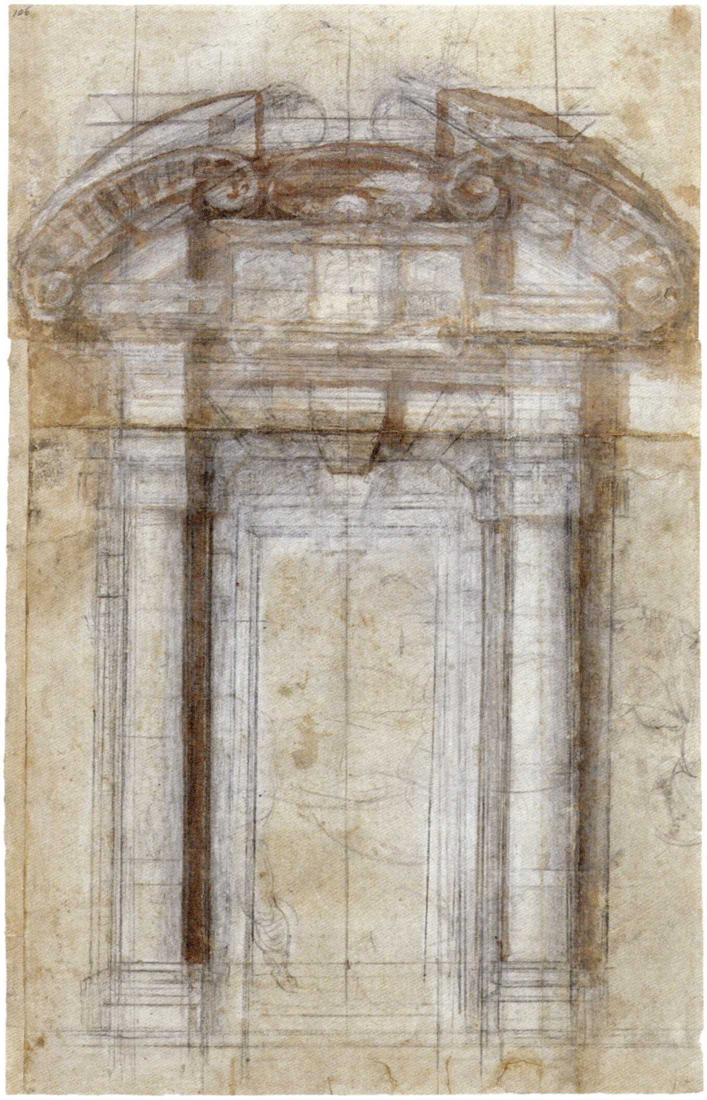

FIG. 33
Michelangelo Buonarroti
Study for the Porta Pia, Rome, c. 1561
Black chalk, pen and ink with watercolor, on paper, 442 × 282 mm
Casa Buonarroti, Florence

if offering itself to touch, and back again into the flatness of the support. The pigment and overlays of drawing media intensifying as the forms push outward (black and red pencil, as well as white-chalk highlights), like the collage of two sheets of paper that make up the drawing, reinforce its "sculpted" artifactual quality as well as its tactility.

The Porta Pia drawing (fig. 33) is likewise a relief-like drawing, and quite unlike those produced by "pure" architects who were concerned with precise contours. This drawing manner has been attributed to Michelangelo's weaker eyesight due to old age and alternatively has been labeled a painterly, impressionistic approach.[33] Yet relief-like is perhaps a more accurate way to describe it, for it hints at the mixed qualities of this hybrid genre that crossed painting and sculpture. While the shadows and washes speak of a painterly sensibility, the absence of firm contours alerts not only to visual impressionism but also to a sculptor's insight. Beside recording Michelangelo's efforts to arrive at a final form by way of layering, the pentimenti cause the frame to seem to vibrate, for its contours are unstable and do not resolve themselves into a single line. This out-of-focus contour also seems to imply the spectator's motion around a three-dimensional object that changes and unfolds as the viewer moves. In fact, it recalls just how much the outlines of a human body—Vasari's *contorni* (contours)—are themselves abstractions when drawn on paper, for the body has no contours, only its shadow does, a fact of which a sculptor would have been keenly aware. And with the intense black shading used to model the forms in his drawings, Michelangelo seems to draw the eye with great force and emphasis precisely to those hidden sides that exist just beyond the contours, and just beyond what the drawing can represent, but which the relief, however flat, is nevertheless able to convey.

This is not to say that painters' drawings do not transcend the flatness of the page and that they did not use every means possible to make them do so that charcoal, ink, washes, and chalks permitted. And both the texture of the paper and the body gesture captured by line give them an immediacy that is profoundly compelling. But they do not have the quality of materiality and physical presence that Michelangelo's drawing conveys and that speaks of a carver's sensibility. Besides, sculptors were quick to note that representation on a flat support (whether painting or drawing) was closely related to the relief. Thus Michelangelo was keenly aware of the importance of the relief as well as of its ambiguity and chose to focus precisely on this site of intersection between sculpture and painting in his response to Varchi's question on the relative nobility of the arts: "... it seems to me that painting is considered good when it approaches the relief, and the relief is considered bad when it approaches painting."[34] Although Vasari did not go so far, for him the relief was nevertheless a hybrid between sculpture and painting, and he described it in these terms at some length in his introduction to sculpture.[35] Elsewhere he connected relief work, goldsmithery, and drawing when he attributed the invention of copper engraving to the translation of niello work into a printing technique by Maso Finiguerra and his follower the goldsmith Baccio Baldini (to whom Vasari unfoundedly claimed the great Italian painter-engraver Andrea Mantegna had apprenticed so as to stress Tuscan primacy in this art).[36] Even as he stressed the presence of *disegno* as the common thread between metalwork and line engraving, he acknowledged hybrids when he related niello and enamel work and defined them as "a flat relief ... a mixture

FIG. 34
Michelangelo Buonarroti
Profile of a column base for the Medici Chapel, San Lorenzo, Florence, 1524–25
Pen and ink with black chalk, on paper, 325 × 145 mm
Casa Buonarroti, Florence

of painting and sculpture," meaning that one was carved into the picture plane and the other built out from it.[37] Vincenzo Borghini, his friend and one of the principal editors of his *Lives*, was more critical, arguing that the relief was the "*dolce amaro*" (bitter sweet) or "*imperfetto*" of the arts.[38] In the nineteenth century Jacob Burckhardt still echoed this evaluation when he identified the relief as the problematic intermedial genre and saw the penetration of painterly elements into Renaissance sculpture as foreshadowing its ultimate corruption (in his eyes) in the Baroque work of Bernini.[39] In the end perhaps Cellini expressed the relation between drawing and the relief most trenchantly when he insisted on the difference between contour and thickness: "true *disegno* is nothing but the shadow of the relief, such that the relief is the father of all *disegni*." And he concluded that because the greatest praise that a painting can receive is to be thought as good as a relief, "therefore the relief is the true father, which is sculpture, and painting is one of its daughters."[40]

This evident desire to turn the paper into a sculpted object emerges just as powerfully from Michelangelo's *modani*—cutout architectural profiles or templates at full scale—for the Medici Chapel and the Laurentian Library (fig. 34). Starting as drawings, they were cut out with scissors into a form of flat architectural model or very thin relief intended as a template to guide the hand of the stonecutter. This was standard architectural practice, and most architects provided such *modani* or *sagome*: Antonio da Sangallo the Younger, Palladio and sculptor-architects like Bartolomeo Ammannati used them as well (the latter for the architectural profiles of the church of San Giovannino in Florence), while Vincenzo Scamozzi illustrated them at large scale in his 1615 architectural treatise. In Ammannati's case these cutouts were collected and bound and may have been intended for his own treatise on architecture described by Raffaello Borghini, his sixteenth-century biographer.[41]

It has been tentatively argued that the sharpness of edges in the architectural details of Michelangelo's Medici Chapel is indebted to the process of cutting the paper and to the scissors as the instrument of their final adjustment, in other words, that in their "objecthood" the *modani* generated design and were not merely working drawings.[42] More substantial and hence more durable models of these profiles for workshop use were also made of sheets of tin and wood, a form of drawing transposed to a range of materials even closer to sculpture. Indeed, these "drawn" relief profiles were "models" just like the full-scale wooden model of one sculpted wall that

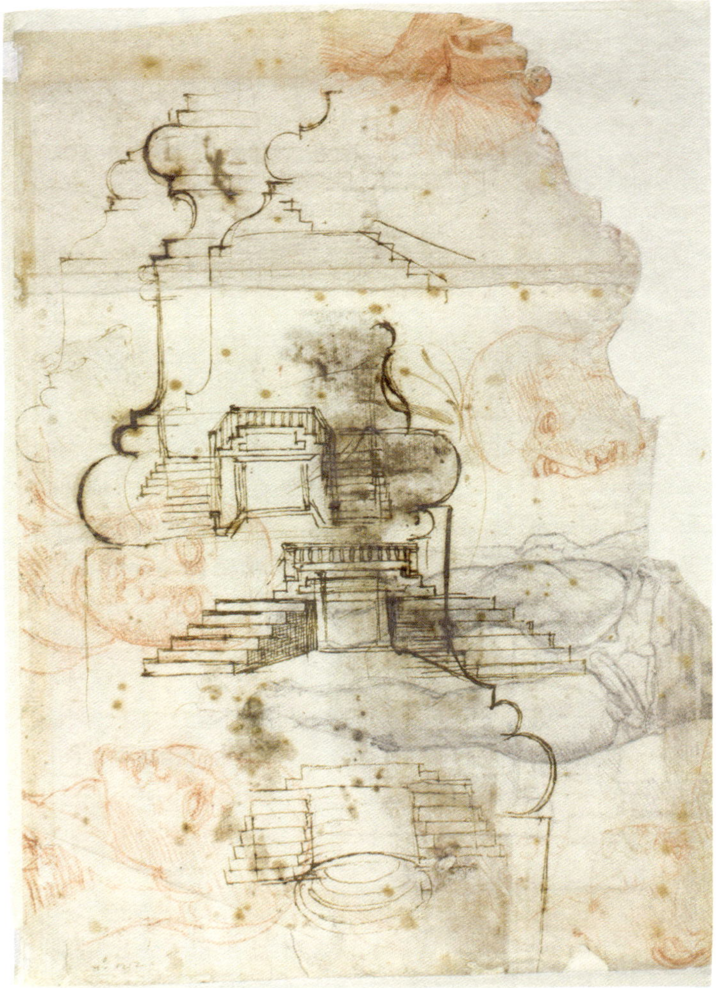

FIG. 35
Michelangelo Buonarroti
Studies of variations to the scale of the vestibule of the Laurentian Library, Florence, c. 1525
Red chalk, pen and brown ink and wash, on paper, 386 × 280 mm
Casa Buonarroti, Florence

Michelangelo had constructed and tried out.[43] Yet once again this translation of a drawing into an object detached from the paper illustrates both the importance and the limitation of drawings: for architectural details precise contours could be drawn; yet they needed to be translated into objects so as to be turned into three-dimensional forms on the stonecutter's table. In some ways this was not that different from the practice of tailors, another set of artisans dealing with the three-dimensional figure in the round rather than its projection, who likewise had to build their garments around the bodies these garments contained. Such an artifactual modification of drawings as seen in the *modani* provided another bridge between architects and sculptors—a bridge that could be crossed in either direction.

But the *modano* presents yet another inflection in the sculptor-architect's relationship to drawing. While it is a compressed model-relief, it is also an outline, a silhouette. And the silhouette or contour as the trace of a three-dimensional object collapsed onto a flat plane was the other direction a sculptor could engage drawing by way of architecture's tools. Clearly, architectural drawings trade in outlines (fig. 35).[44] In fact, the orthogonal set of drawings, "decomposing" as they do the three-dimensional object and

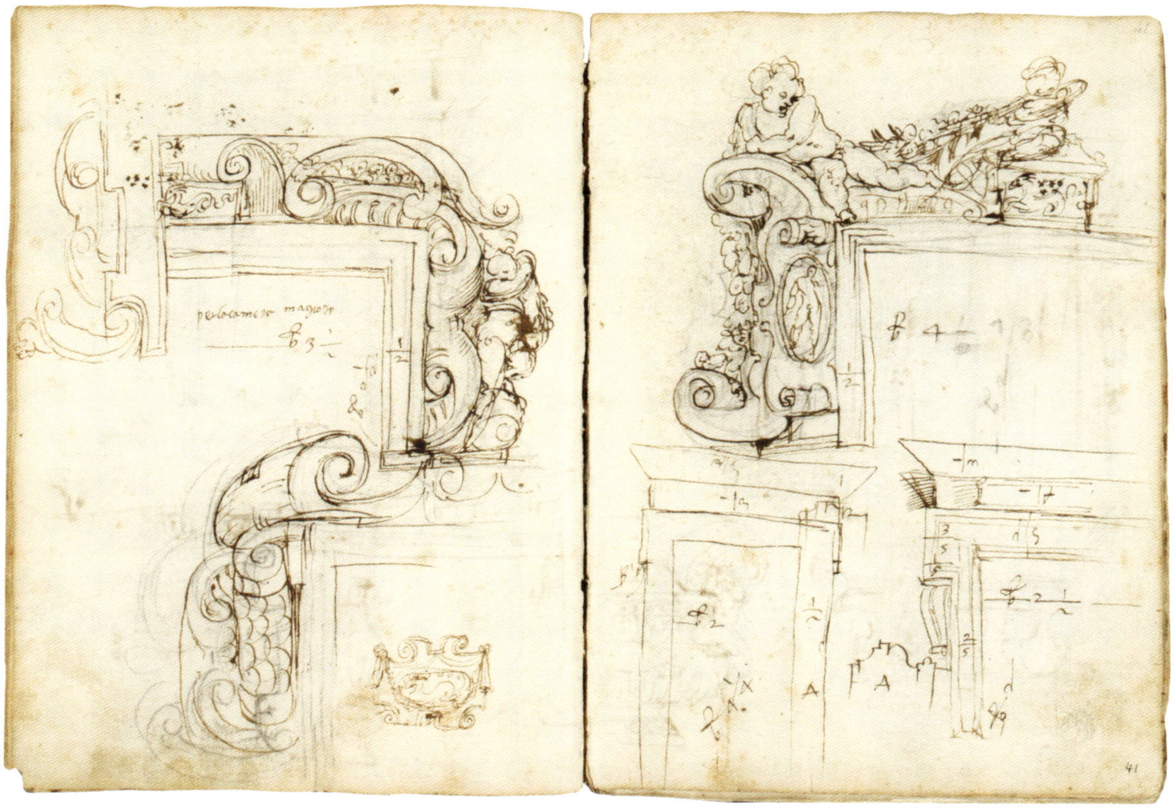

implying each other at all times, increase the awareness of line as notation for depth, as the trace of a slice through an object. An interest in outline is evident in the case of Ammannati, whose drawings of architectural or sculptural ornament are not relief-like in the manner of Michelangelo but retain the quality of silhouette (fig. 36). A freestanding figure in three dimensions does not have a silhouette as such and needs to be comprehended from all sides. But the overall tableau—of a tomb, of a monument, of a funerary chapel, like architectural ornamental details that are seen from a distant vantage point, attached to a wall of which they are the sculptural projection outward—does present that opportunity. Read as reliefs, wall-tombs could also be translated into a continuous line, into a silhouette drawing—into the shadow of the relief, in Cellini's words. This is the case of Giambologna's drawing for the Salviati Chapel (fig. 37) or Guglielmo della Porta's design for Paul III's tomb, just as it is the case of a Renaissance palace or church façade.

FIG. 36
Bartolomeo Ammannati
The Riccardiano notebook: Sketches for a fireplace, c. 1557-61
Pen and brown ink over black pencil
248 × 184 mm
Biblioteca Riccardiana, Florence

What this episodic history of the sculptor-architect begins to suggest is that whereas, in the wake of Vasari, theory claimed that *disegno* alone was the intersection point of the arts, the relief was an equally important convergence point in practice. Ultimately this is also where architectural ensembles-as-reliefs touched painting and drawing: the sculptural "tableau" could be abstracted into a flat plane just as the relief monumentalized the pictorial composition. Alberti had implied as much in his *Della pittura* (which was an important model for Lomazzo) when he recommended the painter take his cue from the Meleager sarcophagus as the most vivid example of an *istoria*

FIG. 37
Giambologna
The Salviati Chapel in San Marco, Florence, 1580s
Brown ink, on paper, 540 × 425 mm
Gabinetto Disegni e Stampe degli Uffizi, Florence

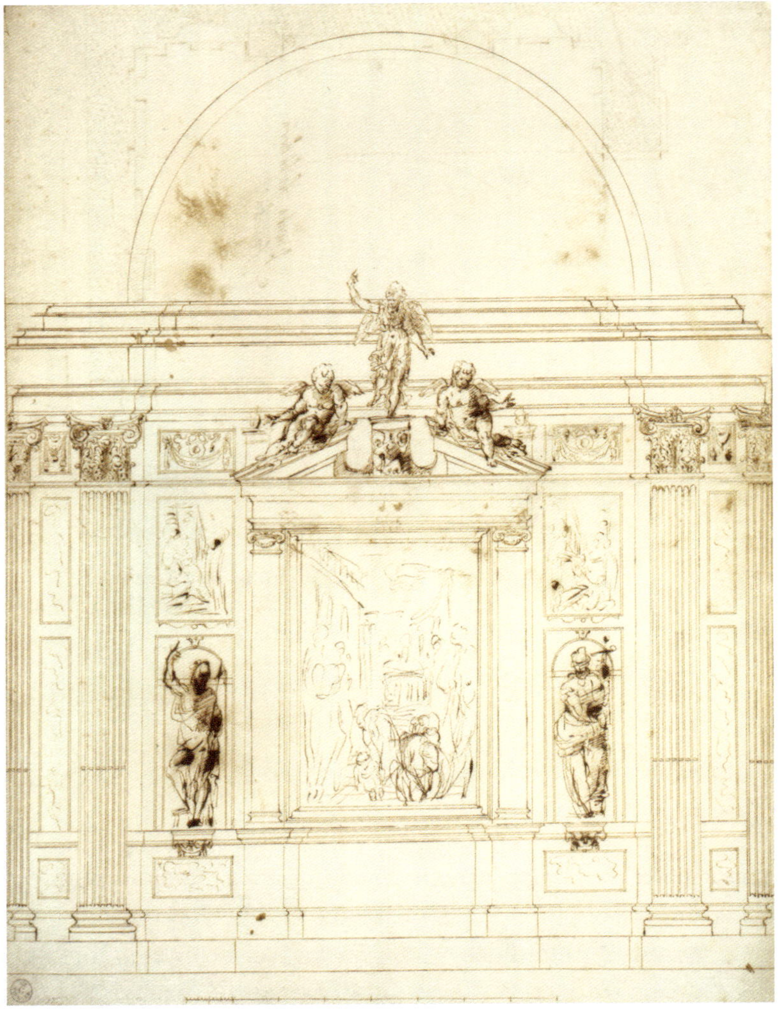

arrangement, in other words, when he recommended a relief as a model for the painter.[45] His view that "pleasing lights [ought to] pass gradually into shadows" in such a painting finds an echo in the connection he implies in *De re aedificatoria* between the surfaces of architecture and the relief. His injunction to combine and bond everything "so that one's gaze might easily flow freely and gently along the cornices, through their recessions, and over the entire exterior and interior face of the work" (IX, 9) describes the scanning of a relief and may well echo Vitruvius's statement that "the sight follows gracious contours."[46] In the final analysis this may well explain Lomazzo's injunction to architects to learn painting as well as why painters and not only sculptors could become architects.

The debate did not end here. "Despite all stylistic differences characteristic of architecture, its object is to unite its forms into a relief effect.... Sculpture undoubtedly emerged from drawing which it pushed into depth, creating the relief. We must conceive of it [sculpture] as the enlivenment of the plane."[47] Thus, more than three centuries later, the sculptor Hildebrand still thought about and claimed just such a unity.

Notes

I am grateful to Michael Cole, David Kim, Maria Loh, and Nicola Suthor for reading and commenting on drafts of this essay. All translations are by myself unless otherwise noted.

1 On the sculptors' reluctance to draw—and the origin of this exhibition—see Cole 2011, in particular pp. 187–91.

2 On the historiography of the relief, see Payne 2011b, pp. 39–64.

3 Vasari-Bellosi and Rossi 1986 (1st ed., 1550), p. 660.

4 Vasari-Bellosi and Rossi 1986 (1st ed., 1550), pp. 59–60 and Vasari-Bettarini 1966 (2nd ed., 1568), vol. 1, p. 111. Vasari did, however, identify *disegno* as the "father of the arts" in his letter to Benedetto Varchi of 1546/47, so the concept of a joint root in drawing was already present during the preparation of the first edition of the *Vite.*

5 Vasari-Bellosi and Rossi 1986 (1st ed., 1550), pp. 45–47.

6 Vasari-Bettarini 1966 (2nd ed., 1568), vol. 1, p. 111.

7 ... *molti scoltori eccellentemente operano che non disegnano in carta niente*: Varchi 1960, p. 30; www.memofonte.it/home/files/pdf/scritti_varchi1.pdf.

8 Vasari-Bettarini 1966 (2nd ed., 1568), vol. 1, p. 112.

9 Varchi 1960, p. 40.

10 Varchi 1960, p. 40. Cellini repeats this view in his treatise: Cellini 1983, vol. 2, pp. 47–48. Documents confirm that Michelangelo made clay models for his architecture projects: Millon 1994, pp. 47–50. Brothers also notes Michelangelo's discomfort with drawing and connects it with his increasing use of washes (rather than perspective) to stress shadows and light: Brothers 2012.

11 In his 1546/47 letter to Varchi Vasari had called *disegno* the mother of the arts. Not so in 1568. On Vasari and Cellini, see Collareta 2003, pp. 161–69.

12 Wittkower 1964; Jacobs 2002, pp. 426–48; Barzman 2000; Ruffini 2011, Chapter 1.

13 Vasari-Bellosi and Rossi 1986 (1st ed., 1550), pp. 19–30.

14 Payne 2007, p. 365; Alberti 1988, pp. 33–35.

15 Grafton 2000, pp. 219–22.

16 Highlighting the importance of architecture for sculpture Cole notes this path in the careers of Ammannati and Giambologna, in particular how focused on architecture they both were in their latter years: Cole 2011, p. 194.

17 Burckhardt 2000 (1st ed., 1867), pp. 19 and 287.

18 Payne 2009.

19 Hildebrand 1913 (first published 1893), pp. 100–101; Berenson 1896, pp. 4–5.

20 Panofsky 1955 (first published 1930), pp. 226–35.

21 Lomazzo 1584, p. 410; Payne 2007, pp. 347–68.

22 For the important argument about the late sixteenth-century Florentine sculptors' relationship to architecture evident in their move toward a form of abstraction as result of their significant involvement with architecture, see Cole 2011, pp. 16–20.

23 Nesselrath 1986; Günther 1988; Frommel and Adams 1994.

24 On Michelangelo and the Codex Coner, see Lotz 1967, pp. 12–19, and more recently Elam 2006, pp. 63–65 and Brothers 2008, pp. 50–64. On the architects' engagement with fragments and assemblage arising from it, see Payne 1998.

25 Chapman 2011, p. 21.

26 This is a different view from Brothers's, who argues that Michelangelo's architectural drawings were behind his reading of the human body in fragments: Brothers 2008, p. 65. On the fragment as *forma mentis* for Renaissance artists, see Barkan 1999, Chapter 3.

27 Alberti 1988, p. 34.

28 Payne 2011a, pp. 3–39.

29 Alberti 1988, pp. 33–35 and 313; on the vast number of lost Renaissance models, see Millon 1994, p. 19.

30 Varchi 1960, p. 30.

31 On the urban implications of sculpture, see Cole 2011, Chapter 7.

32 On the attribution history, see Ruschi 2007, p. 86.

33 Ackerman 1986, p. 251.

34 ... *la pittura mi par più tenuta buona quanto più va verso il rilievo, et il rilievo più tenuto cattivo quanto più va verso la pittura*: Varchi 1960, p. 41. Most recently, using digital technology, Ruschi identifies a "*tumultuosa*" sequence of superimposed designs in the Porta Pia drawings: Ruschi 2012, p. 242.

35 Vasari-Bellosi and Rossi 1986 (1st ed., 1550), pp. 48–49. He describes the *mezzo rilievo* as being similar to painting and the *rilievo stiacciato* as "pure" *disegno* (meaning drawing here).

36 Vasari's definition of niello: *un disegno trattegiato e dipinto su lo argento ... fu trovato da gli orefici*: Vasari-Bellosi and Rossi 1986 (1st ed., 1550), pp. 84–85; Marini 2011, p. 89; Pon 2004, pp. 107–8.

37 Vasari-Bellosi and Rossi 1986, pp. 84–85.

38 Payne 2007, p. 367, and Vasari-Bellosi and Rossi 1986 (1st ed., 1550), p. 48; Varchi and Borghini 1998, pp. 128–29.

39 Burckhardt 2006, pp. 582, 597; Payne 2011b, p. 39.

40 *Il vero disegno non è altra cosa che l'ombra del rilievo, di modo che il rilievo viene a essere il padre di tutti e' disegni ... e la maggior lode che si dà a una bella pittura e' se gli dice: "a par propriamente di rilievo." Addunque il rilievo è il vero padre, che è la scultura, e la pittura è un de' sua figliuoli*: Benvenuto Cellini, "Discorso sopra l'arte del disegno," in Cellini 1973, p. 1930.

41 Cooper 1994; more recently Ruschi 2007, p. 84.

42 Paul Joannides in Androsov and Baldini 2000, pp. 132–34, has tentatively suggested that the contour of Michelangelo's profiles for the Medici Chapel column bases that differs from his drawn profiles resulted in part from the act of cutting the paper templates (used as full-scale "models" by the workshop), which constituted a creative moment in its own right.

43 Cooper 1994, p. 498; Wallace 1994, p. 88; Payne 2009.

44 Already Alberti makes the contours of architectural forms a cardinal point of his theory through the category *finitio* (the third of the triad including *numerus* and *collocatio* in IX, 5) and relates it to *lineamenta* (I, 1): Alberti 1988, pp. 305 and 7, and Payne 2007, p. 364.

45 Alberti 1804, p. 57.

46 Payne 2007, p. 365.

47 Hildebrand 1913, p. 99. *Bei allen Stilunterschieden, welche die Architektur aufweist, bleibt die Aufgabe, ihre Formen als Reliefwirkung zu einigen* (p. 74); ... *der Architektur als Kunst dasselbe Gestaltungsprinzip innewohnt, wie der Plastik und der Malerei* (p. 74). Heinrich Wölfflin picked up and further popularized this view when he identified the "relief style": ... *erst wenn die plastische Figur als ein Flaches wirkt, obschon sie kubisch ist, hat sie künstlerische Form.... Aus diesem Gesichtspunkte ergibt sich als allgemeinste Form künstlerischer Verarbeitung die Reliefauffassung*: Wölfflin 1946, p. 88 (review of Hildebrand's book originally published in *Allgemeine Zeitung*, Munich, no. 157, 11 July 1893).

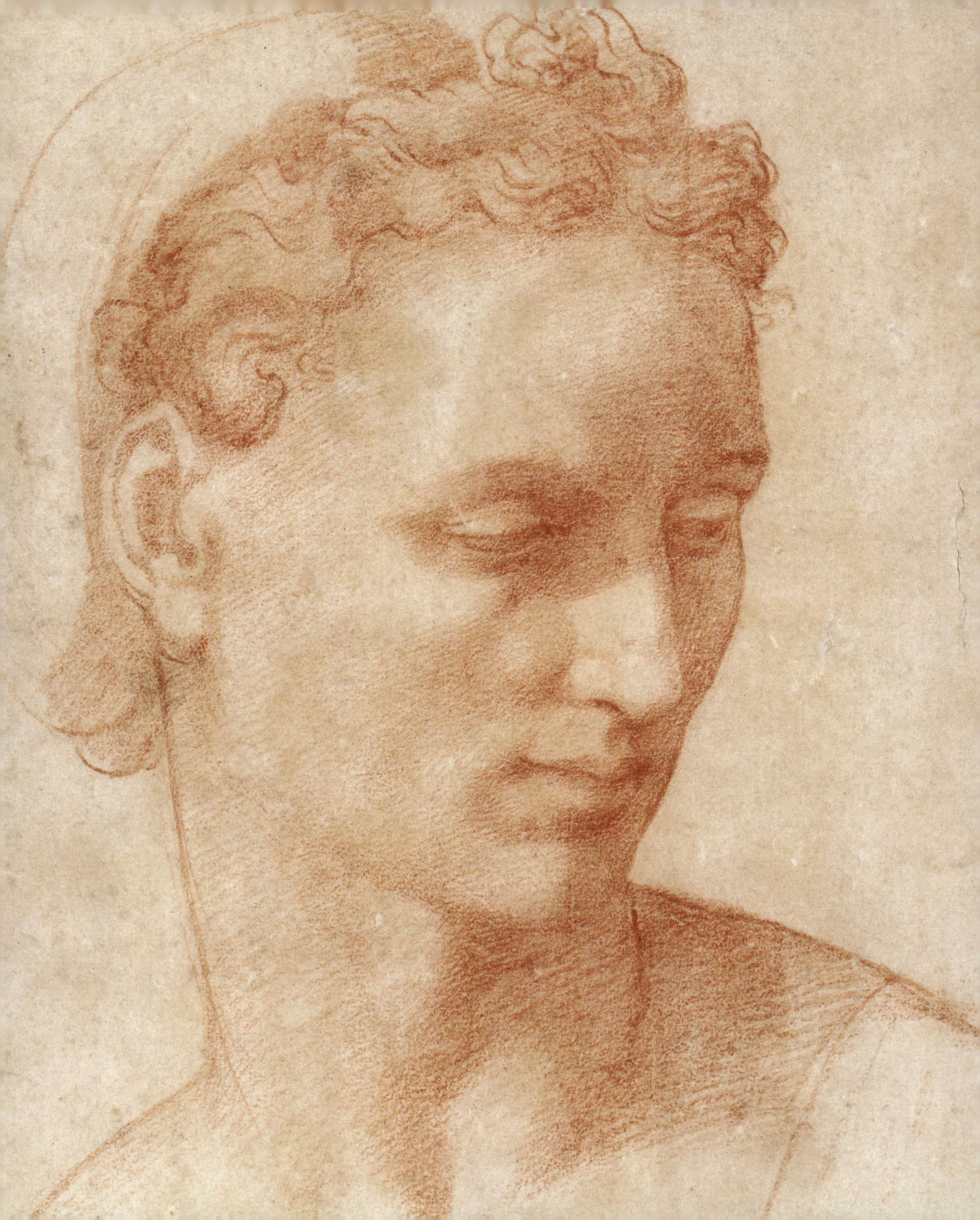

Disegno as *Ritratto:* Drawing in the Biography of Baccio Bandinelli

LINDA WOLK-SIMON

... his drawing, to which it is evident that he gave his attention more than to any other thing, was of such a kind and of such excellence that it atones for his every defect of nature.... We therefore not only count him among our greatest artists, but also have always paid respect to his works, and have sought not to destroy but to finish them and do them honor.... Baccio was in truth one of those who merit honorable praise and eternal fame.[1]

WOVEN INTO THIS PASSAGE from Giorgio Vasari's *Vita* of Baccio Bandinelli is a constellation of themes: the sculptor's disagreeable personality; his overweening ambition, manifested in his tendency to abandon works before seeing them to completion; and the preeminent importance he attached to drawing throughout his career. Though his shortcomings were many, Bandinelli in Vasari's judicious final assessment was not lacking in certain virtues, foremost as a draftsman, and it was in his drawings that his merit and his claim to enduring fame resided.

Offered at the conclusion of a biography that is second in length only to the worshipful account of Michelangelo, this qualified encomium is admirable, for Vasari had a deep antipathy for Bandinelli. His dislike of his subject might cast some doubt on his objectivity as a biographer were it not that various contemporary sources corroborate the essential truthfulness of his largely unflattering portrayal. Letters composed by Bandinelli's patrons and others abound with references to his dilatoriness and his arrogant, querulous, and sycophantic character;[2] documents of the period record the hostile reception accorded many of his public sculptures in Florence and affirm his litigiousness and quick temper;[3] and the sculptor is savaged in the autobiography of his intemperate nemesis Benvenuto Cellini. His advocacy of drawing is recorded in the poet Anton Francesco Doni's dialogue *Disegno*, published in 1549, in which Bandinelli is an interlocutor; in a print depicting the drawing academy he established in Rome (see fig. 43) and more literally in the painted portrait in the Gardner Museum in which he holds up a large, finished red-chalk study (cat. 28); and in the sculptor's fragmentary treatise on drawing, the "Libro del disegno".[4] Some of his letters as well as his purported autobiography, the "Memoriale",[5] record Bandinelli's own perspective on the

CAT. 9 Baccio Bandinelli
Head study (detail)

artistic and cultural milieu in which his career unfolded, narrating various events that Vasari, Cellini, and others also recount and testifying to the truth of his detractors' calumnies in offering correctives to them.

There is ample testimony that Bandinelli's drawings were admired in his own day and long after his death. Vasari not only repeatedly praised his gifts as a draftsman; he also stated that drawings from the sculptor's hand were among the contents of his own "Libro de' disegni". Pietro Aretino, satiric poet, prolific letter-writer, and self-anointed authority in all matters artistic, entreated Bandinelli with his usual orotond bluster for the small token of "at least four or five drawings from your hand," reminding him of their old friendship and of the many favors he had done him in Rome when Bandinelli had dared to promote himself as Michelangelo's rival.[6] Bandinelli himself remarked that Duke Cosimo de' Medici owned a large number of his drawings, and that others were to be found in collections across Italy as well as in Germany and France, the high prices they fetched proof of the esteem in which they were held.[7] And Francesco Bocchi, in his *Ragionamento sopra l'eccellenza del San Giorgio di Donatello*, published in 1584, referred to Bandinelli as the most admired of all draftsmen.[8] A dissenting view was offered by Galileo, who, praising Ariosto over Tasso, likened the latter's verses to a repugnant *Wunderkammer* filled with "'bits of trash'—including, let us say, a petrified crab, a dried chameleon, a fly and a spider preserved in gelatin or amber, some of those earthen puppets that are said to have come from ancient Egyptian tombs; plus the picture collection—some little sketch by Baccio Bandinelli or Parmigianino among countless other pieces of rubbish."[9] But in his condemnation lies proof of the great popularity and status those "little sketches," like the drawings of Parmigianino, another consummate draftsman, enjoyed.

Complementing these abundant written and visual sources are Bandinelli's own drawings, more than 400 surviving sheets representing every stage of his nearly 50-year career. These were augmented by a number of cartoons, now lost. Considerable by any measure—Bandinelli ranks among the most prolific draftsmen of the Cinquecento, with a graphic output rivaling Pontormo's, surpassing Andrea del Sarto's, and far exceeding those of both Rosso Fiorentino and Bronzino—the sizable corpus is remarkable in comparison with the scanty graphic oeuvres of every other sixteenth-century Italian sculptor excepting Michelangelo, who presents a unique and not analogous example.[10] Like his writings and those of his contemporaries, Bandinelli's drawings document his ambitions and limitations, his ideas about artistic theory and practice, including the *paragone* debate over the relative merits of painting and sculpture, and his pursuit of success and fame—biographical tropes each deeply tied to notions of *disegno*. The drawings thus offer primary source material for a concomitant biography of Bandinelli—a *ritratto* that parallels the literary and painted portraits.

Baccio Bandinelli was the son of a distinguished goldsmith, Michelangelo di Viviano da Gaiuole, from whom he received his early instruction. Most Florentine sculptors (and many Florentine painters) of the fifteenth century were themselves goldsmiths or apprenticed to such craftsmen, among them Donatello, Ghiberti, Pollaiuolo, and Verrocchio—a practice that continued into the sixteenth century with artists like Cellini, a goldsmith-turned-sculptor who was a fellow pupil of Bandinelli's father.[11] Bandinelli's formative experience thus followed established conventions of Florentine artistic pedagogy. Training with a marble carver or in a workshop that produced finely wrought gold and silver objects and bronze reliefs entailed thinking in terms of line—the articulation of forms and contours by cutting stone or engraving and incising metal.[12] It is no wonder that so many sculptors' drawings—those of Bandinelli but also of Raffaello da Montelupo to cite but one other example beside the archetypal one of Michelangelo—are executed with hard, incisive outlines and tight webs of hatching and cross-hatching, the short, choppy strokes of the pen evocative of chisel marks (see cat. 18, 20, 22, 32): the graphic idiom suggestively mirrors the sculptor's technique.[13]

This implicit kinship of bronze or stone with drawing—an improbable pairing of unlike media—is not incidental. No less an authority than Donatello averred that drawing lay at the very foundation of the Florentine sculptor's practice. In his 1504 treatise *De sculptura*, the humanist Pomponius Gauricus narrates that "Donatello declared drawing so essential to sculpture that he always told his pupils: the art of sculpture could be taught in one word. Draw. And in that truth is the summit and the basis of all sculpture."[14] It matters little if this report is an accurate transcription of the sculptor's words or a rhetorical invention.[15] By the time Gauricus was writing, a cultivated audience conversant with Alberti's treatises on painting and sculpture and predisposed to accept that artistic practice had an intellectual and theoretical framework would have been persuaded that Donatello gave voice to this utterance.[16] And sixteenth-century artists, patrons, and literati would have discerned in this pronouncement a foreshadowing of the commonplace formulation, articulated by Vasari, Castiglione, and others, of *disegno* as the foundation of all the arts—architecture, sculpture, and painting.[17]

Donatello's drawing of the Massacre of the Innocents (cat. 3)—a virtual relief sculpture in ink—functions both as a specific model of how a sculptor should draw and more generally as a demonstration of the paradigm imputed to him in Gauricus's treatise. This sheet or others like it were conceivably known to artists of Bandinelli's generation; certainly the slashing strokes of Bandinelli's early pen-and-ink drawings recall such a prototype.[18] Reverence for Donatello, an authority often invoked by Bandinelli, and for other forebears in the Florentine pantheon is a persistent theme of the artist's biography.[19] Vasari relates that the young Baccio, as a formative exercise, fashioned wax copies of sculptures by Donatello and Verrocchio. He also recounts that Leonardo da Vinci, whom Bandinelli came to know in the workshop of the sculptor Giovanni Francesco Rustici, his teacher, recommended Donatello as a particularly instructive model upon seeing his drawings and discerning in the young artist an aptitude for working in relief.[20] Several early drawings by Bandinelli that are directly based on or inspired by Donatello's San Lorenzo pulpits and other fifteenth-century Florentine relief sculpture support this narrative (figs. 38, 39).[21] Also instructive in this context is a copy after one of Masaccio's figures in the Brancacci Chapel (a model also for the young Michelangelo), for it testifies to Bandinelli's instinctive responsiveness to painters in the Florentine canon whose works embodied the sculptural property of *rilievo*.[22]

In addition to works by Donatello and Masaccio, Bandinelli industriously copied Michelangelo's *Battle at Cascina* cartoon. This was the practice of many young Florentine artists of his generation, both painters and sculptors, for whom the extraordinary composition abounding with idealized, muscular, heroic male nudes in a variety of straining yet effortless, graceful postures functioned as a virtual *studio d'artefici* or teaching academy.[23] Vasari relates that Bandinelli quickly distinguished himself among all the other artists who set about studying and making drawings after this sublime

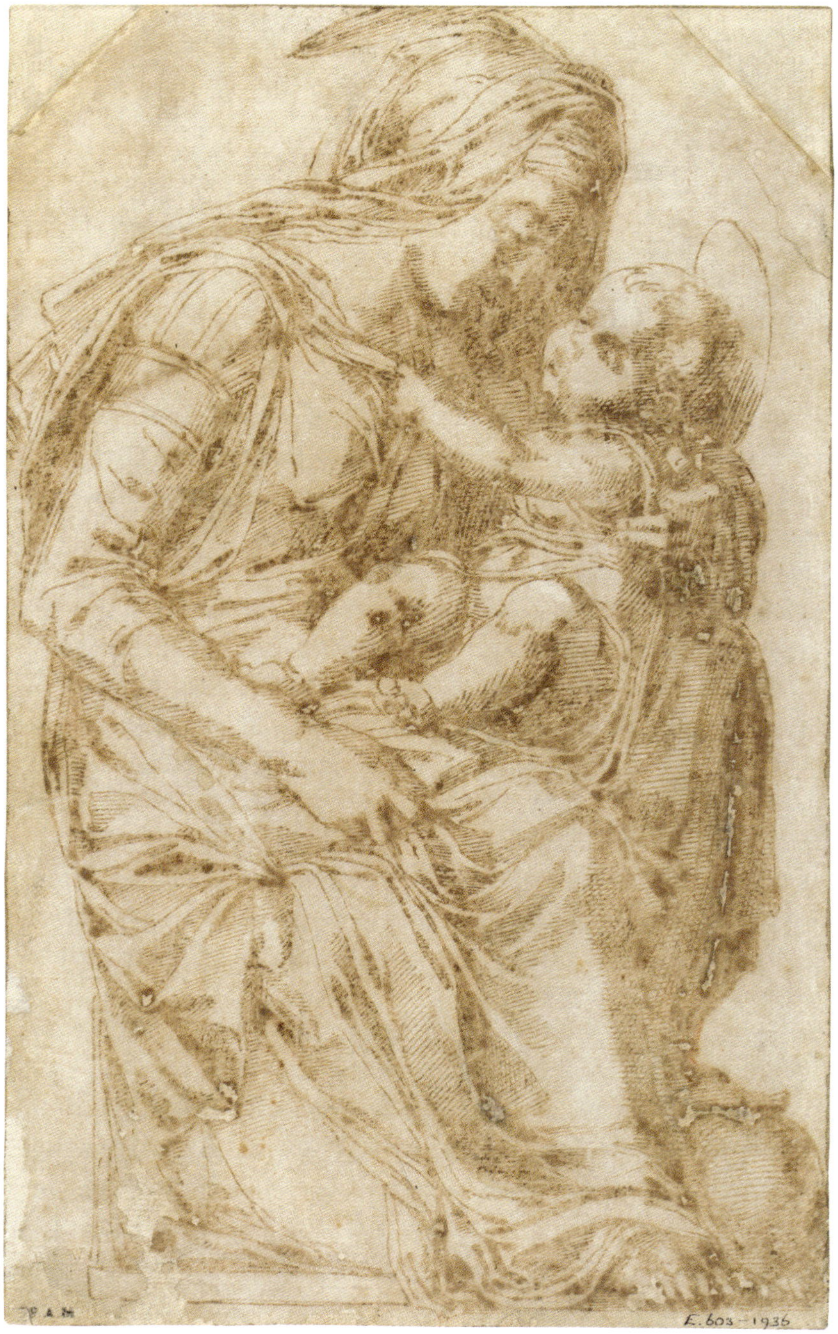

FIG. 38
Baccio Bandinelli
The Virgin and Child (after Desiderio da Settignano's Dudley *Madonna*), c. 1510
Pen and light brown ink, on paper, 244 × 152 mm
Victoria and Albert Museum, London

invention "for the reason that he understood nudes, and outlined, shaded and finished them better than any of the other draftsmen."[24] Several sheets from the 1510s and 1520s, including some directly inspired by the *Cascina* cartoon, demonstrate Bandinelli's command of anatomy, the study of which according to Vasari consumed him for years.[25] Portraying nude figures in a variety of expressive and anatomically accurate poses was acclaimed a supreme artistic virtue in sixteenth-century discourses on art. In Ludovico Dolce's dialogue *Aretino*, both Michelangelo and Raphael are praised in varying degrees for this skill, and Francesco Bocchi, in the above-cited *Ragionamento* on Donatello, singles out Michelangelo's unrivaled powers at describing every nuance of the *corpo umano*. If not always apparent in his sculpture, as his many detractors were quick to observe, Bandinelli's drawings show how successful he was in his singular determination to master anatomy.

Early in his career drawing was for Bandinelli an autodidactic exercise, a means of intensive study undertaken in order to learn and to advance his artistic facility and stature. Vasari repeatedly refers to the zealous industry—fastidious labor antithetical to natural-born, divinely inspired *ingegno*—that was driven by Bandinelli's ambition to "surpass all others who had ever practiced his art" and achieve "honor and excellence." Bandinelli himself, though countering Vasari by claiming that his proclivity for both drawing and sculpture was an "inclination of nature,"[26] likewise gives voice to the proposition that drawing was a means for achieving excellence, recounting that he had "principally applied myself to drawing," in which he was judged "outstanding" by, among others, Michelangelo and Duke Cosimo.[27] On the most fundamental level his sizable corpus of drawings is evidence of that ceaseless industry in the service of self-promotion.

Bandinelli's tireless efforts as a draftsman were fueled by his short-lived and unsuccessful ambition, motivated in part by his devotion to Leonardo, to fashion himself into a painter, or rather a painter-sculptor in the mode of Michelangelo, the ever-superior artistic rival he tediously and tirelessly boasted, to his own perpetual disadvantage, he could surpass.[28] That ambition manifested itself in his clandestine and failed attempt at executing a fresco on the wall of his house, and in his thwarted effort to learn the technique of oil painting while secretly observing Andrea del Sarto at work as he sat for the portrait he had requested from that obliging *amicissimo*. (Detecting Baccio's deceitful purpose, the usually genial master proceeded with such rapidity that all attempts to apprehend his methods of mixing and applying pigments were stymied.) The subterfuge was due to his pride and mendacity rather to any practical necessity, for Bandinelli was connected to Sarto's workshop in the early 1510s, an affiliation that would have afforded him instruction had he sought it.[29]

Considerably more successful was Bandinelli's effort to absorb and emulate Andrea del Sarto's manner as a draftsman, as his red-chalk figure drawings from this period confirm (see cat. 9). The softly modeled forms and suggestion of volume and enveloping space achieved through subtle

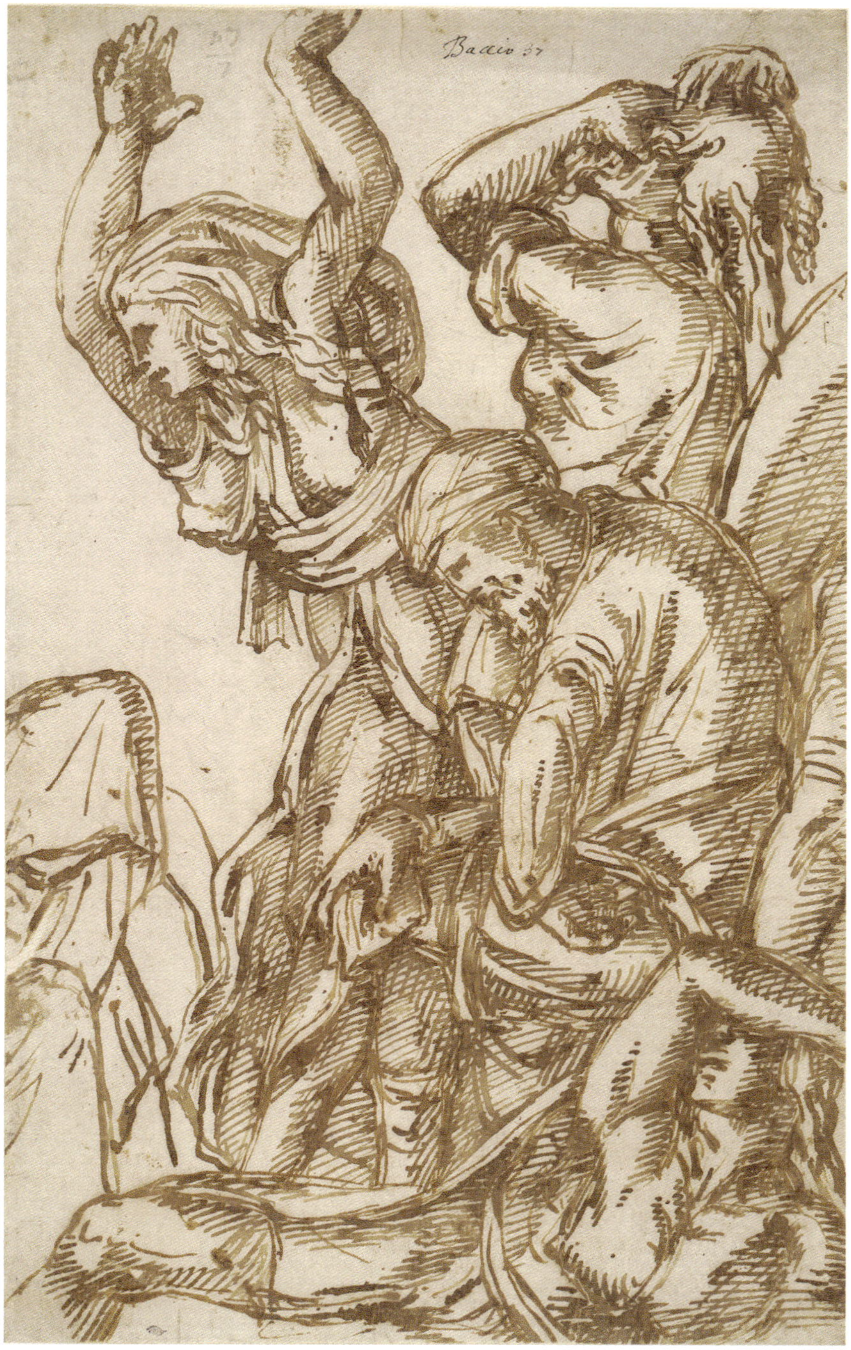

FIG. 39
Baccio Bandinelli
A group of mourners (after Donatello's *Lamentation* relief, pulpit, San Lorenzo, Florence), c. 1515
Pen and brown ink, on paper, 419 × 268 mm
British Museum, London

gradations of light and shadow are indebted to the example of the older artist, as are the occasional quivering outlines and vacant, round eyes seen in certain sheets from this moment (fig. 40). Bandinelli's practice in the late 1510s of producing highly finished red-chalk studies of heads also recalls Sarto's working method (see cat. 9).[30] It is no wonder, given these affinities, that many of the drawings in question were at one time attributed to Andrea del Sarto himself.[31] Far removed from Bandinelli's early pen studies, with their hard, incisive contours and linear, stabbing strokes (see fig. 39), these examples of his draftsmanship are not quintessential sculptors' drawings.

FIG. 40
Baccio Bandinelli
Study for Cleopatra, c. 1514
Red chalk, on paper, 231 × 160 mm
Musée du Louvre, Paris

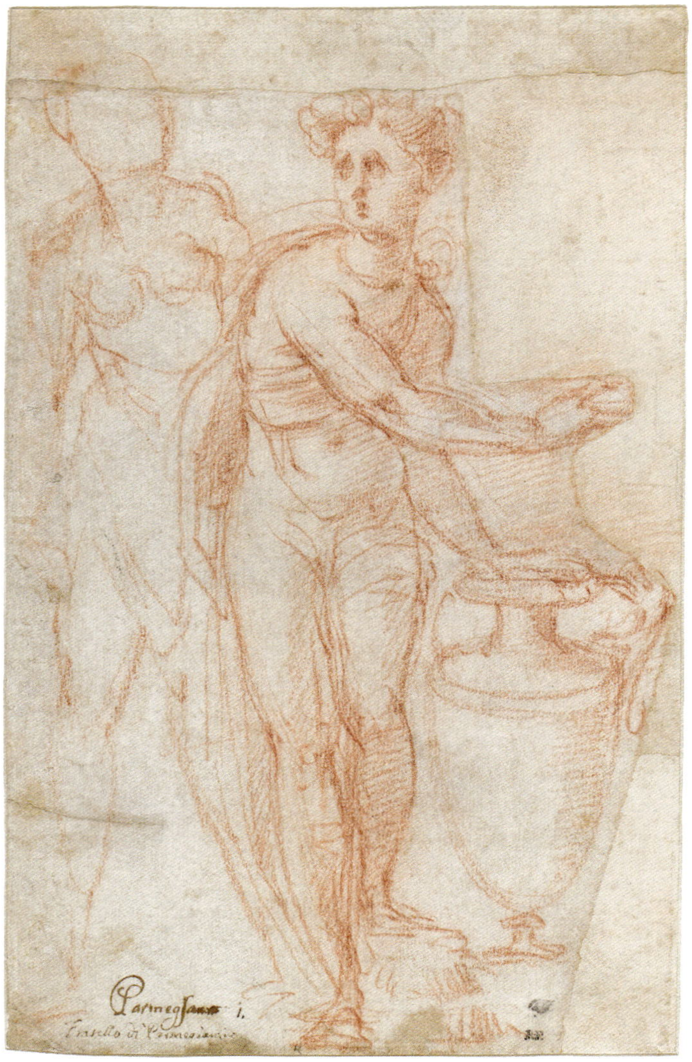

Rather, the affinities lie with drawings by Florentine painters, not only Sarto but also his pupils Pontormo and Rosso. This is a matter of technique as well as style: following Leonardo's innovative demonstrations, red chalk was a medium favored by Florentine painters for its descriptive precision and the warm chromatic range that made it inherently suitable for figure studies.[32] Florentine sculptors, in contrast, seldom used red chalk, finding black chalk, with its cool tonality and shadowy effects, a more efficacious medium for suggesting the properties of marble and bronze (see cat. 12–15, 39).[33] Anamalous for a sculptor, Bandinelli's frequent use of red chalk in the 1510s was a direct corollary of his ambition to become a painter.[34] Though unsuccessful in that pursuit, he had at least learned how painters drew.

A red-chalk drawing of the head of a young woman is a telling record of this moment of Bandinelli's activity (fig. 41).[35] The subject's vague, enigmatic smile and delicately shadowed features descend from Leonardo's female type. Also harking back to the older master are the medium and the manner

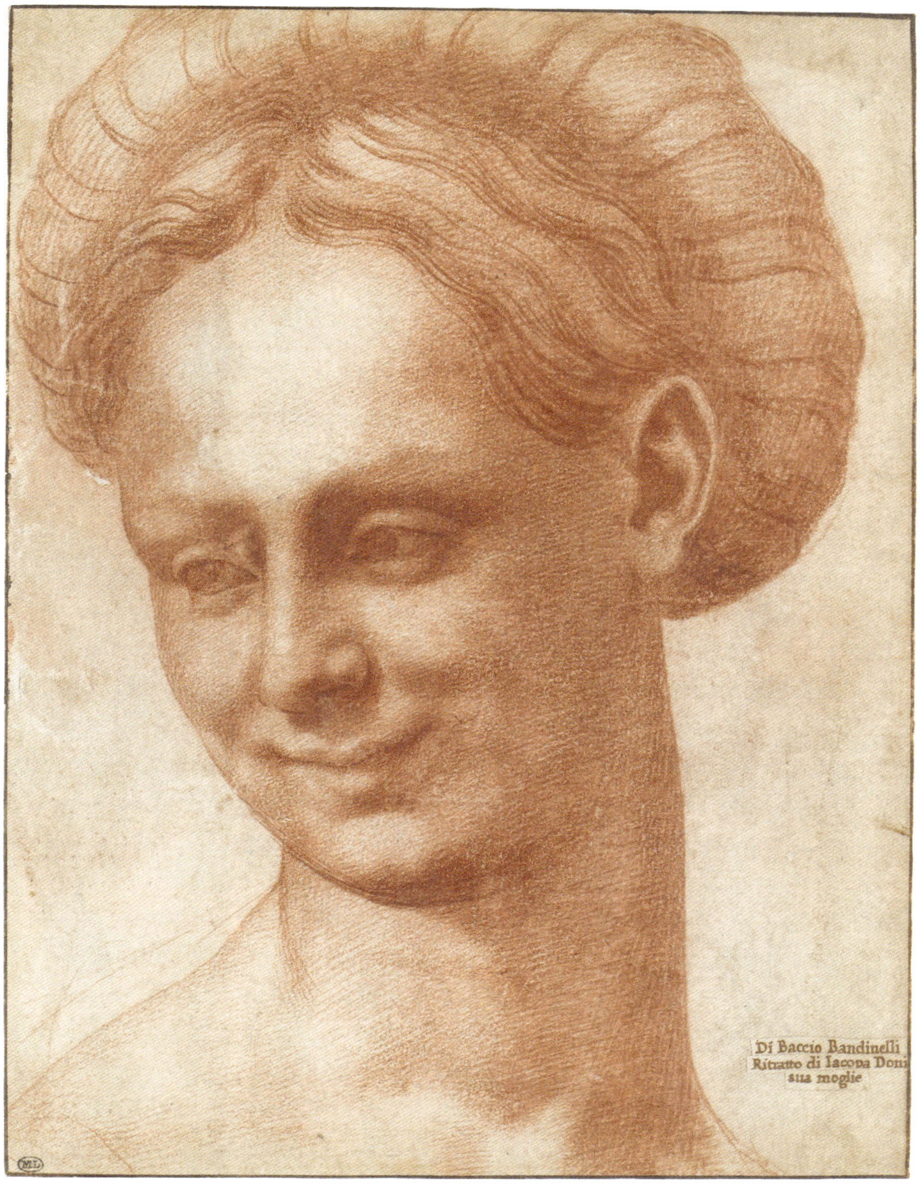

FIG. 41
Baccio Bandinelli
Head of a woman, c. 1516–17
Red chalk, on paper, 242 × 189 mm
Musée du Louvre, Paris

of modeling with dense, tight, continuous strokes. Although the technique may be an attempt to approximate Leonardo's manner of describing an all-enveloping sfumato, the result is a plastic sense of volume and corporeality that counters the carnal softness of the forms described: an attempt to render supple flesh is evident, but so is the ineluctable propensity for plasticity and relief—the property of sculpture—that Leonardo discerned in the young artist's drawings.[36] If Bandinelli in this sheet draws flesh like marble, an inverse transformation is evident in the roughly contemporaneous red-chalk study of a strangely humanoid Torso Belvedere, whose inert marble torso has sprung a head and metamorphosed into breathing flesh (fig. 42).[37] Here is a herald of Bandinelli's ambition to impute to sculpture the properties of painting. As these examples convey, the transferal occurs through the vehicle of *disegno*.

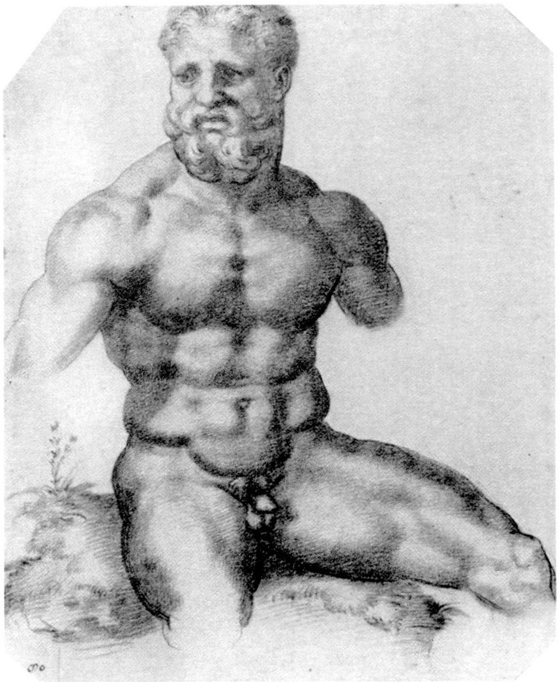

FIG. 42
Baccio Bandinelli
Nude man seated on a grassy bank, c. 1519
Red chalk, on paper, 290 × 232 mm
Private collection

That drawing could be invested by its maker with this agency is an idea embedded in the artist's biography. In 1518–19 Bandinelli worked as an assistant to Andrea Sansovino on the sculptural decoration of the shrine of the Santa Casa in Loreto. He was assigned the relief of the Birth of the Virgin (see cat. 10, fig. 61), for which he received regular payments beginning in June 1518, even in advance of beginning the work.[38] As would be his regrettable tendency, despite collecting his wages, Bandinelli failed to deliver in a timely fashion, and, after protracted interruptions fomented by his quarrelsome disposition and his pursuit of grander undertakings, he abandoned the project. The relief was finally completed more than a decade later, and to no great acclaim, by Raffaello da Montelupo. Of note for this discussion is Bandinelli's strikingly pictorial conception of the scene and the attention lavished on descriptive detail. A well-appointed domestic interior is crowded with attendants, infants, furnishings, draperies, vessels, and a playful dog. The flat, planar space imposed by the relief format is punctured by the orthogonals of receding walls and doorframes, markers of a perspective grid that creates a sense of recession in emulation of a fresco or panel painting. Essentially a painted design carved in stone, the composition and certain of the individual figures descend from Andrea del Sarto's *Birth of the Virgin* fresco in Santissima Annunziata. That Bandinelli, in a reprisal of the painter's practice, evolved the design through an extensive series of preparatory drawings in red chalk and pen and ink (see cat. 9–11) underscores his fundamentally pictorial approach to marble—his resolve to "follow the painter's way."[39]

This recourse to the painter's methods and to painted sources has been interpreted as a sign of Bandinelli's lack of experience as a sculptor. An alternative gloss would be to see the *Birth of the Virgin* relief as a claim for sculpture as the cognate of painting. The foundation of that declaration lies in drawing, as an anecdote pertaining to the relief makes clear. Vasari relates that Bandinelli, who was incapable of praising the work of others, launched a scurrilous attack against Sansovino while working on the Santa Casa commission, charging him with lacking *disegno.* The sculptor's retort was that "works are made with the hands and not with words," and that "*buon disegno* is to be found not in paper, but in the perfection of the finished work in stone."[40] This he followed with the request that Bandinelli accord him respect, to which the insolent Baccio responded "arrogantly and with many abusive words." Sansovino, enraged, lunged at Bandinelli with the intent of killing him (an urge that also seized Cellini years later), after which Bandinelli decamped, with his unfinished relief, to Ancona. Besides highlighting Bandinelli's unattractive temperament, this incident serves to set up a polarity between a mere sculptor, epitomized by the marble carver Sansovino, who thinks only in terms of stone and engages in manual labor—a craftsman who fabricates "works made with the hands"—and a sculptor-draftsman, one adept with stone, but whose ideas and practice have a foundation in the elevated pursuit of drawing, of which Bandinelli casts himself as the archetype. The fundamental correlation between *buon disegno*, with its attendant prized faculty of invention, and good sculpture is one the older master failed to comprehend.[41] For him, all that mattered was the finished work, whereas for Bandinelli *disegno* was preeminent, and the requisite prelude to anything else.[42]

Bandinelli's teacher, the sculptor Giovanni Francesco Rustici, articulated a stance antithetical to Sansovino's championing of stone: "You must first think, then make sketches [*schizzi*], and after that drawings [*disegni*]; which done, you must put them aside for weeks and even months without looking at them, and then, choosing the best, put them into execution."[43] Implicit in this counsel is the primacy of drawing that Bandinelli would enunciate in the Loreto incident. Rustici's words also seem to posit a correlation between and even a certain fusion of drawn sketches and the sculptor's *schizzi* or *modelli* in wax, clay, or plaster (a valid reciprocity given that they shared a common function, both being preparatory to the genesis of a sculpture and both also routinely employed as presentation pieces for securing a patron's approval).[44] The latter synthesis, too, is one that his pupil Bandinelli put into practice, for references to drawings and accompanying models occur more than once in his *Vita* and in documents pertaining to his employment at the ducal court in Florence beginning in the 1540s.

In his youth, Bandinelli copied the works of earlier Florentine sculptors both in drawings and in wax and clay. To gain favor with Emperor Charles V, the enterprising artist in 1529 presented him with a bronze relief of the Deposition, an invention he formulated in a pen-and-ink composition drawing and elaborated in a *modello* known through derivative iterations (see cat. 21). Years later, persuading Duke Cosimo to support the ambitious scheme for the choir of Florence Cathedral, Bandinelli presented him with

FIG. 43
Agostino Veneziano
The Academy of Baccio Bandinelli, 1531
Engraving, 274 × 298 mm
Biblioteca Marucelliana, Florence

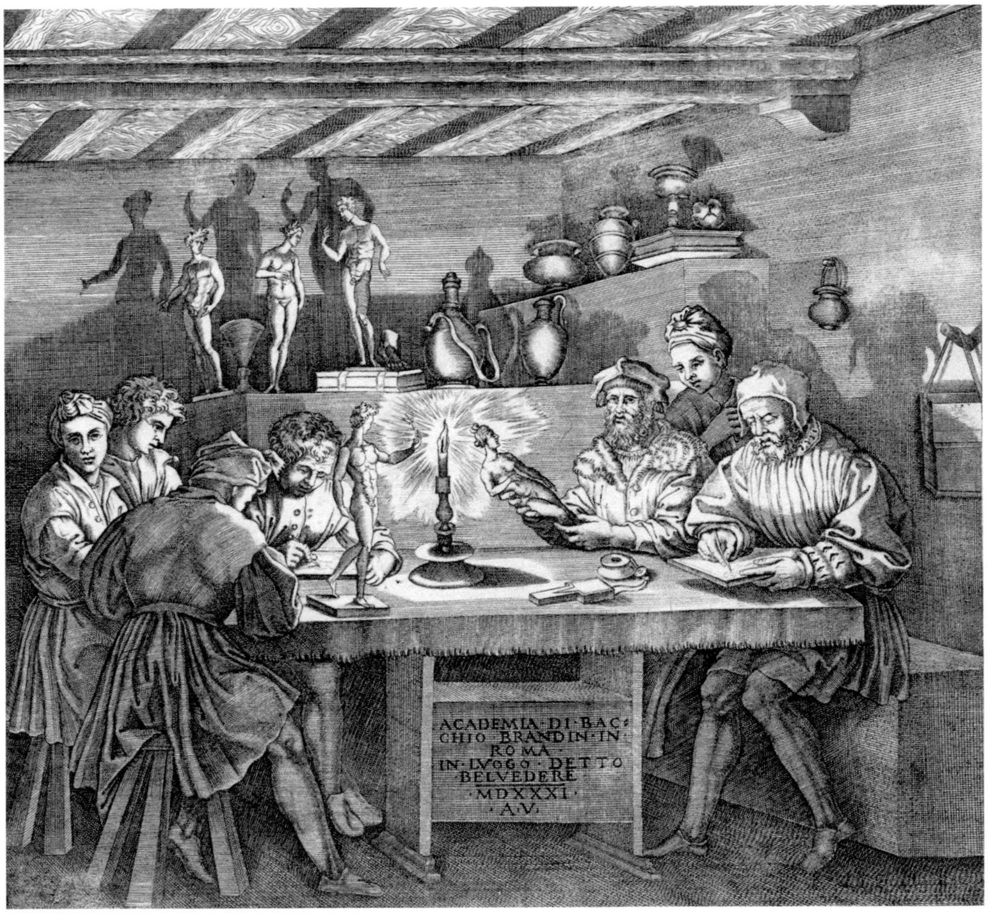

numerous drawings and models; these impressed "both for their variety and number and likewise for their beauty, for the reason that Baccio worked boldly in wax and drew very well."[45] A fountain for the Boboli Garden likewise occasioned a flurry of drawings (including a whole *rinvolto delli disegni*, or roll of drawings)[46] and models. The initial idea was approved by Duke Cosimo and the Duchess Eleonora on the basis of the designs Bandinelli submitted. Further drawings were then solicited by the duke's agent Luca Martini. Bandinelli failed to oblige in a timely fashion and defended his dilatoriness with the pedantic explanation, resonant of Rustici's dictum, that in order to achieve the "variety and invention" he always sought in his drawings it was necessary to have them all before him so as to compare and determine which was the most pleasing.[47] Determined to advance the project, the anxious Martini then urged Bandinelli to provide *piu disegni o modelli*—a request that expressly enunciates the interchangeability, here for reasons of expediency, of drawings and models.[48] The engraving of Bandinelli's academy in Rome already referred to (fig. 43) shows industrious pupils drawing not ancient fragments or corpses or other stock-in-trade implements of the studio but small-scale sculptures—bronze statuettes, perhaps, but more likely the models the artist made for such *bronzetti* in his apartments in the Belvedere (the actual locus depicted in the print) while

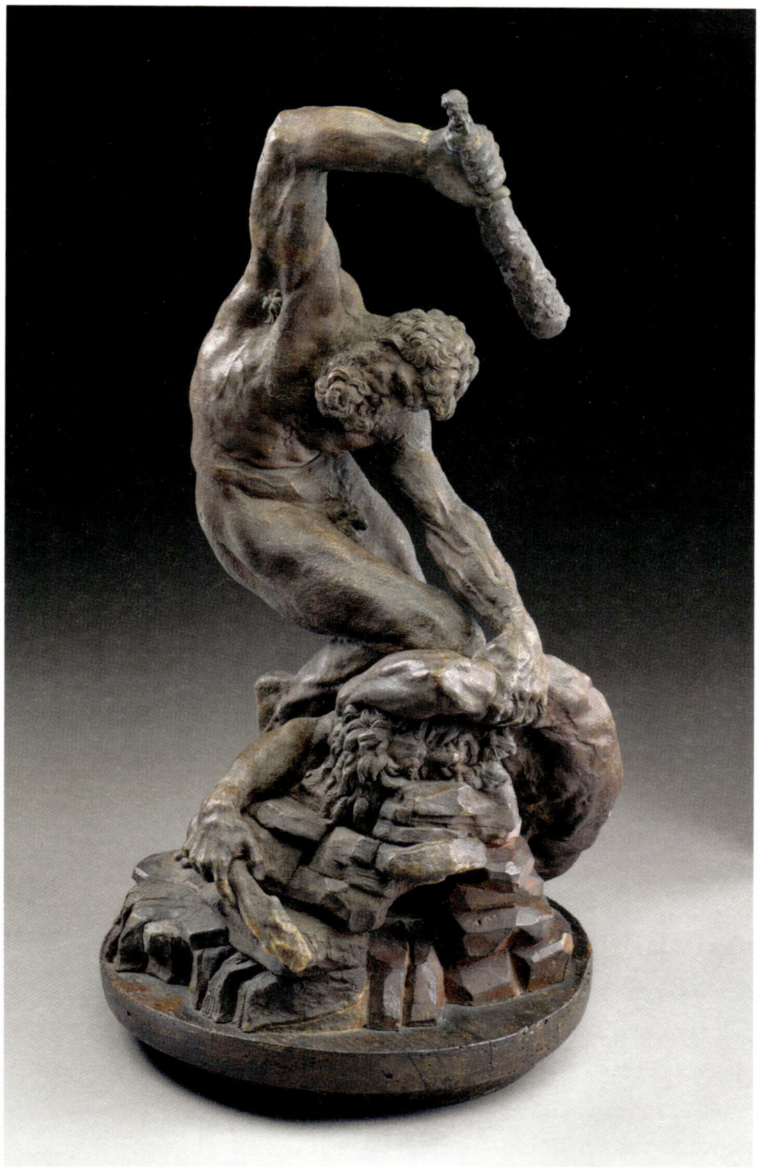

FIG. 44
Baccio Bandinelli
Model for Hercules and Cacus, c. 1525
Wax, 73 cm high
Staatliche Museen, Berlin

resident in the city.[49] And one of the two surviving wax *modelli* by Bandinelli represents Hercules and Cacus (fig. 44),[50] a subject he also treated in drawings—including the one depicted in his painted portrait (see cat. 28).

The most remarkable convergence of drawing and sculpture in Bandinelli's activity occurred when he was charged by Cardinal Giulio de' Medici with carving a copy of the celebrated ancient marble *Laocoön* (a commission that led him to boast that he would not merely equal the original, but surpass it in perfection) in Rome in 1520. In preparation for this enterprise he made drawings of the sculpture (see cat. 20) and a wax model.[51] He also made a full-scale cartoon (as Michelangelo was apprised in a letter from his friend Leonardo Sallaio) in lead white and charcoal.[52] Although this was common practice for fresco painting—Raphael's *School of Athens* cartoon is an iconic example—it was not routine for sculpture. As with the *Birth of the Virgin* relief for the Santa Casa di Loreto, Bandinelli again approached a commission for sculpture in the manner of a painter. Yet there is a fundamental difference between the drawings for *The Birth of the Virgin*, figure and composition studies done in red chalk and pen and ink, and the monumental cartoon for the *Laocoön*, executed in the combination of graphic media supremely suited to describing light and shadow and the plastic volume of forms, that is, for imparting to the design the sculptural property of relief.[53] Here, in the appropriation of the painter's preparatory cartoon for the genesis of a sculpture, was the purest statement of the integral connection of *disegno* and *rilievo*. Painting and sculpture are synthesized through the medium of drawing.

Other episodes of Bandinelli's biography bear out the cartoon's functionality in that artistic edict. In chronicling his feeble efforts as a painter, Vasari adopted a curious pattern of referring in each instance to Bandinelli having first executed a preparatory cartoon. (The medium—charcoal and lead white, as employed for the *Laocoön*—is only specified in one other instance but all must have followed this standard technique.) In this recitation, the cartoon is always praised, while the corresponding painting always derided[54]—a device that establishes a dichotomy between Bandinelli's indisputable gifts as a draftsman, displayed in the cartoon, and his ineptitude as a painter. The perilous chasm between cartoon and painting—between *disegno* and *pittura/colore*—revealed itself most fatefully when Bandinelli undertook a cartoon of the Deposition followed by a painting, which he placed on public display. Among the viewers was Michelangelo who, having closely studied every detail of the work, "marveled that so good a draftsman as Bandinelli should allow a picture so crude and wanting in grace to leave his hands, that he had seen the most feeble painters execute their works in a better manner, and that this was no art for Bandinelli."[55] Francisco de Holanda, in the second of his *Roman Dialogues* recording alleged conversations with Michelangelo, claims to have paid Bandinelli a visit one day when he was trying to paint in oil and found him unable to do so. Regardless of whether this suspect encounter actually took place, the commentary resonates with Michelangelo's words and may reflect information he imparted to the dialogue's author.[56] Vasari concurred with Michelangelo's verdict and used the telling of the *Deposition* anecdote as an opportunity to reiterate that "Bandinelli's drawings were very beautiful but in colors he executed them badly and without grace."[57] Not surprisingly, the narrator of the revisionist "Memoriale" defensively offers a more favorable view of Bandinelli's efforts as a painter—"... though there are some highly praised paintings from my hand, this was never the principal direction of my talent"—then goes on to remark, "I principally applied myself to drawing, in which I was outstanding in the judgment of Michelangelo, of our princes, and of the best people ...." Purging the opprobrium and highlighting the praise, Bandinelli's own telling echoes Michelangelo's judgment that his true penchant was for drawing.[58]

Bandinelli purportedly renounced the act of painting in the wake of Michelangelo's indictment (which, ironically, concurred with Leonardo's earlier and more kindly delivered advice to pursue sculpture), but he did not relinquish the attendant ambitions. Rather, he channeled them into the production of drawings and cartoons, vehicles that allowed him to display the prodigious gifts as a draftsman that his admirers and critics alike extolled. These were given over to executants "who handled colors passing well" to carry out.[59] Even the eminently capable Bronzino was required to follow without deviation a design furnished by Bandinelli when painting an altarpiece of the Lamentation for the Chapel of Eleonora in the Palazzo Vecchio because the duchess was so pleased with the invention. Venturing that he wanted to execute some preparatory drawings before commencing the work, Bronzino was cautioned by Duke Cosimo, "Don't introduce any new ideas, because I like that one [by Bandinelli]."[60]

Reflected in the constraints placed on Bronzino was the staunch belief of both the duke and his consort that Bandinelli was unrivaled when it came to matters of *disegno* and *invenzione*—a claim the sculptor himself regularly pressed on them through his verbal entreaties and the submission of drawings and models for their approval.[61] Cellini and Ammanati may have been permitted to compete with Bandinelli for the commission for the Neptune fountain on the Piazza della Signoria, but the duke remained persuaded that in "ability, judgment and design [*disegno*] Bandinelli was still better than any of the sculptors who were in his service."[62] Although his rivals complained of favoritism, the dearth of drawings by Cellini, Ammanati, Tribolo, Vincenzo Danti, and other sculptors of the Medici court only confirms that the prolific draftsman Bandinelli was indeed the peerless master of *disegno*—author of a bountiful variety of ideas from which the most pleasing solution could be chosen.[63] Affirming Bandinelli's superiority over other contenders for the Neptune fountain, Vasari charitably (and repetitively) remarked that, had Bandinelli not died, the commission would surely have fallen to him because of his superior *disegno e 'l giudicio e la virtù* ("design, judgment, and ability").[64]

The quasi-collaboration with Bronzino forecasted Bandinelli's evolution into the quintessential Cinquecento role of designer—the master who conceives ideas and realizes them in the form of drawings, cartoons, and *modelli*, then leaves the execution of the actual work to assistants (or, alternatively, as was frequently the case with Bandinelli, abandons it entirely).[65] In this practice drawings were the essential vehicle—at once the showcase for invention and the tools for instruction. Thus there exists a payment by the Opera of Santa Maria del Fiore for *3 quaderni di fogli per disegnare per il Cavaliere* [Bandinelli][66]—paper for the drawings that Bandinelli would submit for approval and provide to the assistants who would carve the reliefs for the choir based on those designs from his hand.

As venerable antitypes for his reliance on assistants (a practice at times questioned by Duke Cosimo and for which he was criticized by contemporaries), Bandinelli adduced the praiseworthy examples of Donatello and Ghiberti, master sculptor-draftsmen who each instructed legions of pupils and produced some of the most celebrated works of Florentine art. A letter he penned in December 1547 concerning statues for the choir of Florence Cathedral was an occasion to remind the duke that Donatello always had in his *bottega* at any one time 18 or 20 *garzoni*, without whom he could not have realized such grand creations as the altar of Sant'Antonio in Padua (a model for Bandinelli's own ambitious altar project), and yet the great sculptor never produced a *brutta opera*.[67] Some years later, in a missive discussing the reliefs for the choir, Bandinelli invoked Ghiberti as an even more apposite model for the practice of maintaining a large corps of assistants, praising him as a draftsman and as a teacher: "... to know the true way to create beautiful things, take the example of Lorenzo di Bartolo [Ghiberti] who was an outstanding draftsman: when he was commissioned the [Baptistery] doors, he hired to help him youths who could draw very well, and thus produced two good things: admirable works and good artists."[68] The precedent of Ghiberti's *bottega* was indeed pertinent, for Bandinelli, too, had in his workshop *scarpellini et putti presi per insegnare loro disegnare* (chisellers and boys to teach to draw), as Duke Cosimo himself had once remarked in

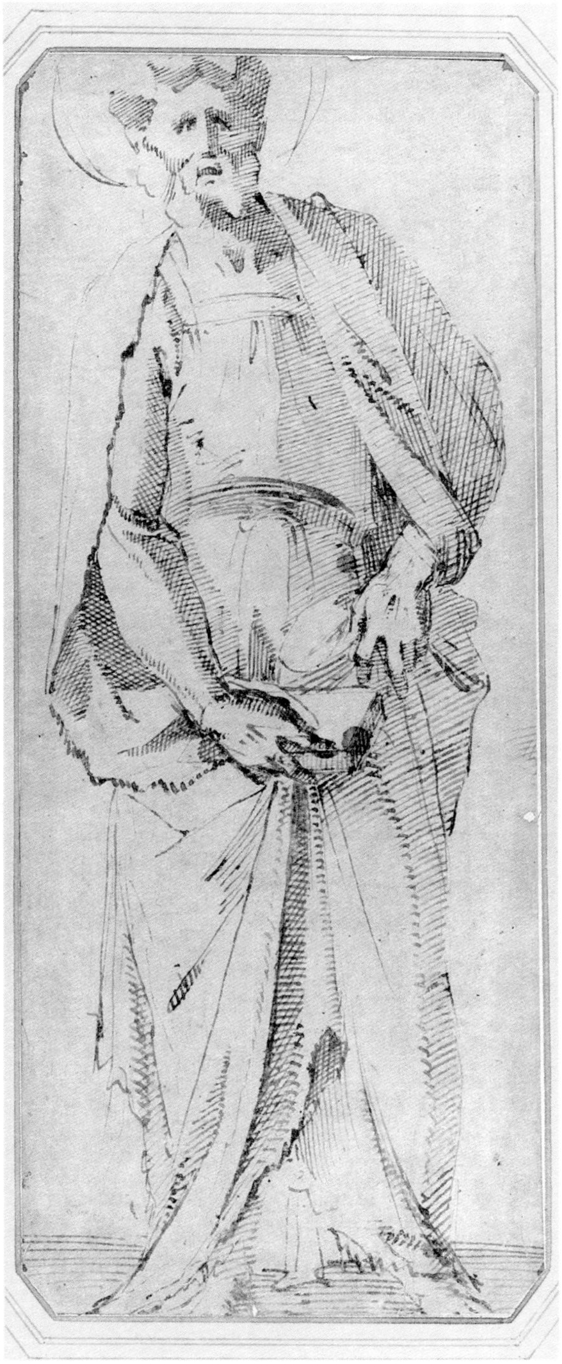

FIG. 45
Giovanni Bandini
Standing Apostle, c. 1560
Pen and brown ink, on paper, 381 × 156 mm
The Metropolitan Museum of Art,
New York, Robert Lehman Collection

an affectionate note to his sculptor.[69] Those assistants not only carried out the labor of marble carving for the choir and other commissions but also learned from their master how to draw, and in that quintessential sculptor-draftsman's manner epitomized in Bandinelli's own drawings (fig. 45).

At the same time, Bandinelli must have known that those lofty comparisons with Donatello and Ghiberti were somewhat disingenuous given the mediocre abilities of some of his assistants and his failure to complete many of the grand projects entrusted to him. In the "Memoriale", he acknowledges that the criticism of Michelangelo, Vasari, and others to this effect was justified, then offers the usual apology:

> ... many people, and particularly the good Buoniaruoti, whose judgment I respected above all others because he was a connoisseur and because he was not motivated by malice, blamed me sometimes because, once I had started and carefully drawn my more important works, I let Rossi, Ammannati, Clemente, and others have a hand in them. I do not deny that in a great measure he was right, because it may be that the works did not come out with that great perfection which they would have had with my own hand, but one must consider that I had, and have always had, many troubles in which, in addition to the illnesses and the family cares of my house my children, my studies had a good part."[70]

Contained in the self-reckoning is the axiomatic statement that it was in his drawings that Bandinelli expended all his effort.

This passage from the "Memoriale" ends with an almost wistful reference to the pursuit of drawing and of the life of the mind that this artist-philosopher—spared the manual labor performed by his assistants and surrounded by his volumes of Petrarch and Pliny—strove to pursue.[71] The engraving of Bandinelli's academy, in which *garzoni* gather around their teacher, industriously drawing small-scale models and statuettes (see fig. 43), offers a similarly Elysian vision of the artist's *équipe*. Some of the pupils cast shadows on the wall—Pliny's explanation for the origins of painting[71]—but none notices the silhouettes or traces their contours. Painting is of no concern in this sculptor-draftsman's studio, from which all implements of the painter's craft have been banished. This academy is devoted to *disegno*. Its members labor to master the sculptural property of *rilievo*—a quality enhanced by the dramatic chiaroscuro of the candlelight flickering in the darkness—that drawing is uniquely capable of describing. Here is a demonstration of the efficacy of the formula for collaboration and instruction practiced by Donatello, Ghiberti, and Bandinelli himself, with drawing as the essential pedagogical tool for producing good sculptors and good draftsmen. And in the pupils' activity is a literal illustration of the ineffable link of sculpture and drawing—of Donatello's maxim that the origins of sculpture reside in *disegno*.[73]

~

The historical legacy of drawing and sculpture as concomitants was integral to Bandinelli's artistic formation, his idiom as draftsman and sculptor alike an expression of the conjoining of *disegno* and *rilievo*.[74] Bandinelli's early studies after Quattrocento sources (see figs. 38, 39) literally copy or approximate reliefs. His many designs for actual reliefs—the base of the Andrea Doria monument, elements of the tomb of Pope Clement VII, the Florence Cathedral choir panels (fig. 46)—masterfully simulate the effects of the sculpture they describe. And although none of his cartoons survives, those monumental monochrome drawings, too, must have been supreme demonstrations of the ability of *disegno* to emulate relief. Conversely, Bandinelli's carved reliefs, with their flat, planar surfaces and incisive, linear contours often have the aspect of a drawing done in stone.

Carved from marble or cast in bronze, relief is the province of sculpture. But in its capacity for describing space and capturing detail, relief sculpture partakes of the properties of painting. Acknowledging those pictorial qualities, Leonardo considered relief to be "a mixture of painting and sculpture,"[75] a tenet Bandinelli demonstrated in *The Birth of the Virgin* (see fig. 61). But, Leonardo continued, the description of *rilievo*—of those traits that an actual relief possesses merely by existing in the illumination created by nature, independent of the sculptor's intervention—is something only the superior art of painting can achieve owing to the painter's expert knowledge of the means to render the qualities of light and shadow. Early in his career Bandinelli, the self-styled disciple of Leonardo, had attempted to demonstrate the painter's mastery. In the privileging of drawing that followed that failed effort, and the forging of a style that was the graphic

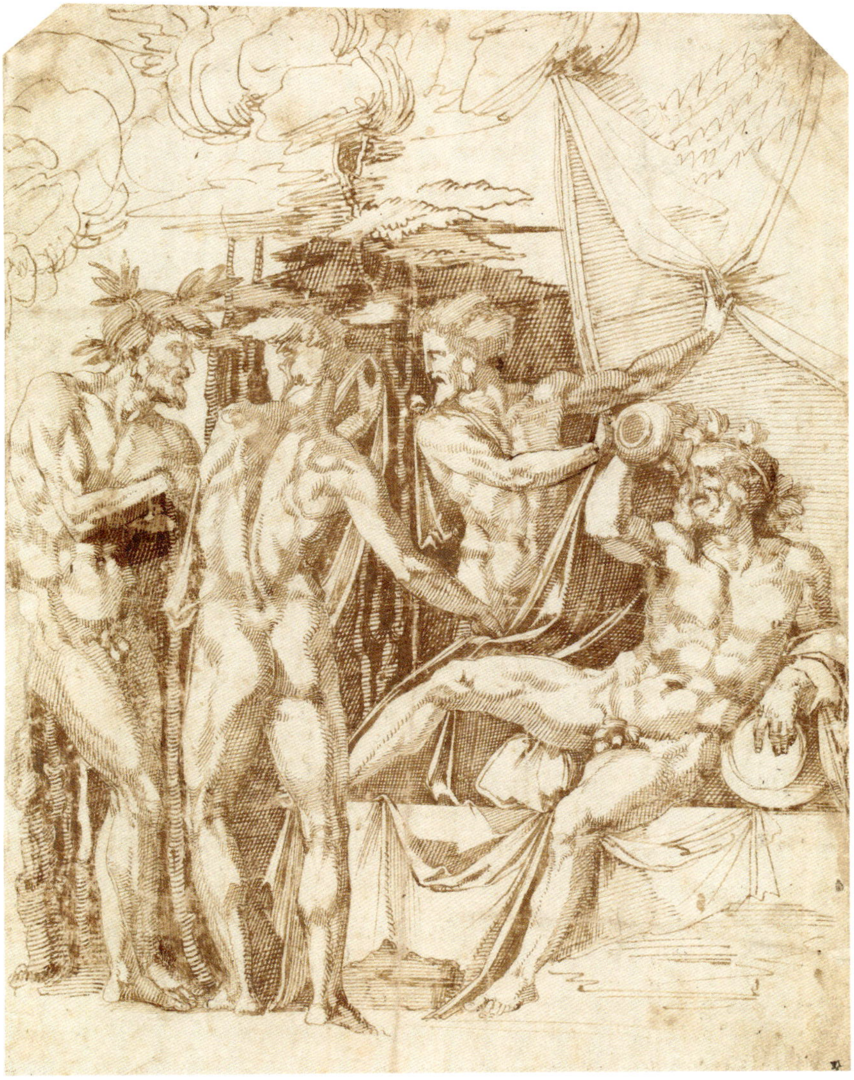

FIG. 46
Baccio Bandinelli
The Drunkenness of Noah, c. 1547–48
Pen and brown ink, over black chalk, on paper, 362 × 287 mm
British Museum, London

analogue of sculpture, he formulated the proposition that *disegno* was the optimal vehicle for describing *rilievo*. Through this appropriation of one of the superior attributes of painting, drawing is interjected into the *paragone* debate, a purveyor of its own merits and a worthy competitor of both painting and sculpture. As though to demonstrate the wondrous variety and capacity of *disegno*—what he in his unfinished treatise hailed as its "disposition of infinite and varied kinds, formed of so many different ways, like the majesty of Nature"[76]—Bandinelli in the design for the Andrea Doria monument transfers to drawing the material characteristics of bronze sculpture (fig. 47). In the study of the dead Christ for the *Lamentation* above the high altar of Florence Cathedral (fig. 48), as in the earlier Belvedere Torso (see fig. 42) and the *Hercules and Cacus* sketch displayed in his self-portrait (see cat. 28), he instead transforms marble into flesh, now appropriating for drawing the animating power of painting.[77] Painting might aspire to imitate sculpture, and sculpture to approximate some of the attributes of painting, but only drawing could rival both painting and sculpture.

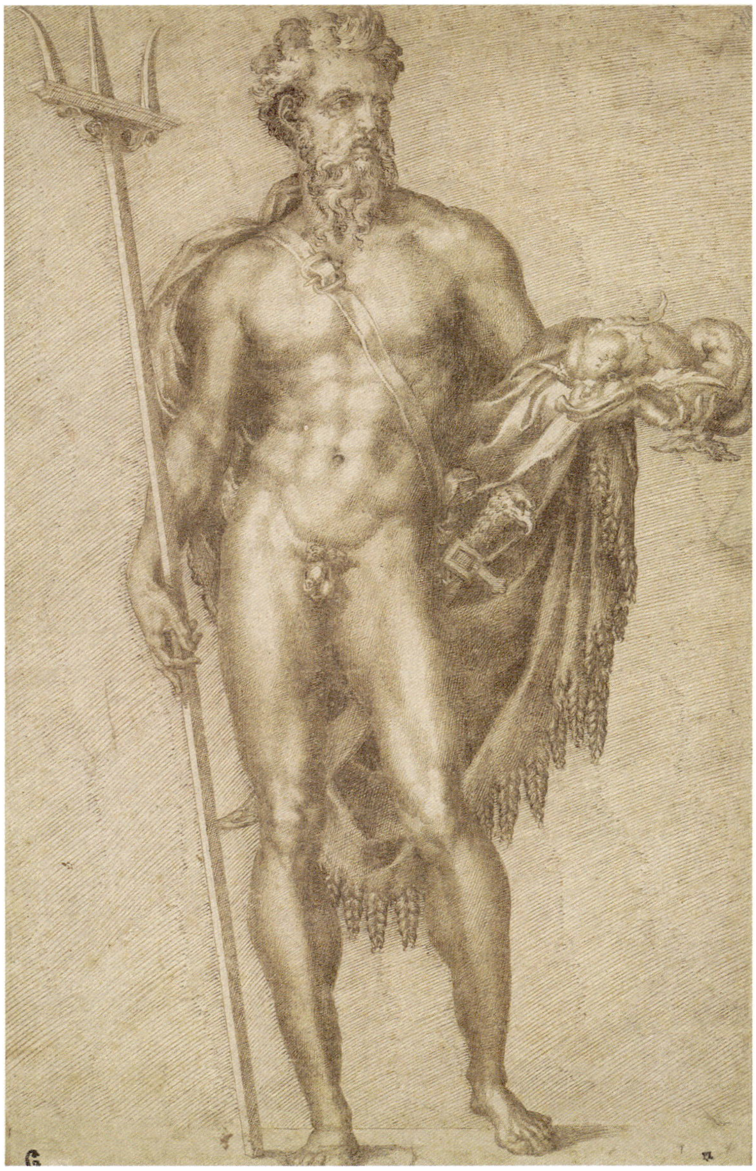

FIG. 47
Baccio Bandinelli
Andrea Doria as Neptune, c. 1529–35
Pen and two tones of brown ink over slight traces of stylus and black chalk underdrawing, on paper, 425 × 275 mm
British Museum, London

In the hands of the true sculptor-draftsman (which Bandinelli alone among his contemporaries, save the always greater Michelangelo, could claim to be) stone could be brought to life, a divine act of creation. This is the message of the painted self-portrait, in which the stately nobleman-artist, sporting the insignia of the chivalric Order of Saint James bestowed on him by the Emperor Charles V, proudly displays a monumental red-chalk drawing of Hercules and Cacus, a subject he also treated in marble. The image is similar but not identical to actual drawings from Bandinelli's hand (see cat. 20). Is this a drawing of a sculpture? A drawing of a red wax or clay model for a sculpture? An idea for a sculpture? Or a drawing of figures who exhibit the sculptural solidity and volume of carved marble, done not as a preparatory exercise but as a demonstration for the implied audience of its creator's abundant gifts? Whatever the case, there could be no clearer statement of drawing as both the foundation and the necessary counterpart of sculpture. Without *disegno*, carved stone remains inert, as the two gray, lifeless *pietra serena* heads near the artist's feet (the bearded and beardless protagonists of the Hercules group shown in the drawing) demonstrate. But through drawing, sculpture comes to life—a claim made by the impudent young artist who challenged Sansovino, and by the older and wiser Bandinelli, the dignified teacher in the portrait who points rhetorically with a stick of red chalk to his own masterful promulgation of this lesson.

In contrast to the engraved portraits of him (see fig. 65),[78] Bandinelli here is not surrounded by sculpture. Rather, he holds up a drawing of a sculpture, done in the graphic manner of a painter. In this is a statement of the nobility of *disegno* and its primacy above all the arts. There could be no more poetic conjuring of Bandinelli's own reflection in the "Memoriale", *tutto il mio intento era nel disegnare*[79]—the essential truth that all he ever wanted to do was draw.

FIG. 48
Baccio Bandinelli
Study for the Dead Christ, c. 1550
Red chalk with traces of stylus underdrawing, on paper, 255 × 407 mm
Musée du Louvre, Paris

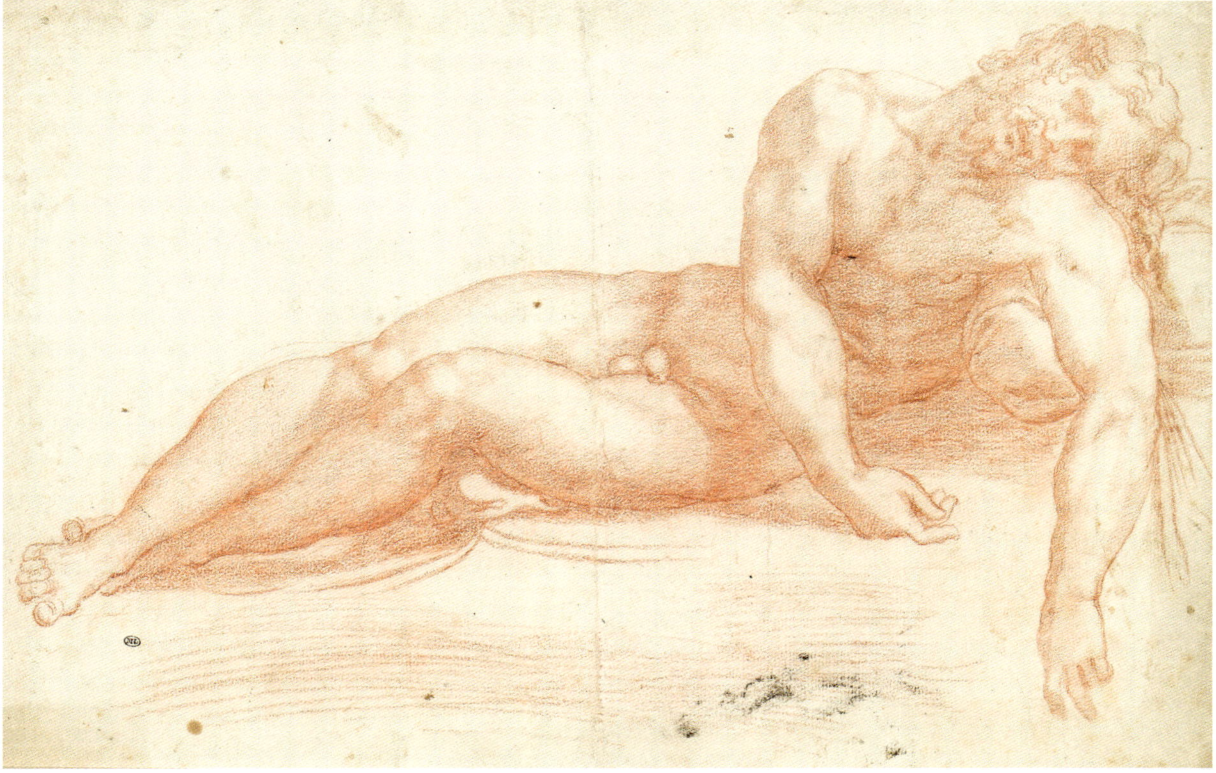

Notes

I wish to thank Michael Cole for encouraging me to think about Bandinelli and for commenting thoughtfully on a draft of this essay. I am indebted to him and to Oliver Tostmann for inviting me to contribute to the present catalogue, and to Elizabeth Reluga for kind assistance with photographs, bibliography, and information on the Gardner Bandinelli portrait. Andrew Butterfield and Sheryl Reiss generously shared their expertise in responding to various queries. Finally, for reading the text and offering numerous insights, I am grateful to Luke Syson.

1 Vasari-Milanesi 1906, vol. 6, p. 195.
2 Baldassare Turini da Pescia, who was responsible for overseeing Bandinelli's work on the Medici papal tombs, disparaged the sculptor as a "greedy, boastful, deceitful, and changeable"; translated and quoted in Poeschke 1996, p. 168.
3 These can be traced in the magisterial corpus of documents pertaining to the artist, cited throughout this essay, published by Louis Waldman (Waldman 2004). Bandinelli, who devoted considerable time and resources to real estate transactions over many years, was involved in a startling number of property disputes (Waldman 2004, passim) and in disagreements with quarrymen and other laborers (Waldman 2004, doc. 269). An epistolary exchange of 7 May 1549 between two of Duke Cosimo's secretaries refers to a vicious altercation with Bandinelli, and in June 1553 the sculptor was fined for hitting a groom with a brass oil lamp (Waldman 2004, pp. 388–89, doc. 665, and 524–25, doc. 950, respectively).
4 The treatise was known only indirectly until the original manuscript, fragmentary and partly in Bandinelli's own hand, was discovered by Louis Waldman (Waldman 2004, pp. 895–909).
5 Published by Colasanti in 1905 (Bandinelli 1905). Long believed to be autograph, the "Memoriale" was recently recognized by Louis Waldman as a "Seicento pastiche" composed by Bandinelli's grandson, Baccio Bandinelli il Giovane (Waldman 2004, p. x). The work, which contains echoes and reflections of the sculptor's own views, functions as a historical corrective and (posthumous) apologia defending Bandinelli against the charges of his detractors.
6 Letter of October 1545; Waldman 2004, p. 320, doc. 520. The unscrupulous Aretino attempted to blackmail Michelangelo after less hostile overtures to procure drawings from him failed. For his letter, see Klein and Zerner 1989, pp. 122–24.
7 Bandinelli 1905; translation from Klein and Zerner 1989, p. 149.
8 Transcribed in Waldman 2004, p. 827, doc. 1521. The text was composed in 1570. A similar sentiment is expressed in Bocchi's *Le Bellezze della città di Firenze* (Bocchi 1677 [first published 1591], p. 52).
9 Galileo Galilei, "Considerazioni al Tasso," in Galilei 1943, p. 96; translated and quoted in Barkan 1999, p. 271; Waldman 2004, p. 858, doc. 1574a.
10 Michelangelo was a painter, a sculptor, and an architect, and his drawings relate to all three categories of his artistic production. Bandinelli, in contrast, showed no aptitude for painting and was inept in matters of architecture, as Vasari repeatedly commented, and unlike Michelangelo can be strictly classified as a sculptor-draftsman. Guglielemo della Porta (a non-Florentine) might also be cited as a contradiction to the contention of my text, but the majority of his drawings are preserved in two sketchbooks from a circumscribed period of his activity, a different category of production than loose sheets executed over the length of an entire career. Nor is the Sienese Francesco di Giorgio an exception. Like Michelangelo, he was a painter and architect as well as a sculptor, and his graphic corpus—which includes drawings relating to his activity as a military engineer—is far smaller than Bandinelli's. Other Cinquecento sculptors not discussed elsewhere in this essay such as Montorsoli and Vincenzo Danti confirm the generalization.
11 To cite the example of only one Florentine Quattrocento painter, Paolo Uccello trained with Ghiberti; see further note 13. The pattern continued into the Seicento, as exemplified by the Florentine draftsman and printmaker Stefano della Bella, who trained in the workshop of goldsmith and sculptor and began his career as a painter.
12 Eisler 1981, n.p.
13 Again this points back to the origination of fifteenth- and early sixteenth-century Florentine sculptors in goldsmiths' shops. In contrast to drawings by Botticelli, Perugino, and Filippino Lippi, *inter alia* (for which see Petrioli Tofani 1992 and Chapman and Faietti 2010), certain of Domenico Ghirlandaio's drawings, with their vigorous cross-hatching, conform to this general characterization of a sculptor's graphic style. Although he was a painter, Ghirlandaio appears to have been trained as a goldsmith (Cadogan 2000, pp. 27–29) and was then attached to the workshop of Verrocchio. His case therefore corroborates rather than contradicts the premise that such tutelage engendered a specific graphic idiom. It could be argued, moreover, that what he imparted to his pupil Michelangelo was the legacy of the goldsmith's, or sculptor-goldsmith's, manner of drawing, which, as Cadogan has remarked with regard to Ghirlandaio, included "above all a facility in drawing, meticulous technique, and versatility of skill" (p. 27). See further Fischer 1994, who remarks that this particular graphic technique "probably originated in Siena as a method for giving bulk to figure drawing," and that "originally it might have been connected with sculpture since it enables the draughtsman to describe with great precision the lay of light and shadow on three dimensional figures" (p. 153). For a panoramic discussion of Renaissance notions of *disegno* particularly in relation to the goldsmiths' art and practice, see Syson and Thornton 2001, "The Value of *Disegno*," pp. 135–81. An exemplary case is Maso Finiguerra, for which see also the discussion by Wright 1994, pp. 133–39.
14 Quoted in Eisler 1981, n.p. The exhortation echoes in Michelangelo's well-known admonition to his hapless pupil Antonio Mini, "Draw Antonio, draw, and don't waste time!" Francisco de Holanda quotes Gauricus's statement about Donatello in the second of his *Dialogues* (Hollanda 1998, p. 92).
15 While the pronouncement may be a rhetorical device, it is also possible that this wisdom was passed down by Bellano or another of Donatello's Paduan pupils to artists like Riccio and Severo da Ravenna, whom Gauricus may well have known in Padua, as Andrew Butterfield has suggested (verbal communication).
16 Ghiberti's *Commentarii* also presaged such ideas in acclaiming *disegno* the "foundation and theory of both painting and sculpture." On this, see Syson and Thornton 2001, p. 136.
17 Castiglione 1959, p. 78; Vasari 1960, p. 205, in language that echoes Ghiberti's premise of the foundational role of *disegno*. Though never expressly mentioned, goldsmiths' art fell into this formulation as well, and it significant that Vasari begins his *Life* of Bandinelli by remarking that "no one was thought to be a good goldsmith who was not a good draftsman" (Vasari-Milanesi 1906, vol. 6, p. 135).
18 Eisler 1981, n.p.
19 For the influence of Donatello's San Lorenzo pulpits on the young Bandinelli, see Shearman 1960; Ward 1988, pp. 23–29, no. 10; Kathleen Weil-Garris Brandt in Darr 1985, pp. 245–46, under no. 93; Fulton 1997,

pp. 174–78; Françoise Viatte in Heikamp and Paolozzi Strozzi 2014, p. 296, under no. 13. Later in his career, Bandinelli more than once invoked Donatello as an efficacious model, as discussed elsewhere in this essay. In addition to the letter cited below (note 68), a discarded draft of a missive of October 1556 to Duke Cosimo concerning the choir project refers to Donatello's work in Padua and the final version of the same letter again cites Donatello, though in a different context, as a model (Waldman 2004, pp. 613–14, doc. 1133, and 615–16, doc. 1135). See further note 21.

20 Vasari-Milanesi 1906, vol. 6, p. 135.

21 See the discussion in Ward 1988, pp. 28–29, under no. 10. An early drawing of St. Jerome in the Wilderness is also significant in this regard for its generally Donatellesque character, as discussed by Ward 1988, pp. 24–25, no. 6. A lingering echo of Donatello's San Lorenzo pulpit reliefs is discernible in a *Crucifixion* drawing by Bandinelli from the 1520s (Albertina, Vienna, 14181; Louis Waldman in Franklin 2005, no. 93).

22 Museo di Capodimonte, Naples, 783; Ward 1988, p. 23, under no. 5; Ward 1982a, no. 251. Vasari recounts that the young Baccio also spent long hours copying Filippo Lippi's frescoes in Prato, but none of those early studies is known (Vasari-Milanesi 1906, vol. 6, p. 136). The young Baccio may have been heeding Alberti's advice that relief is a quality painters should strive for.

23 So described by Vasari in his *Vita* of Michelangelo (Vasari-Milanesi 1906, vol, 7, p. 161). Andrea del Sarto and Rosso Fiorentino are but two of the many artists mentioned in this connection.

24 Vasari-Milanesi 1906, vol. 6, p. 137. Elsewhere, however (vol. 5, p. 590), Vasari anoints Perino del Vaga, a gifted draftsman, as the best among the young artists of the generation who copied the *Cascina* cartoon, so the accolade is to some extent rhetorical.

25 Musée du Louvre, Paris, 93; Tuyll van Serooskerken 2008, no. 11; Viatte 2011, no. 26. An example inspired by *The Battle af Cascina* is a red-chalk drawing in the British Museum of a seated male nude breaking a stick over his knee, a loose quotation in reverse of the figure pulling up his stocking at the lower right of Michelangelo's cartoon, as discussed by Ward 1988, no. 5.

26 Bandinelli 1905; translation from Barkan 1999, p. 398, note 7. The formal instruction arranged by his father followed the revelation of his natural-born instinct for both drawing and sculpture: "Seeing me go around with drawings and paper and working with snow or dirt, as boys do, carving a lion or some other figure, he was able to perceive the energies and inclinations of nature, which rarely fail one if they are encouraged. So he began to instruct me in drawing." Barkan remarks that Bandinelli here presents himself as an "irrepressible" draftsman and "unstoppable sculptor" since childhood (p. 274).

27 Bandinelli 1905; translation from Klein and Zerner 1989, p. 149.

28 Vasari-Milanesi 1906, vol. 6, p. 138. There must also have been an element of competition with his teacher Rustici, who was talented both as a sculptor and as a painter. Indeed, one of Bandinelli's rare paintings was undertaken in a self-styled competition with Rustici (ibid., p. 147). No notice of Bandinelli's matriculation in the Florentine painters' guild (the Arte dei Medici e Speciali) has been found, but in a record of payment on 1 March 1512 he is referred to as "Bartolomeo di Michele Agnolo dipintore" (Waldman 2004, p. 24, doc. 58), and the following year a complaint was filed against him with the guild for failure to carry out work for which he was paid, probably the never-executed fresco in the atrium of Santissima Annunziata (Waldman 2004, pp. 25–26, doc. 61). Bandinelli only matriculated in the Arte dei Fabbricanti (the guild of sculptors, stone-cutters and carpenters) in 1559, at the end of his life (p. 725, doc. 1293).

29 Vasari-Milanesi 1906, vol. 6, pp. 138–39.

30 Parallels are also to be found the practice of Raphael, another quintessential painter-draftsman. For both Sarto and Raphael, the roots of this type of drawing lie in Leonardo, for whom such studies provided the means for exploring a figure's *moti mentali* or "movements of the mind."

31 See the discussion of Ward 1988, pp. 30–31, under no. 12.

32 Naturalism was championed as a superior virtue of painting by its advocates in the *paragone* debate, and red chalk was a graphic medium best suited for describing the warmth of human flesh among other naturalistic properties. The inability of sculpture to portray all of nature, in contrast to the mimetic art of painting, which could render every leaf and cloud as well as light and shadow, was adduced as evidence for painting's superiority by Leonardo, whose views on the *paragone* were expressed in his unfinished *Treatise on Painting.*

33 On Bandinelli's use and handling of red chalk, see Ward 1988, pp. 36–37, under no. 5; Ward 1982b. Most of Michelangelo's red-chalk figure drawings are connected not with marble sculpture but with the Sistine Chapel frescoes and thus do not contradict this generalization. The painter Bronzino is an exception from the painter's side of the equation in his almost exclusive preference, after his apprenticeship with Pontormo, for black chalk. That graphic medium is consistent with the cold, marble-like quality of flesh in his paintings. This is not to suggest that Florentine painters did not use black chalk, as indeed Fra Bartolommeo, Andrea del Sarto, and Pontormo all did (often interchangeably with red chalk)—and as Bandinelli himself did in a few of his early drawings—but to emphasize that red chalk was not the preferred medium of sculptors.

34 Fealty to Leonardo is an explanation Vasari offers for the puzzling and probably untrue story that Bandinelli, in a supreme act of wickedness, was responsible for cutting up Michelangelo's *Battle of Cascina* cartoon (Vasari-Milanesi 1906, vol, 6, p. 138).

35 Tuyll van Serooskerken 2008, no. 5; Viatte 2011, no. 7; Ward 1988, no. 14, for another version now in a New York private collection. The questionable identification of the sitter as Bandinelli's wife, Jacopa Doni, is based on the inscription by Baldinucci on the Louvre drawing.

36 Ward 1988, p. 24, no. 14, has suggested that the subject evokes the "clay heads of smiling women" that, according to Vasari, Leonardo made in his youth. A similar Leonardesque red-chalk drawing by Bandinelli in the Uffizi (491F; Heikamp and Paolozzi Strozzi 2014, no. 46) is conceivably even a study after one such model.

37 For the drawing, see Ward 1988, no. 8; Barkan 1999, p. 308.

38 On the Santa Casa di Loreto, see Weil-Garris 1977. The payments to Bandinelli are cited by Huntley 1971, pp. 117–23; and Waldman 2004, pp. 47–53, doc. 102. The left half of the *Birth of the Virgin* relief was completed much later by Raffaello da Montelupo, and the final payment to Bandinelli was made only on 13 September 1543. A similar, drawn-out, and fraught scenario took place when Bandinelli was commissioned in 1528/29 to cast a bronze sculpture of Andrea Doria in Genoa (see fig. 47), a project for which he was paid handsomely in advance, which dragged on for many years to the increasing ire and despair of his patrons, and which was finally completed in a diminished and underwhelming form (in marble rather than bronze) far removed from the

sculptor's inflated promises and handsome designs. Bandinelli's work on the tombs of Popes Leo X and Clement VII (see further note 42 below) once again followed the same erratic and protracted pattern.

39 In the apt phrase of Weil-Garris 1981, p. 233. The point has also been made and elaborated by Roger Ward, who remarked of the *Birth of the Virgin* relief that Bandinelli's "working process, with its numerous steps of design and elaboration, was analogous to if not identical with that of contemporaneous Florentine painters; in this respect he was completely exceptional amongst sculptors of his generation and practically unique in the history of Renaissance art" (Ward 1988, p. 41, under no. 18). Some of Bandinelli's preparatory drawings for this relief are published by Ward (nos. 17–20), with further discussion of other sheets. See also cat. 9, 10, and 11.

40 Vasari-Milanesi 1906, vol. 6, pp. 142–43.

41 This incident is discussed and analyzed by Weil-Garris 1981, p. 229; and Barkan 1999, pp. 323–34.

42 This was not the only time in his career that Bandinelli found it useful to assail a rival for lacking the faculty of *disegno*. He reiterated the charge against the sculptor Alfonso Lombardo, who had been chosen to execute the tomb of Pope Clement VII (a prestigious commission Bandinelli coveted), appealing to a Medici relation with the claim that he was most worthy and that "Alfonso was a sculptor without the power of *disegno* and without skill and judgment in handling of marble"—twinned virtues he, in contrast, possessed (Vasari-Milanesi 1906, vol. 6, p. 163). His maneuvering was successful, but work on the monument and the pendant tomb of Pope Leo X dragged on to the displeasure of Clement's executors, only to be completed finally, in diminished form, by others. Later, when attempting to thwart Cellini's attempt to insinuate himself into the cathedral choir project, Bandinelli insisted to Duke Cosimo that "Benvenuto had at most the ability to chisel the reliefs, but not to design them" (Poeschke 1996, p. 26). That grand project, too, was never realized in its intended form; indeed, it is a pattern in Bandinelli's career that the self-serving boast of *buon disegno* did not always yield an admirable result.

The idea of the primacy and nobility of drawing that underlies the Sansovino anecdote is a Vasarian construct and might therefore be suspected of being the biographer's interpolation—a retrospective imputing of ideas current in the 1540s and 1550s to events that occurred in 1518/19. Militating against this argument is Vasari's presentation of the event not as a narrative, but, rather, as a dialogue spoken by the actual interlocutors—a rhetorical device that carries significance and is employed by the writer to signal the truthfulness of the account. Moreover, the prolific and autonomous nature of Bandinelli's activity as a draftsman (a good number of his drawings cannot be connected with commissions for sculpture) and his extraordinary establishment of a drawing academy in Rome in the 1530s confirm that he not only shared Vasari's thinking, but, in fact, anticipated it.

43 Rustici added that not everyone could work in the manner he described, especially not those practitioners who labored only for gain (in contrast to his independently wealthy self), and that "works should not be shown to anyone before they are finished, so as to be able to change them as many times and in as many ways as one wants, for whatever reason" (Vasari-Milanesi 1906, vol. 6, pp. 600–601). A survey of Rustici's career is Senechal 2009.

44 Given that the artist quoted here was primarily a sculptor, *schizzi* in this narration (which, given the context, presumably are *primi pensieri*) are assumed to refer to sculptors' models rather than to drawings, which would be redundant with the term *disegni* used in the same passage. The immediately following paragraph refers to Rustici's facility with modeling in terracotta and wax, the function and handling of which in sculptors' models are described by Vasari (Vasari 1960, pp. 148–49). The wax models that Bandinelli himself frequently made (see fig. 44) were *schizzi*. Bernini in the following century posited a certain synthesis of drawings and three-dimensional *modelli* (described as *bozzetti* for the first time in the Seicento, as Michael Cole has alerted me), recording the necessity "always to make sketches and drawings of your different ideas.... Put one thought after the other down on paper, judge them, consider their errors against ancient and modern works, make *modelli* in clay, always preserve that idea even in the most elaborately worked things." The process, he explains, is undertaken "in order to see variations on the idea" (letter to the Swedish architect Nicodemus Tessin the Younger; translation from Tomaso Montanari, "Creating an Eye for Models: The Role of Bernini," in Dickerson, Sigel, and Wardropper 2012, p. 65). Such thinking informs his tandem production of drawings and terracotta models. On the fluidity and fusion of drawing and model in Bandinelli's practice, see further note 61 below.

45 Vasari-Milanesi 1907, vol. 6, p. 179. A letter of 3 November 1549 written by Bandinelli to ducal secretary Jacopo Guidi refers to his design—which was either a drawing or a model—for a *Resurrection* for the predella of the high altar of the cathedral, submitted for the approval of Duke Cosimo "because I do not want to do anything without the good grace of his Excellency" (Waldman 2004, pp. 405–6, doc. 694).

46 A letter from Duke Cosimo's *provveditore* (commissioner or overseer) Luca Martini to Bandinelli dated 5 March 1551 acknowledges receipt of the roll of drawings for the fountain the sculptor sent, though too late to show the duchess (Waldman 2004, pp. 462–63, doc. 798); the first word of the commission is a letter of 15 January 1551 from Martini to Bandinelli written at the behest of Duchess Eleonora asking the sculptor to design a fountain for the Boboli Garden (pp. 454–55, doc. 787). It was not unknown for drawings to be maintained or organized in rolls; another instance of this practice is documented in the workshop of the sixteenth-century Venetian painter Jacopo Bassano.

47 Bandinelli writes, "I have finished another drawing in order to satisfy his Excellency, and I beg that he be willing to hear the reason why at present I have not sent it to him. Namely, that I feel myself disposed to find beautiful *invenzioni*, of which I have now begun yet another; and I do not wish to pause and finish them all. But it is necessary, if I wish to produce variation among the *invenzioni*, that I place all the designs in front of my own eyes, so that each of them illuminates the others helping me to see the truth of the errors in each, because I see by comparisons, and in this manner I will vary and improve my work so that it will please his Excellency, since drawings are made for no other reason than to consider them in comparison to each other" (Waldman 2004, pp. 491–92, doc. 867; translation from Barkan 1999, p. 305). This pronouncement was the disingenuous if polished excuse for what was in reality the lethargy that often set in once favor and a prestigious commission (and the accompanying wages) were procured.

48 *Et quanti più disegni o modelli harà, tanto più presto et meglio farà la resoluzione*; letter of 12 February 1551 (Waldman 2004, pp. 459–60, doc. 794).

49 An inventory of Bandinelli's belongings in Rome drawn up on 14 May 1541 lists one wax *modello* and additional quantities of wax presumably intended for fabricating others (Waldman 2004, pp. 214–15, doc.

351). Vasari says that Bandinelli made models for a series of statuettes in his apartments in the Belvedere (themselves trials or experiments in advance of the creation of never-realized monumental bronzes for Castel Sant'Angelo, and thus another form of *schizzi*), which included "Hercules, Venus, Apollo, Leda, and other fantasies" (Vasari-Milanesi 1906, vol. 6, p. 151). For the Castel Sant'Angelo project, see Lavin 2003. It may well be those actual *modelli* that are represented in the engraving—objects that resemble, and in one instance are identical to, known small bronzes by Bandinelli. (On this little-known aspect of Bandinelli's production, see the discussion by Louis Waldman in Franklin 2005, under no. 96; and now Heikamp and Paolozzi Strozzi 2014, nos. 28–35). Bandinelli's *Jason* statuette, which resembles another one of *Hercules* (Heikamp and Paolozzi Strozzi 2014, nos. 30 and 32), appears to be represented in the drawing academy print to the left of the candle (see fig. 43); however, according to Waldman, that work was cast in Florence only in the mid-1540s—some years after the date of the engraving. The object studied by the pupil must therefore be a model rather than the actual bronze. Similarly, though the statuette held by Bandinelli himself in the print (the bearded, fur-robed figure seated at the right) resembles his bronze *Cleopatra*, it, too, is probably a model since that work likewise was only cast in the mid-1540s. Waldman already observed, though with no further analysis or specific identifications of the works in question, that "countless small models populate many contemporary portraits and self-portraits of Bandinelli, especially the Academy prints" (fig. 43 and cat. 28). Such bronzes by Bandinelli are documented in the ducal Guardaroba in 1552 and in the Tribuna of the Uffizi in the later sixteenth century (Waldman 2004, pp. 535, doc. 977, and 857–58, doc. 1573).

50 Executed in 1525, the *modello* dates from the first, interrupted iteration of the commission for the monumental sculpture that was eventually completed in 1534. It was reproduced in a contemporaneous engraving by Agostino Veneziano (for which see Louis Waldman in Franklin 2005, no. 97; on the sculpture and the commission, see Pope-Hennessy 1986, pp. 363–64; Bush 1980; and Francini and Vossilla 1999). Vasari reports that Bandinelli rejected the original design recorded in the *modello* after determining that the block of marble was too shallow, then produced a number of new models from which his patron, Pope Clement VII, chose the preferred submission (Vasari-Milanesi 1906, vol. 6, p. 151)—an act of *paragone* or comparison among choices carried out in order to determine which was superior that mimics Bandinelli's advocacy of precisely this practice with drawings, for which see note 47 above. Obviously prized, the model eventually became the possession of Cosimo I and is documented in the Palazzo Vecchio by 1553 (Waldman 2004, p. 535, doc. 977) and in the Grand Ducal Guardaroba in 1587 (pp. 854–55, doc. 1563). Bandinelli's other extant wax *modello* is a *Neptune* (Musée Fabre, Montpellier; Heikamp and Paolozzi Strozzi 2014, no. 34); it, too, closely resembles a number of drawings by him.

51 Pope Clement VII's secretary Pier Polo Marzo refers to a *disegno* of the Laocoön in two letters to Bandinelli dated 13 August and 3 October 1531 (Waldman 2004, pp. 114–15, docs. 209 and 210). Two drawings of the *Laocoön* by Bandinelli are known (both in the Uffizi, 14785F and 14786F); the latter, quite unusually for Bandinelli, is executed in a combination of black and red chalks as though to signal that the drawing straddles or claims the properties of both painting and sculpture.

52 In a letter of 11 February 1520 to Michelangelo in Florence, Sellaio wrote from Rome, *Avete a sapere chome Bac[i]o a fatto 1.o chartone d'uno Laochonte* (Waldman 2004, pp. 55–56, doc. 110). The cartoon is also mentioned by Vasari, who describes the medium (Vasari-Milanesi 1906, vol. 6, p. 146).

53 Vasari remarks that in the best cartoons, in which great care has been taken to describe light and shadow, the forms "stand out from the paper in relief" (Vasari 1960, pp. 214–15). Perino del Vaga's demonstrations, lauded by Vasari, confirm that *rilievo* was an essential quality of cartoons (Wolk-Simon 1992, pp. 67–72). Reflected in Bandinelli's highly unusual step of executing a two-dimensional cartoon in preparation for this sculpture in the round (an undertaking that, as usual, dragged on for some years) were not only his propensity for thinking in terms of relief but also increasingly for conceiving even of three-dimensional sculpture as essentially relief-like in having primarily a frontal view.

54 Announcing his ambitions by appropriating a theme and a vehicle associated with Leonardo, Bandinelli executed a cartoon of Leda, then endeavored to show that he had mastered (though without ever having been taught) how to paint in oils. In the eyes of his contemporaries, the resulting work demonstrated just how feeble his mastery really was. A cartoon of the young St. John the Baptist with a lamb was followed by a painting of the subject undertaken in competition with Rustici, a brash and ill-considered demonstration that he, too, could be a painter-sculptor (Vasari-Milanesi 1906, vol, 6, p. 148). Again, the invention realized in the cartoon—the *disegno*—was applauded, while the finished work was derided as "crude and not painted in a beautiful manner." The fulsome praise accorded two other cartoons—a *Cleopatra* (Vasari-Milanesi 1906, vol. 6, p. 138), given as a gift to the gadabout goldsmith Piloto, and a *Lamentation* (ibid., p. 151) produced in connection with an unrealized altarpiece for Cestello (Santa Maria Madelena dei Pazzi)—carried with it the biographer's tacit approval that no corresponding paintings were ever realized. For the recently rediscovered *Leda* painting based on the lost cartoon, see Michela Zurla, in Heikamp and Paolozzi Strozzi 2014, no. 2, with earlier references. On the cartoon as a vehicle for self-promotion and display in Florentine practice, see Wolk-Simon 1992. At least one of Bandinelli's cartoons, the above-mentioned *Cleopatra*, was publicly displayed as a demonstration of its author's virtuosity.

55 Vasari-Milanesi 1906, vol. 6, p. 152.

56 Hollanda 1998, p. 92. Although the comment rings suspiciously like a conceit, it is possible that Francisco de Holanda knew Bandinelli in Rome. The inventory of Bandinelli's possessions in Rome drawn up in 1541 (for which see note 49, above) lists two portraits and three further paintings, one on canvas and two on panel, although whether any was by him is unclear. None of the subjects is identified in the inventory, but a later annotation by Baccio Bandinelli il Giovane indicates that one of the panels represented the Burning of Troy.

57 Vasari-Milanesi 1906, vol. 6, pp. 151–52. Michelangelo's harsh judgment was reported to Bandinelli by their mutual, gossipy friend Piloto. The painting is presumed lost, but a possible fragment was identified by Roger Ward (1982, p. 226; see also Cox-Rearick 1989, p. 56 and p. 55, fig. 20). Vasari's description of the subject is similar but not identical to cat. 21, which Bandinelli may have based on his own earlier invention. A drawing by the artist of The Deposition recorded in the collection of Francesco and Lorenzo Salviati in the late sixteenth century was extolled by Francesco Bocchi as being "of an incredibly rare perfection" (Bocchi 1677; Waldman 2004, p. 861, doc. 1576g). Although his description makes clear he is referring to a drawing, Bocchi calls

this *Deposition* a *quadro,* indicating that it was framed and displayed like a painting. Given this, it is worth considering that the object in question may have been a cartoon.

58 Bandinelli 1905; translation from Klein and Zerner 1989, p. 149. This passage of the "Memoriale" would seem to be a direct response to the relevant section of Vasari's narrative.

59 Vasari mentions two painters in this connection, Agnolo, brother of Franciabigio, and Andrea del Minga. Both, he says redundantly, "handled colors passing well"—the facility Bandinelli lacked (Vasari-Milanesi 1906, vol. 6, pp. 152, 188). The latter was the executant of four paintings of Old Testament subjects that Bandinelli presented as a gift to Eleonora of Toledo in an effort to solicit her support; on these, see Ward 1981 and Michela Zurla in Heikamp and Paolozzi Strozzi 2014, nos. 88, 89, 91, and 92. Bandinelli's practice of providing cartoons for other painters to execute was noted by Cox-Rearick 1993, p. 159.

60 On the commission for the *Lamentation* altarpiece, including Bandinelli's possible attempt to wrest it for himself, and the charge to Bronzino to follow Bandinelli's drawing, see Cox-Rearick 1989 and Cox-Rearick 1993, pp. 155–59. Eleonora's approval of Bandinelli's drawing and Bronzino's requirement to follow the design were communicated to Bandinelli in a letter from Duke Cosimo dated 20 November 1542 (Cox-Rearick 1993, p. 156, doc. 3, and 329; Waldman 2004, p. 244, doc. 399). Bronzino reported Cosimo's satisfaction with Bandinelli's invention and the directive that he should not introduce any changes in a letter of 22 August 1545 to the ducal secretary Pierfrancesco Riccio: *Dissemi che cosi voleva et era acontento ... et di piu ... Sua E[ccellenza] ... dicesse "Non m'entrare in altra inventione, perche quella mi piace"*: transcribed in Cox-Rearick 1993, p. 337, doc. 13.

61 Vasari-Milanesi 1906, vol, 6, p. 177–79, 185 *inter alia*. The practice of submitting drawings and models to powerful patrons was long a part of Bandinelli's method for seeking approval, securing commissions, and currying favor. The following are instances cited in his *Vita* and/or contemporary documentary sources:

DRAWINGS

- *Martyrdom of St. Lawrence*, to Pope Clement VII
- Andrea Doria monument, to Cardinal Hieronimo Doria (Waldman 2004, p. 160, doc. 273, and pp. 164–65, doc. 279)
- *Deposition* altarpiece for the Chapel of Eleonora, to Duchess Eleonora (as reported by Duke Cosimo)
- Façade of the Sala del Cinquecento (Waldman 2004, doc. 396), to Duke Cosimo (request denied)
- Cathedral choir, to Duke Cosimo
- Giovanni delle Bande Nere Monument (*Head of Giovanni delle Bande Nere*), to Duke Cosimo (Waldman 2004, docs. 441 and 442)
- *Resurrection* for the predella of the high altar of Florence Cathedral (Waldman 2004, pp. 405–6, doc. 694; may have been a model; see note 45 above)
- Boboli fountain project, to Duke Cosimo and Duchess Eleonora
- Unknown project, referred to in a letter from Duke Cosimo to Bandinelli, 7 March 1543 (Waldman 2004, p. 252, doc. 416)
- Unknown project/s, to Duke Cosimo (referred to in letter of Ugolino Grifoni cited below)

MODELS

- *David and Goliath*, to Pope Leo X (in collaboration with Rustici; cited by Vasari)
- *Hercules and Cacus*, to Pope Clement VII (see fig. 44)
- *Seven Deadly Sins* for Castel Sant'Angelo, to Pope Clement VII (and, although not documented, possibly also a drawing now in the Musée du Louvre, Paris, 92; Viatte 2011, no. 58, pp. 170–71, and pl. 33)
- Tombs of Leo X and Clement VII, to Clement's datary Baldassare Turini da Pescia and the cardinal-executors of Clement's will
- Tomb of Giovanni delle Bande Nere, to Cosimo I (Waldman 2004, pp. 185–86, doc. 308; pp. 188, doc. 313, 188–89, doc. 314, 203, doc. 332)
- *Resurrection* for the predella of the high altar of Florence Cathedral (Waldman 2004, pp. 405–6, doc. 694; may have been a drawing; see note 45 above)
- Cathedral choir, to Cosimo I
- Boboli fountain project, to Duke Cosimo and Duchess Eleonora
- Terracotta head of Cosimo I (model for proposed marble sculpture, exectured by Bandinelli's son Clemente), to Cosimo I.
- Neptune fountain, to Duke Cosimo
- *Venus,* to Duchess Eleonora (Waldman 2004, p. 719, doc. 1285)

So relentless was Bandinelli in these campaigns that Duke Cosimo on one occasion fled upon glimpsing him approach, instructing his adviser to inform Bandinelli "that there wasn't time to look at drawings even though he, to assure himself a receptive hearing, had let the duke know ... that he had some beauties to show" (letter of Ugolino Grifoni to Pierfrancesco Riccio, 25 November 1543; translated in Cox-Rearick 1993, p. 157).

62 *Conosceva il duca che la virtu e 'l guidicio e 'l disegno di Baccio era ancora meglio*: Vasari-Milanesi 1906, vol. 6, p. 187. His reporting is corroborated in Cellini's account in the autobiography of his extreme frustrations in trying to secure the patronage of Cosimo and Eleonora, who always favored Bandinelli. On Bandinelli and the Neptune fountain, see Vossilla 2010–12.

63 As Bandinelli himself declared in the above-cited letter to Luca Martini concerning the Boboli fountain designs (see note 47, above). Cellini in his autobiography states that he made numerous drawings, a claim not supported by the paltry extant corpus, though accidents of survival need to be factored into any accounting of his and other sculptors' graphic oeuvre. Acts of preservation by heirs (as happened with Michelangelo's and Bandinelli's drawings) or in a workshop through generations meant that a larger body of work was conserved, while the sale of an artist's drawings immediately after his death meant widespread dispersal and higher rate of loss (mitigated if ownership was transferred *en bloc*, optimally to a princely collector whose holdings were passed down by descent to what eventually became a public collection). Even so, it is unarguable that Bandinelli's graphic output vastly exceeded those of any of his sculptor contemporaries.

64 Vasari-Milanesi 1906, vol. 6, p. 193.

65 See Weil-Garris 1981, p. 229, for a different interpretation of this practice.

66 15 October 1554; Waldman 2004, p. 567, doc. 1033.

67 7 December 1547; Waldman 2004, pp. 348–49, doc. 587.

68 Letter of February 1556 to ducal majordomo Tomasso di Jacopo di Lazzero de' Medici concerning the awarding of the commission for the bronze choir reliefs to Cellini (Waldman 2004, pp. 607–8, doc. 1113; translation from Klein and Zerner 1989, p. 166, where the unnamed recipient is said to be Pierfrancesco Riccio). As noted here Bandinelli

was faulted for an overreliance on assistants by Michelangelo among others, a criticism addressed in this letter, which justifies the practice and highlights its positive outcome, and also in the "Memoriale" (translated in Klein and Zerner 1989, p. 150).

69 13 November 1541, in response to a lost letter from the sculptor dated two days earlier in which Bandinelli, it may be inferred, described his "drawing academy" (Waldman 2004, p. 226, doc. 368).

70 Bandinelli 1905; translation from Klein and Zerner 1989, pp. 149–50.

71 This is in essence the "mental fatigue" that according to Leonardo the noble painter experienced, in contrast with the physical fatigue that plagued the less cerebral sculptor (*Treatise on Painting*, quoted in Klein and Zerner 1989, pp. 5–6). While Bandinelli was given to bombast and boasting, the claims for his devotion to study were not hollow: the 1541 inventory of his possessions in Rome referred to earlier lists a volume of Petrarch and another of Pliny, the latter in Latin (Waldman 2004, p. 215, doc. 350).

72 The Plinian conceit was noted by Weil-Garris 1981, p. 247, note 39.

73 The subject of Bandinelli as a designer of prints, which is closely tied to an exploration of the role of drawing in his artistic activity, falls outside the parameters of this discussion, but the following perfunctory synopsis can be offered here: in Rome about 1520, Bandinelli produced a large drawing of the Massacre of the Innocents. The subject had been treated a few years earlier by Raphael and reproduced in an engraving by his gifted collaborator Marcantonio Raimondi, and it was a self-conscious act of emulation when Bandinelli arranged to have his iteration engraved by Marcantonio's disciples Marco Dente and Agostino Veneziano. Showing many nude figures of various ages, male and female, deployed in a range of poses and attitudes—the *varietà* lauded by Alberti in his treatise on painting—the print trumpeted its inventor's knowledge of anatomy and facility as a draftsman, and earned Bandinelli widespread fame. This venture was the prelude to a more ambitious print, *The Martyrdom of St. Lawrence*, engraved this time, at the behest of Pope Clement VII, by Marcantonio himself (who undertook to correct what he regarded as certain deficiencies in Bandinelli's composition). Formulated by Bandinelli in a monumental drawing that Vasari praised for its great subtlety, the elaborate, populous scene was conceived as a design for a fresco in San Lorenzo in Florence. That campaign never came to fruition, but for his masterful invention Bandinelli was awarded a knighthood by the appreciative pope—another measure of the intrinsic link between drawing and fame in the artist's biography. Bandinelli's activity as a designer of prints presages his later role as designer of paintings and sculpture discussed in the last part of this essay. Given that the Massacre of the Innocents was a subject associated with the unsurpassed painter Raphael, and that *The Martyrdom of St. Lawrence* was a design for an unrealized fresco, his activity in this arena should also be seen as a manifestation of his thwarted ambitions to be a painter considered in the preceding pages.

74 A different proposition—the derivation of *disegno* from *rilievo* as a central tenet of Bandinelli's art theory—is contended by Ben Thomas, in Franklin 2005, p. 278, under no. 100. Relief as a defining characteristic of Bandinelli's idiom is also discussed by Weil-Garris 1981. Apposite here is her observation that Bandinelli, in deciding to take up sculpture, naturally gravitated to relief, it "being flatter and involving more drawing and design" (ibid., p. 227).

75 *Treatise on Painting*; translation from Klein and Zerner 1989, p. 8. In his perfunctory contribution to the *paragone* debate, Michelangelo contended instead that "relief is considered bad in proportion as it approaches the effect of painting" (letter to Benedetto Varchi; translation ibid., p. 14). Bandinelli himself was not invited by Varchi to submit a response—a slight that irked him—but as an interlocutor in Anton Francesco Doni's 1549 dialogue *Disegno* he advocates the superiority of sculpture, aligning himself with Michelangelo and pronouncing with Platonic authority that sculpture is to painting as the real is to shadow ("La sesta et ultima parte del Disegno del Doni, La Natura, et l'Arte, Silvio, Pino et il Cavaliere [Bandinelli]," transcribed in Waldman 1995, pp. 889–93).

76 *Disegno è una disposizione di infinite e varie specie, formate in tanti vari modi, come la maestà della Natura per il continuo ci mostra*: Baccio Bandinelli, "Libro del disegno", transcribed in Waldman 2004, pp. 899–907—opening passage of the fragmentary text.

77 It is significant that Bandinelli here employs red chalk, even though this is a study for a marble sculpture, rather than the more obvious black chalk.

78 Dated c. 1544 and 1548, both by Niccolò della Casa; see Fiorentini and Rosenberg 2002, and Tommaso Mozzatti in Heikamp and Paolozzi Strozzi 2014, pp. 524–27, nos. 75 and 76.

79 Bandinelli 1905; transcription in Barkan 1999, p. 306. This idea is repeated elsewhere in the "Memoriale", as when the author announces *averei voluto che tutti attendessi al disegno* (Bandinelli 1905, p. 441).

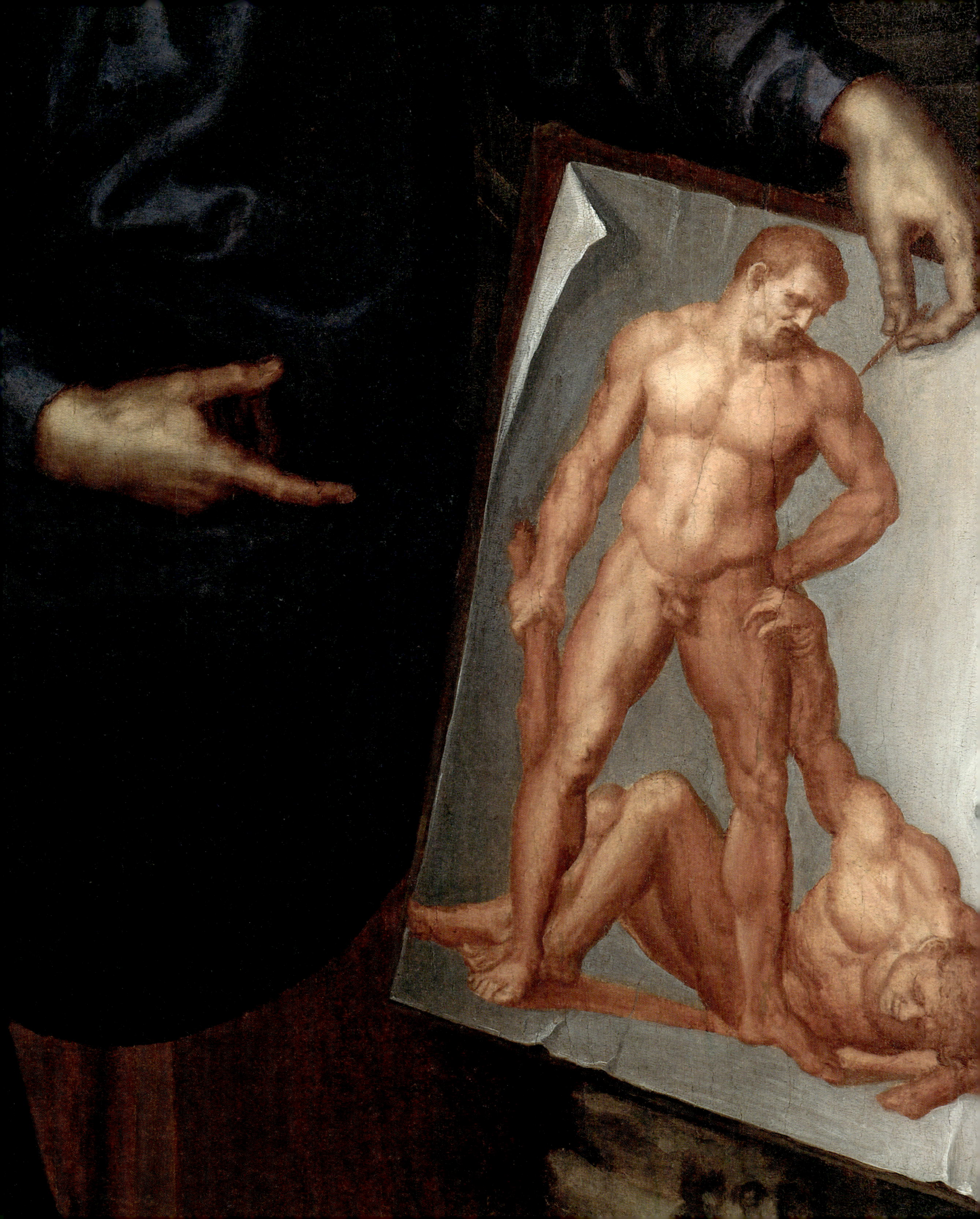

The Sculptor as Draftsman: A Motif in Florentine Portraiture

OLIVER TOSTMANN

IN HIS *Self-Portrait* of about 1545 (cat. 28; detail opposite) Baccio Bandinelli presents himself proudly pointing to a large drawing whose motif alludes to his monumental *Hercules and Cacus* group, a sculpture that resides in the Piazza della Signoria in Florence (fig. 49). The painting raises questions about the importance of drawing within Bandinelli's practice and for Renaissance sculptors more broadly. We know that many sculptors working in the Renaissance created drawings, although only a fraction has survived. One way to gain a better understanding of how and why sculptors drew is to study portraits such as Bandinelli's, which depict sculptors as draftsmen and provide insight into their working practice. Drawings characterized the sitters' virtues and ambitions during a time when sculptors strove to elevate their professional status.

While portraits of painters have captured the interest of scholars and the general public, portraits of sculptors have garnered far less attention.[1] This is in part because the best-known type of artist's portrait is the self-portrait, of which sculptors produced relatively few. Stone and bronze were more expensive than paint and canvas, and sculpting was more time-consuming than painting, making it less feasible for sculptors to experiment with their own likeness. Beyond this, it was difficult to visualize the sculptor's profession iconographically. Starting about 1500, painters were often depicted with brush and/or palette, but what was used to denote a sculptor?[2] If he were shown with a sculpture, the (painted) portrait might be mistaken for that of a collector, and the compass—a standard tool in the sculptor's workshop—represented numerous other professions as well, such as architects, astronomers, and goldsmiths. Drawings provided sculptors with an alternative attribute. Compared with traditional attributes such as the compass and hammer, drawings were able to convey a more individualized message. A quickly executed figural sketch presented the sitter differently than, say, a detailed architectural drawing.[3]

Despite the few that have survived, Renaissance inventories and descriptions reveal that portraits of sculptors, though limited in number,

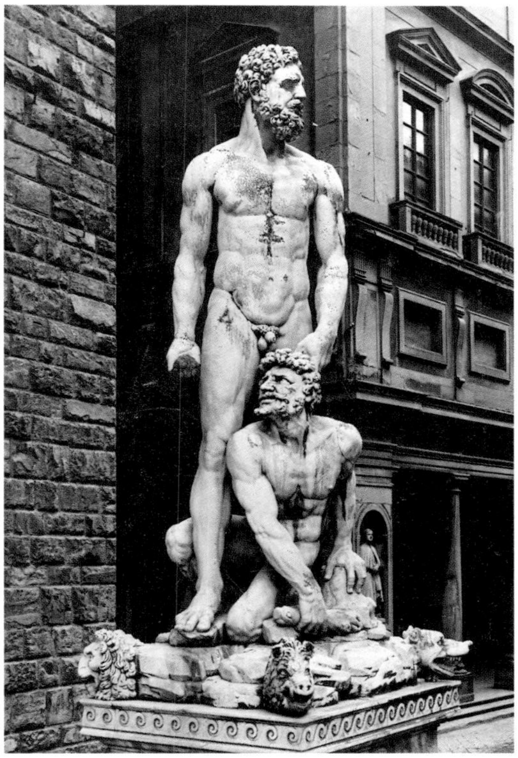

FIG. 49
Baccio Bandinelli
Hercules and Cacus
Marble
Piazza della Signoria, Florence

CAT. 28 Baccio Bandinelli
Self-Portrait (detail)

circulated. According to records, they served representational functions in the homes of sculptors and were much sought after by collectors.[4] This is not entirely surprising, as portraits were a popular medium of (self-) representation during the sixteenth century, a time during which sculptors strove to become recognized as liberal artists. Of the surviving Renaissance portraits of sculptors, several incorporate drawings, pointing to the importance of draftsmanship within many sculptors' practices. Within the broader history of sculptors' portraits, drawings were not a widespread motif; however, it was common in Florence, where the most important sculptors of the sixteenth century were depicted as draftsmen.

What can one learn from portraits of sculptors as draftsmen?[5] What is the role that drawing played in their greater artistic practice? Indeed, why were sculptors interested in being portrayed as draftsmen at all? The present essay brings together six portraits depicting well-known Florentine sculptors to explore these questions. This group of sixteenth-century paintings reveals considerable variation within the genre, demonstrating a broad range of uses for and relationships to drawing.

The universal artist

Owing to its abundance of symbols and early date, Bandinelli's *Self-Portrait* holds a special place in the discussion of representations of sculptors as draftsmen. The large format, the full-length presentation of the artist, and the representation of the sculptor's drawing in such great detail are all unusual for a sixteenth-century sculptor's painted portrait. Trained not only as a sculptor but also as a painter, Bandinelli was exceptional; this work is one of only a few examples of independent self-portraits painted by sculptors.[6] The drawing's prominent placement is unique as well. There is probably no other sculptor's portrait in which a drawing occupies a comparably important place within the composition. While the Hercules and Cacus motif in the drawing alludes to Bandinelli's most famous (and notorious) Florentine sculpture group, the drawing differs significantly from the marble group by depicting a slain Cacus.

If the *Self-Portrait* was executed after the erection of the marble group in 1534 (for a discussion of its dating, see the entry for cat. 28), the motif would highlight the autonomous artistic value of the drawing. It is questionable whether Bandinelli would present himself with a drawing showing an already abandoned version of the group and whether the drawing's composition, Hercules standing upright with Cacus prone at his feet, could have been translated into three dimensions at all.[7] Indeed, Bandinelli appears with a red-chalk holder in his left hand, as if he has just completed the drawing.[8] Rather than a preliminary drawing of an abandoned earlier version, this drawing is most likely a later variant of the famous motif.[9] For Bandinelli it was not unusual to come back to and experiment with earlier motifs. Roger Ward described the conscious repetition and variation of motifs as one of the trademarks of Bandinelli's drafting process.[10] By presenting himself with a markedly different version of Hercules and Cacus Bandinelli points to his *ingegno*, imagination, a quality that is even underscored by his pensive expression.

Red chalk is an unusual medium for a sculptor and testifies to Bandinelli's interest in drawing.[11] The drawing's composition fills the sheet in a well-balanced way and is executed with the utmost care, lacking any hint of preliminary sketching. While Hercules and Cacus are modeled in contrasting shades of light and dark, their impact is softened by the red chalk, rendering the grouping simultaneously virile and elegant. This visual effect, together with the complex composition of the nude figures and the large size of the sheet, characterizes the work as an autonomous drawing.

Bandinelli points to the drawing with his right hand in a sweeping, rhetorical gesture that immediately captures the viewer's attention. The gesture is emphasized by the placement of the hand at the center of the composition and the sharp contrast between its flesh tone and the dark blue of the garment on which it rests. With his left hand, he holds the upper edge of the board to which the drawing is attached. Together, his hands frame the drawing, mimicking an embrace.[12] Next to his newly completed drawing, he presents himself as an inspired and inventive artist. Resting on an elaborately sculpted pedestal, the drawing takes on a sculptural quality, hinting at the artist's multiple skills. Its prominent placement points to the fundamental role of *disegno*, the art of draftsmanship, within Bandinelli's larger artistic practice.[13] Unlike Bandinelli's many other self-portraits (none of which is a painting), this one depicts him as a master of the draftsmanship that enables him to practice multiple disciplines—sculpting and painting.[14]

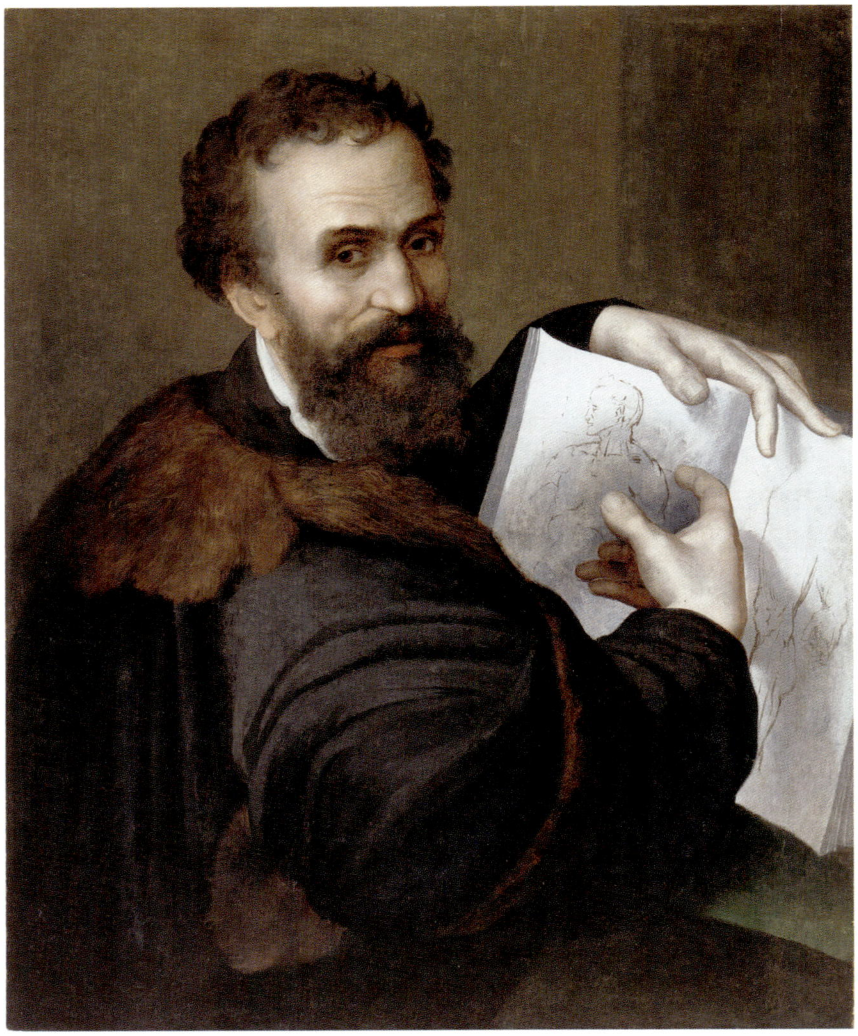

FIG. 50
Sebastiano del Piombo, attributed to
Michelangelo Pointing at His Drawings, c. 1520–25
Oil on panel, 88.5 × 74 cm
Galerie Hans, Hamburg

Disegno plays an equally central role in the portrait of *Michelangelo Pointing at His Drawings*, recently attributed to Sebastiano del Piombo (fig. 50).[15] Dated about 1520, it is one of the earliest examples of a sculptor represented as a draftsman. Michelangelo is seated at a desk, presenting to the viewer an opened book filled with sketches. The three studies shown, executed in ink, demonstrate his dedication to accurate anatomical drawings. According to his biographer Ascanio Condivi, Michelangelo planned a book on anatomy.[16] Could this folio allude to sketches for that book? The exact drawings Sebastiano shows, if they ever existed, are now lost, but similar ones from him and his followers have survived.[17]

Instead of pointing to a finished work, as in Bandinelli's *Self-Portrait*, Michelangelo points to two sheets filled with studies. The body parts, which vary in scale, have been drawn quickly and testify to the informal nature of the work. Michelangelo's momentous turn and lively gesture of pointing correspond with their spontaneous execution. Sebastiano's *Portrait* attests to the importance of figurative drawing within Michelangelo's artistic practice. The sketchy nature of the work hints at their personal use.

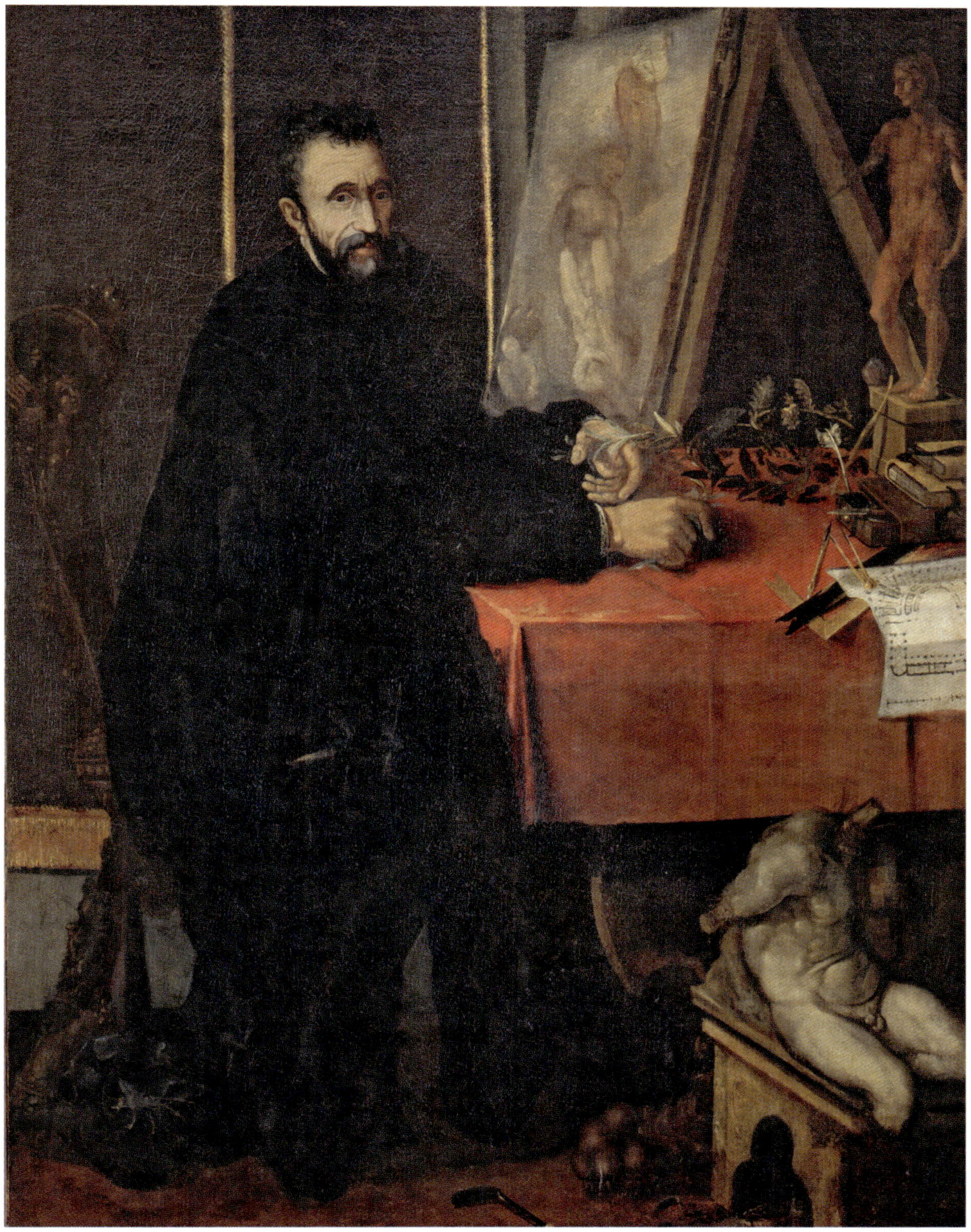

FIG. 51
Pompeo di Giulio Caccini
Michelangelo in His Studio
Oil on canvas, 180 × 140 cm
Casa Buonarroti, Florence

The book documents the esteem accorded to Michelangelo's drawings by his contemporaries, particularly by Sebastiano, to whom he gave many of his works on paper.[18] The drawings in Sebastiano's portrait do not allude directly to any of Michelangelo's sculptural projects. Rather, they demonstrate Michelangelo's dedication to drawing, the medium famously described by him as "the substance of painting and sculpture."[19]

In 1595 Pompeo di Giulio Caccini was commissioned by the Accademia del Disegno to paint a posthumous portrait of Michelangelo (fig. 51). This painting differs from the earlier Sebastiano portrait in its monumentality. It stylizes Michelangelo as the spiritual father of the academy and presents his artistic practice in the larger context of his intellectual studies. Caccini chose a large format, showing Michelangelo full-length, seated at a desk in his study. A canvas *bozzetto*, several statues, books, and tools are arranged haphazardly on, near, and under the desk. A detailed architectural drawing—which has been identified as a plan for the Villa Giulia—hangs precariously over the front edge of his workspace. Assembled around the drawing, one finds a pencil, compass, ruler, and angle meter, instruments that allude to architecture and drawing, and an inkwell with quill is close at hand.[20] Rather than writing or drawing, Michelangelo is intent on braiding a garland to create a wreath, a symbol of the three arts of painting, sculpture, and architecture.[21] Drawing is implied in this portrait through drafting tools, presented in an eye-catching arrangement on the artist's desk and by the room in which Michelangelo sits. The precious wall-hanging, large desk, and intimate nature of the space indicate that the artist works in his study. Michelangelo described a similar room in a floor plan for a house in Florence as a *studiolo*.[22] A *studiolo* was a small, private retreat, ideal for undisturbed studies, which could have also included drawing practice. In this allegorical portrait, Michelangelo represents art based on erudition, an art that takes its beginning literally at the studio desk. This conceit was used in other portraits of Florentine sculptors as well, as we will see.

Whether presenting a carefully completed figurative drawing, figural studies, or a detailed ground plan, the drawings in the portraits of Bandinelli and Michelangelo emphasize artistic capability over production. Drawings are shown as tokens of artistic mastery, characterizing Bandinelli and Michelangelo as "universal artists," exceling in all disciplines. More common, however, are portraits of sculptors with lesser claims, in whose portraits drawings play a more craft role. Sculptors were often depicted during the act of drawing, but such portraits, instead of showing the artist as a draftsman in his own right, identify the sculptor as an architect, busy with conceiving or executing his projects.

The sculptor as architect

In most sculptors' portraits created during the second half of the sixteenth century, the role of drawings (and consequently of sculptors) shifted. Instead of showing them as accomplished draftsmen, these portraits illustrated the artist's working process and often presented sculptors as architects.

The artist is painted seated at a desk, occupied with a more focused task than in previous portraits. Likely the best-known example is the portrait of *Giambologna in His Studio,* recently ascribed to Pieter Candid (see cat. 45). Much like Sebastiano's *Michelangelo*, Giambologna is seated at a workspace in a small room, glancing over his shoulder toward the viewer.[23] Holding a compass in his right hand, with ruler and pens close by, he works on an architectural drawing. A spacious, well-lit studio housing a plaster Oceanus, a model of Florence, and numerous *bozzetti* displayed on shelves is visible through a window or doorway behind his desk. Although the luxuriously dressed Giambologna is drawing in a study, separated from his workshop, the portrait connects his architectural practice to his sculptural work by compressing the spaces, making the sculptures more legible and emphasizing their importance.

Not only are drawing and sculpting assigned two separate spatial spheres, they are accorded different value. It is difficult to imagine the distinguished artist drawing in his dusty workshop. In contrast with the drawings in Bandinelli's and Michelangelo's portraits, the drawing Giambologna is making is not being presented to the viewer as an autonomous work of art but as part of the sculptor's design process. It becomes a means to an end. Indeed, the fact that drawings played a rather secondary role in Giambologna's oeuvre is borne out by his record of drawings, only a handful of which survive.[24] In this portrait, Giambologna is presented as a well-rounded sculptor-architect who uses both drawing and three-dimensional modeling in his artistic practice. This concept gives the portrait its representational character. Possibly, it hung in Giambologna's house in Borgo Pinti in Florence, where it could have been seen by friends and business partners.[25]

From the circle of Giambologna comes another portrait of this type, in which Giambattista Paggi chose a different strategy to depict the sculptor Pietro Francavilla in 1589 (fig. 52).[26] The confined space with desk and drawing tools in proximity to the sitter situates the portrait in the room frequently used for drawing—the studio. As in Giambologna's portrait, drawing tools and three-dimensional modeling are shown together, highlighting the importance of both in Francavilla's working process. In comparison with Giambologna's portrait, however, the picture places greater emphasis on the intellectual aspect of the artist's work. Francavilla sits at his

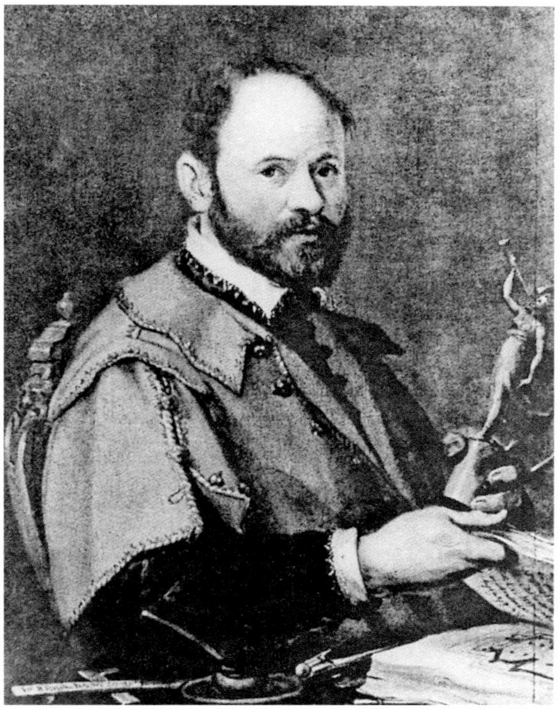

FIG. 52
Giovanbattista Paggi
Pietro Francavilla, 1589
Oil on panel, 76.5 × 59 cm
Private collection, Brussels

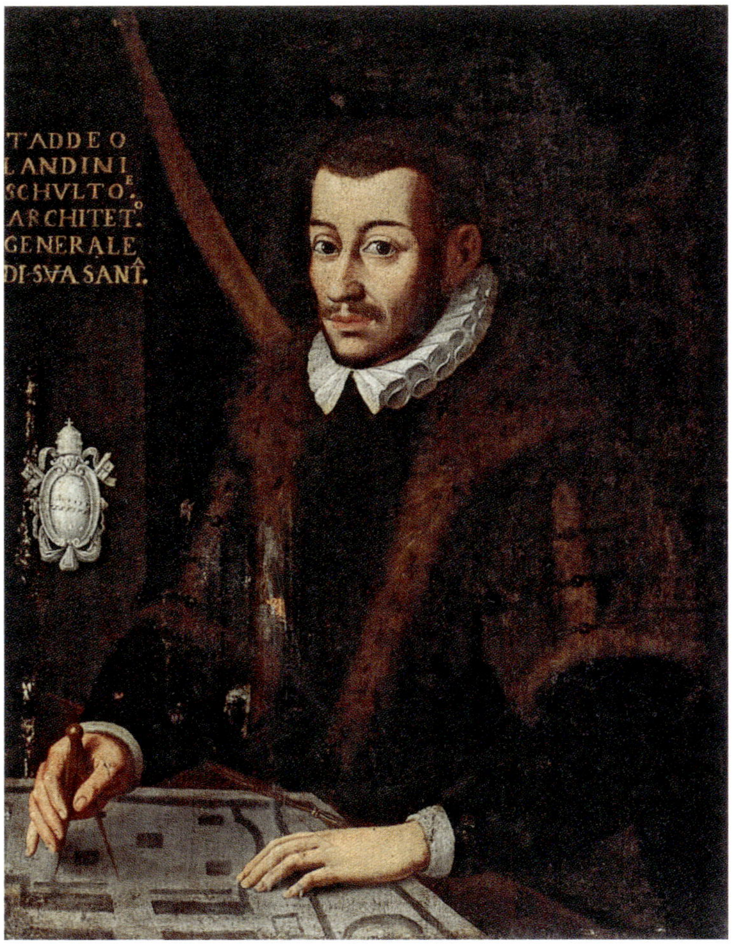

FIG. 53
Roman School
Taddeo Landini, c. 1590
Oil on canvas, 94 × 74.3 cm
Private collection

desk contemplating a book of architectural plans. There is little doubt that these are Francavilla's own designs, as his name is recognizable in them; the portfolio may represent one of his lost treatises.[27] An inkwell, compass, and quill are placed directly next to the book, alluding to Francavilla's abilities as a draftsman, his inventiveness, and his erudition. The biographer Filippo Baldinucci notes that Francavilla invented two new compasses and wrote several treatises.[28] In the portrait Francavilla uses his right hand to turn the pages of the book and in his left he holds a personification of Fame, probably made of wax, pointing to his profession as a sculptor.[29] Contemplation and drawing practice are presented as two interrelated activities carried out in the same space. Here, the sculptor's portrait is conflated with a scholar's portrait. Francavilla is probably depicted in the early stages of his design process, reflecting on old architectural designs. The drawing tools allude to what will follow: he will eventually record his new ideas on paper. Paggi created a successful portrait of Francavilla as sculptor-architect; the painting was owned by Pietro Tacca, a fellow sculptor, and subsequently by Baldinucci, who lauded it profusely in his writings. Its composition was emulated around 1600 by an unknown Flemish painter for a later portrait of Francavilla, commissioned by Cardinal Leopoldo de' Medici.[30] A final example presents this type of portrait in its most simplified form. A portrait of Taddeo Landini, painted about 1590, presents Landini at a desk in an undefined room (fig. 53).[31] Landini, who was trained in Florence, is shown holding a compass and working on a large-scale architectural drawing, possibly commissioned by Pope Clement VIII. The drawing is prominently displayed on a table in the foreground. This could be an architect's portrait, were it not for the clearly legible inscription, which identifies the sculptor-architect Landini and his patron. Landini is presented as a busy artist caught in the midst of his work. The rather generic architectural drawing does not demonstrate the artist's virtuosity, imagination, and learning but serves as proof of his capability to carry out commissions diligently.

It is remarkable that Giambologna, Francavilla, and Landini, three of the greatest Florentine sculptors of the late sixteenth century, are depicted working on architectural projects. Called "my sculptor and architect" by Duke Francesco Medici, Giambologna is also recorded as a sculptor-architect by Baldinucci.[32] In the mid- to late 1580s, when this portrait was painted, Giambologna worked consistently on architectural projects. Although Francavilla and Landini worked occasionally as architects as well, this activity remained minor compared to their work as sculptors.[33] Consequently, in biographies from the early seventeenth century, Landini[34] and Francavilla[35] were referred to exclusively as sculptors in title pages. But to make a sculptor look like an architect was a common strategy in Florentine portraiture of the second half of the sixteenth century. The higher social status of architects was particularly attractive during this time, when sculptors were keen to raise their professional profile.[36]

The sculptor as draftsman proved to be a successful portrait formula for Florentine sculptors of the sixteenth century. Drawings conveyed important information about the sitter's ambitions, demonstrated his mastery of draftsmanship, and pointed to his education and specialization. They offered insight into sculptors' drawing subjects, ranging from figurative drawings to architectural designs, produced for their own sake or as preparatory sketches for larger projects. The motif could present sculptors as contemplative artists, distanced from hard, manual labor. Within its development, however, there was a shift from the sculptor with "universal" aspirations to the sculptor-architect, working at the end of the century.

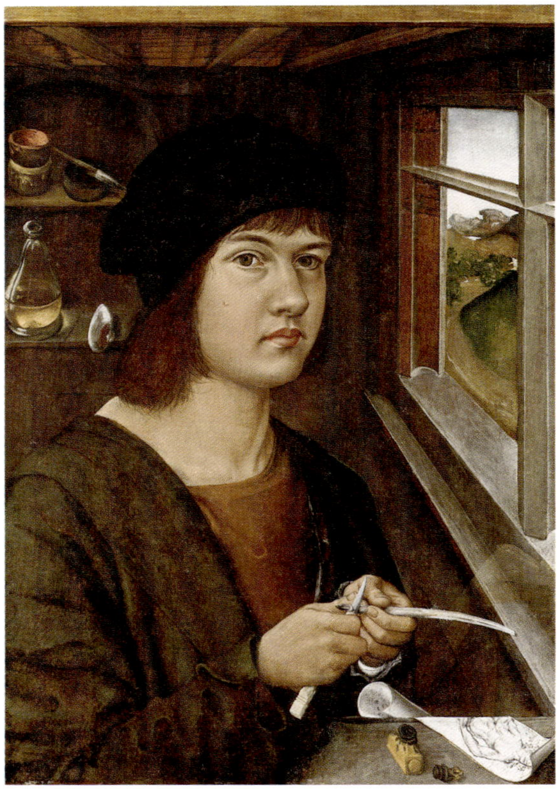

FIG. 54
South German
A young artist, c. 1500
Oil on panel, 45.7 × 32.8 cm
The Art Institute of Chicago

The history of the sculptor-draftsman motif

Sculptors of the sixteenth century were not the first artists depicted as draftsmen; the history of the motif reaches back into the fourteenth century. Beyond book illustrations and informal sketches produced in medieval workshops, the motif first appears in depictions of St. Luke, the patron saint of painters.[37] Portraying St. Luke as a writer emphasized his scholarly attributes, while showing him painting the Madonna underscored his artistic talents. Aside from devotional intentions, both ways of depicting the saint also allowed painters to reflect on themselves. Most famously, about 1435–40 Rogier van der Weyden depicted St. Luke not as a painter but as a draftsman.[38] St. Luke, who works on a portrait of the Madonna, is holding a silverpoint stylus in his right hand and a partially executed sketch in his left. Although Erwin Panofsky has been criticized for his hypothesis that Rogier's painting of St. Luke was a disguised self-portrait, his argument correctly identifies the opportunity this motif gave artists to present and comment on their own profession.[39] St. Luke as draftsman became a frequent motif during this time and helped to promulgate the subject.[40] On occasion, the draftsman also appears before 1500 in informal workshop drawings (for example, by Maso Finiguerra; cat. 4), in prints showing *vedute*, in representations of perspectival apparatus, and, some decades later, in representations of academies (see cat. 38).[41]

A portrait of a young artist in the Art Institute of Chicago is the first known autonomous portrait of an artist depicted with a drawing (fig. 54).[42] In this South German painting of about 1500, the drafting tools serve to set the stage for the artist at work.[43] It shows a young painter sharpening his pen in order to continue working on the study of a figure, tentatively identified as Adam.[44] The choice of this subject demonstrates the young artist's education and enhances the significance of the drawing. Easily recognizable in the back of the room, painter's utensils, including paint pots, conch, and linseed oil, identify the sitter as a painter and showcase the importance of drawing within his work processes. Despite this innovative portrait, it does not seem that painters represented themselves as draftsmen more often than did architects and sculptors throughout the sixteenth century.

In fact, it was architects who were portrayed most frequently as draftsmen. In Piero di Cosimo's 1485 portrait of Giuliano da Sangallo, drawing is represented through the sitter's attributes.[45] Pen and compass lie on a parapet, characterizing the sitter as an architect who draws. And numerous

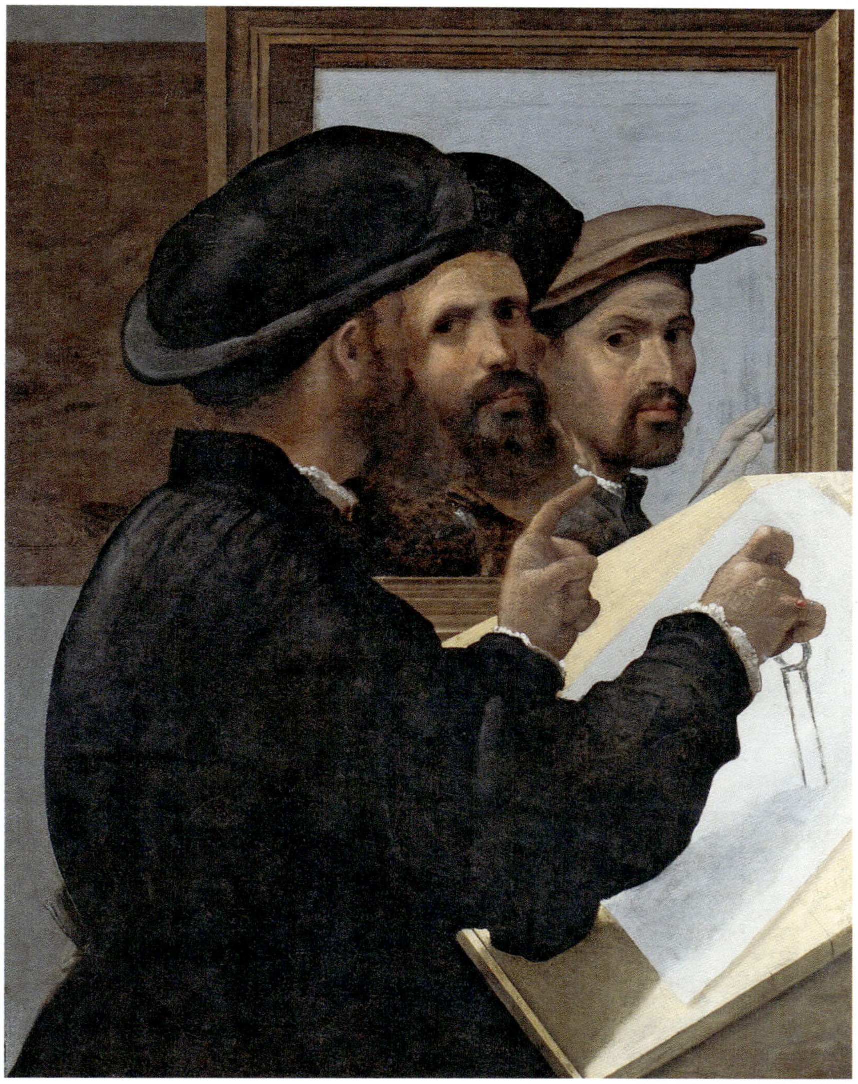

FIG. 55
Bernardino Licinio, attributed to
Two artist friends in front of a mirror
Oil on panel, 81 × 62 cm
Martin-von-Wagner-Museum
der Universität, Würzburg

other portraits of architects with pen and compass were painted during the following decades. The double portrait of two artist friends attributed to Bernardino Licinio about 1530 shows an architect in the foreground working with a drafting compass while he is painted by Licinio, whose reflection is visible in a mirror hanging to one side of the architect (fig. 55).[46] Although the architect's large drawing sheet is at an angle, which makes it visible to the

FIG. 56
Titian
Giulio Romano, c. 1536
Oil on canvas, 102 × 87 cm
Museo Civico di Palazzo Te, Mantua

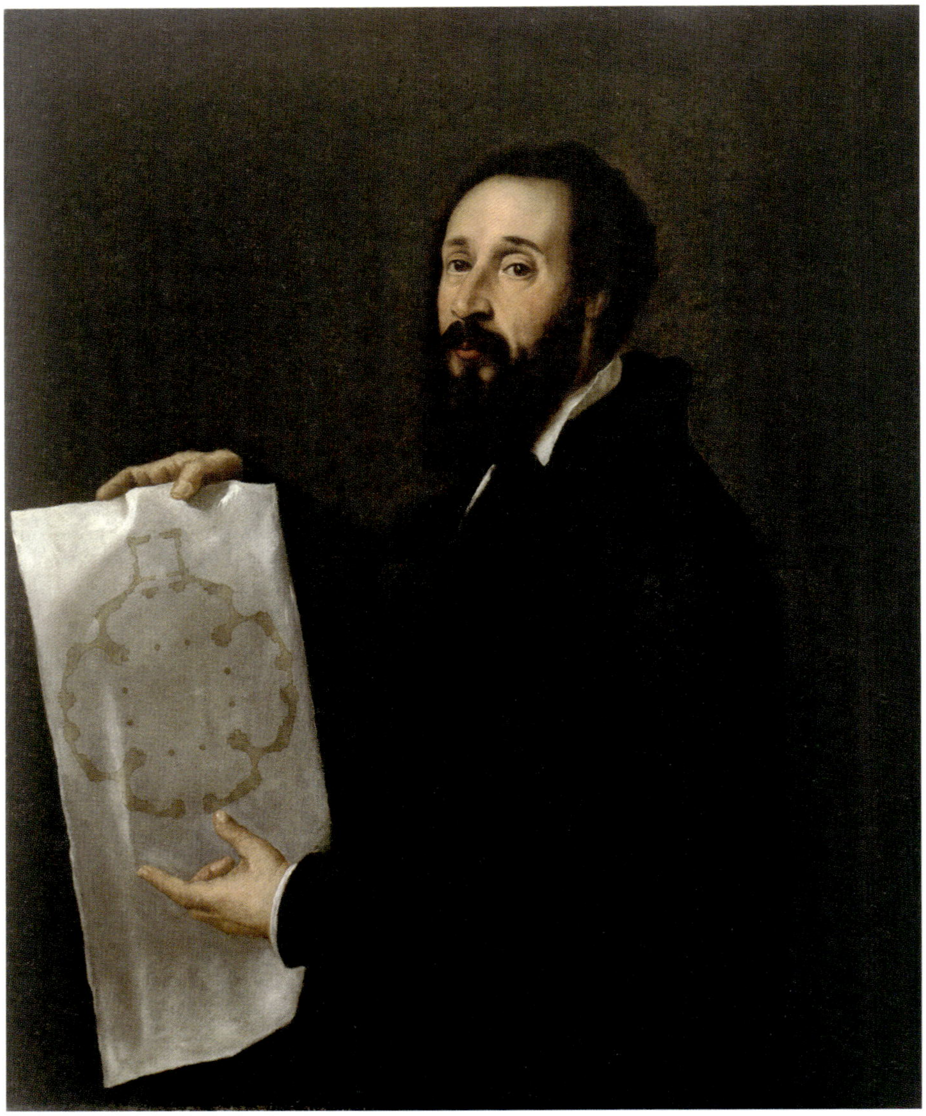

observer, it is blank except for a few hatch marks.[47] The emptiness of the sheet is in marked contrast to the dense composition of the painting—perhaps intended as painter Licinio's praise of his architect friend's imagination.

A couple of years later, about 1536, Titian represented the artist Giulio Romano as an architect, but completely omitted the customary attributes such as compass, ruler, and square (fig. 56).[48] Titian indicates Giulio's profession solely through a detailed architectural drawing that the sitter unfurls with his right hand and points to with his left. His gesture and the prominent placement of the drawing link it to Bandinelli's *Self-Portrait*, as well as to portraits by Agnolo Bronzino and Giorgio Vasari, executed a few years later.[49]

Florentine rulers were also repeatedly portrayed as draftsmen. Jacopo Pontormo's portrait of Alessandro de' Medici, painted in 1534–35, shows a monarch in the act of drawing (fig. 57).[50] Holding a metal stylus, the duke sits in front of a drawing in a wood-paneled interior. Sketched in very few

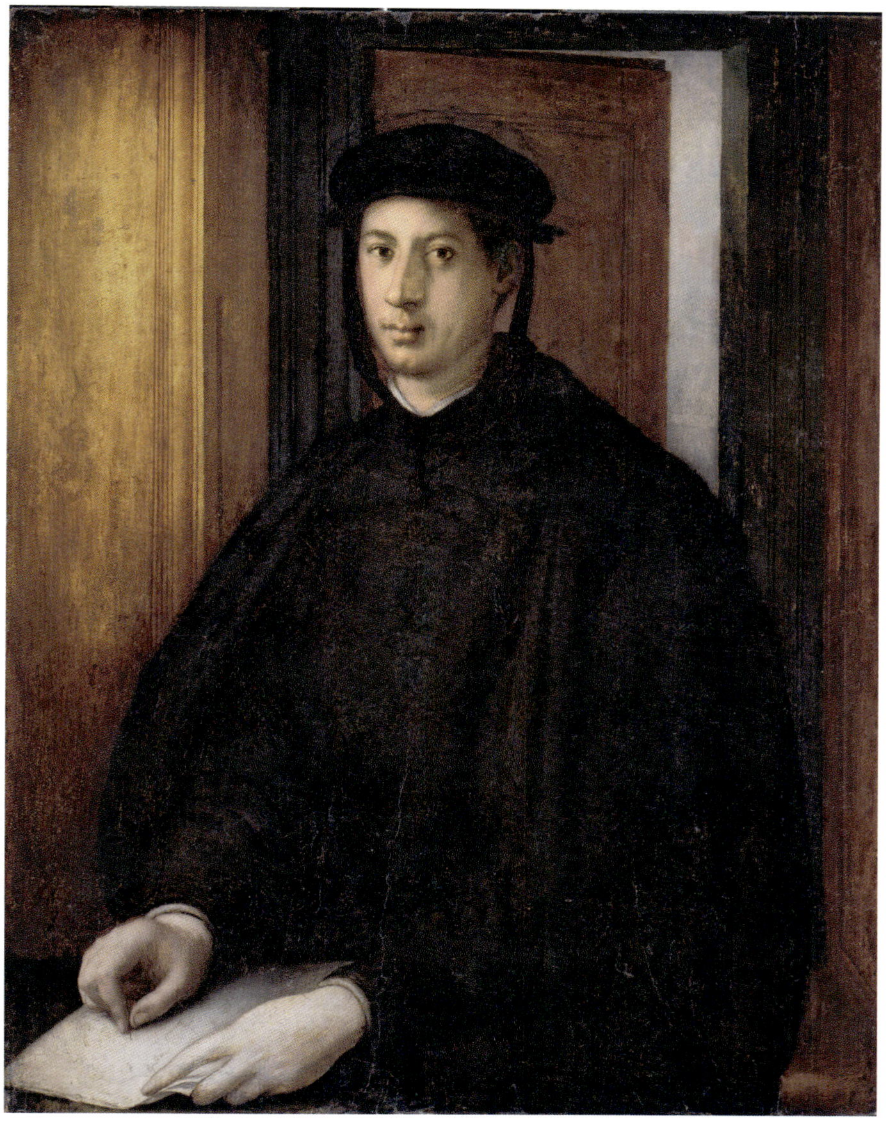

FIG. 57
Jacopo Pontormo
Alessandro de' Medici, 1534–35
Oil on panel, 100.4 × 81.3 cm
Philadelphia Museum of Art

lines, a portrait of a woman in profile is clearly recognizable in the drawing. As Carl Strehlke points out, it is difficult for an amateur to draw with a metal stylus, especially one lacking its holder, as is the case in the duke's portrait. Moreover, in the 1530s, this technique was already archaic.[51] Pontormo's portrait is one of the first to visualize drawing as an aristocratic pastime, and the metal stylus probably alludes to Alessandro's artistic talent. Quite possibly, it refers to a passage in Baldassare Castiglione's 1528 treatise, *Il Cortegiano* (The Book of the Courtier), in which drawing was praised as a noble virtue.[52] Taking on courtly connotations, drawing was to become an important motif in the iconography of Florentine rulers as much as in that of sculptors.[53] Throughout the fifteenth century, sculptors were primarily depicted in medals and busts, formats that dictated a rather restricted iconography.[54] Relief offered greater opportunities to depict a person and his attributes within the context of a larger narrative. So it is not surprising that the first visual reference to sculptors as draftsmen is found in Filarete's

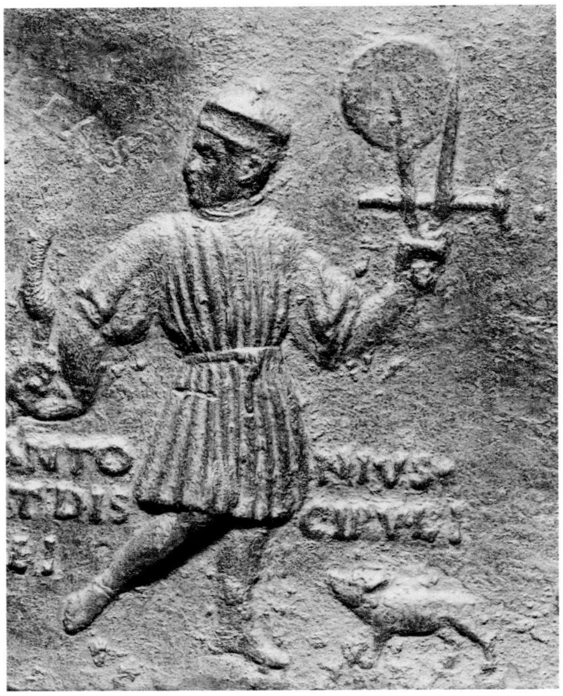

FIG. 58
Filarete
The Doors of St. Peter's Basilica, Rome, completed 1445, detail
Bronze
Vatican City

portrait of himself and his workshop (1445), which is also recognized as one of the earliest Italian self-portraits (fig. 58). Filarete represented himself with his studio workers on the back of the bronze doors that he cast for St. Peter's in Rome. He is seen holding a drafting compass and disk in his left hand, carrying the compass like a banner as he walks ahead of his assistants. The compass, a tool for measuring and design, serves to prove that the sculptor's work is based on theoretical knowledge, thus underscoring Filarete's elevated social status as a learned artist.[55] At this time, the drafting compass served mainly as an architect's attribute.[56] If used by a sculptor, it was in the context of measuring the stone.[57] Here, it transmits a broader meaning, alluding to drawing in general and pointing to Filarete's profession as a sculptor-architect. The fact that the compass also played a definitive practical role in Filarete's drafting process was emphasized in his *Three Books on the Art of Drawing*, in which an entire chapter is devoted to the compass. There it is described as an "indispensable tool for the draftsman," playing a primary role in the design and perspective of drawings.[58] From Filarete onward, compasses were a key attribute in the iconography of artists, underscoring the importance of learning.[59] As such they could also find their place on tombstones of sculptors, as in the case of Andrea Bregno.[60] Eventually, in Cesare Ripa's *Iconologia* of 1603, the compass together with a mirror characterized the personification of *disegno*.[61]

It was painters who created the majority of portraits of Italian sculptors as draftsmen during the sixteenth century, beginning in Italy about 1520.[62] Often, sculptors were depicted holding a statuette, but it is not always easy to distinguish sculptors from other professionals and collectors in such portraits.[63] Even so, this type of a sculptor with a statuette was probably the type most often employed in Italy during the sixteenth century. It was especially used in and around Venice, seemingly less often in Florence. In Giovanni Battista Moroni's portrait of Alessandro Vittoria, the Venetian sculptor is shown with rolled-up sleeves holding an antique torso in both hands (fig. 59).[64] The artist's firm grip of the weighty torso together with his rolled-up sleeves—the physical contact between sculptor and sculpture—indicate physical labor. Conspicuously, this motif accentuates closeness between sculptor and sculpture, contrasting it with the intellectual or conceptual attitude of the drafting sculptor, a type that was more preferred in Florence.

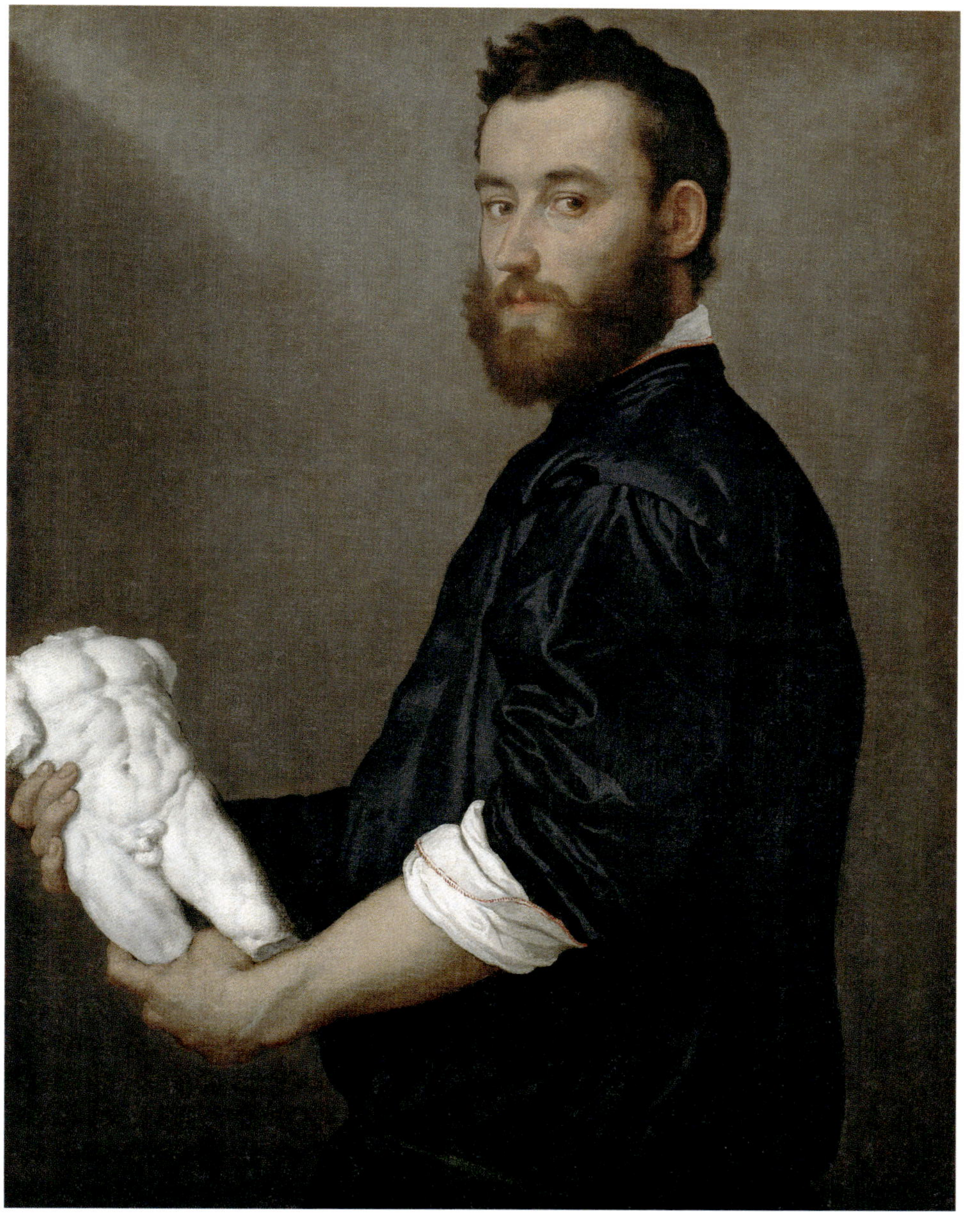

FIG. 59
Giovanni Battista Moroni
Alessandro Vittoria, 1552–53
Oil on canvas, 87.5 × 70 cm
Kunsthistorisches Museum, Vienna

The sculptor in society

For sculptors especially, the motif of drawing was congenial. Owing to its variability, it went beyond the restricted possibilities of traditional attributes such as compass, square, and ruler. Drawings could indicate several achievements and specializations simultaneously, hint at erudition and scholarship, and make statements about the artist's working process. In the fifteenth and sixteenth centuries, as sculptors strove to enhance their professional status from artisan to liberal artist, demonstrating their breadth of skill as draftsmen became increasingly important.

One reason was the larger aesthetic discussion about the concept of *disegno* in Florence during the Renaissance. As early as 1390, Cennino Cennini declared drawing to be the foundation of the arts; moreover, he viewed it as an intellectual activity, praising the experienced artist for "having much drawing in his head."[65] Subsequently, Leon Battista Alberti, Lorenzo Ghiberti, and Leonardo da Vinci championed the primacy of drawings. Related ideas extend all the way to Bandinelli's *Treatise on the Art of Drawing* and culminate in Vasari's concept of *disegno*, which elevates drawing to the status of "father of all arts," placing it above architecture, painting, and sculpting.[66] Moreover, in Vasari's view, drawing embedded a determinative philosophical component. By way of drawing, the artist ultimately gained access to the idea and form of all things. Thus ennobled, *disegno* elevated sculpting, painting, and architecture to the level of the liberal arts.[67] After its founding in 1563, the Accademia del Disegno continued to promulgate this concept among Florentine artists. With the support of the academy, Florentine sculptors experienced an increase of professional recognition. Beginning in 1570, sculptors who were accepted into the academy were officially excused from their traditional guild obligations.

Despite this, sculptors found themselves frequently exposed to comparisons with painters throughout the sixteenth century. The question whether sculpture belonged to the higher liberal arts or to the lower mechanical arts was heatedly discussed until the end of the century.[68] Despite its often sophistic arguments, this debate had clear ramifications for the professional hierarchy of the artists. Most famously, at the end of the fifteenth century, Leonardo da Vinci denigrated sculpting as a mechanical exercise, an *essercizio meccanichissimo*, stressing the physical aspect of working with stone.

> ... for the sculptor in carving his statue out of marble or other stone wherein it is potentially contained has to take off the superfluous and excessive parts with the strength of his arms and the strokes of the hammer—a very mechanical exercise causing much perspiration which mingling with the grit turns into mud. His face is pasted and smeared all over with marble powder, making him look like a baker, and he is covered with minute chips as if emerging from a snowstorm, and his dwelling is dirty and filled with dust and chips of stone.[69]

The dismissal of sculpting as a dirty and physically strenuous activity persisted as a thread running through the discussion regarding the ranking of the arts, a debate that was conducted with special verve in Florence. The argument reemerged in Benedetto Varchi's inquiry among eight leading Florentine painters and sculptors in 1546.[70] It erupted anew on the occasion of the Florentine academy's homage to Michelangelo's death in 1564.[71] Still in 1607 Federico Zuccari (himself a painter) claimed that sculpture was the more robust, less delicate, and hence the less noble art compared with painting.[72] Not surprisingly, therefore, a profession often associated with craftsmanship sought to visualize itself as embracing the concept of *disegno*. Not the dirty laborer in his workshop, but the clean artist in his studio became the more desirable option in depictions of sculptors. Since they were ridiculed as clumsy and rather dull by some of their contemporaries, this was a fitting strategy to correct the nagging prejudice.

Beyond this, the new portrait type reflects the professional shift from the well-rounded sculptor with larger aspirations to the sculptor-architect at the end of the century. Above all, however, it demonstrates the practice of drawing in its various forms to have been common among Florentine Renaissance sculptors.

Notes

I want to thank Michael Cole, Heiko Damm, Elizabeth Reluga, and Linda Wolk-Simon for their invaluable help and countless suggestions.

1 For portraits of sculptors, see Gerstenberg 1937, Fiorentini 1999, Kanzenbach 2007, and Scholten 2008. A general overview is provided by Goldscheider 1936 and Woods-Marseden 1998.

2 See the first painted autonomous Italian self-portrait by Macrino d'Alba, *Self-Portrait*, c. 1495, tempera on panel, 33.5 × 28.5 cm, Museo Civico d'Arte Antica, Turin; Alessandro Allori, *Self-Portrait*, c. 1555, oil on panel, 60 × 47 cm, Uffizi, Florence; Sofonisba Anguissola, *Self-Portrait at the Easel Painting a Devotional Panel*, 1556, oil on canvas, 66 × 57 cm, Museum-Zamek, Lancut. Numerous portraits of painters with brush and palette were painted during the latter half of the sixteenth century in Italy.

3 Kathke and particularly Goffen discuss drawings as an attribute in sixteenth-century portraits. Neither, however, discusses their importance in sculptors' portraits: Goffen 2000, pp. 95–135; Kathke 1997, pp. 194-196. For architects see Severin 1992, pp. 92–97.

4 See Fiorentini 1999, pp. 62, 92; Scholten 2008, pp. 197–204.

5 Kanzenbach does not include this type of portrait in her categories: Kanzenbach 2007, pp. 287–304, 327–32.

6 Apart from Michelangelo's self-portrait in the Sistine *Last Judgment*, there are Francesco Primaticcio, *Self-Portrait*, oil on canvas, 41 × 29 cm, Uffizi, Florence; Willem van den Broecke (Guillelmus Paludanus), *Self-Portrait*, oil on panel, 54 × 45.5 cm, signed and dated 1564, Kunsthistorisches Museum, Vienna. To my knowledge, there is no other safely attributed painted self-portrait by a sixteenth-century sculptor. See Trnek 2004, p. 110.

7 For a contrary opinion, see Heikamp 2001, p. 990.

8 Severin noticed that the holder rests on the contour line, a position that highlights the importance of *disegno*: Severin 1992, p. 93.

9 Hendy, Koortbojian, Woods-Marsden, King, Heikamp, Chong, Hegener, Mozzati, and Ward interpret it as a preparatory drawing. See Hendy 1931, p. 24; Koortbojian 1992, p. 20; Woods-Marsden 1998, p. 144; King 1998, pp. 85–86; Heikamp 2001, p. 998; Chong 2003a, p. 85; Hegener 2008, p. 316; Mozzati 2014, p. 459; Ward 2014, p. 344. Fiorentini sees it as "a typical graphical experiment": Fiorentini 1999, p. 59.

10 Ward 1981, p. 9.

11 See the essay by Wolk-Simon in this volume.

12 This gesture can be found in portraits of friends. See Raphael, *Self-Portrait with a Friend*, c. 1518, oil on canvas, 99 × 83 cm, Musée du Louvre, Paris.

13 As Bandinelli pointed out in his "Memoriale", "All my concentration was fixed on drawings." See Bandinelli 1905, p. 433, quoted in Ward 1988, p. 11. See also Hegener 2008, pp. 66, 72 (with earlier bibliography).

14 In addition, Waźbiński interprets the two columns as a metaphor for Bandinelli's practice as architect: Waźbiński 1987, vol. 1, p. 60. On Bandinelli's self-portraits, see Hegener 2008, p. 291; Mozzati 2014, pp. 453–69.

15 See Barbieri 2007, pp. 107–20.

16 Barbieri 2007, p. 116.

17 Barbieri lists three drawings—in the Biblioteca Reale at Turin, the Moravian Gallery at Brno, and the Fitzwilliam Museum in Cambridge: Barbieri 2007, p. 116.

18 Hirst 1981, p. 41.

19 As reported by Francisco de Holanda in his *Four Dialogues on Painting* (1548); quoted in Barbieri 2007, p. 116.

20 Ragioneri interprets the quill together with the other instruments as a metaphor for Michelangelo's poetry: Ragioneri 2009, p. 43.

21 Ragioneri 2009, p. 42. Compare also Kanzenbach 2007, pp. 327–28.

22 Cole and Pardo 2005, p. 16.

23 Avery noted the resemblance of Giambologna's pose to Baccio Bandinelli's in his self-portrait engraved by Niccolò della Casa, *Self-Portrait of Baccio Bandinelli*, engraving, 289 × 217 mm; see Avery 1987, p. 243, note 8.

24 Krahn 2006, p. 48; Avery 1987, pp. 273–74.

25 Corti 1976, p. 632.

26 See De Franqueville 1968, p. 38; Fiorentini 1999, pp. 100 and 175, Paolozzi Strozzi 2002, pp. 9–11. According to Filippo Baldinucci, who owned and praised the portrait, the recto page in the book shows *PETRUS FRANCEVILLUS BELGIUS etat 42.1589*: Baldinucci 1811, vol. 8, p. 360. The current whereabouts of the portrait are unknown. It was sold in 1936 by the Russian art dealer Vitale Bloch to a private collector.

27 On Francavilla as scholar, see Baldinucci 1811, vol. 8, pp. 362, 369–71; Franqueville 1968, pp. 118–19.

28 On Francavilla as draftsman, see Avery 2000, p. 22. On Francavilla as inventor of compasses, see Baldinucci 1811, vol. 8, p. 369.

29 Baldinucci describes a similar statuette in the later version of this portrait: Baldinucci 1811, vol. 8, p. 361.

30 Baldinucci 1811, vol. 8, p. 360; image in Paolozzi Strozzi 2002, p. 11.

31 Inscribed upper left *TADDEO/LANDINI/ SCHULTOe./ARCHITETo./GENERALE/DESAVA SANTa*; sold Sotheby's New York, 25 May 2000, sale 7481, lot 143. I am grateful to Heiko Damm, who made me aware of this portrait.

32 Quoted in Cole 2010, p. 17; Baldinucci 1811, vol. 8, p. 110.

33 For Francavilla as architect, see Franqueville 1968, pp. 115–16. For Landini, see Schottmüller 1928, p. 297.

34 Baglione 1733, p. 60.

35 Baldinucci 1811, vol. 8, p. 349.

36 See Cole 2010, pp. 158–92; Burioni 2004, pp. 389–408; Warnke 1985, p. 241.

37 Agnolo Gaddi (?), *Study of a Draftsman and Four Heads*, c. 1380–90, Castello Sforzesco, Milan.

38 Rogier van der Weyden, *St. Luke Drawing the Virgin*, c. 1435–40, oil and tempera on panel, 137.5 × 110.8 cm, Museum of Fine Arts, Boston.

39 Asemissen and Schweikhart 1994, p. 40; Panofsky 1953, p. 253.

40 Dieric Bouts, *St. Luke Painting* [sic] *the Virgin*, oil on canvas transferred from panel, 109 x 86.5 cm, Penrhyn Castle, Wales; Israhel van Meckenem, *St. Luke Drawing the Virgin and Child*, c. 1475, engraving, 209 × 138 mm; Jan Gossaert, *St. Luke Drawing the Virgin*, c. 1515, oil on panel, 230 × 205 cm, Národní Galerie, Prague; *St. Luke Drawing the Virgin*, 1520–22, oil on panel, 110 × 82 cm, Kunsthistorisches Museum, Vienna.

41 Schulze Altcappenberg 2007, pp. 10–14.

42 Wolff 2008, pp. 424–30.

43 Compare with Bavarian Master, *Portrait of an Architect*, c. 1480, limewood, 42.9 x 30.5 cm, Kunstmuseum, Basel. See Kemperdick 2006, pp. 48–51. Severin points out the rarity of a drawing in portraits of architects around 1500: Severin 1992, p. 37.

44 Wolff 2008, p. 427.

45 Piero di Cosimo, *Giuliano da Sangallo*, c. 1485, oil on limewood, 47.3 × 33.7 cm, Rijksmuseum, Amsterdam. See Duncan Bull in London 2008, pp. 196–97.

46 For its attribution, see Hansbauer 2004, pp. 263–70. Hansbauer tentatively identifies the architect as Jacopo Sansovino: Hansbauer 2004, p. 278.

47 Shearman 1965, pp. 172–76; Woods-Marsden 1998, p. 143.
48 Bronzino, *Luca Martini*, 1554–55, oil on canvas, 101 × 79 cm, Palazzo Pitti, Florence; Giorgio Vasari, *Self-Portrait*, post 1571, oil on panel, 100.5 × 80 cm, Uffizi, Florence. About this type, see also Severin 1992, p. 92.
49 My thanks to Damian Dombrowski, Würzburg, for this observation.
50 See Strehlke 2004, pp. 112–15.
51 Strehlke 2004, p. 114.
52 Costamagna 1994, p. 224; Warnke 1985, p. 297.
53 See Giorgio Vasari, *Duke Cosimo I in the midst of His Sculptors, Architects and Engineers*, 1559, fresco, Palazzo Vecchio, Florence; *Duke Cosimo I Draws New War Plans*, fresco, Florence, Palazzo Vecchio, Salone del Cinquecento; Burioni 2007.
54 Fiorentini 1999, pp. 6–40; Scholten 2008, pp. 204–9.
55 King 1998, p. 69. In a marked contrast his assistants carry tools used by craftsmen—chisel, stylus, and hammer.
56 See Andrea Pisano (workshop), *Architecture*, marble, 83 × 69 cm, Museo dell'Opera del Duomo, Florence.
57 See Andrea Pisano (workshop), *Sculpture*, marble, 83 × 69 cm, Museo dell'Opera del Duomo, Florence.
58 Filarete-Oettingen 1896, pp. 568 and 600.
59 Schweikhart 2001, p. 233; Kanzenbach 2007, pp. 107–8. Consider Michelangelo's dictum: artistic good judgment is based on the artist having his "compasses in his eyes rather than in his hands": Woods-Marsden 1998, p. 57.
60 Luigo Cappono, tomb of Andrea Bregno, 1506, Santa Maria sopra Minerva, Rome.
61 According to Schweikhart 2001, p. 233.
62 Compare Kanzenbach 2007, pp. 31–45; Fiorentini 1999, p. 113.
63 Compare Kanzenbach 2007, pp. 165–78.
64 See Stefan Morét in Munich 2002, p. 356; Koering in Paris 2009, p. 181.
65 Cennini 2003, p. 71.
66 *Perchè il disegno, padre delle tre arti nostre, Architettura, Scultura e Pittura, procendo dall'intelletto, cava di molte cose un giudizio universale*: Vasari-Bettarini 1966–87, vol. 1, p. 111.
67 Rosand 2002, pp. 24–60.
68 Hessler 2002, pp. 83–91; Poeschke 2006, p. 73.
69 Leonardo 1949, p. 94, no. 37.
70 The participants were the painters Pontormo, Bronzino, and Vasari; the sculptors Cellini, Tribolo, Francesco da Sangallo, and Battista Tasso, with Michelangelo as arbiter. See Mendelsohn-Martone 1982.
71 Giunta 1964, p. 19.
72 *Et io soglio rassomgliare queste due nobilissime professioni* [sculpture and painting] *a due care sorelle generate da un istesso padre, nobile et illustre, ma nate da diverse madri: la prima di prole nobile, delicate & di poco spirito, ma vivace però et ingegniosa; e l'altra sia men nobile, ma più forte e gagliarda*: Federico Zuccari in Barocchi 1960, vol. 1, p. 698.

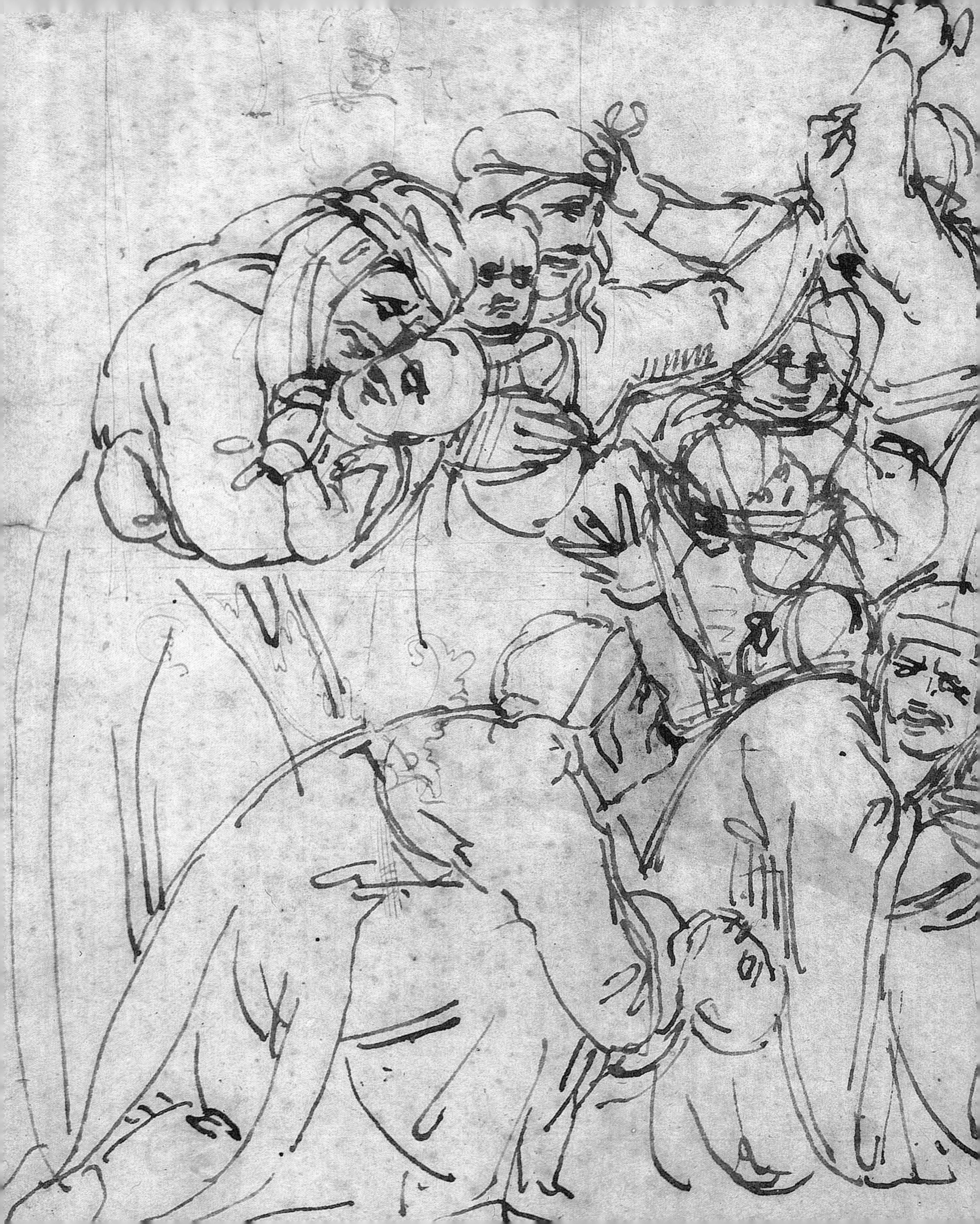

Catalogue

CONTRIBUTORS

C.C.B.	Carmen C. Bambach
R.B.	Rachel Boyd
M.C.	Marco Calafati
R.C.	Raymond Carlson
M.W.C.	Michael W. Cole
H.D.	Heiko Damm
G.E.	Grégoire Extermann
F.F.	Frank Fehrenbach
D.R.F.	Daria Rose Foner
D.G.	Davide Gasparotto
K.H.D.	Kelley Helmstutler di Dio
C.K.	Clare Kobasa
C.K-G.	Claudia Kryza-Gersch
M.L.	Marika Leino
W-D.L.	Wolf-Dietrich Löhr
U.P.	Ulrich Pfisterer
T.M.	Tommaso Mozzati
C.N.	Christina Neilson
J.K.N.	Jonathan K. Nelson
S.F.O.	Steven F. Ostrow
O.T.	Oliver Tostmann
L.W-S.	Linda Wolk-Simon
R.W.	Robert Williams
A.W.	Alison Wright
C.Y.	Carolyn Yerkes

1 & 2

JACOPO DELLA QUERCIA
Siena, c. 1371/74 – Siena, 1438

Design fragment for the left side of the Fonte Gaia in Siena, c. 1415–16

Pen and brown ink, brush and brown wash, over traces of leadpoint and ruling, on vellum, glued onto secondary paper support, 201 × 214 mm (7 15/16 × 8 7/16 in.)
The Metropolitan Museum of Art, New York, Harris Brisbane Fund, 1949 49.141

Design fragment for the right side of the Fonte Gaia in Siena, c. 1415–16

Pen and brown ink, brush and brown wash, over probable traces of leadpoint (untested) and ruling, on vellum, glued onto secondary paper support, 153 × 228 mm (6 × 9 in.)
Inscribed in pen and brown ink at lower right: *Giotto*; and at bottom: *181* (the number of the Dyce inventory)
Victoria and Albert Museum, London Dyce Bequest 181

IN 1408 Jacopo della Quercia was contracted by the magistrates (*signori*) of the republic of Siena to execute the Fonte Gaia ("Fountain of Joy"), a great rectangular basin with figural sculptures in marble, intended to replace a previously existing structure on the northwest edge of the Piazza del Campo, the main public space of the town. The damaged original fragments of the Fonte Gaia are today in Santa Maria della Scala (Siena) but remained in situ until 1858, when the ensemble was substituted with a facsimile copy by Tito Sarrocchi.[1] Eleven years in the making, the Fonte Gaia served practical, symbolic, and aesthetic functions, as part of a larger program of public monuments initiated by the fiercely republican government of the *comune* that rose to power in 1404.[2] It was the principal source of public waters in the center of Siena (a land-locked hill town), serving as a large cistern with several spouts that was supplied from the vast network of subterranean aqueducts, or *bottini*, which had been completed with a 25-kilometer expansion at enormous expense in the late fourteenth century.[3] The documents relating to the Fonte Gaia commission (preserved in the Archivio di Stato of Siena) confirm that drawings produced by Jacopo della Quercia served an important legal purpose, allowing the patrons to discuss and approve the state of the fountain as it progressed. Although much about the two drawing fragments in the Metropolitan Museum of Art and Victoria and Albert Museum has been debated (including their authorship, iconography, and precise purpose), the new visual-archaeological evidence and a critical reading of the documents clearly confirm the attribution to Jacopo della Quercia himself.

On 15 December 1408, the magistrates of the republic established that the total cost of this major civic monument, dedicated to the Virgin as protectress of Siena, was not to exceed 1,700 gold florins.[4] The commission for the Fonte Gaia was authorized and the terms of the contract with Jacopo were stipulated on 22 January 1409. This document refers to a deadline of twenty months for the completion of the fountain, as well as to its dimensions and decoration "with figures, foliage ornament, and marbles that are clearly shown in the above-mentioned drawing" (*cho' le figure, foglame, e marmi che nel disegno soprascritto chiaramente si dimostrano*).[5] A memorandum of 18 January 1415, however, assessed the defects of the design and the incomplete state of the work as it stood: Jacopo della Quercia seems to have begun to produce the sculptures only in 1414; most of the sculptures or their preliminary models may have been complete between 1415 and 1416. The memorandum also noted the need to expand the size of the fountain and to provide for the decoration of the exterior faces of the

PROVENANCE (CAT. 1)

Giorgio Vasari (?) (1511–1574); Alexander Dyce (1798–1869); bequeathed to the Museum in 1869

LITERATURE (CAT. 1)

Dyce Collection 1874, p. 30, no. 181 (anonymous, previously ascribed to Giotto); Reitlinger 1921, p. 4, no. 1 (Sienese, late 14th century); Lány 1927–28, pp. 257–66 (Priamo della Quercia); Kauffmann 1929, p. 9, note 1 (Jacopo della Quercia); Lány 1930, pp. 30, 32–34; Popham 1931, p. 3 (probably by Priamo della Quercia); Foratti 1933, pp. 513–16; Bacci 1936, pp. 142–45; Degenhart 1937, p. 260 (Jacopo della Quercia); Pope-Hennessy 1939, p. 54, note 56 (a drawing after the sculpture, probably of a Veronese artist); Oertel 1940, pp. 263–66 (Jacopo della Quercia); Biagi 1946, pp. 15, 63–65; Krautheimer 1952, pp. 265–74; Pope-Hennessy 1953, p. 278; Pope-Hennessy 1955, p. 214; Coffin Hanson 1964, pp. 11–13, 22–34; Carli 1966, p. 21; Beck 1966, pp. 114–15; Degenhart and Schmitt 1968, vol. 1, pp. xx, 204, no. 113, vol. 3, pl. 162a; Seymour 1968, pp. 93–105; Del Bravo 1970, pp. 24–25, 34; Seymour 1973, p. 45; Ragghianti Collobi 1974, vol. 1, p. 43, vol. 2, fig. 53; Chelazzi Dini and Previtali 1975, pp. 107, 111; Glasser 1977, pp. 126, 412, no. XXI; Bisogni 1977, pp. 108–14; Ward-Jackson 1979, vol. 1, pp. 21–24, no. 17; Conti 1980, p. 148; Ames-Lewis 1981, pp. 128, 130, repr.; Bean 1982, pp. 210–11; Ames-Lewis and Wright 1983, pp. 224–27; Goldner 1989, p. 469; Forlani Tempesti 1991, p. 169, note 9; Beck 1991, p. 374; Symmes 1998a, pp. 35, 190, note 5, fig. 57; Bellosi 2000 [first published in 1983], p. 144; Ferretti 2001; Caciorgna 2001, pp. 71–114; Marilena Caciorgna in Santi and Strinati 2005, p. 144, under nos. 1.16–18; Federica Siddi in Seidel et al. 2010, pp. 68–70, no. A18b; Richter 2010

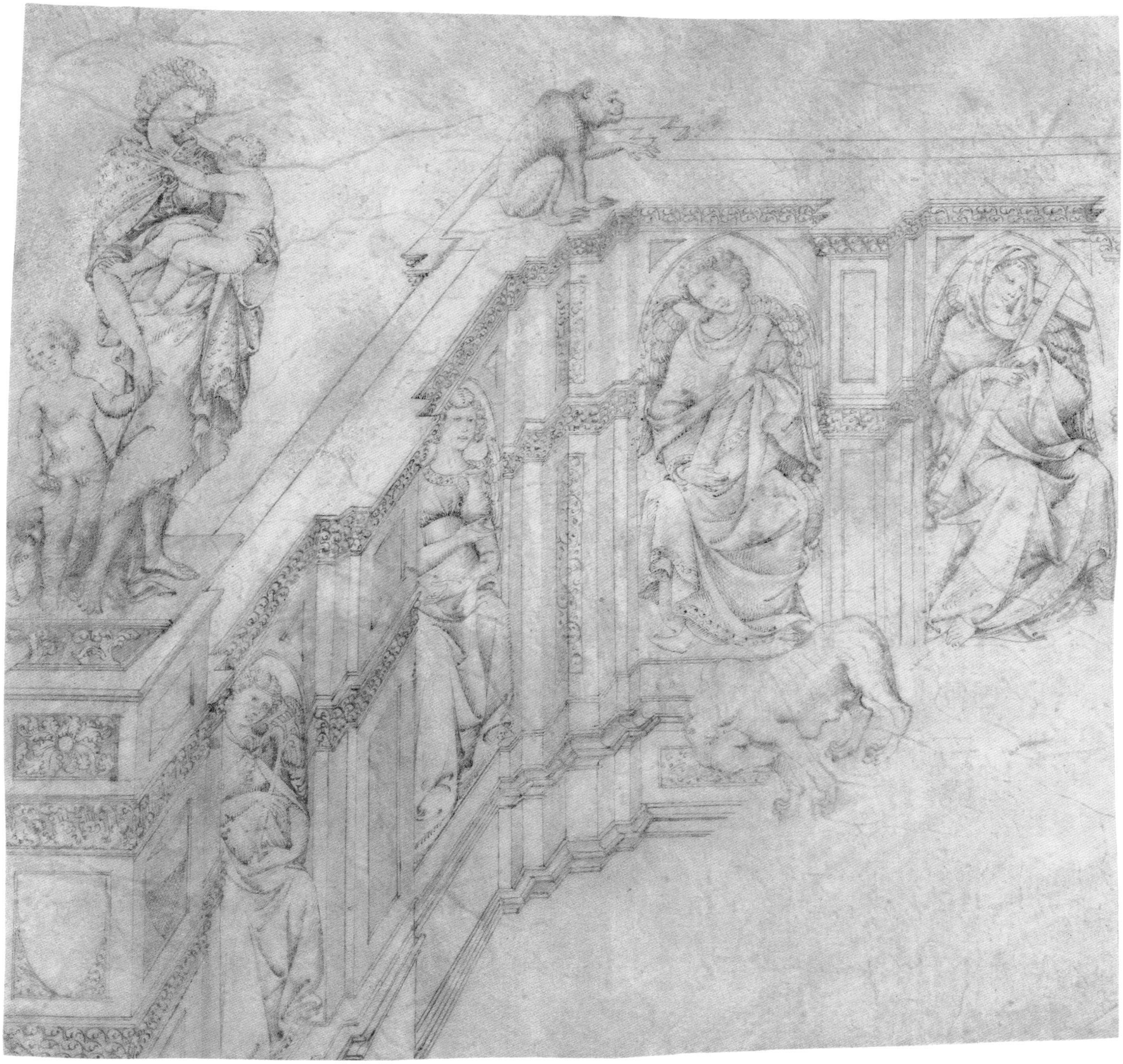

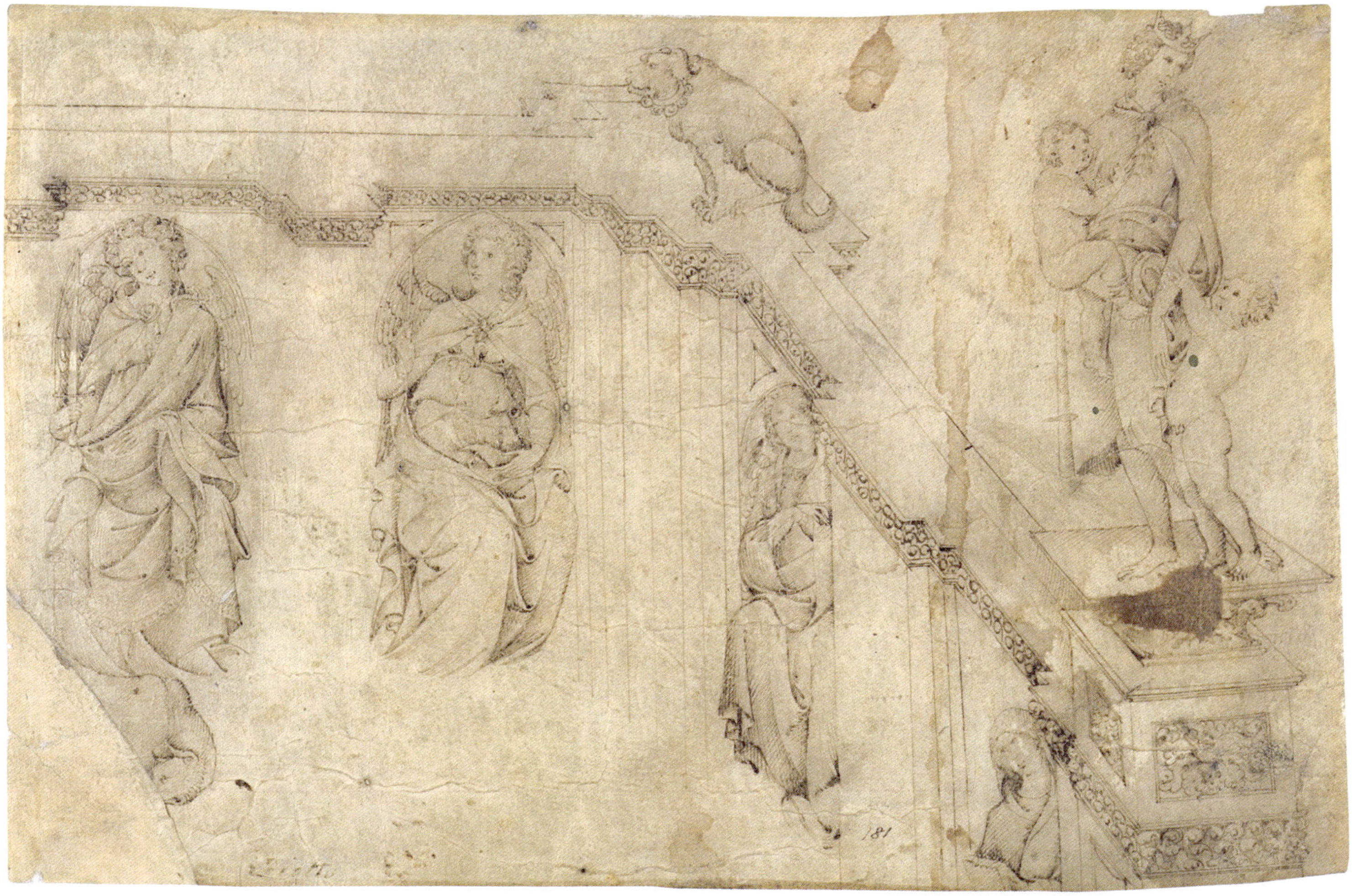

PROVENANCE (CAT. 2)

Giorgio Vasari (?) (1511–1574); Sir Erasmus Philipps (c. 1623–1697); Sir Richard Philipps (1744–1823); Sir John Wynford Philipps (1860–1938); purchased by the Museum in London in 1949

LITERATURE (CAT. 2)

Metropolitan Museum of Art Bulletin 1950, p. 130; Krautheimer 1952, pp. 265–72; Pope-Hennessy 1953, p. 278; Pope-Hennessy 1955, p. 214; Bean 1964, no. 1; Coffin Hanson 1964, pp. 11–13, 22–34; Carli 1966, p. 21; Beck 1966, pp. 114–15; Seymour 1968, passim; Degenhart and Schmitt 1968, vol. 1, no. 112, vol. 3, pl. 161a; Del Bravo 1970, pp. 24–25, 34; Pope-Hennessy 1972, p. 213; Seymour 1973, p. 45; Ragghianti Collobi 1974, vol. 1, p. 43; Chelazzi Dini and Previtali 1975, pp. 107, 110; Glasser 1977, pp. 126, 412, no. XXI; Bisogni 1977, pp. 108–14; Luciano Bellosi in Bellini and Brunetti 1978, p. XX; Ward-Jackson 1979, vol. 1, pp. 21–24, under no. 17; Conti 1980, p. 148; Ames-Lewis 1981, pp. 128, 130; Bean 1982, pp. 210–11, no. 209; Ames-Lewis and Wright 1983, pp. 224–27, no. 46; Goldner 1989, p. 469; Carl Brandon Strehlke in Christiansen, Kanter, and Strehlke 1988, p. 38; Forlani Tempesti 1991, p. 169, note 9; Beck 1991, p. 374; Symmes 1998a, pp. 34–35, 190, note 5, fig. 56; Symmes 1998b, pp. 2–3; Bellosi 2000 [first published in 1983], p. 144; Caciorgna 2001, pp. 71–114; Ferretti 2001; Marilena Caciorgna in Santi and Strinati 2005, p. 144, under nos. 1.16–18; Federica Siddi in Seidel et al. 2010, pp. 68–70, no. A 18a; Richter 2010

basin.[6] On 11 December 1416, a new contract for the Fonte Gaia was drafted, since the prescribed deadline for completion of the monument had also long passed.[7] This document of 1416 refers to a first drawing done in 1408, as well as to a new drawing on a piece of parchment or vellum (*carta edina*) "designed and made by the hand of the said master Jacopo, presented by the lord magistrates themselves in the town council" (*dicti anni MCCCCVIII, secundum formam primi designi facti in Palatio magnificorum dominorum Priorum in sala dicti Palatii tendenti versus Campsum fori, et quod postea fuit facta nova locatio, secundum novum designum factum manu dicti magistri Iacobi . . . et eo modo et forma et prout continetur et designatum est, et apparet in quadam carta edina manu dicti magistri Iacobi designata et facta, presentata per ipsos dominos Regulatores in Consistorio*).[8] The Fonte Gaia was finished with the last payments to Jacopo della Quercia and the cancellation of the previous contracts for the project recorded on October 9 and 20, 1419.[9]

The two surviving fragments at the Metropolitan Museum of Art and the Victoria and Albert Museum pertain to the left and right portions of the Fonte Gaia and originally constituted a large, very detailed single drawing on vellum of which the central portion is lost. The Victoria and Albert fragment has also been cut down substantially along the upper and bottom borders. The minute control of the figural and ornamental details especially evidence Jacopo della Quercia's early training as a goldsmith.[10] Seen close up and in good light, the drawing style of the figures with parallel and cross-hatching is also surprisingly expressive. The general iconography of the Fonte Gaia alludes to the virtues of good government of the republic of Siena, which are also celebrated in the fourteenth-century frescoes of the Palazzo Pubblico, which faced the original fountain across the Piazza del Campo. Two standing female figures, each accompanied by two infants, terminate the design of the fountain at left and right foreground in the present drawing fragments. They represent respectively Acca Larentia (she wears a fur) and Rhea Silvia (she wears a crown), who were the birth and foster mothers of the twins Romulus and Remus, founders of Rome, and according to local legend also the founders of Siena: these figures are much more individualized in the drawings than in the final marble sculptures.[11] In addition to the she-wolf of Rome in the foreground of the Metropolitan Museum fragment, two other symbolic animals adorn the far corners of the low walls, an ape in the Metropolitan Museum fragment and a she-dog in the Victoria and Albert Museum fragment, possibly alluding to the kinds of sinfulness of the Roman twins' mothers.[12] The rows of niches in the interior of the three low walls of the basin house the figures of Christian Virtues.

Of the scientific instrumentation used to examine the Metropolitan Museum drawing fragment, ultraviolet light especially clarifies that the wash modeling in iron-gall ink was originally much more extensive and powerful, and that it has greatly faded with age and light.[13] Hence, the monumentality and overall sculptural quality of the original design, with its graded tonal transitions in the areas with wash and with pen-and-ink hatching in the deepest shadows, have been considerably diminished. The arguments that these drawings are by a painter (Priamo della Quercia, documented 1426–67, brother of Jacopo, being one of the proposed candidates), rather than by a sculptor, therefore fall apart. When the two drawing fragments are seen together side by side, as in the present exhibition and as they were displayed in 1998 and 2010, it becomes clear that they are portions of the same unitary drawing but that the Victoria and Albert portion depicts design elements in a greatly more incomplete state and is of more modest overall conception than the Metropolitan Museum fragment. A possible explanation is that the large original drawing may have represented a kind of visual legal document, or *ricordo*, of the actual state of progress around 1415–16 of the carved monument and the fact that it was largely unfinished in its right half at that point in time. The pilasters and much of the moldings are left unarticulated (almost blank) in the London fragment, while the New York drawing seems only slightly unfinished toward the lower right, where the very summarily sketched outlines indicate a mount projecting forward from the low back wall that provides a ground line for the she-wolf. The moldings at the bottom of the architectural framework toward the right are also drawn in reserve and are therefore blank (this is verified by the view under the microscope and with infrared reflectography). These architectural lines stop quite short of the design of the mount. Close-up examination of both drawing fragments confirms that these passages of apparent unfinish are a matter of intentional facture, not ones due to compromised physical condition: this is not simply a case of the ink being faded in the blank parts of the designs.

The New York and London drawing fragments portray a still fragmentary sculptural ensemble in which the passages of most incomplete execution generally occur in the middle to right portions of the fountain's decoration, although the degree to which the drawings are accurate records of the work in progress may be open to question. The New York and London drawing fragments also provide a greater amount of content and specify details much beyond what the Fonte Gaia documents describe, but represent a much less complex overall design than the fountain that was finally executed in marble by 1419. The drawing fragments therefore must date to 1415–16 or so, roughly speaking during the period of time in which the design of the Fonte Gaia was being reevaluated on the basis of the work in progress, and the new contract and *novum designum* for the greatly modified fountain were being drafted.

The visual conventions of form adopted by Jacopo della Quercia in the New York and London fragments also shed light on the precise function of the monumental original drawing. In both drawing fragments, the detailed design of the precisely ruled architectural framework for the fountain, with its sculpted allegorical figures, animals, and vegetal patterns of ornament, is depicted with precise outlines and modeling in wash in a clearly expository manner so as to indicate the general illusion of the three-dimensional forms receding in space. The figures, animals, and ornament were then further individuated with clarity by the deeper modeling with strokes of spirited hatching. On the two lateral walls, the framing elements of the niches, pilasters, and moldings overlap the forms of the figural sculptures, but the overall design is constructed according to a parallel projection of all diagonal lines, or isometry, rather than a true, pictorial one-point perspective in the Renaissance style pioneered by Filippo Brunelleschi in which orthogonal lines converge on a single vanishing point. These pictorial conventions in the Fonte Gaia design fragments are rooted in Late Gothic practice and fit within a larger typology of architectural-sculptural drawings by Sienese artists from the second half of the fourteenth century onward. Such early Sienese drawings depict carefully ruled architectural ensembles decorated with meticulously drawn figural and ornamental sculpture, and were executed in pen and ink on parchment, as, for example, the drawings for the façade of the Baptistery of Siena and for a lavish, unexecuted pulpit perhaps intended for Orvieto Cathedral (Opera del Duomo, Siena, 20; Opera del Duomo, Orvieto; British Museum, London, 1899,0617.2; and Kupferstichkabinett, Berlin, KdZ 3392).[14]

The result of the early historiography on the Fonte Gaia project has been that the Metropolitan Museum of Art and Victoria and Albert drawing fragments are usually published with a question mark after the attribution to Jacopo della Quercia. While the documents alone should suffice to settle the attribution beyond doubt, the scholarly debates have chiefly arisen from two problems. First, the term *disegno* in Italian embraces the dual meanings of "design" and "drawing," and in making attributions a previous generation of scholars often overly preferred to regard the authorship of the design idea as separate from the actual execution of a drawing. Second, there is a choice of how narrowly or widely one interprets the phrase *manu dicti magistri Jacobi*, "made by master Jacopo's hand." In the Italian vernacular, the phrasing in documents is frequently rendered as *fatto di sua mano*. The phrase *di sua mano*, "by his hand," and like wording have been much better understood by art historians with regard to early paintings and sculptures.[15] The large physical scale of projects often entailed the delegation of labor among collaborators and workshop assistants, which consequently raises nuanced dimensions of authorship in examining a design with respect to its execution. But, one must emphasize, this is more often than not the wrong paradigm for the analysis of early modern drawings. When referring to actual drawings, at least of a reasonably portable scale, the Italian Renaissance artist, patron, and author applied the phrase *di sua mano* in a most literal and practical sense (that was usually also legally binding in the case of contractual documents), to mean that a drawing was physically made by the artist's hand. One must also emphasize that the understanding of the phrase *di sua mano* as that a drawing was physically by the artist's hand went much beyond the sphere of official contractual drawings: the phrase was used in this narrow, literal sense in a variety of written sources of the early modern period —letters, *ricordi*, and writings on art, including Giorgio Vasari's *Vite de' più eccellenti pittori, scultori e architettori*. C.C.B.

NOTES

1 The original fragments of the Fonte Gaia were installed from 1904 to 1989 in the Palazzo Pubblico, Siena, and have undergone conservation treatment from 1989 to the present by the Opificio delle Pietre Dure e Laboratori di Restauro, Florence.
2 Carl Brandon Strehlke in Christiansen, Kanter, and Strehlke 1988, p. 38.
3 Mauro Civai, "I bottini di Siena," in Galluzzi 1991, pp. 272–95.
4 Document transcribed in Beck 1991, vol. 2, pp. 345–46, no. 22, with commentary.
5 Document transcribed Beck 1991, pp. 347–50, no. 25.
6 Document transcribed Beck 1991, pp. 365–66, no. 54.
7 Document transcribed Beck 1991, pp. 371–73, no. 63.
8 Quoted from Beck 1991, vol. 2, p. 372, no. 63.
9 Document transcribed Beck 1991, pp. 391–95, nos. 95, 96.
10 As pointed out by Beck 1991, vol. 1, p. 150.
11 Caciorgna 2001 provides a masterful analysis of the iconography.
12 Caciorgna 2001, pp. 109–12.
13 Examinations with infrared reflectography, microscope, and ultraviolet light were conducted by Marjorie N. Shelley, Conservator in Charge of Paper Conservation Laboratory, Metropolitan Museum of Art, New York, on 7 July 2014. The imaging with infrared reflectography reveals traces of an outline underdrawing in leadpoint.
14 Illustrated and catalogued in Popham and Pouncey 1950, vol. 1, pp. 167–68, no. 268; Degenhart and Schmitt 1968, vol. 1-1, pp. 97–98, nos. 39–42, vol. 1-3, pls. 67–75.
15 The arguments that follow were initially presented in my lecture "'Di sua mano' (from His Hand): Signatures, Authorship and Questions of Originality in Italian Renaissance Drawings," Frick Collection and Museum, New York, 28 January 2013.

3

DONATELLO, attributed to
Florence, c. 1386 – Florence, 1466

The Massacre of the Innocents (recto); *David* (verso), c. 1450

Pen, brown ink and wash over black chalk (recto); pen and ink over black chalk and metalpoint (verso), 288 × 204 mm (11⅜ × 8 in.)
Inscribed in brown ink, on recto, upper left corner (probably by Giorgio Vasari): *buonamico*; on recto, lower right corner: *No. I* (numbering of the Christophe-Paul de Robien collection); on recto, on the mount (in an eighteenth-century hand, perhaps Christophe-Paul de Robien): *Buonamico Buffalmacco fiorentino, citato dal Boccacio, jmparo il disegno da Andrea Taffi visse nel 1340 / Le nom de Donatello ce trouve au revers de ce dessein ce qui feroit juger qu'il seroit de luy.*; on verso, lower right corner (probably by Giorgio Vasari): *donatello*; on verso, lower right corner (in an unidentifiable hand, probably fifteenth-century): *I m q x x* or *ccxxviiii*?
Musée des Beaux-Arts, Rennes 794.1.2501

GIORGIO VASARI inscribed the verso of this sheet with Donatello's name when fitting it into his "Libro de' disegni," the collection of drawings that illustrated the art historical development that he described in the *Vite.* Though Carlo Ragghianti had expressed doubts about Vasari's attribution as early as 1938, it was defended by Bernhard Degenhart and Annegrit Schmitt, who used the sheet as the point of departure for a far-reaching reconstruction of the graphic art of Donatello and his followers. Their influential discussion has shaped the perception of many scholars who have looked at the drawing since, though a number of writers—most forcefully Joachim Poeschke—have resurrected Ragghianti's doubts, concluding that the drawing is a sixteenth-century work with only a loose connection to Donatello.

Questions about the Donatello attribution start with the nature of the evidence Vasari provides. Though Vasari seems to have believed that the verso was by Donatello, he inscribed the recto with the name *buonamico*. This side shows the left half of a Massacre of the Innocents, drawn in part over a metalpoint tabernacle with an angel (of the Annunciation?) in the upper left portion of the page. Some specialists, including most recently Patrick Ramade, have also concluded that it was Vasari who inscribed the first of two lines under the *Massacre*: "The Florentine Buonamico Buffalmacco, who is mentioned by Boccaccio, learned drawing with Andrea Tafi; he lived around 1340." In his Life of Buffalmacco, Vasari wrote of a lost fresco by that artist of the *Massacre,* which "expressed very vividly the emotions both of the murderers and of the other figures."[1] Vasari had no basis for recognizing the drawing style of Buffalmacco, but the Rennes sheet fits this description well, raising the possibility that the *buonamico* inscription indicates not that the drawing was in Buffalmacco's hand but that it replicated a Buffalmacco painting. If this is correct, it bears on the verso as well: Vasari probably had limited direct evidence of how Donatello drew, and he may have linked the drawing to the sculptor on account of the subject matter as much as the style.

A further problem is that to this day no secure drawings by Donatello have been identified, and the few clues we have about Donatello's creative process allow no conclusions about the importance and style of the preparatory drawings he may have made. The earliest indication that Donatello even made drawings comes from Pomponius Gauricus, fifty years after the artist's death: he reported that Donatello daily ordered his students "draw!"[2] Gauricus was writing in Padua, where Donatello had worked, so the anecdote could reflect an oral tradition, passed down through workshops, or it could be the result of a more mythologizing "Donatello Renaissance" around 1500. Either way, it may be that the early association of Donatello with drawing had to do not with the sculptor's graphic output but with circulation of drawings produced after his works. Pisanello drew the putto reliefs on the pulpit of Prato Cathedral very shortly after they were finished. Tommaso Garelli and Giuliano da

PROVENANCE

Giorgio Vasari's "Libro de' disegni" (as Buonamico Buffalmacco and Donatello); Christophe-Paul de Robien (1698–1756); Crozat collection (mentioned in the sale catalogue of 1741); collection of Marquis de Robinet (mentioned in the catalogue of the sequestration, 1793); acquired by the Musée des Beaux-Arts, Rennes, in 1794

LITERATURE

Rennes 1859, p. 54 (Buffalmacco); Rennes 1863, 1871, 1876, 1884 (Donatello for the *Massacre of the Innocents*, following Mariette's attribution); Ragghianti 1938, pp. XXV–XXVI (Bandinelli); Degenhart and Schmitt 1968, vol. 2, pp. 343–65, no. 265 (Donatello); Clark 1970, pp. 262–64 (Donatello); Gardner 1972, p. 32 ("substantially later than Donatello's lifetime"); Collobi Ragghianti 1974, vol. 1, pp. 53–54 (early 16th-century); Bellosi in Bellini and Brunetti 1978, p. XXIV (Antonio Rossellino); Eisler 1981, n.p., no. 2 (Donatello); Bennett and Wilkins 1984, pp. 97–98 (Donatello, tentatively attributed to); Martha L. Dunkelman in Darr 1985, pp. 141–42, no. 34 (Donatello, c. 1445–60); Wohl 1986, p. 566, no. 39 (anonymous early 16th-century); Monbeig-Goguel 1989, pp. 94–95 (Tommaso Garelli); Poeschke 1990 (anonymous early 16th-century); Ramade 1990, pp. 14–17 (Donatello, close to 1445–50); Sciolla 1991, pp. 42–45 (Donatello); Bambach 1999, pp. 188–89 ("Donatello or artist closely influenced by him," probably 1440s); Drogin 2001, p. 153 ("attributed to Donatello"); Randolph 2002, p. 158 ("anonymous [Donatello?], c. 1440")

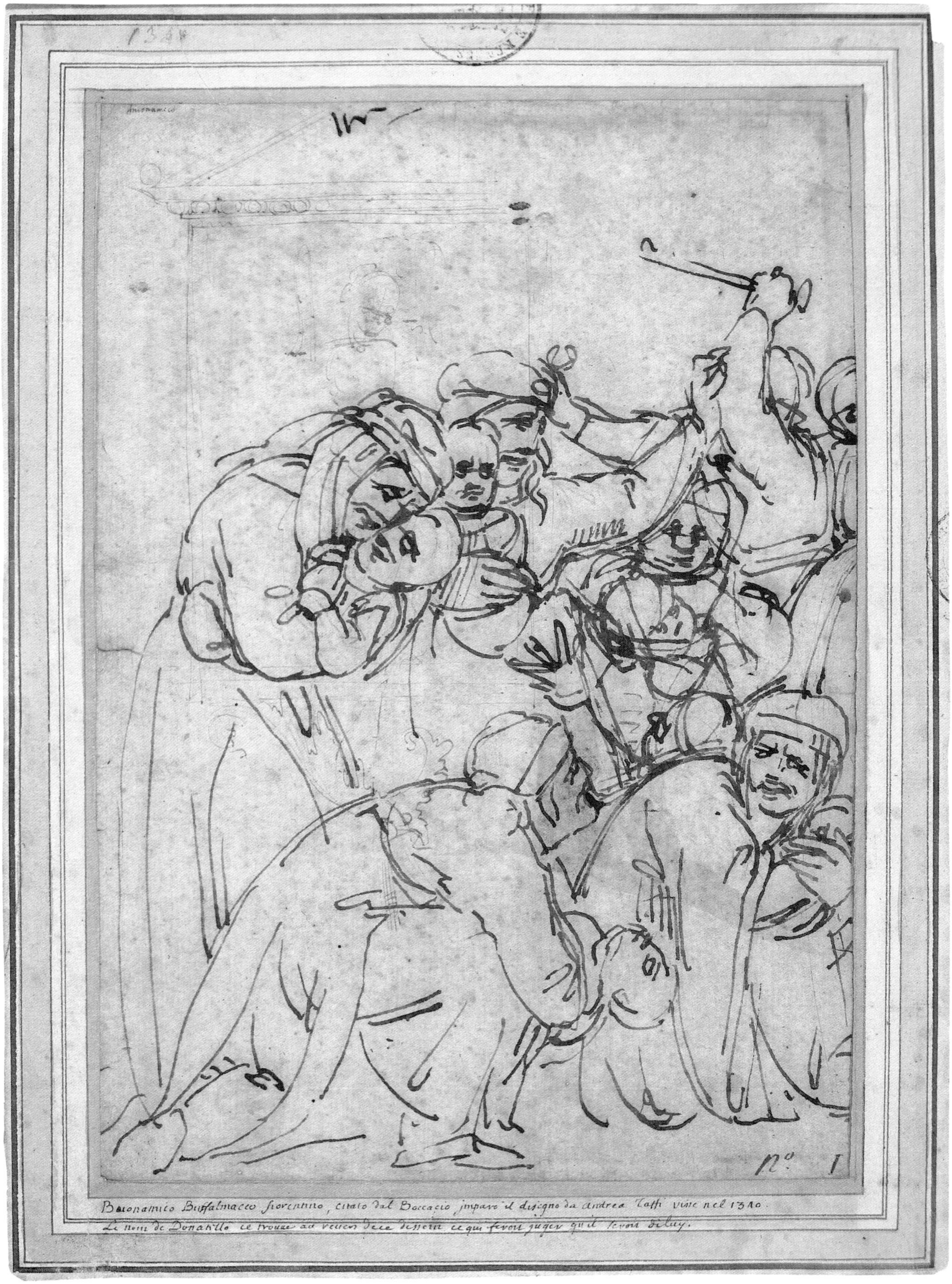
Buonamico Buffalmacco fiorentino, citato dal Boccacio imparò il disegno da Andrea Taffi vine nel 1340.
N.º 1

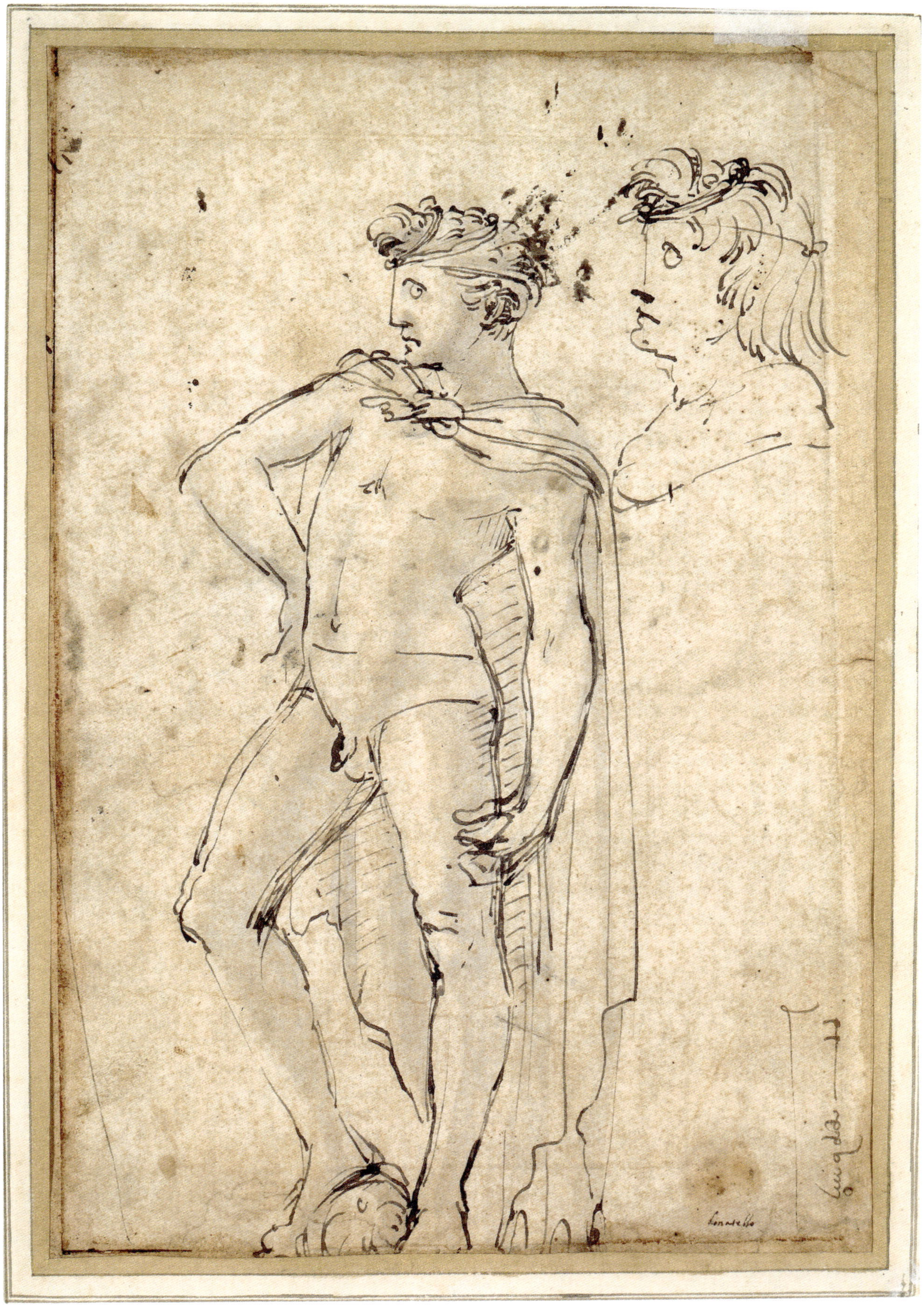

Sangallo both drew after the reliefs of the bronze doors in the Old Sacristy. The high altar in Padua and the pulpits in San Lorenzo appear to have been especially beloved objects of study, drawn by painters in the Raphael circle, by Pontormo, and by Baccio Bandinelli, among others.[3] While important works of painting—such as Giotto's *Navicella* mosaic in Old St. Peter's in Rome—had long been objects of imitation, it was with Donatello that modern sculptures achieved the canonical status of their ancient counterparts and thereby became worthy objects for draftsmen to study.

Another question relates to the sequence of uses to which the sheet was put. The delicate forms of the metalpoint tabernacle, which Poeschke compared to several late fifteenth-century monuments, were drawn first; the *Massacre of the Innocents* was drawn over this and must therefore post-date it. The pen strokes of the *Massacre*, moreover, do not show any consideration of the right edge of the sheet, which cuts through the middle of the scene, allowing the supposition that the sheet was originally twice as large as it is now and that the right half today is missing; given that the tabernacle, too, reaches to the very top edge of the page, the sheet was probably once somewhat higher as well. The main figure on the other side, by contrast, is perfectly placed in the middle of the sheet, which may indicate that the originally larger sheet was either folded or already cut in half when the drawing was made. This might have happened if the page was being used for workshop exercises, a scenario that would make sense both of the copying of an admired fresco and of the drawing of the second head on the right side of the verso. The vertical line that takes the place of the nose and the cut that runs from the back of that head must have provided some sort of guidance for its construction. Comparable motifs appear in student works, produced within the framework of drawing lessons, in the early sixteenth century.

Finally, there is the standing figure itself. Though this does refer unmistakably to Donatello, his figures do not typically incorporate the tension seen here, with head and one foot in profile but right shoulder and arm both rotated sharply to the front. This kind of posture, on the other hand, finds many analogues after the time of Bertoldo di Giovanni and particularly in the age of Michelangelo; the angular form where upper and lower back meet is also common in works from this later period. Degenhart and Schmitt already compared the Rennes figure to Michelangelo's drawing of a David in the Louvre, inv. 714r, as well as to the Pulsky *David* in the same museum, now attributed to Giovanfrancesco Rustici. The Michelangelo commission to which the Louvre drawing is connected was for a statue "like that in the courtyard of the Signoria"—that is, Donatello's early marble *David*—and Rustici was commissioned about 1515 to make a "David similar to the one by Donatello." Those who regard the Rennes drawing as a sixteenth-century work take these formal similarities as evidence that the drawing is a response to these Donatello imitations from around 1500.

Still, none of these arguments is decisive. Vasari was a trained draftsman who knew as much about the history of Italian art as anyone. Though he made mistakes in some of his attributions—Helmut Wohl has suggested that he was off in more than half of the Quattrocento drawings he owned—it is difficult to believe that he could not tell the difference between a drawing made in his own century and one made more than fifty years before. The style of the drawing, moreover, shows many consistencies with drawings from about 1450—the rough, "primitive" forms, the reliance on contour, the use of wash to create volume, the complete absence of cross-hatching. If this is a sixteenth-century drawing, we have to imagine an artist consciously working in an old-fashioned manner. That would be conceivable if something on the sheet were a copy of a historical work, but such a suggestion has been raised only in relation to the Buffalmacco *Massacre,* and there is no evidence to support even that theory. On the contrary, the ink compositions on both recto and verso have underdrawings in charcoal or black chalk as well as some pentimenti, indicating that the artist was thinking actively about his figures, not merely transcribing them.

The forms that constitute the tabernacle, different as they may be from Donatello's few architectural inventions, are conventional elements that alone allow no real conclusions about the sheet's authorship or date. The cutting of the sheet, similarly, tells us nothing about the date the drawings were made, since the centering of the figure on the verso could easily have been a consequence of the cutting rather than a response to it. A drawing by Cellini in the present exhibition (cat. 32) suffered a similar fate, with a later owner trimming the recto so as to center the figure study there, sacrificing part of the drawing on the verso in the process. Such a treatment of the page, in fact, would be all the more understandable if the owner believed that the figure on the verso was by Donatello and the composition on the recto was not. If the text below the *Massacre* was indeed by Vasari, that would be a significant clue at least to the date when the cutting happened. That line and the one below, however, appear to have been written in conjunction and in alignment with one another, on the same scale and in the same ink. The comparable morphology of various letters suggests that they are in the same hand, and the switch to French points to a later collector rather than to Vasari; Degenhart and Schmitt's proposal that the writing is Robien's remains the most plausible hypothesis. If the tabernacle provides a terminus post quem for the recto of the sheet, finally, the text at the bottom right of the verso provides a terminus ante quem for that side. The general consensus is that this is a number, though no one is quite sure what that number is; the script, though, appears to be from the fifteenth century, and if that is so, the drawing must be as well.

There can be little doubt that the figure to which that text relates is for a sculpture, probably—as Poeschke suggested—a work of marble that used the long cape as a brace. Unless we imagine a painter providing a carver with a design, it must also have been by a sculptor. While it is still incomplete in conception—there is no Goliath's head or sword—its pose suggests a David, a subject most commonly found in Florence. True, this David differs markedly from Donatello's bronze, both in its physicality and in its contortion. But Donatello's late bronze *Putto* in the Bargello shows that at the end of his life he was experimenting with more dramatic poses. From the drawing alone, it is impossible to be certain whether the *Massacre* was for a painting or a relief. But if Ockham's Razor allows us to suppose that everything on the Rennes sheet was made by a single person, and if the style and subject of the verso suggest a Florentine sculptor working in the early to mid-fifteenth century, it could be noted that the compression of the figures on the recto, their expressive gestures and deep eyes, all find parallels in Donatello's late works in bronze. That would mean, as Degenhart and Schmitt argued, that artists like Pollaiuolo, Rossellino, and even Michelangelo and Bandinelli responded directly or indirectly to an earlier local graphic practice, the evidence of which has now largely been lost. Gauricus's remark and Michelangelo's Louvre drawing would represent parallel contemporary responses to a real tradition rather than aspects of a Donatello myth.

That leaves the question of why Donatello might have made a sheet like this. The recto is easier to account for, since sculptors regularly turned to drawing in order to conceive reliefs and works of architecture. The figure on the verso is more unusual, though the comparison with Michelangelo's Louvre sheet—whether that is earlier or later—proves that this is a kind of drawing that Renaissance sculptors did make. One possibility is that the drawing was done from life: the lines at the top of the *David*'s thigh and across his stomach may render a pair of short hose; underdrawing on the figure's shoulder suggests that a nude body was sketched in first, and the cape drawn over this. Another possibility is that the drawing was done after a wax or clay model, one to which attributes had not yet been added. In that case, the line across the figure's waist may be related to one that appears to cross the knot of cape on his chest, suggesting a concern with measurement and proportion that continues in the (slightly larger) head at right. Degenhart and Schmitt proposed that the inscrutable text at lower right, which has some kind of bracket above (or below?), might have been a scale; its length corresponds almost exactly to the distance between the lines across stomach and cape. As a drawing by Verrocchio (cat. 7) also illustrates, proportion was a problem that sculptors were apt to work out in a contour drawing on paper, before or after making a model. M.W.C. & U.P.

NOTES

1 Vasari-de Vere 1912–14, vol. 1, p. 138.
2 Gauricus 1969, pp. 72–73: *dicebat, Designate, et Et profecto id est totius Sculpturae caput et fundamentum.*
3 See Vöge 1896; Bertini 1958, p. 65, nos. 517, 518; Darr 1985; Angelini 1986; Bambach 2007, pp. 772–78.

4

MASO FINIGUERRA

Florence, 1426 – Florence, 1464

Young draftsman, 1450s

Pen and brown ink, brown wash over black chalk on white paper, 148 × 100 mm (5¹³⁄₁₆ × 3¹⁵⁄₁₆ in.)
Gabinetto Disegni e Stampe degli Uffizi, Florence 120E

IN HIS HANDBOOK OF PAINTING (about 1400), Cennino Cennini advised his ideal pupil to "draw something every day," and documents show that in the busy Paduan workshop of Francesco Squarcione (1394–1468) the apprentices trained by copying their master's stock of model sheets.[1] It seems that the drawings of the so-called Finiguerra group are the variegated remnants of a similar collection, once a series of at least "fourteen books of drawings … between large and small," documented as belonging to the Florentine goldsmith Tommaso d'Antonio, called Maso Finiguerra.[2] Probably made during the 1450s, when Maso shared a workshop with Piero di Bartolomeo di Sali and the young Antonio Pollaiuolo,[3] the drawings served as a treasure house of forms for the master and as a repository of examples for his apprentices. Although some of these sheets show animals or details of legs, arms, and hands, most of them are dedicated to the entire human figure, studied from the handiest subjects—the *garzoni*, pupils or young assistants whose number attests to the high status of Maso's profession.[4] In fifteenth-century Florence, goldsmiths enjoyed a particular regard among wealthy patrons. Their skill in designing complex, three-dimensional artifacts elevated them to the level of "master draftsman," as Maso was called in the notebooks of the ambitious collector Giovanni Rucellai.[5]

The goldsmith's need to render objects in drawings—objects that were then to be incised, hammered, carved, or cast in various materials—lend the sheets from the Finiguerra group a specific quality. With its unerasable, firm outline, the pen drawing not only provides the clarity that is indispensable for instruction but also prefigures the technique of engraving in metal. Maso was especially famous for his *nielli*—linear designs incised in silver and enhanced with black pigments to achieve an often astonishing plastic effect of *rilievo* or relief. This spatial rendering of multifigure compositions on small plates of metal was praised by Giorgio Vasari, an early collector and admirer of Maso's drawings. The work with the burin—called *intagliare*, just like carving in stone and wood—thus marks the transition between drawing and sculpture.

Although a recent attribution of works in the round to Maso remains a matter of debate, the sheets from his workshop reveal a sculptural approach to drawing.[6] The young assistants mutually study each other like plaster casts, which were frequent props in Florentine and Paduan workshops such as those of Ghiberti and Squarcione.[7] In the Uffizi drawing the application of wash captures effects of light and follows the surface of the garment—especially the hood—as if the paper itself were folded and rolled into an intricate plastic form. The emphasis on plastic qualities evident in the whole Finiguerra group explains why the workshops of Florentine goldsmiths functioned as privileged schools of drawing before the epoch of academies began.[8]

W.-D.L.

PROVENANCE

Collection of Leopoldo de' Medici

LITERATURE

Degenhart and Schmitt 1968, vol. 2, pp. 427, 616; Kubiak 1974, p. 184; Angelini 1986, no. 104; Elen 1995, no. 25; Melli 1995, no. 56; Wolf-Dietrich Löhr in Schulze Altcappenberg and Thimann 2007, no. 14

NOTES

1 Cennini 1936, p. 15 (chapter 28); for Squarcione, see Cassanelli 1998, p. 15, and Hugo Chapman in Chapman and Faietti 2010, p. 27.
2 Carl 1983, p. 550, doc. 26 (of 1507), see docs. 19 and 20; see Melli 2004 for an overview of sources.
3 Melli 1995, pp. 11ff.; Melli 2003.
4 Elen 1995, no. 25; Melli 1995; see Hugo Chapman in Chapman and Faietti 2010, nos. 26 and 27; Whitaker 2012.
5 Rucellai 1960, pp. 23ff.; see Wright 1994, pp. 131–46; Whitaker 1998, p. 46.
6 One attributed bronze is the *Hercules and Antaeus*, 25.2 cm high, collection of Mr. and Mrs. J. Tomilson Hill; see Wengraf 2014, no. 3.
7 Faietti 2012.
8 See the essay by Davide Gasparotto in this volume.

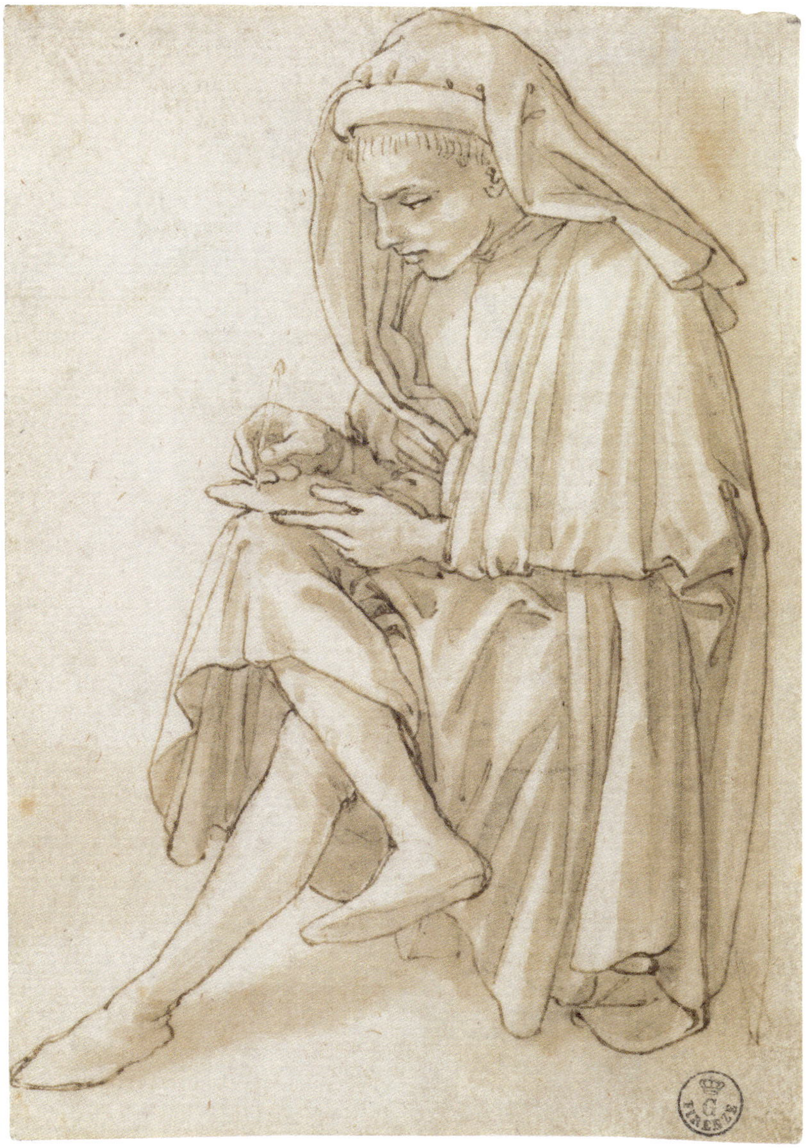
G
FIRENZE

5

ANDREA DEL VERROCCHIO

Florence, 1435 – Venice, 1488

Study for a funerary monument to Doge Andrea Vendramin, 1487–88

Leadpoint, partly reworked in pen and brown ink, brush and brown wash, and some ruling in leadpoint; glued to secondary paper support, 272 × 174 mm (10¾ × 6⅞ in.)
Victoria and Albert Museum, London 2314

THE SUBJECT OF THIS DRAWING is probably a tomb, but it is no ordinary monument. The sarcophagus is rendered like a filigree urn in precious metal, the sort of object that Verrocchio made as a goldsmith.[1] The urn is decorated with ovals on either side displaying cornucopiae and, in the center, the haloed lion of St. Mark holding the Gospel. Two putti, bearing shields and a blank scroll, are seated upon it. Below, three putti standing on a bracket hold up the urn. Surmounting the top is Justice, who holds a sword and scales. Beside her and slightly lower, Victory places a laurel wreath on the scales, while Plenty holds a cornucopia and a palm frond or a sheaf of corn. These allegorical figures resemble in pose and appearance contemporary festival floats, like those that Verrocchio supervised in Florence in 1471 (evoked in Baccio Baldini's engravings of the Twelve Sibyls).[2] At the top of the sheet is a round, coffered arch from which curtains, fastened with rings under the corbels, hang down on either side. Four playful putti holding garlands look down from the arch's capitals. The coat of arms of Doge Andrea Vendramin has been identified on the shield held by the seated putto on the left,[3] a connection strengthened by Giorgio Vasari's comment that Vincenzo Borghini owned a drawing of a doge's tomb by Verrocchio,[4] and by the drawing's emphasis on the quality of justice: Vendramin's motto was *Domi justitiam adeo colui, ut proprio nec pepercerim filio* ("I have cultivated justice in my house to such an extent that I did not spare my own son").[5] A Venetian link is suggested also by the presence of the lion of St. Mark.

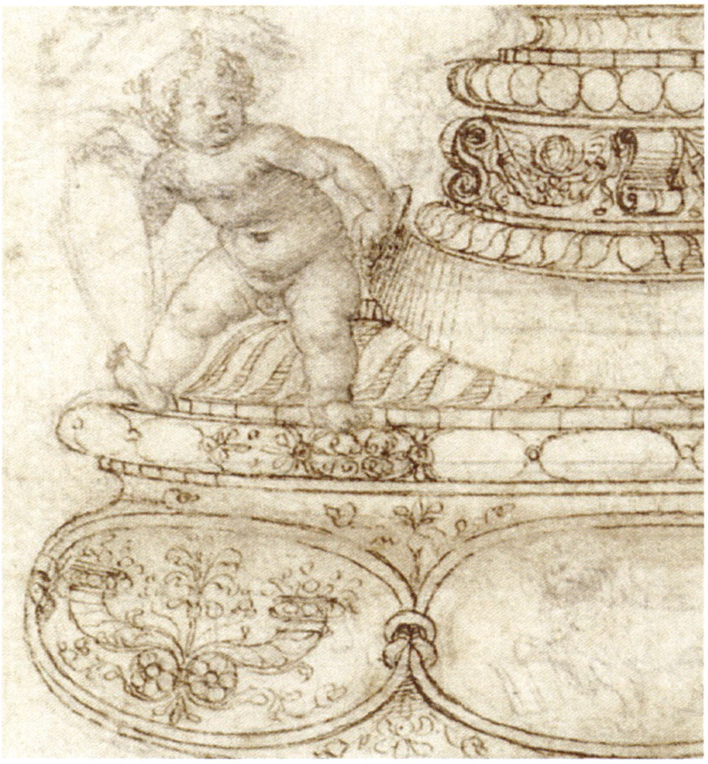

Detail of cat. 5

As a design for a monumental tomb, it is striking that it has no figure representing the deceased. Instead, the personified virtues serve to honor the doge as the embodiment of Venice.[6] In referring to

PROVENANCE

Vincenzo (Maria) Borghini (?), Florence (1515–1580; Lugt under 929); Sir Thomas Lawrence, Bristol and London (1769–1830; Lugt 2445); Samuel Woodburn, London (1786–1853; Lugt 2584, 2591; Suppl. 2378a); Woodburn sale, Christie's, London, 8 June 1860, lot 1053, bought for the museum

LITERATURE

van Marle 1923–38, vol. 9, p. 582 note, vol. 13, p. 269; Dussler 1926, p. 295; Clark 1929, no. 3; Degenhart 1932a; Degenhart 1932b, p. 105, note 65; Berenson 1933–34, pp. 262–63; Middeldorf 1934b, pp. 57–58; Möller 1935, pp. 193–94; Berenson 1938, vol. 1, pp. 68, 75, note 1, vol. 2, p. 73, vol. 3, no. 699 B (Lorenzo di Credi); Valentiner 1950, p. 119 note; Berenson 1961, vol. 1, p. 117, vol. 2, p. 132, no. 699 B (Lorenzo di Credi); Dalli Regoli 1965, p. 41; Dalli Regoli 1966, pp. 133–34, no. 66 (Lorenzo di Credi); Passavant 1969, pp. 60–62 and p. 194, no. D.11 (reworked by another hand); Seymour 1971, pp. 28–29; Grossman 1972, p. 18, fig. 5; Stedman Sheard 1978; Ward-Jackson 1979, pp. 24–26, no. 18 (partly reworked by another hand, Lorenzo di Credi?); Cadogan 1983, pp. 378, 380, 383; Pedretti 1989, p. 33; Stedman Sheard 1992, pp. 78–85; Antonio Natali in Petrioli Tofani 1992, p. 244, under no. 12.4; Butterfield 1997, pp. 185, 191; Rubin and Wright 1999, pp. 146–47, no. 11; Marani 2000, pp. 251, 296, note 51; Carmen C. Bambach in Bambach 2003, pp. 255–58, no. 5; Covi 2005, pp. 231–34

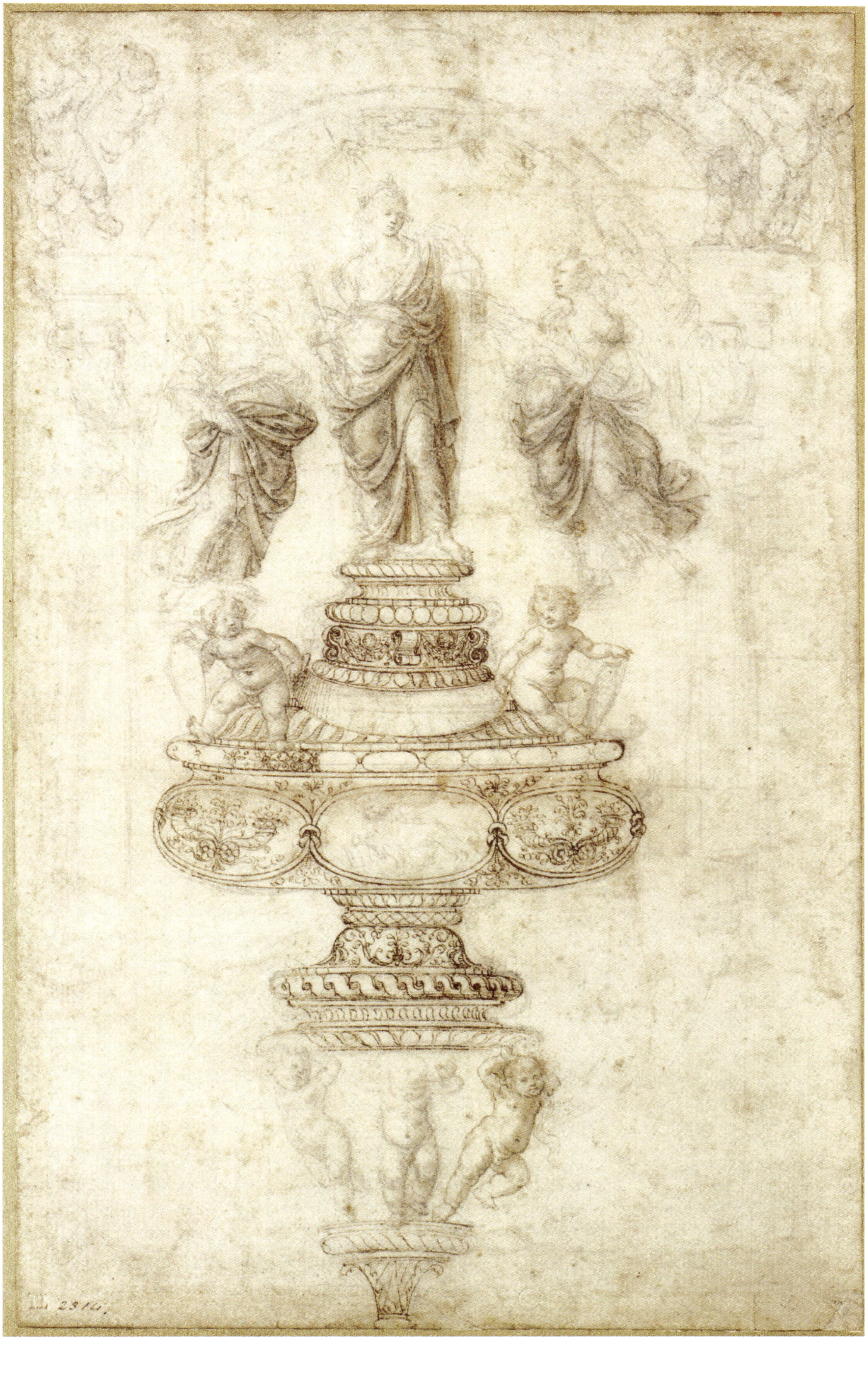
2314

virtues allegorically, the Vendramin design has much in common with Verrocchio's tomb of Giovanni and Piero de' Medici (about 1473, San Lorenzo, Florence), which similarly avoids direct representation of the Medici and alludes to them through symbols and materials.[7] As in the case of the Medici tomb, the artist may have intended Vendramin's monument to be constructed from various materials. It has been plausibly suggested that the urn was to be bronze,[8] and it is possible that the figures were to be of marble, and the curtains and the marble painted, like those for Desiderio da Settignano's Marsuppini tomb in Santa Croce, a commission on which Verrocchio may have worked as an assistant during his youth.[9] The design also bears similarities to Verrocchio's intentions for the Forteguerri cenotaph (1480s, San Zeno, Pistoia), especially the poses and conceit of the three Cardinal Virtues, left unfinished at his death.

In preparing his design, it is likely that Verrocchio depended on sculptured models in wax, wood, or clay after which he made this drawing. This is supported by the resemblance between the left-most putto atop the corbel and one second from left in a drawing of dancing putti (Musée du Louvre, Paris, RF 2, verso), though the latter is turned more to the front and more upright.[10] The similarities suggest they were made after the same (sculptured) model. Verrocchio is known to have made clay sculptures of putti, celebrated by Vasari,[11] and a note survives of a *terracruda* model of a putto that passed from a member of Verrocchio's workshop to another artist.[12] A preparatory terracotta model (Victoria and Albert Museum, London) survives for the Forteguerri cenotaph, the figures for which were carved from marble.

In its design, Verrocchio's drawing speaks to his tendency to work between media and to be inspired in one medium by his production in another. If it had been realized, the Vendramin tomb would have demonstrated the artist's skills as bronze caster, marble carver, architect, and painter. C.N.

NOTES

1 Verrocchio began his career in the shop of Florentine goldsmith Antonio Dei, who mentions him as a shop boy in his 1457 *catasto*: Archivio di Stato di Firenze (ASF), Catasto 793 (S. Spirito, Ferza 1457), 137r; see Carl 1982, p. 162, doc. XXIII. And Vasari praised Verrocchio as a goldsmith: Vasari-Milanesi 1906, vol. 3, pp. 358–59.

2 In 1471 the Medici appointed Verrocchio to make the props for the festival marking the state visit of Galeazzo Maria Sforza: "Per lo adornamento e aparato del ducha Ghaleazo," Biblioteca della Galleria degli Uffizi, Miscellanee Manoscritte, I, c. 3, no. 8; see von Fabriczy 1895, p. 176. On the Baldini prints and festivals, see Dempsey 2012, pp. 144ff.

3 Möller 1935, p. 194.

4 Vasari-Milanesi 1906, vol. 3, p. 364.

5 Möller 1935, p. 194, translated by Stedman Sheard 1978, p. 143.

6 The tombs of doges tended to operate like this. As Doge Francesco Dandolo expressed it in 1339, his tomb was erected *pro honore Ducatus* ("for the honor of Venice"): "Testamento del Doge Francesco Dandolo," October 26, 1339; see Bernardi 1888, p. 10. On this as a feature of late medieval doges' tombs, see Pincus 2000.

7 The materials from which Verrocchio's Medici tomb was constructed would have been understood as expressing virtues. Porphyry, for instance, was said by Francesco Colonna (author of the late fifteenth-century *Hypnerotomachia Poliphili*) to embody the virtue of Patience: Colonna 1980, vol. 1, p. 125, and vol. 2, p. 126.

8 Passavant 1969, p. 61.

9 On the polychromy of Desiderio's tomb, see Weeks 1999 and, most recently, Danti 2012. Verrocchio's design also resembles the cardinal of Portugal's tomb (1460s, San Miniato al Monte, Florence), especially the coffered ceiling, the drawn-back curtains, and the mixed-media ensemble.

10 This was noted by Möller 1935, pp. 193–95.

11 Vasari-Milanesi 1906, vol. 3, p. 375.

12 Pisani 2006, p. 271.

6

ANTONIO DEL POLLAIUOLO

Florence, c. 1432 – Rome, 1498

Design for an equestrian monument, c. 1483–84

Pen and light-brown ink and wash, with darker retouching of the ground; the outlines of the rider, horse, and some of the harness are pricked, 281 × 254 mm (11 1/16 × 10 in.)
Inscribed *GATAMEL* (probably added in the sixteenth century and referring to Donatello's equestrian monument to "Gattamelata" in Padua)
The Metropolitan Museum of Art, New York, Robert Lehman Collection 1975.1.410

EQUESTRIAN STATUES IN BRONZE were the jewels in the crown of a Renaissance sculptor's career and there is no doubt that Antonio del Pollaiuolo wanted such a rare commission very badly. The specificity of the features of the horseman in this drawing and the elaboration of the support suggest this was a design for a monumental work, as opposed to one of the new type of smaller, collectible bronzes. When Pollaiuolo drew this presentation sheet—the more developed of two surviving equestrian drawings in his hand and, to judge by partial pricking apparently from another sheet (fig. 60), one of several trials—he was intent on impressing a potential patron.[1] The honorific profile format, the panache of the pose, the power of the horse are all registered unambiguously through the springy contours of a continuous, well-practiced pen line. Giorgio Vasari, who owned two equestrian drawings by Pollaiuolo in 1568, claimed that both showed the duke of Milan, Francesco Sforza, and that the reclining figure on the second was "Verona."[2] Sforza's features and his diamond ring device on the harness appear in the Munich equestrian design, but the rings are absent here and the domed head and distinctive hooked nose appear to be those of Federigo da Montefeltro, the duke of Urbino, as Caroline Elam first noticed.[3] Pollaiuolo had made a trophy helmet for Federigo after his crushing of Volterra, and it was perhaps to Montefeltro's young son and heir Guidobaldo that the drawing was addressed in the earlier 1480s. The duke had died in 1482, and by 1484 Pollaiuolo would be fully engaged elsewhere on a ten-year bronze project for a papal tomb. A decade later and nearing the end of his life, Pollaiuolo was once again angling for a work to emulate the ancients, and, in a letter to Gentile Virginio Orsini, he tried to extend a commission for a portrait bust to a full-scale horseback monument, which, Pollaiuolo asserted, would make the mercenary captain "eternal."[4] This speaks to the same vaulting ambition and persuasive flair that we find in the present sheet. The drawing anticipates a posthumous glory for its subject, the patron, and the sculptor himself.

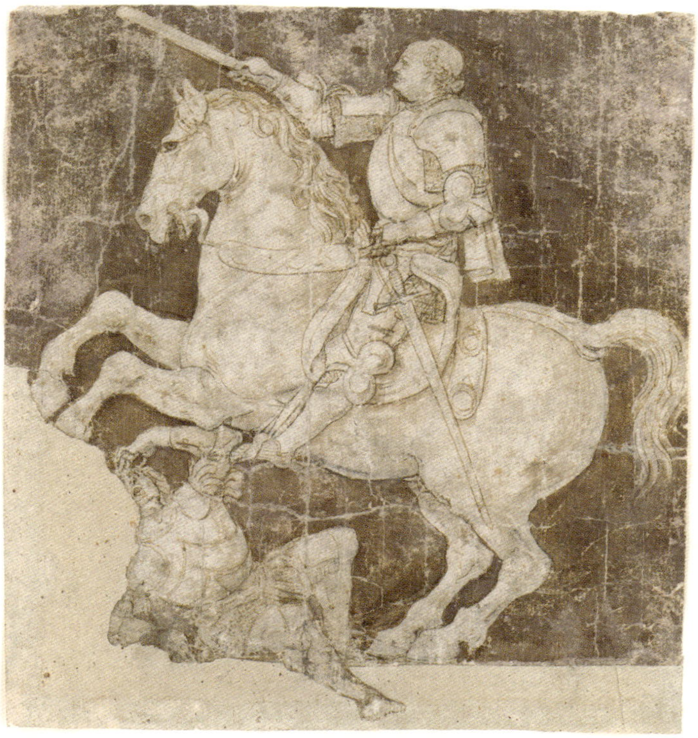

FIG. 60
Antonio del Pollaiuolo
Design for an equestrian monument, 1480–85
Pen and brown ink with brown wash, on paper, 208 × 220 mm
Staatliche Graphische Sammlung, Munich

PROVENANCE

Giorgio Vasari (?); perhaps Simon Meller; Philip Hofer, Cambridge, Massachusetts

LITERATURE

Vasari-Milanesi 1878–85, vol. 3, p. 297; Meller 1934, pp. 76–79, 204–5; Barfucci 1945, p. 170; Degenhart and Schmitt 1964, p. 58; Spencer 1973, pp. 23–35; Ragghianti Collobi 1974, vol. 1, p. 78; Vertova 1976–81, no. 7b; Szabó 1983, no. 12; Wohl 1986, p. 553, note 42; Forlani Tempesti 1991, pp. 197–202; Covi 1995, esp. p. 49; Bambach 1999, pp. 57–58, 328–29; Bambach 2003, pp. 274–77; Wright 2005, pp. 137–43, 510–11

In contrast to earlier monuments that show the horse pacing, Pollaiuolo proposes a rearing animal, which would have presented immense technical difficulties. To support the weight of horse and rider and balance the composition, a larger-than-life naked figure is shown prone the full length of the plinth, her defensive arm and her body wound feebly with some structurally required drapery. The conceit of the screaming woman, the allegory of a vanquished city, is a brutal one that recalls contemporary political poetry; Pollaiuolo's treatment of it is at once awkward and elegant.[5] The awkwardness emerges when one tries to imagine the woman viewed from the other side or from below. The elegance lies in the way, characteristic for Pollaiuolo, that the straining limbs activate the space and are aligned into diagonal rhythms—the horse's body with the nude's extended leg, her arm with the legs of both horse and rider. Her almost balletic pose is strongly reminiscent of Pollaiuolo's work as a painter and especially his dancing nudes in the Lanfredini villa near Florence. Though the sensibility of the sculptor is most obvious in the musculature and relief effects, washed in with dilute ink, or the straining *all'antica* head of the horse, the closest models for Pollaiuolo's design remain Florentine painted monuments. The proportional refinement and formal play of the equestrian frescoes in the cathedral by Uccello and Castagno are here rethought in a heroic mode, both modern and antique, that approaches the dynamism of Leonardo da Vinci's working sketches for the monument to Francesco Sforza. The older artist certainly competed for this commission, and the two Florentines may well have been aware of each other's ambitious ideas. Pollaiuolo's drawing mode in this prospective design is nevertheless more explanatory than exploratory, and the orientation of the figures seems better suited to a wall monument than one freestanding in a piazza. As for Leonardo, though, it was the equestrian drawing itself that secured the posthumous reputation of the designer and not a monumental sculpture, which remained an unfulfilled dream. A.W.

NOTES

1 The other drawing, using the same format, is Staatliche Graphische Sammlung, Munich, 1908.168.
2 Vasari-Milanesi 1878–85, vol. 3, p. 297.
3 See Wright 2005, p. 140.
5 Cruttwell 1907, pp. 256–57; Wright 2005, pp. 3–4 and note 7.
6 Martines 2001, pp. 156–57, 239 and esp. 242, for the sexualized allegory of the city as a woman. The allegory looks generic but might have been intended as Volterra.

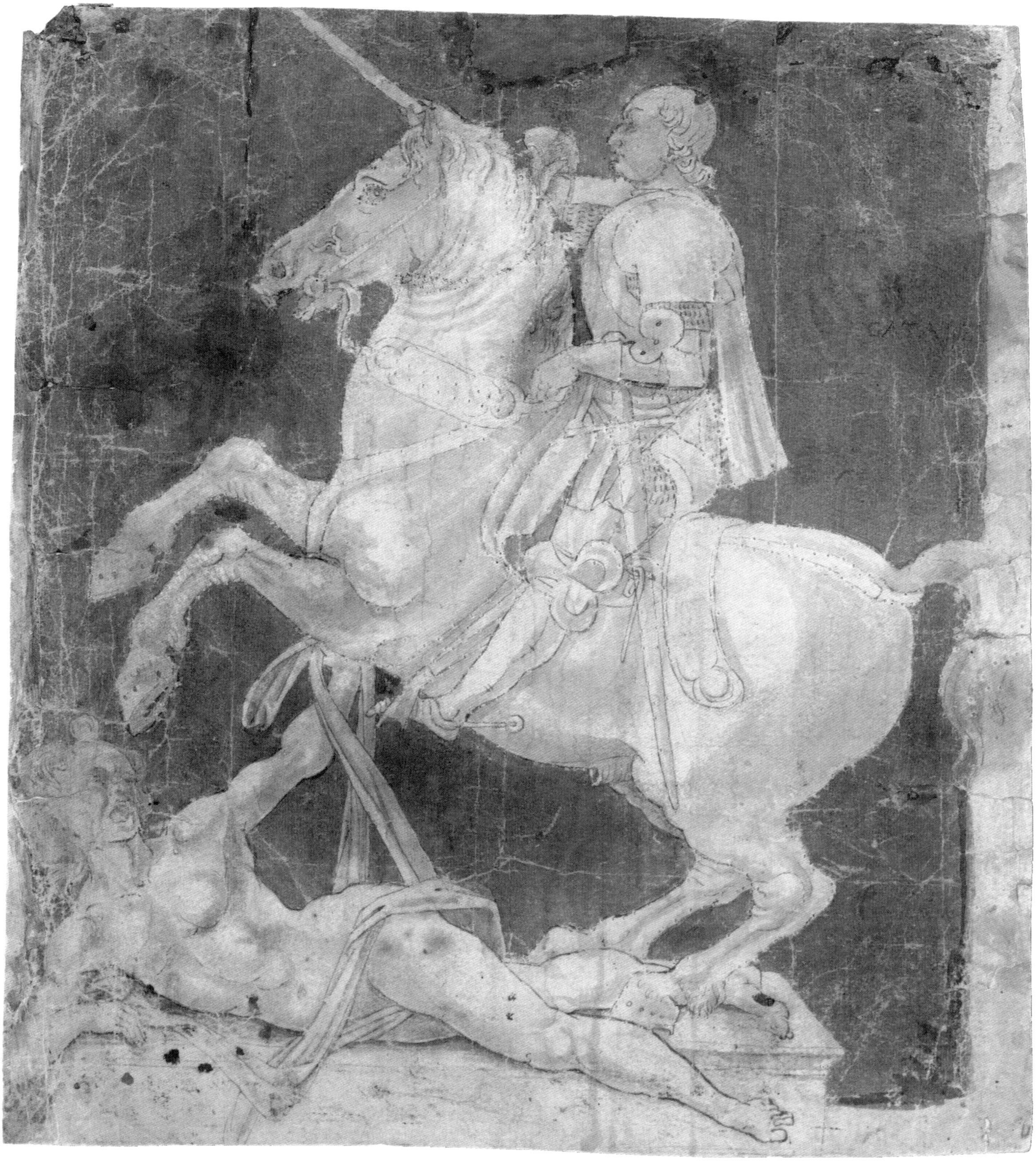

7

ANDREA DEL VERROCCHIO

Florence, 1435 – Venice, 1488

Measured drawing of a horse facing left, 1481–88

Pen and dark brown ink, over traces of black chalk, 249 × 297 mm (9 13/16 × 11 11/16 in.)
Inscribed, from ear to chest ("T" = Testa): *u[na] T 5/16½ | dal osso del orechio insino al petto una testa e cinque sedecimi e mezzo*; from ear to withers: *u[na] T 3 1/6 1/2 | dal orechio al guidalescho un testa e tre sedecimi ½*; from chest to withers: *una T e ½ sedecimo | dal petto al guidalescho una testa e mezo sedecimo*; from chest to front side of upper leg: *sei 1/6 1/2 | dal petto alacchomincio dela ghanba se sedecimi*; from chest to back side of upper leg: *10 sedecimi e nezo* [sic: *mezzo*]*/ dal petto al chomincio de la ghanba dieci sedecimi*; from beginning of front leg to withers: *una T e dua 1 /6 | dal chomincio dela chanba insino al guidalescho una testa e dua sedecimi*; at front left hoof: *tre sedecimi 1/2 3 1/6 1/2*; from front fetlock to knee: *nove sedecimi | da questo nodello al ginochio 9 16*; from front left knee to belly: *undici 16 1/2 | dal ginochio al chomincamento | undici parti e mezzo*; from withers to top of the rump: *una T e 11 1/6 | dal gudalesch a p[r]incipia dela groppa una testa e undici sede-cimi*; from chest to rump: *dua T e 10 1/6 | dal petto alla groppa dua teste e dieci sedecimi*; from top of front leg bone to top of back leg bone: *una T e 4 1/6 | dal ginocho al chomincio dela choscia una testa e quaettro 1 6*; across front thickness of belly: *una T 5 1/6 1/2 | grosso una testa* [cancelled: *e mez*] *e cinque 1/6*; from top of back leg to the rump: *undici 1/6 | da qu al osso dela gropa undici 1 /6*; from rump (or crupper) to tail: *nove 16 | dal gropa alla choda nove 16*; from lower rump to top of tail: *14 16 ½ | da qui alla choda di sop[r]a 14 1/6 e 1/2* ; from top of haunch bone to knee: *u[na] T e 10 1/6 | da questo o dela groppa insino al gnochio una testa e dieci sedecimi*; from top of back leg to knee of back leg: *da questo o insino al ginochio 13 1/6 1/2*; from rear knee to lower rump: *otto sedecimi | dal ginochio a questo 8*; from rear fetlock to above the knee: *dodici 16 | da questa guntura al disop[r]a del ginochio dodici 1/6.*[1] In the lower left corner is inscribed: *And: Verrocchio* in pen and dark brown ink by another hand, presumably Giorgio Vasari.
The Metropolitan Museum of Art, New York, Frederick C. Hewitt Fund, 1917 19.76.5

THIS DRAWING of a horse in profile, executed in pen and dark brown ink over traces of black chalk, and with measurements inscribed along the body, was first attributed to Verrocchio by Strong in 1900.[2] This attribution is supported by the inscription's cursive script, which is identical to Verrocchio's in his 1481 tax declaration.[3] The drawing was probably for a preparatory *modello* for Verrocchio's celebrated Colleoni monument (completed 1494/95, Campo Santi Giovanni e Paolo, Venice). Although the drawing does not appear to replicate the Colleoni horse, it does when the bronze is viewed from the left side, with the difference that the horse faces the other way. The drawing may, therefore, have served as one of several graphic studies from which a sculptured model could be made, not the one from which the bronze was to have been cast, but a model with which Verrocchio could experiment with the pose.

A note by Giorgio Vasari in the *Vite* presents some idea of how the drawing may have functioned: "in our book [Vasari's "Libro de' disegni"] . . . are two horses [by Verrocchio], with the due measures and protractors for reproducing them on a larger scale from a smaller, so that there may not be any errors in their proportions."[4] Here Vasari may have been describing how to make a three-dimensional model from a measured drawing.[5] Leonardo mentions a small wax model of a horse in preparation for casting his Sforza monument.[6] And we know that Verrocchio employed both drawn and sculptured models in preparation for many works, including some intended as visual guides.[7] Verrocchio constructed a life-size model of the Colleoni horse in 1483, possibly in wax, and later made clay models of horse and rider, though he died before the monument was cast.[8] All the finalists for the Colleoni monument made three-dimensional models of the horse: a 1481 letter to Duke Ercole d'Este from his ambassador mentions a life-size competition model made from rags by an unnamed sculptor, and Felix Fabri, a Dominican friar, refers to models by three unnamed sculptors in a 1483 diary entry, one made of wood covered with

PROVENANCE

Giorgio Vasari (1511–1574); Jonathan Richardson Sr. (?) (1667–1745); Earls of Pembroke, Wilton House, near Salisbury, Wiltshire; Sotheby's, London, 5–6, 9–10 July 1917, no. 358

LITERATURE

Strong 1900, pt. 6, no. 58; Berenson 1903, vol. 2, p. 136, no. 1951A (School of Antonio Pollaiuolo); Burroughs 1919, p. 137 (Antonio del Pollaiuolo); Sirén 1928, vol. 2, pl. 81B (Leonardo da Vinci); Suida 1929, pp. 64–65; Valentiner 1933, p. 232; Kurz 1937–38, p. 14; Berenson 1938, vol. 2, p. 271, no. 1947B (School of Antonio Pollaiuolo); Degenhart 1939, pp. 140–41, fig. 57 (Antonio Federighi); Mehring 1942–44, vol. 1, no. 4; *Connoisseur* 1943, p. 151; Berenson 1961, vol. 2, p. 453, no. 1947B (School of Antonio Pollaiuolo); Ragghianti Collobi 1974, vol. 1, p. 82; Beltrame Quattrocchi 1979, pp. 25–26, under no. 7; *Horses of San Marco* 1980, no. 82 (follower of Verrocchio); *I cavalli di San Marco* 1981, no. 47 (follower of Verrocchio); Bean 1982, pp. 264–66 (Verrocchio?); Scaglia 1982, pp. 32–44; Cadogan 1983, pp. 388–89, no. 55; Covi 1983, p. 262, no. 69; Pedretti and Roberts 1984–86, pp. 38–39; Pedretti 1987, p. 44, fig. 31; Kemp and Roberts 1989, pp. 168–69, under no. 92; Kirwin 1995, no. 53, pp. 97–109; Martin Kemp in Ahl 1995, pp. 65–66; Butterfield 1997, pp. 185–191; Clayton 2002, p. 34, under no. 6; Carmen C. Bambach in Bambach 2003, pp. 267–70, no. 9; Covi 2005, pp. 234–37; Galluzzi 2006, pp. 216–17, no. IV, 5B; Carmen C. Bambach in Marani and Fiorio 2007, pp. 59–61, no. 2; Marani 2007, pp. 25–27, no. 2

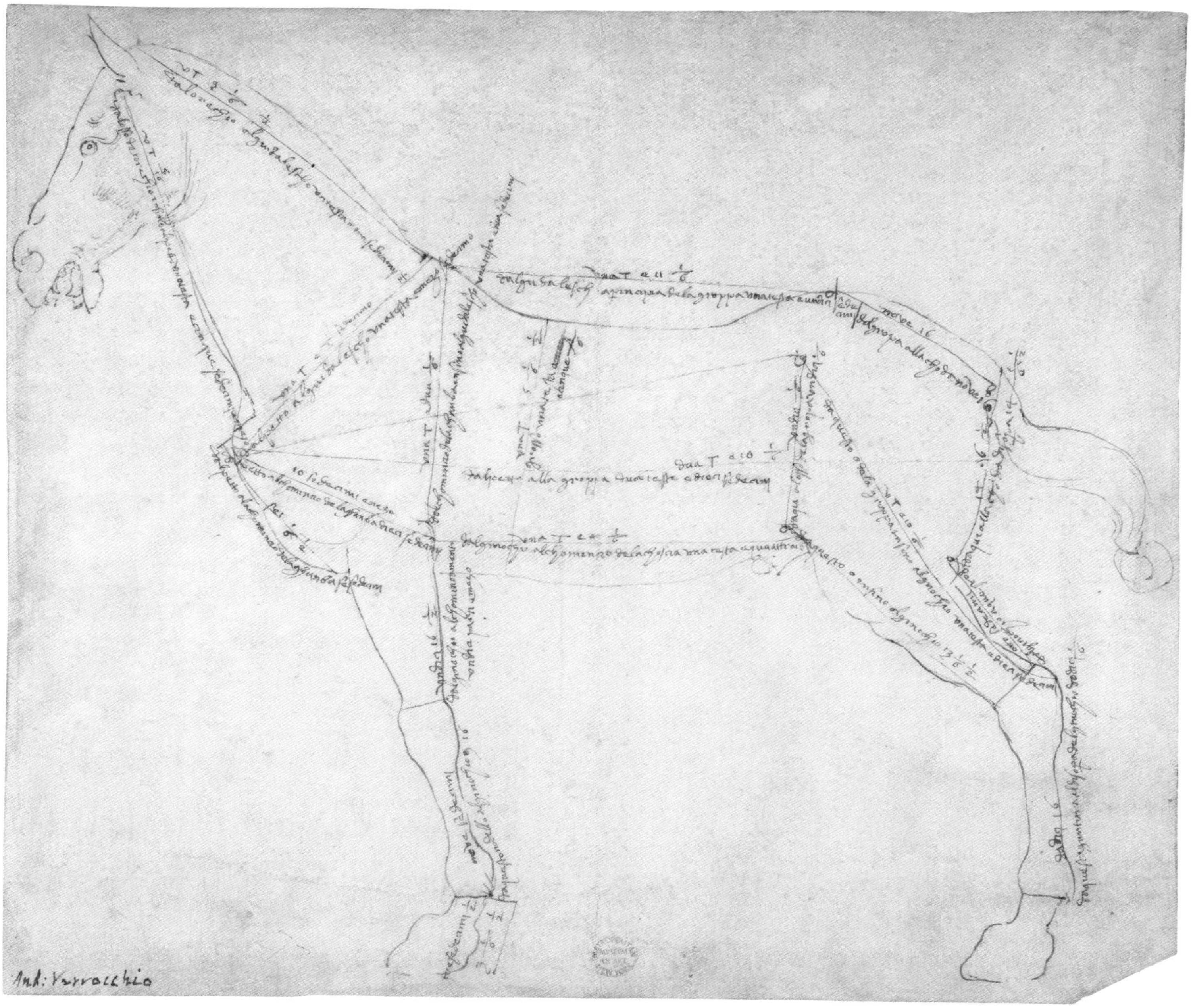
And: Verrocchio

leather, another of terracotta, and one of wax. As the last was the winning entry, it has been presumed that this was Verrocchio's.[9]

Details on the drawing itself suggest several possibilities for its original function. The measurements along the horse's body are not precise (some are longer than the inscriptions would suggest)[10] and they conform to Vitruvius's system of proportions, where the head forms the basic unit (the sixteen sections in Verrocchio's drawing may derive from Vitruvius's model of eight heads to the human body).[11] The divisions may represent an initial plan for the piece molds from which the bronze was to have been constructed.[12] The drawing also includes marks for joints for movement, indicated by lines or circles.[13] These suggest that Verrocchio may have intended to make a jointed wooden model, capable of movement, from which to decide the horse's ideal pose. Antonio Filarete mentioned small mannequins like these in his treatise of 1460–64, though for paintings and not of horses.[14]

Most likely, the drawing was preparatory for a model that Verrocchio used to plan the complex multiple viewpoints present in the final sculpture. A related drawing by Verrocchio (Istituto Nazionale per la Grafica, Rome, F.C. 127615) shows a foreshortened horse from the front and rear that may have served this purpose too.[15] Although other equestrian monuments had several viewpoints, Verrocchio's surpasses them in this regard. From every angle the Colleoni monument satisfies the viewer because the sculptor composed his statue to be seen from every vantage point.[16] This would have required careful planning. The Colleoni monument's success can be judged by the fact that Venetian artists used it around the time the bronze was unveiled as the proof for sculpture's superiority over painting, because it demonstrated several views simultaneously.[17] C.N.

NOTES

1 Bambach 2003, p. 267, no. 9. The transcription and the identification of Verrocchio's and Vasari's hands follows the entry by Carmen Bambach in Marani and Fiorio 2007, pp. 59–61.
2 Strong 1900, pt. 6, no. 58.
3 Scaglia 1982, p. 35.
4 Vasari-Milanesi 1906, vol. 3, p. 364, trans. Vasari-de Vere 1912–15, vol. 3, p. 270. Valentiner connected the drawing with those mentioned by Vasari: Valentiner 1933, p. 232; repr. 1950, pp. 100–101.
5 Scaglia (1982) proposed reading Vasari in this way, though she could not reconcile the discrepancies between the pose of the horse in the drawing and the final bronze.
6 *Per maneggiare la forma grande fane modello della picholla forma* (Royal Collection, Windsor, RN 12350). The existence of Leonardo's model is confirmed by Vasari: Vasari-Milanesi 1906, vol. 4, p. 34; see Kemp 2007, p. 66, no. 7.
7 See, for instance, Neilson 2012.
8 *[E]quo et figura del terra*: ASF, Notarile ante-cosimiano, 20614 (Se Antonio Ubaldini da Firenze, 1486–1493), fols. 33r–v, transcribed in Covi 2005, p. 283, doc. V. 23. The document is a contract by Lorenzo di Credi, drawn up after Verrocchio's death in 1488, to complete the Colleoni monument.
9 The relevant sources are transcribed in Covi 2005, pp. 346–49, doc. 48a–i.
10 Scaglia 1982, pp. 40–41.
11 Bambach 2003, p. 269.
12 In the end, the bronze was cast by Alessandro Leopardi, who sewed separately cast pieces (eight for the horse; eight for Colleoni) with metal threads; several of these pieces appear to have been based on piece molds made by Verrocchio. See Morigi and Morigi 2008, pp. 459–79.
13 Bambach 2003, p. 267.
14 *[U]na figuretta di legname*: Filarete 1972, p. 676, libro xxiv, fol. 184r. A 1450 court proceeding mentions *un modello ligneo coperto di cera* that Donatello had made for Florentines residing in Padua: Archivio di Stato, Sigillo, Padova, B. 348, not. Cristoforo di S. Croce, 9 febbraio 1450; see Herzner 1979, p. 210, no. 323. Wooden models were also preparatory for marble reliefs (see, for instance, that mentioned in relation to Luca della Robbia's altars for the Florentine Duomo: Archivio di Opera del Duomo, Florence, Allog., c. 5 t; see Poggi 1988, vol. 1, pp. 216–17, no. 1080).
15 Carmen C. Bambach in Marani and Fiorio 2007, pp. 59–61, no. 2, pl. 2; Bambach 2003, p. 271, no. 10.
16 This has been noted by Butterfield 1997, pp. 178–79.
17 See Sanudo 1879–1903, vol. 1, p. 96; and Vasari-Milanesi 1906, vol. 4, p. 98.

8

MICHELANGELO BUONARROTI

Caprese, 1475 – Rome, 1564

Project for a wall-tomb of Pope Julius II, c. 1505–6

Pen and brown ink, brush and light brown wash, over extensive underdrawing stylus ruling, incised compass work, and leadpoint, 510 × 319 mm (20 1/16 × 12 9/16 in.)
Watermark: crossed arrows (close to Briquet 6303; Zonghi 1208); Roberts 1988, type "Arrows A"[1]
The Metropolitan Museum of Art, New York, Rogers Fund, 1962 62.93.1

MICHELANGELO'S MOST CELEBRATED PATRON, Julius II della Rovere (1443–1513) was elected pope on 1 November 1503, and in the decade of his controversial pontificate, as a patron of the arts and architecture, he aspired with unprecedented ambition to embellish the city of Rome, while also not neglecting the memorializing project of his tomb.[2] Michelangelo carved the marble funerary monument of Pope Julius II over the course of 40 years, often in conflict with his patron and later with his patron's legal executors. The tomb of Julius II was finally installed in 1545 at the church of San Pietro in Vincoli, the Della Rovere family church in Rome. Much about Michelangelo's design of the tomb of Julius II has been debated by art historians—often unreasonably—including the reconstruction of the various phases in relationship to the extant drawings, letters, *ricordi*, and contractual documents; the iconographic program in its particulars; as well as the attribution of the individual preparatory drawings and some of the sculptures.

The drawing in the Metropolitan Museum of Art entered the Michelangelo literature in 1976. It is dated here to about 1505–6 (rather than 1513 or so, as is more frequent) and is accepted as autograph without question.[3] The variety of changes of the design in the underdrawings of stylus-incised ruling, compass work, and leadpoint (best evident under the microscope and in raking light) with respect to the final pen-and-ink outlines leaves no doubt as to the creative, exploratory nature of the Metropolitan Museum sheet and Michelangelo's authorship. It is the freshest and best preserved of the artist's three large, comprehensive drawings for the tomb of Julius II, but since it is the earliest of his extant ideas for the project, it is also the least adventurous in scale and design. Discovered in 1990, two sketchily drawn fragments showing variations of design closely related to the motifs in the Metropolitan Museum sheet also form part of this earliest phase of planning of the pope's tomb (Musée du Louvre, Paris, 722 verso and 8026 verso).[4] Of these two Louvre sheets, one has a recto with a pen-and-ink study of a nude male figure seen from behind, which was among Michelangelo's first preparatory ideas for *The Battle of Cascina* cartoon, begun in the autumn of 1504. The early date of the Metropolitan Museum tomb design is further affirmed by the style and shorthand notation of the figures, similar to those in the small pen-and-ink jottings on another sheet connected with *The Battle of Cascina* (Uffizi, Florence, 233F).[5] The abbreviation of the faces of the Madonna, Christ Child, and angels with empty eye sockets and triangular noses is also almost exactly that of the figural sketches in the sheet (British Museum, London, 1859,0625.564) associated with the early designs of *The Battle of Cascina* and the Bruges *Madonna*.[6]

Although this is usually overlooked, moreover, the pope's effigy in the present drawing is beardless (see detail p. 149), and, while Julius II is better known bearded from Raphael's much later paintings, in 1505–6 the belligerent Julius was beardless, as depicted in the medal dated 1506 by Cristoforo Caradosso Foppa to celebrate the foundation of the new basilica of St. Peter's (*Templi petri instauracio*), according to Bramante's design. Michelangelo's early work on the tomb of Julius II was repeatedly interrupted by other commissions, and chiefly the frescoes of the Sistine Ceiling, from 1508 to 1512: hence, certain pen-and-ink drawings for the Sistine and the Julius tomb share considerable similarities of style. Following the pope's death on 21 February 1513, his legal executors, Cardinals Lorenzo Pucci and Leonardo Grossi della Rovere, signed a new contract with

PROVENANCE

Hans M. Calmann (1899–1982); acquired by the Museum in 1962

LITERATURE

Hirst 1976; De Tolnay 1975–80, vol. 1, p. 63, under no. 55, vol. 4, p. 27, no. 489; Joannides 1981, p. 680; Bean 1982, p. 141, no. 132; Roberts 1988, pp. 17, 29; Hirst 1988a, pp. 3, 82, 92; Hirst 1988b, pp. 26–28, no. 9; Echinger-Maurach 1991, vol. 1, pp. 225, 290–93; Joannides 1991, pp. 33–42, esp., pp. 36–38; Cordellier 1991, pp. 43–55; Poeschke 1992, p. 20; Bissel 1993, pp. 143–56; William M. Griswold in Griswold and Wolk-Simon 1994, pp. 21–24, 158–59, no. 18; Christoph Luitpold Frommel in Milton and Magnago Lampugnani 1994, pp. 598–99, no. 279; Echinger-Maurach 1998, pp. 294–96, fig. 19; Claudia Echinger-Maurach in Weil-Garris Brandt 1999, pp. 216–17, no. 11; Echinger-Maurach 2002, pp. 257–77; Bredekamp 2004, pp. 61–83; Joannides 2003, pp. 75, 97, 102–7, 128, 137–38, 164, 226, 375, esp. under nos. 14, 15; Kempers 2004, pp. 43–59; Acidini Luchinat 2005, pp. 108, 146; Bambach 2007b, pp. 82, 91–92 and note 40; Zöllner, Thönes, and Pöpper 2007, pp. 61–62, 418, 516; Echinger-Maurach 2009a, p. 103; Echinger-Maurach 2009b, pp. 13–18; Carmen C. Bambach in Franklin 2009, pp. 66–69, no. 1; Bambach 2010, p. 105 and note 38; Gnann 2010, pp. 163–67, no. 45; Frommel 2010, pp. 89–90, 93; Maurer 2012, pp. 33–36; Elam 2012, p. 86; Zanchettin 2012, pp. 102–3; Frommel 2012, pp. 121–23; Poeschke 2013, pp. 32–42; Gnann 2013, pp. 213–14

Michelangelo on 6 May of that year, obliging the artist to finish the tomb in seven years.[7] According to Michelangelo's own version of events in his much later letter of December 1523 to his friend Giovan Francesco Fattucci, he had wished "to enlarge his [the pope's] tomb, that is make a larger work than the drawing that I had made first, and a contract was made" (*volendo acresciere la sua sepultura, cioè far maggiore opera che il disegnio che io avevo facto prima, si fece uno chontracto*).[8] Michelangelo's other two major design drawings for the tomb of Julius II (Uffizi, Florence, 608E; and Kupferstichkabinett, Berlin, KdZ 15305) date from 1513–16 and roughly correspond to the time of the second and third contracts; the very ruined Berlin fragment is more intelligible from a copy by Jacomo Rocchetti in the same museum (Kupferstichkabinett KdZ 15306).[9]

The evenly descriptive, almost diagrammatic clarity of form and carefully precise construction with ruler and compass of the architectural elements in the large Metropolitan Museum sheet are part of the typology of *modelli* (demonstration drawings) produced for presentation of a design to a patron, and for the practical use in the execution of the design by the artist and his assistants. It is even possible it may have had the more formal function of a contractual drawing between patron and artist. These distinctive stylistic features of clarity and constructed precision are also true of Jacopo della Quercia's *Fonte Gaia* drawing fragments of about 1415–16 (cat. 1 and 2), which also had a legal purpose. With regard to the chronology of the design in the Metropolitan Museum drawing, Michelangelo himself first discussed the Julius tomb in a letter from Florence addressed to his friend Giuliano da Sangallo, in Rome, on 2 May 1506.[10] In his role as papal architect, Sangallo had encouraged the pontiff to choose Michelangelo as the sculptor of his tomb, amid the heated artistic jealousies of the papal court.[11] The initial agreements ("*primi pacti*," as Michelangelo called them)[12] for the first design of the tomb probably occurred in March–April 1505, soon after the artist's arrival in Rome.[13] According to Michelangelo's later recollection in 1513, a drawing had specifically provided the basis for negotiating ("*fare merchato*") the price of the monument: "during the first years of Pope Julius, I believe it was in the second year [hence, 1505] that I went to be with him; after [producing] many drawings for his tomb one pleased him, based on which [design] we made the negotiations, and settled to make it for ten thousand ducats" (*Ne' primi anni di papa Iulio, credo che fussi el sechondo anno che io andai a star secho, dopo molti disegni della sua sepultura uno gniene piaque, sopra 'l quale facemo el merchato, e ·ctolsila a fare per dieci mila duchati*).[14] The revised contractual documents of May 1513 and July 1516 between Michelangelo and the pope's executors all refer to demonstration drawings and models for work on the tomb being convened (*secondo el disegno et modello hovero figura de essa sepulture*).[15]

Michelangelo envisioned the design of about 1505–6 in the Metropolitan Museum drawing as a deeply projecting wall-tomb, three stories high, in which the general architectural framework evoked that of an ancient Roman triumphal arch. In the first story of the edifice, the male figures sketched in profile at either side provide a visual yardstick from which to extrapolate the general proportions of the tomb in plan, since the protrusion of the architectural ensemble from the wall is the same measurement as that of the end bays at left and right with the niches housing the sculptures of the Christian Virtues. In a departure from tradition, the pope's effigy is seen frontally within the tall arched niche, or *cappelletta*, as it is called in the Julius tomb documents, and angels raise his body from the antique-style sarcophagus toward the Virgin and Child: the concept of the pope's effigy in the act of being raised did not change in some of Michelangelo's later designs and is thus portrayed in an outline sketch of about 1515–17 showing a side view of the tomb (Casa Buonarroti, Florence, 43A verso).[16] The conception of the wall-tomb in the Metropolitan Museum of Art sheet differs with respect to the design drawings Uffizi 608E and Berlin KdZ 15305 most radically in the lower parts. It is missing the large podium with molding on which the entire architectural ensemble was intended to stand, because the paper is cropped at the bottom. It also omits the classicizing figures of the slaves and herm pilasters seen in the Uffizi and Berlin drawings, and the nearly square relief at center offers an inventive portrayal of the Gathering of Manna (Exodus 16:4, 16–36; Numbers 11:7–9), with acorns falling from an oak tree, in allusion to the heraldic device of the Della Rovere family (in Italian, *rovere* means oak). The Della Rovere acorns also fill a footed cup between the two reclining river gods at lower center, and they decorate the finials of the thrones of the Sibyl and Prophet on the second story of the monument. Allegorical figures of Charity and Faith stand within the niches to the left and right on the lower story.

Michelangelo's wall-tomb design in the Metropolitan Museum of Art sheet is of the type that had been traditional in Tuscany and

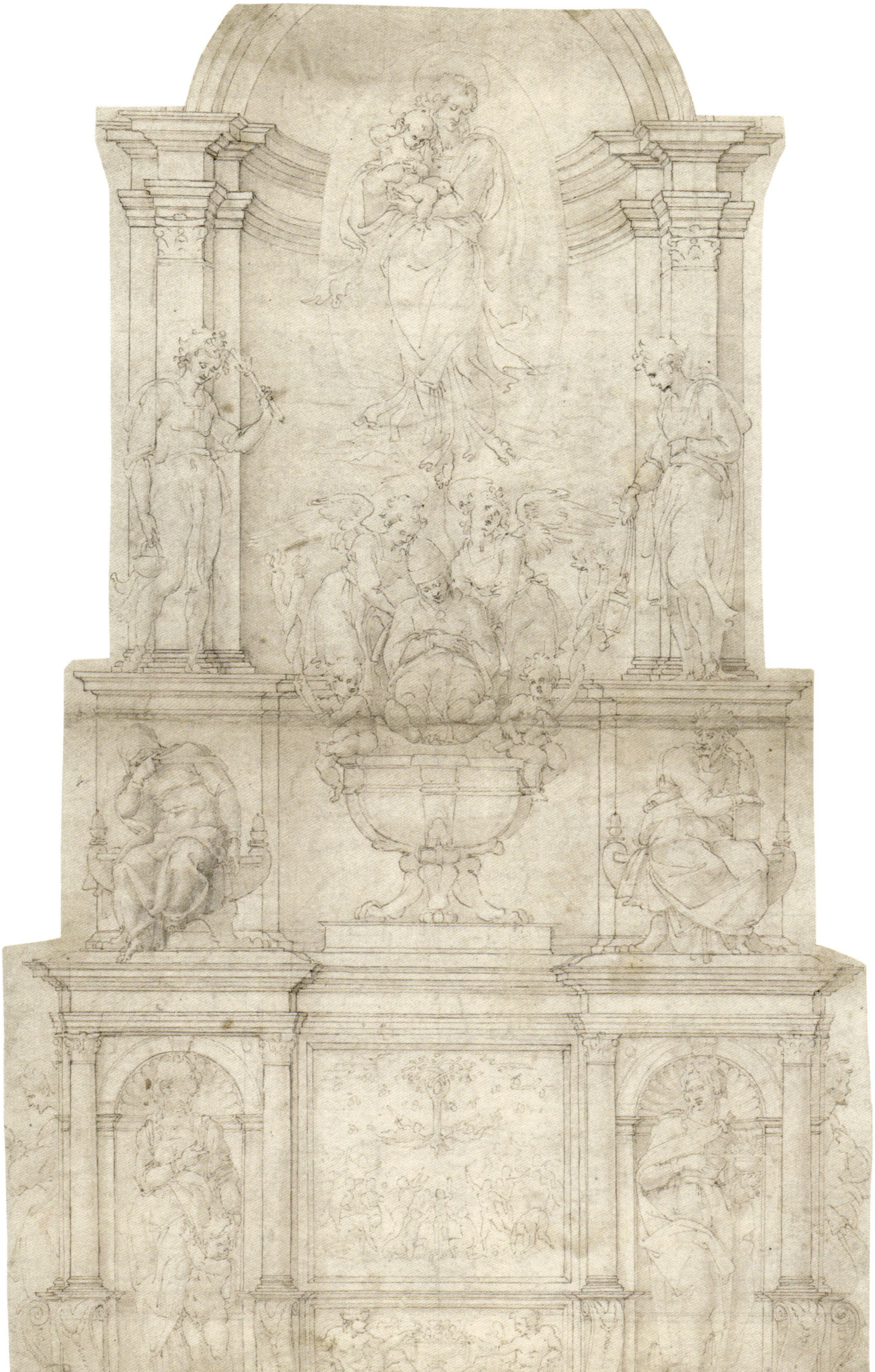

Rome since the second half of the fifteenth century.[17] A hitherto neglected passage in Condivi's biography of Michelangelo suggests that the still unfinished choir of the old basilica of St. Peter's (which had been begun before 1455 during the pontificate of Nicholas V) was the very first intended site of the Julius tomb.[18] In my opinion, this intended location could explain why the Metropolitan Museum sheet displays a tomb of relatively modest design and dimensions (compared to the drawings Uffizi 608E and Berlin KdZ 15305), in a traditional Quattrocento architectural style with a subtly pictorial illusionism, as well as the frontal pose of the pope's effigy. These elements seem adjusted for a terminal structure to be seen from a long vantage point, which the end wall of the unfinished Nicholas V choir, begun by Bernardo Rossellino, could have provided. [19] Most scholars have instead linked Michelangelo's drawing with the choir of the new St. Peter's as being designed by Bramante.[20] By 1506 or so, however, Michelangelo's ambitions—and possibly also the pope's—were for an immense freestanding mausoleum to be installed in the crossing of the new basilica of St. Peter's projected by Bramante to replace the ruinous Constantinian building. The 1568 edition of Vasari's biography of Michelangelo describes some details of the Julius monument in this later, grandiose conception, "which in its beauty and splendor, and in its great ornament and wealth of statues, surpassed all ancient and imperial tombs" (*che di bellezza e di superbia e di grande ornamento e richezza di statue passava ogni antica et imperiale sepoltura*).[21] In contrast to the wall-tomb in the Metropolitan Museum drawing, the new monument was to be a multiple-storied, freestanding architectural ensemble richly detailed with niches, antique-style terms, moldings, and cornices, and its overall shape diminished "step-like" (*in gradi*) to the top. Condivi in 1553 and Vasari in 1568 note that this grand monument was to include 40 marble sculptures. Elaborating on Condivi, Vasari alluded to the allegorical figures of captives (*prigioni*), Virtues, the Liberal Arts, four larger figures (the Active and Contemplative Lives, St. Paul, and Moses), as well as to an upper frieze with narrative scenes in bronze, while mentioning that the top of the ensemble culminated with the personifications of heaven (*cielo*) and Cybele (goddess of the earth). An oval chamber within the edifice (accessed from the sides of the first story) contained the casket with the pope's body. The projects described in the contracts after Pope Julius's death, however, represent a gradual scaling down of ideas from the gargantuan conception, and a return to the design of a wall-tomb, as seen in the design drawings Uffizi 608E and Berlin KdZ 15305.
C.C.B.

NOTES

1 Roberts 1988, p. 17.
2 For a biography and the quotation by a contemporary, see Pastore 2001.
3 In agreement with Hirst 1988b, pp. 26–28, no. 9.
4 Illustrated and discussed in Cordellier 1991, pp. 43–55; Joannides 2003, pp. 102–7, nos. 14, 15.
5 Illustrated and discussed in Hirst 1988b, p. 18, no. 6.
6 Illustrated and discussed in Wilde 1953, pp. 10–14, no. 5; Chapman 2005, pp. 76, 91, 285, no. 14.
7 See Bardeschi Ciulich 2005, pp. XXI–XXIX, XL–LII, for a summary of the contractual documents for the tomb of Julius II.
8 Quoted from Barocchi and Ristori 1965–83, vol. 3, p. 9.
9 On these drawings, compare De Tolnay 1975–80, vol. 1, pp. 63–65, nos. 55, 56; Gnann 2010, pp. 168–70, no. 46; and Carmen C. Bambach in Franklin 2009, pp. 66–69, under no. 1, with new archaeological evidence.
10 See Barocchi and Ristori 1965–83, vol. 1, pp. 13–14, no. VIII (for transcription), and *Appendice*, pp. 360–62, no. VII (for additional discussion).
11 Compare Vasari-Bettarini 1966, vol. 4, pp. 144–45.
12 Quoted from Michelangelo's *ricordo* of April 1508 in Bardeschi Ciulich and Barocchi 1970, p. 1, doc. 1.
13 See Barocchi and Ristori 1965–83, vol. 1, p. 360.
14 Quoted from the document of before 6 May 1513, Bardeschi Ciulich 2005, p. 41, no. XVIII.
15 Transcribed in Bardeschi Ciulich 2005, pp. 45–80 (quotation on p. 49), 56–80, nos. XX–XXIX.
16 De Tolnay 1975–80, vol. 4, p. 38, no. 501 verso.
17 Esp. Frommel 2010.
18 Condivi 1998, p. 25: *Visto questo disegno, il papa mandò Michelagnolo in San Pietro a veder dove comodamente si potesse collocare. Era la forma della chiesa allora a modo d'una croce, in capo della quale papa Nicola Quinto aveva cominciato a tirar sù la tribuna di nuovo, e già era venuta sopra terra, quando morì, all'altezza di tre braccia. Parve a Michelagnolo che tal luogo fusse molto a proposito, e tornato al papa, gli spose il suo parere, aggiungendo che, se così paresse a Sua Santita, era necessario tirar sù la fabrica e coprirla.*
19 For a documented article on Rossellino's career in Rome, see esp. Caglioti 1992.
20 Frommel in Milton and Magnago Lampugnani 1994; Joannides 2003, p. 105; Frommel 2010, p. 89; Frommel 2012, pp. 125–29.
21 Vasari-Bettarini 1966, vol. 6 (text 1568 edn), p. 26.

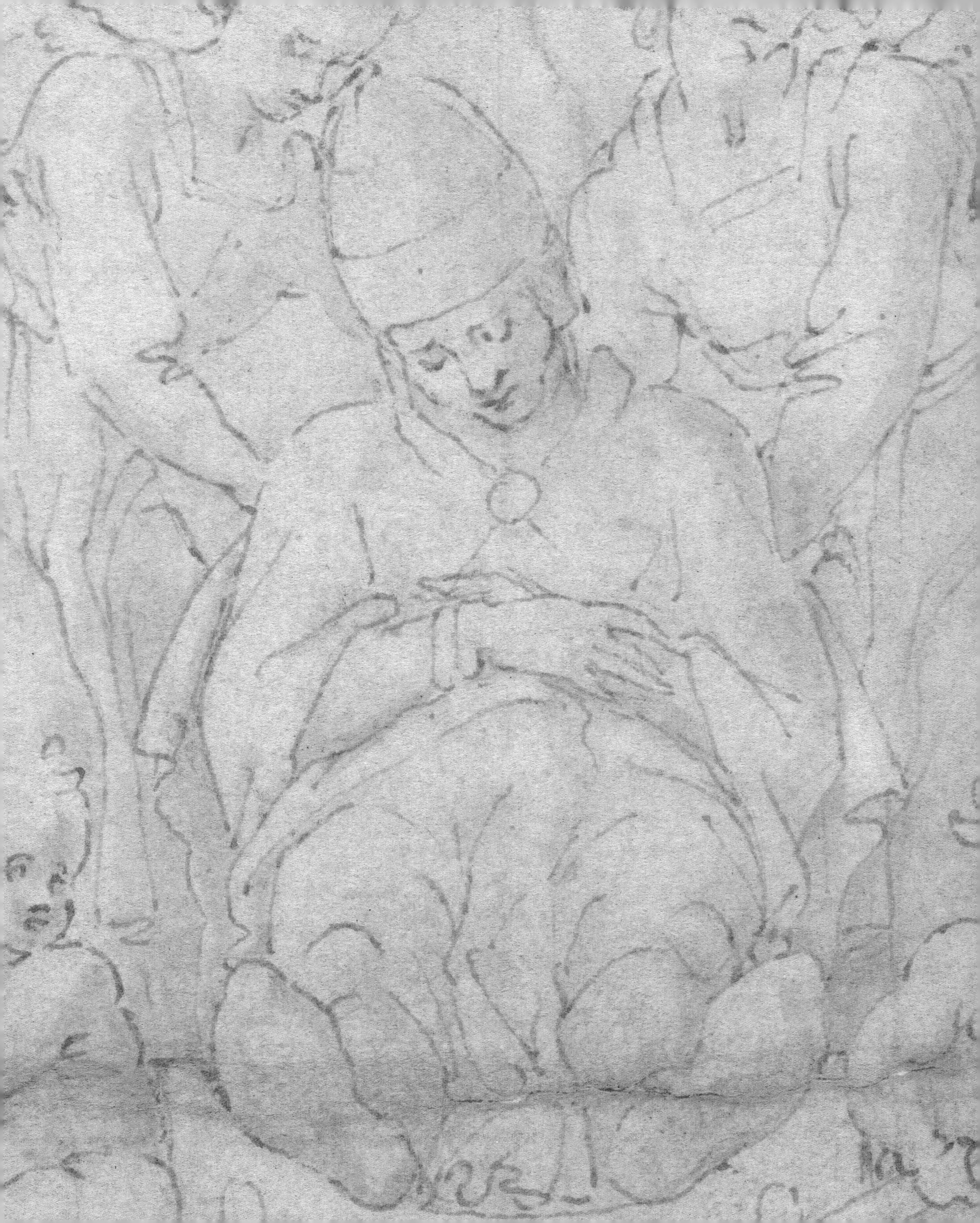

9

BACCIO BANDINELLI

Florence, 1493 – Florence, 1560

Head study, 1510–20

Red chalk, 307 × 219 mm (12$\frac{1}{16}$ × 8$\frac{5}{8}$ in.)
Inscribed in pen and ink in lower right corner by later hand: *Michaele Angelo Buonaroti.*
Ashmolean Museum, Oxford, Presented by a Body of Subscribers, 1846 WA1846.19

BANDINELLI likely produced this drawing between 1510 and 1520, the period to which most of his red-chalk heads date. He derived the idea of drawing heads in chalk from Leonardo da Vinci and Andrea del Sarto, whose work he had studied as a young artist in Florence.[1] With this medium, he emphasized the fall of light and shadow in overlapping patches of controlled, tightly spaced hatching and quick but determined contours that highlight the relief quality of the figure.

More than half a century ago, Brophy suggested that the drawing may depict a man rather than a woman, as it is otherwise catalogued. Although no recent writer has picked up on the proposal, it merits serious consideration. The ambiguity in the Ashmolean drawing becomes visible when it is compared to other Bandinelli head studies. Three of them, once misidentified as portraits of his wife, Jacopa Doni, show rounder faces and curving chins with exaggerated smiles and carefully styled hair.[2] Perhaps, in making the present drawing, Bandinelli sketched a *garzone* in his workshop, then adjusted the nose, cheeks, and lips of the face to let it serve a new function. A similar process of transformation can be seen elsewhere in his work; there is a series of drawings for his 1518–19 relief of the Birth of the Virgin for the Santa Casa in Loreto, for example, in which Bandinelli worked out poses with *garzoni* in the studio and then incorporated them as women into compositional drawings.[3] This conforms with the practice of contemporaries such as Rosso Fiorentino and Michelangelo.

Ward tentatively suggested a connection to the same Santa Casa relief, for which Bandinelli also made a least one other head study; even if the present drawing does not align with any specific head in the relief as executed, the similarities in pose and modeling of the two heads strengthen the possibility of this sheet's preparatory function.[4] Earlier in the decade, in 1512, Bandinelli had also briefly worked in collaboration with Sarto on an uncompleted fresco commission for the Marriage of the Virgin in the courtyard of the Santissima Annunziata, although it was Franciabigio who carried out the painting in 1513. Bandinelli developed various compositions for which a thoughtful female head could be of use, and the sheet shows his attention to this single element. C.K.

PROVENANCE

Jeremiah Harman; Sir Thomas Lawrence; Samuel Woodburn (sold in 1843)

LITERATURE

Oxford Galleries 1846, no. 21 (as Michelangelo); Robinson 1870, p. 69, no. 56 (ascribed tentatively to Michelangelo); Berenson 1903, no. 1719; Brinckmann 1925, pp. 62, 91 (as Andrea del Sarto); Parker 1936, p. 44 (as Daniele da Volterra); Berenson 1938, p. 238, no. 1719; Parker 1956, pp. 46–47, no. 77; Brophy 1963, p. 136, pl. 16; Bacon and Viatte 1974, no. 6; Monbeig-Goguel 1979, no. 8 (ascribed tentatively to Daniele da Volterra); Berti 1980, pp. 70–71, no. 74; Ward 1982a, pp. 334–35, no. 273; Byam Shaw 1983, p. 33, no. 25; Ward 1988, pp. 42, 103, no. 19

NOTES

1 Costamagna 2005, pp. 274–91.
2 Musée du Louvre, Paris, 81 (Viatte 2011, pp. 111–14, no. 7); Frits Lugt Collection, Paris, 9316 (Byam Shaw 1983, pp. 33–34, pl. 25); Uffizi, Florence, 492F (Petrioli Tofani 1991, pp. 210–11).
3 Ward 1982a, p. 125.
4 On the relief, see Weil-Garris 1977, pp. 40–45, which does not, however, discuss the present drawing. The single known head study for the relief is in the Jean Bonna Collection (Ward 1988, pp. 40–41, no. 18).

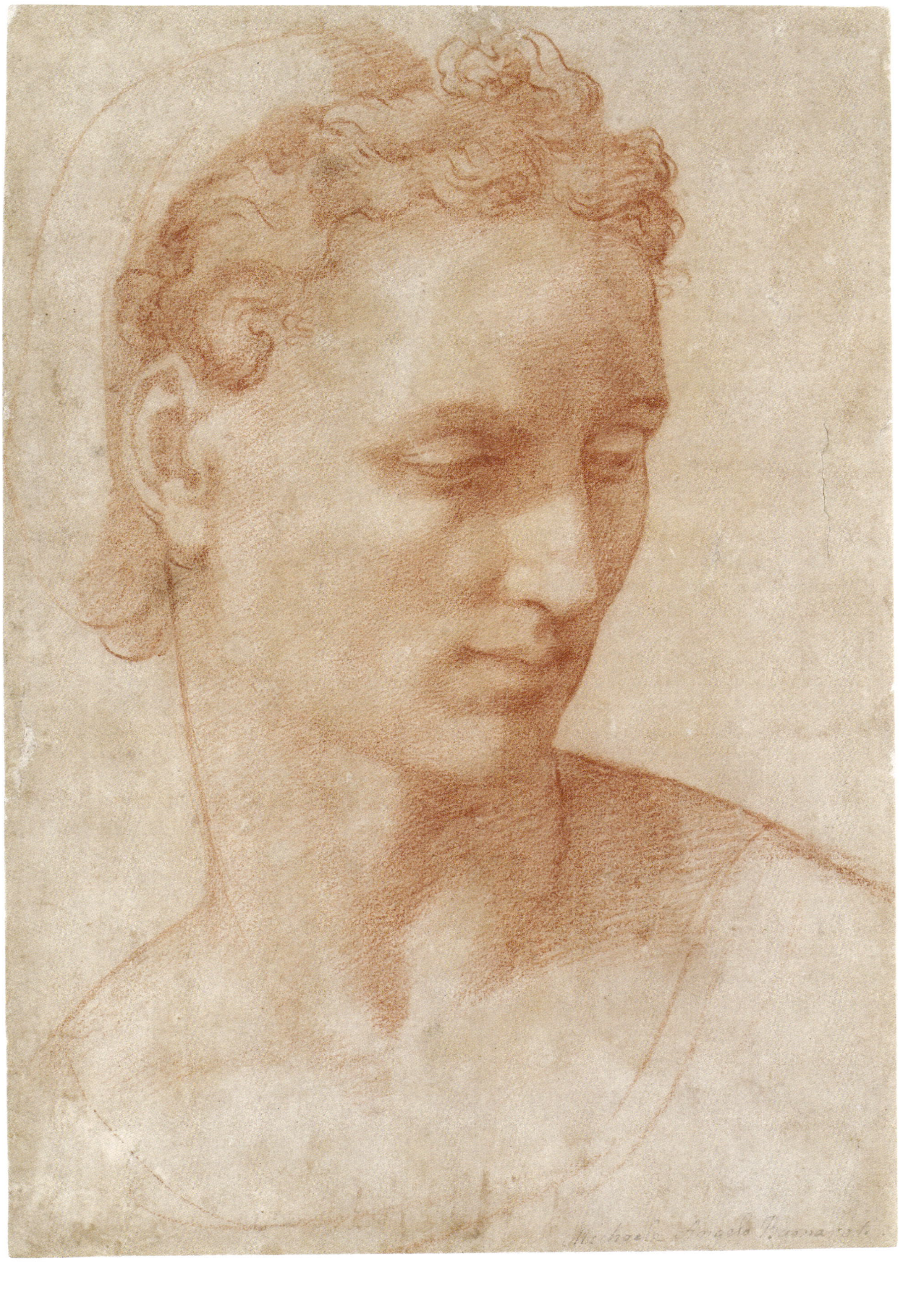

10

BACCIO BANDINELLI

Florence, 1493 – Florence, 1560

Young man raising a curtain, 1518–19

Red chalk, 329 × 197 mm (12 15/16 × 7 3/4 in.)
Inscribed in brown ink at lower right: *Empoli*
British Museum, London 1885-5-9-35

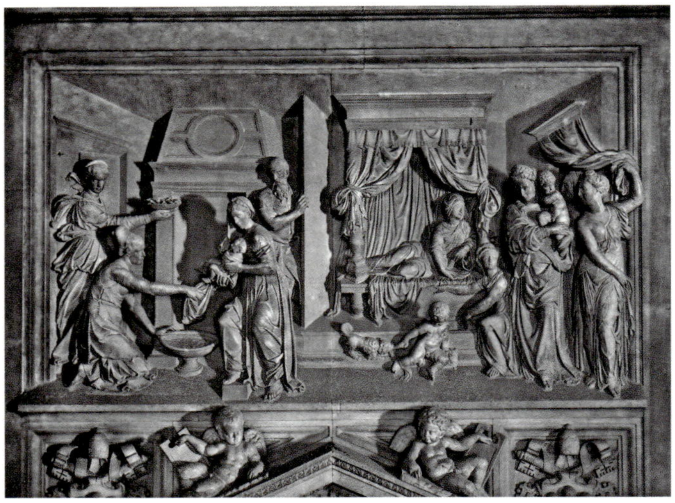

FIG. 61
Baccio Bandinelli
The Birth of the Virgin
Marble relief
Basilica della Casa Santa,
Loreto

THIS DRAWING is likely a study for the figure who appears at far right in Baccio Bandinelli's *Birth of the Virgin* relief at the Santa Casa di Loreto (fig. 61).[1] Bandinelli worked at Loreto under the supervision of Andrea Sansovino from 1518 to 1519, so the drawing may reasonably be dated to this period.[2] Only the right-hand half of the relief—St. Anne reclining in bed, accompanied by four women, two male children, and a dog—was carried out by Bandinelli himself, although he seems to have begun work on the left side as well.[3] The relief was finished by Raffaello da Montelupo more than a decade later, in 1533.[4]

Roger Ward has proposed that this beautiful red-chalk study was made at a middle stage in Bandinelli's design process. According to Ward, Bandinelli first made a group of compositional drawings that included a red-chalk sketch of the right half of the relief (Ackland Art Museum, Chapel Hill, NC, 77.55.1) and a pen-and-ink sketch of the entire composition (Uffizi 710E).[5] He then selected certain figures and groups to study in more detail: the present red-chalk drawing elaborates and fixes, through study of a live model, a pose earlier imagined in a quickly drawn pen-and-wash sketch of two women (Veste Coburg Z.2419-K91).[6] The rectangular block upon which the studio assistant rests his right foot is clearly visible, and the figure's clenched fist suggests that the model held a suspended rope in order to support his pose for the draftsman's extended examination. His left hand is unconvincingly assimilated with the only summarily defined curtain, the contours of which seem to have been drawn, perhaps from the artist's imagination, only after his careful study of the figure. As Ward has demonstrated, the pose of the figure underwent substantial revision before its inclusion in the finished relief.[7]

The outfit depicted here—tight-fitting trousers and a bodice worn atop a shirt with voluminous sleeves—is repeated in another red-chalk study of a live model (perhaps the very same *garzone*) holding a dish (Kunstmuseum der Stadt Düsseldorf, Kupferstichkabinett, FP 17). Ward understands the Düsseldorf sheet, too, to have been drawn in connection with the *Birth of the Virgin* relief and notes that it is derived from Andrea del Sarto's 1514 fresco of the same subject in the Chiostro de' Voti of the church of the Santissima Annunziata in Florence.[8] Bandinelli too had been commissioned to paint a fresco in Santissima Annuziata in 1512, but it was never finished.[9] Bandinelli's ties to Sarto's workshop in the second decade of the sixteenth century explain both his imitation of Sarto's finished compositions and his extensive use of red chalk, which the older painter favored especially for figure studies.[10] Bandinelli's drawing thus demonstrates his application to sculptural design of a preparatory process pioneered by painters. R.B.

PROVENANCE

William Russell (1800–1884; Lugt 2648); Alphonse Wyatt Thibaudeau (c. 1840–c. 1892; Lugt 2473)

LITERATURE

Popham and Wilde 1949, p. 189, under no. 85; Weil-Garris 1977, pp. 132–33; Ward 1978, pp. 18–19, no. 9; Ward 1981, pp. 10–11, pl. 13; Ward 1982a, no. 192; Ward 1982b, p. 25 and no. 16; Turner 1986, p. 123, no. 86; Ward 1988, pp. 39–40, no. 17; Koshikawa and Kurita 1996, pp. 52–53, no. 12; Strasser 2010, under no. 19

NOTES

1 Popham and Wilde 1949, p. 189. See also Ward 1988, pp. 39–40.
2 Ward 1988, p. 39; Waldman 2004, doc. 102.
3 Ward 1982a, p. 126; Ward 1988, p. 39.
4 Fattorini 2013, p. 102; Ward 1982a, p. 126; Weil-Garris 1977, p. 110.
5 Ward 1982a, p. 126; Ward 1988, p. 39.
6 Ward 1988, p. 39.
7 Ward 1988, pp. 39–40.
8 Ward 1988, p. 40.
9 See docs. 58 and 61 in Waldman 2004.
10 Middledorf 1937, p. 297; on Sarto's use of chalk, Franklin 2005, p. 26.

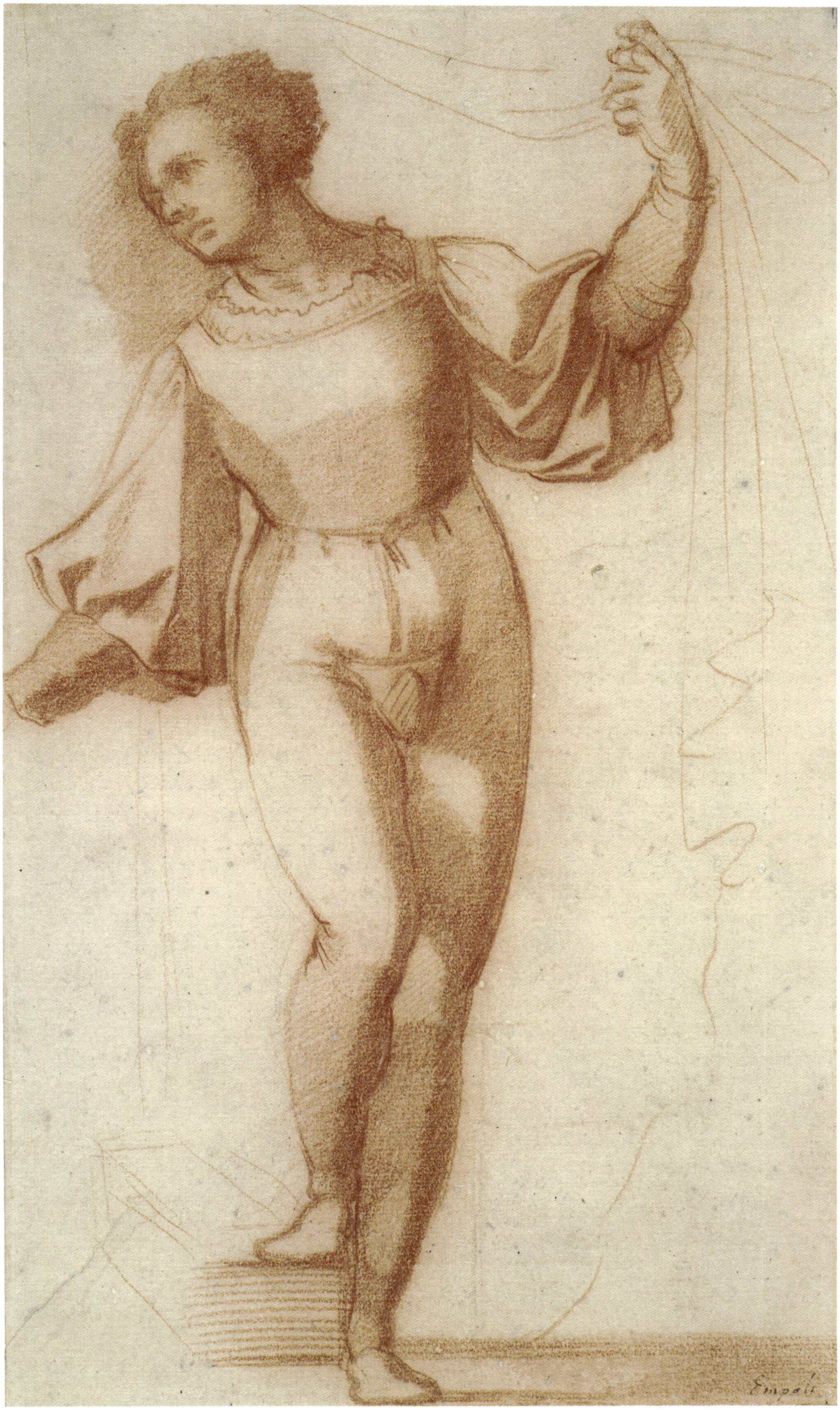
Empoli

11

BACCIO BANDINELLI

Florence, 1493 – Florence, 1560

Standing male figure, 1518–19

Red chalk, 381 × 262 mm (15 × 105⁄16 in.)
Inscribed in brown ink at lower right: *Andrea del Sarto* and *Donato Creti*; in brown ink on verso: *LN*
The Metropolitan Museum of Art, New York, Rogers Fund, 1996 1996.177

THIS DRAWING is closely related to cat. 10 in subject, medium, and perhaps function. Both sheets are beautifully drawn in red chalk and depict what appears to be the same model wearing the same costume.

If, as Roger Ward has proposed, both drawings were made by Baccio Bandinelli himself in connection with his work at Loreto, it is intriguing to consider the artist's motivation for the creation of two so similar figure studies.[1] That the positions from which the model is observed are slightly different suggests that Bandinelli wished to experiment with the angle from which to depict the figure at far right in the Loreto relief *The Birth of the Virgin*: the British Museum sheet (cat. 10) implies a viewpoint to the left of and slightly higher than that in the present Metropolitan Museum sheet.

On the whole, the Metropolitan sheet captures the model's pose with greater nuance and energy. If Bandinelli made both, it seems likely that the Metropolitan sheet was drawn first, as Bandinelli took the time to capture finer gradations in shade and additional details of the model's costume.[2] The volume of the model's upper torso and the buttons and loops of his trousers, for example, are described much more precisely here than in the British Museum sheet. The British Museum drawing, then, could be a second study made primarily in order to edit the model's pose.

An alternative scenario is that Bandinelli and another artist working with him drew from the same model at the same time, akin to the scene depicted in Agostino Veneziano's engraving *The Academy of Baccio Bandinelli* (fig. 43), but with a live model rather than a statuette. Certain inconsistencies between the two sheets, if not simply evidence of the range of Bandinelli's graphic language, support the possibility that they were drawn by different hands. First, while the Metropolitan drawing captures the full extension of the model's right arm, its hand is abruptly cut off at the left edge of the British Museum drawing. This seeming lack of forethought is surprising from Bandinelli, an experienced and prolific draftsman. Despite this, the contours of the model's costume are drawn with more self-assurance in the British Museum sheet. This difference is visible especially in the upper hem of the bodice: while the hem is drawn confidently with two rapid, parallel strokes in the British Museum sheet, the line defining its lower edge falters in the Metropolitan sheet.

The most fundamental difference is in the hatching itself. Strong, confident parallel lines block out the model's left arm and hand and the front of the block in the British Museum sheet, while the Metropolitan sheet relies on narrower and softer lines to define the figure's right arm and torso. The volume of the model's right thigh in the Metropolitan drawing, furthermore, is suggested by gently curved hatching of a sort that does not appear in the British Museum sheet.

A third possibility—although one that would not explain the slight difference in viewpoint—is that Bandinelli or a member of his studio reimagined in the British Museum drawing the pose first captured in the Metropolitan drawing, perhaps in conjunction with a project in which a similar arrangement of limbs was envisioned.[3]

The model's general pose is one that engaged Bandinelli throughout his career. A similar combination of a raised left arm and extended right arm is visible, for example, in his painting *Leda* of about 1510–11 (Collection du Rectorat, Université de Paris Sorbonne, Paris), in a female figure at upper right in his *Massacre of the Innocents* engraving, in a figure at center right in his compositional study for *The Martyrdom of St. Lawrence* (Musée du Louvre, Paris), in a prophet sculpted in relief on his choir enclosure for Santa Maria del Fiore, and in a nude statuette included in his pen-and-ink self-portrait (Uffizi, Florence).[4] In Niccolò della Casa's engraving after Bandinelli's self-portrait, this figure in fact becomes a kind of personal emblem: with his raised arm, he points to Bandinelli's name. These examples demonstrate Bandinelli's continued interest in the pose recorded here, and they raise the possibility that both this and cat. 10 were used as models for other compositions beyond the Loreto relief. R.B.

PROVENANCE

Stanislas d'Albuquerque

LITERATURE

George Goldner in Metropolitan Museum 1996, p. 13; Strasser 2010, under no. 19; Ward 2014, p. 336

NOTES

1 On the attribution to Bandinelli of the Metropolitan drawing, known only since 1996, see Ward 2014, p. 336. Ward lists this sheet and cat. 10 as preparatory for the Loreto relief in his "Regesto dei disegni preparatori" in Heikamp and Paolozzi Strozzi 2014, p. 608.
2 I am indebted to George Goldner for this observation.
3 As Middeldorf noted (1937, p. 291), "a flood of copies and imitations" of Bandinelli's drawings was produced both during and after his career.
4 *The Massacre* was engraved by Marco Dente da Ravenna after a design by Bandinelli; the similarity of the woman's pose in the engraving to the pose in the Loreto relief and to a possibly related pen drawing in Chicago was noted by Roger Ward in McCullagh 2012, p. 37.

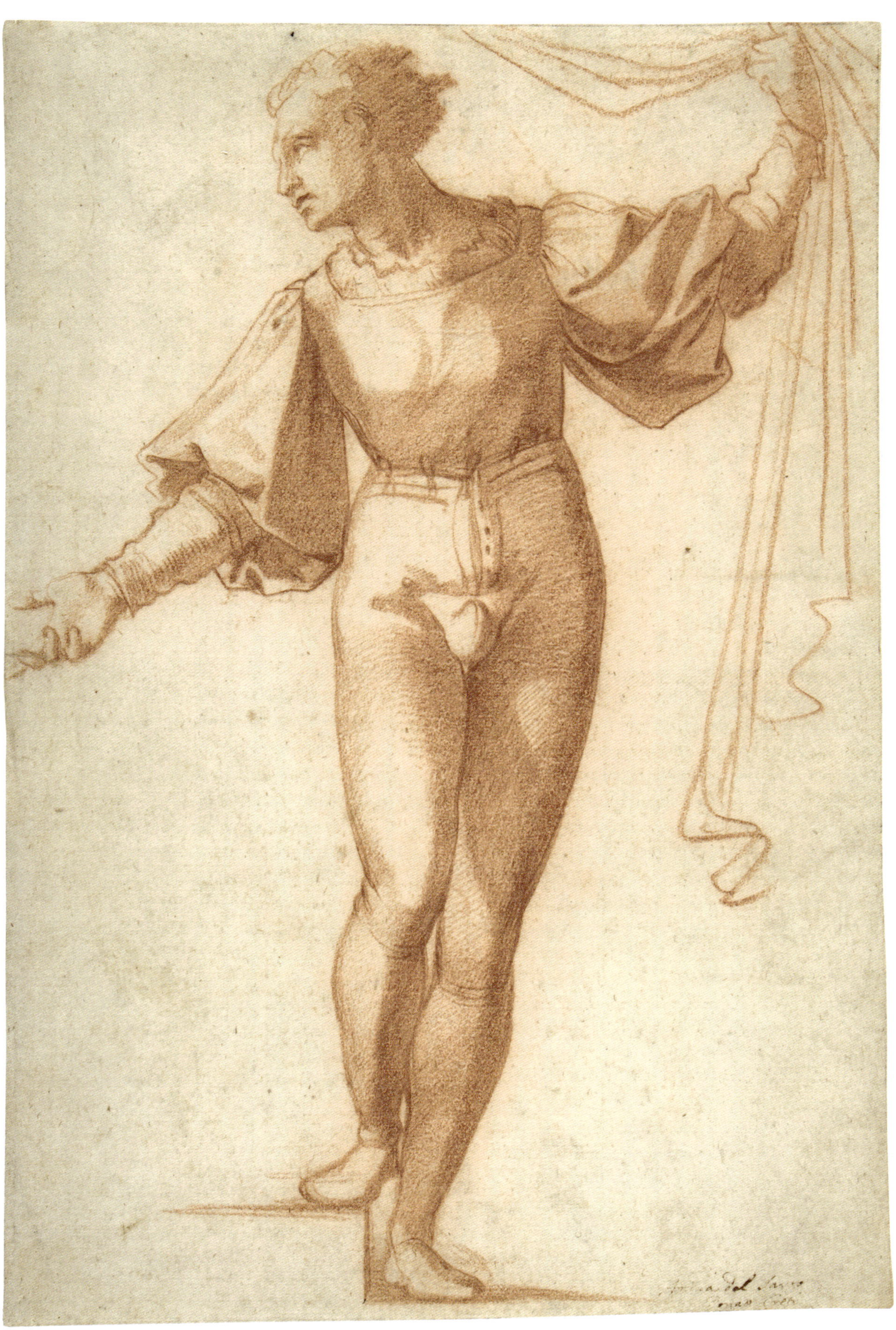

12–15

MICHELANGELO BUONARROTI

Caprese, 1475 – Rome, 1564

Four drawings of an antique nude *Venus*

12. *Torso of a nude Venus in strict profile views, seen from the right and left*, c. 1523–26

Black chalk, on thin off-white paper (now darkened); the sheet is glued onto a secondary paper support and exhibits mat burn, as well as brown stains, 201 × 146 mm ($7^{15}/_{16}$ × $5^{3}/_{4}$ in.) (maximum, slightly irregular lower boder)
Casa Buonarroti, Florence 41 F

THE ANATOMY OF THE HUMAN BODY in unabashed nudity was for Michelangelo a primary means of artistic expression. He therefore returned frequently to particular figural types, poses, and motifs as compositional devices (not repetitions), in re-creating his vocabulary of painting and sculpture over the course of his career. Relatively little discussed in the literature, these four studies after the torso of an antique nude Venus date from 1523–26 or so, during Michelangelo's work on the Medici Chapel (New Sacristy) at San Lorenzo in Florence, to judge from their bold drawing style and handling of the grayish black chalk of almost silvery hue.[1] While the drawings are today divided between the Casa Buonarroti and the British Museum, they were until 1858–59 in the possession of the great artist's descendants in Florence and Settignano: the noticeable disparity in their physical state of preservation is due to late nineteenth- and twentieth-century episodes in their history.[2] They are listed and discussed here in a proposed order of execution by the artist.[3] They were almost certainly either fragments from the same original sheet[4] or from successive leaves in the same sketchbook. Though of slighter appearance, their drawing style and technique are exactly comparable to the very sketchy, little modeled passages toward the margins in the very famous life studies for the allegorical times of day in the Medici Chapel, particularly *Day* and *Night*.[5] This stylistic relationship to the Medici Chapel life drawings disqualifies any of the possible doubts by some scholars about the attribution of the *Venus* studies to Michelangelo himself. Even in the most finished of the studies of the female nude torso (cat. 13 and 14), the modeling is somewhat schematic, so as to emphasize the sculptural values of the forms, and while the outlines are vigorously drawn and expressive, their tonal quality is overall quite soft.

Michelangelo's drawings were inspired by the same ancient Roman sculpture, presumably a *Venus*, seen from five different points of view, whose headless torso was thick, S-curved, and pear-shaped with a relatively narrow chest, very small, high breasts, high waist, and robust hips and thighs. The artist also seems to have animated the drawings further, re-creating life-likeness, and probably also observing parts of the somewhat masculine female body from an independent living model or a three-dimensional sketch in clay or wax. A fifth study very closely related to the torso of *Venus* drawings and in the identical medium and technique (Musée du Louvre 725) is on paper containing a watermark that confirms the date of about 1523–26 for the series, since some dated documents by the artist also possess this watermark.[6] The fascinating Louvre sheet shows the powerful nude female figure from behind, in a stiffer, slightly more erect pose. Michelangelo enlivened the woman's form in the Louvre drawing by adding the head with a fantastic, intricately detailed coiffure and allowing her left arm and expressive hand to hang somewhat limply by the side of her nude body, while a quickly sketched swath of cloth falls from her right upper arm. Almost twenty years earlier, Michelangelo had studied a similar sculpture of *Venus* in a sheet of about 1500–1504 (Musée Condé, Chantilly, 35 [29]),[7] executed in pen and brown ink with the cross-hatching technique of pliant strokes closely following the form that immediately anticipates his early drawings for *The Battle of Cascina*. The Chantilly sheet in pen and ink depicts the fragmentary sculpture of the nude female figure in a much fuller length, and with a slightly bent-forward torso in contrapposto, framed at left by a cloak falling from her left shoulder (hence, differently from the Louvre drawing of almost twenty years later). In the Chantilly sheet, the woman's fully revealed naked body is shown from a rear and profile views, with an intact head and headdress, shoulders, torso, and legs down to slightly below the knees. A crude, more or less contemporary copy in Oxford by an artist in Michelangelo's circle (Ashmolean 1846.133 recto [KP II 412]),[8] also drawn in pen and ink, represents

PROVENANCE

Estate of Michelangelo, and by descent in his family

LITERATURE (selected)

Gotti 1875–76, vol. 2, p. 190; Thode 1902–13, vol. 3, no. 81 (rejected); Wilde 1953, p. 80, under nos. 43–44; Dussler 1959, no. 432 (rejected as "apocryphal"); Barocchi 1962–64, vol. 1 (*testo*), p. 92, no. 70; Tolnay 1975–80, vol. 2, pp. 52–53, no. 231 recto; Agosti and Farinella 1987, pp. 75–76, no. 29; Hirst 1988a, p. 61; Paul Joannides in Falletti and Nelson 2002, pp. 150–51, no. 2; Joannides 2003, pp. 128–31, under inv. 725; Chapman 2005, pp. 64, 66–67, 301–2, nos. 92, 93; Joannides 2007, p. 283, under no. 58

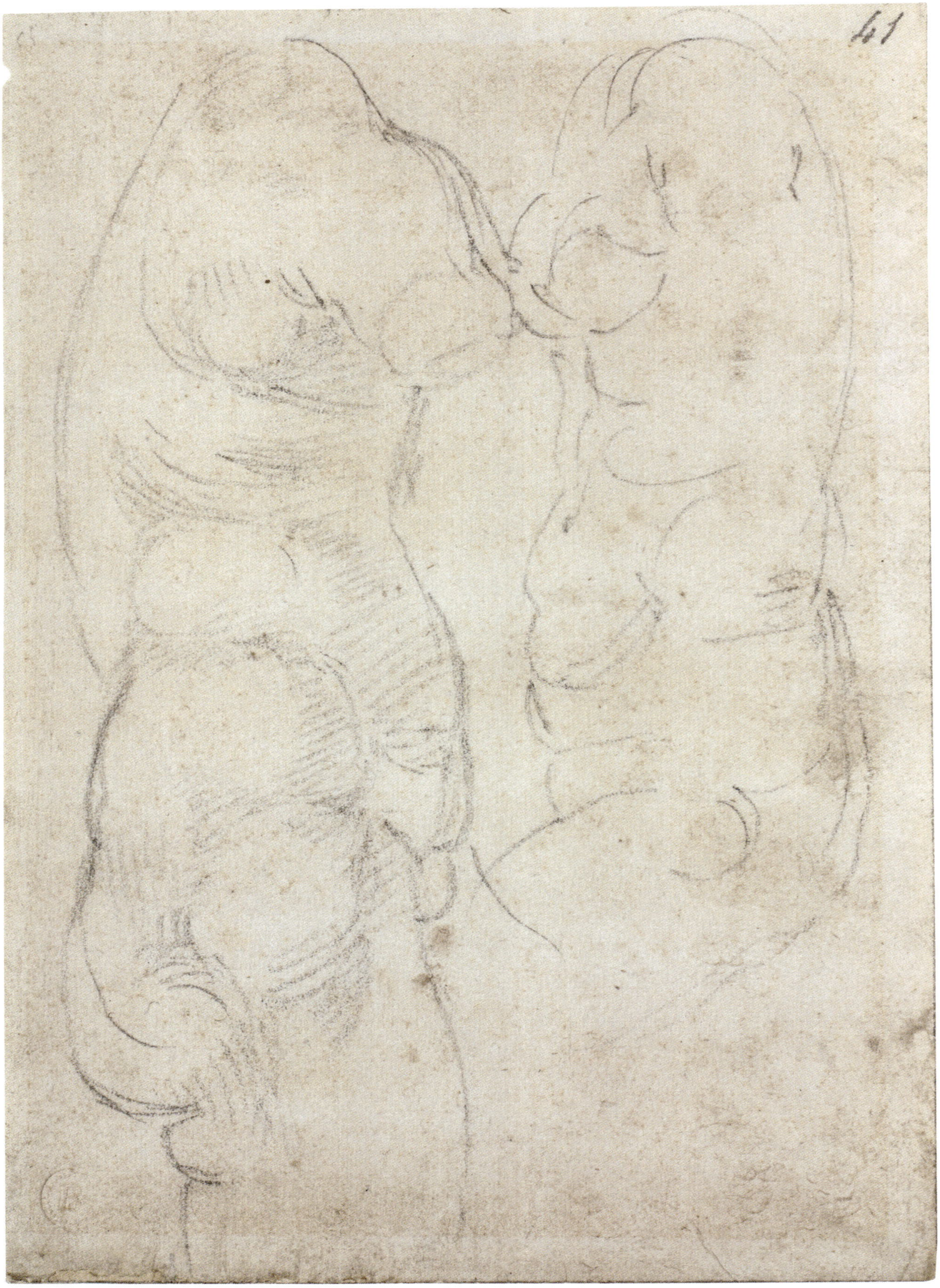
41

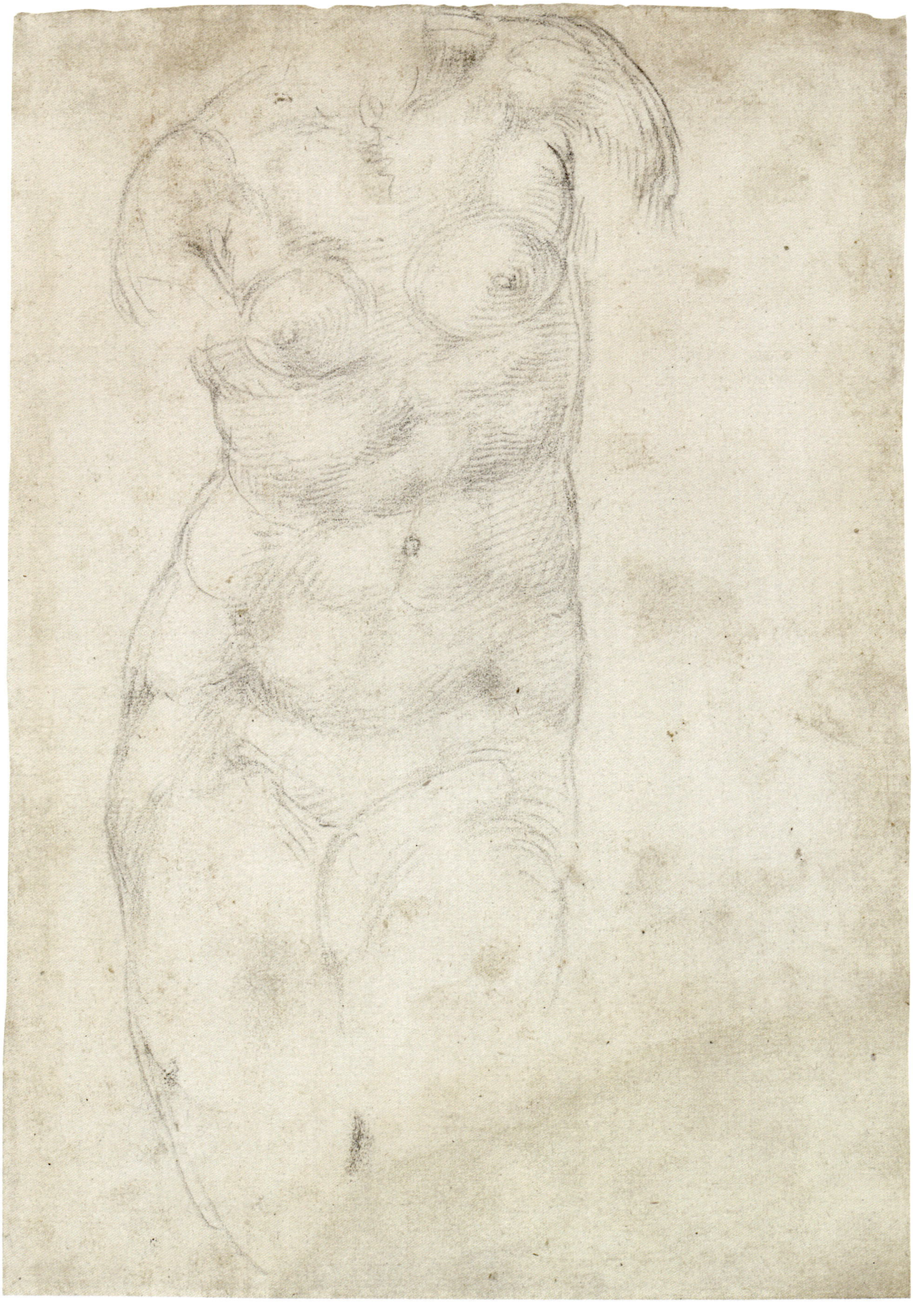

13. *Torso of a nude Venus seen from the front, in a slight turn toward the right*, c. 1523–26

Black chalk, 256 × 181 mm (10 1/16 × 7 1/8 in.) (maximum, lower right corner made up)
British Museum, London 1859,0625.570 recto

the same female statue in an almost straight frontal view, such as is not found in Michelangelo's Chantilly sheet, but includes as well two profile views from the same side of the sculpture, including her intact head and headdress, those being the motifs that are closely dependent on the autograph Chantilly sheet.[9] It is therefore not possible to argue that the female figure in Michelangelo's Chantilly sheet is a transgendered design modeled on the headless marble torso of the Apollo Saurocthonos (Museo Archaeologico, Naples), which in the early sixteenth century was exhibited in a niche with his back facing the viewer in the courtyard of the Casa Sassi in Rome.[10] The comparison of details in all these drawings also suggests to this writer that Michelangelo was referring to two different versions of a similar female sculptural type, representing Venus, in the respective sheets of about 1500–1504 and about 1523–26, contrary to the assumption of some scholars, who maintain the drawings are all based on one and the same classical female torso.[11]

The precise antique sources for Michelangelo's *Venus* drawings are open to question, however, because they subtly transform the design with respect to the possible ancient marble sculptures available to him and to other closely related Renaissance drawings and copies in which the artist adapted the models for his own creative purposes. In my opinion, Michelangelo's most probable sources were Roman copies (or casts thereof) after a sculpted Greek original of a standing Venus Anadyomene type (as implied by the Greek term, the goddess born from the foam of the sea is seen rising in unashamed nakedness), an invention sometimes imprecisely attributed to Polycharmes, but which is known in numerous versions of design —entirely naked or with some drapery—and in great variations of size from tiny to monumental, dating from the late 2nd century BCE and later.[12] Such a model would have appealed to Michelangelo, who unabashedly extolled the nudity of the male and female body rather than obscuring it with devices for the sake of modesty. The particular Anadyomene exemplar studied by Michelangelo in the

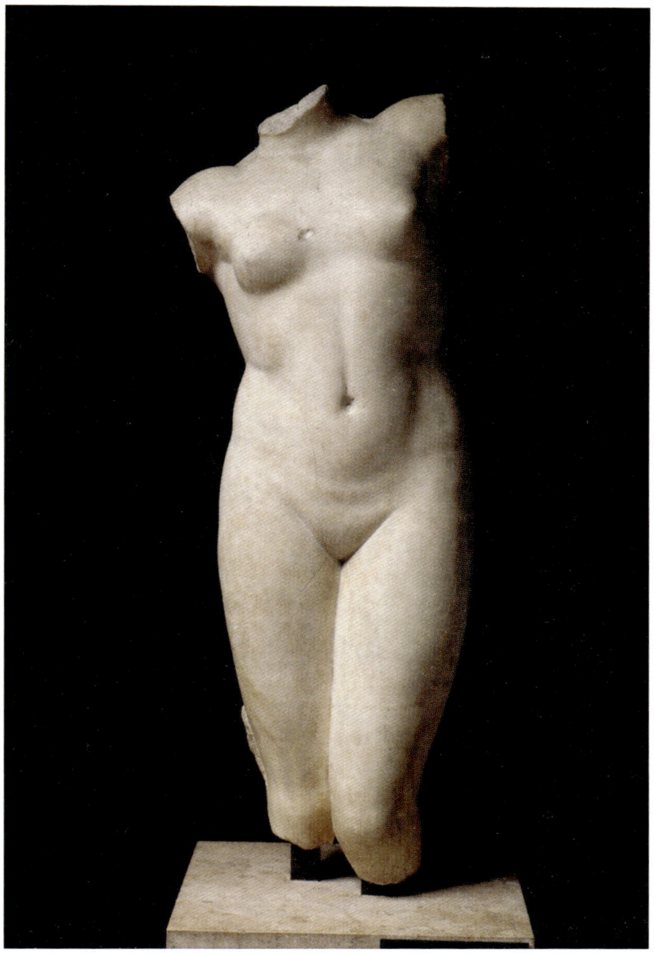

FIG. 62
Roman copy after the
Venus Anadyomene type
2nd century BCE
Marble, 96 cm high
Musée du Louvre, Paris

PROVENANCE

Estate of Michelangelo, and by descent in his family

LITERATURE (selected)

Thode 1902–13, vol. 3, no. 313 (rejected); Berenson 1938, vol. 2, p. 231, no. 1686 ("Michelangelo School, possibly by Bartolomeo Ammannati"); Wilde 1953, pp. 79–80, no. 43; Berenson 1961, vol. 2, p. 386, no. 1686 (*forse di Bartolomeo Ammannati*); Tolnay 1975–80, vol. 2, p. 53, no. 232 recto; Agosti and Farinella 1987, p. 75, nos. 29–30a; Hirst 1988a, p. 61, pl. 112; Paul Joannides in Falletti and Nelson 2002, pp. 150–51, no. 4; Chapman 2005, pp. 64, 66–67, 301–2, nos. 92, 93; Joannides 2007, p. 283, under no. 58

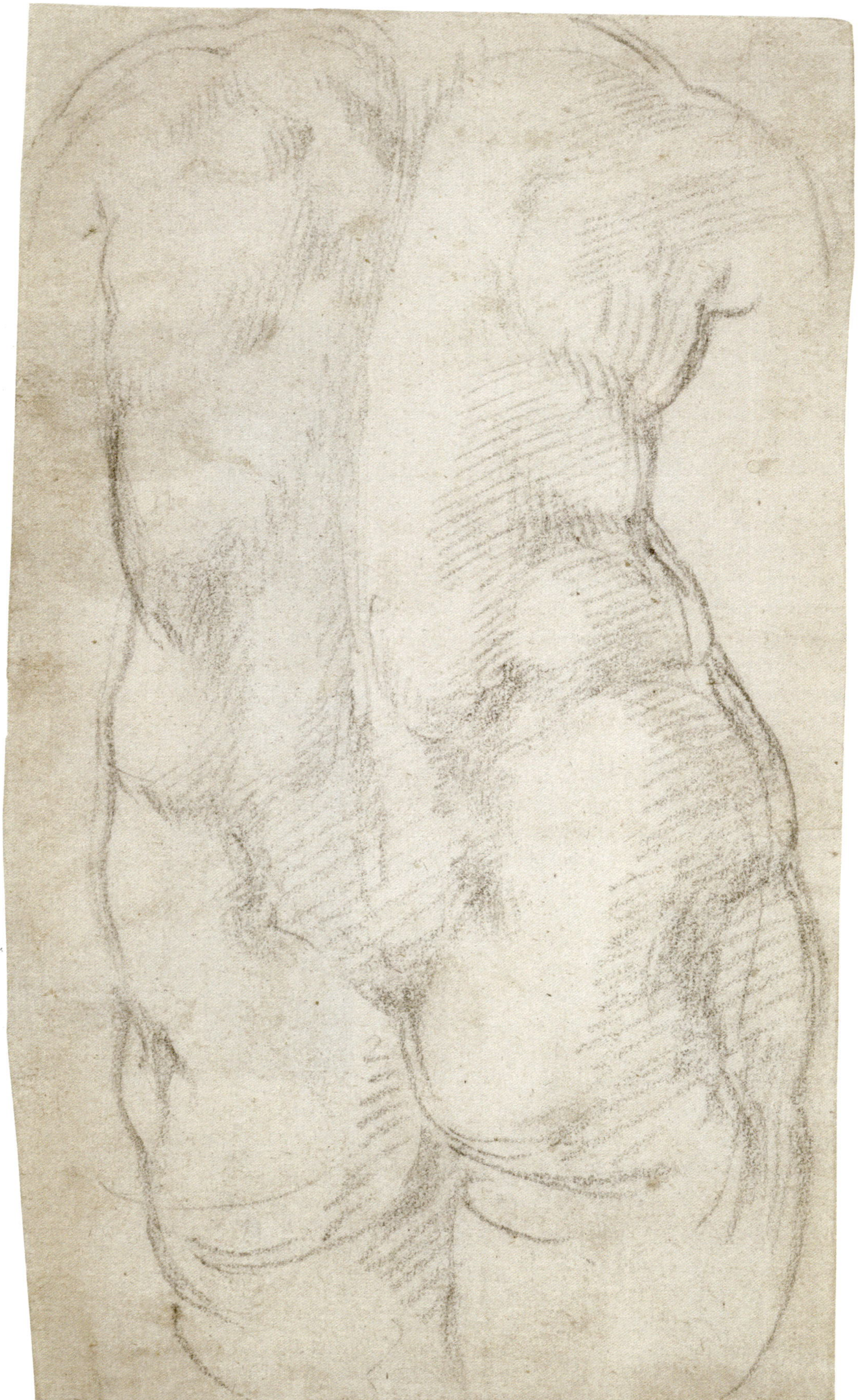

14. *Torso of a nude Venus seen from behind, in a slight turn toward the right*, c. 1523–26

Black chalk, over preliminary stylus indentations, 201 × 106 mm (7¹⁵⁄₁₆ × 4³⁄₁₆ in.)
British Museum, London 1859,0625.571 recto

1520s was a headless and armless torso with legs cropped at the knee or slightly below it, like the type here illustrated (fig. 62). It has also been not unreasonably suggested that Michelangelo's model for the 1520s drawings was a Roman copy after a sculpted Greek original of a Venus of Cnidian type by Praxiteles, but in such representations the goddess is seen in a modest, or *pudica*, pose,[13] as in the famous Capitoline Venus (Musei Capitolini, MC0409), the Venus de' Medici (in the Tribuna of the Uffizi, Florence, 1914, no. 224), or the Ludovisi Venus (Museo Nazionale Romano, Palazzo Altemps, 8619), sculptures which themselves were not known in Michelangelo's lifetime though their general figural formula had been disseminated through lesser examples.[14] Less convincingly, it has also been argued that Michelangelo re-created in the drawing at Chantilly the interchangeable details from the Three Graces marble that since 1502 had been a centerpiece in the Piccolomini Library at Siena Cathedral, and in the case of the Venus drawings of the 1520s that Michelangelo worked from a reduced plaster cast of a Roman marble original.[15]

The earliest of Michelangelo's studies after the torso of the nude Venus was probably the most tentative, least finished sheet in the Casa Buonarroti (cat. 12), depicting the two strictly descriptive side views of the sculpture, left and right, facing one another almost touching. The execution is relatively prosaic for Michelangelo, since these views of the carved fragment were probably the least interesting to him. He thus did little more than quickly and very lightly sketch the forms with summary strokes: the preliminary state of the two designs is virtually that of an abandoned underdrawing on the paper. Nevertheless, the self-assured, almost gestural crudeness of the contours and sparse patches of modeling with only a few lines of parallel hatching reveal a sculptor's virtuosic ability to encapsulate fully the plasticity of forms, this with the utmost economy of means. It is probable that Michelangelo first drew the motif of the statue at left, which is more awkward. The quicker and smaller sketch at right has no internal modeling to speak of, but is volumetrically more precise than the drawing at left, which is overly and roughly parallel-hatched. The drawing at left also exhibits fairly clumsy anatomy and is more belabored in the contours. Comparison of the two designs shows that by the time Michelangelo turned to draw the view of the sculpture at right, his hand had loosened as he worked on the paper, and his eye was sufficiently exercised in the morphology of the statue that the drawing fluently poured forth with a greater mastery of anatomy. While this drawing at right is less finished, the contours of the figure here are greatly more spontaneous and animated. This drawing of two side views of the *Venus* torso demonstrates clearly that both arms, left and right, were similarly broken off slightly below the shoulders. The profiles along the back, hips, and buttocks of the figure in both sketches are extremely awkward, and consequently Michelangelo's attention focused closely on redesigning this backside of the figure in the later *Venus* drawings (cat. 14, 15 and Louvre 725).

Following the two side views, the artist then concentrated on the frontal view of the sculpted torso in cat. 13, first blocking out the figure with fine, very light outlines on the paper and then building up the final contours with a thicker point of the black-chalk stick and softly calibrating the areas of chiaroscuro by working up the drawing with pliant strokes of parallel hatching and cross-hatching, in which the lines, though closely woven together, are not rubbed in for a pictorial *sfumato*, but rather preserve the quality of a sculptural process as if a toothed chisel had coursed through the surface, hatching and grooving for a carefully descriptive effect. This frontal view of the statue gently communicates the sensuous "*figura serpentinata*," or S-curve, of the overall outlines of the woman's nude body, without sacrificing the intricacies of her nearly masculine muscularity, and at the same time seems to exude the suppleness of living flesh.

The view of the woman's torso from behind was perhaps the most interesting for Michelangelo, however, as three of the surviving drawings of the 1520s concern themselves with this aspect of the fragmentary sculpture. The back view of the *Venus* torso is gently

PROVENANCE

Estate of Michelangelo, and by descent in his family

LITERATURE (selected)

Thode 1902–13, vol. 3, no. 313 (rejected); Berenson 1938, vol. 2, p. 231, no. 1686A ("Michelangelo School, possibly by Bartolomeo Ammanati"); Wilde 1953, p. 80, no. 44; Berenson 1961, vol. 2, p. 386, no. 1686A (*forse dell'Ammannati*); Tolnay 1975–80, vol. 2, p. 53, no. 233 recto; Agosti and Farinella 1987, p. 75; Hirst 1988a, p. 61; Paul Joannides in Falletti and Nelson 2002, pp. 150–51, no. 5; Chapman 2005, pp. 64, 66–67, 301–2, nos. 92, 93; Joannides 2007, p. 283, under no. 58

15. *Torso of a nude Venus seen from behind, in a three-quarter turn toward left*, c. 1523–26

Black chalk, on very thin off-white paper (now slightly darkened), the silhouetted sheet inlaid on a secondary paper support, 133 × 81 mm (5¼ × 3³⁄₁₆ in.) (maximum, the sheet is cut tightly around the body of the figure)
Casa Buonarroti, Florence 16F

animated into a relatively upright pose, seen almost straight on, in cat. 14. Here, the modulations of tone and detail in the areas of the buttocks and the lower back region of the figure with its delicately articulated spine and adjoining muscles (the *lumbodorsal fascia* and *erector spinae*) seem sufficiently naturalistic as to suggest the good possibility that Michelangelo enhanced his study of this anatomy from life by actually posing a (male) model in the studio in a stance similar to that of the sculpture. Be this as it may, the last of the drawings of the *Venus* series here exhibited, cat. 15 depicts the powerfully expressive torso of the nude goddess seen from behind, in a three-quarter turn toward the left. The way the heavily cutout drawing is mounted today onto the secondary paper support misleadingly makes the body appear to lean further forward than it should. Michelangelo returned here to the chiseled sculptural values of the figure, and it is just possible that he enhanced these also by observing similar forms from a separate clay or wax three-dimensional model of male anatomy. Again be this as it may, he applied the chalk more forcefully onto the paper than in the other sheets, with hatching that follows closely the anatomical forms, and he abandoned the more softly naturalistic technique of flesh-like finish he had employed in drawing the back view in cat. 14. This impressive study of the back of the *Venus* torso, though sadly damaged by the darkened secondary support and the cutting up of the original sheet close to the body of the figure, searches for her pose with bold, dynamic reinforcement outlines. The drawing is greatly more worked up than cat. 12 and seems more monumental, but the figure is actually in a slightly smaller body scale. In the back view (cat. 15), the understanding of her body's anatomy still retains enough of the life-like observed in cat. 14 while amplifying the sculptural monumentality of her forms. The pentimenti outlines on the breast, rib cage, and hips show that Michelangelo began drawing lightly on the paper and gradually refined the torso into slenderer proportions. For example, he drew the first contour at left of the rib cage finely, and then reworked it toward the right by 3 or 4 mm; other outlines display smaller changes. He especially sketched and reworked contours a few times to indicate the disappearing edges of the foreshortened shoulders. He also drew the figure's arm at left as an undefined stump, true to the physical condition of the antique sculpture in his lifetime: a partial outline within the shoulder area seems to indicate vaguely the rim of the break in the marble. The final drawing in the series of *Venus* drawings was probably Louvre 725, not exhibited here, in which the view of the woman's nude figure is humanized beyond that of a statuary fragment and the pose is readapted in a more pictorial way with the addition of several details, as described above, perhaps with the intention of using her design in a painting.

The precise final purpose of Michelangelo's black-chalk studies of the nude torso of a Venus is not clear. Although the drawings have been connected to his ideas for the unexecuted allegorical figures that were to adorn the tabernacles in the tombs of the Dukes Giuliano and Lorenzo di Piero de' Medici in the New Sacristy,[16] none of the recorded documents, or surviving autograph designs, or direct copies after these by artists from Michelangelo's circle seems to bear out such a claim in a concrete way. Rather, especially because the *Venus* drawings represent a sequence of multiple, descriptive views of the figure, it suggests to my mind that the studies were most likely destined by Michelangelo to serve him as general repertory material of the nude female form, for reference in his creative process. It is possible that his studies in black chalk after the antique *Venus* were later enlisted in order to assist another artist with designs in executing a sculpture. A dynamic *bozzetto* in light gray clay (cat. 16) attributed to the great master himself by Johannes Wilde and a number of other scholars, who attempted to identify it as a preparatory sketch for the lost allegorical figure of Terra (Earth), a sculpture that was to be executed by il Tribolo for the Medici Chapel based on Michelangelo's

PROVENANCE

Estate of Michelangelo, and by descent in his family

LITERATURE (selected)

Gotti 1875–76, vol. 2, p. 188; Thode 1902–13, vol. 3, no. 26 (rejected); Wilde 1953, p. 80, under nos. 43–44; Dussler 1959, no. 418 (rejected as "apocryphal"); Barocchi 1962–64, vol. 1 (*testo*), pp. 91–92 , no. 69; Tolnay 1975–80, vol. 2, p. 53, no. 234 recto; Agosti and Farinella 1987, pp. 75–77, no. 30; Hirst 1988a, p. 61; Paul Joannides in Falletti and Nelson 2002, pp. 150–51, no. 3; Joannides 2003, pp. 128–31, under inv. 725; Chapman 2005, pp. 64, 66–67, 301–2, nos. 92, 93; Joannides 2007, p. 283, under no. 58

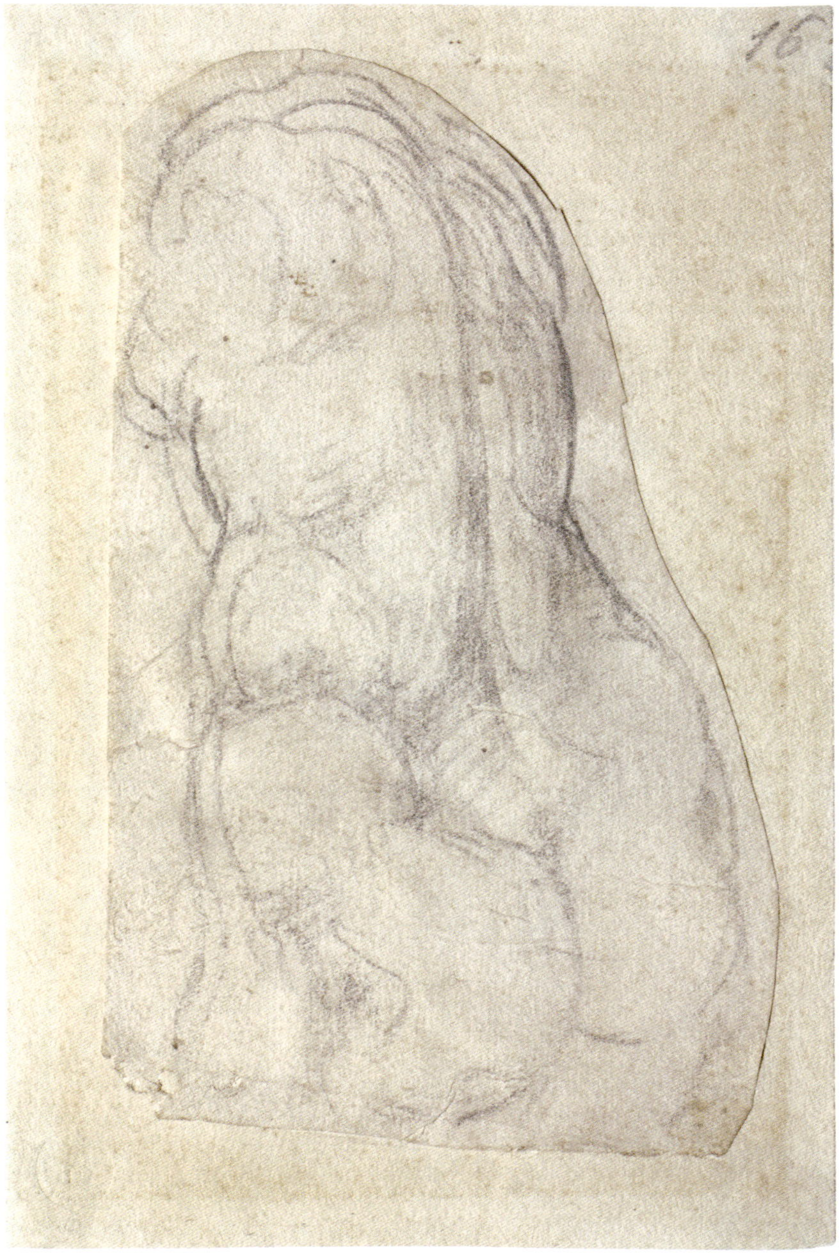

two small clay models, "*dua modelli picholi*," being finished for Tribolo on 15 October 1533.[17] This *bozzetto* in clay portrays a muscular female figure with the same physical type as the antique *Venus* torso drawn by Michelangelo in cat. 12. A third sheet with sketches in the Casa Buonarroti (53F recto), dating to the mid- to late 1520s, done in red chalk with some stylus ruling, but which is of questionable attribution, portrays a large design of a full-length female nude of elegantly elongated proportions standing on a base.[18] This woman's figure is clearly meant to depict a statue with supporting struts. Her torso also recalls that of the securely autograph Venus studies in cat. 12–15, but the technical execution of these sketches in red chalk is very delicate, hesitant, and ultimately awkward, when compared with Michelangelo's securely autograph drawings of this time (preserved in the same museum collection and thus easily compared in the originals). The intended sculpture of the female figure is surrounded by three much smaller sketches in red chalk also inspired by the antique—a servant carrying a vessel in a dance-like pose, a Hercules and Antaeus, and the Bed of Polyclitus. The verso of this sheet includes a large copy in red chalk after a well-known drawing of the grotesque head of a satyr or devil (Städel Museum 392),[19] and thus the recto of the Casa Buonarroti sheet may be by the same hand. C.C.B.

NOTES

1 Dating essentially in agreement with Wilde 1953. Paul Joannides in Falletti and Nelson 2002, pp. 150–51, under nos. 2–4, has, however, dated these drawings c. 1520; the evidence of the watermark on the related sheet (Musée du Louvre, 725), discussed below, contradicts this.
2 See Thornton and Warren 1998, on the acquisition of the British Museum drawings from the Buonarroti family in 1858.
3 A different sequence of execution is stated in Hirst 1988a, p. 61, pls. 112–15, also terming the drawings "copies of an antique torso of Venus," rather than studies.
4 First noted hesitantly in Wilde 1953, p. 80, under nos. 43–44; affirmed by Paul Joannides in Falletti and Nelson 2002, pp. 150–51, under nos. 2–4.
5 The relevant life studies for the Medici Chapel are Ashmolean Museum, Oxford, 1846.55 [KP II 309] and 1846.56 [KP II 310]; Teylers Museum, Haarlem, A30, A33, A33bis, A36; British Museum, London, 1859,625.566 verso; British Library, London, Add. MS 21907, fol. 1; and Uffizi, Florence, 18719F.
6 This Louvre drawing is discussed and illustrated in Joannides 2003, pp. 128–31, no. 23. The watermark on the paper is catalogued and illustrated in Roberts 1988, p. 20, "type C: eagle in circle: medium-sized"; Ariane de La Chapelle in Joannides 2003, p. 414, fig. 11.
7 Discussed and illustrated in Lanfranc de Panthou and Peronnet 1995, pp. 126–29, no. 38.
8 Discussed and illustrated in Joannides 2007, pp. 281–85, no. 58, with full literature, though with an unconvincing attribution to Piero d'Argenta.
9 The upper part of the non-autograph sheet, Casa Buonarroti 28F recto, contains four feeble copies in pen and ink after the copies of the female sculpture depicted in the Ashmolean sheet discussed above.
10 *Contra* Ekserdjian 1993, pp. 390–91, who does not mention the Ashmolean drawn copy partly based on Michelangelo's Chantilly sheet, which demonstrates the model to be a female statue.
11 Wilde 1953, p. 80; Lanfranc de Panthou and Peronnet 1995, p. 127, under no. 38.
12 See Wardle 2010, on the typologies of the Venus Anadyomene, with 365 catalogued examples. The standing pose is the most common for the Venus Anadyomene (ibid., p. 7).
13 Wilde 1953, p. 80, under nos. 43–44; Paul Joannides in Falletti and Nelson 2002, pp. 150–51, under nos. 2–4.
14 The head, arms, lower legs, drapery, and jug of the Ludovisi Venus were restored by Ippolito Buzzi (1562–1632).
15 As proposed in Tolnay 1975–80, vol. 1, pp. 42–47, no. 24, and vol. 2, pp. 52–53, nos. 231–34.
16 Wilde 1953, p. 80, under nos. 43–44.
17 Quotation from Michelangelo's letter to Battista Figiovanni of 15 October 1533 (Barocchi and Ristori 1965–83, vol. 4, p. 55, no. CMXXXVI). For the attribution, see Wilde 1953, p. 80, under nos. 43–44; Jonathan K. Nelson in Falletti and Nelson 2002, pp. 154–55, no. 7.
18 This drawing was attributed to Michelangelo by Wilde 1953, p. 80, under nos. 43–44; Tolnay 1975–80, vol. 2, no. 229bis; Paul Joannides in Falletti and Nelson 2002, pp. 152–53, no. 6.
19 Sonnabend 2009.

16

MICHELANGELO BUONARROTI

Caprese, 1475 – Rome, 1564

Nude female figure, c. 1530

Light gray terracotta, height 350 mm (13¾ in.)
Casa Buonarroti, Florence 193

THE TERRACOTTA, part of a larger collection of small sculptures, was rediscovered in the Casa Buonarroti in the middle of the nineteenth century, when Rosina Vendramin, wife of the last heir of the Buonarroti family, opened one of the cabinets of the palace study by chance.[1] Earlier inventories of the Florentine residence, nevertheless, had already referred to a collection of "Michelangelo's models" preserved there—explicitly in the so-called Descrizione buonarrotiana of 1684 and indirectly in a notarial act completed between 8 November and 18 December 1799, which noted the presence of "two walnut cabinets … containing things of the Museum."[2]

Among the various small figures that came to light as a result of that chance discovery, the slim female nude may be the one that has had the least stable critical fortune. Although Michelangelo's authorship of the work has only rarely been questioned (for example by Balas 1992), there has been less consensus on the terracotta's function, date, and place in the artist's oeuvre. The work has convincingly been connected to a group of drawings that are now divided between the Casa Buonarroti and the British Museum (cat. 12--15), though Wilde (1953) believed them to be parts of a single original folio. In these, Michelangelo compulsively experimented with an ancient fragment that appears to have been close in its anatomy to the present piece: the various views document a classical torso of Venus, lacking arms and probably the lower extremities as well, in a pose that suggests a more dynamic version of Praxiteles's Cnidian Venus or, as Carmen C. Bambach claims in her entry to cat. 12–15 in this volume, a version of the Venus Anadyomene. No one has been able to identify the archaeological discovery that Michelangelo so enthusiastically analyzed, but it must have been an object of great fascination, since it seems also to be reflected in several other sheets by Michelangelo (Casa Buonarroti, Florence, 53F; Musée du Louvre, Paris, 725 recto), in a number of studies from his workshop (among them a copy after an original by the artist in the Casa Buonarroti, 28F recto, and one of the drawings on the wall in the New Sacristy), and in sketches by Domenico Beccafumi (Musée du Louvre, Paris, 255) and Giovan Ambrogio Figino.

Henry Thode, in 1913, connected the terracotta to the genesis of the great tomb of Pope Julius II, seeing it in relation to the Victories imagined for that imposing structure. Wilde, by contrast, took the work to be a model executed by Michelangelo for the allegorical figures that were to be placed at the sides of the effigies of Lorenzo and Giuliano de' Medici in the tombs of the New Sacristy, more specifically the personifications of Heaven and Earth meant to flank Giuliano. He based this suggestion on Vasari's *Lives*, which in fact reports that Michelangelo delegated the execution of those sculptures to Tribolo.[3] Neither of these proposals—taken up again in recent contributions like those of Johannes Myssok (1999) or Paul Joannides (2002)—is fully convincing, in view of the more developed drawings Michelangelo made for these two monumental projects. It is difficult to see, moreover, how the Casa Buonarroti figure, with its incomplete state and small dimensions, could have served as a true "model" for any sculpture that had been delegated to a different artist to carve.

The terracotta might thus better be read as a three-dimensional version of the above-mentioned studies on paper, with the further ambition of reintegrating the ancient female torso with a complex pose. As a famous passage from Pietro Bembo's *Prose della volgar lingua* attests,[4] Cinquecento artists copied from the antique using both graphic and plastic media. The idea of firing the material after the

---

PROVENANCE

Studio of the artist (?); documented in the Casa Buonarroti from 1684

LITERATURE

Fabbrichesi 1865, p. 18, no. 4; Casa Buonarroti 1891, p. 22, no. 4; Bode 1892–1905, vol. 9, p. 174; "Galleria Buonarroti in Firenze. Inventario della suppellettile artistica", 1896, p. 32, no. 416; Thode 1902–13, vol. 3, p. 265, vol. 4, p. 158, no. XVIII, vol. 6, p. 280, no. 583; von Fabriczy 1909, esp. p. 40, note 144; Brinckmann 1923–24, vol. 1, p. 38; Maclagan 1924, esp. pp. 12, 15, note 15; Popham, Wilde, and Pouncey 1953, p. 80, no. 44; De Tolnay 1954, p. 158, no. 6; Goldscheider 1957, p. 11; Goldscheider 1962, n.p.; Procacci 1965, p. 188; Barocchi and Ristori 1965–83, vol. 4, p. 55, no. CMXXXVI; Weinberger 1967, vol. 1, pp. 211, 263–64, 339–40, vol. 2, figs. 114.1, 114.2, 115.1; Hartt 1969, pp. 15, 140; De Tolnay 1970, pp. 6, 54; Le Brooy 1972, pp. 19, 126, 128, 143 note 3, 147; Baldini 1973, p. 113, note 67; Wittkower 1977, pp. 130–31; Parronchi 1981, pp. 30, 108–10; Hartt 1987, pp. 64–65; Ragionieri 1987, p. 42, no. 2; Balas 1992, p. 72; Goldscheider 1996, p. 273; Schmidt 1996, esp. p. 125, note 40; Myssok 1999, pp. 281–84, 358–59; O'Grody 1999, pp. 262–66, no. 8; Jeannine A. O'Grody in Ragionieri 2000, pp. 48–53; Boucher 2001, pp. 41–42; Paul Joannides in Falletti and Nelson 2002, pp. 152–53; Jonathan K. Nelson in Falletti and Nelson 2002, pp. 154–55

statuette had been modeled could then be interpreted as a decision to preserve an invention that Michelangelo held to be particularly successful and potentially useful in future projects. Such a procedure would not have been foreign to Michelangelo's creative practices. One other clay preserved in the Casa Buonarroti can be understood in the same way, the group of two wrestlers sometimes said to be the model for a statue to go beside the marble *David* in the Piazza della Signoria or a project connected to the tomb of Julius II.[5] This group, which shares the overall dimensions and the level of finish of the Venus, could be interpreted as a *primo pensiero* that was then transformed in the furnace into a lasting reference point, rather than as a proper model conceived for a literal translation into marble. To follow the contemporary literature, true models should measure two *palmi*, about sixty centimeters.[6]

A dating to the 1530s, keyed to the scant internal information present in the related drawings,[7] is not inconsistent stylistically with the exuberant and rough elegance of Michelangelo's creations in those years, precisely within the workshop of the New Sacristy. T.M.

NOTES

1 Ragionieri 2000, pp. 15–16.
2 Ragionieri 2000, pp. 12–14.
3 Vasari-Bettarini 1966, vol. 5, pp. 204–5.
4 Bembo 1966, III.1.
5 Ragionieri 2000, pp. 45–46.
6 See for example Cellini 1568/69, p. 57.
7 Paul Joannides in Falletti and Nelson 2002, pp. 152–53.

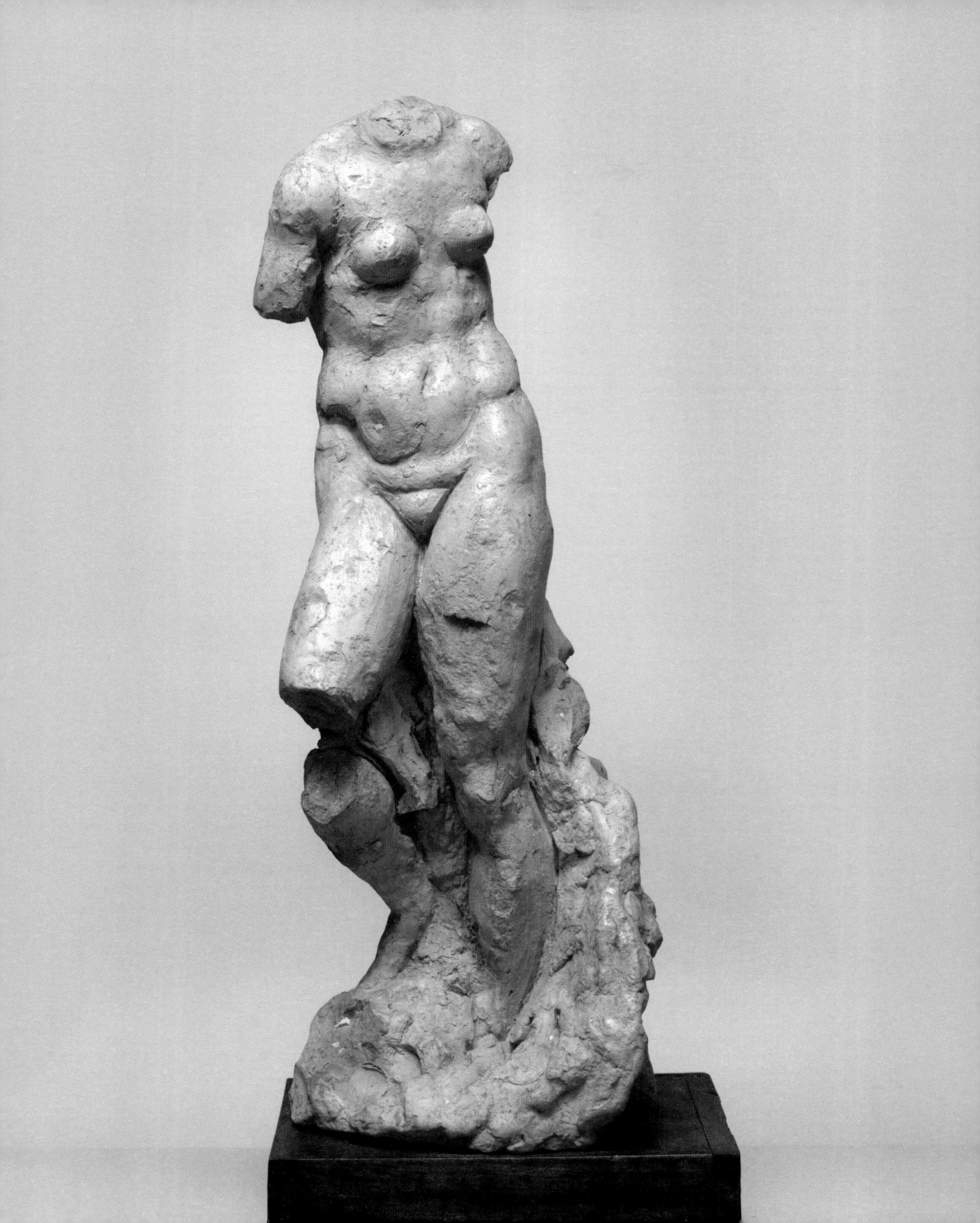

17

FRA MATTIA (MARCO) DELLA ROBBIA

Florence, 1468 – Montecassiano, 1534

Design and contract for a tondo of the Virgin and Child (recto); *Sketches and notes for a tondo of the Virgin and Child* (verso), 1524

Black chalk with Indian ink wash and pen and brown ink on white paper, 405 × 292 mm (15 15/16 × 11½ in.)
Inscribed in brown ink on recto, below a design for a tondo: *Die Quarta junii 1524 ~ Fr[ater] Mathias Andree de Flore[n]tia or[di]nis S[anc]ti D[o]m[inici sponte etc. promisit etc. d[on] alberto ~~p[raese]nti etc.~~ / Serra Curie Ca[usa]r[um] Came[re] ap[ostoli]ce not[ar]io p[raese]nti etc. d[omi]no meo, ei construere et facere figurans figuras supra designatas / de terra dicta Creta Cocta Invittriata et Smaltata de bonis et finis ac sufficientibus coloribus jux[t]a predesignatum / dessignum et melius in apparentia, ita q[uo]d vanum ~~suae va~~ sit latitudinis Palmor[um] trium et Festonis cum / Cherubinis sit alterius palmi cum uno quarto et quas Figuras promisit facere de terra bona infra Quindecim / dies et Illas ostendere factas ex fresco infra idem tempus ac subinde easdem invittriare smaltare, coquere / & perficere ac eidem d[on] Alberto hic in urbe ad domum habi[tatio]nis sue consignare infra unum aliu[m] mensem / cum dimidio ex inde seque[n]tem al[ia]s teneri voluit ad restitutionem infra[scrip]te pecunie ad et ad penam dupli al ac o[mn]ia / damna etc. Et Premissa fecit et facere promisit dictus Fr[ater] Mathias pro pretio et solutione duor[um] ducator[um] / auri de ~~Camera~~ largor[um] quos dictus d. Albertus eidem solvit in pr[aesen]tia testium etc. et de quibus etc. Pro quibus etc. sed / etiam ea que in g[e]n[er]ali obligatione non veniunt nec comprehenduntur et sub penis Cam[er]e ap[osto]lic[ae] obligavit / Cum iura[men]to et consti[tutio]ne procur[atorum] et in se omnes suscepit cens[ur]as ecc[lesiasti]cas cum mandato exequtivo etc. contra / eum decernen[do] etc. Act[um] Rom[a]e in off[icio] etc. pr[ese]ntibus gerardo poerssom* [ink from the other side has eaten through the sheet] *cl[er]ico Tullen[sis] dioc[esis] et / Waltero Regis cl[er]ico tullen[sis] dioc[esis] testibus etc.* (4 June 1524. Fra Mattia, son of Andrea, of Florence of the holy order of St. Dominic, voluntarily promised to my master, Don Alberto Serra of the apostolic chamber of the Curia Causarum, in the presence of a notary, to construct for him and to make the figures drawn above out of earth called *creta*, that has been fired, glazed, and enameled, out of good and fine and satisfactory colors, together with the predesignated design, and better in appearance [than the design], so that the interior space is of three *palmi*, and the festoon with cherubs is of another one and a quarter *palmi*; and which figures he promised to make out of good earth, within fifteen days, and to display them, having been made from fresh clay, within the same time; and also immediately thereafter, he promised to glaze, enamel, fire, and complete the same ones, and to consign them to the same Don Alberto here in the city, at his place of residence, within one and a half additional months. He wanted the others to be held for the payment of the money written below, and at the penalty of twice as much, and all damages etc. And the aforementioned Fra Mattia made the things which were set forth previously and he promised to make, for the price and payment of two large gold ducats, which the aforementioned Don Alberto paid to the same person [i.e., Fra Mattia], in the presence of witnesses, etc., and from whom, etc. In return for this, etc., he pledged even those things which do not come into general obligation and are not included, under penalty of the papal court, with the oath and the agreement of the procurators, and he took onto himself all the ecclesiastical expenses, with the executive mandate, etc., to be decreed against him. Done in Rome in the offices etc., in the presence of the cleric Gerardo Poerssom, of the diocese of Toul, and Walter Rex, a cleric of the diocese of Toul, and witnesses, etc.); in brown ink, on recto below the text of the contract: *Ita est fr[ater] mathias, manu propria* (Thus it is [written by] Fra Mattia, in his own hand); in brown ink, on verso, upper left: *pro d[on] Alberto Serra* (for Don Alberto Serra); in brown ink, on verso, middle left: *p[ro] figuris cedula / f[rat]ris Mathie d[ella] robbia* (Contract for figures / Fra Mattia della Robbia); in brown ink, on verso, lower left, below another design for a tondo: *palmi di roma[na] tre largo e lungo / tondo, el vano senza el festono / la madonna, lo figlio, san giovanni / una monacha di santo sixto con / un breve per mano dira, / sit mens sana in corpore sano, / Di bone e belle figure, con belli colori* (Three Roman *palmi* wide and high, round, the interior space without the festoon. The Madonna, the Son, St. John, a nun of St. Sixtus with a banderole in her hand will say: "let there be a healthy mind in a healthy body." Of good and beautiful figures, with beautiful colors).[1]
Ashmolean Museum, Oxford, Presented by the Art Fund, 1936 WA1936.46

THIS OBJECT IS REMARKABLE in at least two respects: not only does it contain the only secure drawings by any member of the three-generation Della Robbia workshop, but it is also a rare example of Renaissance drawings that survive together with a contract for a work of art.[2] Study of these drawings in connection with the related language of the contract, therefore, provides exceptional, if limited, insight into the process of commissioning sculpture in the Italian Renaissance.

The sheet is inscribed and drawn on both sides. On the recto, the Latin text of the contract, written in Rome on 4 June 1524, appears beneath a highly finished drawing of the glazed terracotta tondo that Fra Mattia della Robbia agrees to make for his client, the apostolic notary Alberto Serra. Both the language of the text and its orientation on the page indicate that it was composed after the making of the drawing, which in turn is an integral part of the contractual document: in the second line, Fra Mattia promises "to construct and to make the figures drawn above" ("*construere et facere figuras supra designatas*"). This language helps to explain the painstaking composition of the drawing. Ink wash is used to model the bodies of the central figures and the heads of the cherubs, and even the individual leaves of the botanical garland are delineated. The two circular frames, furthermore, were outlined with the assistance of a compass in order to make their

PROVENANCE

Cav. Gian-Carlo Rossi (Lugt 2212); Gutekunst sale, Stuttgart, 17 March 1886, lot 1450; John Postle Heseltine (Lugt 1507); Henry Oppenheimer (Lugt 1351); Christie, Manson & Woods sale, London, 13 July 1936, lot 162

LITERATURE

Gutekunst 1886, pp. 104–5, lot 1450; Gnoli 1889, pp. 82–85; Cruttwell 1902, p. 256; Marquand 1928, pp. 23–29; Christie, Manson & Woods 1936, lot 162; Parker 1956, pp. 361–62, no. 669; Annamaria Petrioli Tofani in Berti 1980, p. 112, no. 201; Ian Wardropper in Eisler 1981, no. 4; Gentilini 1992, vol. 2, p. 375; Olson 1993, pp. 41–43; Alfredo Bellandi in Gentilini 1998, p. 324; Olson 2000, pp. 69–70

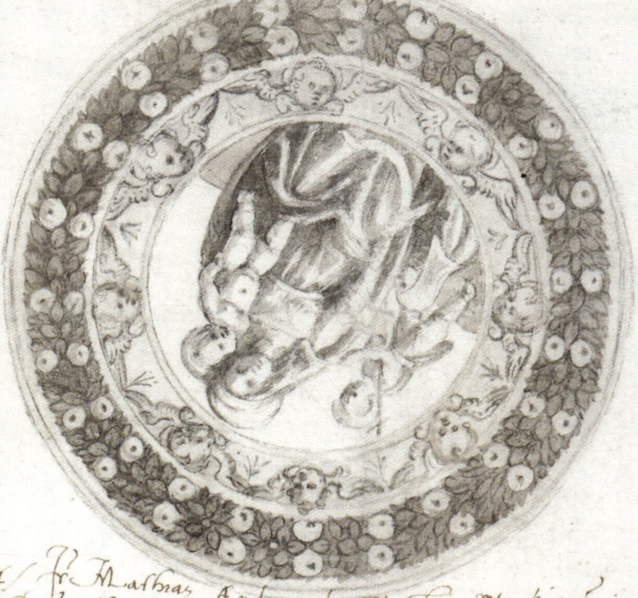

Die quarta Junii 1524 / Fr. Mathias Andree de Florentia or.ms S. Dnci sponte promisit d. Alberto ~~[illegible]~~
Serra Curie Car. Came ap.ce ~~[illegible]~~ [illegible] meos ei construere et facere ~~figuras~~ figuras supra designatas
de terra dicta Creta Cocta inuitriata et Smaltata de bonis +et finis ac sufficientibus coloribus juxta predesignatum
designum et melius in apparentia, ita quod vanum ~~[illegible]~~ sit latitudinis Palmorum trium et festonus cum
Cherubinis sit alterius palmi cum uno quarto et quas figuras promisit facere de terra bona infra quindecim
dies et illas ostendere factas ex fresco. infra idem tempus ac subinde easdem inuitriare smaltare coquere
et perficere ac eidem d. Alberto hic in urbe ad domum habi.nis sue consignare infra unum alium mensem
cum [illegible] exinde sequentem alias teneri voluit ad restitutionem infrascripte pecunie ~~ad~~ et ad penam dupli alias ac omnia
damna et Q + Premissa fecit et facere promisit dictus Fr. Mathias pro pretio et solutione ducatorum duodecim
auri de ~~Camera~~ largorum quos dictus d. Albertus eidem solvit in pnta [illegible] et de quibus [illegible] Pro quibus [illegible]
etiam ea que in generali obligatione non veniunt nec comprehenduntur et sub penis Came aplice obligavit
cum jurato et consti.ne procuratorum et in se omnes suscepit clausulas ecc.as cum mandato executivo contra
eum decernendo [illegible] Actum Rome in off.o [illegible] Dnis Gerardo [illegible] clerico [illegible]
[illegible] Reg[illegible] clerico [illegible] testibus

Jta est fr. mathias manu propria

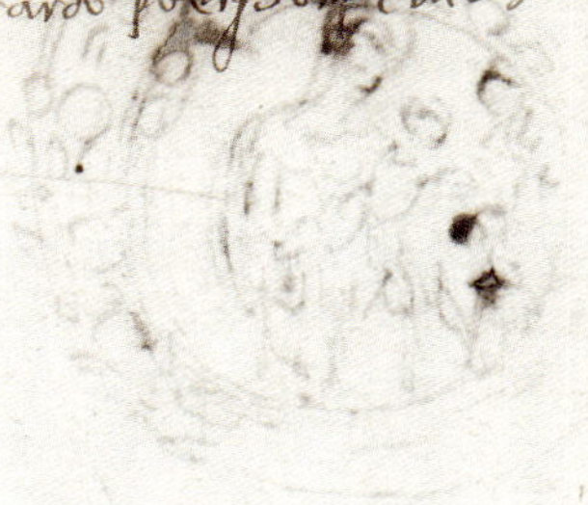

dimensions precise. This level of detail not only gave the patron a clear idea of what his sculpture would look like but also assured him of a minimum level of accomplishment in the finished sculpture. The presence of a finished drawing also meant that the contract need not address the details of the object's appearance in formal language. Not mentioned in the contract, for example, are the number, identity, and arrangement of the figures to be included in the tondo, likely because these issues are already made clear in the drawing above and in the notes on the verso.

The verso contains two smaller sketches as well as text in Italian. Near the top of the sheet is a chalk drawing of a portion of the double frame, which corresponds with the outlines of the frame on the recto. It seems possible that the borders of the frame were sketched first on the verso and then traced through on the recto, where Fra Mattia then drew a slightly different arrangement of fruit and foliage. This order of drawing would explain the strange disposition of the tondo as drawn on the recto: if Fra Mattia began the process of drawing on the recto by tracing through the portion of the frame that he had already drawn on the verso, it seems likely that he would orient the sheet so that the portion to be traced through was facing his own body.

On the bottom left of the verso is another depiction of the tondo, quickly drawn in pen and ink. This freer sketch seems to precede the more formal composition on the recto. The frames are briefly suggested and uneven in width, and the figures are only summarily defined. An inscription in Italian below identifies the size of the tondo and the figures to be included: "The Madonna, the son, St. John the Baptist, a nun of St. Sixtus." The nun is to hold a scroll with a quotation from Juvenal's *Satires*: *sit mens sana in corpore sano* ("let there be a healthy mind in a healthy body").

Both these words and the inclusion of a nun from a contemporary Roman church are unprecedented in a Della Robbia tondo. That the patron insisted on such specific features from a member of a workshop known for mass-producing glazed terracotta Virgin and Child reliefs may help explain the very existence of these drawings: Fra Mattia likely had no similar existing sculptures to use as visual models for his client's wishes.

The Italian inscription on the verso identifies the nun as *una monacha di Santo Sixto*, presumably referring to the community of St. Sixtus in Rome.[3] This was a Dominican order that dated to about 1220, when it was founded in Rome by St. Dominic himself.[4] It seems likely, therefore, that the tondo bears a connection to this order. Perhaps Serra had ties to the convent and commissioned the work, now lost, as a donation to the nuns' church. His choice of artist would be especially appropriate in this context: born Marco della Robbia, the sculptor took the name Fra Mattia when in 1496 he became a Dominican friar at the convent of San Marco in Florence.[5]

R.B.

NOTES

1 My transcriptions and translations are based primarily on firsthand examination of the document in the Ashmolean. I have also consulted the different transcriptions published in Marquand 1928, pp. 27–29, and Parker 1956, pp. 360–61, and the translation by Ian Wardropper in Eisler 1981, n.p. I would like to thank Barbara Weiden Boyd and Michael Cole for their kind advice and assistance with the transcriptions and translations.

2 On the general scarcity of extant plastic or drawn models that can securely be connected with specific contracts, see O'Malley 2005, p. 197, and Glasser 1977, p. 121.

3 Roberta Olson has interpreted the nun instead as a Franciscan (Olson 2000, p. 70).

4 The order was the first convent to follow the Rule of St. Sixtus (McOmber 1997, p. 34) and was housed originally in the Church of St. Sixtus, now known as San Sisto Vecchio (Pagano 1994, pp. 7–8).

5 According to the *Liber vestitionum dal 1491 al 1681* in the Archivio di San Marco, Marco della Robbia became Fra Mattia in 1496. The relevant passage is transcribed in Marquand 1928, p. 3.

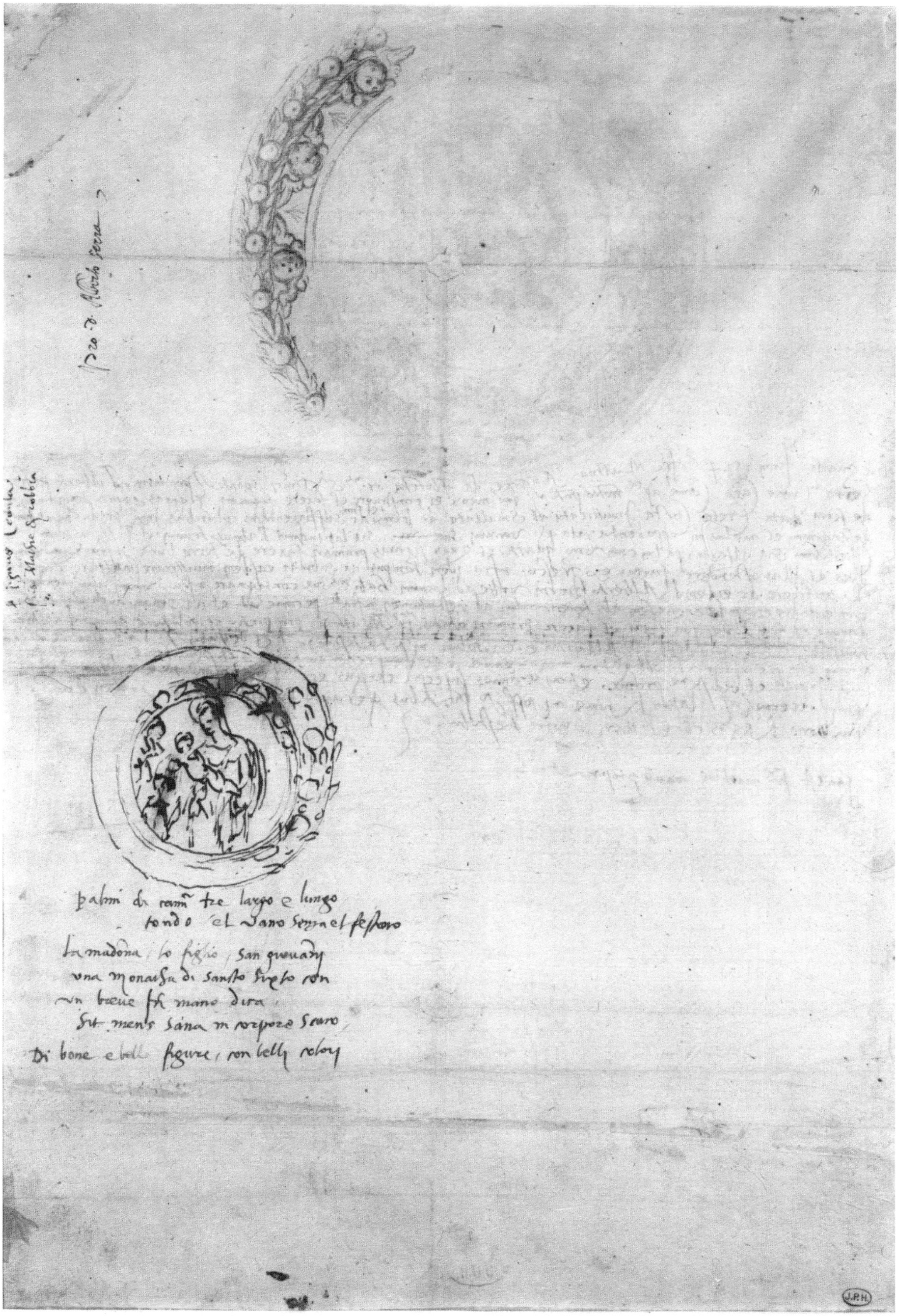
palmi di ram̃ tre largo e lungo
tondo el vano serra el fessoro
la madona, lo figlio, san giovanni
una monacha di sancto sixto con
un breue in mano dira
sit mens sana in corpore sano
Di bone e belle figure, con belli colori

18

BACCIO BANDINELLI

Florence, 1493 – Florence, 1560

Hercules (recto); *Two studies of Hercules' head* (verso), 1525–26

Pen and brown ink with rubbed red chalk on verso, 384 × 220 mm (15⅛ × 8¹¹⁄₁₆ in.)
Paper reinforcements on verso
Inscribed in the hand of Jonathan Richardson, Sr., on a piece of mount attached at the bottom of the drawing on the recto: *B. Bandinelli*; inscribed in the hand of William Gibson on the verso: *di Baccio Bandinelli* and *8.3* (a possible reference to the drawing's price in crowns)[1]
Christ Church Picture Gallery, Oxford 0085

IN 1523 Bandinelli entered into a contract for a block of Carrara marble that he would eventually carve into the *Hercules and Cacus* installed outside the Palazzo Vecchio (fig. 49).[2] Bandinelli's initial design, known from a surviving wax model in Berlin, showed Hercules subduing Cacus under his knee and raising his club to deal the fatal blow (see fig. 44).[3] During the marble block's tumultuous transport to Florence, Bandinelli discovered that it was too small to accommodate his intended composition.[4] According to Vasari, he made new models to present to his patron, Pope Clement VII, and "one pleased the Pope more than the others, in which Hercules had Cacus between his legs, and grabbing him by the hair he held him in the guise of a prisoner."[5]

The Christ Church drawing belongs to this new phase of sculptural designs, as it shows the figure of Hercules in a pose that correlates to the completed sculpture.[6] Its authorship has not been questioned since a reference to it was first published in 1914, and Christopher Lloyd dated the drawing between 1525 and 1526, after the marble block arrived in Florence but before the Medici were exiled from the city in 1527.[7]

The recto of the sheet shows Hercules with a wide stance as he wields a club in his right hand. Here Bandinelli continued to negotiate Hercules' pose, leaving his arm incomplete below the bicep. Curvilinear strokes and hatching above Hercules' left shoulder indicate the cancellation of earlier contour lines. Michael Wiemers raised the possibility that these curved lines suggest a cape, which seems unlikely, as it would cover Hercules' heroic nudity from behind.[8]

Roger Ward has rightly argued that the Christ Church drawing develops an idea from a red-chalk drawing in the Louvre (156), previously considered a copy but more recently deemed autograph.[9] The Louvre sheet shows Hercules in a similar pose but with several short lines near his left hand, which Ward has interpreted as a rope, concluding that Bandinelli may have envisaged a bound Cacus.[10] If Vasari is correct that Clement VII chose from multiple models, the Louvre sheet could, alternatively, represent a preparatory design for a different model. Whatever the case, Bandinelli reconceived it to formulate Hercules' pose in the Christ Church sheet. The incompleteness of Hercules' arm suggests that Bandinelli had not yet decided how to situate Cacus.[11] The horizontal hatches above Hercules' feet imply the positioning of a base but do not indicate its actual shape.

On the verso of the sheet Bandinelli represented Hercules' head twice, recalling the numerous adjacent studies of heads in his oeuvre, a technique that allowed Bandinelli to test poses and consider different aspects of a sculpture.[12] The head on the left is carefully resolved with hatching. The head on the right is composed of looser lines and minimal hatching, but it faithfully replicates the head adjacent to it, evidenced in the fine lines along the brow and cheeks. Both heads show Hercules' downward-oriented gaze, which Bandinelli changed to an outward orientation in the final sculpture.[13] R.C.

PROVENANCE

William Gibson (d. 1703; Lugt Suppl. 2885); Jonathan Richardson, Sr. (1665–1745; Lugt 2184); General J. Guise

LITERATURE

Bell 1914, p. 27, no. C4; Lloyd 1969, pp. 373–74; Byam Shaw 1976, vol. 1, pp. 58–59, no. 89, vol. 2, pls. 69, 70; Bush 1980, p. 179, note 68; Ward 1982a, pp. 343–44; Ward 1988, pp. 49–51, no. 26; Myssok 1999, pp. 250, 252; Wiemers 2000, pp. 247–48; Viatte 2011, pp. 152, 155, 157

NOTES

1 Byam Shaw 1976, vol. 1, p. 59.
2 Waldman 2004, pp. 66–68.
3 On this model, see Schmidt 1996, pp. 100–103; Greve 2008, pp. 123–31.
4 Vasari-Milanesi 1906, vol. 6, p. 150. The transport of the block to Florence, its fall into and recovery from the Arno River, and Bandinelli's visit to Rome are described in contemporary documents (Waldman 2004, pp. 78–79, 81–83).
5 *Fatti addunque più modelli, uno più degli altri ne piacque al Papa, dove Ercole aveva Cacco fra le gambe, e presolo pe' capelli, lo teneva sotto a guisa di prigione*: Vasari-Milanesi 1906, vol. 6, p. 151. Vasari's description coincides with the final version of the sculpture, unveiled in 1534.
6 Ward (1982a, p. 344) has identified two copies after this drawing in the Kupferstich-kabinett, Dresden (C.66), and in the Musée du Louvre (182).
7 Lloyd 1969, pp. 373–74, note 7. Lloyd assigns 1526 as a terminus post quem for the drawing on the basis of Vasari's report that Bandinelli had begun carving the statue before the Medici were exiled.
8 Wiemers 2000, p. 248.
9 Ward 1988, p. 50. Cf. Viatte 2011, pp. 152–54.
10 Ward 1988, p. 50.
11 Lloyd 1969, p. 373.
12 Ward has brought attention to a drawing in the Stockholm Nationalmuseum (128) that shows a similar-looking pair of adjacent faces (1993, pp. 395–96).
13 Ward 1988, p. 51.

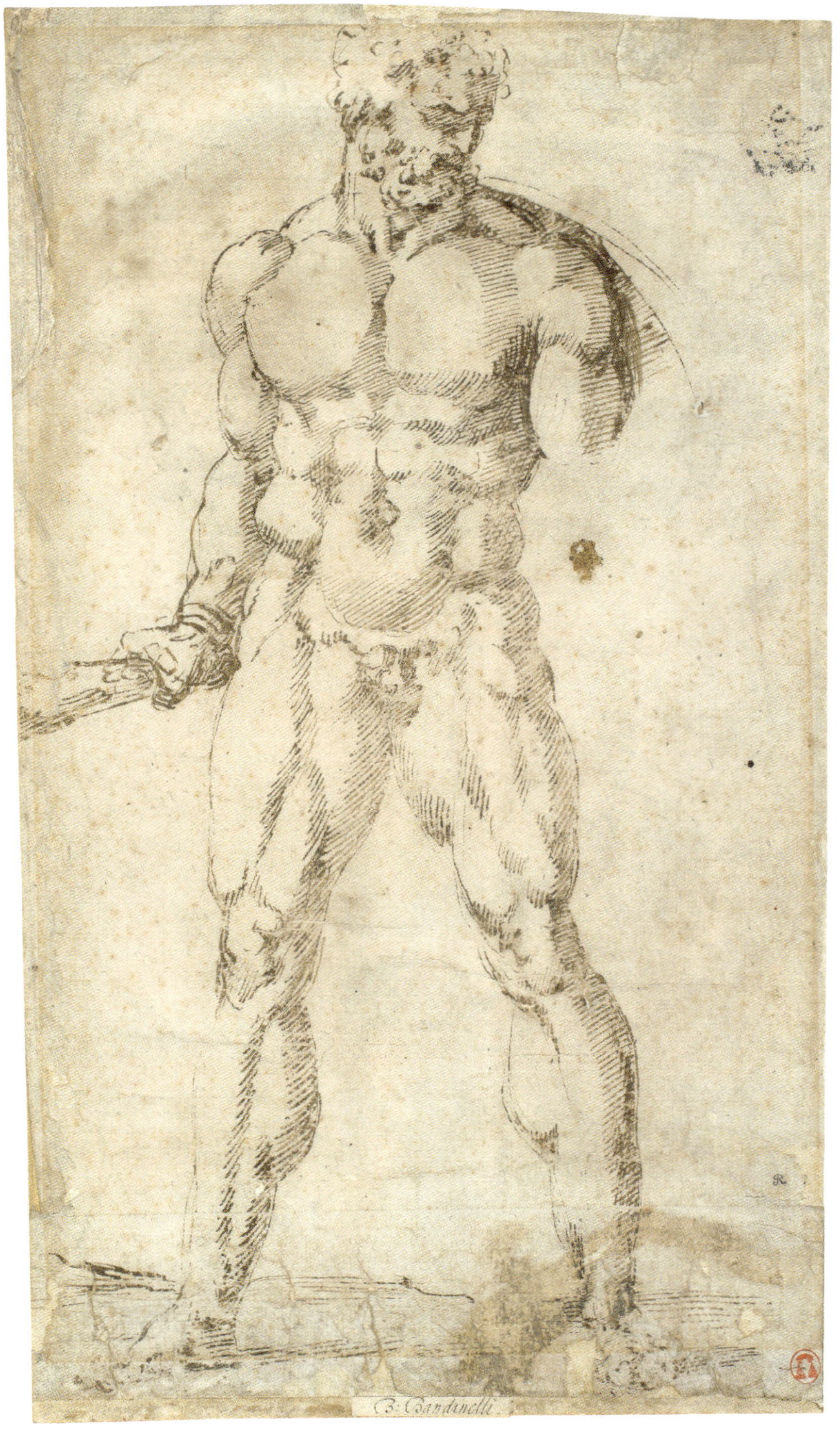
B: Bandinelli

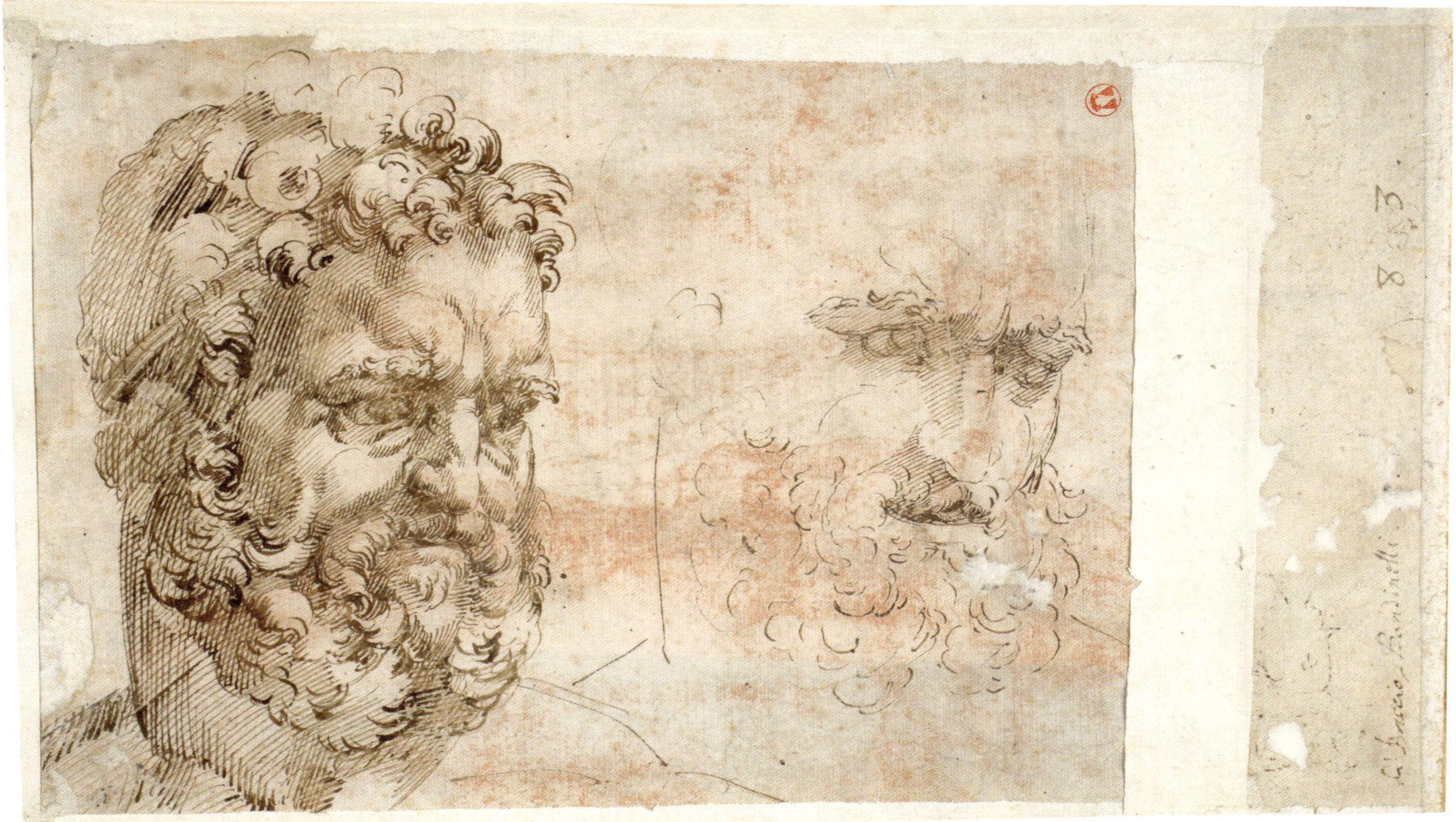

19

BACCIO BANDINELLI

Florence, 1493 – Florence, 1560

Hercules from a side view, 1525–26

Red chalk, 403 × 196 mm (15⅞ × 7¾ in.)
Gabinetto Disegni e Stampe degli Uffizi, Florence 520F

IN THIS STUDY for the *Hercules and Cacus* sculptural group (see also cat. 18 and 20), Bandinelli explored the hero's pose from a side view. An oblong shape represents the club in Hercules' unseen right hand, while a few short, curved lines adjacent to Hercules' left hand evoke a tuft of Cacus's hair—visible in the completed sculpture—implying the position of his vanquished opponent.[1]

Made using red chalk, the drawing has boldly rendered contour lines, as well as broad sections of even hatching that establish unmodulated shadows. The rapidity of execution in red chalk and the numerous lines around the figure's contours give credence to Johannes Myssok's suggestion that this drawing was made from a live model.[2] A separate sheet in pen and ink refines the musculature and shading of Hercules' legs from this viewpoint.[3] The vertical and horizontal lines made with a straightedge indicate a preoccupation with balancing the figure, as Roger Ward has rightly noted.[4]

Ward has proposed that this is the earliest extant drawing associated with Bandinelli's approved design for the *Hercules and Cacus* commission.[5] It seems more likely that Bandinelli first conceived the rather flat stance of Hercules from a frontal view in the Louvre and Christ Church sheets (see cat. 18). When incorporating Cacus and the Hercules together in a different drawing in the Uffizi (cat. 20), Bandinelli recognized the need to extend Hercules' left leg backward to create space for his defeated foe. This side-view drawing, in turn, elaborated the solution of Hercules' forward stance to accommodate Cacus. It seems probable that Bandinelli returned to a live model in order to render Hercules' amended pose accurately. R.C.

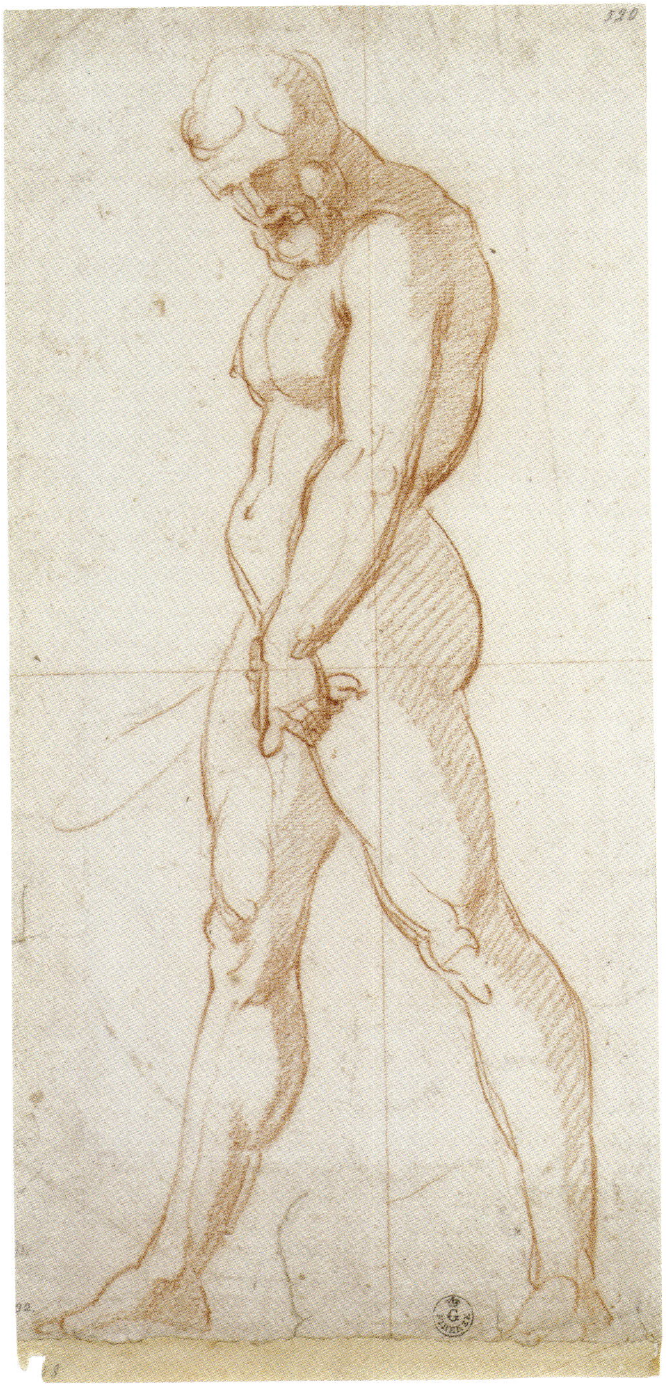

LITERATURE

Ciardi Duprè 1966, p. 169, note 34; Bush 1980, p. 179, note 68; Ward 1982a, p. 220; Ward 1988, p. 50; Myssok 1999, pp. 249–50; Wiemers 2000, p. 248

NOTES

1 Wiemers 2000, p. 248.
2 Myssok 1999, p. 249.
3 Ward 1982a, pp. 220–21.
4 Ward 1988, p. 50.
5 Ward 1988, p. 50; see also Bush 1980, p. 179, note 68; Myssok 1999, pp. 249–50.

20

BACCIO BANDINELLI
Florence, 1493 – Florence, 1560

Hercules and Cacus (recto); *Studies of three heads and two arms* (verso), 1525–26

Pen and brown ink, 399 × 281 mm (15¾ × 11¹/₁₆ in.)
Inscribed on verso in pencil, pen and brown ink: *6* and *Bandinelli* and *Bandinelli 714E*
Gabinetto Disegni e Stampe degli Uffizi, Florence 714E

THIS SHEET shows an advanced design for Bandinelli's sculpture of *Hercules and Cacus.*

The interlocking figures on the recto correspond closely to the final version of the sculpture, suggesting that this is a relatively late-stage preparatory drawing for the model that the pope would subsequently approve.[1] Bandinelli's authorship of the drawing has gone largely unchallenged, and Roger Ward dated it to 1526.[2]

The recto of the Uffizi sheet unites separately developed designs for Hercules and Cacus, such as the figure of Hercules in the Christ Church sheet (cat. 18). A wiry line near Hercules' left arm indicates that Bandinelli shifted the arm and Cacus's head closer to Hercules' body, creating a more closed composition, as presumably necessitated by the marble block.[3] The drawing corresponds to a diagonal viewing axis roughly from the northwest corner of the Piazza della Signoria, which was considered the primary viewpoint of both the Palazzo Vecchio and its adjacent sculptures throughout the Renaissance.[4]

Bandinelli may have established the poses shown in this drawing with the use of sculptural or live models (or both).[5] The image reveals a careful attempt to reconcile the frontal view of Hercules elaborated in drawings with the three-dimensional form the sculpture would ultimately take. Hercules seems to have first been drawn with fine contour lines, after which point Cacus was added. These contour lines are most visible in areas where the figures overlap. Hercules' left foot is unresolved, as it would occupy the area that belongs to Cacus's hand. The drawing reveals the problem created by Hercules' relatively flat stance once Bandinelli opted to position Cacus between his legs.

The verso of the sheet shows three studies of Cacus's head from various perspectives.[6] At the base of the sheet are two arms that correspond to the figure of Cacus on the recto: the extended arm is similar to his right arm, while the arm bent backwards may be related to his left arm. These arms seem to derive from artworks Bandinelli made shortly before designing the *Hercules and Cacus* sculpture. Bandinelli had carved a marble copy of the ancient Roman sculptural group *Laocoön and His Sons*, and the bent arm in the drawing is a close approximation of the left arm of Laocoön.[7] The extended arm and its adjoining musculature seem a direct quotation of a figure in the right foreground of Bandinelli's design for *The Martyrdom of St. Lawrence*, preserved in prints but never executed.[8] The development of Cacus's arms in the sheet is not final; in the completed sculpture, Cacus holds a club in his right hand and rests his left hand on a tree stump. R.C.

LITERATURE

Ferri 1890, p. 30; Venturi 1901, vol. 10-2, p. 199; Delacre 1938, pp. 96–97; *Mostra del Cinquecento* 1940, pp. 169–70; Barocchi et al. 1963, pp. 19–20, no. 7; Ciardi Duprè 1966, p. 169, note 34; Weinberger 1967, vol. 1, p. 248; Lloyd 1969, pp. 373–74; Monbeig-Goguel 1971, pp. 87–88; Weil-Garris 1974, p. 80, note 247; Bush 1976, pp. 128–29; Byam Shaw 1976, vol. 1, p. 59; Carroll 1976, vol. 2, p. 541; Bush 1980, p. 179; Ward 1982a, pp. 260–61; Ward 1988, pp. 50–51; Myssok 1999, pp. 251–52; Wiemers 2000, p. 253; Viatte 2011, p. 152

NOTES

1 Ward 1988, p. 50.
2 Ward 1982a, p. 261. Virginia Bush labels the drawing "After (?) Bandinelli" (1980, fig. 22).
3 Myssok 1999, p. 249.
4 Weinberger 1967, p. 248; Ward 1988, p. 50. On the importance of this diagonal view of the Piazza della Signoria, see Trachtenberg 1997, pp. 87–147.
5 In a different pen-and-ink drawing in the Uffizi (518F), Bandinelli renders Cacus in a related pose from both the front and back; Myssok suggests this drawing was made from a sculptural model (1999, p. 251). Ward proposes that the Christ Church sheet is likely based on a sculptural model. See Ward 1982a, p. 260; Ward 1988, p. 50.
6 Ward 1982a, p. 260.
7 Vasari reports that Bandinelli's sculpture of *Laocoön and His Sons* was installed in Palazzo Medici in 1525 (Vasari-Milanesi 1906, vol. 6, p. 146).
8 For the prints by Marcantonio Raimondi and others, see Bartsch 1978, vol. 26, pp. 135–38. In the prints, the figure is oriented in the inverse direction of the arm in the Uffizi sheet. A drawing of disputed authorship in the Uffizi (526F) thought to be related to *The Martyrdom of St. Lawrence* shows a similarly extended arm (Ciardi-Duprè 1966, p. 169; Ward 1982a, pp. 221–22; Louis Waldman in Franklin 2005, p. 258).

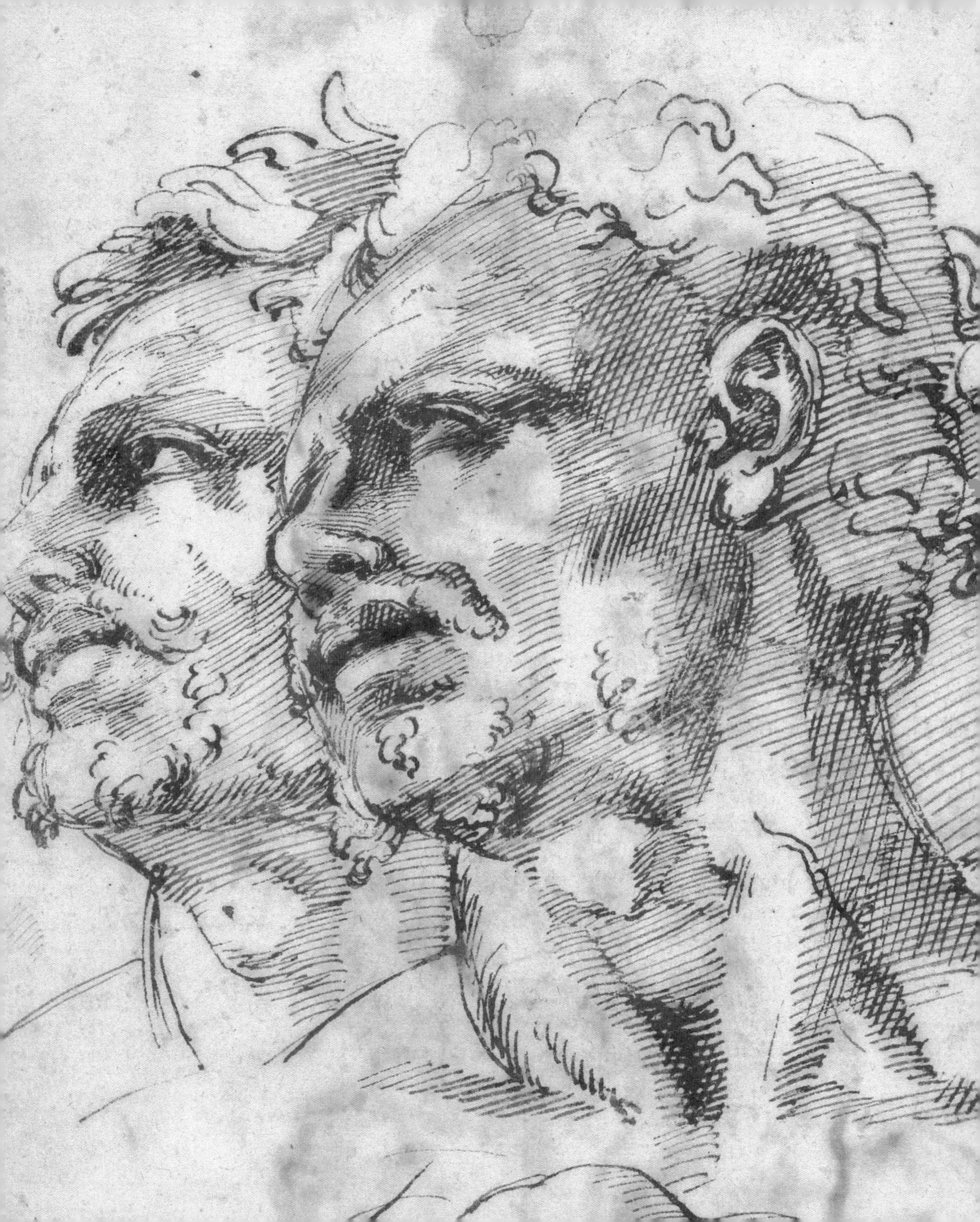

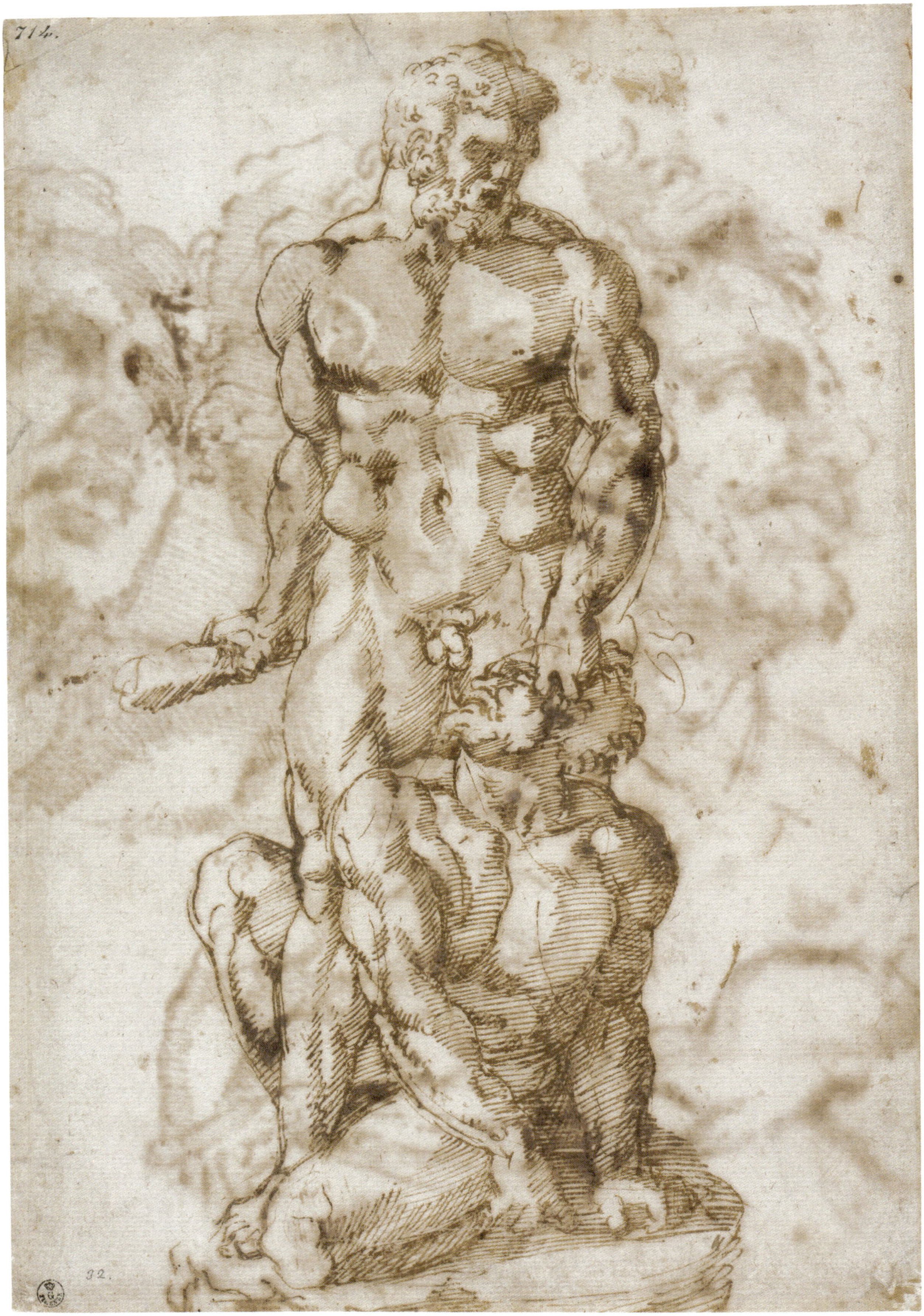
714.
32.

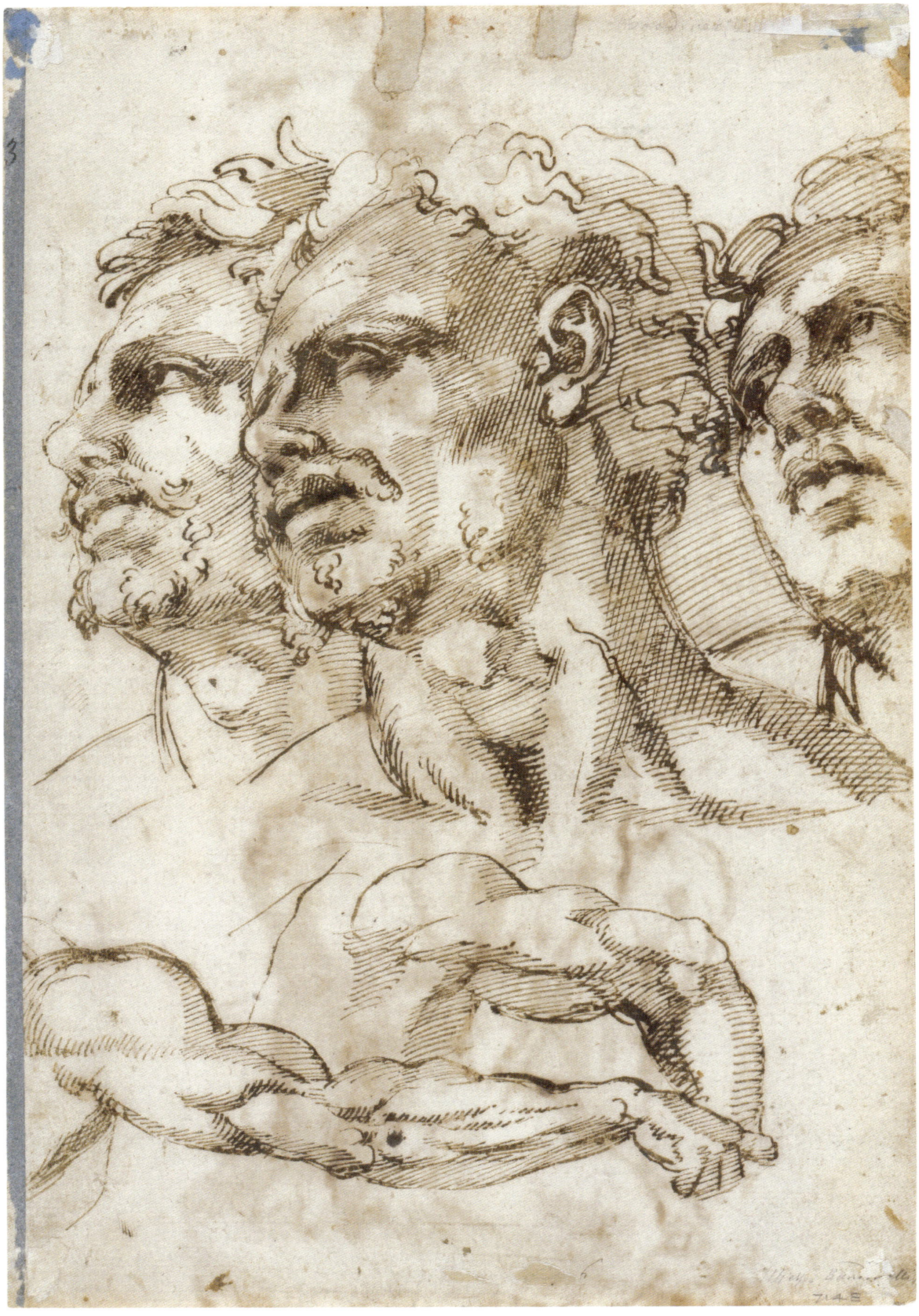

21

BACCIO BANDINELLI

Florence, 1493 – Florence, 1560

The Deposition, 1525–30

Pen and light and dark brown ink, brush and gray wash, 383 × 281 mm (15⅛ × 11 1/16 in.)
Inscribed, lower right, in pen and ink: *hı* (?), probably the shelf mark of Lord John Somers (Lugt 2981), and *amc*, the collector's mark of Arthur Melville Champernowne (Lugt 153); also stamped with the marks of Nicholas Lanier (Lugt 2885), Pierre-Jean Mariette (Lugt 1852), and Sir Joshua Reynolds (Lugt 2364); inscribed at center of mount in pen and brown ink: *Baccio Bandinelli*
Private collection, New York

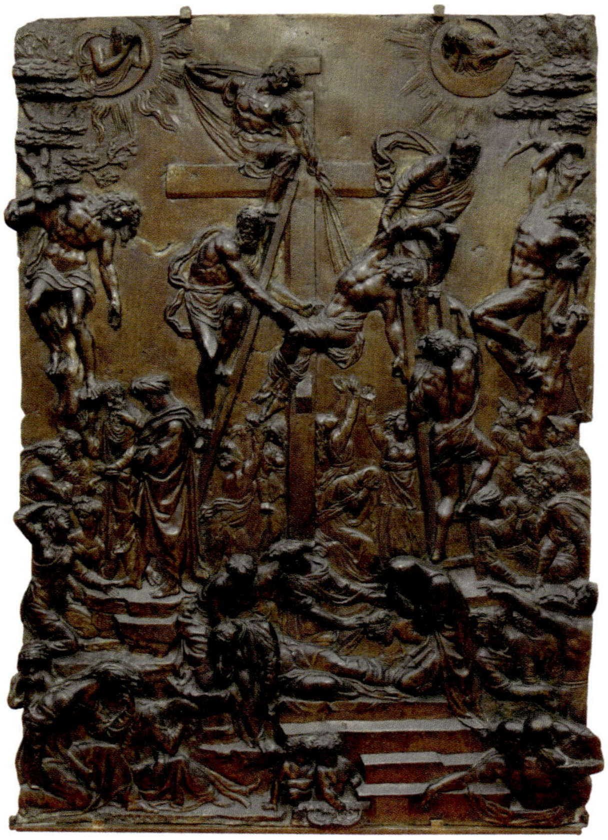

IN THIS DRAWING, two figures strain to support Christ's lifeless body from behind the cross; a third, possibly John the Evangelist, perched precariously on the adjacent ladder, extracts the nail securing Christ's feet. Three women appear on the left, while the Virgin sits firmly planted at the base of the cross. Vasari refers to three projects from the second half of the 1520s to which the drawing may relate: two cartoons Bandinelli made in preparation for non-extant paintings, one of the dead Christ surrounded "by the Marys, with Nicodemus and other figures" and another of "Christ taken down from the Cross" with an angel who holds "the Nails and the Crown of Thorns," as well as a bronze relief for Charles V.[2] Although that relief does not survive, either, a bronze copy by Antonio Susini and Girolamo Portigiani in the Louvre (fig. 63) and a plaster *modello* presumed to be by Bandinelli in San Marino (fig. 64) do.[3]

Though this drawing is usually connected with the project for Charles V, neither the oblique viewpoint (possibly inspired by Donatello's *Lamentation* relief on the north pulpit of San Lorenzo,

FIG. 63
Antonio Susini and Girolamo Portigiani
after Baccio Bandinelli
The Deposition, 1578–79
Bronze, 65 × 46.5cm
Musée du Louvre, Paris

PROVENANCE

Nicholas Lanier, London (1588–1666); Cardinal Gaspare Antonio Cavaliere (?), bishop of Capua; Padre Sebastiano Resta (1635–1714); Lord John Somers (1651–1716); probably his sale, Motteux of Covent Garden, London, 16 May 1717; bought by an agent (?) of Pierre Crozat, Paris (1665–1740); Pierre-Jean Mariette, Paris (1694–1774); Sir Joshua Reynolds, London (1723–1792); Arthur Melville Champernowne, Totnes, South Devon (1871–1946); private collection; sale, Sotheby's, London, 9 April 1981, lot 74; P. & D. Colnaghi and Co. Ltd., London; Daniel Katz Ltd., London; W.M. Brady & Co., Inc., New York, 1998[1]

LITERATURE

Colnaghi 1982, no. 4; Ward 1982a, pp. 305–6, no. 224; Ward 1982b, pp. 26, 29, 37ff.; Kathleen Weil-Garris in Darr 1985, p. 244; Ward 1988, p. 112, no. 27; Cox-Rearick 1989, pp. 53, 56; Cox-Rearick 1993, pp. 173–75; Brady 1999, no. 2; Sørensen 1999, pp. 200, 202; Rhoda Eitel-Porter in Grasselli and Robison 2007, pp. 173–75; Hegener 2008, pp. 290, 341 ff., 369–70, 624, no. 46; Gregory 2012, p. 188

NOTES

1 Ward 1982a, p. 305, and Rhoda Eitel-Porter in Grasselli and Robison 2007, pp. 173–75.
2 Vasari-de Vere 1912–15, vol. 2, pp. 277–79; Vasari-Milanesi 1878–85, vol. 6, pp. 151–54.
3 On these reliefs, see most recently Viatte 2011, pp. 284–87, and Heikamp and Paolozzi Strozzi 2014, pp. 298–301.
4 Ward has noted a connection with a Marcantonio Raimondi engraving after a Raphael painting (Bartsch 1978, vol. 26, p. 47, no. 32), and Weil-Garris, Cox-Rearick, and Eitel-Porter noted precedents in Donatello's sculpture. See Ward 1982a, p. 305; Kathleen Weil-Garris in Darr 1985, pp. 244–46; Cox-Rearick 1993, pp. 173–75; and Rhoda Eitel-Porter in Grasselli and Robison 2007, pp. 173–75.

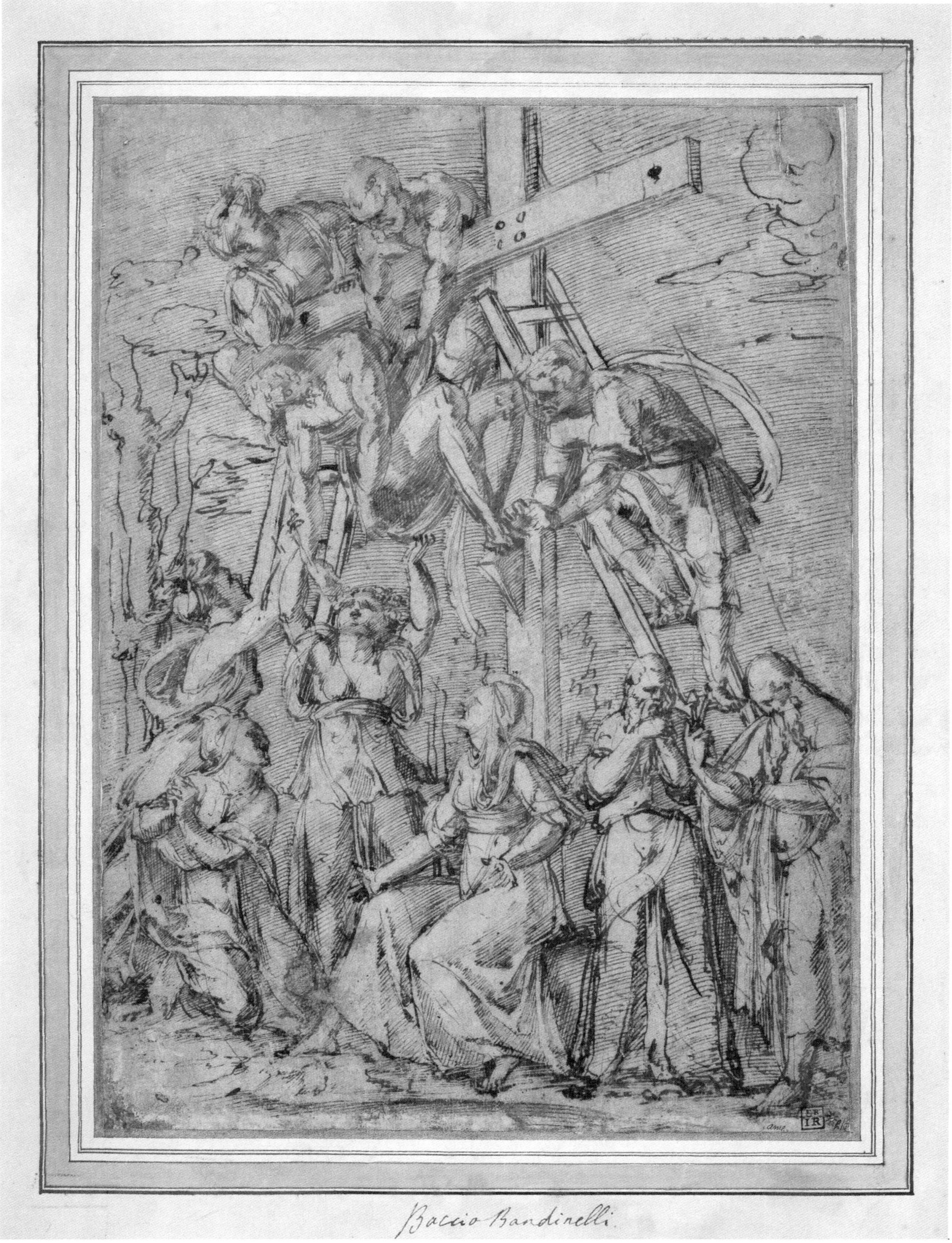
Baccio Bandinelli

Florence) nor the figures' poses correspond to the surviving reliefs.[4] The two women who raise their arms on the drawing's left are most closely related to the bronze, though even they differ in their dress, hair, and pose. Certain elements, moreover, resemble those that seem to have been part of the cartoons but do not appear in the finished reliefs, notably the figures (here Nicodemus and Joseph of Arimathea rather than an angel) who contemplate the instruments of the Passion. Bandinelli's use of gray wash (in the wooden crossbeam and elsewhere) further distances the work from the sculptural project. And although the sheet appears to have been cut down, it remains unlikely that it was originally large enough to include the penitent and unrepentant thieves, stepped foreground, and multitude of teeming figures contained in the Louvre and San Marino reliefs.

However, Bandinelli does fill almost the entire sheet with hatched lines that eliminate depth and evoke the solidity of a sculptural plane. The use of two shades of ink—a light brown for the diagonal hatching and a darker brown for the contours—suggest the juxtaposition of high and low sculptural relief, as well as the metallic sheen of bronze. The hatched lines seem to have been added after those conveying contours, perhaps indicating that Bandinelli only decided to use the drawing as a study for sculptural purposes after he had resolved the composition. D.R.F.

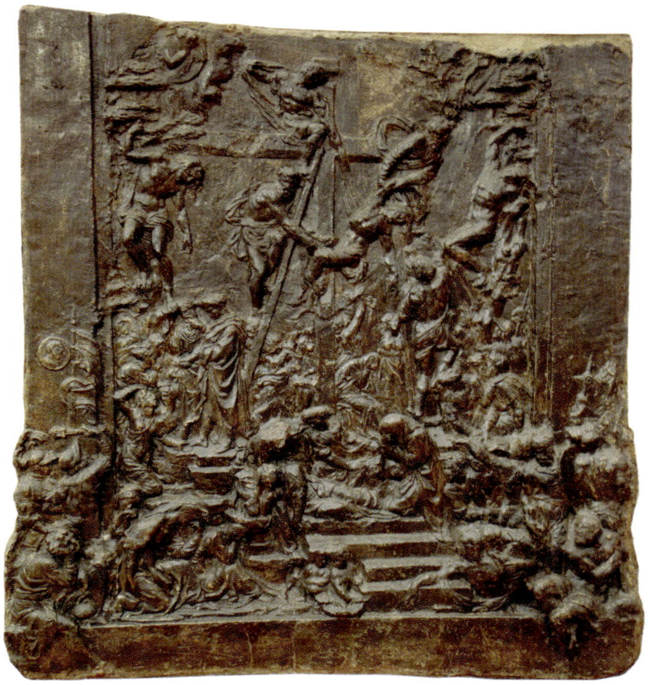

FIG. 64
After Baccio Bandinelli
The Deposition, 16th century
Plaster cast with traces of original bronzing, 76.8 × 74.5 cm
Museo di Stato della Repubblica di San Marino

22

ITALIAN, 16TH CENTURY (RAFFAELLO DA MONTELUPO?)
Montelupo Fiorentino, 1505 – Orvieto, c. 1567

Studies of a male torso, c. 1525–40

Pen and brown ink on gray-blue paper; 257 × 203 mm (10⅛ × 8 in.)
Annotated in two shades of pen and brown ink (the lighter ink showing signs of water damage), partly in lobed field, across lower edge of sheet: *perché da un amore facto o mai / si certo [q]ual manifesta cer / tanza ne può senza tentar / san pena* [?]. . . ~~*chon parole esc.*~~ / *con parole escolto* [*ascolto*] *disscerco* [?] / *angelo*
National Gallery of Art, Washington, D.C., Andrew W. Mellon Fund 1978.52.1

THE MUSCULAR NUDE MALE TORSO drawn twice on this sheet is probably a fragment of an antique sculpture (it loosely recalls but is not identical to the Apollo Belvedere) or, conceivably, a small-scale model based on an ancient prototype. Similar torsos litter the ground in an engraved portrait of Bandinelli by Niccolò della Casa dated 1548 (fig. 65), and variants, limbless but not decapitated, appear in Della Casa's earlier engraved portrait of the sculptor[1] and in Enea Vico's print of Bandinelli's Academy (cat. 38). As a principal component of their instruction the pupils in this academy made drawings after such models, both entire figures and fragments: they are shown industriously engaged in this task in Vico's print and in an earlier engraving of Bandinelli's academy by Agostino Veneziano (see fig. 43), and the large surviving, widely dispersed corpus of drawings of nude figures, heads, and dismembered body parts—some examples by Bandinelli himself and numerous others generically classified as "school of Bandinelli"—is material testimony of this practice.[2]

The torso at the left has what appears to be a hole at the top of the sternum. If the object is a model, this could be the aperture for an internal support that would have enabled it to be displayed upright (as some of the models are seen in the earlier of the two Della Casa engraved portraits and in Vico's print). Following this interpretation, the lobed forms below may be a quick sketch of the outline of the model's base, the circles in the center and the right side indicating recesses for inserting vertical support rods.[3] Alternatively, the profile may represent a plaque or cartouche intended to be affixed to the bust at the top of the breastbone, where a *cartellino*-like ornament with a central link or hole and a suspended pendant or medallion (?) is indicated. Inscribed within the field in the same ink as the drawing and presumably in the draftsman's hand are the partially legible verses of a convoluted love sonnet, written—as the use of *chon* for *con* signals—in Tuscan.[4] That the lines of verse are only partly accommodated within the field suggests that this base or frame was drawn first and the

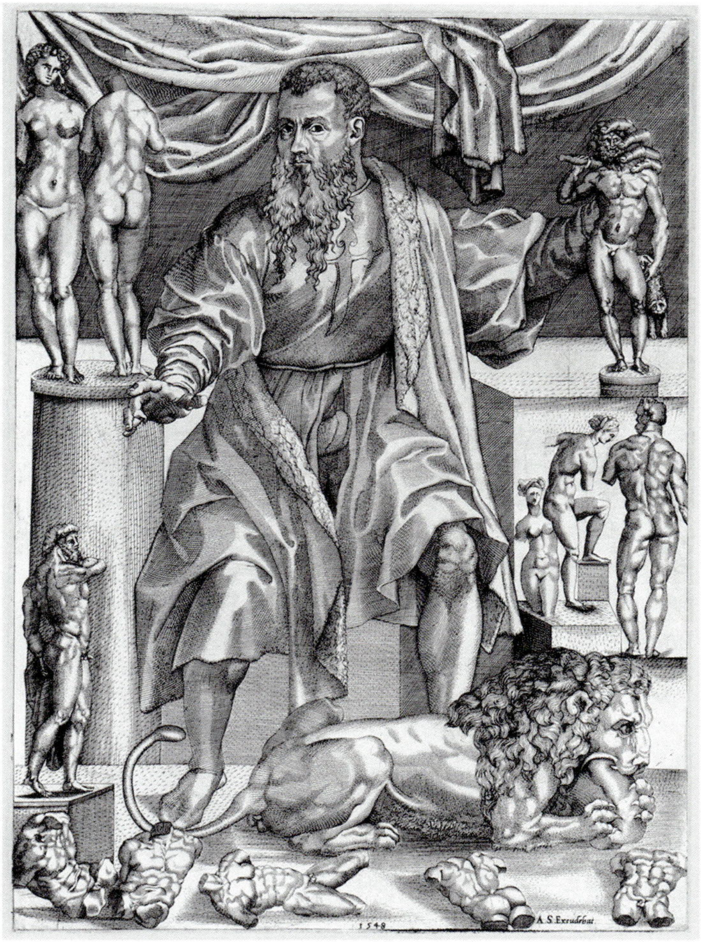

FIG. 65
Niccolò della Casa
Baccio Bandinelli, 1548
Engraving, 412 × 304 mm
Los Angeles County Museum of Art

PROVENANCE

Mrs. E.E. James; sale, Sotheby's, London, 16 May 1962, lot 161, as Bandinelli; bought by Williams; Hans Calmann, London, by 1965; David Daniels, New York, 1965 (sale, Sotheby's, London, 25 April 1978, lot 16); David Tunick, New York, from whom purchased by the National Gallery of Art

LITERATURE

Pillsbury 1974, no. 10

words added in and around it. Although the fragmentary sonnet has no immediately obvious relation to the image, the power of ancient sculpture—and specifically an idealized fragmentary torso—to fuel amatory passion was something of a poetic conceit in the sixteenth century, evidenced in an account of Michelangelo having fallen in love with the Belvedere torso.[5] The inscription *angelo* in what appears to be a different, perhaps slightly later hand, and in a different colored ink, at the lower edge of the sheet may record an old (untenable) attribution of the drawing, or perhaps the poem, to Michelangelo himself.

The hard, angular contours and webs of short, choppy strokes evocative of chisel marks, as well as the manner in which the neutral space around the torsos is filled in with incisive hatching that serves to highlight the plasticity of the drawn forms, are tell-tale indications that this sheet, whoever its author, is a sculptor's drawing.[6] (The former attribution to Bandinelli corroborates this supposition.) One possible candidate is the sculptor and architect Raffaello da Montelupo, a pupil and occasional assistant of Michelangelo who also worked in Bandinelli's orbit at times during his long career. In his fragmentary autobiography, Raffaello recounted that, like Michelangelo and the painter Sebastiano del Piombo, he was by nature left-handed, but unlike them and much to their astonishment (in a departure from accepted practice of the time) was allowed to write and draw with his left hand in addition to being trained to use his right.[7] Some of the small number of surviving drawings by Raffaello reflect this manual dexterity in having both left-handed and right-handed hatching—a feature evident in the present sheet and which provides grounds for a tentative attribution to him advanced here. The practiced *corsiva* script of the inscription differs from the informal and hurried handwriting seen in the sculptor's draft autobiography, but it is not impossible that the writing is by the same hand.

Close examination of the study of the torso at the left reveals passages where a second layer of dense hatching (some of it left-handed) has been added to give heightened definition to the anatomical forms. This is most evident around the right pectoral, the proper left side of the abdomen, and the uppermost part of the truncated left leg. With a few crude, quick strokes the torso was also made ithyphallic, a lewd detail partly obscured by the vigorous hatching. L.W-S.

NOTES

1 For which see Tommaso Mozzati in Heikamp and Paolozzi Strozzi 2014, pp. 524–25, no. 75.

2 An example of the former is a sheet of studies by Bandinelli in the Yale University Art Gallery depicting unrelated limbs and extremities together with two male heads (1975.101.10; see Boorsch and Marciari 2006, no. 2, repr.). A group of drawings in the Musée du Louvre, Paris, classified as "school of Bandinelli" (Viatte 2011, nos. 82–98)—presumably the production of this mysterious academy—are copies after such fragments and small-scale models.

3 As suggested by Luke Syson (verbal communication).

4 I owe this observation to Frank Dabell (written communication), who kindly corrected and clarified my transcription of the inscription. Further clarifications and interpretations of the hard-to-decipher text were offered by Michael Cole and Diletta Gamberini.

5 As pointed out by Ulrich Pfisterer (verbal communication).

6 As noted by Pillsbury 1974, no. 10, whose tentative attribution to Cellini can be rejected on stylistic grounds. Further militating against his authorship is the presence here of left-handed hatching, which is never present in Cellini's drawings, and the fact that the handwriting does not appear to be his, as Diletta Gamberini has confirmed (written communication).

7 Transcribed in Gatteschi 1998, p. 121.

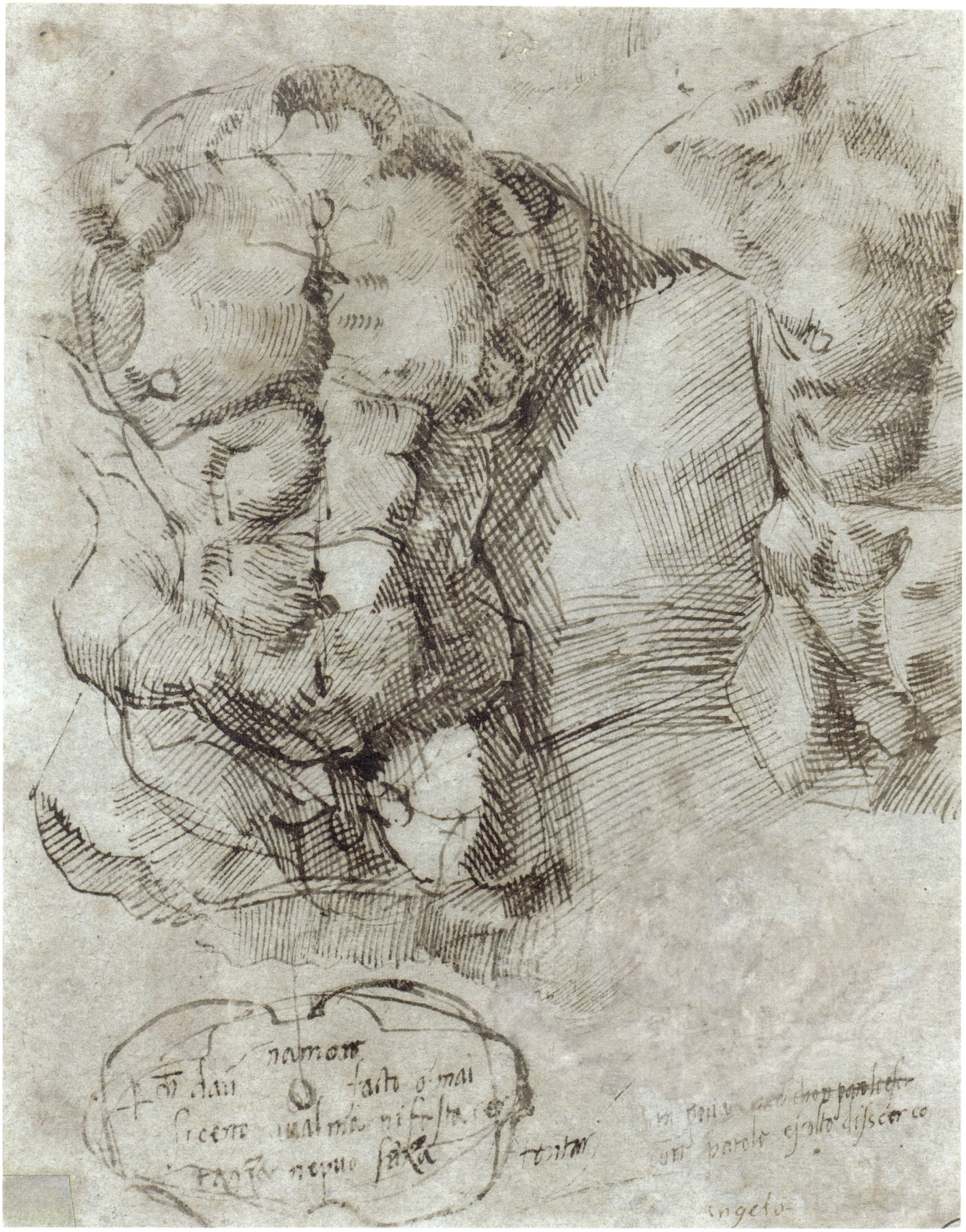

23

MICHELANGELO BUONAROTTI

Caprese, 1475 – Rome, 1564

The Pietà, 1540

Black chalk, on paper, 289 × 189 mm (11⅜ × 7 7/16 in.)
Inscribed (cut off at the top): *nonuisipensaquantosang* … [*Non vi si pensa quanto sangue costa* ("They do not think how much blood it costs"), Dante, *Paradiso*, Canto 29, 91]
Isabella Stewart Gardner Museum, Boston 1.2.0.16

THIS HIGHLY FINISHED GIFT DRAWING, executed by Michelangelo for his friend and patron Vittoria Colonna in 1540, is one of three such works by the artist depicting religious themes. Vittoria Colonna, the marchesa of Pescara, was one of the most learned women of her period. She and Michelangelo shared a religious sensibility, regularly exchanging letters and poems, and this drawing, with its conflation of two events from Christ's Passion, highlights their spiritual synergy.[1] The Virgin seeks consolation over the dead body of her son, while Christ takes meditative precedence at the front of the composition, echoing the visual and redemptive tradition of the Man of Sorrows. The inscription, now partly cut off, is taken from Canto 29 of Dante's *Paradiso* and refers to the scarcely acknowledged effort and pain of martyrs and others in spreading the true Gospel. Here, however, it can be seen to allude to Christ's blood and points to Michelangelo's and Colonna's belief in redemption through Christ's sacrifice.[2] Both were in close contact with Catholic Reformation thinkers. Colonna followed the popular preacher Bernardino Ochino and was an intimate of Cardinal Reginald Pole, who acted as her spiritual adviser. Though she remained a Catholic throughout her life, these drawings by Michelangelo reflect Colonna's fascination with Reformation ideas about personal faith as a means to salvation. Michelangelo had an ongoing fascination with the subject of the Pietà, beginning with his youthful marble version in St. Peter's in Rome (1499). His sculpted "Florentine" *Pietà* (1547–53), carved a few years after he made the Colonna drawing, demonstrates his continuing rethinking and reworking of the theme.[3]

The immediate appeal of this drawing, along with the others made for Colonna, and its importance to Michelangelo are evident both in the fact that Michelangelo made sure the gift was recorded in detail by his biographer Ascanio Condivi, and also in the number of copies that were made after it. The drawing was reproduced in several prints by such artists as Giulio Bonasone (1546) and Nicholas Béatrizet (1547), the design was also used in many paintings, and versions were made in marble and bronze,[4] ensuring its enduring popularity.

The relationship of the drawing with the versions in other media is not straightforward, and it is likely that the design was disseminated by allowing one or two other artists access to the original drawing, with their reproductions acting as channels for other versions to be made, often without any direct knowledge of the original. This is evident in the widely varying quality and accuracy of the copies.[5] Much like the many versions in multiple media made after the mythological presentation drawings Michelangelo had executed nearly a decade earlier, in 1532–33, for his young friend Tommaso de' Cavalieri,[6] the copies of Colonna's drawings demonstrate the byways by which Michelangelo's designs fed into, for example, small bronze production (cat. 24). Colonna's *Pietà* was primarily intended for her contemplation and pleasure, but multiple copies made in varying media ensured that Michelangelo's fame spread beyond the elite circles around her. M.L.

PROVENANCE

Vittoria Colonna, 1540; Casa Buonarroti, Florence; M. Brunet, Paris; Sir Thomas Lawrence (1769–1830); Samuel Woodburn (1780/5–1853), purchased 1834; Ensor, purchased 1860; Mr. Brooks; Francis Turner Palgrave (1827–1897), 1884; Sir John Charles Robinson (1824–1913), purchased 1886; purchased by Isabella Stewart Gardner through the dealer Thomas Agnew & Sons, London, 13 May 1902

LITERATURE

Woodburn 1836, p. 23, no. 64 (as a copy after Michelangelo; Condivi 1887, p. 202; Berenson 1938, vol. 2, p. 235 (as a copy after Michelangelo); De Tolnay 1953 (as Michelangelo); Hadley 1968, pp. 12–15, no. 7; Hartt 1970, p. 323, no. 455; Hausherr 1971, p. 10; Hadley 1981, pp. 64–65; Brandt 1991, pp. 10–30; Goldfarb 1991, p. 11; Goldfarb 1992, pp. 41–43; Harrmann Fiore, pp. 96–104; Goldfarb 1995, pp. 78–80; Nagel 1997; Ferino-Pagden 1997, pp. 426–28, no. IV.36; Schurr 2001, p. 133; Ciulich and Ragionieri 2002, p. 70; James M. Saslow in Chong and Lingner 2003, pp. 80–83; Chapman 2005, pp. 249–57; Ragionieri 2005, pp. 151–55; Forcellino 2009, pp. 64–75; Forcellino 2011

NOTES

1 James M. Saslow in Chong and Lingner 2003, pp. 80–83. Concerning gift giving between Mighelangelo and Colonna, see Nagel 1997, esp. pp. 649–55.
2 Nagel 1997, esp. pp. 661–65. James M. Saslow in Chong and Lingner 2003, p. 81, suggests that the scene reflects Michelangelo's and Colonna's shared belief in spiritual salvation through the contemplation of sacred events, in this case Christ's death, which ultimately brings joy in the hope of redemption.
3 Museo dell'Opera del Duomo, Florence. See also Michelangelo's Rondanini *Pietà* in the Castello Sforzesco in Milan, on which he worked until the end of his life in 1564; see Wasserman 2003.
4 De Tolnay 1953. Antonio Forcellino (Forcellino 2011) argues that one of these paintings, generally believed to be by Marcello Venusti, is in fact by Michelangelo.
5 This issue is discussed in more detail in cat. 24 below.
6 These were *The Fall of Phaeton*, *The Rape of Ganymede*, and *Tityus*. They were much admired at the time by leading figures, and Cardinal Ippolito de' Medici was so enamored of them that he ordered copies of the drawings to be executed in crystal by Giovanni Bernardi. See Leino 2013, pp. 69–72, with literature.

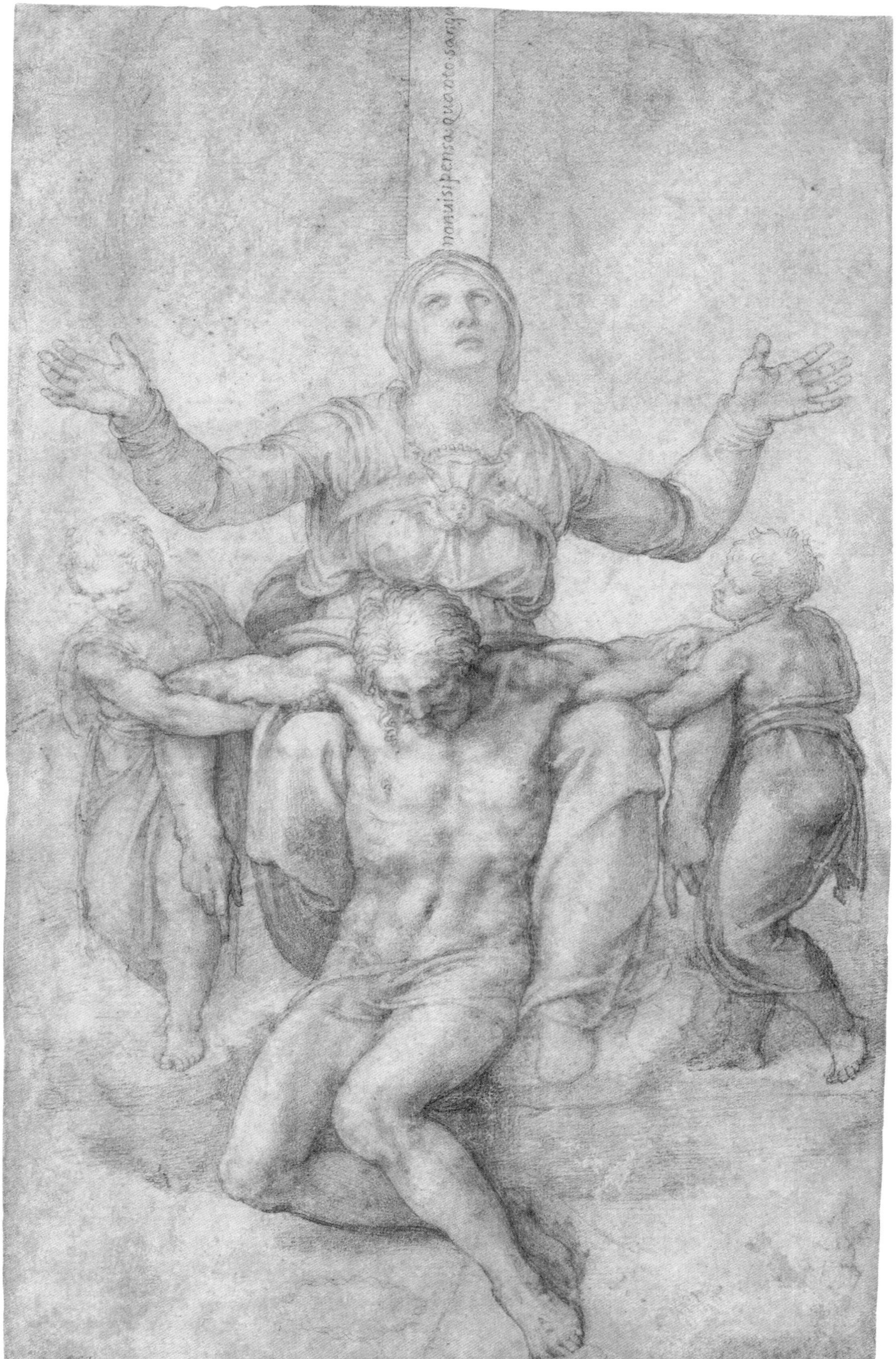
nonuisipensa quanto sangu

24

ITALIAN, 16TH CENTURY

The Pietà, second half of 16th century

Bronze, 129 × 89 mm (5 1/16 × 3 1/2 in.)
National Gallery of Art, Washington, D.C., Widener Collection 1942.9.231

THIS BRONZE PLAQUETTE is ultimately based on a drawing of the Pietà by Michelangelo, either the one he made for his friend and spiritual soulmate Vittoria Colonna in 1540 (see cat. 23) or another, now-lost drawing.[1] As Charles de Tolnay pointed out in his thorough article on the design behind this plaquette, there seem to be two strands of composition from which prints and paintings on the one hand and marble and bronze reliefs on the other depend. It is clear from many differences in design and detail that the present plaquette is not a direct copy of Colonna's drawing. For example, in the drawing the putto on the right looks inward to Christ, while in the plaquette both putti are frontal. Similarly, many features, such as the overlapping feet of Christ, are not so clearly defined in the bronze. The small bronze reliefs have the same the arrangement of a marble relief in the Vatican,[2] suggesting that perhaps the plastic versions are actually based on a drawing different from the Colonna *Pietà*, which in turn seems to be the model for the many prints and paintings of the subject.

Plaquettes of this type exist in two different sizes and many are still encased in frames, which highlight their original use as paxes or private devotional pieces. For example, a gilt-bronze version in the Princeton University Art Museum has an elaborate scrollwork frame with heads of cherubs at the top and bottom. On the reverse it has a handle, suggesting its use.[3] While the present plaquette is not framed, it is likely that it too originally sported some framing element. This may explain the piercings at the corners, though it is also possible that they were made later. It is not clear whether the bronze relief is directly based on the supposed lost Michelangelo drawing or whether it draws from the many other versions of this design. In a print of 1547, for example, Nicolas Béatrizet added an elaborate architectural surround to the group, which is reminiscent of the frames of the *Pietà* paxes. These correlations in ideas between the drawing, prints, and plaquettes, with similar surrounds but subtly different arrangement of the figures,[4] make determining the exact chain of imitation difficult.

It seems that, while plaquettes can on occasion be related to a drawing, there is rarely a direct connection. Indeed, as only a handful of drawings for plaquettes exist, and these seem not to be by the plaquette artist, it is clear that models for these small reliefs were sought elsewhere. More often, plaquette artists used as their sources intermediary objects: casts of a crystal engraving, for example, or prints. In this instance, as stated above, the design source is ultimately a drawing, probably a lost one, by Michelangelo, maybe obtained through an agent. Gift drawings such as *The Pietà* were kept in elite collections, hidden away to be viewed by invited audiences, and as such were not available to many artists directly. Copies were both a means for Michelangelo to spread his fame and for "Michelangelo designs" to be owned by those who could not obtain original artworks by the master. M.L.

PROVENANCE

Oscar Hainauer (d. 1894), Berlin; his wife, Julie Hainauer, Berlin; acquired 1906 by Duveen Brothers, London and New York; by exchange 21 October 1920 to Joseph E. Widener; gift 1942 to National Gallery of Art

LITERATURE

De Tolnay 1953; Lewis 1992, pp. 189–90; Marani 1992, pp. 408–9, no. 118; Leino 2013, pp. 183–85

NOTES

1 There are differing opinions on the number of autograph drawings of this subject, and some believe that Cardinal Reginald Pole, Colonna's spiritual adviser, owned another version, on the basis of a letter of 12 May 1546 in which he offered to give his drawing of *The Pietà* to Ercole Gonzaga should he want it, saying he could obtain another from the marchesa: De Tolnay 1953, p. 48. Antonio Forcellino (2011) believes Pole to have been in the possession of a painting, not a drawing.

2 Marani 1992, pp. 406–7, no. 117; De Tolnay 1953, p. 58.

3 De Tolnay 1953, esp. pp. 58–59; Lewis 1992, pp. 189–90; Leino 2013, p. 184.

4 De Tolnay 1953, pp. 45, note 3, and 50, figs. 2 and 3. For the Bonasone print, see Marani 1992, p. 410, no. 119.

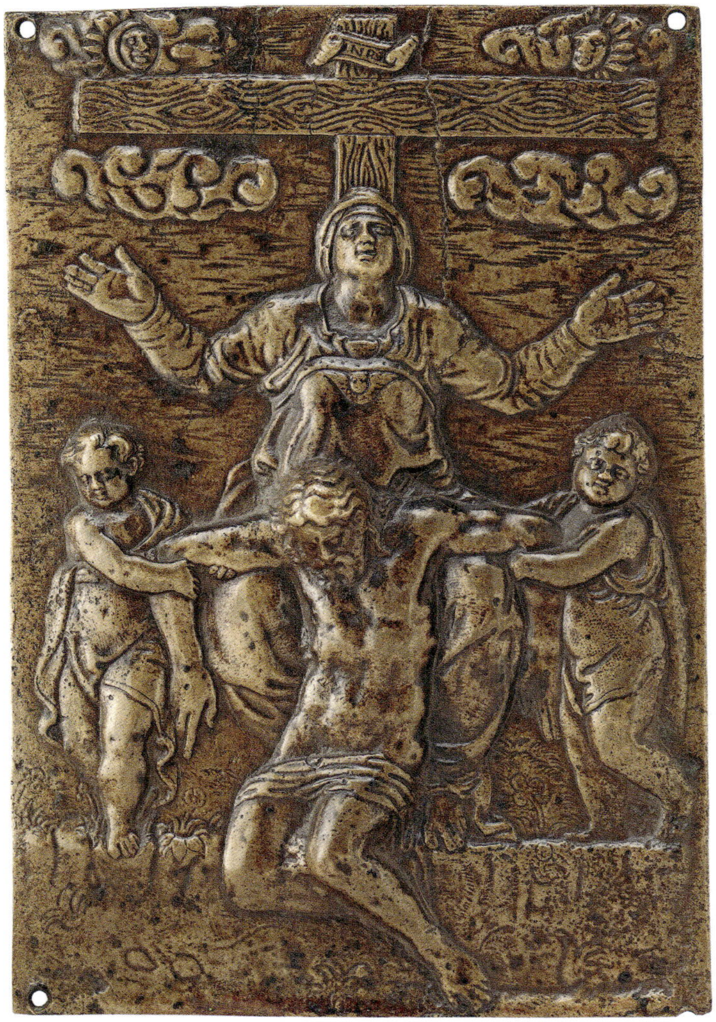

25

LEONE LEONI

Arezzo, c. 1509 – Milan, 1590

Four studies for the head of Andrea Doria, three sketches of a horse tamer and pen tests (recto); *study of Andrea Doria, a centaur, and Medici emblem* (verso), 1541

Pen and brown ink (recto); pen and brown ink with red chalk (verso), 151 × 198 mm (5 15/16 × 7 13/16 in.)
Inscribed in brown ink at upper right: *andreae doriae*
The Pierpont Morgan Library and Museum, New York, Purchased as the gift of the Fellows 1960.11

THE PORTRAITS ON THIS SHEET are unmistakably those of the man whose name is inscribed in a sixteenth-century hand on the recto, the admiral who had been elected as "censor" for life of Genoa, Andrea Doria. Because one of those portraits has been framed in a circle, the drawing has always been taken to contain studies for a medal. Most scholars have consequently connected it to the best-known medals portraying Doria, those produced by the Aretine sculptor Leone Leoni (fig. 66). Leoni had been working in Rome when in 1540 he was convicted of assaulting another goldsmith and sentenced to servitude on a galley. Several months later, Doria liberated him, and in 1541 Leoni made three medals for his new protector. Jacob Bean and Felice Stampfle, the earliest scholars to give real attention to the drawing, hesitated in the Leoni attribution, since there are no other drawings that can safely be given to the artist. Philip Attwood, who in 1994 accepted Leoni's authorship, has more recently (2003) urged caution as well. The traditional attribution, nevertheless, has merit for a number of reasons.

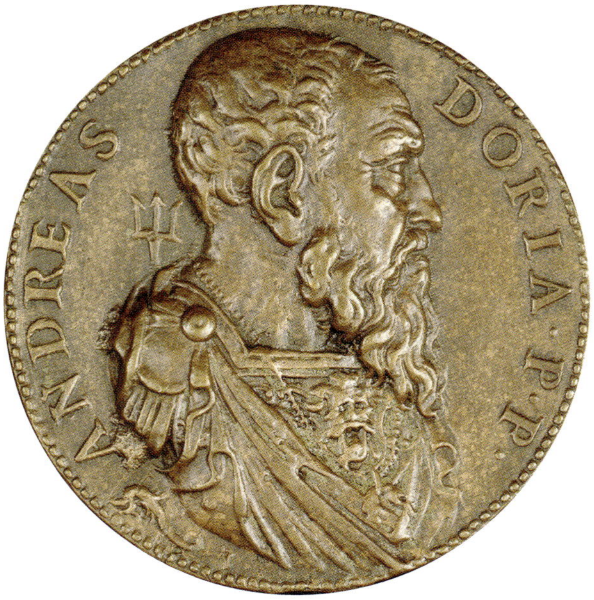

FIG. 66
Leone Leoni
Andrea Doria, 1541, obverse
Bronze, 4.2 cm diameter
National Gallery of Art, Washington D.C.,
Samuel H. Kress Collection

The drawing in the circle shows its subject slightly from behind, a view one would sooner expect an artist to have captured when observing the ruler engaged in daily activities than to have derived from a formal sitting or another portrait. The similar costume of the two portraits at left allows the possibility that they, too, were made from life, on the same occasion: the medalist may have followed a procedure much like Pisanello's a century before, when he sketched Emperor John Paleologos at an official event then adapted his drawings into an image suitable for the permanent record.[1] It cannot be ruled out, nevertheless, that the draftsman also consulted an exisiting portrait, particularly when producing his pure profile views. At least half a dozen sixteenth-century portraits of Doria in profile, wearing a similar hat, have survived, and while none that are well known date as early as 1541, the artist made have seen a prototype in Doria's own city or household.[2] One oddity of all the images with the hat on the Morgan sheet is that they also include the contours of the head that hat would have covered. The pentimenti in the contours of two of the drawings suggest uncertainty on the draftsman's part: could it be that he was trying to imagine the head beneath the hat, rather than adding a hat to a previously drawn head? Perhaps these show the artist attempting to convert the image he encountered of the man in the hat to the more classicizing form he would need for

PROVENANCE

Hans M. Calmann, London (1960); Paul Adamidi bey Frasheri (Lugt 4019)

LITERATURE

Stampfle (unsigned) in Adams 1960, pp. 48–50; Bean and Stampfle 1965, p. 3; Jones 1979, p. 59; Gealt 1983, pp. 28–29, 116–17; Philip Attwood in Scher 1994, p. 159; Attwood 1997, pp. 3–5; Attwood 2003, pp. 87 and 94–96; Boccardo 1989, p. 117; Pollard and Luciano 2007, p. 490, no. 489

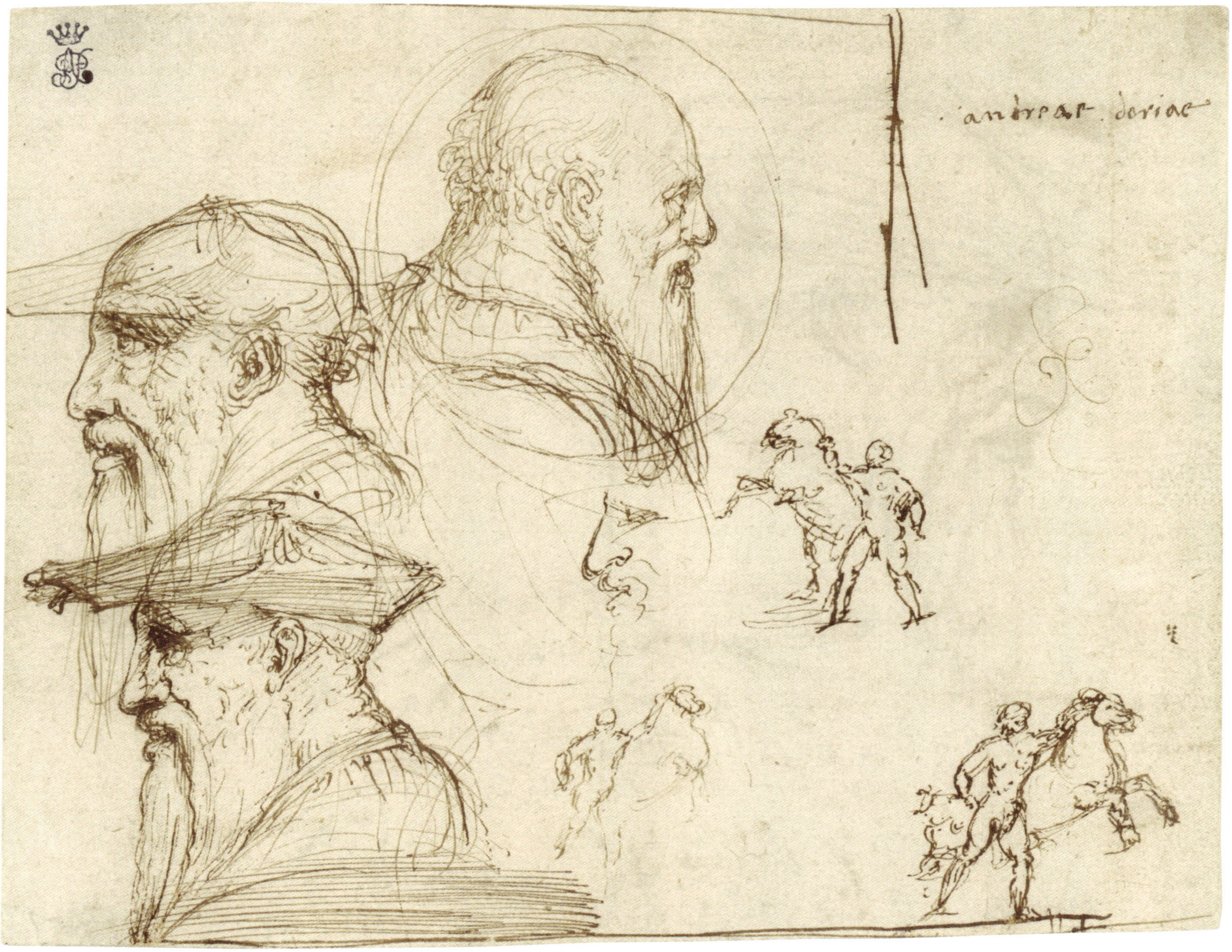
andreas doriae

a medal. All three of Leoni's drawn portraits show a hatless Doria, younger and with more hair than the 75-year-old man Leoni would have met in 1541, and they show him in armor rather than a chemise.[3] The lines drawn through the hat would illustrate the process of converting one kind of appearance into another, just as the drawing in the middle of the recto shows the artist reshaping the round nose of the other portraits into the more aquiline feature that would appear on Leoni's medals.

Leoni was not the only medalist to portray Doria. A medal by the German sculptor and goldsmith Christoph Weiditz shows an apparently younger Doria facing left with a full head of more closely cropped hair and a tighter beard. A later print suggests that another medal, by Alfonso Citadella, once existed, showing a three-quarter view of a nude Doria.[4] Leoni, nevertheless, is the only known medalist to have portrayed Doria facing right; to make the die for such medals, he would have needed a design that faced left, as he produced in most of the drawings on the Morgan sheet.[5] The recto of the sheet shows the Dioscuri, the colossal horse tamers that counted among the greatest antiquities of Rome. Leoni was fascinated with antiquities, and he would later assemble a great personal collection in his Milanese house. He had been in Rome in the very years Michelangelo was proposing a reconfiguration of the Campidoglio, with the Dioscuri at its entrance; he was interested enough in that site that he later placed a cast of the *Marcus Aurelius*, its centerpiece, in the middle of his courtyard.[6] The versions of the Dioscuri on the page, nevertheless, may not have been made after the Roman monuments themselves but after the obverse of a medal produced by Giovanni da Cavino in Padua sometime between 1532 and 1565.[7] Leoni had worked in Padua in 1537; it may even have been in Padua that he produced his own first medal.

The verso of the sheet shows a portion of the Medici device of a diamond ring with three feathers over a shield with the Medici *palle*. Variants of the *diamante* were widely used by generations of the family; in Rome, Leoni might well have seen it on the tomb of Pope Clement VII, in the stuccos of the Villa Madama, and on the shutters in the Stanza d'Eliodoro.[8] As Bean and Stampfle observed, the motif on the Morgan sheet appears to be a counterproof, transferred (perhaps unintentionally) from the wet ink of another drawing. The centaur was probably taken from a battle scene on an ancient sarcophagus.[9] With the exception of the portrait studies, then, all the drawings on the sheet may have been made after relief sculptures.

M.W.C.

NOTES

1 Syson and Gordon 2001, pp. 30–34.
2 The hat appears in several earlier state portraits of Doria, most famously those by Sebastiano del Piombo and Jan Massys.
3 In a letter of 23 March 1541, Leone writes of the hospitality Doria showed him in Genoa. See Bottati-Ticozzi, vol. 5, pp. 251–53, cited in Plon 1883, p. 15 and Attwood 2003, p. 87. Boccardo 1989, p. 117, proposes that Bronzino, by contrast, may have made his portrait without direct access to Doria. Attwood (1993, p. 154) noted the difference in dress in the Morgan drawing and the known Leoni medals.
4 Boccardo 1989, p. 117.
5 A woodcut in the *Prontuario delle medaglie de' più illustri, & fulgenti huomini & donne* (Rouillé 1553), p. 229, shows Doria facing right and in a hat, but there is no reason to believe that this medal ever existed.
6 For Leoni's collection, see Helmstutler 2000; for the *Marcus Aurelius*, p. 186.
7 Illustration and discussion in Pollard and Luciano 2007, vol. 1, p. 452.
8 Janet Cox-Rearick illustrates and discusses many examples of the motif in Cox-Rearick 1984. I have not been able to locate a version of the device that combines the ring, feathers, and shield with acanthus leaves, as here.
9 The twisted torso, outstretched arm, and collapsed hind legs all bear comparison to motifs from the friezes illustrated in Bober and Rubinstein 1986, nos. 145 and 146.

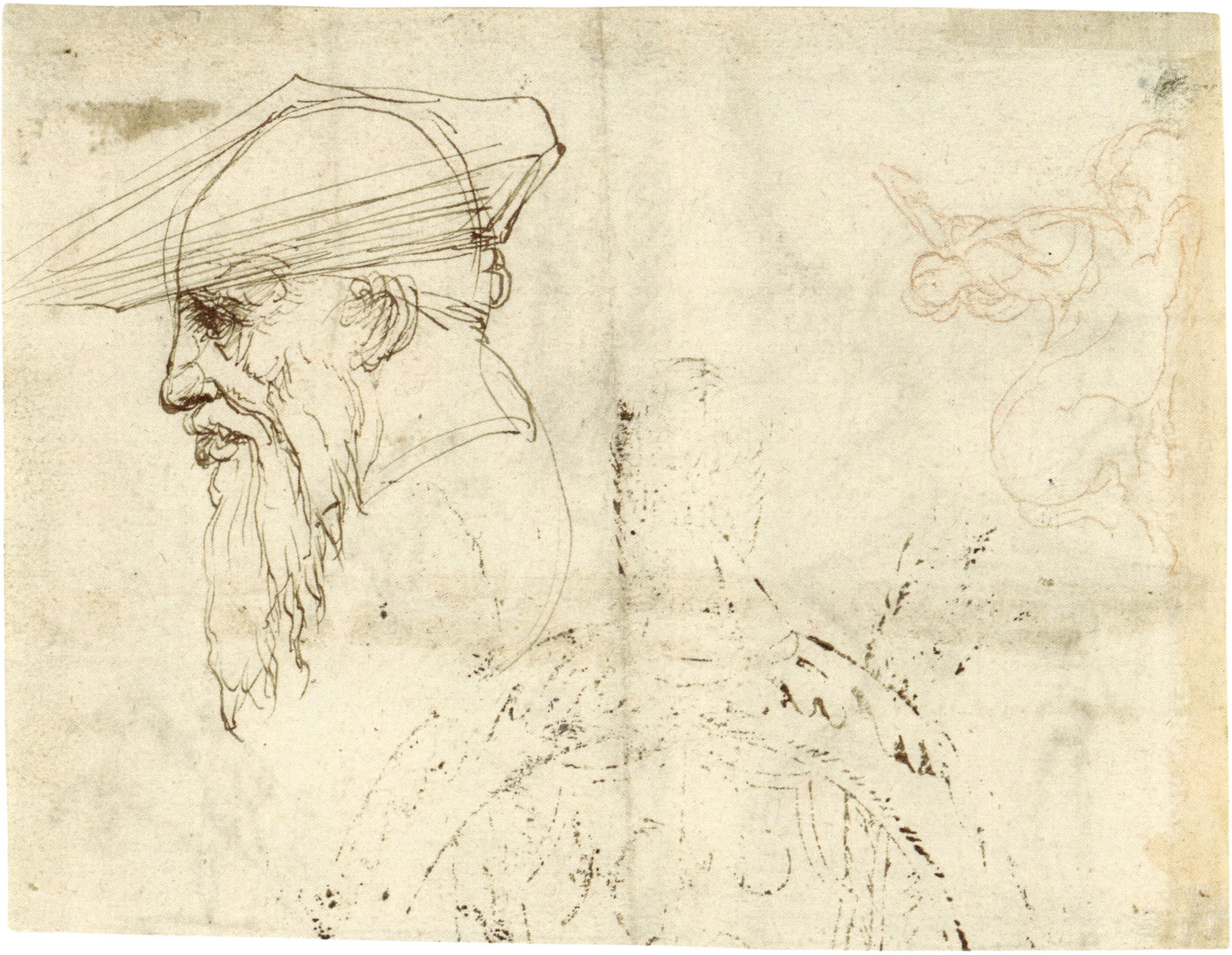

26 & 27

BENVENUTO CELLINI

Florence, 1500 – Florence, 1571

Satyr, 1543–45

Pen and brown ink, brown and white washes, black chalk, on paper, 416 × 203 mm (16⅜ × 8 in.)
Inscribed by the artist in brown ink at lower right: *alla porta di fontana / Bellio . di bronzo p[er] piu / di dua volte il vivo b[raccia] 7 / erano dua variati*
National Gallery of Art, Washington, D.C., Woodner Collection, Patron's Permanent Fund 1991.190.2

Satyr, 1543–45

Bronze, 56.8 cm (22⅜ in.)
The J. Paul Getty Museum, Los Angeles 85.SB.69

THE DRAWING AND THE BRONZE record the intended appearance of one of the supporting figures envisioned by the Florentine goldsmith Benvenuto Cellini during his sojourn at the French court (1540–45)[1] for the Porte Dorée, the main entrance of the castle of Fontainebleau, King François I's favorite retreat. Cellini's highly innovative and meaningful design for embellishing the already existing gateway comprised essentially a large relief of the Nymph of Fontainebleau as a reclining nude woman embodying the name-giving source of the hunting lodge, which was to be placed in the lunette above the doorway, and two colossal figures representing armed Satyrs as guardians of the door, which were depicted as if carrying the lintel.[2] When Cellini left France abruptly in 1545, the project was left unfinished. Only the reliefs of the Nymph and of two Victories for the spandrels above the lunette, as well as some decorative elements, had been executed, while the two Satyrs had reached only the stage of full-size clay models, ready to be cast in bronze.[3] The drawing in Washington, which shows how the figure would have held above the head something like an abacus, depicts one of these models, namely the Satyr for the left side of the door. Since the inscription is given in the past tense, it seems that Cellini had brought the sheet with him back to Florence, where he labeled it at an unknown date.[4] The drawing itself must have been executed in France, however, as a record of the full-size model, which measured around 350 cm.[5] That Cellini's model for this drawing was of such a colossal size can be gathered from the fact that the head of the figure is seen from below, while the feet are looked upon from above, indicating that the eye of the viewer must have been approximately at the level of the Satyr's genitals.

The sheet, which is superbly executed, does not represent a sketch documenting the creative process but is rather a record of the final artistic solution. Great care is devoted not only to the modeling of the nude body but also to its contour, which is rendered by a sharp line,[6] drawn with remarkable certainty, as if to emphasize the clearly defined shape and factuality of sculpture. It is furthermore notable that the figure casts a shadow that indicates that the Satyr is standing against a wall as if already in situ. How cleverly Cellini wanted to install the finished sculpture is demonstrated by the Getty bronze, which is hollow and partly open at the back. Sections of the figure's proper right thigh, torso, and raised upper arm appear to have been

PROVENANCE (CAT. 26)

John Barnard (d. 1784), London; Sir Thomas Lawrence (1769–1830), London; Samuel Woodburn (1786–1853), London; Hans M. Calmann (1899–1982), London; William H. Schab Gallery, New York; purchased by Ian Woodner (1903–1990), New York, 1959; by inheritance to his daughters, Dian and Andrea Woodner, New York, 1990; purchased by the National Gallery of Art, 1991

LITERATURE (CAT. 26)

Gerdts and Gerdts 1960, no. 25; Bean and Stampfle 1965, p. 55, no. 82; Heikamp 1966, p. 53; Grodecki 1971, pp. 61, 63; Perrig 1977, pp. 48–49; Avery and Barbaglia 1981, p. 90, no. 33; Pope-Hennessy 1982, p. 409; Pope-Hennessy 1985, pp. 135–36; Herrig 1992, p. 169; Perrig 2003, pp. 128–29; Cole 2003, pp. 45–46; Marsden and Bassett 2003, pp. 552, 557, 559; Denise Allen in Franklin 2005, pp. 282–83, no. 102; Grasselli 2009, pp. 24–25, no. 3

PROVENANCE (CAT. 27)

Windsor Castle, 1875/76; Aaron S. Drey Gallery, Munich; purchased by August Lederer (1857–1936), Vienna, 1918; by inheritance to his widow, Serena Lederer (1867–1943), Vienna, 1936; seized by the National Socialist government, 1938; under the control of Allied Russian troops, 1945; restituted by the Allied Forces to the Austrian government, 1946; restituted by the Austrian government to Serena's son, Erich Lederer (1896–1985), Geneva, 1948; by inheritance to his widow, Elisabeth Lederer, Geneva, 1985; purchased by The J. Paul Getty Museum, Los Angeles, 1985

LITERATURE (CAT. 27)

Pope-Hennessy 1982, p. 409; Pope-Hennessy 1985, pp. 135–36; Avery 1986, p. 62; Radcliffe 1988, p. 930; Scalini 1995, p. 21; Nova 1996, pp. 141–42; Paolucci 2000, p. 25; Peggy Fogelman in Fogelman and Fusco 2002, pp. 38–42; Bliss 2003, pp. 77–81; Marsden and Bassett 2003, pp. 552–63; Jestaz 2003, pp. 107–9, 117–18; Denise Allen in Franklin 2005, pp. 285–86, no. 103; Jonathan Marsden in Heard and Whitaker 2011, p. 232

sliced off, in order to facilitate attaching it to a flat background. In the drawing these "sliced-off parts" correspond exactly to those passages of the body that cast a shadow against the backdrop. The Satyr was thus modeled indeed, as Cellini tells in his autobiography, as a very high relief, which can be seen not only at the back of the Getty bronze but also when looking at it from the left side (a point of view that would be impossible in the archway of the Porte Dorée), where the foreshortening of the figure's compressed chest becomes apparent, while the drawing depicts the Satyr from that point of view from which the illusion of it being a fully three-dimensional sculpture works best. The Getty bronze is furthermore not modeled like a statuette, for which artists usually built up the shape of the figure around a doll-like iron armature, but was created out of a thick sheet of wax, which is only partly closed on the back (a telling detail can be found on the back of the bronze, where the artist pinched the edges of the wax sheet together with his fingers to shape the neck). It seems thus that Cellini tried to adapt his favorite goldsmith's technique of hammering out a figure from a sheet of metal (repoussé)[7] for his first monumental sculpture in bronze. The only element in the door's ensemble of reliefs that is modeled fully in the round is therefore all the more remarkable: it is the head of the stag in the center of the lunette. While the Nymph surrounded by peaceful animals represents the ideal of a fertile and harmonious garden of Eden, the stag is the alter ego of François I.[8] The fact that the king is thus the only figure who is fully present in three dimensions makes him the only "real" thing, while the mythic inhabitants of the woods surrounding Fontainebleau are contained in the illusionistic fabric of the reliefs. To represent the king in the round is also a fitting although probably unintended homage to the patron, who enabled Cellini's all-important professional move from goldsmith to sculptor.

It was only recently that the companion of the Getty *Satyr* was discovered in the Royal Collection, London.[9] Also fashioned as a relief with open back, it represents a slightly younger Satyr in a pose that is similar to but not identical with that of the Getty bronze. This discovery is of crucial importance for the evaluation of Cellini's authorship of the Getty *Satyr*, which was considered by many to be a later relic cast made after the artist had left France in order to preserve his wax model from perishing.[10] Marsden and Bassett were able to demonstrate that the bronze in London dates almost exactly from the years when Cellini was at work on the Porte Dorée and that both *Satyr*s had once been together in the Royal Collection, where they presumably also received their mutilating fig leaves. The role of these bronzes within the design process was established by Allen, who argued convincingly that they were made when the final appearance of the Satyr-Atlantes was fully worked out and Cellini wanted to test the skills of the local founders.[11] Indeed, as is indicated by the fact that the Getty bronze is a direct cast while his companion in London was produced by the indirect method,[12] it seems that Cellini wanted to find out specifically which of these two techniques was better suited for executing the large *Satyr*s. The use of different casting methods speaks furthermore against the theory of their being relic casts, as such technical experimenting is most likely to have occurred only with Cellini still being present. All arguments that criticize the facture of the Getty bronze as not fastidious enough to be by Cellini are thus missing the essential point, namely that Morellian comparisons with his finished masterpieces are not the way to approach this very special creation. These two *Satyr*s are not "small bronzes" produced for the French king as a sort of "preview" and something he could place in his collection—like the more finished small bronze model *Perseus* (Bargello, Florence)—but testimonies of Cellini's exploration of casting techniques. Usually the evidence of such experimenting has not survived, and it may not be a coincidence that we also have no drawings by Cellini documenting his creative struggles. As a consummate master of self-promotion, he did not want to reveal that even he sometimes simply had to try what would work best. While the drawing in Washington can be considered an authorized testimony of Cellini's design for the Porte Dorée, the two bronze *Satyr*s offer, so to speak, a rare unofficial glance at how the great artist arrived at his masterpieces. C.K-G.

NOTES

1 Cellini's famous golden saltcellar (Kunsthistorisches Museum, Vienna), also executed for François I, is the only surviving example of his work as a goldsmith and attests to his sublime craftsmanship in this field.

2 For Cellini's account of this project, see his autobiography: Symonds 1889, pp. 327–28.

3 The *Nymph of Fontainebleau* (Musée du Louvre, Paris) is the only executed part of the Porte Dorée that has survived. Of the *Victories* only plaster casts (Musée du Louvre) have come down to us; see Grodecki 1971; Pope-Hennessy 1985, pp. 132–61; Jestaz 2003, pp. 99–119. That the Satyrs were the only parts "left uncast, but in a state ready for casting" is reported by Cellini in his *Treatise on Sculpture*.

4 Denise Allen in Franklin 2005, p. 282; Grasselli 2009, p. 24.

5 Marsden and Bassett 2003, p. 559; on the height of the original models see ibid., p. 557, note 12, and Jestaz 2003, p. 113.

6 Denise Allen in Franklin 2005, p. 283, insightfully compares this line to the reinforced contours of designs executed in repoussé relief, a typical goldsmith's technique.

7 Cellini made the figures on top of the saltcellar by this method, as well as the monumental silver candlestick representing Jupiter.

8 For the stag as symbol of the king and an analysis of the Porte Dorée as access to an ideal place of peace and pleasure, see Herrig 1992, p. 142–72. Compare also Vickers 1986.

9 Marsden and Bassett 2003.

10 After Pope-Hennessy had proposed the attribution in 1982, it was questioned by Avery 1986, p. 62; Radcliffe 1988, p. 930; Scalini 1995, p. 21; Paolucci 2000, p. 25; Peggy Fogelman in Fogelman and Fusco 2002, p. 40; Jestaz 2003, pp. 107–8.

11 Denise Allen in Franklin 2005, pp. 285–86.

12 For an explanation of the direct and the indirect casting methods, see Stone 1981.

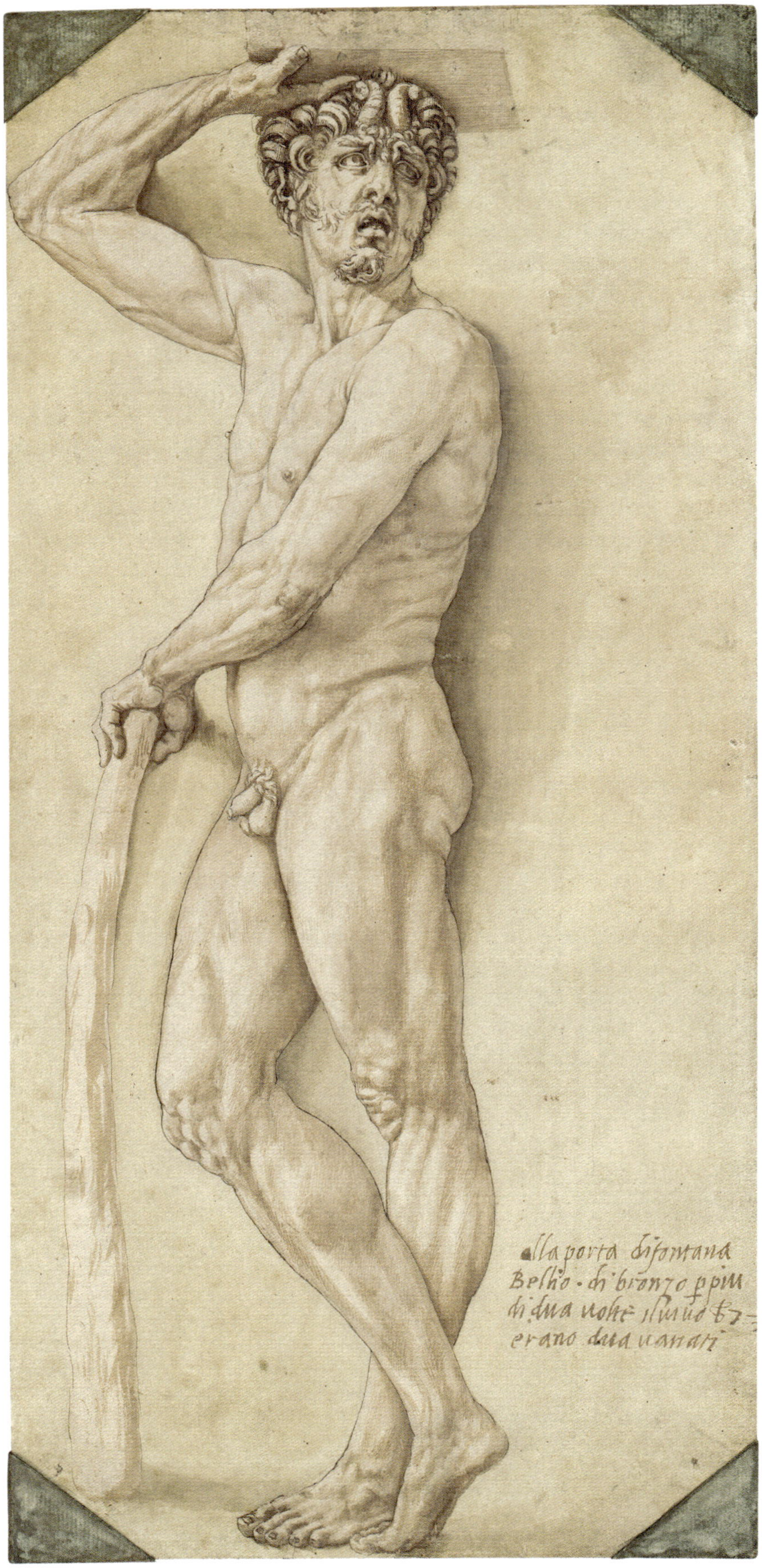
alla porta difontana
erano dua

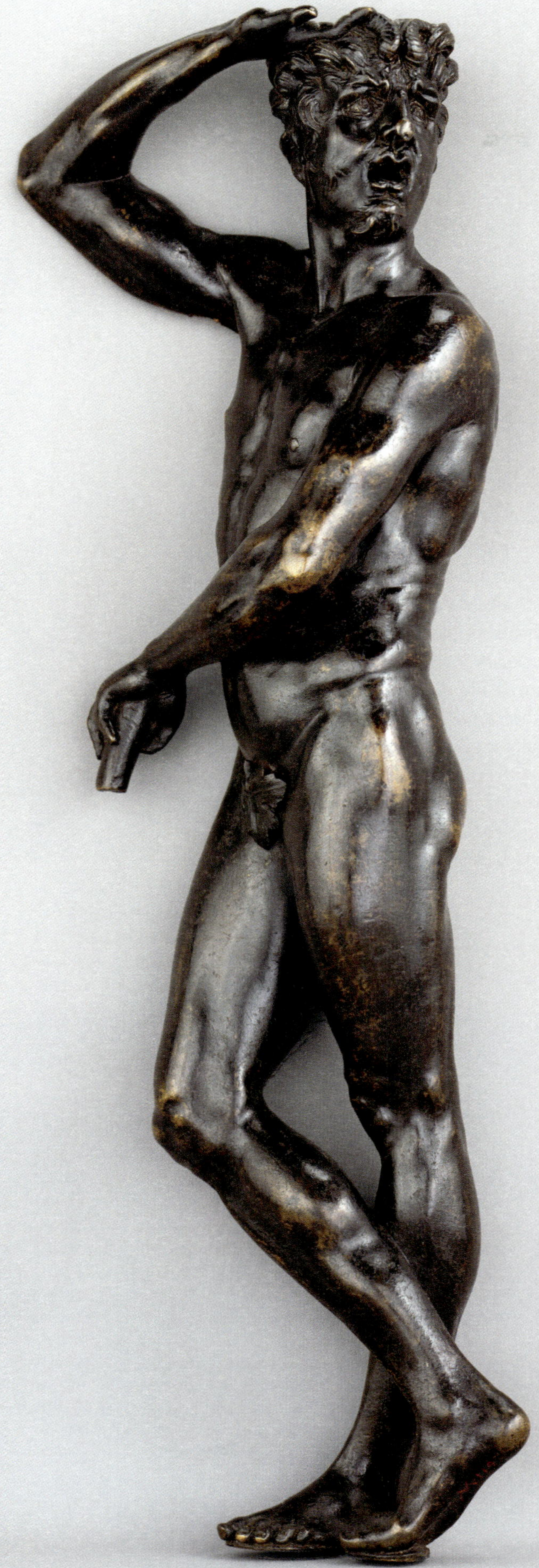

28

BACCIO BANDINELLI

Florence, 1493 – Florence, 1560

Self-Portrait, c. 1545

Oil on panel, 142.5 x 113.5 cm (56⅛ × 44 ¹¹⁄₁₆ in.)
Isabella Stewart Gardner Museum, Boston P26e22

BACCIO BANDINELLI'S *Self-Portrait* is one of the most ambitious and innovative artists' portraits ever created. With its grand format and its sitter depicted at full length before two stately columns, it owes its inspiration to state portraits, developed earlier in the sixteenth century.[1] In contrast to his other portraits, this celebrates Bandinelli as a universal artist, whose sculpture is based on *disegno*.[2] Opinions are still divided about the authorship of the painting, the date of its execution, and the nature of the drawing in the portrait.[3]

Giorgio Vasari and Francisco de Holanda both remarked on Bandinelli's efforts to paint.[4] Bandinelli himself claimed in his "Memoriale" that his paintings were admired by his contemporaries and mentioned a self-portrait.[5] Though most scholars accept the fundamental veracity of these reports and regard Bandinelli as the primary painter involved with the Gardner picture, some argue for the presence of a second hand as well,[6] and still others suggest that it was executed entirely by another artist.[7] Undisputed is the terminus post quem for this *Self-Portrait*: it must have been painted after February 1530, when Emperor Charles V most likely bestowed on Bandinelli the Order of Santiago.[8] The artist wears the order's shell emblem on a gold chain conspicuously around his neck.

The large drawing that Bandinelli is holding relates the painting to his famous *Hercules and Cacus* group, erected in front of the Palazzo Vecchio in Florence in 1534. Contested is whether the portrait was painted before or after the statue's completion.

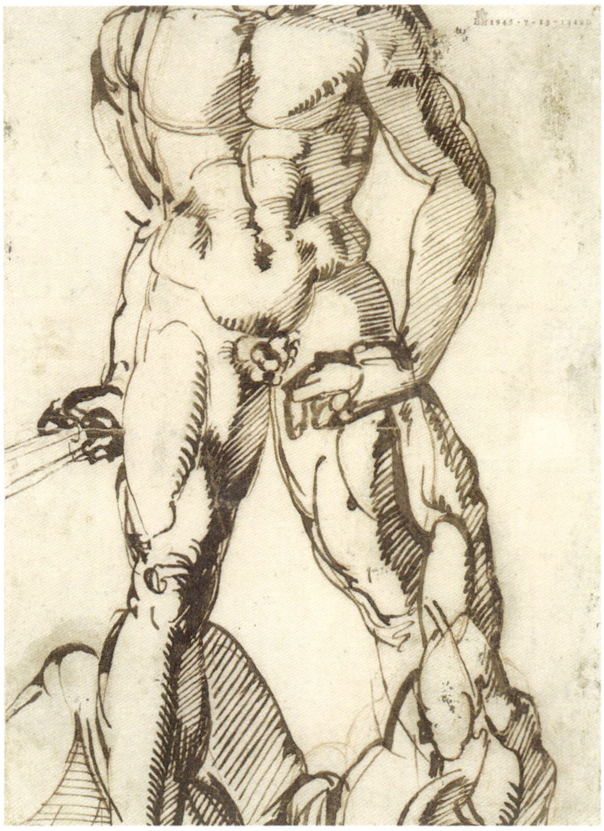

FIG. 67
Baccio Bandinelli
Study of nudes, 1525–26
Pen and brown ink, over red chalk, on paper, 297 × 218 mm
British Museum, London

PROVENANCE

Cesare Bandinelli?; Ignazio Hugford, Florence; sale M. Lapeyrière, Paris, 14–16 March 1825; sales of Alexis Delahante, London, 19–20 May 1826 (not sold), 8–9 July 1828 (not sold), 29–30 June 1830; George Vivian, Claverton (as Andrea del Sarto); Ralph Vivian, Claverton; S.T. Gooden; bought in January 1899 from Colnaghi & Co. of London by Isabella Stewart Gardner (as portrait of Michelangelo by Sebastiano del Piombo)

LITERATURE

Bandinelli 1905, p. 433; *Serie degli uomini più illustri* 1772, vol. 5, p. 83, note 2 (Francesco Salviati); Waagen 1854–57, vol. 3, p. 176 (Sebastiano del Piombo); Schubring 1880, p. 169 (Baccio Bandinelli); Berenson (7 December 1898) in Berenson and Gardner 1987, vol. 1, pp. 255–63 (Sebastiano del Piombo); Fischel 1908, p. 440 (Sebastiano del Piombo or Francesco Salviati); Hendy 1931, pp. 22–26 (Bandinelli); Goldscheider 1936, no. 114 (Bandinelli); Zeri 1948, pp. 182–83, note 2 (Jacopino del Conte); Freedberg 1963, vol. 1, pp. 58–59, notes 2–3; Detlef Heikamp in Vasari-Della Pergola, Grassi, and Previtali 1964, vol. 6, p. 19, note 1 (Bandinelli); Hadley 1966, pp. 17–24 (Bandinelli and assistant, Andrea del Minga?); Fredericksen and Zeri 1972, p. 14 (Bandinelli); Hendy 1974, p. 12 (probably Bandinelli); Weil-Garris 1981, p. 237 (not Bandinelli); Waźbiński 1987, p. 60 (Bandinelli); Natali 1988, p. 29 (not Bandinelli); Koortbojian 1992, p. 20 (Bandinelli); Mortari 1992, pp. 141–42 (Francesco Salviati); Severin 1992, pp. 92–93 (Bandinelli); Goldstein 1996, p. 14 (Bandinelli); Kathke 1997, p. 195 (Bandinelli); Woods-Marsden 1998, pp. 139–47 (Bandinelli); King 1998, p. 85 (Bandinelli); Fiorentini 1999, pp. 156–57, note 36 (Bandinelli); Goffen 1999, p. 771 (Bandinelli); Myssok 1999, p. 286, note 940; Wiemers 2000, p. 235 (Bandinelli); Brown 2000, pp. 103–4 (Bandinelli); Heikamp 2001, pp. 983–1006 (Bandinelli); Goffen 2002, pp. 362–64 (Bandinelli); Vossilla 2002, p. 193 (not Bandinelli); Chong and Lingner 2003, p. 85 (Bandinelli); Chong 2003, p. 252 (Bandinelli); Béguin and Costamagna 2003, pp. 11–13 (Bandinelli and Jacopino del Conte); Waldman 2004, p. 866; Müller Hofstede 2004, pp. 208–11 (Bandinelli); Thomas 2005, p. 278; Bredekamp 2007, pp. 55–56 (Bandinelli); Hegener 2008, pp. 315–24, 615, note 9 (Bandinelli and Jacopino del Conte or Angelo di Cristofano); Stimato 2008; Greve 2008, pp. 338–42 (Bandinelli); Morford 2009, p. 88 (Bandinelli); Donati 2010, pp. 162–63 (Bandinelli and Andrea del Minga); Tostmann in Heikamp and Paolozzi Strozzi 2014, pp. 514–16 (Bandinelli and assistant); Mozzati 2014, pp. 453–69 (Bandinelli); Ward 2014, p. 343 (Bandinelli)

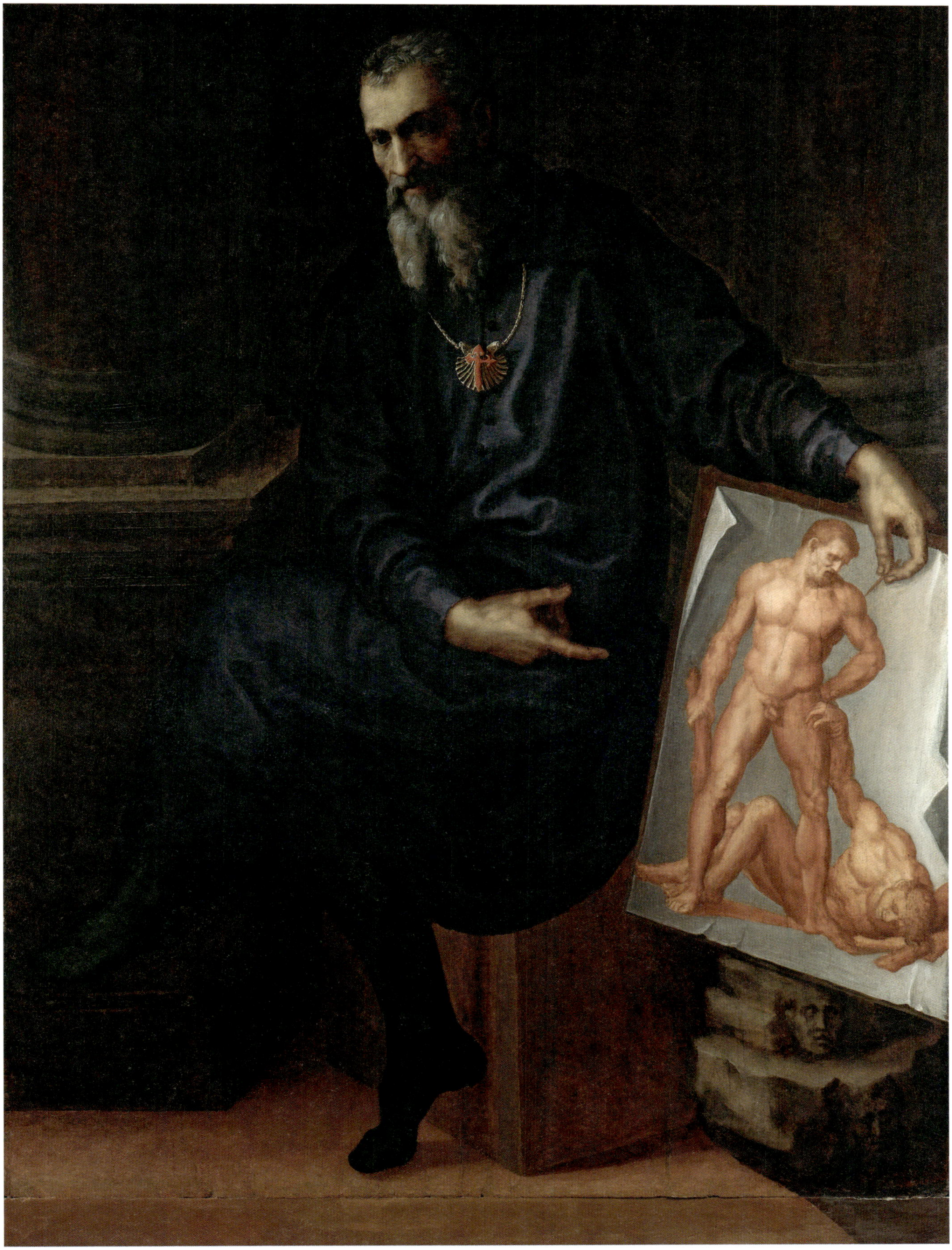

FIG. 68
Infrared digital photograph of Baccio Bandinelli's *Self-Portrait* (detail)

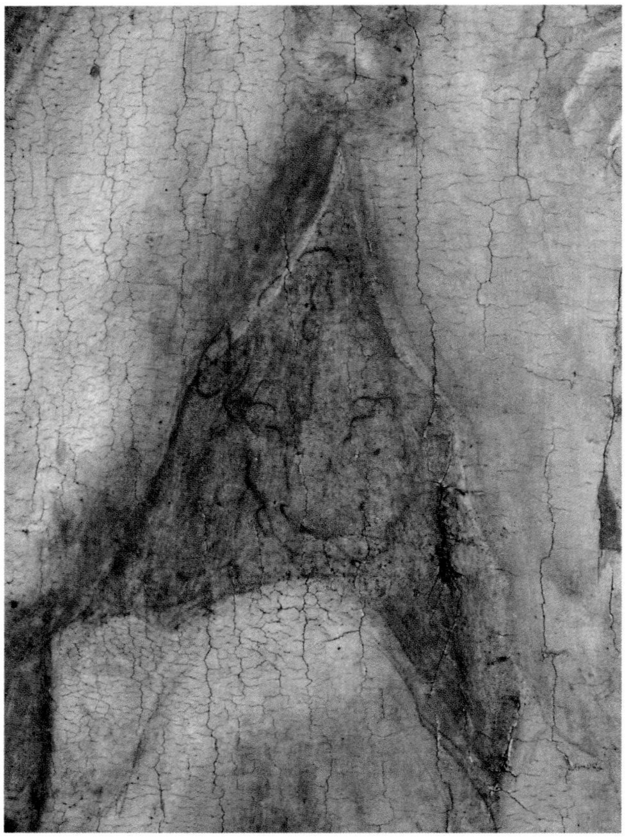

The interpretation of the drawing has been a key argument for an earlier dating, before 1534. Cacus is lying dead at the feet of Hercules, a motif that differs strikingly from that in the finished marble group, where Cacus is shown still alive. For this reason, the drawing has often been taken to represent an earlier, eventually abandoned version of the group.[9] The red-chalk drawing, if ever executed, is lost, but a related version from the British Museum has survived (fig. 67).[10] Executed in ink on a much smaller scale, it also shows Cacus lying dead beneath Hercules. Roger Ward convincingly dated the London drawing to 1525–26, a period when Bandinelli did not yet know the actual size of the marble block from which he would have to carve the group, and connected it with the drawing in the Gardner portrait.[11]

A dating after 1534 is supported by the advanced age of the sitter, the creation of a prototype for this portrait by Giorgio Vasari as late as 1534, and the ambitious portraits of the 1540s.[12] In addition, there was a heated debate about the supremacy of the arts in Florence during the mid-1540s, and this portrait could have served as a painted commentary.[13] Others, however, argue for an even later date, during the late 1550s or the early seventeenth century.[14]Recent infrared reflectography has revealed a number of previously unknown compositional changes throughout the image, such as slight alterations to the sitter's proper left eye and proper right foot. Most important is the underdrawing in the painted drawing.[15] A lion's head, rendered in fine black chalk, is clearly legible between Hercules' legs (fig. 68). This Herculean attribute does not appear in the London drawing, in other preparatory drawings related to this motif, or in the figure in the later sculpture group.[16] Although we do not know why Bandinelli inserted the lion's head, it shows another significant alteration from the London drawing to which it has been linked. This discovery makes it unlikely that the depicted drawing represents an intermediate preparatory design for the Hercules and Cacus group. In fact, the pentimento indicates that this drawing was never executed, and that it is a fictive drawing.

Nevertheless, the painted drawing highlights the sculptor's superb draftsmanship and most prominent commission, while stressing his ingenuity by showing a variant on the famous motif. If executed in the mid-1540s, Bandinelli could have speculated that most viewers of this portrait would be able fully to appreciate the differences between the marble group and the autonomous drawing. It may be that Bandinelli decided not to include the lion's head so as to ensure recognition of the motif even as he provoked the viewer to marvel at his new variation on it. Probably this self-portrait hung for representational purposes in Bandinelli's house in Florence.[17] O.T.

NOTES

* My thanks to Gianfranco Pocobene, John L. and Susan K. Gardner Chief Conservator, who kindly discussed the recent technical findings of the painting with me.

1 Béguin and Costamagna convincingly suggested Giorgio Vasari's *Portrait of Duke Alessandro de' Medici*, 1534, Galleria Palatina (Palazzo Pitti, Florence) as a source for Bandinelli's *Self-Portrait*: Béguin and Costamagna 2003, p. 1. Hegener correctly identified the *impresa* of Emperor Charles V, *Plus Ultra*, as another source for Bandinelli's portrait: Hegener 2008, pp. 322–24.

2 On Bandinelli's portraits see Hegener 2008, pp. 291–419.

3 Tostmann in Heikamp and Paolozzi Strozzi 2014, pp. 514–16.

4 Vasari-Milanesi 1906, vol. 6, p. 138; de Hollanda 1899, pp. 60–61 (in Hegener 2008, p. 61).

5 *Avvertendovi ancora che se bene si veggono alchune pitture di mia mano stimatissime, con tutto ciò non ci sono stato molto dedico, come più volte lo dissi e scrissi a loro Eccellentie, e fra queste vi prego a tenere conto del quadro che vi lascio in Casa, ove col mezzo di una spera dipinsi me stesso; conservandolo, di me ricordiate e preghiate per l'anima mia*: Bandinelli 1905, p. 433.

6 For an ascription to Bandinelli alone, see Schubring 1880, p. 169; Hendy 1931, pp. 22–26; Goldscheider 1936, no. 114; Heikamp 1964, p. 19, note 1; Fredericksen and Zeri 1972, p. 14; Hendy 1974, p. 12; Waźbiński 1987, p. 60; Koortbojian 1992, p. 20; Severin 1992, p. 92; Goldstein 1996, pp. 14–15; Kathke 1997, p. 195; King 1998, p. 85; Woods-Marsden 1998, pp. 139–47; Fiorentini 1999, pp. 156–57, note 36; Goffen 1999, p. 771; Wiemers 2000, p. 235; Brown 2000, p. 103; Heikamp 2001, p. 983; Goffen 2002, pp. 362–64; Chong and Lingner 2003, p. 85; Chong 2003, p. 252; Béguin and Costamagna 2003, pp. 12–13; Müller Hofstede 2004, pp. 208–11; Bredekamp 2007, pp. 55–56; Greve 2008, pp. 338–42; Morford 2009, p. 88; Mozzati 2014, p. 458. Others suggest a second hand involved in the execution: Hadley 1966, p. 24; Tostmann in Heikamp and Paolozzi Strozzi 2014, p. 516. Hegener 2008, p. 320, points to Angelo di Cristofano (or Jacopino del Conte). Donati 2010, p. 163, suggests Andrea del Minga.

7 For Jacopino del Conte, see Zeri 1948, pp. 182–83, note 2. Béguin and Costamagna 2003, pp. 12–13, suggest Jacopino del Conte; Donati more recently argued against an ascription to him: Donati 2010, p. 163. For Francesco Salviati see *Serie degli uomini più illustri* 1772, vol. 5, p. 83, note 2; Fischel 1908, p. 440; Mortari 1992, pp. 141–42. For Sebastiano del Piombo, see Waagen 1854–57, vol. 3, p. 176; Berenson (1898) in Berenson and Gardner 1987, vol. 1, pp. 255–63; Fischel 1908, p. 440. Weil-Garris doubts Bandinelli's authorship: Weil-Garris 1981, p. 237. Natali suggests a Florentine artist from the sixteenth century: Natali 1988, p. 29. Vossilla ascribes the work to an artist from the early seventeenth century: Vossilla 2002, p. 193.

8 Hegener 2008, p. 735.

9 See Hendy 1931, p. 24; Koortbojian 1992, p. 20; Woods-Marsden 1998, p. 142; King 1998, pp. 85–86; Heikamp 2001, p. 998; Chong 2003, p. 85; Hegener 2008, p. 316; Mozzati 2014, p. 459; Ward 2014, p. 344.

10 Ward 2014, p. 343, fig. 12.

11 Ward 2014, pp. 343–44.

12 Compare Hegener 2008, pp. 616–18.

13 Hadley 1966, p. 23; Béguin and Costamagna 2003, p. 11; Vossila 2002, p. 193.

14 Donati 2010, p. 163; Vossilla 2002, p. 193.

15 Infrared digital photography conducted by Jessica Chloros and Gianfranco Pocobene.

16 For a reconstruction of the preliminary designs for the Hercules and Cacus group, see Myssok 1999, pp. 228–52; Viatte 2011, pp. 152–56, and with an alternative proposal Carlson 2014, p. 175. The head of a lion is carved in one of the four corners of the pedestal of the marble group.

17 Bandinelli 1905 p. 433; see also Waldman 2004, p. 866.

29 & 30

GUGLIELMO DELLA PORTA

Porlezza, beside Lake Lugano, c. 1510 – Rome, 1577

Rear elevation of the tomb of Pope Paul III (recto); *Fragmentary sketch of three heads* (verso), 1551

139 × 142 mm (5½ × 5⅝ in.)
Victoria and Albert Museum, London, Purchased with the assistance of the Art Fund E.501-1966

Right side elevation of the tomb of Pope Paul III (recto); *Fragmentary sketch of three heads on a clouded base* (verso), 1551

152 × 142 mm (6 × 5⅝ in.)
Victoria and Albert Museum, London, Purchased with the assistance of the Art Fund E.502-1966

THESE TWO DRAWINGS show a variant of the first version of Guglielmo della Porta's tomb of Pope Paul III, the *opus magnum* of his career and the first sepulture placed in the new Basilica of St. Peter.[1] The pages were purchased by the architect and collector John Talman (1677–1726), who also managed to obtain other significant projects by Della Porta, probably with the help of Giuseppe Ghezzi (1634–1721). One of Talman's aims was to make an "ideal gallery of papal monuments,"[2] and for the Farnese tomb he could acquire a third drawing, also conserved in the Victoria and Albert Museum, showing the final version of the tomb—as a parietal monument intended for a niche.[3]

Our drawings present a freestanding monument with a base and a two-level corps decorated with eight allegorical figures reclining on scrolls, presented alternatively from the front and back. Above, an odd trapezoidal bronze structure with putti and satyrs forms a pedestal for the papal effigy. This Della Porta reused from another work, the tomb of Francisco de Solis, also documented in an autograph drawing (Biblioteca Reale, Turin).[4] The papal effigy on the top was the most celebrated technical challenge undertaken by Della Porta and was the first colossal bronze statue to be cast in Rome during the sixteenth century.

Herbert Siebenhüner and Philip Ward-Jackson considered the drawings to be autograph works from the initial phase of the project, but Werner Gramberg, Clare Robertson, and Christina Riebesell have asserted that they were workshop products dating to the final phase, i.e., 1574–75. The first proposal is undoubtedly correct. The use of parallel hatching for casting shadows is recurrent in Della Porta's work, including the drawing of the De Solis tomb. The highly stylized masks between the scrolls are also characteristic of his style, and studies of the reclining figures and escutcheon abound in the artist's surviving sketchbooks in Düsseldorf.[5] The verso presents a study for a reliquary, with three busts of God, Christ, and the Virgins, united atop a base of clouds. This curious design, traced with a nervous graphic line, is typical of Della Porta and is corroboration of his documented activity in the field of liturgical goldsmithery: we know that he made the models for a series of reliquary busts cast by Antonio Gentili da Faenza and Pierantonio di Benvenuto Tatti in 1571 (probably sent to the monastery of Bosco Marengo in Piedmont),[6] and some of his designs were also offered by his son Teodoro della Porta to the Chapter of St. Peter for the reliquary of the Holy Face and the Sacred Spear.[7]

Della Porta discontinued work on four of the eight allegories after 1553, possibly to save time. The presence of eight reclining figures establishes that the drawings were completed before 1553. Furthermore, as Ward-Jackson notes, the figures in the drawings do not correspond to those on the tomb: they have one or both legs extended (like Michelangelo's allegories in the New Sacristy or most of Perino's figures in the Palazzo Doria in Genoa), whereas the statues on the tomb bend both legs. This "unusual pose"[8] may have been functional, in order to follow the angle of the freestanding monument—a formal expedient we find in reduced scale with the two reclining figures on the piédouche of the bust of Paul III at Naples.[9]

PROVENANCE

John Talman (Lugt 2462); Sotheby's, London, November 1960, lot 91; Victoria and Albert Museum, London, since 1966

LITERATURE

Gregorovius 1932, fig. 64; Hülsen 1933, p. 38; Montini 1957, fig. 127; Siebenhüner 1962, pp. 238–39; Gramberg 1964, Textband, p. 56, no. 60; Ward-Jackson 1979, pp. 126–27, nos. 252–53; Gramberg 1984, pp. 276, 358–59, no. Z6; Robertson 2004, pp. 210–12; Giometti 2008, p. 173; Riebesell 2008, p. 199, fig. 4

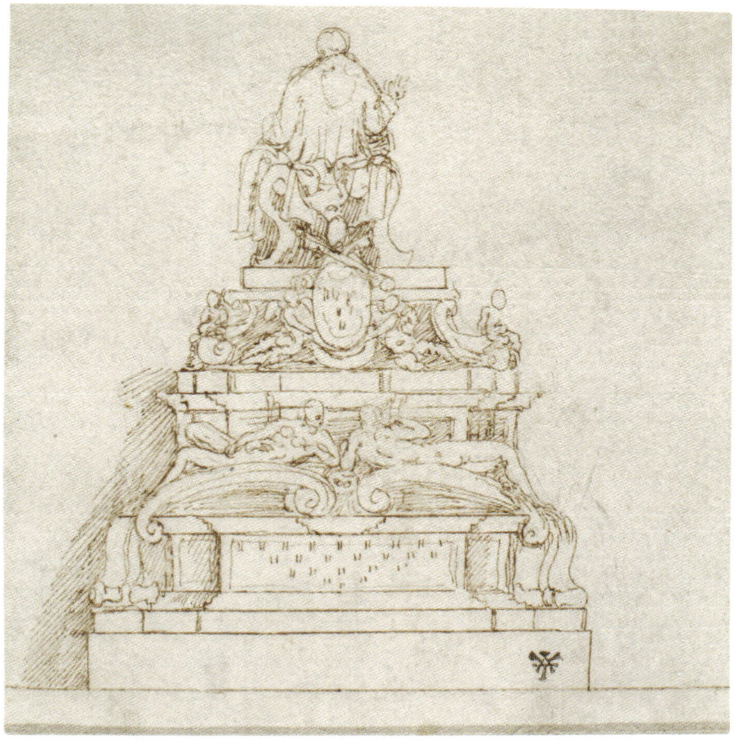

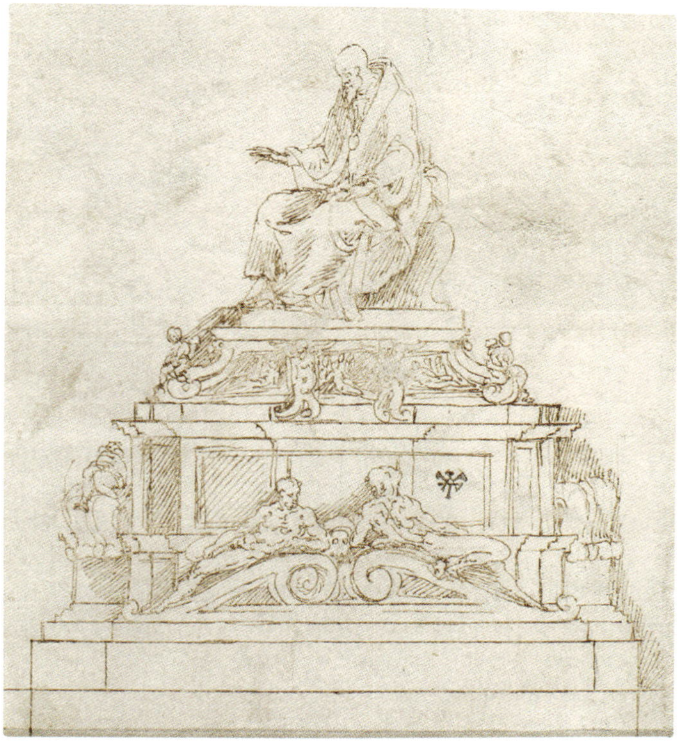

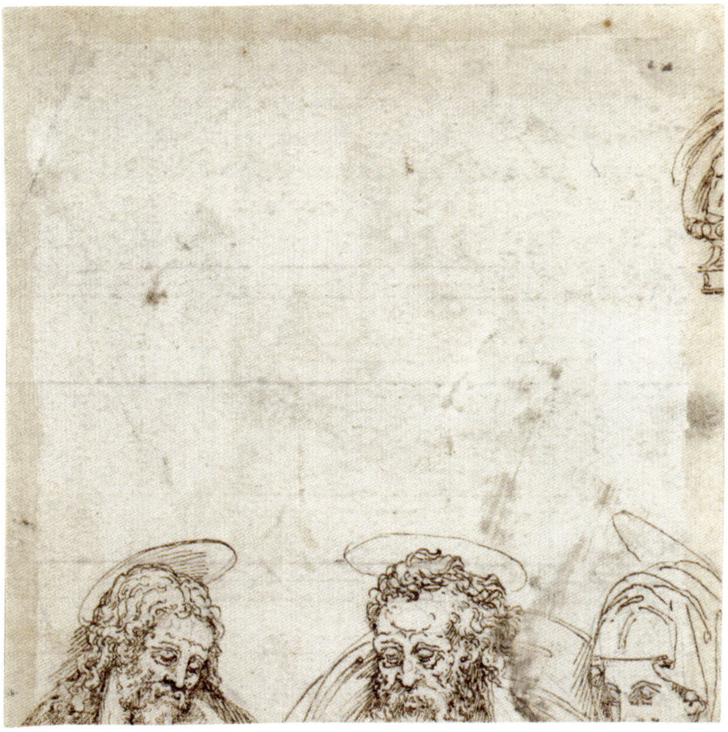

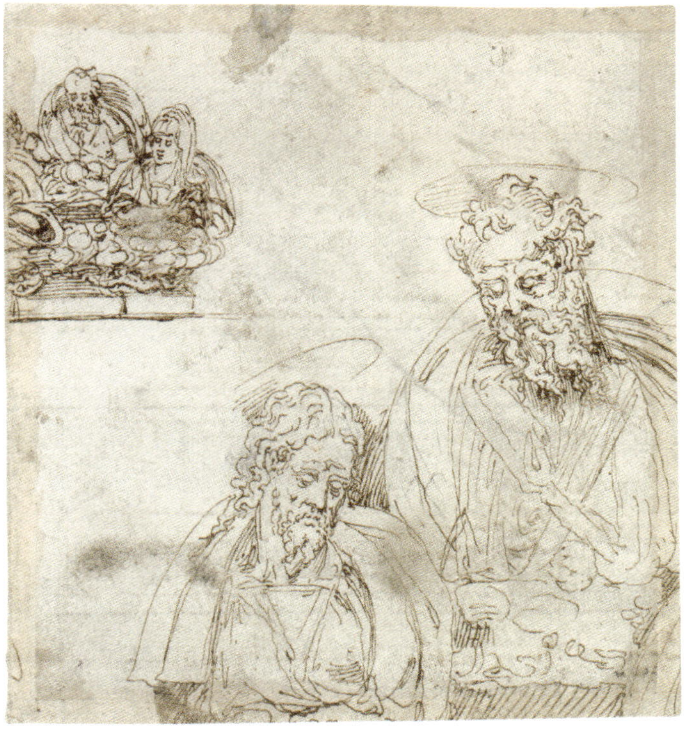

To date the drawings more precisely, we must observe that the tomb differs in some ways from the original project of about 1550, evidenced in a sketch and in two descriptions by Annibale Caro.[10] The original design had a higher corps to contain a sepulchral chamber and was decorated with eight atlantes and two sarcophagi on the lateral sides. This project generated much criticism for its profane character, its disorganic composition, and above all its placement under the eastern arch of the crossing of the basilica, a proposition that provoked the fierce hostility of Michelangelo. Hoping to placate the chorus of protests, Annibale Caro suggested in a letter of 5 August 1551 that Della Porta construct a simpler tomb: still freestanding, but without a sepulchral chamber, and consequently without atlantes and sarcophagi. Our drawing is evidently the illustration of Caro's proposal and must therefore be dated to the summer of 1551. Caro's attempt at *captatio benevolentiae* by suggesting a lower monument ("due to its elevated dimensions, we have concerns about putting it in St. Peter," he wrote) was totally ineffective in appeasing critics. Despite strong opposition, Della Porta completed the main parts of the tomb in 1558, but, for unclear reasons, work stopped in 1559 and restarted only in 1573. The final version, erected in 1575, was no longer a freestanding, but a parietal tomb, as indicated in the third Talman drawing.[11]

Della Porta was a prolific draftsman, likely a result of his collaboration with Perino del Vaga on some important commissions in Genoa (Palazzo Doria) and Rome (Cappella Massimi). However, we know of very few presentation drawings for clients, like those of the Farnese or De Solis tombs. The eccentricity of his sketches, which use elongated, almost skeletal figures and lack depth, was perhaps too personal for official taste, and it is significant that for the presentation of his most ambitious projects (the church of San Silvestro, the Carafa Chapel and perhaps the mausoleum for Charles V) Della Porta relied on the drawings of Giovanni Antonio Dosio, an artist whose cold objectivity and patient exactitude was the opposite of his own style.[12] In fact, Della Porta seems to have used drawing mainly as a first step to stimulate his imagination, "bubbling over with ever new ideas."[13] Thus his graphic production may reveal a quite particular character, yet the artist was aware of and perhaps proud of that fact; on sending a work to Giovanni Gaddi (*The Fall of the Giants* now in the Pierpont Morgan Library; cat. 36), Della Porta specified that it was made "*alla scultoresca*."[14] G.E.

NOTES

1 For a survey of the tomb, see Steven Ostrow in Pinelli 2000, pp. 613–15, no. 771.
2 Giometti 2008, p. 173.
3 Ward-Jackson 1979, pp. 128–29, no. 256.
4 Bertini 1958, p. 26, no. 137.
5 See Gramberg 1964, nos. 13, 20, 21, 28, 38, 49, 55, 56, 58, 60, 65, 66.
6 Natale 2002, p. 88.
7 Archivio della Reverenda Fabbrica di San Pietro, I, B, 14, fasc. 78, fol. 250.
8 Ward-Jackson 1979, p. 129.
9 Museo Nazionale di Capodimonte, Naples, 10521.
10 Kupferstichkabinett, Berlin, 79D1 (Gramberg 1984, p. 357, no. Z1); for both letters of Annibal Caro (before July 1550 and 5 August 1551): ibid., pp. 340–41, 343–44, nos. II, IV.
11 The documents of 1573–74 published by Robertson (2004) show that the final version of the tomb was parietal and not freestanding, as Grimaldi erroneously wrote in 1620 (Grimaldi 1972, p. 470 verso). Divergent opinion in Riebesell 2008, pp. 199–201.
12 Extermann 2012, pp. 61–67.
13 Middeldorf 1976, p. 158.
14 Gramberg 1964, Textband, p. 102, no. 191.

31

PIERINO DA VINCI (Pier Francesco di Bartolomeo da Vinci)
Vinci, c. 1529 – Pisa, 1553

Pisa Restored, c. 1552

Pen and ink, 186 × 288 mm (7⁵⁄₁₆ × 11⁵⁄₁₆ in.)
Gabinetto Disegni e Stampe degli Uffizi, Florence 13371F

THIS DRAWING and a more finished sheet in Chatsworth (fig. 69) were recognized by Middeldorf as preparatory studies for a marble relief by Pierino da Vinci in the Vatican, carved in about 1552 (fig. 70).[1] The Chatsworth drawing once formed part of Vasari's book of drawings, and the surviving fragment of the original mount bears the inscription *Piero da Vinci Scult: Fior*. This very early attribution establishes the work as a touchstone for our understanding of Pierino as a draftsman.

In his 1568 Life of the artist, Giorgio Vasari described the sculpture as representing "Pisa restored by the duke [Cosimo I de' Medici], who is in the work present in the city and at its restoration, which is being urged on by his presence. Surrounding the duke his virtues are portrayed, in particular a Minerva, represented because of the Wisdom and the Arts which had been revived by the duke in the city of Pisa. Pisa is surrounded by many evils and natural deficiencies of the place, which in the manner of enemies besiege her all round and afflict her. From all these the city has since been freed by the above-mentioned virtues of the duke." In the relief, Cosimo stands near a river god who represents the Arno. The duke looks forward, scepter in hand, as Emperor Hadrian does in a coin inscribed *Restitutor Italiae*.[2] In his lively interpretation of an ancient theme, Pierino shows the restoration of Pisa as taking place before our eyes. Led by the Duke in the center, the Virtues move in from the left as the Vices exit on the right. The two related drawings correspond to the relief in its overall design and most details. Both sheets, however, show Cosimo as literally lifting up the figure of Pisa; her pose closely recalls the *Fiesole* (Bargello, Florence) by Pierino's teacher Tribolo. In the relief, Pierino added Minerva among the Virtues as well as several portraits,

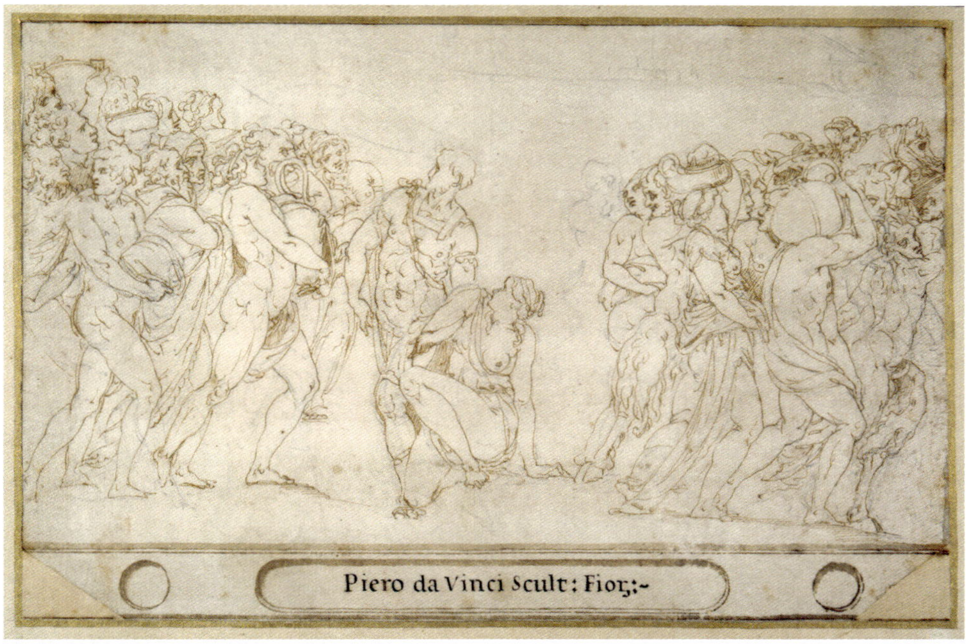

FIG. 69
Pierino da Vinci
Pisa Restored, c. 1552
Pen and brown ink, on paper,
165 × 293 mm
Devonshire Collection, Chatsworth

LITERATURE

Middeldorf 1938–39, p. 9; Collareta 1995, pp. 36–37; Cianchi 1995a, pp. 52–53; Kusch-Arnhold 2008, p. 243, no. Z.2

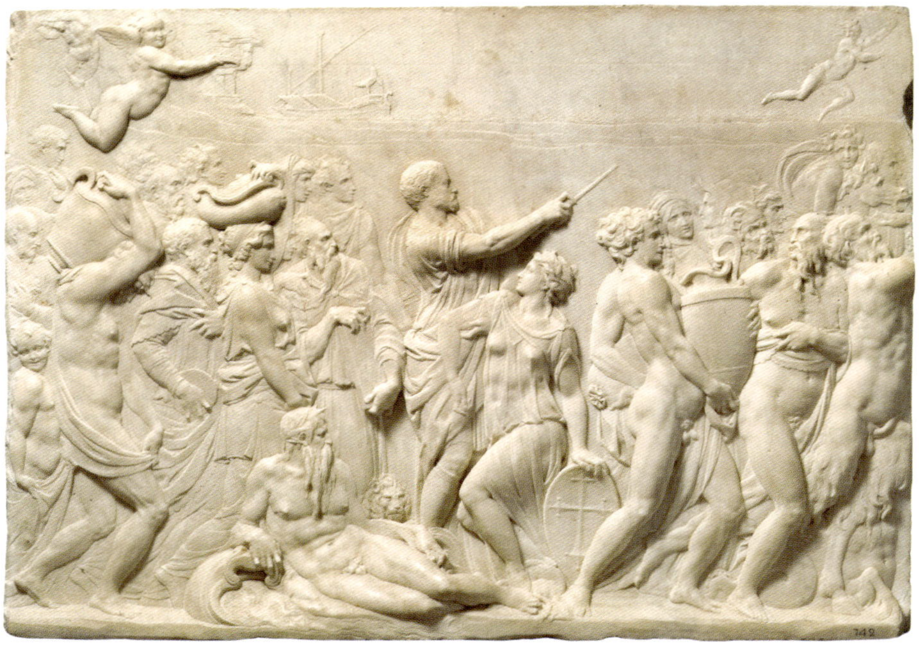

FIG. 70
Pierino da Vinci
Pisa Restored, c. 1552
Marble, 74 × 108 cm
Museo Pio Clementino, Vatican City

including those of Tribolo and Michelangelo and made the figure of Pisa more urgent.

The iconography must have been suggested by Luca Martini, who discovered Pierino and commissioned most of his works. The relief was probably commissioned by Martini, either as a gift for Cosimo or to decorate his own study. As Cosimo's principal representative in the city, Martini directed the Office of Canals, established in 1547, and supervised the draining of pestiferous marshes. He appears in the center of the left-hand group, and in the relief he holds a compass and astrolabe. These instruments refer to Martini's work in surveying the Pisan countryside, also reflected in a portrait by Bronzino (Galleria Patatina, Florence). In the upper part of the relief, a distant ship probably refers to Martini's role in Pisa. Some sketchy lines in a similar location of the present drawing (but not the one in Chatsworth) may indicate a seashore.

Cianchi argued convincingly that the light touch in the Florence drawing, in striking contrast to the Chatsworth sheet, indicates not a different moment in the artist's short career, as Middledorf had suggested, but a different function: this is an early compositional sketch.[3] Moreover, the highly finished quality of the Chastworth sheet distinguishes it not only from all other drawings by Pierino[4] but also from those made by his contemporaries in preparation for sculptures. Perhaps Pierino wanted to emulate the celebrated drawings created by Michelangelo as special gifts. Certainly, as noted by Johannes Wilde, the lack of continuous recession in Pierino's relief reflects the lessons he learned from drawings like Michelangelo's *Archers* (Royal Collection, Windsor). In both "the contrast between the majority of very flat forms and a few projecting ones is essential for the effect, and with both the distribution of the higher relief has been determined by compositional considerations only."[5] It would be fitting if Pierino made this "presentation drawing" for Martini, who had a particular interest in reliefs. Martini not only commissioned several examples but played a major role in collecting letters for Benedetto Varchi from Michelangelo and other artists on the debate over the relative merits of painting and sculpture. J.K.N.

NOTES

1 Middeldorf 1938–39, p. 9.
2 Collareta 1995, pp. 36–37.
3 Middeldorf 1938–39, p. 9; Cianchi 1995a, pp. 52–53.
4 For Pierino's drawings, see now Kusch-Arnold 2008.
5 Wilde 1978, p. 152.

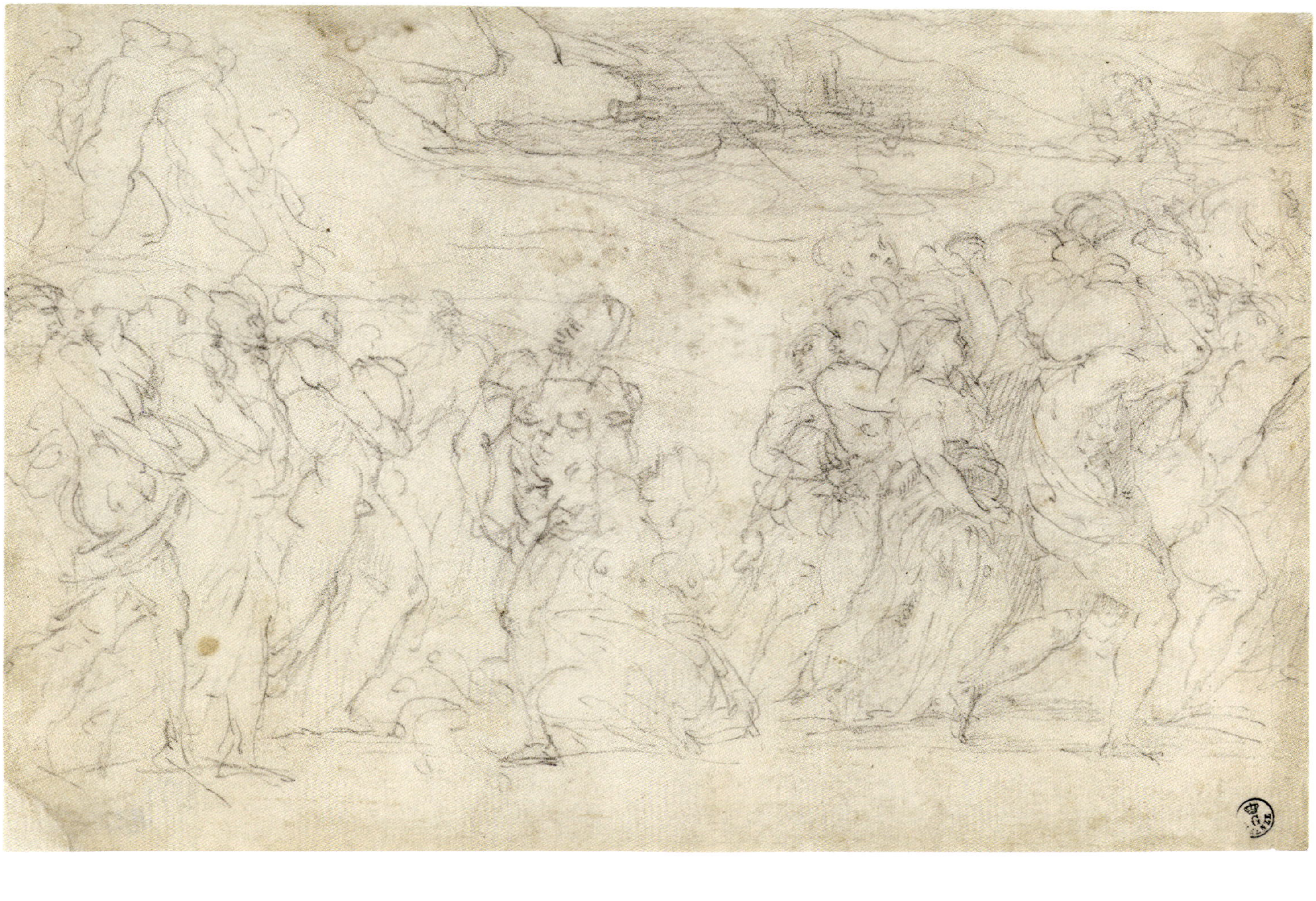

32

BENVENUTO CELLINI

Florence, 1500 – Florence, 1571

Mourning woman (recto); *Design for the seal of the Accademia del Disegno* (verso), 1552 and 1563–69

Pen and brown ink over black chalk, sheet subsequently cut down, 300 × 125 mm (11 13/16 × 4 15/16 in.)
Musée du Louvre, Paris 2752

DETLEF HEIKAMP first recognized the verso of this drawing, previously catalogued as a work by Baccio Bandinelli, to be a design by Cellini for the seal of the Accademia del Disegno in Florence. Its imagery is very close to that in the British Museum drawing (cat. 40), the main differences being that the personified "idea of nature" here wears wings on her head and a look of concentration on her face, rather than radiating light. Her lower half is more herm-like, and the diamond frame that contains her is surrounded by an oval border.

Matthias Winner, the earliest scholar to give close attention to the recto of the drawing, noted the connection between the figure Cellini drew there and the artist's portrayal of Andromeda's mother Cassiopeia in his bronze relief *Perseus Rescuing Andromeda* (cat. 33). Winner also noted, however, that the relief was complete by 1554, whereas the Florentine Academy was only founded in 1563; finding it unlikely that the drawings on recto and verso were separated by nine years or more, he tentatively proposed that the draped woman represented the Virgin Mary. Subsequent scholars (Monbeig-Goguel, Pope-Hennessy) have tended to find the connection to the relief persuasive enough to ignore the dating problem, and several considerations allow cautious support of this theory. The ground line in the drawing, rising from the right before dipping again at left, corresponds closely to its counterpart in the relief, suggesting that Cellini already had some idea of the space into which the figure would fit but had not yet finalized the pose. Cellini may well have proceeded here like many painters in his day, working out a general idea for the composition, then isolating and reworking important individual figures. Also significant is the fact that Cellini determined to consider this figure on paper rather than relying exclusively on a model. Such a decision would be less surprising if he knew that he would ultimately have to depict Cassiopeia in low relief, to set her back in space. In the bronze panel, Cellini gave Cassiopeia a different pose from that in the drawing, turning her feet into profile and raising her arms to her face. He may have done this after deciding instead to arrange Andromeda's father Cepheus with hands at hip and feet oriented downward, necessitating a variation for the mother. This, too, would mean that the drawing preceded Cellini's conception of the final composition.

The drawing appears to have been cut down by a later collector, who regarded the figure, not the seal design, as the most important element on the sheet. M.W.C.

PROVENANCE

Acquired for the Cabinet du Roi, 1671, from Everhard Jabach

LITERATURE

Winner 1968, pp. 301–3; Monbeig-Goguel 1972, pp. 45–46, no. 22; Pope-Hennessy 1985, p. 278–79; Scalini 1995, p. 70; Flemming 2003

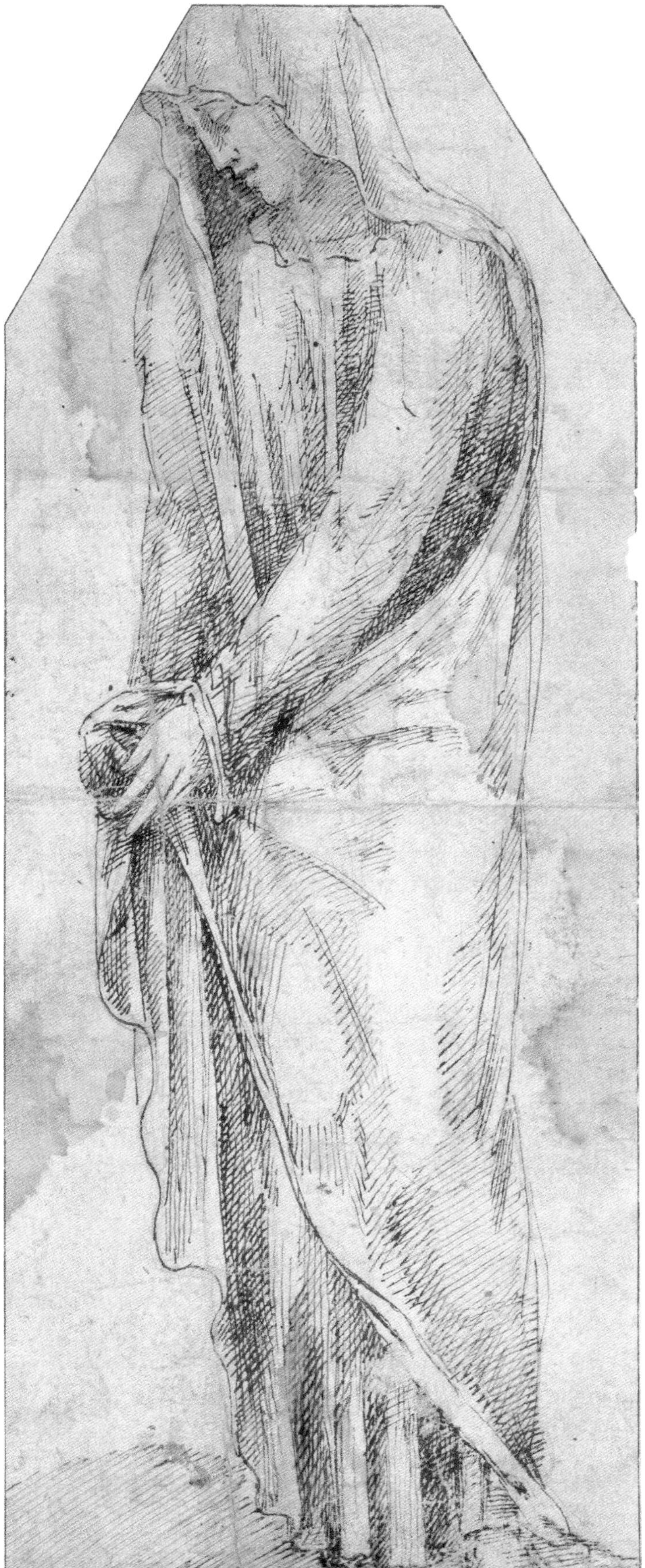

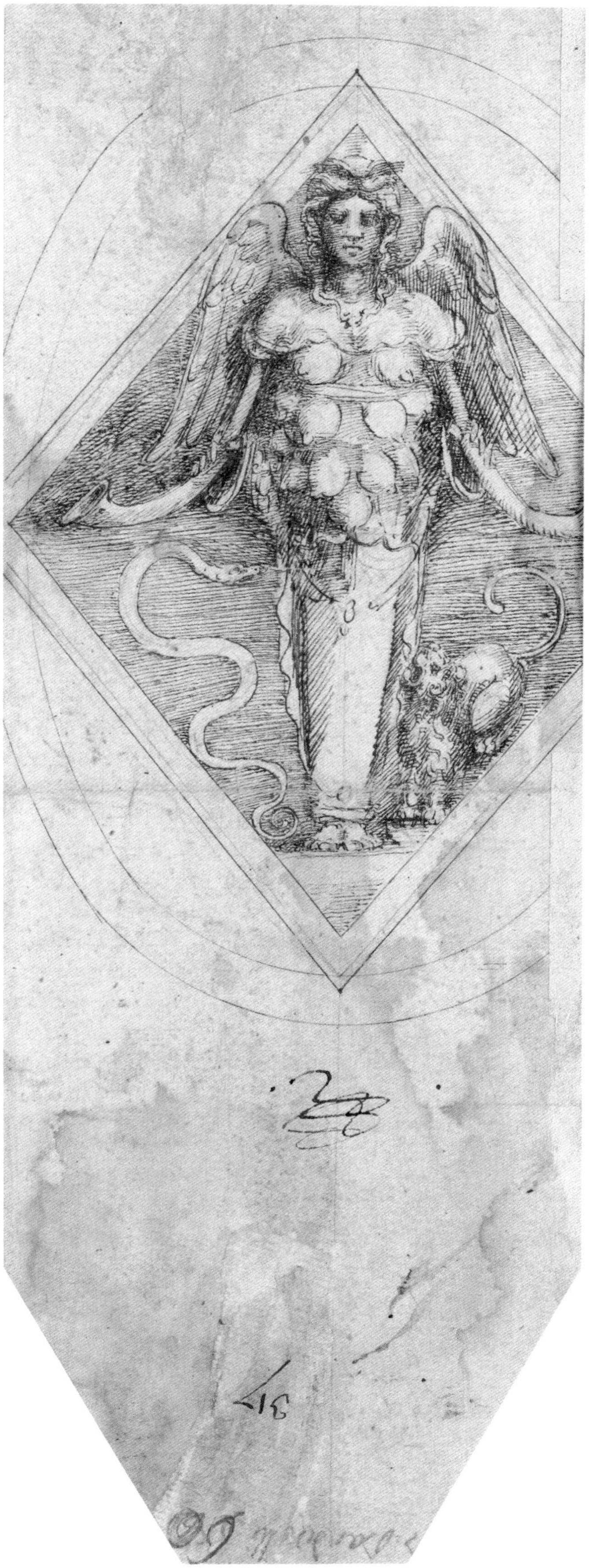

33

BENVENUTO CELLINI

Florence, 1500 – Florence, 1571

Perseus and Andromeda, 1552–53

Bronze, 81 × 90 cm (31 ⅞ × 35 ½)
Museo Nazionale del Bargello, Florence, 483B

ON 20 AUGUST 1552, Bernardo Minerbetti wrote that he had seen in Cellini's workshop "two bronze panels in low relief, which have not been cast but for which the wax is almost complete."[1] One of these must have been the *Perseus and Andromeda,* which was cast by the bellfounder Nardo Calderaio in May 1553 and finished by the goldsmith Cesare da Bagno before its installation on the base of Cellini's *Perseus and Medusa* in early 1554.[2] If Cellini's autobiography is to be believed, the *Andromeda* did not originate with a request from the sculptor's employer, Duke Cosimo I; rather, Cellini undertook the work on his own initiative as he attempted to expand a commission that initially involved only the freestanding bronze figures above.

Cellini distinguished his main characters—the flying figure of Perseus, the dragon he is about to strike, the bound Andromeda, and Andromeda's anxious parents—by executing them in the highest relief. He might well have conceived several of these using separate wax figures: the complex pose of Perseus, who appears at once to plunge downward toward the monster and to halt his flight, twisting to look at Andromeda, corresponds to a model depicted in two contemporary portraits of Cellini.[3] Other details of the composition, moreover, emphasize the physical presence of the protagonists. The wall to which Andromeda was chained in the Perseus myth is transformed in the relief into a kind of pedestal, reminding us that Ovid compared her to a statue. The subsidiary figures are arranged in a way that suggests multiple points of view: at the far right, a little dog goes so far as to poke his head out and around Andromeda's father to get a better perspective on the scene.[4]

At the same time, Cellini seems to have set out to demonstrate that he also understood the flattened, more illusionistic style of relief that descended from Donatello. This brought Cellini's work as a sculptor closer to that of the draftsman. Charles Avery has remarked, for example, that several elements in the relief, notably the running man at the center, appear to have been generated by drawing into the wax model with a sharp instrument. Gwendolyn Trottein has further observed that contemporaries associated Cellini's relief sculpture with drawing: when Cellini attempted to win the commission of another series of relief projects from Baccio Bandinelli, Bandinelli groused that Cellini's figures were full of errors because he did not know how to draw.[5] Cellini's sense that the *Andromeda* panel provided an opportunity to exhibit his skills in draftsmanship may help explain the curious insertion of the battling horsemen at the top right, figures that have no evident connection to the Andromeda story. As Pope-Hennessy recognized, this passage, along with the figure of the bald-headed, shouting man, must allude to Leonardo da Vinci's *Battle of Anghiari.* That work made a deep impression on Cellini when he was learning his craft in the early years of the century. In his autobiography, Cellini writes that "our admirable Lionardo had chosen to depict a battle of horses, with the capture of some standards"—a description that might work for the detail in Andromeda scene as well. Leonardo's design, which Cellini writes that he knew as a cartoon rather than as a painting, was "admirably beautiful." Together with Michelangelo's cartoon *The Battle of Cascina,* it served as a "school of the world."[6] M.W.C.

PROVENANCE

Originally part of the base of the *Perseus* monument in Piazza della Signoria, Florence

LITERATURE

Plon 1883, p. 218; Supino 1901, pp. 24–25; Focillon 1911, p. 101; Camesasca 1955, pp. 23, 45; Braunfels 1961 [first published in 1948], p. 15, fig. 13; Pope-Hennessy 1963, vol. 1, p. 69; Venturi 1967, pp. 479–82; Davis 1976, pp. 8, 14–17; Avery and Barbaglia 1981, pp. 97–98; Weil-Garris Brandt 1983, pp. 410, 414; Pope-Hennessy 1985, pp. 174, 181–82; Hirthe 1988a, pp. 199–200, 204–5, 212–14; Poeschke 1993, p. 215; Meller 1994, p. 14; Mandel 1996a, pp. 374–75; Mandel 1996b; Vossilla 1997, pp. 284–99; Avery 1998, p. 116; Cole 2002, pp. IV, 68, 74–75, 125–45; Wolf 2003, pp. 328–35; Trottein 2004, pp. 144–45; Scalini 1995, p. 70; Pegazzano 2005, pp. 52–53; Trottein 2009, pp. 55–73; Cammarella Falsitta and Falsitta 2009, p. 119

NOTES

1 Barocchi 1971–77, vol. 2, p. 1200: *due tavole di bronzo di basso relievo, le quali non sono gettate, ma quasi fatte di cera.*
2 For the casting, see the document transcribed in Milanesi 1857 p. 256. For the cleaning, see Biblioteca Riccardiana, Florence, MS 2789, 3 right, payment of 3 April 1554.
3 Meller 1994, p. 14, who first observed this, also proposed that the model derives from a lost work by Michelangelo.
4 See the discussion in Cole 2002, esp. pp. 131–32.
5 Trottein 2009, p. 60, cites the passage in conjunction with the *Andromeda* relief.
6 Cellini 1971, p. 82.

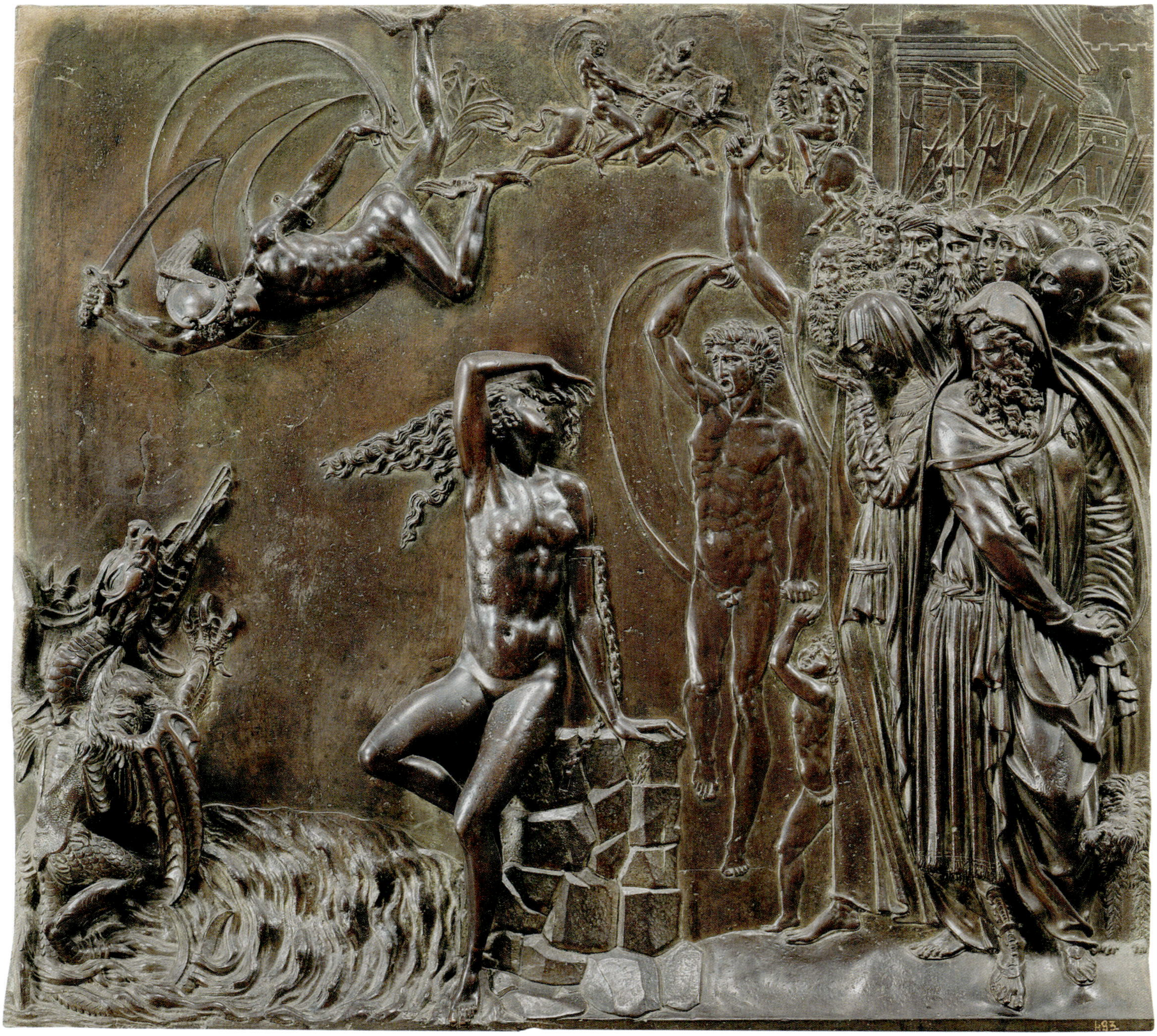

34

GUGLIELMO DELLA PORTA

Porlezza, beside Lake Lugano, c. 1510 – Rome, 1577

The Banquet of the Gods, c. 1560–70

Pen and brown ink, over black chalk; 123 × 166 mm (4 5/16 × 6 9/16 in.)
The Metropolitan Museum of Art, New York, Rogers Fund, 1963 63.103.3

LIKE CELLINI, Guglielmo della Porta worked in both a monumental and a miniature idiom (though unlike Cellini he was not trained as a goldsmith). To the latter category belongs a series of sixteen oval and octagonal-shaped reliefs depicting scenes from Ovid's *Metamorphoses.* These were designed by Guglielmo and modeled by his assistant Jacob Cobaert (c. 1535–1615). Bronze plaquettes were cast by a number of different artists at the end of the sixteenth century, some years after the sculptor's death.[1] This sprightly drawing of the Banquet of the Gods formulated for an oval-shaped field is a design for one of these small-scale reliefs (see cat. 35).[2] Recognizable among the assembled Olympians are the languidly reclining Apollo with his lyre; Mercury holding a caduceus; Venus, with a clinging Cupid, at the left; and, flanking her, Mars, sporting a helmet, and Hercules, grasping a club. Another helmeted figure at the right is probably Minerva. The male and female figures reaching across the table with impossibly long arms can plausibly be identified as Jupiter and Juno.

The drawing's precise narrative subject is ambiguous. It may depict the marriage banquet of Peleus and Thetis. However, the defining episode of that Greek myth (retold by Ovid), the awarding of the golden apple of discord by Eris, is not shown. Similar banquet scenes in the Villa Farnesina in Rome by Raphael's workshop and the Palazzo Te in Mantua by Giulio Romano depict the marriage feast of Cupid and the mortal nymph Psyche from the *Golden Ass* (originally entitled *Metamorphoses*) by the Roman poet Apuleius.[3] If this is the subject, the diminutive servant is Ganymede, who bears the drink of immortality for Psyche (probably the seated female at his left). The plaquettes diverge from and clarify elements of Guglielmo's somewhat jumbled composition and, as a result, seem more clearly to represent that particular banquet. The possibility also exists that this is a generic Olympian feast (hence the portrayal of Cupid as an irrepressible toddler rather than an adolescent bridegroom) that was transformed into a specific *storia* by Cobaert.

The slender, attenuated figures with tiny heads and claw-like hands are typical of Guglielmo della Porta's distinctive manner as a draftsman, as are the trembling line and abbreviated hooked strokes that serve as shorthand notations for suggesting hair and musculature. Also typical of the artist is the manner of filling in space with tight, striated vertical hatching. Suggesting a flat, solid background from which forms emerge, the technique evokes the properties of a relief. Rarely do the figures in his drawings exhibit a concomitant sculptural volume or plasticity, however. Instead, their insubstantial, lumpy forms have an oozing quality, as though formed of wet clay. The legacy of Guglielmo's presumed formative activity in the workshop of Perino del Vaga as a *stuccatore* (stucco worker), a specialized practitioner expert at modeling in the soft, malleable medium of stucco, may inform this aspect of his graphic style. L.W-S.

PROVENANCE

"Pseudo-Crozat" (unidentified collector, formerly mistaken for Pierre Crozat; Lugt 474); John F. Keane; sale, Sotheby's, London, 21 May 1963, lot 55

LITERATURE

Bean and Stampfle 1965, no. 111

NOTES

1 The only complete set is the series of sixteen bronze plaques once in the Este collection in Modena and now in the Kunsthistorisches Museum, Vienna (Planiscig 1919, nos. 395–410; Coppel Aréizaga et al. 2012, pp. 40–43). See further cat. 37.
2 Bean and Stampfle 1965, no. 112.
3 Ovid's *Metamphoses* is invariably cited as the literary source of Guglielmo's designs in accordance with an autograph notation in one of his sketchbooks: *in questo libro schizzero le storie de hovidio per l'ornamento dele tavole orientale* (Gramberg 1964, Textband, p. 100, no. 180). However, the present scene is not self-evidently based on that text, and its source may instead be the *Golden Ass.*

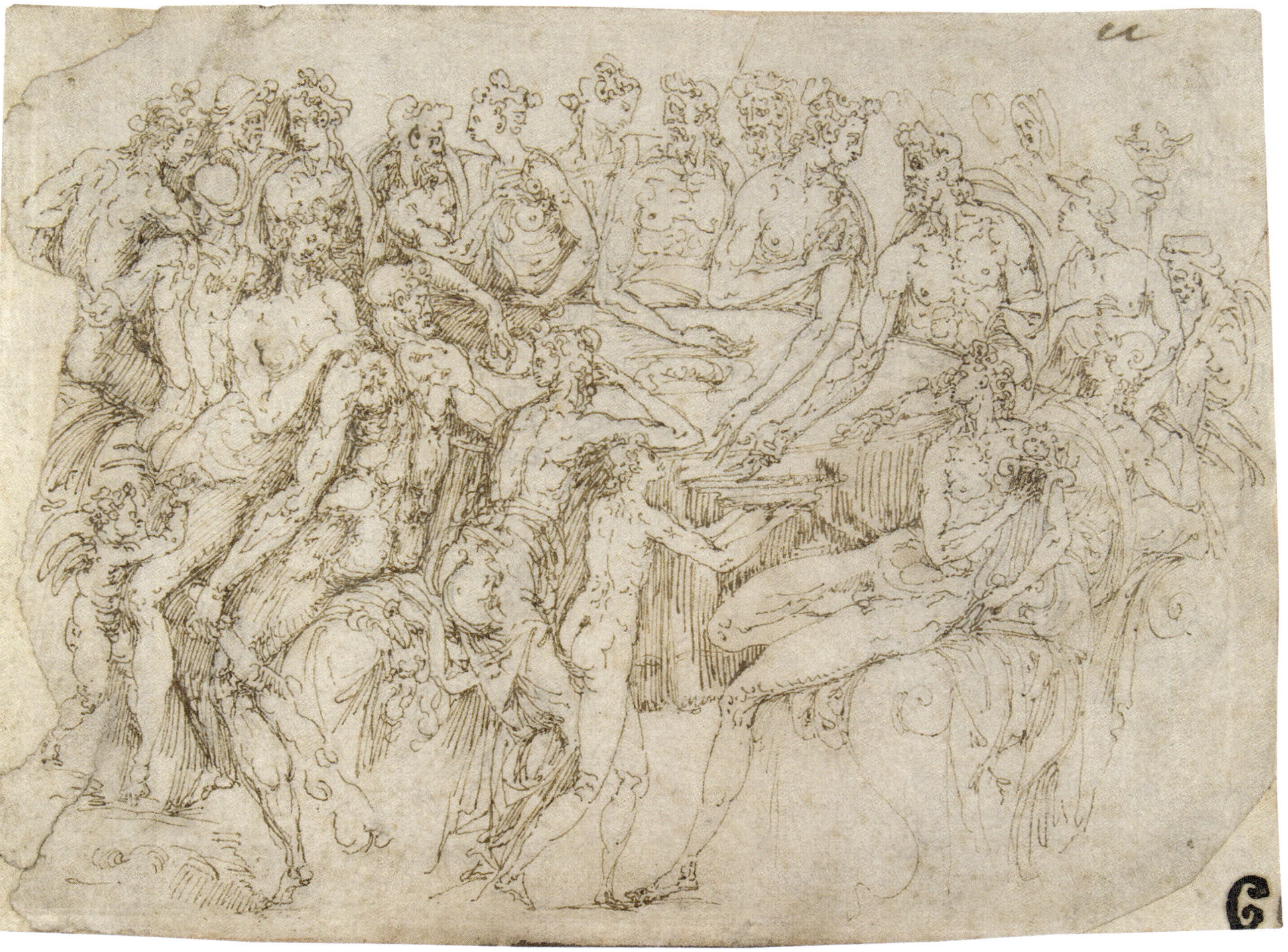

35

CESARE TARGONE, attributed to
active in Rome and Florence, 1575–90

The Banquet of the Gods, c. 1580–1600

Gold, lapis lazuli, carnelian, and slate, 140 × 244 mm (5½ × 9⅝ in.)
The Metropolitan Museum of Art, New York, Rogers Fund, 1912 12.135.5

THIS PRECIOUS RELIEF derives from an invention by the great sculptor Guglielmo della Porta, as indicated by a drawing also in the Metropolitan Museum (cat. 34) and by a series of bronze plaquettes. (The most complete version of this series, which consists of sixteen reliefs—eight oval and eight octagonal—is preserved in the Kunsthistorisches Museum in Vienna.) The relief exhibited here is part of a series of specimens executed in precious metal that reproduces the eight oval compositions. Six of the other reliefs in this group are in Berlin; one is in a private collection.[1]

When Guglielmo was designing this series of reliefs with mythological scenes taken from Ovid's *Metamorphoses*, he was already thinking about the translation of models into gold or silver plaquettes. This is evident in a letter datable to about 1575, in which Guglielmo proposed to a Spanish correspondent that he would make "sixteen Greek moral stories of low relief in silver and gold for the adornment of tables and cabinets."[2]

The relief was acquired by the museum as a work of Benvenuto Cellini, an attribution that Joseph Breck mantained in 1912. In 1939 John Goldsmith Phillips proposed a new attribution to Antonio Gentili da Faenza, one of the most important goldsmiths active in Rome in the second half of the sixteenth century. His reasons were to be found primarily in the documents of a 1609 lawsuit, which indicate that Antonio and Guglielmo were "very close friends" and that, after Guglielmo's death in 1577, Antonio kept the models of the Ovidian myths in his workshop.[3] Gentili, however, was principally an "*orefice grossiere*,"[4] a goldsmith who worked on large-scale objects, often cast in silver, as his documented works well attest. We can probably attribute to him two embossed silver reliefs today in the Biblioteca Apostolica Vaticana with reproductions of Guglielmo's inventions (*The Fall of the Giants* and *Perseus and Phineus*), works once attributed to Cellini[5] and later to Guglielmo's assistant, Jacob Cobaert.[6] But the friendship and collaboration between Guglielmo and Antonio do not represent, in my opinion, sufficient reason to attribute the series of gold reliefs to Antonio. These required an artisan with a technical ability and a specialization substantially different from that of Antonio. The ideal candidate is a different goldsmith, Cesare Targone, as Ann Gabbart suggested several decades ago.[7]

The nephew of a Venetian jeweler celebrated by Cellini, Targone was characterized by the biographer Giovanni Baglione as a goldsmith "who made large-scale objects into small ones, and formed noble figurines, little stories in gold, and very well made compositions of precious stone."[8] In 1585 Cesare worked in Florence together with Antonio Susini on a series of reliefs in gold repoussé based on Giambologna's wax models.[9] These reliefs were destined for a *studiolo* of Francesco I de' Medici. The waxes and the surviving incised metal molds make it possible to understand the technique used by Targone: the process, which Cellini also described in his treatise on goldsmithery, called for the working of a thin gold leaf first from the back—pressing it into a mold or using a tool freehand—and then from the front, using other tools to shape the surface.[10] The finished object was then welded to a ground, generally a colored hard stone (lapis lazuli, ardesia).

What is most noteworthy is that a few undisputed works by Targone, including his signed masterpiece in the Getty Museum,[11] are clearly connected to inventions and drawings by Guglielmo della Porta, as Ulrich Middeldorf demonstrated.[12] The fact that Targone was employed by the Medici to execute objects of this singular type demonstrates that he was considered at the time to be a specialist in this technique. The very close affinities between the technical features of Targone's documented works and the drawings and compositions by Guglielmo della Porta present a powerful case in favor of Targone's authorship of the eight gold reliefs of Ovid's *Metamorphoses*. D.G.

PROVENANCE

Julius Böhler, Munich; Rogers Fund 1912

LITERATURE

Breck 1912, pp. 192–93; Breck 1913, pp. 75–77, no. 75-A; Phillips 1939; Gramberg 1960, pp. 45–48; Gabhart 1968–69, pp. 35–39

NOTES

1 Bange 1922, pp. 2–3, nos. 8–13; Christie's, London, King Street, Sale 7889, 9 December 2010, lot 285.
2 Gramberg 1964, Textband, p. 108, no. 200.
3 Bertolotti 1881, p. 145.
4 Baglione 1649, p. 109.
5 Plon 1883, p. 278.
6 Gramberg 1968, p. 74.
7 Gabhart 1968–69, pp. 35–39.
8 Baglione 1649, p. 329.
9 See B. Bertelli in Paolozzi Strozzi and Zikos 2006, pp. 226–31, nos. 33–35.
10 Cellini 1857, pp. 71–98.
11 See Cambareri in Fogelman and Fusco 2002, pp. 108–15.
12 Middeldorf 1976; Middeldorf 1977.

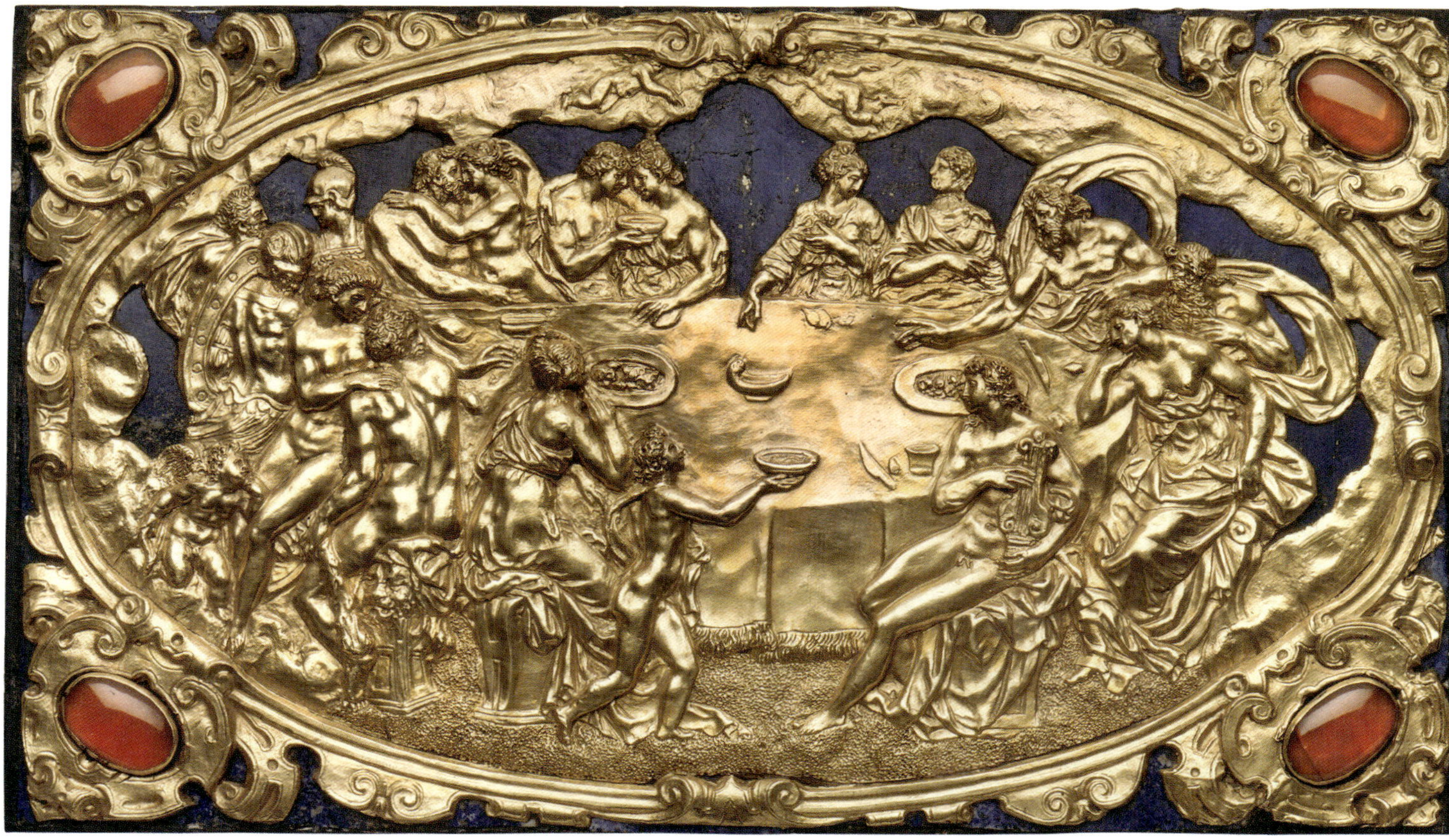

36

GUGLIELMO DELLA PORTA

Lugano, c. 1500 – Rome, 1577

The Fall of the Giants, c. 1560–70

Pen and brown ink, over black chalk, 179 × 258 mm (7 1/16 × 10 3/16 in.)
The Pierpont Morgan Library and Museum, New York I, 33

LIKE THE *Banquet of the Gods* (cat. 34), this drawing is a study by Guglielmo della Porta for one of sixteen bronze plaquettes illustrating moralizing stories from Ovid's *Metamorphoses* (see cat. 37), versions of which were cast after the sculptor's death from models by his pupil Jacob Cobaert.[1] The subject is the Fall of the Giants—the apocalyptic battle between the Olympian deities and a race of titans who challenged their dominion. With the aid of Hercules the giants were vanquished by Jupiter, who hurled his flaming thunderbolts at them as they attempted to scale Olympus. Cast down to the underworld, they became the source of earthquakes and volcanoes.

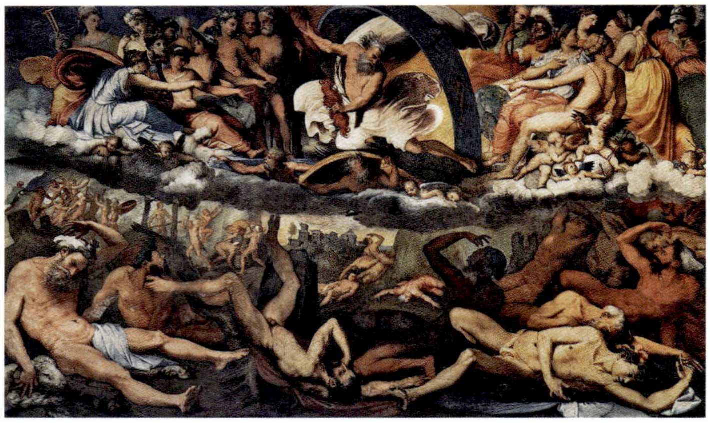

FIG. 71
Perino del Vaga
The Fall of the Giants, c. 1529–30
Fresco
Palazzo Doria, Genoa

Recognized here are Jupiter with his thunderbolt and eagle at the center, Mercury with the caduceus, and, at the far left—a spectator more than an avenger—Hercules with his club. Seated on his lap with her arm draped around him, a crescent moon on her head, is the goddess Diana. Contrasting with this ordered row of deities is the collapsed, jumbled heap of giants below. Although the composition is incomplete at the right and no framing contour line is indicated, the two tiers of figures are arranged in a loosely ovoid field that suggests the intended shape of the corresponding plaquette. On the verso is an unrelated study for a silver-gilt cup. The present sheet may be the *schizzo della fulminatione dell giganti* ("sketch of the fulmination of the giants") that the sculptor in 1574 gave to the Florentine collector Niccolo Gaddi, then resident in Rome.[2]

The wiry figures with implausibly small heads and elongated limbs are familiar aspects of Guglielmo's graphic style. Also typical of his draftsmanship are the quivering, spidery line and a claustrophobic sense of horror vacui, manifest in the condensed compression of forms and cramped, shallow space, and the tendency to fill every void with long, tight, hatched strokes. The corresponding plaquette retains the somewhat illegible character of the present, populous design, which proved to be an overly ambitious idea for a small-scale invention.[3] This lapse is accounted for by its derivation from a monumental source, Perino del Vaga's *Fall of the Giants* ceiling fresco in the Palazzo Doria (fig. 71), which was well known to Guglielmo from his years in Genoa. If not entirely successful, the appropriation nonetheless testifies to a fluidity between the monumental and the miniature—the elastic inflating and shrinking of forms and motifs—that informs mid-sixteenth-century Central Italian art. L.W-S.

PROVENANCE

Possibly Niccolo Gaddi, Florence; "Pseudo-Crozat" (unidentified collector, formerly mistaken for Pierre Crozat; Lugt 474); Jonathan Richardson, Sr., London (1665–1745; Lugt 2183); John Barnard, London (d. 1784; Lugt 1419); Sir Thomas Lawrence, London (1769–1830; Lugt 2445); Brooke sale, London, Sotheby, Wilkinson and Hodge, 20 June 1891, lot 216, as Benvenuto Cellini; Charles Fairfax Murray, London; from whom purchased by J. Pierpont Morgan in 1910

LITERATURE

Bean and Stampfle 1965, no. 112

NOTES

1 In addition to the references cited in cat. 37, see also Phillips 1939 on the plaquettes, particularly *The Fall of the Giants* to which the present drawing relates.
2 In one of Guglielmo's Düsseldorf sketchbooks there is a draft letter to Giovanni Antonio Dosio dated 24 May 1574, which records the sculptor's intention to send a drawing of this subject to Gaddi as a gift; see Bean and Stampfle 1965, no. 112.
3 Reproductive prints and copy drawings based on this widely circulated design all clarify and make more legible the murky composition. Among other examples, see, i.e., the reproductive engraving ascribed to Matthias Greuter of c. 1581–86, an impression of which is in the British Museum (1861,0713.1211), and an anonymous copy drawing in the Art Institute of Chicago (1922.154). Greuter's engraving provides a terminus ante quem for the plaquette, on which it is based.

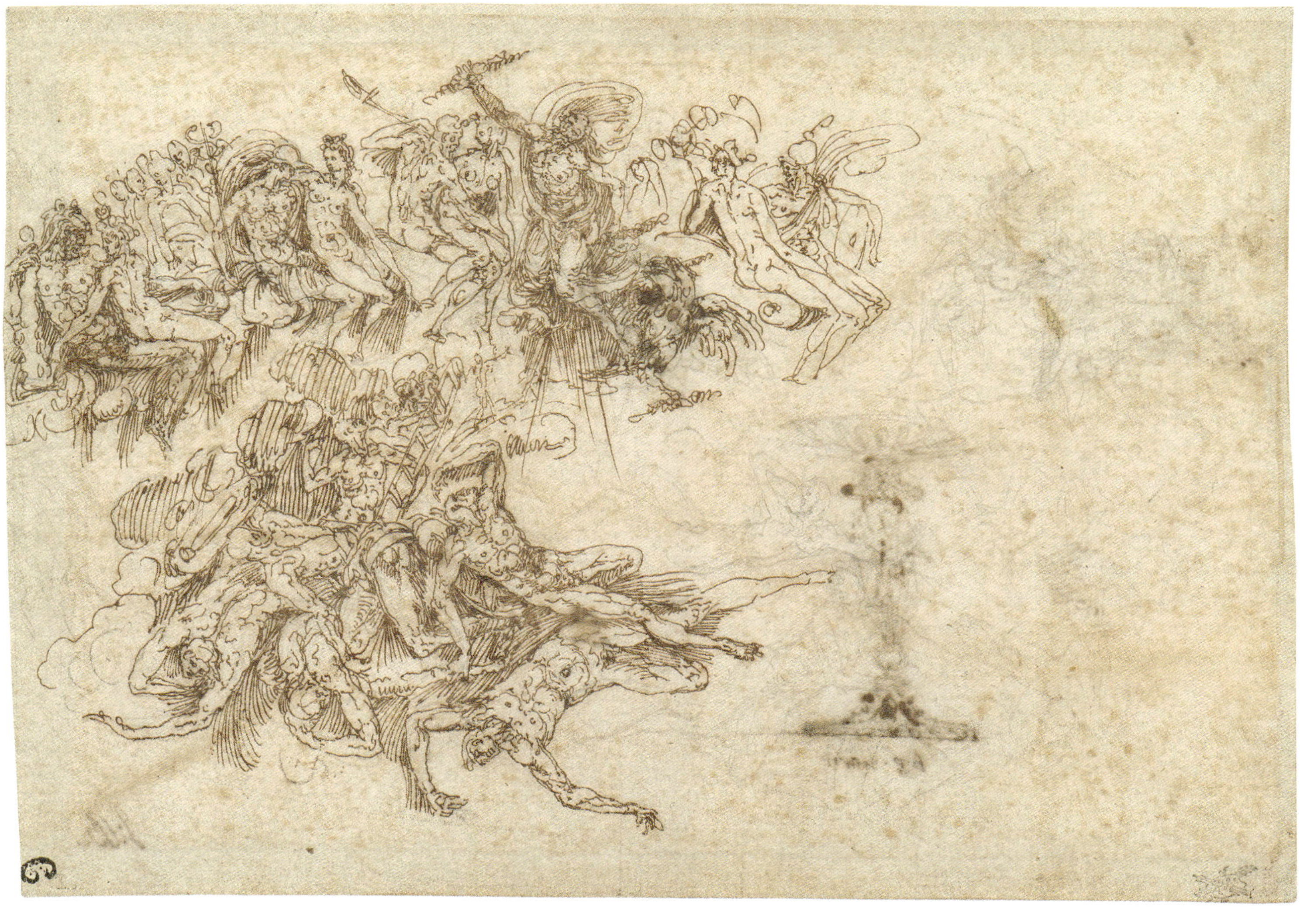

37

FIDIA DELLA PORTA

after 1538 – after 1589

The Fall of the Giants, c. 1560–70

Bronze, 143 × 222 mm (5⅝ × 8¾ in.)
Inscribed, on the reverse: *FIDIA F[ecit]*
The Metropolitan Museum of Art, New York, Rogers Fund, 1938 38.152.13

THIS PLAQUETTE (signed on the reverse) is the only known work by Fidia della Porta, the illegitimate son of the sculptor Guglielmo della Porta.[1] It is an object of greater historic than artistic interest, as it helps in understanding the workings of Guglielmo's workshop.

Fidia's plaquette is a rough, simplified copy of an invention by his father attested to by the drawing in the Morgan Library and Museum of New York exhibited here (cat. 36) and by other bronze casts of varying quality. The relief by Guglielmo with the Fall of the Giants is from a series of sixteen reliefs representing episodes from Ovid's *Metamorphoses* (see also cat. 34, 35). Eight of the reliefs are in an oval format (*The Battle between Perseus and Phineas*, *Meleager and the Calydonian Boar*, *Scene of Satyrs*, *Dance of Nymphs*, *Bacchanal*, *Massacre of the Niobids*, *Banquet of the Gods*), and eight are octagonal (*Hermaphroditus and Salmacis*, *Diana and Callisto*, *Venus and Mars*, *The Fall of Phaeton*, *Apollo and Marsyas*, *The Judgment of Paris*, *Venus and Adonis*, *Liriope and Narcissus*). A complete set is found in the Kunsthistorisches Museum in Vienna.[2]

Rudolf Berliner identified the series with that described by the biographer Giovanni Baglione as a work by Jacob Cobaert,[3] a Flemish sculptor and goldsmith who worked in the Roman workshop of Guglielmo della Porta.[4] The studies of Ulrich Middeldorf and Werner Gramberg have rightly reframed Cobaert's role as an executor of graphic models made by Guglielmo.[5] The authorship of the original compositions is confirmed in a series of sheets undoubtedly by the hand of Guglielmo (cat. 34, 36), as well as in a few annotations in the sculptor's notebooks in Düsseldorf, and finally in various letters Guglielmo sent to potential clients in which the reliefs with the "stories of Ovid" were designated as "for the adornment of tables and of *studioli*."[6]

In the Victoria and Albert Museum in London there are two models in terracotta representing Meleager and the Calydonian Boar and a dance of nymphs, probably by Jacob Cobaert.[7] Four other terracotta models, in the Museo Nazionale di Palazzo Venezia in Rome, considered autograph works by Guglielmo,[8] are in my opinion later replicas, given that they are smaller than the bronze plaquettes and entirely lack the plastic definition of the London models. The success and circulation of Guglielmo's inventions lasted long after his death, as a set of legal documents from 1609 attests.[9]

Fidia's plaquette can be considered a workshop exercise of the young and not very talented son of Guglielmo. Fidia—just like Cobaert—had to realize a three-dimensional model from the invention of his father; this model was the source of the bronze exhibited here, which was likely also made as a workshop exercise. Fidia, however, translated the complexity and elegance of the original composition with rather less success than the Flemish goldsmith demonstrated. D.G.

PROVENANCE

New York, Herman Falkenberg; Rogers Fund, 1938

LITERATURE

Phillips 1939, p. 150; Gramberg 1960, p. 49

NOTES

1 On Guglielmo della Porta, see Brentano 1989.
2 Planiscig 1919, pp. 188–92, nos. 395–410.
3 Berliner 1921–22, p. 134
4 Baglione 1649, p. 100.
5 Middeldorf 1935; Gramberg 1960; Gramberg 1964.
6 Gramberg 1964,Textband, p. 100, no. 180.
7 Gramberg 1960, pp. 42–43.
8 Cannata 1982, pp. 72–76.
9 See the present author's essay in this volume.

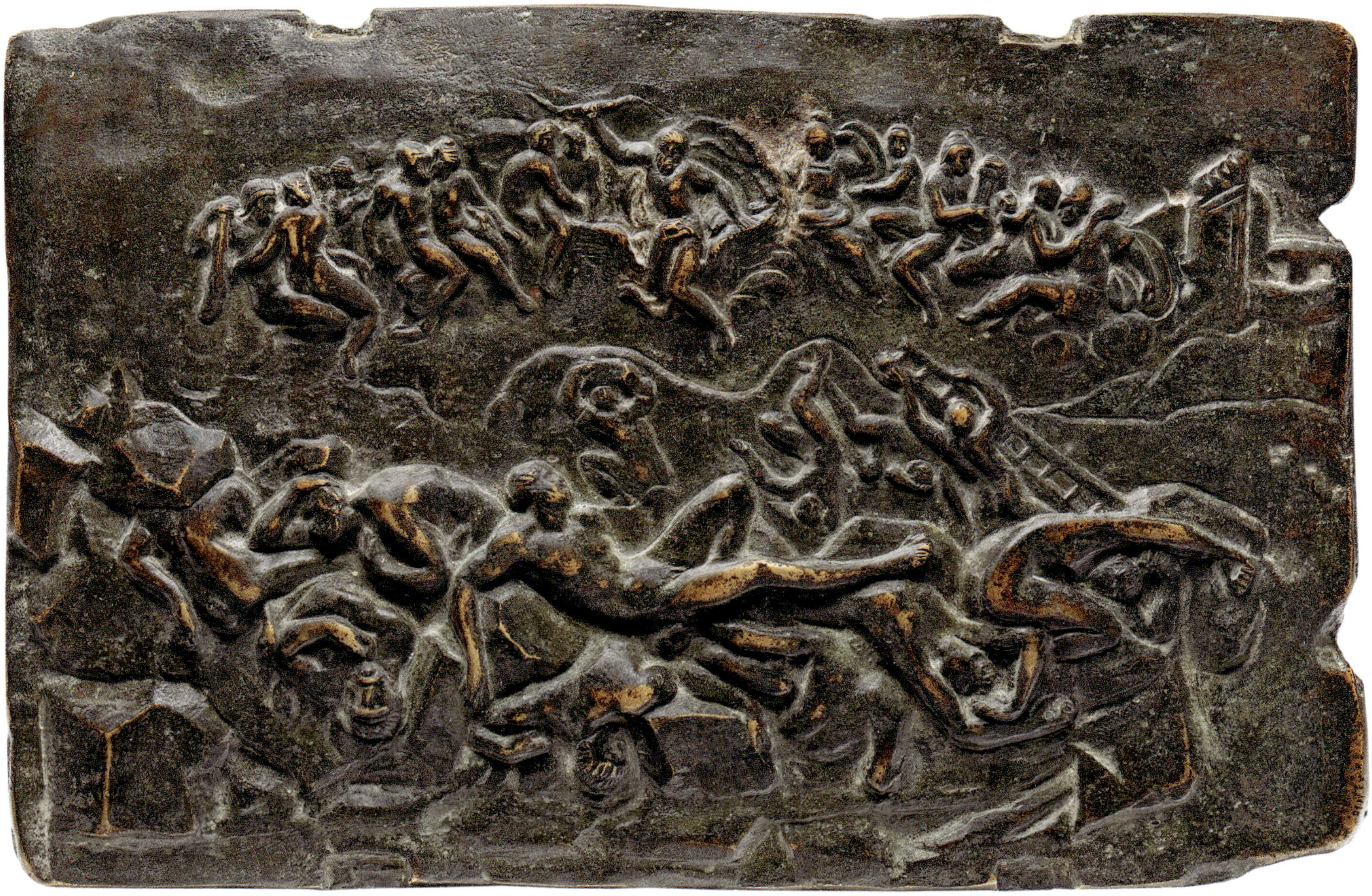

38

ENEA VICO

Parma, 1523 – 1567, Ferrara

The Academy of Baccio Bandinelli, c. 1561–62

Published by Pietro Paolo Palumbo (Italian, active in Rome, 1563–86 [?])
Engraving (second state);[1] 306 × 479 mm (12 × 18⅞ in.)
Inscribed on left-hand page of open book at upper right: *Baccius/ Bandi/ nellus/ invent.*;
on right-hand page: *Enea uigo Parmegiano sculpsit*; at lower edge: *Romae Petrus Paulus Palumbus formis*
Museum of Fine Arts, Boston, Fund in memory of Horatio Greenough Curtis 1976.611

THIS IMAGE of young draftsmen toiling by firelight and candlelight is one of two engravings depicting Bandinelli's academy, the name given to the informal drawing sessions taught by the sculptor. The earlier print by Agostino Veneziano (see fig. 43), which bears the date 1531, records that these gatherings took place in Bandinelli's apartments in the Belvedere in the Vatican. While various academies and sodalities existed in Rome—most notably the humanist Academia Romana established in the fifteenth century by Pomponio Leto—Bandinelli's was the first devoted solely to artistic instruction.[2] His model may have been the Giardino di San Marco, the informal academy established by Lorenzo de' Medici in Florence and presided over by the sculptor Bertoldo, where drawing after sculpture in the Medici collection was among the pedagogical exercises.

Vico's engraving incorporates numerous elements of the earlier composition and expands on that source. Lacking the ceiling beams that create a sense of spatial recession, the room is larger and includes a fireplace—a second light source that vies with the bright flame of the candle on the table. Augmented by a classical bust and by skulls and other skeletal remains, the models or statuettes here, in contrast to the intact examples in Veneziano's print, are almost all missing limbs. Their fragmentary state conveys that these are antiquities rather than modern works by Bandinelli himself. Although the room is littered with these familiar trappings of an artist's studio, none is the object of the young draftsmen's attention or study: they are assiduously drawing (or discoursing on drawing, or ruminating on drawing), but the act does not proceed from observation; rather, it is an idea that originates in the mind (the province of the weighty tomes stacked on the shelf). Drawing is thus presented as an abstract, intellectual formulation—what later sixteenth-century artistic theory would propound as *disegno interno*—rather than an empirical practice grounded in the study of art and nature.[3]

In the Veneziano print, Bandinelli—the bearded figure seated at the table holding a statuette—is portrayed as a *maestro del disegno*, the accomplished teacher who instructs the diligent young draftsmen gathered around him. But in Vico's engraving, where he appears at the far right, he is an ancillary bystander—an irrelevant observer rather than an active participant in his own academy (here, perhaps, an academy in Florence rather than the earlier Roman iteration).[4] His short hair and long beard are consistent with his appearance as recorded in various portraits and self-portraits, but it is primarily through the insignia of the Order of Santiago emblazoned on his tunic, which recurs on the shield above the mantelpiece, that his identity is communicated. (Bandinelli was awarded this knighthood by Emperor Charles V in 1530 and thereafter signed himself a Knight

---

LITERATURE

Landau and Parshall 1994, p. 286; Waldmann 2001, pp. 233–37; Clifton 2005, pp. 86–88, no. 21; Thomas 2005; Ben Thomas in Franklin 2005, pp. 278–79, no. 100; Ulrich Pfisterer in Berlin 2007, pp. 106–13, no. 25; Hegener 2008, pp. 405, 625–26, no. 52; Mozzati 2014, pp. 530–31, no. 78

NOTES

1 The existence of a third state of this print was established by Thomas 2005, p. 13.

2 See Pevsner 1940, pp. 33–66, for a survey of early Italian art academies. The so-called academy that Leonardo da Vinci established in Milan (the Achademia Leonardo da Vinci) seems to have been a gathering of poets, musicians, and humanists rather than an artist's teaching academy, though Bandinelli—a great admirer of the older artist—may well have had this "academy" in mind as well, as the self-conscious appropriation of that resonant word for his venture suggests. Ulrich Pfisterer has noted that Bandinelli treats the subject of academies in his unfinished treatise "Libro del disegno" (2007, p. 108).

3 Significantly, two of the interlocutors in Anton Franceso Doni's 1549 dialogue *Disegno* are Art and Nature—testimony that drawing as conceptualized by Bandinelli (whose views are articulated in Doni's dialogue) in the 1540s was founded on these two pillars.

4 As suggested by Louis Waldmann in Haines 2001. Correspondence exchanged between Bandinelli and Duke Cosimo de' Medici in the 1540s and 1550s contains references to the sculptor instructing his students in drawing, though the academy nomenclature is not used.

5 Ideas explored in greater depth by Thomas 2005 and Thomas in Franklin 2005, p. 278, no. 100.

6 Thomas in Franklin 2005, p. 278, no. 100, and Pfisterer 2007, who further notes that two different and unrelated perspectival systems have been employed for the left and right halves of the disjointed composition. Thomas, ibid., also traces the publication history of the print (an approximate terminus post quem for which is provided by the beginning of Palumbo's activity as a publisher in Rome) and proposes that the author of the design may have been Vico himself.

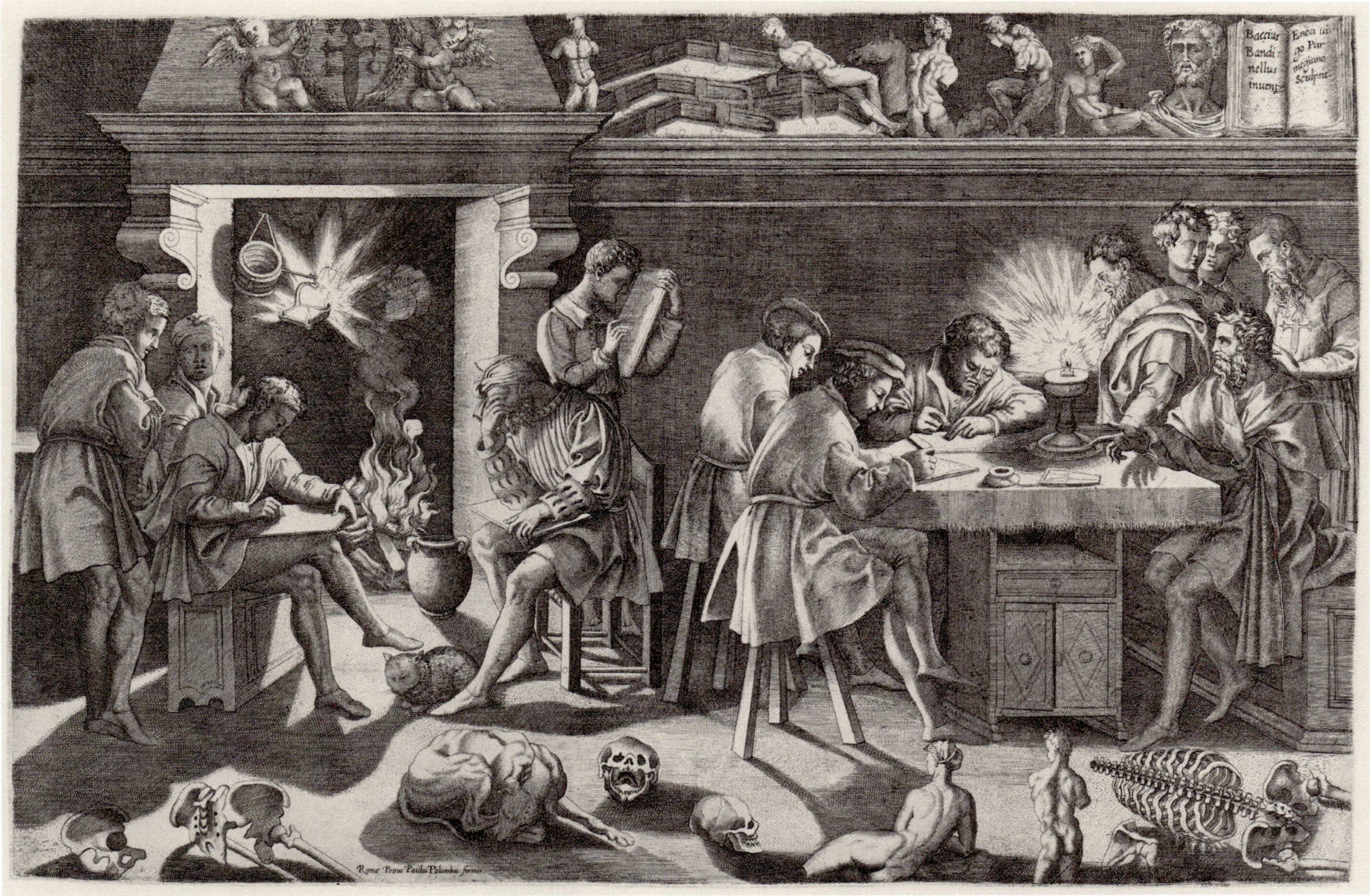

of Saint James.) While Veneziano's print depicts a seemingly real-life tableau, Bandinelli instructing his pupils, Vico's engraving is pre-eminently about an idea, the nobility of drawing—here portrayed as a theoretical and intellectual pursuit—and its corollary, the nobility of the artist. Lacking an inscription identifying the specific locus, the image may in fact represent not an actual drawing academy presided over by Bandinelli (hence his curiously marginal status), but an ideal academy such as the artist himself imagined in his writings, authentic and spurious. These twinned conceits also inform the presentation of Bandinelli's ideas in Anton Francesco Doni's 1549 dialogue *Disegno*, the painted portrait in the Gardner Museum (see cat. 28), and the purported autobiography (in fact, a posthumous compilation) known as the "Memoriale".[5] Presenting Bandinelli as a gifted draftsman and learned pedagogue, those literary and visual accounts all serve as counterweights—and, in the case of the *Memoriale*, a historical corrective—to the negative portrayals put forth by Cellini, Vasari, and other contemporaries.

It was long assumed that Vico's print was based on a design by Bandinelli and produced during his lifetime. However, recent scholarship has posited that the invention, like the *Memoriale*, is a posthumous pastiche—an assemblage of figures and motifs appropriated from disparate sources (including drawings by Bandinelli himself) and awkwardly fused into a composition that is spatially and thematically incoherent.[6] That some of the theoretical ideas about drawing expressed here would have been anachronistic for the 1540s but were current in the 1560s, when the Florentine Accademia del Disegno was founded, supports this contention. L.W-S.

39

VINCENZO DE' ROSSI

Fiesole, 1525 – Florence, 1587

Fountain with the Labors of Hercules, c. 1562

Black chalk over stylus, 433 × 253 mm (17 1/16 × 9 15/16 in.)
Inscribed in brown ink in a later hand: *Bacchio 46*
Cooper-Hewitt National Design Museum, Smithsonian Institution, New York 1942-36-1

WHEN BACCIO BANDINELLI DIED in 1560, his former student Vincenzo de' Rossi, then in Rome, saw a new opportunity for himself in Florence. He wrote to Duke Cosimo, hoping to submit a proposal for the Neptune fountain Bandinelli could no longer complete. The duke instead held a competition for that project and ultimately awarded it to Bartolomeo Ammannati. Still, Vincenzo's admirer and supporter Giorgio Vasari reported that Cosimo soon thereafter brought Vincenzo to Florence, commissioning "the Labours of Hercules in figures of marble larger than life and in the round."[1] An inscription on the verso of a drawing by Vincenzo in the Musée du Louvre (inv. 1573) further informs us that the statues were to have narrative reliefs in bronze below. The present drawing, as Detlef Heikamp first recognized, must have been made by Vincenzo in conjunction with this project.

To create the drawing, which shows the fountain from a high vantage point, Vincenzo incised the basic architectural forms into the page with a stylus and straightedge, then drew the primary features over this in black chalk. The use of chalk to make such a careful and detailed rendering of a complex figural and architectural project was rare in Renaissance Italy. Vincenzo must have learned the technique from Bandinelli, to whom the drawing was originally attributed. That Vincenzo made the drawing fairly early in his design process is evident from the fact that none of the marbles as executed (fig. 72) hew very closely to their chalk counterparts. Perhaps the drawing served as an example of what Ward, describing Bandinelli's practice, called an "intermediate *modello*": a kind of transitional drawing in which disparate preliminary figure studies "are united in an organized and clearly articulated whole and thus present (for the benefit of both patron and artist) a reasonable idea for the projected appearance of the finished work of art."[2] Just how reasonable an idea this drawing

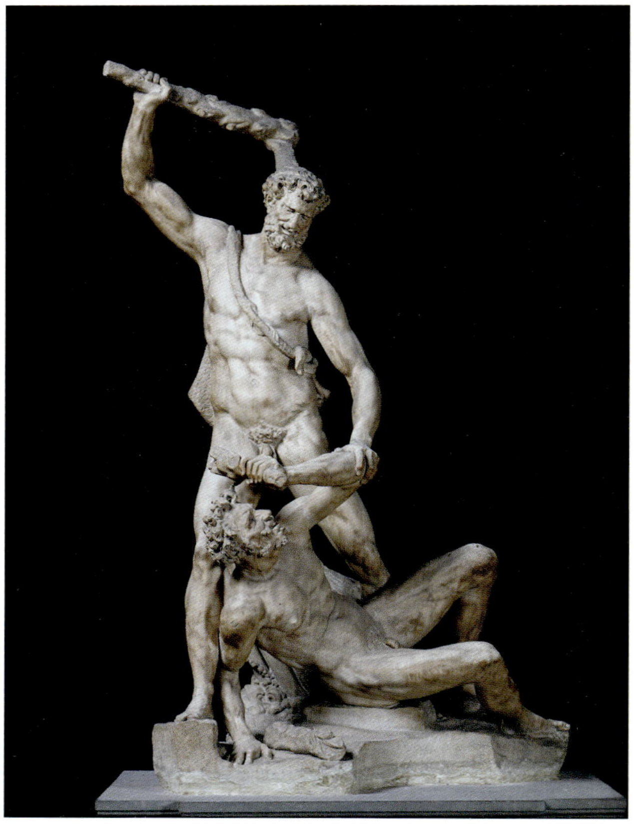

FIG. 72
Vincenzo de' Rossi
Hercules and Cacus, c. 1570
Marble
Palazzo Vecchio, Florence

PROVENANCE

Sir Joshua Reynolds (Lugt 2364); purchased by the Cooper Union Museum from P. & D. Colnaghi and Co., London, 1942 (with attribution to Baccio Bandinelli)

LITERATURE

Maser 1957, p. 21, no. 15 (artist unknown, Italy, about 1540); Wunder 1959, p. 6, no. 3 (unknown Florentine artist about 1540–50); Heikamp 1964; Utz 1971; Eisler 1981, n.p., no. 15; Cox-Rearick 1984, pp. 186–87; Miller 1988, p. 69; Heikamp 1997, p. 356; Avery 1998, p. 117; Fiorani 2005, p. 37

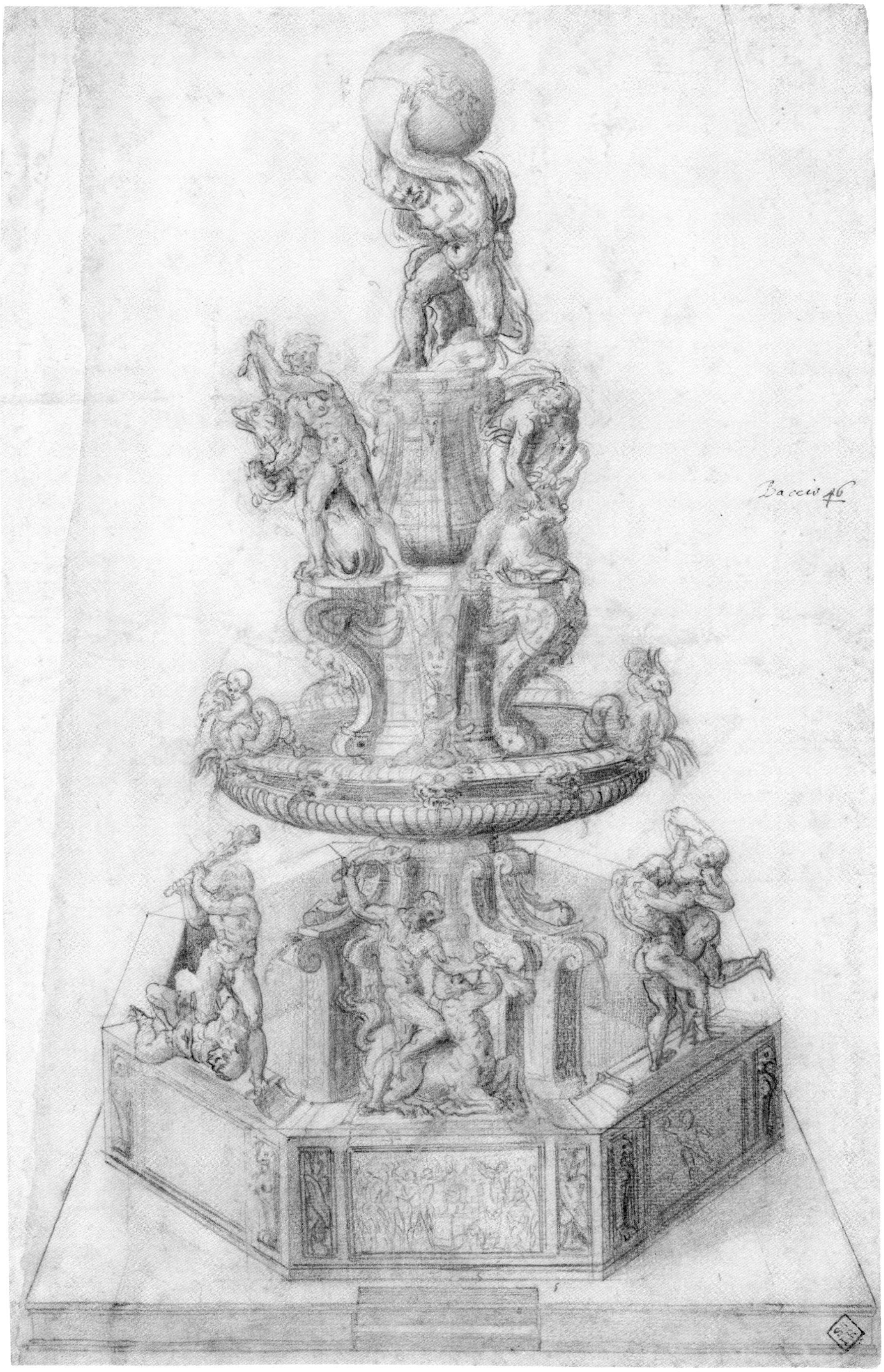
Baccio 46

proposed, nevertheless, is a question: it is difficult to imagine the installation of fragile, multi-ton carvings, years in the making, on elevated projecting platforms.

Heikamp's understanding was that the Vincenzo's three marble statues of Hercules and Cacus, Hercules and the Centaur, and Hercules and Antaeus were "calculated from a frontal viewpoint," yet it is not immediately obvious what the front of each statue is, and the drawing shows two of his three preliminary ideas for the statues from above and to the side. It may even be that the artist drew rotated clay models he had made for these figures, a traditional approach that would have made it easier to render the foreshortened figures on paper. If the statue groups were indeed planned for a fountain, their impression of planarity may simply reflect the requirement that they stand on a shallow balustrade. The polygonal form of the Neptune fountain in Piazza della Signoria, a project Vincenzo certainly had in mind as he worked, had been expressly conceived so as to address viewers coming to the site from different routes.[3] Earlier Tuscan fountains of this "candelabrum" type were made for gardens, and that may have been the intention behind Vincenzo's drawing as well. In imagining this towering monument, he must have been aware that Francesco Camilliani, another Bandinelli disciple five years his junior, had completed an impressive fountain with more than a dozen marble figures outside Florence in 1555.

Vincenzo's variation on the "candelabrum" form seems conceived to accommodate all twelve of Hercules' labors, with five more on the lower octagonal balustrade and one more hidden from view on the second tier. It is conceivable that he decided not to show more because that would have compromised the clarity of the drawing. Alternatively, the drawing may give a sense of what Vincenzo had modeled by the early 1560s: we know that by 1568 at the latest, he had finished the *Hercules and Cacus*, the *Hercules and the Centaur*, and the *Hercules and Antaeus*,[4] precisely the groups that appear on the lower level of the fountain. He must have been aware that Bandinelli's own *Hercules and Cacus* was his most famous public work and that Ammannati had recently completed a monumental (bronze) *Hercules and Antaeus*, also for a fountain. The fact that Vasari mentions no fountain when describing the project for Vincenzo in 1568 may indicate that by the time of his writing the statues had already been repurposed. Of the four *Hercules* groups that Vincenzo roughed out or completed between 1568 and 1584, only one—*Hercules with the Globe*—appears in Vincenzo's drawing.

In the end, Vincenzo did not complete the series. In 1592 seven of his more-or-less finished statues were placed on bases in the Sala dei Cinquecento; six of them remain in the hall today. M.W.C.

NOTES

1 Vasari-de Vere 1912, p. 888.
2 Ward 1982a, p. 137. Among the most relevant examples Ward gives of a Bandinelli "intermediate *modello*" is a black-chalk drawing in the Musée du Louvre (122) for a Neptune fountain (Ward 1982a, pp. 138 and 374–75). Heikamp believed this to be by Vincenzo.
3 Cole 2011, p. 250.
4 Utz 1971, pp. 347–48.

40

BENVENUTO CELLINI

Florence, 1500 – Florence, 1571

Design for an emblem of the Accademia del Disegno, with "hieroglyphic" alphabet and explanatory essay, 1563–69

Pen and ink with brown wash, 332 × 218 mm (13 × 8⁹⁄₁₆ in.)
British Museum, London 1860, 0616.18
Havendo io considerato quanto queste nostre arti che procedono dal disegno siano grandi, non potendo l'huomo alcuna cosa perfettamente operare senza riferirsi al disegno, dal quale egli trae sempre i miglior consigli, e perché io crederrei benissimo far capaci tutti gl'huomini con vive ragioni a le quali non si potrebbe contra[d] dire, essere verissimo, che il disegno essendo veramente origine e principio di tuttte le azzioni dell'huomo, e solo quella Iddea vera della Natura che fu dagli Antiqui con molte poppe figurata per significare ch'ella nutrisce ogni cosa, come sola e principale ministra di Dio, che di erra sculpì e creò il primo huomo ad imagine e similitudine di sé, e che per consequenza non possono i professori dell'arti del disegno havere per suggello e per impresa loro niuna cosa né più somigliante al vero né più propria degli esercizii loro che la detta Iddea della Natura, come più largamente dimostrarei, senza ristringermi a tanta brevità, se io non conoscessi voi tanti artefici nobilissimi non meno esercitati in discorrere le meravigliose opere della Natura che virtuosissimi et excellenti nelle cose che dal disegno procedono. Hora quanto de la forma similmente del nostro suggello, havendomi voi fatto degnio di dire il parer mio fra voi bellissimi ingegni, che riaccendete il gran lume poco manco che spento di una così grande et honorata scuola com' è la nostra, et aiutati dalla divina et immortal virtù del nostro illustrissimo et gloriosissimo Duca Cosimo de' Medici amatore del vero bene, cioè principalmente di Dio, e poi della virtù. Io dico che per mio gi[u]dicio nulla forma è più somigliante che la quadra, prima perché tutte le cose che si fanno dalla Natura, la quale noi cerchiamo imitare, sono di quattro cose composte e non di più né di manco. Secondariamente quattro sono l'arti principali, che dal disegno dependano, la scultura, la quale c'insegnò i[d]Dio, facendo l'huomo con le proprie mani; la pittura, che da quella scultura si trasse; e l'architettura, che dallo stesso Dio s'imparò nella meravigliosa fabbrica di questo mondo. Doppo questo havendo l'huomo signor di tutte le cose terrene ritrovati i metalli, e fra questi l'oro e l'argento sopra tutti gli altri nobilissimi, egli pensò anche di quegli cavarne diverse figure mediante la scultura, dando loro diverse forme. Ma perché questi due metalli, come avanzano gli altri di nobiltà e di excellenza, non essendo contaminati né dal fuoco, né dal tempo, né da qual si voglia cosa creata da la Natura, così meritavano nell'essere lavorati qualche privilegio, non volsero gli Antiqui lavorargli come 'l rame e lo stagno e 'l piombo si lavora; però diedero all'oro et all'argento varie forme non col getto ma col martello e col cesello, la quale arte chiamarano gli Antiqui celatoria, onde aggiunsero a le tre sopradette questa quarta nobilissima arte del cesello, che compie il numero come si vede de le quattro principali arti del disegno. E perché quei primi inventori ponevano dagli due lati de la imagine de la Iddea della Natura un cane e dall'altro un cervio per quella cagione che era a proposito dell'intelletto loro, noi in cambio di quegli animali potremo porre da una parte la imagine del leone, che oltre a la fortezza è segno della nostra città, e dal l'altra il serpente, che oltre al la prudenza è una delle imprese del nostro excellentissimo Signor Duca, che è prudentissimo e fortissimo, come vede e sa hoggi tutto il mondo. A queste cose aggiugnerò che havendo gli Egyptii fatto uno alphabeto di caratteri e lettere a lor modo, et uno altro i Greci diverso di quello, e gli Hebrei i[l] loro anchora differente da tutti, come ancho quello dei Latini e così tutte le altre nazioni sono differenti, non sarebbe se non cosa capricciosa e lodevole che noi havessimo anchora uno alphabeto diverso dagli altri; la onde io ho fatto quello che voi vedete sotto la nostra impresa di tutti quegli istrumenti che si adoperano nell'esercitare queste nostre arti nobilissime et utilissime; Rimettendomi sempre e . . .[1]
At bottom of r. [in another hand]: *di Benvenuto Cellini*
In Cellini's hand, beside design: *La tromba della nostra fama viene da le braccia*

THE PRESENT SHEET is one of six from Cellini's hand containing versions of his proposed designs for an emblem of the Florentine Academy of Design (Accademia del Disegno). The contest for the design of the seal began at the time of the foundation of the academy in 1563, and Cellini's drawings date to the period 1563–69. The academy made no choice of design, however, until 1597, when an arrangement featuring three intertwined wreaths—representing the interrelation of the three arts of painting, sculpture, and architecture, and their dependence on the principle of design (*disegno*)—was officially adopted.

The present design features a figure of the Artemis Polymastia, also known as the Artemis or Diana of Ephesus, a figure type that Cellini, like other Renaissance artists and writers, understood to be a personification of nature, the *Iddea della Natura*, the word *iddea* suggesting both "idea" (*idea*) and "goddess" (*dea*). Cellini had made prominent use of the motif on the elaborately embellished pedestal of his most important statue, the *Perseus*, completed in 1554. The lion, he goes on to explain in the essay, is a symbol of Fortitude but also of Florence, while the snake, a symbol of Prudence, is also a symbol of Duke Cosimo I de' Medici, ruler of the city and patron of the academy. The lozenge-shaped frame is meant to indicate that the arts of design consist not just of the three arts of painting, sculpture, and architecture but include a fourth, gold- and silversmithery, which he calls *celatoria*. Trumpets issue from the arms of Nature, a motif that Cellini explains with a marginal inscription beside the drawing: "the trumpet of our fame comes from the [work of our] arms."

PROVENANCE

Francesco Maria Niccolò Gabburri (?); Sir Thomas Lawrence; William Young Ottley; Samuel Woodburn

LITERATURE

Calamandrei 1971 (essay originally published in 1956); Kemp 1974, esp. pp. 220–24; Pope-Hennessy 1985, pp. 275–80; Turner 1986, p. 163; Wazbinski 1987, vol. 1, pp. 168–72; Alexander Perrig in Güse and Perrig 1997, pp. 152–55; Cole 2002, esp. pp. 121–27; Flemming 2003; British Museum research website: http://www.britishmuseum.org/research/collection_online/collection_object_details/collection_image_gallery.aspx?assetId=1188779&objectId=716447&partId=1#more-views

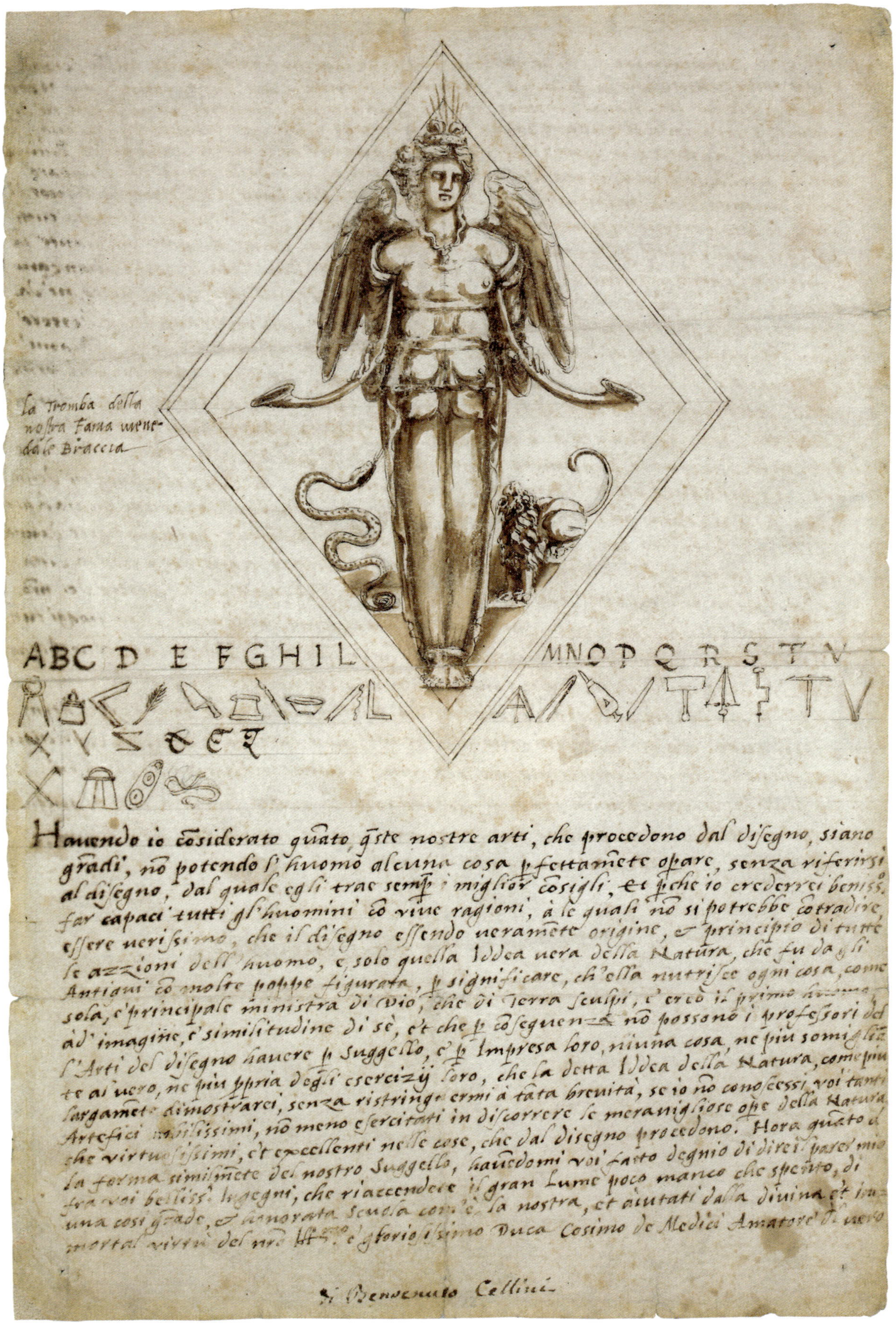
La Tromba della nostra Fama viene dalle Braccia

ABC D E FGHIL MNOPQRSTV

Hauendo io cosiderato quato qste nostre arti, che procedono dal disegno, siano
gradi, no potendo l'huomo alcuna cosa pfettamete opare, senza riferirsi
al disegno, dal quale egli trae semp i miglior cosigli, Et pche io crederrei beniss.
far capaci tutti gl'huomini co viue ragioni, à le quali no si potrebbe cotradire,
essere uerissimo, che il disegno essendo ueramete origine, et principio di tutte
le azzioni dell'huomo, e solo quella Iddea uera della Natura, che fu dagli
Antiani co molte poesie figurata, p significare, ch'ella nutrisce ogni cosa, come
sola, e principale ministra di Dio, che di Terra sculpsi, e creo il primo huomo
ad'imagine, e similitudine di sè, et che p consequenza no possono i professori del
l'Arti del disegno hauere p suggello, e p Impresa loro, niuna cosa, ne piu somiglia
te al uero, ne piu ppria degli esercizij loro, che la detta Iddea della Natura, come piu
largamete dimostrarei, senza ristringermi à tata breuità, se io no conoscessi voi tanti
Artefici nobilissimi, no meno esercitati in discorrere le merauigliose ope della Natura
che virtuosissimi, et excellenti nelle cose, che dal disegno procedono. Hora quato à
la forma similmete del nostro Suggello, hauedomi voi fatto degnio di direi pareri mio
fra voi bellissi. Ingegni, che riaccendere il gran Lume poco manco che spento, di
una cosi grade, et honorata Scuola com'è la nostra, et aiutati dalla diuina et im
mortal virtù del nro Illmo. e gloriosissimo Duca Cosimo de Medici Amatore di uero

Benvenuto Cellini

bene, ciò è, principalmẽte di Dio, è poi della virtù. Io dico che per mio giudicio nulla forma
è più somigliante, che la quadra; prima perche tutte le cose che si fanno dalla Natu-
ra, laquale noi cerchiamo imitare, sono di quattro cose composte, & nõ di più, nè di
manco: Secõdariamẽte quattro sono l'Arti principali, che dal Disegno dependano, la
Scultura, laquale c'insegnò i Dio, facendo l'huomo cõ le proprie mani: la Pittura
che da quella Scultura si trasse: Et l'Architettura, che dallo stesso Dio s'imparò
nella merauigliosa fabbrica di q̃sto Mondo. Dopo q̃sto hauendo l'huomo Signor di
tutte le cose terrene, ritrouati i Metalli, & fra questi l'Oro, è l'Argento sopra tutti
gl'altri nobilissimi; egli pensò anche di quegli cauarne diuerse figure mediante la
Scultura, dando loro diuerse forme: Ma perche questi due Metalli, come auanzano
gl'altri di nobiltà, & di Excellenza, nõ essendo cõtaminati, ne dal fuoco, nè dal
Tempo, ne da qual si voglia cosa creata dalla Natura, così meritauano nell'essere
lauorati qualche priuilegio, non volsero gl'Antiqui lauorargli, come'l Rame,
è lo Stagno è'l Piombo si lauora; però diedero à l'Oro, & à l'Argẽto varie forme
nõ col getto, ma col Martello, è col Cesello, laquale Arte chiamarano gl'Antiqui
Celatoria, onde aggiunsero à le trè sopra dette questa quarta nobilissima Arte
del Cesello, che compie il numero, come si vede delle quattro principali Arti del dise-
gno. Et perche quei primi Inuentori poneuano dagli due lati della Imagine della
Iddea della Natura un Cane, & dall'altro vn Ceruio, per quella cagione che era à pro-
posito dell'Intelletto loro: Noi in cambio di quegli Animali, potremo porre da una
parte la Imagine del Leone, che oltre à la fortezza è segno della nostra Città,
& da l'altra il Serpente, che oltre à la Prudenza, è vna delle Imprese del nostro
Ecc.mo S.or Duca, che è prudentissimo, & fortissimo, come vede, & sà hoggi tutto
il Mondo. A questo ancò aggiugnerò, che hauendo gli Egyptij fatto vno Alpha-
beto di Caratteri & Lettere à lor modo, & vno altro i Greci diuerso da quello,
& gli Hebrei i loro anchora differente da tutti, come ancho quello dei Latini,
& così tutte le altre nazioni sono differenti; non sarebbe se non cosa capricciosa
& lodeuole, che noi hauessimo anchora vno Alphabeto diuerso dagli Altri;
La onde io ho fatto quello che voi vedete sotto la nostra Impresa di tutti quegli
istrumenti, che si adoperano nell'esercitare queste nostre Arti nobilissime, et
vtilissime; Rimettendomi sempre, & Cet.

8

2

The row of tools with the letters of the alphabet above them are identified by Cellini on a closely related, earlier sheet that once belonged to Piero Calamandrei as *hieroglifici*, a term used in the Renaissance to denote any kind of pictographic writing. He explains that since the Greeks, Hebrews, and Latins each invented their own alphabets, different from one another, it would be "imaginative and praiseworthy [*capricciosa e lodevole*] if we had another alphabet different from the others," so he offers one of his own invention, composed "of all the tools that are used in practicing these most noble and useful arts of ours." Cellini must have imagined it as a kind of code, perhaps for use in documents to be read only by initiates, yet as such it would have been unwieldy, if not unworkable. Nevertheless, the serious idea that it might be said to express is similar to that implied by the trumpets issuing from the arms of Nature: that the communicative efficacy of the visual arts is simultaneously like and unlike that of language, and by extension, perhaps, that the concepts of art theory, no matter how abstract, are based on artisanal practice.

That each craft has its own language—*nomi propi e vocaboli particolari*—had been emphasized in the 1540s by the Florentine philosopher Benedetto Varchi in his effort to differentiate between "arts" (*arti*) and "sciences" (*scienze*). Dependence on special terminology—subliterate workmen's slang—meant that the different crafts do not share common concepts: one can thus excel at a certain craft without understanding any others. Practitioners of the sciences, by contrast, seldom master one without having knowledge of others, an indication that they operate with comprehensive principles of a more elevated, fully rational kind.[2] Cellini's alphabet would seem to oppose the hierarchy implicit in Varchi's distinction, to insist upon the positive value of the knowledge specific to the arts, even on the "secret" quality of their lore, and to insist that such knowledge calls for the protective veil of code, as the original hieroglyphs were believed to protect the sacred wisdom of the ancient Egyptians. At the same time, emphasizing the discursivity of tools and the practices associated with them may be Cellini's attempt to reconcile his craftsmanly orientation with the more rationalistic approach appropriate to an academy.

The fact that Cellini's designs were rejected is not surprising. He was heartily detested by the two most powerful members of the Accademia del Disegno, Duke Cosimo's official representative to the group, the scholar Vincenzo Borghini, and the duke's most trusted artist, Giorgio Vasari. Cellini's ideas also jarred with the emerging theoretical orthodoxy that Borghini and Vasari were working to establish. His belief, stated at the beginning of the essay, that all human activities depend on *disegno*, was commonplace,[3] but his insistence that *celatoria* was of equal importance to the other three arts of design would have struck Borghini and Vasari as both shamelessly self-promoting and a challenge to one of their own fundamental principles: the prioritization of painting, sculpture, and architecture was a conspicuous achievement of Vasari's *Lives of the Most Excellent Painters, Sculptors and Architects*, published in 1550, and would be further consolidated and justified in the second edition, published in 1568. In that second edition, Vasari—almost certainly with Borghini's help—took care to provide an unprecedentedly precise definition of *disegno* as a faculty of mind and practice of hand.[4] Cellini's insistence on the superiority of sculpture to painting would lead to an open break with Vasari and Borghini on the occasion of Michelangelo's funeral in the summer of 1564.[5]

Some modern scholars have seen the craftsmanly tradition evident in Cellini's ideas as one that circumvents Vasari[6]—or that Vasari and Borghini sought to elevate and transform—and that reappears in later theorists, such as Federico Zuccaro,[7] or even in Annibale Carracci's remark to his brother Agostino, that "we painters have to speak with our hands."[8] R.W.

NOTES

1 The text of the essay on the British Museum sheet seems never to have been published in its entirety until now. It may be translated as follows: "Having considered how great these arts of ours are that proceed from design, and that man can do nothing perfectly without having recourse to design, from which he always gets the best guidance, and convinced that with lively and incontrovertible reasons I could persuade all men of the truth that since design is truly the origin and principle of all the actions of man and that since the true Goddess of Nature was represented by the ancients with many breasts in order to signify that she alone nourishes everything as the unique and principal ministress of God—who sculpted and created the first man from earth in the image and likeness of himself —it follows that those who profess the arts of design could have for their seal and emblem nothing either in greater conformity to the truth nor more proper to their practices than the said Goddess of Nature, something I would demonstrate at greater length without limiting myself to such brevity if I did not know you noble artists to be as practiced in discussing the marvelous works of nature as you are most accomplished and excellent in the things that proceed from design. Now as regards the shape of our seal, since you have made me worthy to share my opinion in the midst of your most beautiful minds – which are rekindling the great light, all but spent, of our great and honored school, aided by the divine and immortal virtue of our most illustrious and glorious Duke Cosimo de' Medici, lover of the true good, that is, first, God, and then virtue—I say that in my judgment no shape is more appropriate than the square, first because all things made by nature—which we seek to imitate—are composed of four things, neither more nor less, and secondly because the principal arts that depend upon design are four: sculpture, which God taught us, making the first man with his own hands; painting, which is taken from sculpture; and architecture, which is learned from the same God in the marvelous building of the world. After man, as lord of all earthly things, discovered metals, and among them gold and silver, nobler than the rest, he thought also to extract from them diverse figures by means of sculpture, giving them diverse forms. But because these two metals surpass the others in nobility and excellence, being corrupted neither by fire nor by time nor by any other thing created by nature, they deserved to be given some privilege in the way they are worked, so the ancients chose not to work them as copper or brass or lead is worked; rather, they gave various forms to gold and silver not by casting but with the hammer and chisel, to which art they gave the name *celatoria*, so that to the three above-mentioned is added this fourth most noble art of the chisel, completing, as one sees, the number of the four principal arts of design. And because those first inventors put beside the image of the Goddess of Nature a dog and on the other a deer, since it seemed appropriate to their way of thinking, we can put, instead of those animals, the lion on one side, since in addition to strength it is the sign of our city, and on the other the serpent, since in addition to prudence it is one of the emblems of our most excellent Lord Duke, who is most prudent and most strong, as the whole world today knows. To these things I will add that the Egyptians having made an alphabet of characters and letters in their way, and the Greeks another, which was different, and the Hebrews, theirs, different yet again from the others, as is that of the Latins as well, and thus all the other nations, it would be something imaginative and praiseworthy if we, too, had one different from the rest, for which reason I have made the one that you see beneath our emblem, composed of all the tools that are used in practicing these most noble and useful arts of ours. Submitting myself always and. . . ."

2 "Della Maggioranza e nobiltà dell'arti, disputa prima," in Barocchi 1960–62, vol. 1, pp. 24–25.

3 According to the Venetian painter Paolo Pino, whose *Dialogo di pittura* was published in 1548, "smiths cannot even make a ladle without *disegno*": Barocchi 1960–62, vol. 1, p. 106. An even bolder statement of the same idea is found in the *Dialogues* of the Portuguese painter and theorist, Francisco de Holanda, published in 1548: Hollanda 1928, p. 36; Hollanda 1984, p. 264.

4 Vasari-Bettarini 1966, vol. 1, p. 111. For a thorough account, see Roggenkamp 1996; see also Williams 1997, pp. 29–72.

5 Cellini argued his position in a letter to Varchi in 1546, then again in treatises written in response to the Michelangelo funeral controversy: see Barocchi 1960–62, vol. 1, pp. 80–81; Cellini 1971, pp. 807–26. On Michelangelo's funeral, see Giunta 1964.

6 See Cole 2002, esp. pp. 118–48.

7 Zuccaro 1961. The relation of Zuccaro's ideas to Cellini's is emphasized by Kemp 1974.

8 *Noi altri Dipintori habbiamo da parlare con le mani*. For a learned and perceptive study of Annibale's ideas that sheds unexpected light on the significance of the remark, see Dempsey 1977.

41

GIAMBOLOGNA

Douai, 1529 – Florence, 1608

Design for a fountain, c. 1571–75

Pen and brown ink over black chalk and stylus indentations; two areas on each side have been excised, 205 × 330 mm (8¹⁄₁₆ × 13 in.)
Inscribed, by Giambologna, in the same brown ink as the drawing: *figura b 5 ½* (the measurements of Oceanus); *bracio dondice in cerco* (the diameter of the basin); *b 8 in cerco* (the radius from the basin to the pavement); *b 2* (the height of the parapet)
Ashmolean Museum, Oxford, Purchased, 1954 WA1954.29

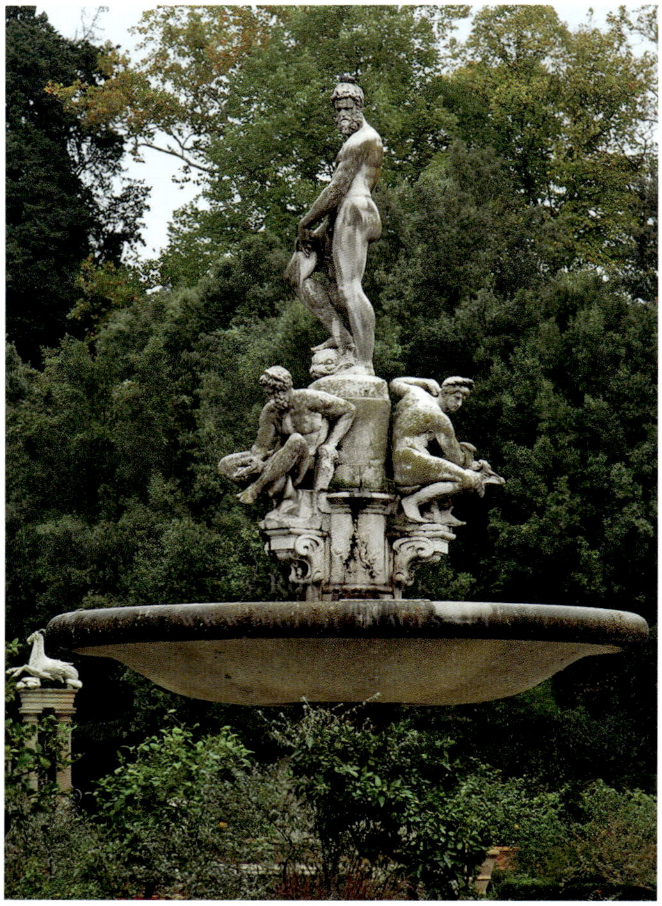

FIG. 73
Giambologna
Oceanus fountain
Marble
Boboli Gardens, Florence

THE DRAWING shows Giambologna's ideas for the installation of the *Oceanus*, three *River gods*, and six merman sculptures for the fountain in the Boboli gardens behind Palazzo Pitti in Florence (fig. 73).[1] In the drawing, Giambologna records the measurements of the basin as well as those of *Oceanus*. Giambologna was responsible for the sculpted figures and their installation, whereas the basin had been brought from Elba at great cost and labor.

The sculptor Niccolò Tribolo wrote in 1550 that he had been sent to Elba to find granite for two fountain basins, "one for Pitti and the other for the piazza of His Excellency [Piazza della Signoria], both of granite," and added that "one cannot go anywhere but Elba, where the ancients quarried their granite fountains."[2] Vasari, in his 1568 *Life* of Tribolo, states that the artist

> was sent by His Excellency to the Island of Elba, not only to see the city and port [the duke] had built there, but also so that he could order the transport of a round piece of granite 12 braccia in diameter from which a basin was to be made for the large field of the Pitti.[3]

In his preface to the *Lives*, in the section on architecture, Vasari insinuated that the basin was carved from a block during the time of Duke Cosimo.[4]

Some scholars have construed these statements to mean that Tribolo's mission to Elba was to find granite to carve a new basin and that the basin of the Oceanus fountain was carved by him.[5] However, Vasari does not specify that it was done by Tribolo, and he does not seem to have been completely informed about the basin's origins. Unpublished documents in the Archivio di Stato, Florence, suggest that it is an ancient Roman basin.[6] The date of its discovery is unknown and may be before or after Tribolo's death on 7 September 1550. A letter from 1 March 1553 described "that basin that was found" and its Latin inscriptions on the inside and outside of the lip.[7] Another letter from 18 March included measurements.[8]

PROVENANCE

Formerly in the collection of Henry Oppenheimer, London (Christie's sale, 10 July 1936, lot 35); purchased by the Ashmolean in 1954

LITERATURE

Popp 1927, p. 23; Parker 1956, p. 65, no. 118; Dhanens 1956, p. 167; Avery 1987, p. 273, no. 168; Campbell 1991, pp. 90–97; Acidini Luchinat 2002, p. 314, no. 171

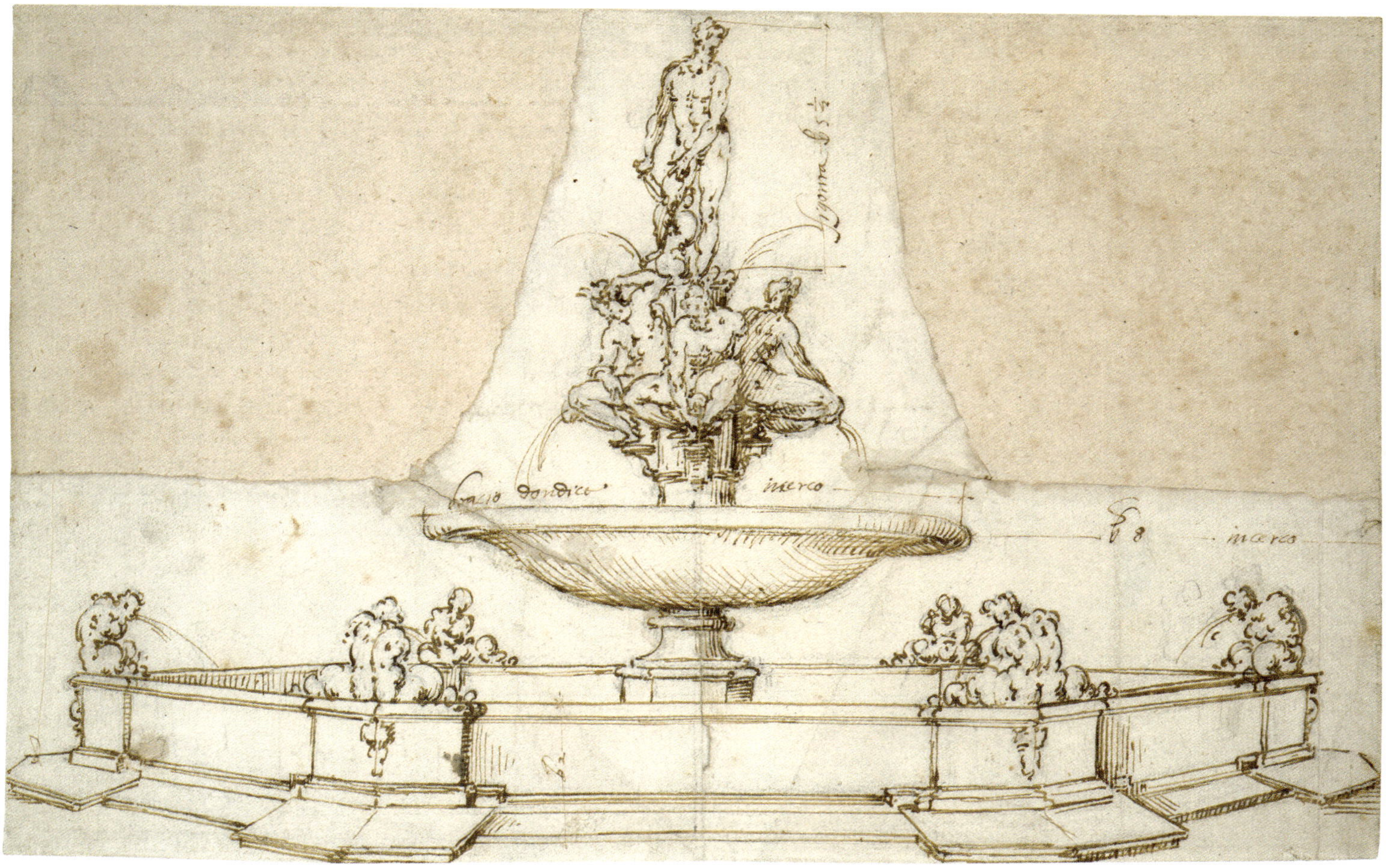

The subsequent series of letters between the duke's secretary and the men in Portoferraio detail the difficulties and risks of transporting such a large and heavy basin. Before it even left the shores of Elba, the Turks attacked the troops there. Giovanni Battista Vettori reported to Cosimo that fortunately there had been no injury either to them or to the *tazza di Vostra Eccelenza*. New armatures had to be made at least twice; it had to be pulled slowly to the shore, then onto a galley, one that had previously been used to transport Spanish troops to La Spezia and Genoa. The *tazza* was loaded onto the galley on 17 September 1566 and it was in Livorno by 4 October.[7] It finally arrived in Florence on 17 July 1567. Even its transport from the outside the city walls to Palazzo Pitti proved challenging. Lapini recorded:

> On Thursday, 17 July, the beautiful granite basin was placed in Florence in the beautiful Palazzo de' Pitti. And to bring it to Florence, it was necessary to break and enlarge the Porta del Prato on each side because it was so large that it could not otherwise fit. It came from Elba and is 35 *braccia* and the city that is in the said Elba, called Cosmopoli, was founded by Cosimo de' Medici, second duke of Florence and Siena, and the said duke had the basin brought here.[9]

Giambologna was commissioned by Cosimo I to make a suitable figure for such a grandiose and important basin. Baldinucci recorded that the Grand Duke instructed Giambologna:

> I have had this rock extracted, as you see, to make a beautiful fountain for the Boboli gardens. Make it your intention to make this fountain in such a way that the basin brings honor to you and your work [honors] the basin.[10]

The marble for the figures was procured in April 1571. By October 1572 Giambologna had completed a full-scale model, which was placed in the gardens to see how the final installation would look. The sculpture of Oceanus was blocked out in 1572–73 and payments record its progress from 1574 to 1576. The figures were moved from Giambologna's workshop beginning on 25 June 1575.[11] The fountain was moved in 1618 to a site near the Grotta della Madama and then again in the 1630s to its current location, the Isolotto.

The Ashmolean drawing may date to this moment or to an earlier planning stage, perhaps 1571, when Giambologna's commission was initiated. The hexagonal base with satellite figures of mermen or sea monsters was never executed. K.H.D

NOTES

1 Popp 1927, p. 23, first identified the drawing as relating to Giambologna's Oceanus fountain. Oceanus/Neptune is the central figure; the subsidiary figures represent the Nile, the Euphrates, and the Ganges. The drawing shows satellite figures at the corners of a hexagonal basin. Neither the basin nor the figures were executed. See Parker 1956, p. 65.

2 Archivio di Stato, Florence (hereafter ASF), Guardaroba medicei, 780, c. 877, 21 April 1550: Niccolò Tribolo in Pisa to Pierfrancesco Riccio, Florence: *Stamatina mi parto e vo a Livorno a sua ecelenzia. E anni comeso loro ecelezie io vadi al Ebba. E la chausa s'é che se risolut* [lacuna] *si chavi dua vasi pe le fonte, una de piti e laltra pe la piazza di sua ecelenzia chosti di granito, e ttale opere non se puo chavare datronde se non e' nel E[l]ba dove li antichi* [lacuna] *chavorno le loro fonti di granito.*

3 *...fu mandato il Tribolo da sua eccellenza nell'isola dell'Elba ... perché desse ordine di condurre un pezzo di granito tondo di dodici braccia per diametro, del quale si aveva a fare una tazza per lo prato grande de' Pitti.* Agostino del Riccio, *Istoria delle pietre*, 1597, fols. 12 verso–14 recto (Del Riccio 1979), in his section XII, "Del Granito dell' Elba," recorded that the large basin had been brought (*fece condurre*) from Elba to the gardens at Palazzo Pitti but does not mention Tribolo's role in it at all. He remarks that Elba is where the Romans had long quarried their best granite and the Grand Duke was following suit.

4 See Vasari-Milanesi 1878–85, vol. 1, p. 95. There the author commented on the Romans' frequent use of granite from Elba, citing the granite columns in the portico of the Pantheon, and mentioned the use of granite from Elba in modern Tuscany: *Di questo granito bigio è dotata la Italia in molte parti, ma le maggiori saldezze che si trovino sono nell'isola dell'Elba, dove i Romani tennero di continuo uomini a cavare infinito numero di questa pietra; e di questa sorte ne sono parte le colonne del portico della Ritonda, D'un pezzo della qual sorte pietra che era staccato dal masso, n'ha cavato il duca Cosimo una tazza tonda di larghezza di braccia dodici per ogni verso, et una tavola della medesima lung[h]ezza per lo palazzo e giardino de' Pitti.*

5 For example, Avery 1987, p. 215, remarks that Tribolo had "shaped" the basin. Campbell 1991, p. 90, similarly says that "it is probable that the bowl was largely shaped by Tribolo" and compares it with the basin Tribolo made for the Hercules fountain at the Villa Reale di Castello. Lazzaro 1990, p. 194, writes that the *tazza* was a "great, simple basin chosen by Tribolo," which suggests that Lazzaro understood that Tribolo had not, in fact, carved the basin but selected an already complete basin from Elba. Given the archival documentation presented here, it seems unlikely that Tribolo carved the basin from a rough block as Campbell and Avery suggest, but it is possible that Tribolo may have reshaped or restored the basin in some way. I think this unlikely, however, given his declining health at that point.

6 My colleague Fabrizio Nevola and I discovered this series of documents and made the connection to the basin of the Oceanus fountain while we were fellows at the Medici Archive Project in 2000. ASF, Mediceo del Principato, 419, fol. 512 (1 March 1553), Giovanni Camerini in Portoferraio to Cosimo I in Florence: ... *La pila o tazza che s'é trovato é di granito la quale é braccia* [page loss, proposed reading: *1*] *1, 4 di diametro 3,5 di braccio lavorata ragionevole e consumata la pelle di fuora al quanto che con poco tempo si ripulirebbe, ma detta pila sotto l'orlo, atorno circa la quarta parte della sua circunferenze, a un pezo asai boni latino che passa drento et fuora, tale che piccole per cossa penso che assai lo fondessi.* I have not had the opportunity to examine the basin to see if these inscriptions are still legible.

7 ASF, Mediceo del Principato, 503a, fol. 1172 (18 March 1563/64): *misure della gira la tazza braccia 34½, l'altezza del tutto nel mezzo della tazza, braccia 1,16; la testa di detta palmi dodici; la faccia di sopra largha palmi quindici; el più sottile della tazza presso all'orlo palmi sedici; lo sverzato o scarnatura del corpo di dentro palmi due e ½; la sboncellatura dell'orlo palmi uno; el concavo di detta palmi undici; el più grosso nel mezo della taza tratto il fondo di mezo, braccia 1, e 5 palmi.*

8 ASF, Mediceo del Principato, 225, fol. 57 (4 October 1566), Cosimo I in Florence to Iacopo VI Appiani d'Aragona in Piombino: *L'arrivo della tazza di granito a Livorno ci é stato gratissimo.*

9 Lapini 1900, p. 157: *A dí 17 di luglio in giovedì si messe in Firenze la bella tazza di granito che é nel bel Palazzo de' Pitti. E per metterle in Firenze bisognó rompere et allargare la Porta del Prato di qua e di lá, perché era tanto larga che non vi entrava, venne dall'Elba. La qual tazza gira braccia 35. E la cittá che é nella detta Elba, che si chiama Cosmopoli, la fondó Cosimo de' Medici, duca secondo di Firenze e Siena e detto duca fe' condure la detta tazza.* See also Dhanens 1956, p. 167, note 2, where she first noted the information from Lapini's account about the arrival of the basin.

10 Baldinucci 1974, vol. 2, p. 559: *Aveva il granduca in questo tempo fatto cavare nell'Elba uno smisurato sasso di granito per farne una gran tazza ad una fonte nel giardino di Boboli, ed avuto a sé Gio. Bologna, cosí gli parló: Io ho fatto cavar questo sasso, come tu vedi, per fare una bella fonte per lo giardino, sia dunque tuo pensiero il fare essa fonte in modo, che la tazza faccia onore a te, e l'opere tue alla tazza.* Baldinucci does not say by whom or when the basin was carved.

11 Marble for the figures was purchased in April 1571. In October 1572 the model of Oceanus was taken to the garden to try it out. In the same year, the figures were blocked out. Cosimo I died on 21 April 1574, but the project was continued under Francesco I. Payments for the figures run from 1574 to 1576. On 25 June 1575 a porter was paid for help in moving the figures for the fountain to their place in the garden. From 31 October to 5 November men were hired to move the basin. On 29 November the bronze pipes for the fountain were purchased. On 21 March 1576 bronze spikes and rivets for attaching the figures and reliefs were purchased. On 15 May, the large pipe for the granite basin was bought. On 30 October another bronze spike and two rivets to fasten the figure of Oceanus were acquired. By the end of 1576, the installation of the statuary and the plumbing was complete. See Gaye 1839–40, vol. 3, pp. 404–5. The *Oceanus* was taken to the Bargello in 1907 and was substituted by a copy.

42

BARTOLOMEO AMMANNATI

Settignano, 1511 – Florence, 1592

Project for the interior side elevation of the church of San Giovannino, Florence, early 1580s

Pen and ink, 280 × 420 mm (11 × 16½ in.)
Inscribed in brown ink in Ammannati's hand: *alto il palcho braccia 2½*
Gabinetto Disegni e Stampe degli Uffizi, Florence 2944A

ON 13 APRIL 1592, Bartolomeo Ammannati died in his house in via della Stufa in Florence, to be buried in the church of San Giovannino with his wife, Laura Battiferri, who had passed away three years earlier. Beginning in 1572, both Laura and Bartolomeo had begun financially supporting the Company of Jesus, which had been introduced to Florence by Duchess Eleonora of Toledo in contact with the General of the Order, Ignatius of Loyola. In 1579 the construction site opened for the restructuring of the college and two years later that for the reconstruction of the church.[1] The testaments of Ammannati and Battiferri of 16 February 1581 named the Jesuits as their universal heirs.[2] Bartolomeo served both as the designer and the supervisor of construction, discussing the most important decisions, participating in the surveys that sought to identify an appropriate location, and enthusiastically considering compositional solutions. The chronicles of the Jesuits and the account books related to the construction register the beginning of the decorations in 1581 in the front part of the church, corresponding to the first three chapels used for liturgical functions. At the end of 1583 the zone up to the apse was also covered, and the chapels were decorated with paintings, stucco, and gold.

Combining architecture and decoration, this drawing represents a true study for the interior longitudinal elevation of the church, probably the left side: the second chapel at right could possibly correspond to Ammannati and Battiferi's own chapel.[3] The wall is articulated with tall Ionic pilasters in a sequence of regular bays linked with rhythmic trusses. It is among the few studies known by Ammannati for the outfitting of an interior. The surfaces extend in a clear but articulated way and are animated by variegated decorative elements. While the altars within the arches resemble those that Ammannati designed for the church of the Umiltà in Pistoia, the zones between the pilasters are linked above by balustrated terrace-choirs that recall those of the ground-floor windows on the garden façade of Palazzo Giugni. At the level of the attic-clerestory, the abstract, synthetic, simplified architectural order—a departure from any recognizable, proper order, in the manner of Giulio Romano at Palazzo Stati Maccarani—is another citation from Palazzo Giugni, this time from the third story of the courtyard.[4] Such shaped frames were widely employed by Ammannati, and the cartouches below the paintings—which represent such recognizable subjects as the *Noli me tangere*—are analogous to those in marble on the bridge at Santa Trinita or on the portal of the Orazio Rucellai palace. The sumptious cornice at the extreme upper left of the sheet delimits a flat, wooden, coffered ceiling, as the inscription *alto il palco*, written vertically at the lower left of the sheet, confirms. The design of the cornice thus alludes to a flat roof, and a quick sketch evokes woodwork. Ultimately, the church was built with a vaulted ceiling; in this respect, its design history echoes that of the Gesù in Rome, with Ignatius initially seeking a flat ceiling for acoustical reasons and the patron insisting on a vault. With respect to the design and the wall surfaces that were actually carried out, the drawing exhibits an attenuation of decorative elements in pursuit of a more severe decorum, conforming to the Counter-Reformation climate that motivated Ammannati's letter to his fellow academics in 1582.[5] The configuration of the walls with a wood ceiling imposed above was taken up again in the church of Santa Maria in Gradi in Arezzo, designed by Ammannati and constructed in 1591. M.C.

PROVENANCE

From a group of drawings and papers bequeathed by Bartolomeo Ammannati to the College of the Jesuits and then dispersed, now in the Gabinetto Disegni e Stampe degli Uffizi and in the Archivio di Stato, Florence

LITERATURE

Fossi 1969, p. 135; Kiene 1995b, p. 140; Belluzzi 2009, p. 121

NOTES

1 Concerning Ammannati's project, see Archivio di Stato di Firenze (ASF), Compagnie Religiose Soppresse da Pietro Leopoldo, 1037, ins. 241, c. 199v; Bösel 1985, pp. 78–89; Carmagnini and Matracchi 1986, pp. 295–347; Matracchi 1988, pp. 105–12; Boccia 1988, pp. 95–104; Kiene 1995a, pp. 187–94; Kiene 1995b, pp. 136–45; Hurx 2005, pp. 151–71; Belluzzi 2009, p. 91; Gómez Leon 2011, pp. 232–33; Gómez Leon 2014.

2 Kirkham 2000, p. 344.

3 For reflections on the chapel and the relation between Ammannati and the Jesuits, see Cole 2011, pp. 229–33.

4 Calafati 2011.

5 Ammannati's entry into the world of the Jesuits pushed him toward a deep religious sensibility, which brought with it a repudiation of the secular works of his youth: in the *Lettera di Messer Bartholomeo Ammannati Architetto e Scultore fiorentino. Agli ornatissimi Accademici del Disegno* (published by Bartolimeo Sermattei in Florence on 22 August 1582), he distanced himself from mythological nudes, which were not consonant with his new principles of religious austerity, and in a letter he wrote about 1590 he asked Grand Duke Ferdinando I de' Medici not to make him "sculpt or paint nude things."

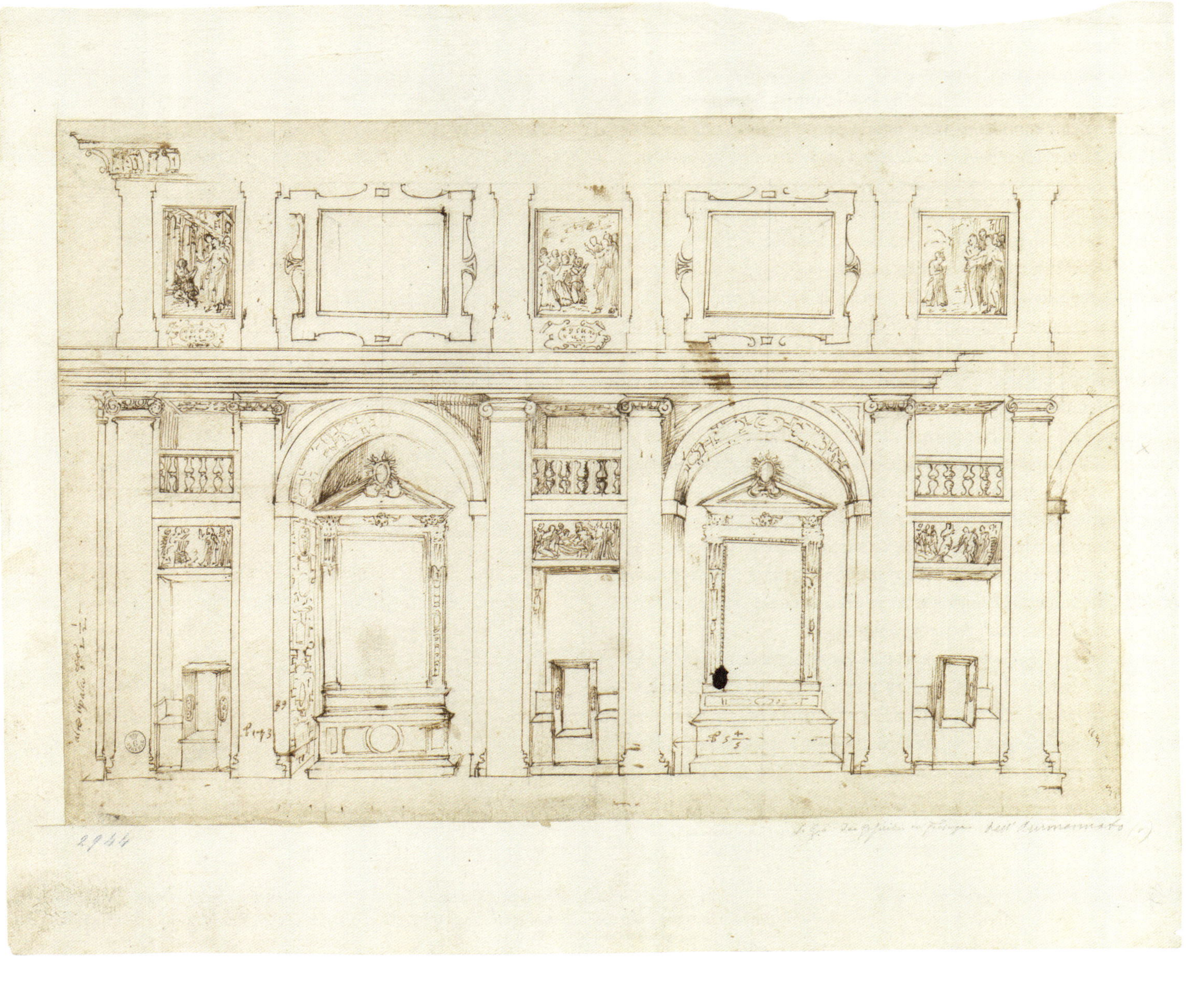
2944

43 & 44

PIETRO FRANCAVILLA

Cambrai, 1548 – Paris, 1615

Record drawings of Giambologna's models for the Apennines, the fountain of Samson and a Philistine, and a fountain of Neptune, 1580–1602

Pen and brown ink over black chalk, on paper, 138 × 100 mm (5 7/16 × 3 15/16 in.)
Victoria and Albert Museum, London, purchased with the assistance of the Murray Bequest and the Art Fund
E.696-1993 and E.695-1993

FIVE DRAWINGS on these two sketchbook sheets signed by Pietro Francavilla depict study models made by his teacher and employer Giambologna.[1] Drawn at the top of the recto of cat. 43, the terracotta model of the crouching figure for the Apennines is still extant (fig. 74). The other models depicted on this sheet, one for the supporting figural bracket of the fountain of Samson and a Philistine, shown below the Apennines model at the bottom of the recto, and another for a fountain of Neptune, shown on the verso, are not. The models for two variations of the fountain of Samson and a Philistine, drawn on the recto and verso of cat. 44, do not survive, either. Yet the drawings evidently show models, not only because they differ from Giambologna's completed works, but also because they include the wooden bases that once served as supports for the studies.[2] That Francavilla incorporated this information in his drawings reveals his concern to show that their subjects were models and not finished sculptures. This is relatively rare in the history of Renaissance artists making studies after models. In the mid-sixteenth century, it is more common to find drawings of architectural models—particularly of those models made for complex building projects like St. Peter's or by prominent architects such as Michelangelo—than it is to find drawings of figural models for sculptures. By revealing the preparatory nature of his subjects, Francavilla helps document the importance of models to Giambologna's working method.[3]

In the oeuvre of Giambologna, a sculptor whose bronze and marble works were often finished by assistants, the preparatory model held special status as an object that preserved the artist's original creative impulses.[4] Giambologna displayed models in his house, was depicted with models in portraits, and occasionally depicted models in his

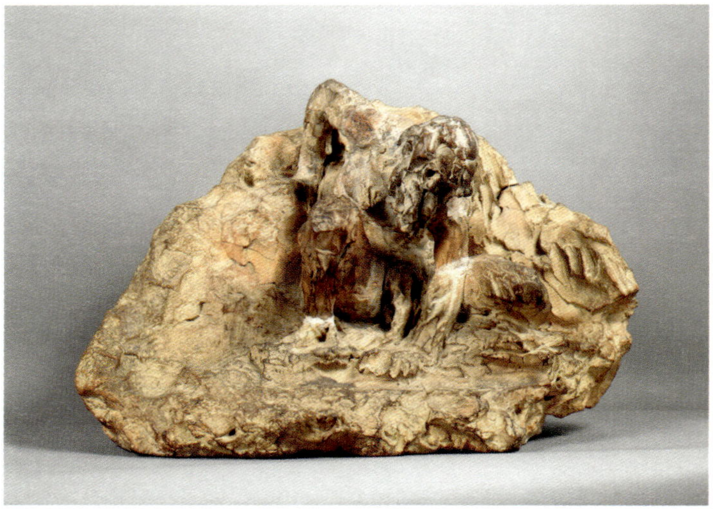

FIG. 74
Giambologna
Model for the Apennines, 1580
Terracotta, 33 × 51 cm
Museo Nazionale del Bargello, Florence

LITERATURE

Avery 2000, pp. 22–26; Krahn 2006, pp. 70–101

NOTES

1 Avery 2000, pp. 22–26.
2 The wooden bases that Giambologna presumably used as supports for most of his terracotta models are not always extant. For example, the model for the Apennines, now in the Bargello (see fig. 74), today lacks the base that appears in Francavilla's drawing. Similarly, the terracotta model for *Florence Triumphant over Pisa* (1565), which is in the Victoria and Albert Museum, has visible marks that suggest it was once attached to a wooden plinth or board (see Avery 1987, p. 66, fig. 74).
3 On this point, see Cole 2011, pp. 21–25.
4 For Giambologna's use of models, see Cole 2011, pp. 21–50, Avery 1987, pp. 63–70, and Krahn 2006.
5 This wax relief is now in the Bargello. There is a gold-leaf and amethyst relief of the same subject from the Studiolo Nuovo of Francesco I in the Museo degli Argenti, Palazzo Pitti, Florence.
6 In addition to the absence of a base on Giambologna's terracotta model (see note 2 above), Francavilla's drawing differs from that model in another way: the drawing shows a grotto-like backdrop extending above the figure—a form that does not appear in the model, where the clay stops just below the figure's elbow. The sketchiness of this section of the drawing implies that Francavilla exaggerated his depiction of the model, in the same way that he added water to the verso drawing of the model for a fountain of Neptune.

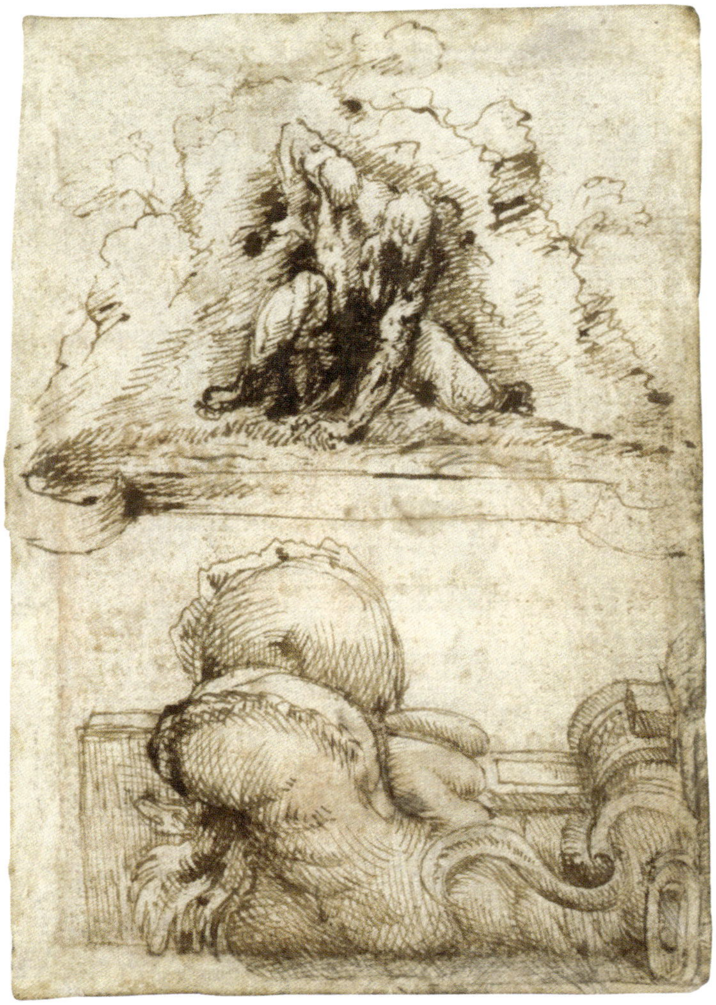

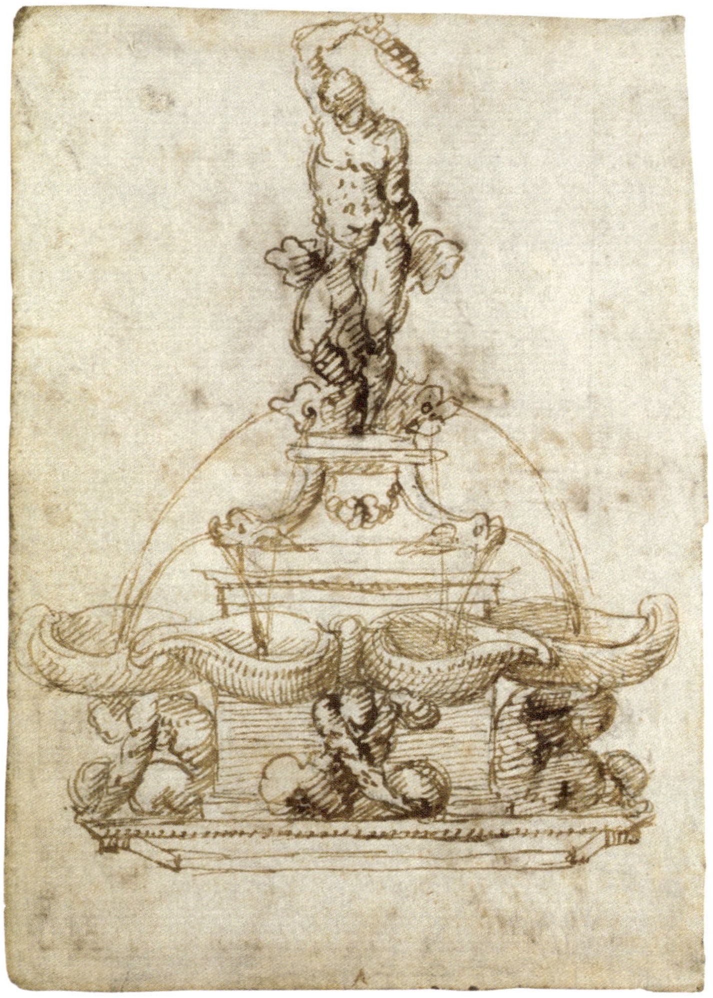

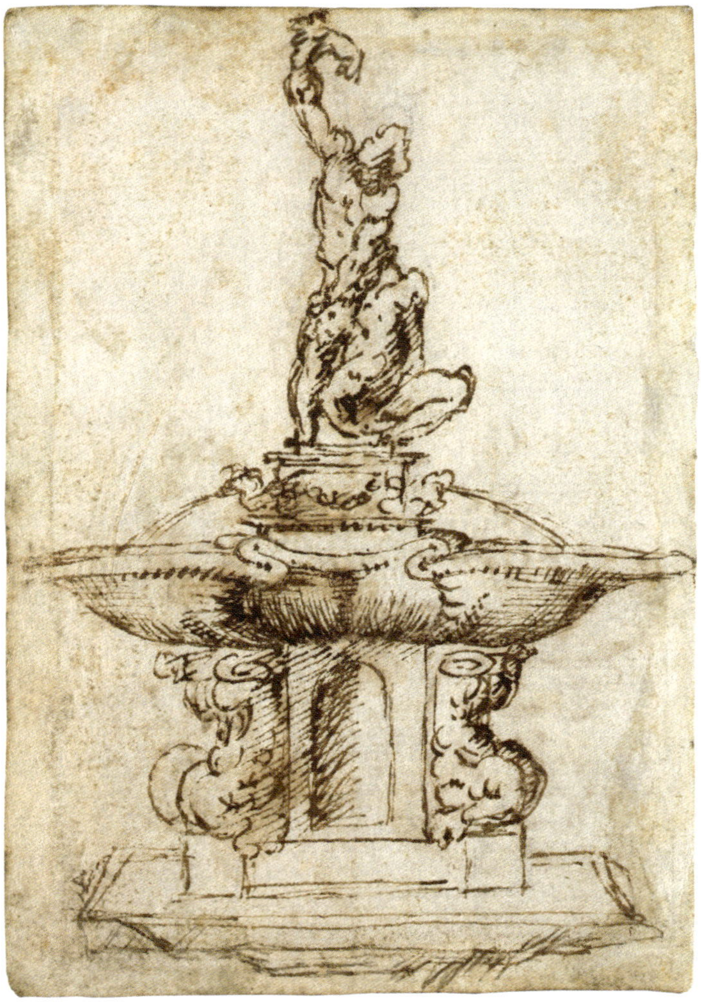

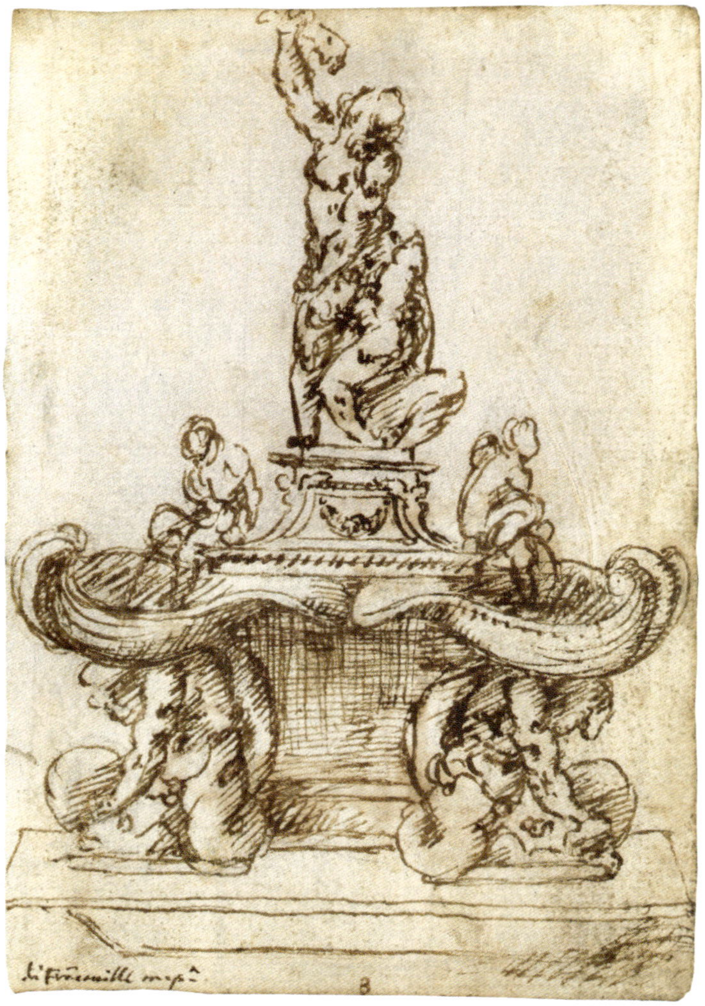

works, as in the wax relief *Giambologna Presenting a Model of a Fountain to Francesco I de' Medici in the Gardens of the Villa Medicea di Pratolino.*[5] Francavilla's drawings of Giambologna's models highlight their elevated status, as well as his own understanding of their role in the artist's process. Giambologna's bronze figurines proliferated in part because they could be recast, but terracotta sketch models could not be copied so easily. Although drawing allowed him to copy an object that could not otherwise be replicated, Francavilla could not render the other essential qualities that distinguish a study model from a final sculpture—scale, finish, and materiality.

But Francavilla turned this limitation to his advantage. As they appear in the drawings, the model supports provide an architectonic contrast to the figural bodies portrayed in a state of arrested motion. The relationship between the softer bodily masses and their supports differs in all five models. In the model for the Apennines, the figure pushes away from its plinth: the base contributes to the apparent play between equal and opposite forces pressing against each other.[6] Instead of a horizontal foundation, the base in the bracket model for the fountain of Samson and a Philistine provides a vertical axis, an anchor for the bulbous masses curled on either side. In the models for a fountain of Neptune and for the fountain of Samson and a Philistine variations, each base acts only as a tray, a datum for the composition. In the sculptural models, Giambologna experimented with torsion, exploring how a body twists under an applied weight. The models' bases, by contrast, served the opposite purpose, transferring the weight of those figures to the ground through simple statics. By choosing to show the bases in his drawings, Francavilla heightened the tension between the bases and the figures and thus emphasized the virtuosity of the sculptural subjects. C.Y.

45

PETER CANDID, attributed to
Bruges, c. 1548 – Munich, 1628

Portrait of Giambologna in His Studio, c. 1585–88

Oil on canvas, 138.8 × 101.8 cm (54¾ × 40 1/16 in.)
Private collection, on loan to the National Gallery of Scotland, Edinburgh

THE PAINTING connects a precise rendering of the artist's features with a convincing representation of his work environment. It has frequently been illustrated. but the authorship, dating, and purpose of this portrait of the Flemish sculptor and architect Giambologna have been debated. The sculptor is portrayed sitting on a stool in front of a table covered with a red cloth. He turns to look over his shoulder directly at the beholder, his right hand concealing a drawing he has just created. The upper right corner of the picture provides a view into a spacious workshop, illuminated by two large windows; a side entrance, shown in the background, indicates the dimensions of this space.

There can be no doubt about the identity of the sitter, for Giambologna's appearance is documented in a number of portraits.[1] His biographer Filippo Baldinucci described him as "small in stature, yes, but fleshy and solid."[2] We know from the inventory of his estate drawn up in 1608 that Giambologna kept not only an art collection but also numerous pictures of himself in his residence in Borgo Pinti.[3] Given its dimensions (2 × 1 ½ ells), the work itemized there as a "portrait of the Signor Cavaliere when he was young" could certainly be the Edinburgh painting.[4]

More important than the concrete location of the depicted spaces[5] is the idealized division of the interior into *studio* and *bottega*.[6] While the view into the workshop shows productive disorder, its chalky color suggesting dust in the air, noble textiles predominate in the study room. The elegantly dressed artist has left the hard work of sculpture behind him and now dedicates himself in a relaxed way to the creative act of drawing, symbolized in the tools—a square, pencil holder, quill, inkwell, and not least the compass, which his right hand stands playfully on the table surface.

Whether this is a drawing compass or a pair of dividers is unclear. What can be said is that the instrument, which could be employed in various ways, connoted such concepts as rule, proportion, and "right measure."[7] It associates Giambologna with a particular kind of art, referring to his reason, method, reflectiveness, and process of creation. Contemporaries connected measuring and drawing with learning and judgment, though on a more practical level the compass was essential for the replication of statues, as well as for the systematic study of architectural proportion. For this reason, it appears as a professional attribute in numerous portraits of sculptors and architects.[8] The Edinburgh portrait visibly connects hand and intellect, *manus* and *mens*, to one another; the artist's illuminated forehead refers to his inspiration while the drawing he has just completed shows the materialization of his ideas.

Though it is true that Giambologna's powerful hand allows only a limited view of what he has drawn, one can see that the page, covered right to the edges, treats a ground plan, even if the few recognizable elements cannot easily be aligned with a specific project. Still, the portrait here hints unmistakably at Giambologna's competence in architecture, to which he began dedicating himself in the 1570s and which, like her sister art, sculpture, grounded itself in the mastery of *disegno*.[9] The picture associates the artist not with graphic bravura but rather with calculated planning and a command of proportion.[10] The painting shows the kind of art that even nobles found suitable because it allowed the avoidance of labor.

PROVENANCE

Marchesa Guadagni, Florence; William Spence, Florence; bought by Alexander Lindsay, 25th Earl of Crawford, c. 1864; since 1988 on loan to the National Gallery of Scotland, Edinburgh

LITERATURE

Desjardins 1883, p. 54, no. 4; Dubrulle 1912, p. 335; Gramberg 1936, pp. 124–25 (Francavilla, 1574/75); Heiden 1970, pp. 147–48, 181, no. A7 (Hans von Aachen, c. 1585); Charles Avery in Avery, Radcliffe, and Leithe-Jasper 1978, pp. 286–88, no. 216 (attributed to Hans von Aachen); Herrmann-Fiore 1983, pp. 32–34; Avery 1987, pp. 27–28 (attributed to Francavilla, c. 1570); Foucart 1987, p. 314 (Fleming, 16th-century, active in Florence; based on Roberto Longhi); Kathke 1997, pp. 227–28, no. 856 (attributed to Bartolomeo Passarotti, based on Francis Russell); Cecchi 1998, p. 142, no. 18 (Peter Candid); Fiorentini 1999, pp. 92–98 and 167–68, no. 50 (Passarotti, 1571–72); Hugh Brigstocke in Weston-Lewis 2000, p. 104, no. 32 (Flemish, close to Cornelis Ketel, between 1563 and 1575); Jacoby 2000, p. 236 (presumably Flemish, c. 1574); Laschke 2000, pp. 65–67, 84 (Passarotti, c. 1575/76; based on Corinna Höper); Zikos 2002, pp. 360–61; Cole and Pardo 2005, pp. 18–19 (Passarotti [?], c. 1580); Krahn 2006, p. 70, fig. 1 (Passarotti); Warren 2006, p. 137 (Flemish [or Passarotti]); Kanzenbach 2007, p. 325 (Flemish [Hans von Aachen?], c. 1585); Zikos 2008, p. 183 (attributed to Passarotti, c. 1570); Cecchi 2009, p. 28 (Candid, c. 1585); Volk-Knüttel 2010, p. 18, note 36 (leaning toward Passarotti); Cole 2011, pp. 162–65, 187 (Candid, c. 1580, based on Alessandro Cecchi)

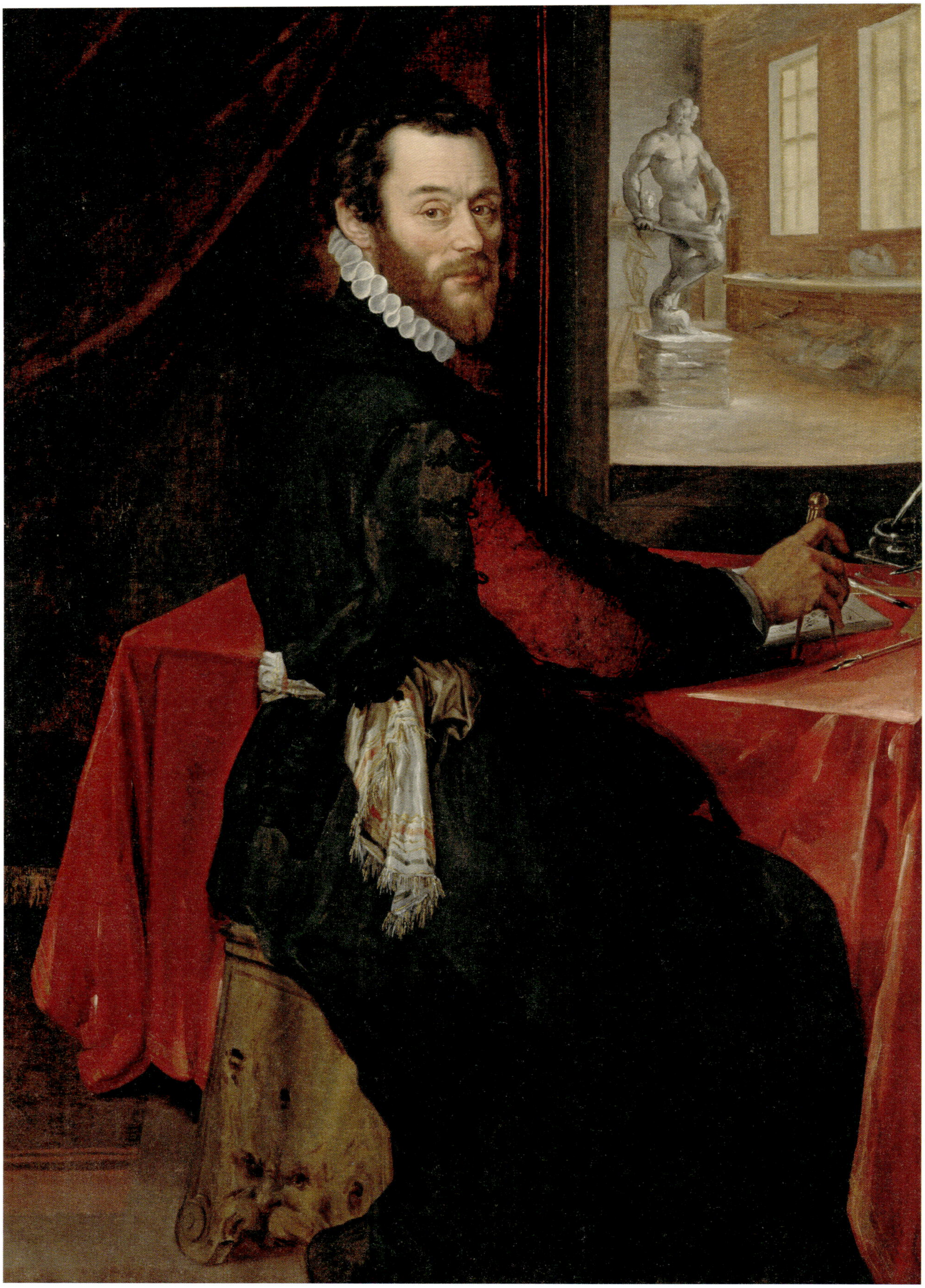

At the same time, the picture's view into the workshop thematizes the concrete process of making sculpture. Especially prominent here is a gray, Herculean form on a masonry sockel, easily identifiable as the plaster model for the sea god *Oceanus*. In October 1572 Giambologna had erected such a model as a test on the monumental fountain basin in the Boboli Gardens (see cat. 41). Now the turning figure, more than four meters high, "rules" over the studio; his baton establishes a parallel between the control of the world sea and the power and virtue of the duke.[11] Behind the *Oceanus*, on a tripod, is a notably smaller female figure, likewise a Medici commission. The pose of this model corresponds to that of the bronze *Florence* of about 1571–72, a Venus-like beauty made for the fountain of the Labyrinth of the Villa of Castello, where she wrung out her wet hair and brought the garden flowers to blossom with her water.[12]

Further *bozzetti* of stucco, clay, or wax are distributed on the two shelves; they document different phases of the works' genesis.[13] One fragment, until now unnoticed, lies somewhat segregated at the far right, under the window. Despite the summary portrayal, one suspects this to be a plaster cast of the bent right arm of Michelangelo's *Victory*. Is it an accident that the *Oceanus*, bursting with energy, directs his gaze in the direction of this eloquent body fragment? Michelangelo's tense figure group was a key work of Mannerist sculpture, one with which the generation of Florentine sculptors born about 1530 engaged intensively;[14] in 1565 the young Giambologna himself had placed the stucco model of his *Triumph over Pisa* opposite this in the Sala dei Cinquecento in the Palazzo Vecchio, interpreting Michelangelo's concept of playfully contained force in a new way. It is not to be excluded that the construction of the atelier in our portrait shows a similar measuring of sculptural power.[15]

The perfectly preserved canvas owes its effect, however, not primarily to such eloquent details but to the commandingly staged contrast between the artist's dark silhouette and the desaturated, streaming red colors of the sculptor's workshop, the masterful shift between energetic facture and the rendering of detail, as well as the altogether fluent and notably thin laying of pigment, which in many places allows the ground to shimmer through. A connection to the work of the Bolognese painter Bartolomeo Passarotti (1529–1592), the attribution favored by various scholars, is not in the end convincing.[16] The rhythm of the contours and the peculiarity of the facture speak clearly for Pieter de Witte, called Candid, of Bruges, as the portrait's author.[17]

Interestingly, the handling of the Edinburgh portrait especially resembles Candid's works from the period immediately after his move to the court of the Wittelsbach duke Wilhelm V. Suffice it to refer to the crumpled sash with its colorful pattern of stripes, which reappears on the hip of an archer in a masterpiece of the painter, *The Martyrdom of St. Ursula* (1588) in the Jesuit church of St. Michael in Munich. The striking modeling of hands is likewise to be found there.[18] The Giambologna portrait must thus have been made either shortly before Candid's departure from Florence in 1586, or only in Munich, perhaps in gratitute for his invitation to serve as court painter there, which Giambologna had arranged.[19]

Against this one could counter that the portrayed artist seems too young for such a dating.[20] Partially visible contour lines refer to a transfer process. It is very possible, then, that Peter Candid, in my opinion the single creator of the picture, made use of a likeness of Giambologna from the 1570s, integrating this into his image of the atelier.[21] H.D.

NOTES

1 For other portraits of Giambologna, see Desjardins 1883, p. 54; Corti 1976, p. 632; Giambologna 1978, pp. 227–31, 283–88, nos. 143–47, 212–16; Fiorentini 1999, pp. 172ff., nos. 51–55.
2 Baldinucci 1845–47, vol. 2, p. 579.
3 Corti 1976; Fiorentini 1999, p. 92; Zikos 2002.
4 Corti 1976, pp. 632–33.
5 While Fiorentini 1999, pp. 92–93, sees Giambologna's workrooms in Borgo Pinti represented, Zikos 2002, pp. 360–61, locates the scene in a workshop in the second (eastern) court of the Palazzo Vecchio, which the artist used between 1566 and 1587. The bright background could conceivably also have resembled the space in the country house outside the Porta Romana that the artist owned.
6 Fiorentini 1999, p. 94; Cole and Pardo 2005, p. 17.
7 To follow the Greek myth, the compass was invented by a nephew of Daedalus, with which he, "in turning the hand," allowed the drawing of the most perfect geometric figure, time and again bound up with the idea of divine propotion, cosmic originary form, and act of creation. Compare Göricke 2000, esp. pp. 278–88 ("Zwischen Idee, Abbild und Konstruktion: Der Zirkel").
8 For corresponding representations compare, for example, Schweikhart 2001, on the compass here pp. 232–34. In Cesare Ripa's *Iconologia* the compass is employed in the following emblems: *Dissegno*, *Economia* (*Il compasso insegna quanto ciascuno debba misurare le sue forze, & secondo quelle governarsi, tanto nello spendere come nelle altre cose*"), *Giuditio*, *Liberalità*, *Matematica*, *Misura*, *Operatione perfetta*, *Parsimonia* (*Il compasso significa l'ordine, & misura in tutte le cose*), *Perfettione*, *Legge naturale*, *Prattica*, *Teoria*. On this, compare again Göricke 2000, p. 281.
9 Compare Borghini 1584, pp. 588–89. In July 1579, after Giambologna had already made his mark with fountain projects and with the *Altare della Libertà* in Lucca Cathedral (1577–79), he signed the contract for the building of the Cappella Grimaldi in Genoa; soon thereafter there began under his direction the work on the Salviati Chapel in San Marco in Florence. Released by the Grand Duke from his court duties for these demanding assignments (Dhanens 1956, p. 253), he was probably supported professionally in the planning by Giovanni Antonio Dosio (Spinelli 1992, pp. 237–38). On Giambologna's collaboration with Dosio on the decoraton of the assembly room of the Accademia del Disegno in the Cestello, see also Pacini 2001, pp. 11–13.
10 "The portrait proposes that it was *as* an architect that Giambologna produced his models; the depicted models represent skills that an architect like the one shown at the table might cultivate": Cole 2011, p. 165. On Giambologna's drawn elevation for the Cappella Salviati, in which he specified relative proportions of wall division, sculpture, and painted panels, see Morrogh 1985, pp. 123–26, no. 63, und Karwacka Codini 2003.
11 On the circumstances and meaning of the *Oceanus*, see Campbell 1991 and Laschke 2000. The Giambologna drawing for that project in this exhibition (cat. 41) counts among the few secure drawings that Giambologna made.
12 On *Fiorenza* (or *Venus genitrix* as protector of garden flora), made as a replacement for a fountain figure by Tribolo, see Herbert Keutner in Giambologna 1978, p. 80, idem in Krahn 1995, pp. 358–61, no. 111, and Michael Cole in Chiarini, Darr, and Giannini 2002, pp. 214–15, no. 74.
13 Their preservation is confirmed in the already mentioned inventory published by Corti 1976. On Giambologna's use of models, see Avery 1987, pp. 63–70, Krahn 2006, and Cole 2011, pp. 33–44. In 1753 the heirs of his student Ferdinando Tacca, who took over Giambologna's house and atelier in 1609, sold *molti modelli di Gio. Bologna*; see Lankheit 1962, pp. 243–44.
14 See Cole 2001.
15 ... *avendo una ambizione estrema d'arrivare Michelangelo et a molti giudiziosi par già che l'abbi arrivato e vivendo sii per avanzarlo e tale opinione ha il Gran Duca ancora*: Simone Fortuna in Florence to the Duke of Urbino, 27 October 1580, cited after Barocchi and Gaeta Bertelà 1993, p. 181. On the relationship Giambologna–Michelangelo, see Keutner 1966, Möseneder 1985, and Schmidt 1994, esp. p. 139, note 147. On the *Victory* as "challenger" for Giambologna's *Triumph over Pisa*, see Strunck 2000, esp. pp. 267–71.
16 There is in fact a portrait of Giambologna that in my opinion can be attributed to Passarotti, in the Kunsthistorisches Museum, Vienna, GG9826. The two artists' acquaintance presumably went back to Giambologna's stay in Bologna during his work on the Neptune fountain there, 1563–64 and 1565–67; the picture, however, has been connected with Passarotti's stay in Florence in 1575: Laschke 2000, p. 66.
17 So Cecchi already observed (1998, p. 142, note 18). Cecchi strengthened this attribution in the catalogue of the Volterra Candid exhibition in 2009; Brigitte Volk-Knüttel refers to it skeptically in her monograph, which appeared shortly thereafter; see Cecchi 2009, pp. 26ff., and Volk-Knüttel 2010, p. 18, no. 36.
18 Cf. Volk-Knüttel 2010, nos. G17 and G18, pp. 136–40.
19 Volk-Knüttel 2010, p. 18. Cecchi rightly noted the rupture between the *feinmalerisch* modeling of the head and collar and the visible facture of the upper picture surface. To conclude from this, however, that a second hand participated in the making of the picture appears in no way necessary to me, for the application of color remains equally thin, allowing the underpainting of the face to shine through. The open painting technique appears first in the background of Candid's *Entombment* of c. 1585 in the Pinacoteca of Volterra.
20 Above all in comparison to the portrait drawing by Joseph Heintz (National Gallery of Art, Washington, D.C., 1984.3.11), which probably served as the model for the 1589 engraving by Gijsbert van Veen; see Kaufmann 1982, pp. 152–53, no. 55, and Zimmer 1988, pp. 117–19, no. A16.
21 The author of this entry is preparing a more detailed article on this painting and on Peter Candid's activity as a portraitist.

46

ALESSANDRO ALGARDI

Bologna, 1598 – Rome, 1654

Christ on the Cross, 1647

Pen and brown ink over red chalk on laid paper; drawing 484 × 328 mm (19 1/16 × 12 15/16 in.), support/mount 562 × 409 mm (22 1/8 × 16 1/8 in.)
Inscribed, upper right in brown ink (by a later hand): *Alessandro Algardi Delinea*[cut off]/*Roma 1647*; on mount across bottom in brown ink (by a later hand): *questo disegno e fatto dal Cav Algardi, lo fece pel comm^r Lonte del Pozza di Verona, lo acquisto in Roma il Comm^r Conte Isola e passo al conte Miroglio/di Rosignano 1795. Questo disegno lo comprai in Casale assieme ad altri disegni e libri Santo Varni. Vedi la stessa descrizione ch'io trovai sulla/ dietro al disegno sopra* [illegible]; on verso, on mount at upper center in brown ink (by a later and different hand): *Questo disegno è fatto dal Cav^re Algardi lo fece pel Commendatore Lonte Del Pozzo/ di Verona, lo aquisto in Roma il commendatore Cte Isola e passo al Conte Miroglio/ di Rosignano—1795—/ N.B. questo disegno lo comprai in Casale assieme a molti altri disegni e libri, e dietro/ sopra il cortone che lo chiudessa nella cornice vi si leggero la sopra inscrizione**
National Gallery of Art, Washington, D.C., Ailsa Mellon Bruce Fund 1992.42.1

OVER THE COURSE OF HIS CAREER, Alessandro Algardi and his workshop produced a number of crucifixes, in a variety of media. The most significant versions are the life-size "Alamandini Crucifix," commissioned about 1641, known from the painted clay model in the Vatican and the bronze cast in Genoa, featuring Christ dead on the cross, and the smaller (approx. 70 cm) silver crucifix, with a living Christ, made about 1646 for Innocent X, which is lost but known from numerous casts and later copies.[1] The Washington drawing, inscribed with the date of 1647, similarly depicts a living Christ. Rapidly sketched in pen over red chalk—the sculptor's preferred graphic media—it presents the figure from a slightly oblique angle, looking up to the left, his head surrounded by a glory of light. His elongated but muscled body curves gently to the right, its movement accentuated by the *perizonium* spiraling up to the right, while blood streams from the wounds in his hands and feet. In keeping with all of Algardi's crucifixes, it shows the figure attached to the cross with four nails.

As Wittkower first observed, the drawing is closely related to a bronze crucifix in the Palazzo Rospigliosi-Pallavicini, with which it shares a living Christ, elongated proportions, four nails, and a "flying piece of drapery."[2] On the basis of this comparison, Wittkower tentatively attributed the so-called Pallavicini Crucifix to Algardi, an attribution subsequently embraced by all scholars, the majority of whom identified the sheet as a preparatory study, the first idea for the sculpture.[3] Among them was Johnston, who also drew attention to two other drawings of a living Christ, one in Modena, the other in Florence, attributing them to Algardi and proposing that they followed the Washington sheet as preparatory studies for the Pallavicini bronze.[4]

In 1985 Montagu noted that the Pallavicini bronze was only one of several fine casts after the original model made for the silver crucifix for Innocent X; one example is that in the Art Institute of Chicago (fig. 75). Following Johnston, she connected the three drawings to this model and clarified the fact that the sculptor's name and date on the recto of the Washington sheet were not autograph.[5] However, in the catalogue accompanying the 1999 Algardi exhibition in Rome, Johnston revised her original argument. Based on the pictorial qualities of the image—the oblique viewing angle, the dripping blood, the glory of light around Christ's head, the shadow projected by the body—she proposed that the Washington drawing was likely made in preparation for a print. Although no print after the drawing is known, Johnston's proposal is suggestive, especially when one compares the more dramatic expression and greater sense of movement of the Christ in the drawing to the more classical and restrained figure in the many versions of the bronze. More likely, however, is that the sculptor made the drawing as a meditative reflection on his *Cristo vivo* crucifix—which Montagu has called "undoubtedly the most popular and influential of all of Algardi's works"[6]—made either as an autonomous study or, perhaps, in preparation for another sculpture.

PROVENANCE

Commendatore Conte del Pozzo, Verona; Commendatore Conte Isola; Conte Miroglio di Rosignano, 1795; Santo Varni; Claudio Argentieri (Lugt 486b); Pier Giulio Breschi (Lugt 2079b); private collection; sold Sotheby's, London, 15 June 1983, lot 61, to David Tunick, New York, for James S. Deely, New York; David Tunick, New York; National Gallery of Art, Washington, D.C. purchase in 1992

LITERATURE

Varni 1879, p. 52; Labò 1930, p. 1398; Vitzhum 1963, p. 76; Wittkower 1966, pp. 231–32; Nava Cellini 1967, p. 42; Johnston 1968, pp. 459–60; Heimbürger Ravalli 1973, p. 160; Negri Arnoldi 1974, pp. 70–71; Stock 1984, p. 19; Montagu 1985, vol. 2, pp. 328, 479, no. 9; Jennifer Montagu in Montagu 1999, p. 166, no. 33; Catherine Johnston in Montagu 1999, pp. 288–89, no. 93; Virginia Tuttle Clayton in *Art for the Nation* 2000, pp. 172–73; Boucher 2006, pp. 50, 95, note 4; Grimaldi and Mascii 2011a, pp. 13–15, 37, and 38; Grimaldi and Mascii 2011b, pp. 14, 17–19, and 27; Denise Allen in Wengraf 2014, p. 236

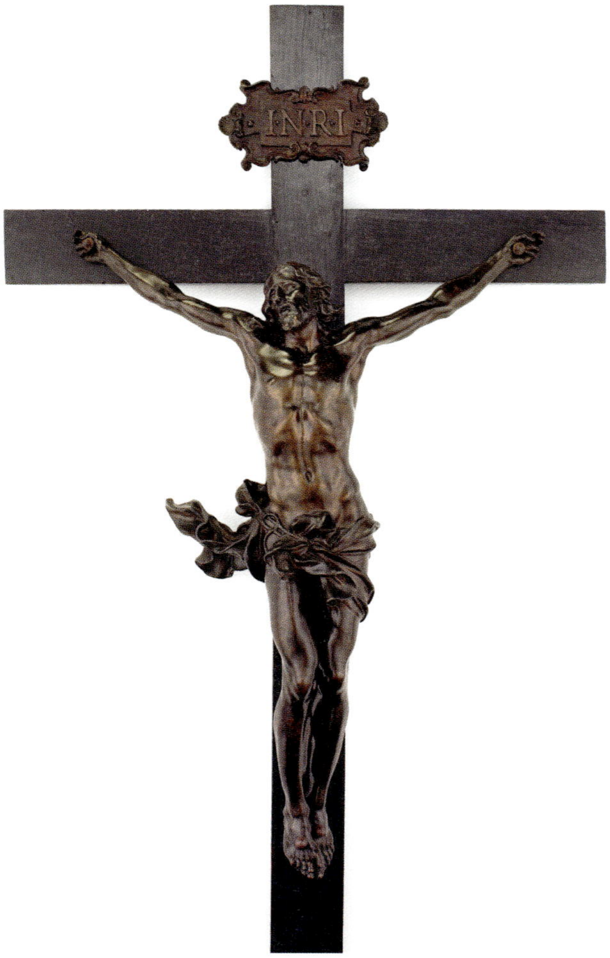

FIG. 75
Alessandro Algardi
Crucifix, c. 1646
Bronze, pearwood with ebonizing and staining, 188.9 × 75.6 cm
The Art Institute of Chicago

By virtue of its inscribed date, the Washington sheet is a precious document among Algardi's drawings. It is also unique in featuring, both on its recto and verso, its early provenance, beginning with "Commendatore Conte del Pozzo," who can likely be identified as Francesco Bartolomeo Dal Pozzo (1637–1722), a knight of Malta and biographer of Veronese artists, who indeed owned a bronze crucifix by Algardi.[7] Although its second owner, "Commendatore Conte Isola," remains a mystery, "Conte Miroglio di Rosignano" can be tentatively identified as a member of the Miroglio family from Rosignano Monferrato in the Piedmont, a town adjacent to Casale Monferrato. And it was in Casale that its next owner, Varni, tells us he purchased it in 1859.[8] Following Varni, and before its sale at Sotheby's in 1983, the drawing was owned by the publisher Claudio Argentieri (1891–1956) and the journalist Pier Luigi Breschi, well-known collectors of mostly Bolognese drawings. S.F.O.

NOTES

1 See Montagu 1985, vol. 2, pp. 315–41. On the dating of the Alamandini Crucifix, see Mazzarelli 2013, in which, on the basis of new documents, she establishes 1641 as the likely date of the commission.
2 Wittkower 1966, pp. 231–32.
3 Nava Cellini 1967, p. 42; Johnston 1968, pp. 459–60; Heimbürger Ravalli 1973, p. 160; Negri Arnoldi 1974, pp. 70–71; Stock 1984, p. 19; Virginia Tuttle Clayton in *Art for the Nation* 2000, p. 172; Boucher 2006, pp. 50, 96, note 4. Recently, Grimaldi and Mascii (Grimaldi and Mascii 2011a and Grimaldi and Mascii 2011b) have unconvincingly attributed an ivory crucifix (in a private collection) to Algardi, dating it to c. 1625; on the basis of what they call the "perfect coincidence" (in form and conception) between the ivory and the Washington drawing, they argue that Algardi produced the latter from the ivory, wanting to "redraw analytically" his earlier work.
4 Johnston 1968. The Modena drawing (Galleria Estensen 980) was formerly attributed to Giovanni Maria Tamburini, a pupil of Guido Reni; the Florentine drawing (Uffizi 3427) had been attributed to Guido Reni. Negri Arnoldi 1974, p. 71, note 47, rejected Johnston's attribution of the Modena drawing, calling it a *ripresa ottocentesca*.
5 Heimbürger Ravalli 1973, p. 160, wrote that the sheet was *firmato Alessandro Algardi e datato 1647*; Montagu 1985, vol. 2, p. 479.
6 Montagu 1985, vol. 2, p. 329.
7 The inscription on the recto of the mount is in the hand of Santo Varni (who purchased the drawing in 1859), as can be confirmed by comparing it with his dedicatory inscription on the copy of his *Ricordi di alcuni fonditori in bronzo* in the library of the National Gallery of Art, Washington, D.C. As Catherine Johnston noted in Montagu 1999, p. 288, Varni copied the early provenance from the late eighteenth-century inscription on the mount's verso. She also identified the first owner as Conte Bartolomeo Dal Pozzo, but—given his age (ten years old) at the time the drawing was made—rightly discounted the idea that the drawing was made for him and suggested that it could have been drawn for another (older) member of his family. Algardi's bronze crucifix in the Art Institute of Chicago (a fine version of the Pallavicini type) bears, on its back, the stamp of Francesco Bartolomeo Dal Pozzo, who confirmed his ownership of the work, as well as of two bronze *angeletti* by Algardi, in his *Le vite de' pittori, de gli scultori, et architetti veronesi*, p. 309. See Boucher 2006, p. 50, who sees the inscription on the Washington drawing as "link[ing] the crucifix's history with the dal Pozzo family."
8 Varni 1879, p. 52.

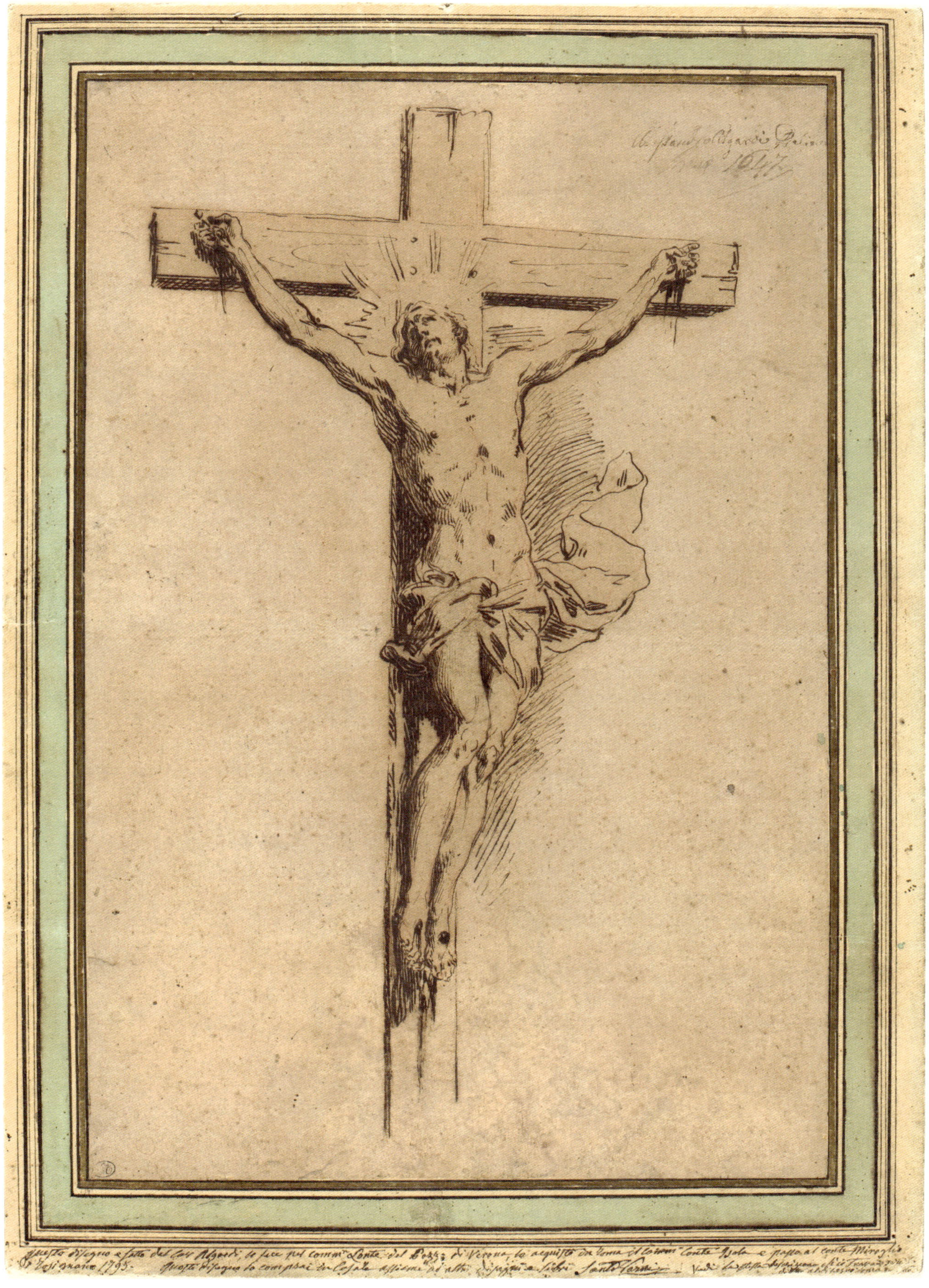
1647
1795
Santo Varni

47

GIAN LORENZO BERNINI AND WORKSHOP

Naples, 1598 – Rome, 1680

Sea deity with a dolphin, 1652–53

Pen, ink and wash with traces of chalk, 406 × 273 mm (16 × 10¾ in.)
Victoria and Albert Museum, London, Bequeathed by Constantine Alexander Ionides CAI.416

IN 1652 Francesco I d'Este commissioned Bernini to design multiple wall fountains for his residence in Sassuolo. After inquiring by letter as to the precise requirements of the space, Bernini recommended that their execution be entrusted to Antonio Raggi, who journeyed to Sassuolo the following year and assisted there in the creation of a stucco statue still displayed today in the monumental court of the palace, across from its main entrance.

The sculptor himself relates that he began by sketching multiple variants of the same motif side by side.[1] Preparatory drawings that would document his *primo pensiero* for Sassuolo have not survived; comparable sheets show, however, that Bernini first sketched the contours from a central viewpoint with vigorous pen strokes, paying little attention to surface texture, spatial context, or tonal contrast. In a second preparatory stage peculiar to Bernini, the figure or figural group was rendered loosely in chalk on the sheet, emphasizing volume. This stage is represented in a drawing for Sassuolo now at the J. Paul Getty Museum in Los Angeles, in which Bernini emphasizes the sculpture's overall three-dimensional appearance: undulating pentimenti strengthen the expansive force of bodily forms, making the figures communicate with their surroundings while also appearing strangely weightless, like a cloudy mass.

In a later preparatory stage, which conveyed a more precise idea of the execution to the commissioner and often involved heavy workshop participation, Bernini gave fixed substance to the plastic surfaces and more strongly separated the figures from their surroundings. This is the stage seen in the present drawing, in which a few repetitive internal contours betray some workshop involvement. While the contours are rendered in precise pen strokes, it is the wash, built up in multiple tonal layers, that works to accentuate the chiaroscuro dramatically, lends outer surfaces a nearly metallic hardness, and indicates the shadows cast by bodies. The points of contact of limbs and rocks, hands and fish, are now depicted with great precision.

The drawing thematizes the sculptural polarities of formlessness and organic form, heaviness and lightness, statuesqueness and ostensive movement. As is frequently the case with Bernini, the figure appears to be pushed to the side by the almost physical impact of light,[2] an aspect that could not have been entirely conveyed by Bernini's plastic model. (Two of Raggi's *modelli* for the fountain are preserved in Milan and Modena.)[3] The sea creature, probably a triton, presents himself powerfully on a crumbling stone arch and heaves a floundering fish over his right shoulder. Lifted violently from its element and squeezed by powerful arms, the animal spouts a large stream of water indicated with determined brushstrokes. Bernini's fountains are often construed as a form of antagonism; sometimes, water itself seems to undermine the stability of the architectural setting.[4] With the natural stone arch, the seated position of the triton, and the rock ledge that virtually slips down beneath his right leg, Bernini paraphrases his Four Rivers fountain and fountain of the Moor, completed just a short time earlier, while the struggle between the triton and the slippery fish recalls his contemporary Fontana del Moro (both Piazza Navona, Rome).

The never-completed *concetto* to which the Sassuolo fountain originally belonged would have staged a twofold opposition or contrapposto (see drawings in Windsor Castle and in the British Museum, London). The central fountain would have juxtaposed the theme of instability and violence with the erotic encounter of Neptune and Amphitrite or the sovereign balance of the standing Neptune, and a counterpart to the Triton fountain would have been offered by the peaceful sleep of a Nereid carried by a dolphin. F.F.

PROVENANCE

Earl Spencer; H. Reveley (sale, Christie's, London, 11 May 1852); C.A. Ionides Bequest 1901

LITERATURE

Brauer and Wittkower 1931, p. 53; Wittkower 1966, p. 267; Desmond Shawe-Taylor in Weston-Lewis 1998, pp. 139–40; Bacchi 2004, pp. 47–54; Wardropper 2012, pp. 29–30

NOTES

1. Chantelou 1985, p. 19 (6 June 1665).
2. See Fehrenbach 2005, pp. 11–24.
3. See C.D. Dickerson and Anthony Sigel in Dickerson, Sigel, and Wardropper 2012, pp. 182–87.
4. See Fehrenbach 2008, pp. 130–33.

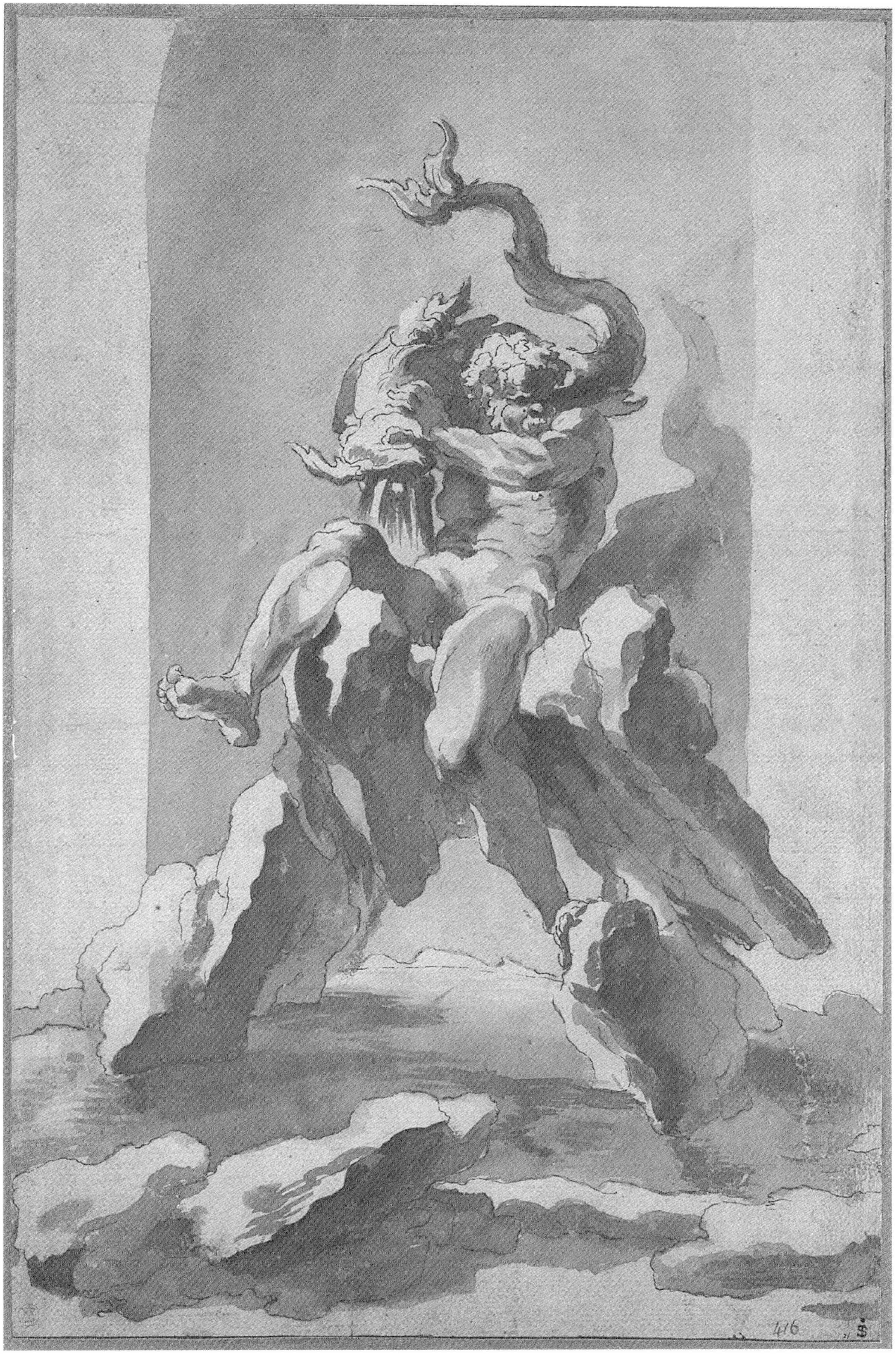

Bibliography

ACIDINI LUCHINAT 2002
Cristina Acidini Luchinat, ed., *The Medici, Michelangelo, & the Art of Late Renaissance Florence*, exh. cat., Palazzo Strozzi, Florence; Art Institute of Chicago; Detroit Institute of Arts; New Haven and London 2002

ACIDINI LUCHINAT 2005
Cristina Acidini Luchinat, *Michelangelo Scultore*, photographs by Aurelio Amendola, Milan 2005

ACKERMAN 1986
James S. Ackerman, *The Architecture of Michelangelo,* Harmondsworth 1986

ADAMS 1960
Frederick B. Adams, Jr., *Tenth Report to the Fellows of the Pierpont Morgan Library*, New York 1960

AGOSTI AND FARINELLA 1987
Giovanni Agosti and Vincenzo Farinella, *Michelangelo e l'arte classica*, exh. cat., Casa Buonarroti, Florence, 1987

AHL 1995
Diane Cole Ahl, ed., *Leonardo da Vinci's Sforza Monument Horse: The Art and the Engineering*, Bethlehem, Pa., and London 1995

ALBERTI 1804
Leon Battista Alberti, *Della pittura e della statua*, Milan 1804

ALBERTI 1988
Leon Battista Alberti, *On the Art of Building in Ten Books,* translated by Joseph Rykwert with Neil Leach and Robert Tavernor, Cambridge, Mass., 1988

AMES-LEWIS 1981
Frances Ames-Lewis, *Drawing in Early Renaissance Italy*, New Haven and London 1981

AMES-LEWIS AND WRIGHT 1983
Frances Ames-Lewis and Joanne Wright, eds., *Drawing in the Italian Renaissance Workshop*, exh. cat., University Art Gallery, Nottingham, and Victoria and Albert Museum, London; London 1983

AMMIRATO 1594
Scipione Ammirato, *Discorsi sopra Cornelio Tacito*, Florence 1594

ANDROSOV AND BALDINI 2000
Sergej Androsov and Umberto Baldini, eds., *L'adolescente dell'Ermitage e la Sagrestia Nuova di Michelangelo*, exh. cat., Casa Buonarroti, Florence, and Hermitage Museum, St. Petersburg; Pistoria 2000

ANGELINI 1986
Alessandro Angelini, ed., *Disegni italiani del tempo di Donatello*, exh. cat., Gabinetto Disegni e Stampe degli Uffizi, Florence, 1986

ARETINO 1957
Pietro Aretino, *Lettere sull'arte*, commentary by Fidenzio Pertile, ed. Ettore Camesasca, 3 vols., Milan 1957–60

ART FOR THE NATION 2000
Art for the Nation: Collecting for a New Century, exh. cat., National Gallery of Art, Washington, D.C., 2000

ASEMISSEN AND SCHWEIKHART 1994
Hermann Ulrich Asemissen and Gunter Schweikhart, *Malerei als Thema der Malerei*, Berlin 1994

ATTWOOD 1997
Philip Attwood, "Self-Promotion in Sixteenth-century Florence: Baccio Bandinelli's Portrait Medal," *The Medal*, vol. 30, 1997, pp. 3–9

ATTWOOD 2003
Philip Attwood, *Italian Medals c. 1530–1600 in British Public Collections*, London 2003

AVERY 1986
Charles Avery, "The Pope's Goldsmith," [review of Pope-Hennessy 1985], *Apollo*, vol. 124, 1986, pp. 61–63

AVERY 1987
Charles Avery, *Giambologna: The Complete Sculpture*, Oxford and Mt. Kisco, NY, 1987

AVERY 1998
Charles Avery, "Drawing in the Work of Renaissance Sculptors," *Drawing*, vol. 19, 1998, pp. 113–17

AVERY 2000
Charles Avery, "Pietro Francavilla's Drawings of Giambologna's Models," *Apollo*, vol. 152, no. 463, 2000, pp. 22–26

AVERY AND BARBAGLIA 1981
Charles Avery and Susanna Barbaglia, *L'opera completa del Cellini*, Milan 1981

AVERY, RADCLIFFE, AND LEITHE-JASPER 1978
Charles Avery, Anthony Radcliffe, and Manfred Leithe-Jasper, eds., *Giambologna 1529–1608: Ein Wendepunkt der europäischen Plastik*, exh. cat., Royal Scottish Museum, Edinburgh; Victoria and Albert Museum, London; and Kunsthistorisches Museum, Vienna; Vienna 1978

BACCHI 2004
Andrea Bacchi, "Sculture e apparati decorativi," in Filippo Trevisani, ed., *Il Palazzo di Sassuolo, Delizia dei Duchi d'Este*, Parma 2004, pp. 41–54

BACCI 1936
Pèleo Bacci, *Francesco di Valdambrino, emulo del Ghiberti e collaborator di Jacopo della Quercia, con 50 illustrazioni e 103 documenti*, Siena 1936

BACOU AND VIATTE 1974
Roseline Bacou and Françoise Viatte, *Italian Renaissance Drawings from the Musée du Louvre, Paris: Roman, Tuscan, and Emilian Schools, 1500–1575*, exh. cat., Metropolitan Museum of Art, New York, 1974

BAGLIONE 1649
Giovanni Baglione, *Le vite de' pittori, scultori et architetti dal pontificato di Gregorio XIII fino a tutto quello d'Urbano VIII*, Rome 1649

BAGLIONE 1733
Giovanni Baglione, *Le vite de' pittori, scultori, architetti, ed intagliatori*, Naples 1733

BALAS 1992
Edith Balas, "The Iconography of Michelangelo's Medici Chapel: A New Hypothesis," *Gazette des Beaux-Arts*, vol. 120, 1992, pp. 117–26

BALDINI 1973
Umberto Baldini, *L'opera completa di Michelangelo scultore*, Milan 1973

BALDINUCCI 1811
Filippo Baldinucci, *Notizie de' professori del disegno*, 12 vols., Milan 1811

BALDINUCCI 1845–47
Filippo Baldinucci, *Notizie dei professori del disegno da Cimabue in qua*, ed. Ferdinando Ranalli, 5 vols., Florence 1845–47

BALDINUCCI 1974–75
Filippo Baldinucci, *Notizie dei professori del disegno da Cimabue in qua,* ed. Paola Barocchi and Antonio Boschetto, 7 vols., Florence 1974–75

BAMBACH 1999
Carmen C. Bambach, *Drawing and Painting in the Italian Renaissance Workshop: Theory and Practice, 1300–1700*, Cambridge 1999

BAMBACH 2003
Carmen C. Bambach, ed., *Leonardo da Vinci, Master Draftsman,* exh. cat., Metropolitan Museum of Art, New York; New Haven 2003

BAMBACH 2007A
Carmen C. Bambach, "A New Drawing by the Young Raphael and its Source in Donatello," *The Burlington Magazine*, vol. 149, 2007, pp. 772–78

BAMBACH 2007B
Carmen C. Bambach, "Tuscan Drawings of the Quattrocento and Cinquecento in the Metropolitan Museum of Art 1998–2005," in Nicoletta Baldini, ed., *Invisibile agli occhi: Atti della giornata di studio in ricordo di Lisa Venturini*, Florence 2007, pp. 77–95

BAMBACH 2010
Carmen C. Bambach, "Berenson's Michelangelo," *Apollo*, vol. 171, 2010, pp. 100–17

BANDINELLI 1905
Arduino Colasanti, ed., "Il *memoriale* di Baccio Bandinelli," *Repertorium für Kunstwissenschaft*, vol. 28, 1905, pp. 406–43

BANGE 1922
Ernst Friedrich Bange, *Die italienischen Bronzen der Renaissance und des Barock*, vol. 2: *Reliefs und Plaketten*, Berlin 1922

BARBIERI 2007
Costanza Barbieri, "'Chompare e amicho karissimo': A 'Portrait of Michelangelo' by His Friend Sebastiano," *Artibus et Historiae*, vol. 28, 2007, pp. 107–20

BARDESCHI CIULICH 2005
Lucilla Bardeschi Ciulich, *I contratti di Michelangelo*, Florence 2005

BARDESCHI CIULICH AND BAROCCHI 2005
Lucilla Bardeschi Ciulich and Paola Barocchi, eds., *I ricordi di Michelangelo*. Florence 1970

BARFUCCI 1945
Enrico Barfucci, *Lorenzo de' Medici e la società artistica del suo tempo*, Florence 1945

BARKAN 1999
Leonard Barkan, *Unearthing the Past: Archaeology and Aesthetics in the Making of Renaissance Culture*, New Haven and London 1999

BARKAN 2010
Leonard Barkan, *Michelangelo: A Life on Paper*, Princeton 2010

BAROCCHI 1960–62
Paola Barocchi, ed., *Trattati d'arte del Cinquecento*, 3 vols., Bari 1960–62

BAROCCHI 1962–64
Paola Barocchi, *Michelangelo e sua scuola: I disegni di Casa Buonarroti e degli Uffizi*, 3 vols., Florence 1962–64

BAROCCHI 1971–77
Paola Barocchi, ed., *Scritti d'arte del Cinquecento*, 3 vols., Milan and Naples 1971–77

BAROCCHI ET AL. 1963
Paola Barocchi et al., eds., *Mostra di disegni dei fondatori dell'Accademia delle Arti del Disegno nel IV centenario della fondazione*, exh. cat., Galleria degli Uffizi, Florence, 1963

BAROCCHI AND GAETA BERTELÀ 1993
Paola Barocchi and Giovanna Gaeta Bertelà, *Collezionismo mediceo: Cosimo I, Francesco I e il Cardinale Ferdinando: Documenti 1540–1587*, Modena 1993

BAROCCHI AND RISTORI 1965–83
Paola Barocchi and Renzo Ristori, eds., *Il carteggio di Michelangelo*, 5 vols., Florence 1965–83

BARTSCH
The Illustrated Bartsch, ed. Walter L. Strauss, 104 vols., New York 1978–

BARZMAN 2000
Karen-Edis Barzman, *The Florentine Academy and the Early Modern State*, Cambridge 2000

BATTAGLIA 1961–2002
Salvatore Battaglia, ed., *Grande dizionario della lingua italiana*, 21 vols., Turin 1961–2002

BEAN 1964
Jacob Bean, *100 European Drawings in the Metropolitan Museum of Art*, Greenwich, Conn., 1964

BEAN AND TURCIC 1982
Jacob Bean, with Lawrence Turčić, *15th and 16th Century Italian Drawings in the Metropolitan Museum of Art*, New York 1982

BEAN AND STAMPFLE 1965
Jacob Bean and Felice Stampfle, *Drawings from New York Collections*, vol. 1: *The Italian Renaissance*, exh. cat., Metropolitan Museum of Art, New York; Greenwich, Conn., 1965

BECK 1966
James H. Beck, review of Coffin Hanson 1964, *Art Bulletin*, vol. 48, 1966, pp. 114–15

BECK 1991
James H. Beck, *Jacopo della Quercia*, 2 vols., New York 1991

BÉGUIN AND COSTAMAGNA 2003
Sylvie Béguin and Philippe Costamagna, "Nouvelles considerations sur Baccio Bandinelli peintre; la redécouverte de la Léda et le Cygne," *Les cahiers d'histoire de l'art*, vol. 1, 2003, pp. 7–18

BELL 1914
Charles Francis Bell, *Drawings by the Old Masters in the Library of Christ Church, Oxford*, Oxford 1914

BELLINI AND BRUNETTI 1978
Fiora Bellini and Giulia Brunetti, eds., *I disegni antichi degli Uffizi: I tempi del Ghiberti*, exh. cat., Gabinetto Disegni e Stampe degli Uffizi, Florence, 1978

BELLANDI 1998
Alfredo Bellandi, "Marco della Robbia (Fra Mattia)," in Gentilini 1998, pp. 322–25

BELLOSI 1980
Luciano Bellosi, "A proposito del disegno dell'Albertina (dal Ghiberti a Masolino)," in Giulia Brunetti, ed., *Lorenzo Ghiberti nel suo tempo*, Florence 1980, vol. 1, pp. 135–45

BELLOSI 2000
Luciano Bellosi, "La 'Porta Magna' di Jacopo della Quercia" (1983), republished in Bellosi, *Come un prato fiorito: studi sull'arte tardogotica*, Milan 2000

BELTRAME QUATTROCCHI 1979
Enrichetta Beltrame Quattrocchi, *Disegni toscani e umbri del primo rinascimento dalle collezioni del Gabinetto Nazionale delle Stampe*, exh. cat., Villa alla Farnesina alla Lungara, Rome, 1979

BELTRAMINI, GASPAROTTO, AND TURA 2013
Guido Beltramini, Davide Gasparotto, and Adolfo Tura, eds., *Pietro Bembo e l'invenzione del Rinascimento*, exh. cat., Palazzo del Monte di Pietà, Padua; Venice 2013

BEMBO 1966
Pietro Bembo, *Prose e rime*, ed. Carlo Dionisotti, Turin 1966

BENNETT AND WILKINS 1984
Bonnie A. Bennett and David G. Wilkins, *Donatello*, Mt. Kisco, NY, 1984

BERENSON 1896
Bernard Berenson, *The Florentine Painters of the Renaissance*, New York 1896

BERENSON AND GARDNER 1987
Rollin van N. Hadley, ed., *The Letters of Bernard Berenson and Isabella Stewart Gardner, 1887–1924: with Correspondence by Mary Berenson*, Boston 1987

BERENSON 1903
Bernard Berenson, *The Drawings of the Florentine Painters Classified, Criticised and Studied as Documents in the History and Appreciation of Tuscan Art*, 2 vols., London 1903

BERENSON 1933
Bernard Berenson, "Verrocchio e Leonardo, Leonardo e Credi," *Bollettino d'Arte*, vol. 27, 1933, pp. 241–64

BERENSON 1935
Bernard Berenson, "I disegni di Raffaello da Montelupo," *Bollettino d'Arte*, vol. 3, 1935, pp. 105–20

BERENSON 1938
Bernard Berenson, *The Drawings of the Florentine Painters: Amplified Edition*, 3 vols., Chicago 1938

BERENSON 1961
Bernard Berenson, *I disegni dei pittori fiorentini*, translated by Luisa Vertova Nicolson, revised and enlarged edition, 3 vols., Milan 1961

BERLINER 1921–22
Rudolf Berliner, "Eine Plakettenfolge von Jakob Cobaert," *Archiv für Medaillen- und Plaketten-Kunde*, vol. 3, 1921–22, pp. 134–35

BERNARDI 1882–93
Jacopo Bernardi, *Antichi testamenti tratti dagli archivi della congregazione di Carità di Venezia*, Venice 1882–93

BERTI 1980
Luciano Berti, ed., *Il primato del disegno*, exh. cat., Palazzo Strozzi, Florence, 1980

BERTINI 1958
Aldo Bertini, *I disegni italiani della Biblioteca Reale di Torino*, Rome 1958

BERTOLOTTI 1881
Antonino Bertolotti, *Artisti lombardi a Roma nei secoli XV, XVI e XVII: Studi e ricerche negli archivi romani*, Milan 1881

BIAGI 1946
Luigi Biagi, *Jacopo della Quercia*, Florence 1946

BIGI IOTTI 2008
Alessandra Bigi Iotti, "Andrea Sansovino and the Design for a Funerary Monument for Leo X," *The Burlington Magazine*, vol. 150, 2008, pp. 757–59

BISOGNI 1977
Fabio Bisogni, "Sull'iconografia della Fonte Gaia," in Giulietta Chelazzi Dini, ed., *Jacopo della Quercia fra gotico e rinascimento: Atti del Convegno di Studi, Facoltà di Lettere e Filosofia 2–5 ottobre 1975*, Florence 1977, pp. 109–18

BISSELL 1993
Gerhard Bissell, "Beobachtungen zum Werden des Juliusgrabs bis 1513," in Volkmar Greiselmayer, ed., *Musis et Litteris: Festschrift für Bernhard Rupprecht zum 65. Geburtstag*, Munich 1993, pp. 143–56

BLISS 2003
Joseph R. Bliss, "Benvenuto Cellini's Satyrs for the Porte Dorée at Fountainebleau," in Peta Motture, ed., *Large Bronzes of the Renaissance* (Studies in the History of Art 64), New Haven 2003, pp. 73–93

BOBER AND RUBINSTEIN 1986
Phyllis Pray Bober and Ruth Rubinstein, *Renaissance Artists & Antique Sculpture: A Handbook of Sources*, London 1986

BOCCARDO 1989
Piero Boccardo, *Andrea Doria e le arti: committenza e mecenatismo a Genova nel Rinascimento*, Rome 1989

BOCCHI 1677
Francesco Bocchi, with Giovanni Cinelli, *Le bellezze della città di Firenze*, Florence 1677

BODE 1906
Wilhelm von Bode, *The Collection of Oscar Hainauer*, London 1906

BOORSCH AND MARCIARI 2006
Suzanne Boorsch and John J. Marciari, *Master Drawings from the Yale University Art Gallery*, exh. cat., Yale University Art Gallery, New Haven, 2006

BORGHINI 1584
Raffaele Borghini, *Il Riposo*, Florence 1584

BOTTARI AND TICOZZI 1822
Giovanni Gaetano Bottari and Stefano Ticozzi, *Raccolta di lettere sulla pittura, scultura e architettura*, 8 vols., Milan 1822–25

BOUCHER 1991
Bruce Boucher, *The Sculpture of Jacopo Sansovino*, 2 vols., New Haven and London 1991

BOUCHER 2001
Bruce Boucher, "Italian Renaissance Terracotta: Artistic Revival or Technological Innovation?," in *Earth and Fire: Italian Terracotta Sculpture from Donatello to Canova*, exh. cat., ed. Bruce Boucher, Museum of Fine Arts, Houston, and Victoria and Albert Museum, London; New Haven and London 2001

BOUCHER 2006
Bruce Boucher, "Crucifix. Notable Acquisitions at the Art Institute of Chicago," *Art Institute of Chicago Museum Studies*, vol. 32, 2006, pp. 50–51 and 95

BOYLE 1977
Leonard E. Boyle, O.P., *San Clemente Miscellany I: The Community of Ss. Sisto e Clemente in Rome, 1677–1977*, Rome 1977

BRADY 1999
Old Master Drawings, New York 1999

BRAUER AND WITTKOWER 1931
Heinrich Brauer and Rudolf Wittkower, *Die Zeichnungen des Gianlorenzo Bernini* (Römische Forschungen der Bibliotheca Hertziana, 9 and 10), 2 vols., Munich 1931

BRAUNFELS 1948
Wolfgang Braunfels, *Benvenuto Cellini: Perseus und Medusa,* Berlin 1948

BRECK 1912
Joseph Breck, "Renaissance Metalwork," *The Metropolitan Museum of Art Bulletin*, vol. 7, 1912, pp. 191–94

BRECK 1912
Joseph Breck, *Catalogue of Romanesque, Gothic, and Renaissance Sculpture* (Metropolitan Museum of Art), New York 1913

BREDEKAMP 2004
Horst Bredekamp, "Ende (1545) und Anfang (1505) von Michelangelos Juliusgrab: Frei – oder Wandgrab?" in Horst Bredekamp and Volker Reinhardt, eds., *Totenkult und Wille zur Macht*, Darmstadt 2004, pp. 61–83

BREDEKAMP 2007
Horst Bredekamp, *Galilei der Künstler: Der Mond, die Sonne, die Hand*, Berlin 2007

BRENTANO 1989
Carrol Brentano, "Guglielmo della Porta," in *Dizionario Biografico degli Italiani*, vol. 37, Rome 1989, in *Teccani.it, L'enciclopedia italiana*, online: http://www.treccani.it/enciclopedia/guglielmo-della-porta_(Dizionario-Biografico)/

BRINCKMANN 1923–24
Albert Erich Brinckmann, *Barock-Bozzetti*, 4 vols., Frankfurt am Main 1923–24

BRINCKMANN 1925
Albert Erich Brinckmann, *Michelangelo Zeichnungen*, Munich 1925

BROPHY 1963
John Brophy, *The Face in Western Art*, London 1963

BROTHERS 2008
Cammy Brothers, *Michelangelo, Drawing and the Invention of Architecture*, New Haven and London 2008

BROTHERS 2012
Cammy Brothers, "Designing What You Cannot Draw: Michelangelo and the Laurentian Library," in Nova and Maurer 2012, pp. 133–46

BROWN 2008
Katherine T. Brown, *The Painter's Reflection: Self-Portraiture in Renaissance Venice 1458–1625*, Florence 2000

BURCKHARDT 2000
Die Baukunst der Renaissance in Italien, Munich and Basel 2000

BURCKHARDT 2006
Jacob Burckhardt, "Randglossen zur Sculptur der Renaissance," in *Jacob Burckhardt Werke: kritische Gesamtausgabe*, vol. 16: *Die Kunst der Renaissance*, Part 1, Munich and Basel 2006

BURIONI 2004
Matteo Burioni, "Die Architektur: Kunst, Handwerk oder Technik? Giorgio Vasari, Vincenzo Borghini und die Ordnung der Künste an der Accademia del Disegno im frühabsolutistischen Herzogtum Florenz," in Gisela Engel and Nicole C. Karafyllis, eds., *Technik in der Frühen Neuzeit – Schrittmacher der europäischen Moderne*, Frankfurt am Main 2004, pp. 389–408

BURIONI 2007
Matteo Burioni, "Der Fürst als Architekt. Eine Relektüre von Giorgio Vasaris Bildnis Cosimos I.," in Ulrich Oevermann, Johannes Süssmann, and Christine Tauber, eds., *Die Kunst der Mächtigen und die Macht der Kunst: Untersuchungen zu Mäzenatentum und Kultur Patronage*, Berlin 2007

BURNS, COLLARETA, AND GASPAROTTO 2000
Howard Burns, Marco Collareta, and Davide Gasparotto, eds., *Valerio Belli Vicentino c. 1480–1546: Scultore della luce*, Vicenza 2000

BURROUGHS 1919
Bryson Burroughs, "Drawings from the Pembroke Collection," *The Metropolitan Museum of Art Bulletin*, vol. 14, 1919, pp. 136–40

BUSH 1976
Virginia Bush, *The Colossal Sculpture of the Cinquecento*, New York 1976

BUSH 1980
Virginia Bush, "Bandinelli's 'Hercules and Cacus' and Florentine Traditions," *Memoirs of the American Academy in Rome*, vol. 35, 1980, pp. 163–206

BUTTERFIELD 1997
Andrew Butterfield, *The Sculptures of Andrea del Verrocchio*, New Haven and London 1997

BYAM SHAW 1976
James Byam Shaw, *Drawings by Old Masters at Christ Church, Oxford*, 2 vols., Oxford 1976

BYAM SHAW 1983
James Byam Shaw, *The Italian Drawings of the Frits Lugt Collection*, Paris 1983

CACIORGNA 2001
Marilena Caciorgna, "Moduli antichi e tradizione classica nel programma della Fonte Gaia di Jacopo della Quercia," *Fontes*, vols. 4–5, 2001–2, pp. 71–142

CADOGAN 1983
Jean K. Cadogan, "Verrocchio's Drawings Reconsidered," *Zeitschrift für Kunstgeschichte*, vol. 46, 1983, pp. 367–400

CADOGAN 2000
Jean K. Cadogan, *Domenico Ghirlandaio: Artist and Artisan*, New Haven and London 2000

CAGLIOTI 1992
Francesco Caglioti, "Bernardo Rossellino a Roma, II: Tra Giannozzo Manetti e Giorgio Vasari," *Prospettiva*, vol. 65, 1992, pp. 31–43

CAGLIOTI 1997
Francesco Caglioti, "Sui primi tempi romani d'Andrea Bregno: un progetto per il Cardinale Camerlengo Alvise Trevisan e un San Michele Arcangelo per il Cardinal Juan de Carvajal," *Mitteilungen des Kunsthistorischen Institutes in Florenz*, vol. 41, 1997, pp. 213–53

CAGLIOTI 2005
Francesco Caglioti, "La Cappella Piccolomini nel Duomo di Siena, da Andrea Bregno a Michelangelo," in Alessandro Angelini, ed., *Pio II e le arti: la riscoperta dell'antico da Federighi a Michelangelo,* Milan 2005, pp. 387–481

CALAMANDREI 1971
Piero Calamandrei, "Il Sigillo e i caratteri dell'Accademia," in Carlo Cordié, ed., *Scritti e inediti celliniani*, Florence 1971, pp. 123–46

CAMERLINGI 1999
Lia Camerlingi, "Alessandro Vittoria Trentino," in Andrea Bacchi et al., eds., *La Bellissima maniera: Alessandro Vittoria e la scultura veneta del Cinquecento*, Trent 1999, pp. 47–57

CAMESASCA 1955
Ettore Camesasca, *Tutta l'opera del Cellini*, Milan 1955

CAMMARELLA FALSITTA AND FALSITTA 2009
Loretta Cammarella Falsitta and Alessandro Falsitta, *Cellini, Bandinelli, Ammannati: La fontana del Nettuno in Piazza della Signoria a Firenze*, Milan 2009

CAMPBELL 1991
Malcolm Campbell, "Giambologna's Oceanus Fountain: Identifications and Interpretations," *Boboli*, vol. 90, 1991, pp. 90–97

CAMPBELL, FALOMIR, FLETCHER AND SYSON 2008
Lorne Campbell, Miguel Falomir, Jennifer Fletcher and Luke Syson, eds., *Renaissance Faces. Van Eyck to Titian*, exh. cat., National Gallery, London; New Haven and London 2008

CANNATA 1982
P. Cannata, *Rilievi e placchetti dal XV al XVIII secolo*, Rome 1982

CAPPELLI 2011
Adriano Cappelli, ed., *Dizionario di abbreviature latine ed italiane: usate nelle carte e codici specialmente del medio-evo riprodotte con oltre 14000 segni incisi*, Milan 2011

CARL 1982
Doris Carl, "Zur Goldschmiedefamilie Dei, mit neuen Dokumenten zu Antonio Pollaiuolo und Andrea Verrocchio," *Mitteilungen des Kunsthistorischen Institutes in Florenz*, vol. 26, 1982, pp. 129–66

CARL 1983
Doris Carl, "Documenti inediti su Maso Finiguerra e la sua bottega," *Annali della Scuola Normale Superiore di Pisa*, series III, vol. 13, 1983, pp. 507–54

CARLI 1966
Enzo Carli, review of Coffin Hanson 1964, *Renaissance News*, vol. 19, Spring 1966, pp. 20–22

CARO 1957
Annibale Caro, *Lettere familiari*, ed. A. Greco, 3 vols., Florence 1957–61

CARPI 1930
Piera Carpi, "Nuove notizie e documenti intorno a Giovanni Minello e all'arte del suo tempo," *Bollettino del Museo Civico di Padova*, vol. 23, 1930, pp. 40–91

CARROLL 1976
Eugene Carroll, *The Drawings of Rosso Fiorentino*, 2 vols., New York 1976

CASA BUONARROTI 1891
Guide to the Buonarroti Gallery, Florence 1891

CASSANELLI 1998
Roberto Cassanelli, "Artisti in bottega: luoghi e prassi dell'arte alle soglie della modernità," in Roberto Cassanelli, ed., *La bottega dell'artista tra Medioevo e Rinascimento*, Milan 1998, pp. 7–29

CASTIGLIONE 1959
Baldassarre Castiglione, *The Book of the Courtier*, translated by Charles S. Singleton, Garden City, NY, 1959

CECCHI 1998
Alessandro Cecchi, "La casa e bottega di Giambologna in Pinti," in Roberto Paolo Ciardi, ed., *Case di artisti in Toscana*, Cinisello Balsamo, pp. 139–43

CECCHI 2009
Alessandro Cecchi, "Pietro Candido fra Firenze e Volterra: La formazione e l'attività fiorentina, 1568–1586," in *Pieter de Witte – Pietro Candido: Un pittore del Cinquecento tra Volterra e Monaco*, exh. cat., ed. Mariagiulia Burresi and Alessandro Cecchi, Palazzo dei Priori, Volterra; Cinisello Balsamo 2009, pp. 17–35

CELLINI 1568/69
Benvenuto Cellini, *Due trattati, uno intormo alle otto principali arti dell'oreficeria, l'altro in materia dell'arte della scultura; dove si veggono infiniti segreti nel lavorar le figure di marmo, & nel gettarle di bronzo*, Florence 1568/69

CELLINI 1857
Benvenuto Cellini, *I trattati dell'oreficeria e della scultura*, ed. Gaetano Milanesi, Florence 1857

CELLINI 1910
Benvenuto Cellini, *The Life of Benvenuto Cellini*, ed. Robert H. Hobart Cust, London 1910

CELLINI 1967
Benvenuto Cellini, *The Treatises of Benvenuto Cellini on Goldsmithing and Sculpture*, translated by C.R. Ashbee, New York 1967

CELLINI 1971
Benvenuto Cellini, *Opere*, ed. Giuseppe Guido Ferrero, Turin 1971

CELLINI 1973
Benvenuto Cellini, "Discorso sopra l'arte del disegno," in Barocchi 1971–77, pp. 1930–40

CELLINI 1980
Benvenuto Cellini, *Opere di Benvenuto Cellini*, ed. Giuseppe Guido Ferrero, Turin 1980

CELLINI 1983
Benvenuto Cellini, *Due trattati*, Modena 1983

CENNINI 1936
Cennino Cennini, *Il libro dell'arte – The Craftsman's Handbook*, translated by Daniel V. Thompson, New Haven 1936

CENNINI 2003
Cennino Cennini, *Il libro dell'arte*, ed. Fabio Frezzato, Venice 2003

CERIANA 2004
Matteo Ceriana, ed., *Il camerino di alabastro: Antonio Lombardo e la scultura all'antica*, exh. cat., Castello di Ferrara; Milan 2004

CHADOUR 1982
Anna Beatriz Chadour, "Der Altaraufsatz Antonio Gentilis von St. Peter in Rom," *Wallraf-Richartz Jahrbuch*, vol. 43, 1982, pp. 133–94

CHAMBERS AND MARTINEAU 1981
David Chambers and Jane Martineau, *Splendours of the Gonzaga*, exh. cat., Victoria and Albert Museum, London, 1981

CHANTELOU 1985
Paul Fréart de Chantelou, *Diary of the Cavaliere Bernini's Visit to France*, ed. Anthony Blunt, annotated by George C. Bauer, translated by Margery Corbett, Princeton 1985

CHAPMAN 2005
Hugo Chapman, *Michelangelo Drawings: Closer to the Master*, exh. cat., Teyler Museum, Haarlem, and British Museum, London; London 2005

CHAPMAN 2010
Hugo Chapman, "Introduction," in Chapman and Faietti 2010, pp. 15–75

CHAPMAN 2011
Hugo Chapman, "Il disegno italiano del Quattrocento," in Faietti, Griffo, and Marini 2011

CHAPMAN AND FAIETTI 2010
Hugo Chapman and Marzia Faietti, eds., *Fra Angelico to Leonardo: Italian Renaissance Drawings*, exh. cat., British Museum, London, and Galleria degli Uffizi, Florence; London 2010

CHELAZZI DINI AND PREVITALI 2002
Giulietta Chelazzi Dini and Giovanni Previtali, eds., *Jacopo della Quercia nell'arte del suo tempo*, exh. cat., Museo Civico, Siena; Florence 1975

CHIARINI, DARR, AND GIANNINI 2002
Marco Chiarini, Alan P. Darr, and Cristina Giannini, eds., *L'ombra del genio: Michelangelo e l'arte a Firenze 1537–1631*, exh. cat., Palazzo Strozzi, Florence; Art Institute of Chicago; Detroit Institute of Arts; Milan 2002

CHONG 2003
Alan Chong, "The Afterlife of Cellini's bust of Bindo Altoviti," in *Raphael, Cellini & A Renaissance Banker*, exh. cat., ed. Alan Chong, Isabella Stewart Gardner Museum, Boston, 2003, pp. 237–62

CHONG AND LINGNER 2003
Alan Chong and Richard Lingner, eds., *Eye of the Beholder: Masterpieces from the Isabella Stewart Gardner Museum*, Boston 2003

CHRISTIANSEN, KANTER, AND STREHLKE 1988
Keith Christiansen, Laurence B. Kanter, and Carl Brandon Strehlke, eds., *Painting in Renaissance Siena: 1420–1500*, exh. cat., Metropolitan Museum of Art, New York, 1988

CHRISTIE, MANSON & WOODS 1936
Catalogue of the Famous Collection of Old Master Drawings Formed by the Late Henry Oppenheimer, Esq., F.S.A., of 9 Kensington Palace Gardens, W.8, which (By Order of the Trustees) Will be Sold at Auction by Messrs. Christie, Manson & Woods, sale cat., Christie, Manson & Woods, London, 10, 13 and 14 July 1936

CIANCHI 1995
Marco Cianchi, ed., *Pierino da Vinci*, Florence 1995

CIARDI DUPRÈ 1966
Maria Grazia Ciardi Duprè, "Per la cronologia dei disegni di Baccio Bandinelli fino al 1540," *Commentari*, vol. 17, 1966, pp. 146–70

CLARK 1929
Kenneth Clark, "Florentine Sculptor," *Vasari Society*, vol. 10, 1929, pp. 7–9

CLARK 1970
Kenneth Clark, "The Genesis of Italian Drawing: A Major Contribution to the History of Art" [review of Degenhart and Schmitt 1968], *Apollo*, vol. 91, 1970, pp. 260–65

CLAYTON 2002
Martin Clayton, *Leonardo da Vinci: The Divine and the Grotesque*, exh. cat., The Queen's Gallery, Edinburgh, and The Queen's Gallery, London; London 2002

CLIFTON 1985
James Clifton, with contributions by Leslie Scattone and Andrew C. Weislogel, *A Portrait of the Artist, 1525–1825: Prints from the Collection of the Sarah Campbell Blaffer Foundation*, exh. cat., Museum of Fine Arts, Houston, 1985

CLIFFORD 2002
Timothy Clifford, "A Candelabrum by Michelangelo: A Discovery in the Cooper-Hewitt, National Design Museum, New York," *The Burlington Magazine*, vol. 146, 2002, pp. 30–40

COFFIN HANSON 1964
Anne Coffin Hanson, *Jacopo della Quercia's Fonte Gaia*, Oxford 1964

COLE 1999
Michael W. Cole, "Cellini's Blood," *Art Bulletin*, vol. 81, 1999, pp. 215–35

COLE 2001
Michael W. Cole, "The Figura Sforzata: Modeling, Power and the Mannerist Body," *Art History*, vol. 24, 2001, pp. 520–51

COLE 2002
Michael W. Cole, *Cellini and the Principles of Sculpture*, Cambridge 2002

COLE 2003
Michael W. Cole, "'Am Werkzeug erkennen wir den Künstler': Waffen und Wappen in der Zeit Cellinis,'" in Nova and Schreurs 2003, pp. 39–58

COLE 2011
Michael W. Cole, *Ambitious Form: Giambologna, Ammanati, and Danti in Florence*, Princeton 2011

COLE AND PARDO 2005
Michael W. Cole and Mary Pardo, eds., *Inventions of the Studio: Renaissance to Romanticism*, Chapel Hill and London 2005

COLLARETA 1995
Marco Collareta, "Pierino da Vinci e Pisa," in Cianchi 1995, pp. 35–38

COLLARETA 2003
Marco Collareta, "Benvenuto Cellini e il destino dell'oreficieria," in Nova and Schreurs 2003, pp. 161–70

COLLARETA 2006
Marco Collareta, "The Historian and the Technique. On the Role of Goldsmithery in Vasari's *Lives*," in Michael. W. Cole, ed., *Sixteenth-Century Italian Art*, Oxford 2006, pp. 291–300

COLLARETA 2008
Marco Collareta, "Il primato del disegno: un percorso attraverso le arti minori," in *L'eredità di Giotto: Arte a Firenze 1340–1375*, exh. cat., ed. Angelo Tartuferi, Galleria degli Uffizi, Florence 2008, pp. 56–65

COLLARETA 2010
Marco Collareta, "Dalle 'diverse arti' alle 'arti del disegno': un tracciato," in *Arte in terra d'Arezzo: il Medioevo*, ed. Marco Collareta and Paola Refice, Arezzo 2010, pp. 233–40

COLLARETA 2012
Marco Collareta, "L'ultima età dell'oro," in *Bagliori dorati: Il gotico internazionale a Firenze 1375–1440*, exh. cat., ed. Antonio Natali, Enrica Neri Lusanna and Angelo Tartuferi, Galleria degli Uffizi, Florence 2012, pp. 63–69

COLLARETA 2013
Marco Collareta, "Oreficeria e scultura nell'arte fiorentina del Quattrocento," in Paolozzi Strozzi and Bormand 2013, pp. 97–101

COLLARETA AND CAPITANIO 1990
Marco Collareta and A. Capitanio, *Museo Nazionale del Bargello: Oreficeria sacra italiana*, Florence 1990

COLLEZIONE FARNESE 1996
Musei e Gallerie Nazionali di Capodimonte: La collezione Farnese. Le arti decorative, Naples 1996

COLNAGHI 1982
Exhibition of Old Master Drawings, P. & D. Colnaghi and Co. Ltd., London, 1982

COLONNA 1980
Francesco Colonna, *Hypnerotomachia Poliphili*, ed. Giovanni Pozzi and Lucia A. Ciapponi, 2 vols., Padua 1980

CONDIVI 1998
Ascanio Condivi, *Vita di Michelagnolo Buonarroti*, ed. Giovanni Nencioni, Florence 1998

CONNOISSEUR 1943
"Some Italian Drawings in The Metropolitan Museum," *Connoisseur*, vol. 110, January 1943, p. 151

CONTI 1980
Alessandro Conti, "Un libro di disegni della bottega del Ghiberti," in Giulia Brunetti, *Lorenzo Ghiberti nel suo tempo*, Florence 1980, vol. 1, pp. 147–64

COOPER 1994
Tracy Cooper, "*I Modani:* Template Drawings," in Millon and Lampugnani 1994, pp. 494–500

COPPEL AREIZAGA ET AL. 2012
Rosario Coppel Aréizaga et al., *Guglielmo della Porta: A Counter-Reformation Sculptor*, exh. cat., Coll & Cortés Fine Arts, Madrid, 2012

CORDELLIER 1991
Dominique Cordellier, "Fragments de jeunesse: deux dessins inédites de Michel-Ange au Louvre," *Revue du Louvre and des Musées de France*, vol. 41, 1991, pp. 43–55

CORDELLIER AND MARINI 1996
Dominique Cordellier and Paola Marini, eds., *Pisanello: le peintre aux sept vertus,* exh. cat., Musée du Louvre, Paris, 1996

CORTI 1976
Gino Corti, "Two early seventeenth-century inventories involving Giambologna," *The Burlington Magazine*, vol. 118, 1976, pp. 629–34

COSTAMAGNA 1994
Philippe Costamagna, *Pontormo*, Milan 1994

COSTAMAGNA 2005
Philippe Costamagna, "The Formation of Florentine Draftsmanship: Life Studies from Leonardo and Michelangelo to Pontormo and Salviati," *Master Drawings*, vol. 43, 2005, pp. 274–91

COVI 1983
Dario A. Covi, "Verrocchio and Venice," *Art Bulletin*, vol. 65, 1983, pp. 253–73

COVI 1995
Dario A. Covi, "The Italian Renaissance and the Equestrian Monument," in Ahl 1995, pp. 40–63

COVI 2005
Dario A. Covi, *Andrea del Verrocchio: Life and Work*, Florence 2005

COX-REARICK 1984
Janet Cox-Rearick, *Dynasty and Destiny in Medici Art: Pontormo, Leo X, and the Two Cosimos*, Princeton 1984

COX-REARICK 1989
Janet Cox-Rearick, "From Bandinelli to Bronzino: The Genesis of the 'Lamentation' for the Chapel of Eleonora di Toledo," *Mitteilungen des Kunsthistorischen Institutes in Florenz*, vol. 33, 1989, pp. 37–83

COX-REARICK 1993
Janet Cox-Rearick, *Bronzino's Chapel of Eleonora in the Palazzo Vecchio*, Berkeley 1993

CRUTTWELL 1902
Maud Cruttwell, *Luca & Andrea della Robbia and Their Successors*, London 1902

CRUTTWELL 1907
Maud Cruttwell, *Antonio Pollaiuolo,* London 1907

DALLI REGOLI 1965
Gigetta Dalli Regoli, "Problemi di grafica crediana," *Critica d'Arte*, vol. 12, 1965, pp. 25–45

DALLI REGOLI 1966
Gigetta Dalli Regoli, *Lorenzo di Credi*, Milan 1966

DAL POZZO 1718
Francesco Bartolomeo Dal Pozzo, *Le vite de' pittori, de gli scultori, et architetti veronesi*, Verona 1718

DANTI 2012
Cristina Danti, "Scultura e affresco: Novità dal restauro del monument Marsuppini," in Maria Cristina Improta, ed., *Il restauro dei materiali lapidei* (Le antologie di OPD restauro, vol. 8), Florence 2012, vol. 1, pp. 55–73

DARR 1985
Alan Phipps Darr, ed., *Italian Renaissance Sculpture in the Time of Donatello*, exh. cat., Detroit Institute of Arts, and Kimbell Art Museum, Fort Worth; Detroit 1985

DAVIES 1994
Paul Davies, "A Project Drawing by Jacopo Sansovino for the Loggetta in Venice," *The Burlington Magazine*, vol. 136, 1994, pp. 487–97

DAVIS 1976
Charles Davis, "Benvenuto Cellini and the Scuola Fiorentina," *North Carolina Museum of Art Bulletin*, vol. 13, 1976, pp. 1–70

DAVIS 2008
Charles Davis, "Disegno, lo scultore all'opera: delineare, inquadrare, progettare," in *I grandi bronzi del Battistero: l'arte di Vincenzo Danti, discepolo di Michelangelo*, exh. cat., ed. Charles Davis and Beatrice Paolozzi Strozzi, Museo Nazionale del Bargello, Florence, 2008, pp. 221–71

DAVIS 2013
Charles Davis, "Michelangelo or Tribolo? – Drawings for Sculpture," in Echinger-Maurach, Gnann, and Poeschke 2013, pp. 189–99

DEGENHART 1932A
Bernhard Degenhart, "Di alcuni problemi dello sviluppo della pittura nella bottega del Verrocchio, di Leonardo e di Lorenzo di Credi," *Rivista d'arte*, vol. 14, 1932, pp. 263–300, 403–44

DEGENHART 1932B
Bernhard Degenhart, "Die Schüler des Lorenzo di Credi," *Münchner Jahrbuch der bildenden Kunst*, vol. 9, 1932, pp. 95–161

DEGENHART 1937
Bernhard Degenhart, "Zur Graphologie der Handzeichnungen: die Strichbildung als stetige Erscheinung innerhalb der italienischen Kunstkreise," *Römisches Jahrbuch für Kunstgeschichte*, vol. 1, 1937, pp. 223–343

DEGENHART 1939
Bernhard Degenhart, "Unbekannte Zeichnungen Francescos di Giorgio," *Zeitschrift für Kunstgeschichte*, vol. 8, 1939, pp. 117–50

DEGENHART AND SCHMITT 1964
Bernhard Degenhart and Annegrit Schmitt, "Methoden Vasaris bei der Gestaltung seines 'Libro,'" in Wolfgang Lotz und Lise Lotte Möller, eds., *Studien zur toskanischen Kunst: Festschrift für Ludwig Heinrich Heydenreich*, Munich 1964, pp. 45–64

DEGENHART AND SCHMITT 1968
Bernhard Degenhart and Annegrit Schmitt, *Corpus der italienischen Zeichnungen, 1300–1450*, Part 1: *Süd- und Mittelitalien*, Berlin 1968

DELACRE 1938
Maurice Delacre, *Le dessin de Michel-Ange*, Brussels 1938

DEL BRAVO 1970
Carlo Del Bravo, *Scultura senese del Quattrocento*, Florence 1970

DIEULEVIN AND HABERT 2009
Vincent Dieulevin and Jean Habert, eds., *Titien, Tintoret, Véronèse: Rivalités à Venise*, exh. cat, Musée du Louvre, Paris, 2009

DEL RICCIO 1979
Agostino Del Riccio, *Istoria delle pietre*, ed. Paola Barocchi, Florence 1979

DEMPSEY 1977
Charles Dempsey, *Annibale Carracci and the Beginnings of Baroque Style*, Glückstadt 1977

DEMPSEY 2001
Charles Dempsey, *Inventing the Renaissance Putto*, Chapel Hill 2001

DEMPSEY 2012
Charles Dempsey, *The Early Renaissance and Vernacular Culture*, Cambridge, Mass., and London 2012

DESJARDINS 1883
Abel Desjardins, *La vie et l'œuvre de Jean Boulogne, d'après les manuscrits inédits receuillis par Foucques de Vagnonville*, Paris 1883

DE TOLNAY 1953
Charles De Tolnay, "Michelangelo's Pietà Composition for Vittoria Colonna," *Record of the Art Museum Princeton University*, vol. 12, 1953, pp. 44–62

DE TOLNAY 1954
Charles De Tolnay, *Michelangelo*, vol. 4: *The Tomb of Julius II*, Princeton 1954

DE TOLNAY 1970
Charles De Tolnay, *Casa Buonarroti: The Sculptures of Michelangelo and the Family Collections*, Florence 1970

DE TOLNAY 1975–80
Charles De Tolnay, *Corpus dei disegni di Michelangelo*, 4 vols., Novara 1975–80

DHANENS 1956
Elisabeth Dhanens, *Jean Boulogne: Giovanni Bologna Fiammingo*, Brussels 1956

DI LORENZO AND FRANGI 2007
Andrea Di Lorenzo and Francesco Frangi, eds., *La raccolta Mario Scaglia: dipinti e sculture, medaglie e placchette da Pisanello a Ceruti*, exh. cat., Museo Poldi Pezzoli, Milan; Cinisello Balsamo 2007

DICKERSON 2008
C.D. Dickerson, "The 'Gran Scuola' of Guglielmo della Porta, the Rise of the 'Aurifex Inventor', and the Education of Stefano Maderno," *Storia dell'arte*, vol. 21, no. 121, 2008, pp. 25–72

DICKERSON, SIGEL, AND WARDROPPER 2012
C.D. Dickerson, Anthony Sigel, and Ian Wardropper, eds., *Bernini: Sculpting in Clay*, exh. cat., Metropolitan Museum of Art, New York, and Kimbell Art Museum, Fort Worth; New Haven 2012

DONATI 2010
Andrea Donati, *Ritratto e figura nel manierismo a Roma: Michelangelo Buonarroti, Jacopino del Conte, Daniele Ricciarelli*, San Marino 2010

DROGIN 2001
David Drogin, "'Lo spirito di Donato': Young Michelangelo and the Sculpture of Donatello," in Lars R. Jones and Louisa C. Matthew, eds., *Coming About: A Festschrift for John Shearman*, Cambridge, Mass., 2001, pp. 149–56

DUBRULLE 1912
Augustin A. Dubrulle, "Un portrait ignoré de Jean de Bologne," *Gazette des Beaux-Arts*, vol. 8, 1912, pp. 333–36

DUSSLER 1926
Luitpold Dussler, "Verrocchio, Andrea del," in Thieme Becker 1907–50, vol. 34, 1926, pp. 292–98

DUSSLER 1959
Luitpold Dussler, *Die Zeichnungen des Michelangelo: Kritischer Katalog*, Berlin 1959

DYCE COLLECTION 1874
Dyce Collection: A Catalogue of the Paintings, Miniatures, Drawings, Engravings, Rings and Miscellaneous Objects Bequeathed by the Reverend Alexander Dyce (South Kensington Museum), London 1874

ECHINGER-MAURACH 1991
Claudia Echinger-Maurach, *Studien zu Michelangelos Juliusgrabmal*, 2 vols., Hildesheim, Zurich, and New York 1991

ECHINGER-MAURACH 1998
Claudia Echinger-Maurach, "Zu Michelangelos Skizze für den verlorenen Bronze David und zum Beginn der gran maniera degli ignudi in seinem Entwurf für den Marmordavid," *Zeitschrift für Kunstgeschichte*, vol. 61, 1998, pp. 301–38

ECHINGER-MAURACH 2002
Claudia Echinger-Maurach, "Zwischen Quattrocento und Barock: Michelangelos Entwurf für das Juliusgrabmal in New York," in Joachim Poeschke, ed., *Praemium Virtutis. Grabmonumente und Begräbniszeremoniell im Zeichen des Humanismus*, Münster 2002, vol. 1, pp. 257–77

ECHINGER-MAURACH 2009A
Claudia Echinger-Maurach, *Michelangelos Grabmal für Papst Julius II (mit Aufnahmen von Andrea Jemolo)*, Munich 2009

ECHINGER-MAURACH 2009B
Claudia Echinger-Maurach, "La sepoltura di Giulio II dai primi progetti alla realizzazione," in *Michelangelo architetto a Roma*, exh. cat., ed. Mauro Mussolin and Clara Altavista, Musei Capitolini, Rome; Cinisello Balsamo 2009, pp. 100–13

ECHINGER-MAURACH, GNANN, AND POESCHKE 2013
Claudia Echinger-Maurach, Achim Gnann, and Joachim Poeschke, eds., *Michelangelo als Zeichner: Akten des Internationalen Kolloquiums Wien, Albertina-Museum, 19.–20. November 2010*, Münster 2013

EISLER 1981
Colin Eisler, *Sculptors' Drawings Over Six Centuries 1400–1950*, exh. cat., The Drawing Center, New York [1981]

EKSERDJIAN 1993
David Ekserdjian, "Parmigianino and Michelangelo," *Master Drawings*, vol. 31, 1993, pp. 390–94

ELAM 2006
Caroline Elam, "Funzione, tipo e ricezione dei disegni di architettura di Michelangelo," in *Michelangelo e il disegno di architettura*, exh. cat., ed. Caroline Elam, Centro internazionale di studi Andrea Palladio, Vicenza, and Casa Buonarroti, Florence; Venice 2006, pp. 42–73

ELAM 2012
Caroline Elam, "The Significance of the Profile in Michelangelo's Architectural Drawings," in Nova and Maurer 2012, pp. 85–99

ELEN 1995
Albert Jan Elen, *Italian Late-Medieval and Renaissance Drawing-Books from Giovannino de' Grassi to Palma Giovane: A Codicological Approach*, Leiden 1995

ETTLINGER 1950
Leopold David Ettlinger, "The Pictorial Source of Ripa's 'Historia,'" *Journal of the Warburg and Courtauld Institutes*, vol. 13, 1950, pp. 322–23

EXTERMANN 2012
Grégoire Extermann, "Il ciclo della Passione di Cristo di Guglielmo Della Porta," in Walter Cupperi, Grégoire Extermann, and Giovanna Ioele, eds., *Scultura nella seconda metà del Cinquecento: protagonisti e problemi*, San Casciano in Val di Pesa 2012, pp. 59–111

FABBRICHESI 1865
Angiolo Fabbrichesi, *Guida della Galleria Buonarroti*, Florence 1865

VON FABRICZY 1895
Cornelius von Fabriczy, "Andrea del Verrocchio ai servizi de' Medici," *Archivio storico dell'arte*, vol. 1, 1895, pp. 163–76

VON FABRICZY 1909
Cornelius von Fabriczy, "Kritisches Verzeichnis toskanischer Holz- und Tonstatuen bis zum Beginn des Cinquecento," *Jahrbuch der Königlich Preussischen Kunstsamlungen*, vol. 30, 1909, pp. 1–88

FAIETTI, GRIFFO, AND MARINI 2011
Marzia Faietti, Alessandra Griffo, and Giorgio Marini, eds., *Figure, memorie, spazio: la grafica del Quattrocento: appunti di teoria, conoscenza e gusto*, exh. cat., Gabinetto Disegni e Stampe degli Uffizi, Florence, 2011

FAIETTI 2012
Marzia Faietti, "Giovani pensierosi. Intrecci tra Natura e Antico," in Michael W. Kwakkelstein and Lorenza Melli, eds., *From Pattern to Nature in Italian Renaissance Drawing: Pisanello to Leonardo*, Florence 2012, pp. 103–19

FALLETTI AND NELSON 2002
Franca Falletti and Jonathan K. Nelson, *Venere e amore: Michelangelo e la nuova bellezza ideale/ Venus and Love: Michelangelo and the New Ideal of Beauty*, exh. cat., Galleria dell'Accademia, Florence, 2002

FATTORINI 2013
Gabriele Fattorini, *Andrea Sansovino*, Trent 2013

FEHRENBACH 2005
Frank Fehrenbach, "Bernini's Light," *Art History*, vol. 28, 2005, pp. 1–42

FEHRENBACH 2008
Frank Fehrenbach, *Compendia Mundi: Gianlorenzo Berninis Fontana dei Quattro Fiumi und Nicola Salvis Fontana di Trevi*, Munich 2008

FERRETTI 2001
Massimo Ferretti, *Fonte Gaia di Jacopo della Quercia*, Siena 2001

FERRETTI 2006A
Emanuela Ferretti, "La casa-studio di Giambologna in Borgo Pinti," in Paolozzi Strozzi and Zikos 2006, pp. 315–20

FERRETTI 2006B
Emanuela Ferretti, "Giambologna architetto: le esperienze architettoniche e la fortuna critica," in Paolozzi Strozzi and Zikos 2006, pp. 321–26

FERRI 1890
Pasquale Nerino Ferri, *Catalogo riassuntivo della raccolta di disegni antichi e moderni posseduta dalla R. Galleria degli Uffizi di Firenze,* Rome 1890

FILARETE 1896
Filarete [Antonio Averlino], *Tractat über die Baukunst*, ed. Wolfgang von Oettingen, Vienna 1896

FILARETE 1972
Filarete [Antonio Averlino], *Trattato di Architettura*, ed. Anna Maria Finoli and Liliana Grassi, 2 vols., Milan 1972

FIORANI 2005
Francesca Fiorani, *The Marvel of Maps: Art, Cartography and Politics in Renaissance Italy*, New Haven 2005

FIORENTINI 1999
Erna Fiorentini, *Ikonographie eines Wandels: Form und Intention von Selbstbildnis und Porträt des Bildhauers im Italien des 16. Jahrhunderts*, Berlin 1999

FISCHEL 1908
Oskar Fischel, "Bandinelli, Bartolomeo," in Thieme-Becker 1907–50, vol. 2, Leipzig 1908, pp. 439–40

FISCHER 1994
Chris Fischer, "Ghirlandaio and the Origins of Cross-Hatching," in Elizabeth Cropper, ed., *Florentine Drawing at the Time of Lorenzo the Magnificent*, Bologna 1994, pp. 245–53

FLEMMING 2003
Victoria von Flemming, "Gezähmte Phantasie: Cellinis Entwürfe für das Akademie-Siegel," in Nova and Schreurs 2003, pp. 59–98

FOCILLON 1911
Henri Focillon, *Benvenuto Cellini, biographie critique*, Paris 1911

FOGELMAN AND FUSCO 2002
Peggy Fogelman and Peter Fusco, *Italian and Spanish Sculpture: Catalogue of the J. Paul Getty Museum Collection*, Los Angeles 2002

FORATTI 1933
Aldo Foratti, "Quercia, Jacopo della," in Thieme-Becker 1907–50, vol. 27, 1933, pp. 513–16

FORCELLINO 2009
Maria Forcellino, *Michelangelo, Vittoria Colonna e gli "spirituali": Religiosità e vita artistica a Roma negli anni Quaranta*, Rome 2009

FORCELLINO 2011
Antonio Forcellino, *The Lost Michelangelos*, translated by Lucinda Byatt, Cambridge 2011

FORLANI TEMPESTI 1991
Anna Forlani Tempesti, *The Robert Lehman Collection*, vol. 5: *Italian Fifteenth- to Seventeenth-Century Drawings*, Princeton 1991

FRANCINI AND VOSSILLA 1999
Carlo Francini and Francesco Vossilla, *Baccio Bandinelli's Hercules and Cacus*, translated by Anne T. Rocchiccioli, Florence 1999

FRANKLIN 2005
David Franklin, ed., *Leonardo da Vinci, Michelangelo, and the Renaissance in Florence*, exh. cat., National Gallery of Canada, Ottawa, 2005

FRANKLIN 2009
David Franklin, ed., *From Raphael to Carracci: The Art of Papal Rome*, exh. cat., National Gallery of Canada, Ottawa, 2009

FRANQUEVILLE 1968
Robert de Franqueville, *Pierre de Franqueville: Sculpteur des Médicis et du Roi Henri IV (1548–1615)*, Paris 1968

FREDERICKSEN AND ZERI 1972
Burton B. Fredericksen and Federico Zeri, *Census of Pre-Nineteenth-Century Italian Paintings in North American Public Collections*, Cambridge, Mass., 1972

FREEDBERG 1963
Sydney Joseph Freedberg, *Andrea del Sarto*, 2 vols., Cambridge, Mass., 1963

FROMMEL 2010
Christoph Luitpold Frommel, "La scultura funeraria a Roma fra Andrea Bregno e Michelangelo," in *La forma del Rinascimento: Donatello, Andrea Bregno, Michelangelo e la scultura a Roma nel Quattrocento*, exh. cat., ed. Claudio Crescentini and Claudio Strinati, Palazzo di Venezia, Rome; Soveria Mannelli 2010, pp. 87–93

FROMMEL 2012
Christoph Luitpold Frommel, "La tomba di Giulio II e gli inizi dell'architettura trionfale di Michelangelo (1505–1516)," in Nova and Maurer 2012, pp. 120–39

FROMMEL AND ADAMS 1994
Frommel, Christoph, general editor, and Nicholas Adams, ed., *The Architectural Drawings of Antonio Sangallo the Younger and His Circle*, 2 vols., Cambridge, Mass., 1994

FULTON 1997
Christopher Fulton, "Present at the Inception: Donatello and the Origins of Sixteenth-Century Mannerism," *Zeitschrift für Kunstgeschichte*, vol. 60, 1997, pp. 166–99

GABHART 1968–69
Ann Gabhart, "A Sixteenth-century Gold Relief," *The Journal of the Walters Art Gallery*, vols. 31–32, 1968–69, pp. 28–39

GALILEI 1943
Galileo Galilei, *Scritti letterari*, ed. Alberto Chiari, Florence 1943

GALLI 1998
Aldo Galli, "Nel segno di Ghiberti," in Sylvie Béguin, Roberto Cassanelli et al., eds., *La bottega dell'artista tra Medioevo e Rinascimento*, Milan 1998, pp. 87–108

GALLUZZI 1991
Paolo Galluzzi, *Prima di Leonardo: Cultura delle macchine a Siena nel Rinascimento*, exh. cat., Magazzini del Sale, Siena; Milan 1991

GALLUZZI 2006
Paolo Galluzzi, *La mente di Leonardo: Nel laboratorio del Genio Universale,* exh. cat., Galleria degli Uffizi, Florence, 2006

GARDNER 1972
Julian Gardner, review of Degenhart and Schmitt 1968, *The Burlington Magazine*, vol. 114, 1972, pp. 32–34

GASPAROTTO 2003
Davide Gasparotto, "Parmigianino, le arti decorative e la 'maniera'," in *Parmigianino e il manierismo europeo*, exh. cat., ed. Silvia Ferino Pagden and Lucia Fornari Schianchi, Cinisello Balsamo 2003, pp. 143–51

GASPAROTTO 2006
Davide Gasparotto, "Cavalli e cavalieri. Il monumento equestre da Giambologna a Foggini," in Paolozzi Strozzi and Zikos 2006, pp. 88–105

GATTESCHI 1993
Riccardo Gatteschi, *Baccio da Montelupo: Scultore e architetto del Cinquecento,* Florence 1993

GATTESCHI 1998
Riccardo Gatteschi, *Vita di Raffaello da Montelupo*, Florence 1998

GAURICUS 1969
Pomponius Gauricus, *De sculptura*, translated by André Chastel and Robert Klein, Geneva 1969

GAYE 1839–40
Johannes Gaye, ed., *Carteggio inedito d'artisti dei secoli XIV, XV, XVI,* 3 vols., Florence 1839–40

GEALT 1983
Adelheid M. Gealt, *Italian Portrait Drawings, 1400–1800, from North American Collections*, exh. cat., Indiana University Art Museum, Bloomington, Ind., 1983

GENTILINI 1992
Giancarlo Gentilini, *I Della Robbia: La scultura invetriata nel Rinascimento*, 2 vols., Florence 1992

GENTILINI 1998
Giancarlo Gentilini, ed., *I Della Robbia e l'*arte nuova *della scultura invetriata*, exh. cat., Fiesole, Florence, 1998

GERDTS AND GERDTS 1960
Elaine Evans Gerdts and William Gerdts, *Old Master Drawings*, exh. cat., Newark Museum; Newark, 1960

GERSTENBERG 1960
Kurt Gerstenberg, "Bildhauerbildnis," in *Reallexikon zur Deutschen Kunstgeschichte*, vol. 2, 1947, cols. 614–22

GHIBERTI 1998
Lorenzo Ghiberti, *I commentarii (Biblioteca Nazionale Centrale di Firenze, II, I, 333)*, ed. Lorenzo Bartoli, Florence 1998

GILLHAM AND WOOD 2001
Carol C. Gillham and Carolyn H. Wood, *European Drawings from the Collection of the Ackland Art Museum*, Chapel Hill 2001

GIOMETTI 2008
Cristiano Giometti, "John Talman and the Roman Art World," in Cinzia Maria Sicca, ed., *John Talman: An Early-Eighteenth-Century Connoisseur*, New Haven and London 2008, pp. 159–88

GIUNTA 1964
Jacopo Giunta, *The Divine Michelangelo: The Florentine Academy's Homage on his Death in 1564*, introduced, translated, and annotated by Rudolf and Margot Wittkower, London 1964

GLASSER 1977
Hannelore Glasser, *Artists' Contracts of the Early Renaissance*, New York 1977

GNANN 2010
Achim Gnann, *Michelangelo: The Drawings of a Genius*, exh. cat., Albertina, Vienna; Osfildern 2010

GNANN 2013
Achim Gnann, "Neue Vorschläge zur Datierung verschiedener Michelangelo-Zeichnungen," in Echinger-Maurach, Gnann, and Poeschke 2013, pp. 210–36

GNOLI 1889
Domenico Gnoli, "Fra Mattia della Robbia," *Archivio Storico dell'Arte*, vol. 2, 1889, pp. 82–85

GOFFEN 1999
Rona Goffen, "La Lucrezia di Lorenzo Lotto," *Renaissance Quarterly*, vol. 52, 1999, pp. 742–81

GOFFEN 2002
Rona Goffen, *Renaissance Rivals: Michaelangelo, Leonardo, Raphael, Titian*, New Haven and London 2002

GOLDNER 1989
George Goldner, "A Drawing by Desiderio da Settignano," *The Burlington Magazine*, vol. 131, 1989, pp. 469–73

GOLDSCHEIDER 1936
Ludwig Goldscheider, *500 Selbstporträts*, Vienna 1936

GOLDSCHEIDER 1957
Ludwig Goldscheider, *Michelangelo's Bozzetti for Statues in the Medici Chapel*, London 1957

GOLDSCHEIDER 1962
Ludwig Goldscheider, *A Survey of Michelangelo's Models in Wax and Clay*, London 1962

GOLDSCHEIDER 1996
Ludwig Goldscheider, *Michelangelo: Paintings, Sculpture, Architecture*, London 1996

GOLDSTEIN 1996
Carl Goldstein, *Teaching Art: Academies and Schools from Vasari to Albers*, Cambridge 1996

GONZALEZ-PALACIOS 1988
Alvar Gonzalez-Palacios, "Itinerario da Roma a Firenze," in *Splendori di pietre dure: L'arte di corte nella Firenze dei Granduchi*, exh. cat., ed. Annamaria Giusti, Florence 1988, pp. 43–52

GÖRICKE 2000
Jutta Göricke, "Zur Ikonographie mathematischer instrumente," in Hans Holländer, ed., *Erkenntnis, Erfindung, Konstruktion: Studien zur Bildgeschichte von Naturwissenschaften und Technik vom 16. bis zum 19. Jahrhundert*, Berlin2000, pp. 255–95

GOTTI 1875–76
Aurelio Gotti, *Vita di Michelangelo Buonarroti, narrata con l'aiuto di nuovi documenti*, 2 vols., Florence 1875–76

GRAFTON 2000
Anthony Grafton, *Leon Battista Alberti: Master Builder of the Italian Renaissance,* New York 2000

GRAMBERG 1936
Werner Gramberg, *Giovanni Bologna: Eine Untersuchung über die Werke seiner Wanderjahre (bis 1567)*, Libau 1936

GRAMBERG 1960
Werner Gramberg, "Guglielmo della Porta, Coppe Fiorentino, und Antonio Gentili da Faenza," *Jahrbuch der Hamburger Kunstsammlungen*, vol. 5, 1960, pp. 31–52

GRAMBERG 1964
Werner Gramberg, *Die Düsseldorfer Skizzenbücher des Guglielmo della Porta*, 3 vols., Berlin 1964

GRAMBERG 1968
Werner Gramberg, "Vier zeichnungen des Guglielmo della Porta zu seiner Serie mythologischer Reliefs," *Jahrbuch der Hamburger Kunstsammlungen*, vol. 13, 1968, pp. 69–94

GRAMBERG 1981
Werner Gramberg, "Notizen zu den Kruzifixen des Guglielmo della Porta und zur Entstehungsgeschichte des Hochaltarkreuzes in S. Pietro in Vaticano," *Munchner Jahrbuch der bildenden Kunst*, vol. 32, 1981, pp. 95–114

GRAMBERG 1984
Werner Gramberg, "Guglielmo della Portas Grabmal für Paul III. Farnese in San Pietro in Vaticano," *Römisches Jahrbuch für Kunstgeschichte*, vol. 21, 1984, pp. 154–262

GRASSELLI 2009
Margaret Morgan Grasselli, ed., *Renaissance to Revolution: French Drawings from the National Gallery of Art, 1500–1800*, exh. cat., National Gallery of Art, Washington, D.C., 2009

GRASSELLI AND ROBISON 2007
Margaret Morgan Grasselli and Andrew Robison, eds., *Private Treasures: Four Centuries of European Master Drawings*, exh. cat., Morgan Library and Museum, New York, and National Gallery of Art, Washington, D.C.; Aldershot 2007

GREGOROVIUS 1932
Ferdinand Gregorovius, *Le tombe dei papi,* ed. Christian Hülsen, Rome 1932

GREGORY 2012
Sharon Gregory, *Vasari and the Renaissance Print*, London 2012

GREVE 2008
David Greve, *Status und Statue: Studien zum Leben und Werk des Florentiner Bildhauers Baccio Bandinelli,* Berlin 2008

GRIMALDI 1972
Giacomo Grimaldi, *Descrizione della Basilica antica di S. Pietro in Vaticano, 1619–20*, ed. Reto Niggl, Vatican City 1972

GRIMALDI AND MASCII 2011A
Floriano Grimaldi and Massimo Mascii, *Alessandro Algardi: Il Crocifisso Borghese*, Alezio 2011

GRIMALDI AND MASCII 2011B
Floriano Grimaldi and Massimo Mascii, eds., *Alessandro Algardi: Sul Crocifisso Borghese*, Trent 2011

GRISWOLD AND WOLK-SIMON 1994
William M. Griswold and Linda Wolk-Simon, eds., *Sixteenth-Century Italian Drawings in New York Collections*, exh. cat., Metropolitan Museum of Art, New York, 1994

GRODECKI 1971
Catherine Grodecki, "Le séjour de Benvenuto Cellini à l'Hôtel de Nesle et la fonte de la nymphe de Fontainebleau d'après les actes des notaires parisiens," *Bulletin de la Société de l'histoire de Paris et de l'Ile-de-France*, vol. 98, 1971, pp. 45–80

GROSSMAN 1972
Sheldon Grossman, "An Anonymous Florentine Drawing and the 'So-Called Verrocchio Sketchbook,'" *Master Drawings*, vol. 10, 1972, pp. 15–19

GÜNTHER 1988
Hubertus Günther, *Das Studium der Architektur in den Zeichnungen der Hochrenaissance*, Tübingen 1988

GÜSE AND PERRIG 1997
Ernst-Gerhard Güse and Alexander Perrig, eds., *Zeichnungen aus der Toskana: Das Zeitalter Michelangelos*, Munich 1997

GUTEKUNST 1886
H.G. Gutekunst, *Catalog der reichhaltigen und ausgezeichneten Sammlung von Kupferstichen, Radierungen & Holzschnitten sowie Original-Zeichnungen hervorragender Meister des 15.–17. Jahrhunderts des Herrn Dav. Gian-Carlo Rossi in Rom,* Stuttgart 1886

HADLEY 1966
Rollin Hadley, "A Portrait of Bandinelli," *Fenway Court*, vol. 1, 1966, pp. 17–24

HAINES 1983
Margaret Haines, *La Sacrestia delle Messe del Duomo di Firenze*, Florence 1983

HANSBAUER 2004
Severin Hansbauer, "Bernardino Licinios Künstlerfreunde vor dem Spiegel," *Zeitschrift für Kunstgeschichte*, vol. 67, 2004, pp. 263–78

HARTT 1969
Frederick Hartt, *Michelangelo: The Complete Sculpture*, New York 1969

HARTT 1987
Frederick Hartt, *David by the Hand of Michelangelo: The Original Model Discovered*, New York 1987

HEARD AND WHITAKER 2011
Kate Heard and Lucy Whitaker, eds., *The Northern Renaissance: Dürer to Holbein*, exh. cat., The Queen's Gallery, Edinburgh, and The Queen's Gallery, London, 2011

HEGENER 2008
Nicole Hegener, *DIVI IACOBI EQUES: Selbstdarstellung im Werk des Florentiner Bildhauers Baccio Bandinelli*, Munich and Berlin 2008

HEIDEN 1970
Rüdiger an der Heiden, "Die Porträtmalerei des Hans von Aachen," *Jahrbuch der Kunsthistorischen Sammlungen in Wien*, vol. 66, 1970, pp. 135–226

HEIKAMP 1964
Detlef Heikamp, "Vincenzo de' Rossi disegnatore," *Paragone*, vol. 169, 1964, pp. 38–42

HEIKAMP 1966
Detlef Heikamp, "In margine alla 'Vita di Baccio Bandinelli' del Vasari," *Paragone*, vol. 191, 1966, pp. 51–62

HEIKAMP 1997
Detlef Heikamp, "Sulla scultura fiorentina fra Maniera e Controriforma," in Cristina Acidini Luchinat et al., eds., *Magnificenza alla corte dei Medici: Arte a Firenze alla fine del Cinquecento*, Milan 1997, pp. 346–69

HEIKAMP 2001
Detlef Heikamp, "Zum Herkules und Kakus von Baccio Bandinelli," in Raffaele Torella, ed., *Le parole e i marmi*, 2001, pp. 983–1006

HEIKAMP AND PAOLOZZI STROZZI 2014
Detlef Heikamp and Beatrice Paolozzi Strozzi, eds., *Baccio Bandinelli: Scultore e Maestro (1493–1560)*, exh. cat., Museo Nazionale del Bargello, Florence, 2014

HEIMBÜRGER RAVALLI 1973
Minna Heimbürger Ravalli, *Alessandro Algardi scultore*, Rome 1973

HELMSTUTLER 2000
Kelley Helmstutler [Di Dio], "To Demonstrate the Greatness of his Spirit: Leone Leoni and the Casa degli Omenoni," Ph.D. diss., Rutgers University, 2000

HENDY 1931
Philip Hendy, *The Isabella Stewart Gardner Museum: Catalogue of the Exhibited Paintings and Drawings*, Boston 1931

HENDY 1974
Philip Hendy, *European and American Paintings in the Isabella Stewart Gardner Museum*, Boston 1974

HERRIG 1992
Dorothee Herrig, *Fontainebleau: Geschichte und Ikonologie der Schloßanlage Franz I.*, Munich 1992

HERRMANN-FIORE 1983
Kristina Herrmann-Fiore, "Due artisti allo specchio: un doppio ritratto del Museo di Würzburg attribuito a Giovanni Battista Paggi," *Storia dell'arte*, vols. 47–49, 1983, pp. 29–39

HERZNER 1979
Volker Herzner, "Regesti donatelliani," *Rivista dell'Istituto Nazionale d'archeologia e storia dell'arte*, vol. 2, 1979, pp. 169–228

HESSLER 2002
Christiane J. Hessler, "Maler und Bildhauer im sophistischen Tauziehen. Der Paragone in der italienischen Kunstliteratur des 16. Jahrhunderts," in Mai and Wettengl 2002, pp. 82–97

HILDEBRAND 1913
Adolf von Hildebrand, *Das Problem der Form in der bildenden Kunst*, Strassburg 1913

HIRST 1965
Michael Hirst, "Tibaldi around Perino," *The Burlington Magazine*, vol. 107, 1965, pp. 569–71

HIRST 1976
Michael Hirst, "A project of Michelangelo's for the Tomb of Julius II," *Master Drawings*, vol. 14, 1976, pp. 375–82

HIRST 1981
Michael Hirst, *Sebastiano del Piombo*, Oxford 1981

HIRST 1988A
Michael Hirst, *Michelangelo and His Drawings*, New Haven and London 1988

HIRST 1988B
Michael Hirst, *Michelangelo Draftsman*, exh. cat., National Gallery of Art, Washington, D.C., 1988

HIRTHE 1988
Thomas Hirthe, "Die Perseus-und-Medusa-Gruppe des Benvenuto Cellini in Florenz," *Jahrbuch der Berliner Museen*, vols. 29–30, 1987/88 (1988), pp. 197–216

HÖFLER 1992
Janez Höfler, "New Light on Sansovino's Journey to Portugal," *The Burlington Magazine*, vol. 134, 1992, pp. 234–38

HOLDERBAUM 1957
James Holderbaum, "Notes on Tribolo – II: A Marble Aesculapius by Tribolo," *The Burlington Magazine*, vol. 99, 1957, pp. 368–73

HOLLANDA 1928
Francisco de Hollanda, *Four Dialogues on Painting*, translated by Aubrey F.G. Bell, London 1928

HOLLANDA 1984
Francisco de Hollanda, *Da pintura antiga*, introduction and notes by Angel González Garcia, Lisbon 1984

HOLLANDA 1998
Francisco de Hollanda, *Dialogos em Roma: Conversations on Art with Michelangelo Buonarroti*, ed. Grazia Dolores Folliero-Metz, translated by Aubrey F.G. Bell, Heidelberg 1998

HOLMAN 1997
Beth Holman, *Disegno: Italian Renaissance Designs for the Decorative Arts*, exh. cat., Dubuque, Iowa, 1997

HOLMAN 2000
Beth Holman, "A 'subtle artifice': Giulio Romano's 'Salt Cellar with Satyrs' for Federico Gonzaga," *Quaderni di Palazzo Te*, vol. 8, 2000, pp. 57–67

HORSES OF SAN MARCO 1980
The Horses of San Marco, supplementary exhibition catalogue, Metropolitan Museum of Art, New York, 1980

HOWARD 1987
Deborah Howard, *Jacopo Sansovino: Architecture and Patronage in Renaissance Venice*, New Haven and London 1987

HÜLSEN 1933
Christian Hülsen, ed., *Das Skizzenbuch des Giovannantonio Dosio im Staatlichen Kupferstichkabinett zu Berlin*, 2 vols. Berlin 1933

HUNTLEY 1971
G. Haydn Huntley, *Andrea Sansovino, Sculptor and Architect of the Italian Renaissance* (1935), repr. Westport, Conn., 1971

JACOBS 2002
Fredrika Jacobs, "(Dis)assembling: Marsyas, Michelangelo and the *Accademia del disegno*," *Art Bulletin*, vol. 84, 2002, pp. 426–48

JACOBY AND SONNABEND 2012
Joachim Jacoby and Martin Sonnabend, eds., *Raphael: Drawings*, Munich 2012

JAFFÉ 1994
Michael Jaffé, *The Devonshire Collection of Italian Drawings*, 4 vols., London 1994

JEROMACK 1996
Paul Jeromack, "Duo Bandinellis," *The Art Newspaper*, vol. 64, November 1996, p. 8

JESTAZ 2003
Bertrand Jestaz, "Benvenuto Cellini et la Cour de France (1540–1545)," *Bibliothèque de l'Ecole des Chartes*, vol. 161, 2003, pp. 71–132

JOANNIDES 1981
Paul Joannides, "Ch. De Tolnay, Corpus dei Disegni di Michelangelo," *Art Bulletin*, vol. 63, 1981, pp. 679–87

JOANNIDES 1991
Paul Joannides, "La chronologie du tombeau de Jules II a propos d'un dessin de Michel-Ange découvert," *La Revue de Louvre*, vol. 41, 1991, pp. 33–42

JOANNIDES 2003
Paul Joannides, *Musée du Louvre: Inventaire general des dessins italiens*, vol. 6: *Michel-ange: Élèves et copistes*, Paris 2003

JOANNIDES 2007
Paul Joannides, *The Drawings of Michelangelo and His Followers in the Ashmolean Museum*, Cambridge, New York, and Melbourne 2007

JOHNSON 1995
Geraldine Johnson, "Activating the Effigy: Donatello's Pecci Tomb in Siena Cathedral," *Art Bulletin*, vol. 77, 1995, pp. 445–59

JOHNSTON 1968
Catherine Johnston, "Drawings for Algardi's 'Cristo Vivo,'" *The Burlington Magazine*, vol. 110, 1968, pp. 454–60

JONES 1979
Mark Jones, *The Art of the Medal*, London 1979

KANZENBACH 2007
Annette Kanzenbach, *Der Bildhauer im Porträt: Darstellungstraditionen vom 16. bis zur Mitte des 19. Jahrhunderts*, Munich and Berlin 2007

KARWACKA CODINI 2003
Ewa Karwacka Codini, "The plans and the work-site of Sant'Antonino's chapel in St. Mark's in Florence – the work of Giambologna – in a manuscript in the Salviati Archives," *Proceedings of the First International Congress on Construction History*, vol. 2, 2003, pp. 1215–23

KATHKE 1997
Petra Kathke, *Porträt und Accessoir: Eine Bildnisform im 16. Jahrhundert*, Berlin 1997

KAUFFMANN 1929
Hans Kauffmann, "Eine Ghibertizeichnung im Louvre," *Jahrbuch der Preußischen Kunstsammlungen*, vol. 50, 1929, pp. 1–10

KAUFMANN 1982
Thomas DaCosta Kaufmann, ed., *Drawings from the Holy Roman Empire 1540–1680: A Selection from North American Collections*, exh. cat., Art Museum, Princeton; National Gallery of Art, Washington, D.C.; Pittsburgh Museum of Art; Princeton 1982

KAUFMANN 1984
Thomas DaCosta Kaufmann, "A Drawing by Adriaen de Vries in Gdansk," *Biuletyn Historii Sztuki*, vol. 46, 1984, pp. 203–9

KEMP 1974
Wolfgang Kemp, "Disegno: Beiträge zur Geschichte des Begriffs zwischen 1547 und 1607," *Marburger Jahrbuch für Kunstwissenschaft*, vol. 19, 1974, pp. 219–40

KEMP 1995
Martin Kemp, "Leonardo's Drawings for 'Il Cavallo del Duca Francesco di Bronzo': The Program of Research," in Ahl 1995, pp. 65–66

KEMP 2007
Martin Kemp, "Leonardo e il modello di cera di un cavallo ben proporzionato," in Marani and Fiorio 2007, pp. 47–55

KEMP AND ROBERTS 1989
Martin Kemp and Jane Roberts, *Leonardo da Vinci*, exh. cat., Hayward Gallery, London; London 1989

KEMPERDINK 2006
Stephan Kemperdick, ed., *The Early Portrait: From the Liechtenstein Collections and the Kunstmuseum, Basel*, exh. cat., Kunstmuseum Basel; Munich, Berlin, London, and New York 2006

KEMPERS 2004
Bram Kempers, "Die Erfindung eines Monuments: Michelangelo und die Metamorphosen des Juliusgrabmals," in Horst Bedekamp and Volker Reinhardt, eds., *Totenkult und Wille zur Macht*, , Darmstadt 2004, pp. 41–59

KEUTNER 1965
Herbert Keutner, "Niccolò Tribolo und Antonio Lorenzi: Der Äskulapbrunnen im Heilkräutergarten der Villa Castello bei Florenz," in Kurt Martin et al., eds., *Studien zur Geschichte der europäischen Plastik: Festchrift, Theodor Müller,* Munich 1965, pp. 235–44

KEUTNER 1967
Herbert Keutner, "Giovanni Bologna und Michelangelo," in *Stil und Überlieferung in der Kunst des Abendlandes: Akten des 21. Internationalen Kongresses für Kunstgeschichte in Bonn 1964*, vol. 2: *Michelangelo*, Berlin 1967, pp. 128–34

KEUTNER 1987
Herbert Keutner, "La statua del Giambologna," in Cristina Acidini Luchinat, ed., *Fiorenza in villa*, Florence 1987, pp. 43–46

KING 1998
Catherine King, "Italian Self-Portraits and the Reward of Virtue," in Schweikhart 1998, pp. 69–92

KIRWIN 1995
William Chandler Kirwin, "The Bubble Reputation: In the Cannon's and the Horse's Mouth (or The Tale of Three Horses)," in Ahl 1995, pp. 87–110

KLEIN AND ZERNER 1989
Robert Klein and Henri Zerner, *Italian Art 1500–1600, Sources and Documents*, Englewood Cliffs 1989

KOERING 2009
Jérémie Koering, "L'art en personne(s)," in Dieulevin and Habert 2009, pp. 158–77

KOORTBOJIAN 1992
Michael Koortbojian, *Self-Portraits*, London 1992

KOSHIKAWA AND KURITA 1996
Michiaki Koshikawa and Hidenori Kurita, eds., *Italian 16th and 17th Century Drawings from the British Museum*, exh. cat., National Museum of Western Art, Tokyo, and Aichi Prefectural Museum of Art, Nagoya; Tokyo 1996

KRAHN 1995
Volker Krahn, ed., *Von allen Seiten schön. Bronzen der Renaissance und des Barock*, exh. cat., Skulpturensammlung Staatliche Museen zu Berlin; Heidelberg 1995

KRAHN 2006
Volker Krahn, "Die Entswurfmodelle Giambolognas," in *Giambologna: Triumph des Körpers*, exh. cat., ed. Wilfried Seipel, Kunsthistorisches Museum, Vienna; Milan 2006, pp. 70–101; also published in Italian as "I Bozzetti del Giambologna," in Paolozzi Strozzi and Zikos 2006, pp. 45–61

KRAUTHEIMER 1952
Richard Krautheimer, "A Drawing for the Fonte Gaia in Siena," *Metropolitan Museum of Art Bulletin*, vol. 10, 1952, pp. 265–74

KRAUTHEIMER AND KRAUTHEIMER-HESS 1982
Richard Krautheimer and Trude Krautheimer-Hess, *Lorenzo Ghiberti*, Princeton 1982

KRISTELLER 1951–52
P.O. Kristeller, "The Modern System of the Arts. A Study in the History of Aesthetics," *Journal of the History of Ideas*, vol. 12, 1951, pp. 496–527; vol. 13, 1952, pp. 17–46

KUBIAK 1974
John Richard Kubiak, "Maso Finiguerra", Ph.D. diss., University of Virginia, 1974

KURZ 1937–38
Otto Kurz, "Giorgio Vasari's 'Libro de' Disegni,'" *Old Master Drawings*, vols. 11–12, 1937–38, pp. 1–15

KUSCH-ARNHOLD 2008
Britta Kusch-Arnhold, *Pierino da Vinci*, Münster 2008

LABÒ 1930
Mario Labò, "La cappella dell'Algardi nei Santi Vittore e Carlo a Genova," *Dedalo*, vol. 2, 1930, pp. 1392–1405

LANDAU AND PARSHALL 1994
David Landau and Peter Parshall, *The Renaissance Print: 1470–1550,* New Haven 1994

LANFRANC DE PANTHOU AND PERONNET 1995
Caroline Lanfranc de Panthou and Benjamin Peronnet, *Dessins italiens du musée Condé à Chantilly. I: Autour de Pérugin, Filippino Lippi et Michel-ange*, exh. cat., Musée Condé, Château de Chantilly; Paris, 1995

LANGDALE 2002
Shelley Langdale, ed., *Battle of the Nudes: Pollaiuolo's Renaissance Masterpiece*, exh. cat., Cleveland Museum of Art, 2002

LANKHEIT 1962
Klaus Lankheit, *Florentinische Barockplastik. Die Kunst am Hofe der letzten Medici, 1670–1743*, Munich: Bruckmann, 1962

LÁNY 1927–28
Jenö Lány, "Den Entwurf zur Fonte Gaia in Siena," *Zeitschrift für Bildende Kunst*, vol. 61, 1927–28, pp. 257–66

LÁNY 1930
Jenö Lány, "Quercia-Studien," *Jahrbuch für Kunstwissenschaft*, 1930, pp. 25–63

LAPINI 1900
Agostino Lapini, *Diario Fiorentino dal 252 al 1596*, ed. Giuseppe Corazzini, Florence 1900

LASCHKE 1993
Birgit Laschke, *Fra Giovan Angelo da Montorsoli: Ein Florentiner Bildhauer des 16. Jahrhunderts*, Berlin 1993

LASCHKE 1998
Birgit Laschke, "Alessandro Vittoria: il progetto di una fontana per Trento," *Studi trentini di scienze storiche*, vol. 74, 1995 (1998), pp. 5–27

LASCHKE 2000
Birgit Laschke, "Un ritratto di Giovanni Bologna e la Fontana di Oceano nel Giardino di Boboli," in Sabine Eiche, ed., *Giambologna tra Firenze e l'Europa: Atti del Convegno Internazionale, Firenze, Istituto Universitario di Storia dell'Arte* (1995), Florence 2000, pp. 65–86

LAZZARO 1990
Claudia Lazzaro, *The Italian Renaissance Garden: From the Conventions of Planting, Design, and Ornament to the Grand Gardens of Sixteenth-Century Italy*, New Haven 1990

LE BROOY 1972
Paul James Le Brooy, *Michelangelo Models Formerly in the Paul von Praun Collection*, Vancouver 1972

LEINO 2013
Marika Leino, *Fashion, Devotion and Contemplation: The Status and Functions of Italian Renaissance Plaquettes,* Oxford 2013

LEONARDO 1949
Leonardo da Vinci, *Paragone: A Comparison of the Arts*, with an introduction and English translation by Irma A. Richter, London, New York, and Toronto 1949

LEONARDO 1993
Leonardo da Vinci, *Il Paragone delle arti*, ed. Claudio Scarpati, Milan 1993

LEWIS 1992
Lewis, Douglas, "Genius Disseminated: The Influence of Michelangelo's Works on Contemporary Sculpture," in Marani 1992, pp. 179–99

LLOYD 1969
Christopher Lloyd, "Four Drawings by Bandinelli at Christ Church," *The Burlington Magazine*, vol. 111, 1969, pp. 371–74

LOMAZZO 1584
Giovanni Paolo Lomazzo, *Trattato dell'arte della pittura,* Milan 1584

LOTZ 1951
Wolfgang Lotz, "Antonio Gentili or Manno Sbarri?," *The Art Bulletin*, vol. 33, 1951, pp. 260–62

LOTZ 1967
Wolfgang Lotz, "Zu Michelangelo's Kopien nach dem Codex Coner," in *Stil und Überlieferung in der Kunst des Abendlandes*, Berlin 1967, vol. 2, pp. 12–19

LUCHS 2010
Alison Luchs, *Mermaids of Venice: Fantastic Sea Creatures in Venetian Renaissance Art,* London 2010

LUCIANO 2011
Eleonora Luciano, with Denise Allen and Claudia Kryza-Gersch, *Antico: The Golden Age of Renaissance Bronzes*, exh. cat., National Gallery of Art, Washington, D.C., and Frick Collection, New York; London 2011

LUZIO AND RENIER 1893
A. Luzio and R. Renier, *Mantova e Urbino. Isabella d'Este ed Elisabetta Gonzaga nelle relazioni familiari e nelle vicende politiche*, Turin 1893

MCCULLAGH 2012
Suzanne Folds McCullagh, ed., *Capturing the Sublime: Italian Drawings of the Renaissance and Baroque*, exh. cat., Art Institute of Chicago; New Haven 2012

MACLAGAN 1924
Eric Maclagan, "The Wax Models by Michael Angelo in the Victoria and Albert Museum," *The Burlington Magazine,* vol. 44, 1924, pp. 4–16

MCOMBER 1997
Christina Morris McOmber, "Recovering Female Agency: Roman Patronage and the Dominican Convent of SS. Domenico e Sisto," Ph.D. diss., University of Iowa, 1997

MADONNA 1993
Maria Luisa Madonna, ed., *Roma di Sisto V: le arti e la cultura*, exh. cat., Palazzo Venezia, Rome, 1993

MAI AND WETTENGL 2002
Ekkehard Mai and Kurt Wettengl, *Wettstreit der Künste: Malerei und Skulptur von Dürer bis Daumier*, exh. cat., Haus der Kunst, Munich, 2002

MANDEL 1996A
Corinne Mandel, "Mythe, mariage et métamorphose: Piazza della Signoria," in Alain Laframboise and Françoise Siguret, eds., *Andromède ou le héros à l'épreuve de la beauté*, Paris 1996, pp. 365–85

MANDEL 1996B
Corinne Mandel, "Perseus and the Medici," *Storia dell'Arte*, vol. 87, 1996, pp. 168–87

MANETTI 1992
Antonio Manetti, *Vita di Filippo Brunelleschi*, ed. Carlachiara Perrone, Rome 1992

MARANI 1992
Pietro C. Marani, ed., *The Genius of the Sculptor in Michelangelo's Work*, exh. cat., Montreal Museum of Fine Arts, 1992

MARANI 2000
Pietro C. Marani, *Leonardo da Vinci: The Complete Paintings*, New York 2000

MARANI 2007
Pietro C. Marani, "Leonardo, l'antico, il rilievo e le proporzioni dell'uomo e del cavallo," in Marani and Fiorio 2007, pp. 17–27

MARANI AND FIORIO 2007
Pietro C. Marani and Maria Teresa Fiorio, eds., *Leonardo: Dagli studi di proporzioni al Trattato della Pittura*, exh. cat., Castello Sforzesco, Milan, 2007

MARINI 2011
Giorgio Marini, "Vasari e 'il principio dell'intagliare le stampe' nella Firenze del Quattrocento," in Faietti, Griffo, and Marini 2011, pp. 89–107

VAN MARLE 1923–38
Raimond van Marle, *The Development of the Italian Schools of Painting*, 19 vols., The Hague 1923–38

MARQUAND 1928
Allan Marquand, *The Brothers of Giovanni della Robbia: Fra Mattia, Luca, Girolamo, Fra Ambrogio,* Princeton 1928

MARSDEN AND BASSETT 2003
Jonathan Marsden and Jane Bassett, "Cellini's other Satyr for the Porte Dorée at Fontainebleau," *The Burlington Magazine*, vol. 145, 2003, pp. 552–63

MARTINES 2001
Lauro Martines, *Strong Words: Writing and Social Strain in the Italian Renaissance*, Baltimore 2001

MASER 1957
Edward A. Maser, *Fontinalia: The Art of the Fountain and the Fountain in Art*, Lawrence 1957

MASETTI ZANNINI 1972
Gian Ludovico Masetti Zannini, "Notizie biografiche di Guglielmo della Porta in documenti notarili romani," *Commentari*, vol. 23, 1972, pp. 299–305

MAURER 2012
Golo Maurer, "Fatiche su carta: Michelangelo disegnatore di architettura," in Nova and Maurer 2012, pp. 33–51

MAZZARELLI 2013
Carla Mazzarelli, "New Documents for Algardi's Alamandini 'Crucifix', 'a beautiful and famous thing,'" *The Burlington Magazine*, vol. 150, 2013, pp. 769–73

MEHRING 1942–44
Walter Mehring, *European Drawings from the Collections of The Metropolitan Museum of Art: A Portfolio of Collotype Reproductions*, 3 vols., New York 1942–44

MELLER 1934
Simon Meller, "I progetti di Antonio Pollaiuolo per la statua equestre di Francesco Sforza," in *Hommage à Alexis Petrovics*, Budapest 1934, pp. 76–79, 204–5

MELLER 1994
Peter Meller, "Geroglifici e ornamenti 'parlanti' nell'opera del Cellini," *Arte Lombarda*, vols. 3–4, 1994, pp. 9–16

MELLI 1995
Lorenza Melli, *Maso Finiguerra: I disegni*, Ospedaletto 1995

MELLI 2003
Lorenza Melli, "Antonio del Pollaiolo orafo e la sua bottega 'magnifica ed onorata in Mercato Nuovo,'" *Prospettiva*, vol. 109, 2003, pp. 65–75

MELLI 2004
Lorenza Melli, "Finiguerra, Maso," in *Saur. Allgemeines Künstler Lexikon*, vol. 40, Munich and Leipzig 2004, pp. 126–28

MENDELSOHN-MARTONE 1982
L. Mendelsohn-Martone, *Benedetto Varchi's "Due Lezzioni": Paragoni and Cinquecento Art Theory*, Ann Arbor 1982

METROPOLITAN MUSEUM OF ART 1950
"The Metropolitan Museum of Art 1940–1950: A Report to the Trustees on the Buildings and the Growth of the Collections," *The Metropolitan Museum of Art Bulletin*, vol. 8, 1950

METROPOLITAN MUSEUM OF ART 1996
Annual Report of the Trustees of the Metropolitan Museum of Art (1 July 1995–30 June 1996), no. 126, 1996, pp. 6–23

MIDDELDORF 1932
Ulrich Middeldorf, "Unknown Drawings of the Two Sansovinos," *The Burlington Magazine*, vol. 60, 1932, pp. 236–45

MIDDELDORF 1933
Ulrich Middeldorf, "Eine Zeichnung von Andrea Sansovino in München," *Münchner Jahrbuch der bildenden Kunst*, vol. 10, 1933, pp. 139–46

MIDDELDORF 1934A
Ulrich Middeldorf, "Two Sansovino Drawings," *The Burlington Magazine*, vol. 64, 1934, pp. 159–64

MIDDELDORF 1934B
Ulrich Middeldorf, review of *The Unfinished Monument by Andrea del Verrocchio to the Cardinal Niccolò Forteguerri at Pistoia*, by Elizabeth Wilder, *Zeitschrift für Kunstgeschichte*, vol. 3, 1934, pp. 54–58

MIDDELDORF 1935
Ulrich Middeldorf, "Two wax reliefs by Guglielmo della Porta," *Art Bulletin*, vol. 17, 1935, pp. 90–96

MIDDELDORF 1937
Ulrich Middeldorf, "A Group of Drawings by Baccio Bandinelli," *Print Collector's Quarterly*, vol. 24, 1937, pp. 290–304

MIDDELDORF 1938–39
Ulrich Middeldorf, "Pierino da Vinci," *Old Master Drawings*, vol. 13, 1938–39, pp. 9–11

MIDDELDORF 1976
Ulrich Middeldorf, "A Renaissance Jewel in a Baroque Setting," *The Burlington Magazine*, vol. 118, 1976, pp. 157–58

MIDDELDORF 1977
Ulrich Middeldorf, 'In the wake of Guglielmo della Porta,' *The Connoisseur*, vol. 194, 1977, pp. 75–84

MILANESI 1854–56
Gaetano Milanesi, ed., *Documenti per la storia dell'arte senese*, 3 vols., Siena 1854–56

MILLER 1988
Naomi Miller, "Fountains as Metaphor," in Symmes 1988a, pp. 57–73, 191–92

MILLON 1994
Henry A. Millon, "Models in Renaissance Architecture," in Millon and Lampugnani 1994, pp. 19–72

MILLON AND LAMPUGNANI 1994
Henry A. Millon and Vittorio Lampugnani, eds., *The Renaissance from Brunelleschi to Michelangelo: The Representation of Architecture*, New York 1994

MÖLLER 1935
Emil Möller, "Verrocchio's Last Drawing," *The Burlington Magazine*, vol. 66, 1935, pp. 192–95

MONBEIG-GOGUEL 1971
Catherine Monbeig-Goguel, *Il manierismo fiorentino*, Milan 1971

MONBEIG-GOGUEL 1972
Catherine Monbeig-Goguel, *Vasari et son temps; maîtres toscans nés après 1500, morts avant 1600,* Paris 1972

MONBEIG-GOGUEL 1979
Catherine Monbeig-Goguel, *Maestri toscani del Cinquecento* (Biblioteca di disegni 22), Florence 1979

MONBEIG-GOGUEL 1989
Catherine Monbeig-Goguel, commentary, in Giorgio Vasari, *Les Vies des meilleurs peintres, sculpteurs et architectes*, ed. André Chastel, vol. 12: *Du texte à l'image: Dessins du 'Libro'*, Florence 1979

MONBEIG-GOGUEL AND HOCHMANN 1998
Catherine Monbeig-Goguel and Michel Hochmann, eds., *Francesco Salviati (1510–1563) o la bella Maniera*, exh. cat., Villa Medici, Rome, and Musée du Louvre, Paris, 1998

MONTAGU 1985
Jennifer Montagu, *Alessandro Algardi*, 2 vols., New Haven and London 1985

MONTAGU 1999
Jennifer Montagu, ed., *Algardi: L'altra faccia del barocco*, exh. cat., Palazzo delle Esposizioni, Rome 1999

MONTINI 1957
Renzo Uberto Montini, *Le tombe dei papi*, Rome 1957

MORFORD 2009
Michael Morford, "Carving for a Future: Baccio Bandinelli Securing Medici Patronage through His Mutually Fulfilling and Propagandistic Hercules and Cacus," Ph.D. diss., Case Western Reserve University, Cleveland 2009

MORIGI AND MORIGI 2008
Giovanni and Lorenzo Morigi, "Note tecniche sul restauro del monument a Bartolomeo Colleoni di Andrea del Verrocchio," in Matteo Ceriana and Victoria Avery, eds., *L'industria artistica del bronzo del rinascimento a Venezia e nell'Italia settentrionale: Atti del Convegno Internazionale di Studi Venezia, Fondazione Giorgio Cini, 23 e 24 ottobre 2007*, Verona 2008, pp. 459–79

MORROGH 1985
Andrew Morrogh, *Disegni di architetti fiorentini 1540–1640*, exh. cat., Gabinetto Disegni e Stampe degli Uffizi, Florence, 1985

MORTARI 1992
Luisa Mortari, *Francesco Salviati*, Rome 1992

MÖSENENDER 1985
Karl Möseneder, "Werke Michelangelos als Movens ikonographischer Erfindung," *Mitteilungen des Kunsthistorischen Institutes in Florenz*, vol. 29, 1985, pp. 347–84

MOSTRA DEL CINQUECENTO 1940
Mostra del Cinquecento toscano in Palazzo Strozzi, Firenze, aprile-ottobre 1940, exh. cat., Palazzo Strozzi, Florence, 1940

MOZZATI 2014
Tommaso Mozzati, "'Dicendo come scultore non lo meritassi': Ritratto, autoritratto e conformismo sociale nella carriera di Baccio Bandinelli," in Heikamp and Paolozzi Strozzi 2014, pp. 453–69

MÜLLER HOFSTEDE 2007
Ulrike Müller Hofstede, "Emotion und Agon, Modell und Zeichnung: Benvenuto Cellini und Baccio Bandinelli," in Hannah Baader, Ulrike Müller Hofstede, Kristine Patz, and Nicola Suthor, eds., *Im Agon der Künste: Paragonales Denken, ästhetische Praxis und die Diversität der Sinne*, Munich 2007, pp. 195–230

MYSSOK 1999
Johannes Myssok, *Bildhauerische Konzeption und plastisches Modell in der Renaissance*, Münster 1999

NAGEL 1997
Alexander Nagel, "Gifts for Michelangelo and Vittoria Colonna," *Art Bulletin*, vol. 79, 1997, pp. 647–68

NATALI 1988
Antonio Natali, "Studio Portraits," in *Painters by Painters*, exh. cat., National Academy of Design, New York, and Museum of Fine Arts, Houston, 1988, pp. 28–34

NATALE 2002
Vittorio Natale, "'Mi commise che io gli facessi in Fiorenza una tavola:' Vasari e i suoi a Bosco," in Fulvio Cervini and Carlenrica Spantigati, eds., *Santa Croce di Bosco Marengo*, Alessandria 2002, pp. 76–101

NAVA CELLINI 1967
Antonia Nava Cellini, "Note per l'Algardi, il Bernini e il Reni," *Paragone*, no. 207, 1967, pp. 35–52

NEGRI ARNOLDI 1974
Francesco Negri Arnoldi, "Origine e diffusione del Crocifisso barocco con l'immagine del Cristo vivente," *Storia dell'arte*, vol. 20, 1974, pp. 57–79

NEILSON 2012
Christina Neilson, "Rediscovered Photographs of Two Terracotta Modelli by Verrocchio," *The Burlington Magazine*, vol. 154, 2012, pp. 762–67

NESSELRATH 1986
Arnold Nesselrath, "I libri di disegni di antichità: Tentativo di tipologia," in *Memoria dell'antico nell'arte italiana*, vol. 3: *Dalla tradizione all'archeologia*, Turin: Einaudi, 1986, pp. 87–147

NOVA 1996
Alessandro Nova, "Cellini, Benvenuto", in Jane Turner, ed., *The Dictionary of Art*, New York and London 1996, vol. 6, pp. 139–50

NOVA AND MAURER 2012
Alessandro Nova and Golo Maurer, eds., *Michelangelo e il linguaggio dei disegni di architettura*, Venice 2012

NOVA AND SCHREURS 2003
Alessandro Nova and Anna Schreurs, eds., *Benvenuto Cellini: Kunst und Kunsttheorie im 16. Jahrhundert*, Cologne 2003

OERTEL 1940
Robert Oertel, "Wandmalerei und Zeichnung in Italien: Die Anfänge der Entwurfszeichnung und ihre monumentalen Vorstufen," *Mitteilungen des Kunsthistorischen Institutes in Florenz*, vol. 5, 1937, pp. 217–314

O'GRADY 1949
Jeannine A. O'Grody, "'*Un semplice modello*': Michelangelo and his Three-Dimensional Preparatory Works," Ph.D. diss., Case Western Reserve University, 1999

OLSON 1993
Roberta Olson, "Lost and Partially Found: The Tondo, a Significant Florentine Art Form, in Documents of the Renaissance," *Artibus et historiae*, vol. 14, 1993, pp. 31–65

OLSON 2000
Roberta Olson, *The Florentine Tondo*, Oxford 2000

O'MALLEY 2005
Michelle O'Malley, *The Business of Art: Contracts and the Commissioning Process in Renaissance Italy*, New Haven and London 2005

OXFORD GALLERIES 1848
Catalogues of Original Designs by Michael Angelo and Raffaelle in the University Galleries, exh. cat., Oxford University Galleries, Oxford, 1848

PACINI 2001
Piero Pacini, *Le sedi dell'Accademia del Disegno: al "Cestello" e alla "Crocetta,"* Florence 2001

PAGANO 1994
Sergio Pagano, *L'archivio del convento dei Ss. Domenico e Sisto di Roma*, Vatican City 1994

PANOFSKY 1953
Erwin Panofsky, *Early Netherlandish Painting: Its Origins and Character*, 2 vols., Cambridge, Mass., 1953

PANOFSKY 1955
Erwin Panofsky, "Excursus: Two Façade Designs by Domenico Beccafumi and the Problem of Mannerism in Architecture," in Panofsky, *Meaning in the Visual Arts*, Garden City, NY, 1955, pp. 226–35

PAOLOZZI STROZZI 2002
Beatrice Paolozzi Strozzi, "Note in margine all'iconografia del Francavilla e al tema del Giasone," in Pegazzano 2002, pp. 9–14

PAOLOZZI STROZZI AND BORMAND 2013
Beatrice Paolozzi Strozzi and Marc Bormand, eds., *La primavera del Rinascimento: La scultura e le arti a Firenze 1400–1460*, exh. cat. Palazzo Strozzi, Florence, and Musée du Louvre, Paris; Florence 2013

PAOLOZZI STROZZI AND ZIKOS 2006
Beatrice Paolozzi Strozzi and Dimitrios Zikos, eds., *Giambologna: gli dei, gli eroi: Genesi e fortuna di uno stile europeo nella scultura*, exh. cat., Museo Nazionale del Bargello, Florence, 2006

PAOLUCCI 2000
Antonio Paolucci, *Cellini*, Florence 2000

PARKER 1936
Karl T. Parker, "Daniele da Volterra," *Old Master Drawings*, vol. 9, 1936, p. 44

PARKER 1956
Karl T. Parker, *Catalogue of the Collection of Drawings in the Ashmolean Museum*, vol. 2: *The Italian Schools*, Oxford 1956

PARMA 2001
Elena Parma, ed., *Perino del Vaga tra Raffaello e Michelangelo*, exh. cat., Palazzo del Te, Mantua; Milan 2001

PARRONCHI 1981
Alessandro Parronchi, *Opere giovanili di Michelangelo*, vol. 3: *Miscellanea michelangiolesca*, Florence 1981

PASSAVANT 1969
Günter Passavant, *Verrocchio: Sculptures, Paintings, and Drawings: Complete Edition*, translated by Katherine Watson, London 1969

PASTORE 2001
Alessandro Pastore, "Giulio II, papa," in *Dizionario biografico degli italiani*, vol. 57, Rome 2001 (http://www.treccani.it/enciclopedia/papa-giulio-ii_, accessed August 25, 2014

PAYNE 1998
Alina Payne, "Creativity and *Bricolage* in Architectural Literature of the Renaissance," *RES: Journal of Anthropology and Aesthetics*, vol. 34, 1998, pp. 20–38

PAYNE 2007
Alina Payne, "Alberti and the Origins of the 'Paragone' between Architecture and the Figural Arts," in Arturo Calzona, Francesco Paolo Fiore, and Alberto Tenenti, eds., *Leon Battista Alberti: Teorico delle arti e gli impegni civili del "De re aedificatoria,"* Florence 2007, vol. 1, pp. 347–68

PAYNE 2009
Alina Payne, "Materiality, Crafting and Scale in Renaissance Architecture," *Oxford Art Journal*, vol. 32, 2009, pp. 365–86

PAYNE 2011A
Alina Payne, "Architecture: Image, Icon or *Kunst der Zerstreuung?*", in Andreas Beyer et al., *Das Auge der Architektur*, Munich 2011, pp. 55–91

PAYNE 2011B
Alina Payne, "On Sculptural Relief: *Malerisch*, the Autonomy of Artistic Media and the Beginnings of Baroque Studies," in Helen Hills, ed., *Rethinking the Baroque*, London 2011, pp. 39–64

PEDRETTI 1987
Carlo Pedretti, ed., *The Drawings and Miscellaneous Papers of Leonardo da Vinci in the Collection of Her Majesty the Queen at Windsor Castle*, vol. 2: *Horses and Other Animals*, London and New York 1987

PEDRETTI 1989
Carlo Pedretti, "A Proem to Sculpture," *Achademia Leonardo da Vinci: Journal of Leonardo Studies and Bibliography of Vinciana*, vol. 2, 1989, pp. 11–39

PEDRETTI AND ROBERTS 1984
Carlo Pedretti and Jane Roberts, *Leonardo da Vinci: Drawings of Horses and other Animals from the Royal Library at Windsor Castle*, exh. cat., Palazzo Vecchio, Florence; National Gallery of Art, Washington, D.C.; Museum of Fine Arts, Houston; Fine Arts Museums of San Francisco; New York 1984

PEGAZZANO 2002
Donatella Pegazzano, ed., *Il Giasone di Palazzo Zanchini*, exh. cat., Museo Nazionale del Bargello, Florence, 2002

PEGAZZANO 2005
Donatella Pegazzano, *Benvenuto Cellini*, Rome 2005

PEROCCO 1981
Guido Perocco, ed., *I cavalli di San Marco*, exh. cat., Palazzo Reale, Milan, 1981

PERRIG 1977
Alexander Perrig, *Michelangelo-Studien*, vol. 4: *Die "Michelangelo" Zeichnungen Benvenuto Cellinis*, Frankfurt 1977

PETRIOLI TOFANI 1991
Annamaria Petrioli Tofani, ed., *Inventario: Gabinetto Disegni e Stampe degli Uffizi*, vol. 2: *Disegni di figura*, Florence 1991

PETRIOLI TOFANI 1992
Annamaria Petrioli Tofani et al., *Il disegno fiorentino del tempo di Lorenzo il Magnifico*, exh. cat., Gabinetto Disegni e Stampe degli Uffizi, Florence; Cinisello Balsamo 1992

PEVSNER 1940
Nikolaus Pevsner, *Academies of Art, Past and Present*, Cambridge 1940

PFISTERER 2002
Ulrich Pfisterer, *Donatello und die Entdeckung der Stile, 1430–1445*, Munich 2002

PFISTERER 2007
"Der Kontrakt des Zeichners. Barent Fabritius und die disegno-Theorien der Frühen Neuzeit", in Schulze Altcappenberg und Michael Thimann 2007, pp. 45–53

PFISTERER AND VON ROSEN 2005
Ulrich Pfisterer and Valeska von Rosen, *Der Künstler als Kunstwerk: Selbstporträts vom Mittelalter bis zur Gegenwart*, Stuttgart 2005

PHILLIPS 1939
John Goldsmith Phillips, "Guglielmo della Porta – His Ovid Plaquettes," *Bulletin of The Metropolitan Museum of Art*, vol. 34, 1939, pp. 148–51

PILLSBURY 1974
Edmund Pillsbury, ed., *Sixteenth-Century Italian Drawings: Form and Function*, exh. cat., Yale University Art Gallery, New Haven, 1974

PINCUS 2000
Debra Pincus, *The Tombs of the Doges of Venice*, Cambridge 2000

PINCUS AND COMTE 2006
Debra Pincus and Barbara Shapiro Comte, "A Drawing for the Tomb of Dante Attributed to Tullio Lombardo," *The Burlington Magazine*, vol. 148, 2006, pp. 734–46

PINELLI 2000
Antonio Pinelli, ed., *La Basilica di San Pietro in Vaticano* (Mirabilia Italiae 10), 4 vols., Modena 2000

PISANI 2006
Linda Pisani, "The Exchange of Models in Florentine Workshops of the Quattrocento: A Sheet from the 'Verrocchio Sketchbook,'" *Journal of the Warburg and Courtauld Institutes*, vol. 67, 2006, pp. 269–74

PLANISCIG 1919
Leo Planiscig, *Die Estensische Kunstsammlung, Kunsthistorisches Museum Wien*, Vienna 1919

PLON 1883
Eugène Plon, *Benvenuto Cellini, orfèvre, médailleur, sculpteur; recherches sur sa vie, sur son œuvre et sur les pièces qui lui sont attribuées*, Paris 1883

PLON 1887
Eugène Plon, *Les maîtres italiens au service de la maison d'Autriche: Leone Leoni, sculpteur de Charles-Quint, et Pompeo Leoni, sculpteur de Philippe II*, Paris 1887

POESCHKE 1990
Joachim Poeschke, "Donatello als Zeichner," in Stefan Kummer and Georg Satzinger, eds., *Studien zur Künstlerzeichnung: Klaus Schwager zum 65. Geburtstag*, Stuttgart 1990, pp. 20–30

POESCHKE 1992
Joachim Poeschke, *Die Skulptur der Renaissance in Italien*, vol. 2: *Michelangelo und seine Zeit*, Munich 1992

POESCHKE 1993
Joachim Poeschke, *Donatello and His World: Sculpture of the Italian Renaissance*, translated by Russell Stockman, New York 1993

POESCHKE 1996
Joachim Poeschke, *Michelangelo and His World: Sculpture of the Italian Renaissance*, translated by Russell Stockman, New York 1996 (English translation of Poeschke 1992)

POESCHKE 2006
Joachim Poeschke, "Virtus und Status des Bildhauers in der Renaissance," in Poeschke, Weigel, and Kusch-Arnhold 2006, pp. 73–82

POESCHKE 2013
Joachim Poeschke, "Michelangelo-Zeichnungen in der Diskussion," in Echinger-Maurach, Gnann, and Poeschke 2013, pp. 11–49

POESCHKE, WEIGEL, AND KUSCH-ARNHOLD 2006
Joachim Poeschke, Thomas Weigel, and Britta Kusch-Arnhold, *Die Virtus des Künstlers in der Italienischen Renaissance*, Münster 2006

POGGI 1988
Giovanni Poggi, *Il Duomo di Firenze: Documenti sulla decorazione della chiesa e del campanile tratti dall'archivio dell'Opera*, reprinted with notes by Margaret Haines, 2 vols., Florence 1988

POLANO 1989
Sergio Polano, ed., *Giulio Romano*, exh. cat., Palazzo del Te and Palazzo Ducale, Mantua; Milan 1989

POLLARD AND LUCIANO 2007
John Graham Pollard and Eleonora Luciano, eds., *Renaissance Medals*, 2 vols., Washington, D.C.: National Gallery of Art, 2007

PON 2004
Lisa Pon, *Raphael, Dürer, and Marcantonio Raimondi: Copying and the Italian Renaissance Print*, New Haven 2004

POPE HENNESSY 1939
John Pope-Hennessy, *Sassetta*, London 1939

POPE HENNESSY 1953
John Pope-Hennessy, "Recent Research," *The Burlington Magazine*, vol. 95, 1953, pp. 277–81

POPE HENNESSY 1955
John Pope-Hennessy, *Italian Gothic Sculpture*, London 1955

POPE-HENNESSY 1963
John Pope-Hennessy, *Italian High Renaissance and Baroque Sculpture*, New York 1963

POPE HENNESSY 1972
John Pope-Hennessy, *Italian Gothic Sculpture*, rev. ed., London and New York 1972

POPE HENNESSY 1982
John Pope-Hennessy, "A Bronze Satyr by Cellini," *The Burlington Magazine*, vol. 124, 1982, pp. 406–12

POPE-HENNESSY 1985
John Pope-Hennessy, *Cellini*, London 1985

POPE-HENNESSY 1986
John Pope-Hennessy, *Italian High Renaissance and Baroque Sculpture*, rev. ed., Oxford 1986

POPHAM 1931
Arthur E. Popham, *Italian Drawings Exhibited at the Royal Academy*, exh. cat., Burlington House, London, 1931

POPHAM AND POUNCEY 1950
Arthur E. Popham and Philip Pouncey, *Italian Drawings in the Department of Prints and Drawings in the British Museum: The Fourteenth and Fifteenth Centuries*, London 1950

POPHAM AND POUNCEY 1952
Arthur E. Popham and Philip Pouncey, "Supplement to the Catalogue of Italian Drawings, XIV-XV Centuries," *British Museum Quarterly*, vol. 17, 1952, pp. 61–63

POPHAM AND WILDE 1949
Arthur E. Popham and Johannes Wilde, *The Italian Drawings of the XV and XVI Centuries in the Collection of His Majesty the King at Windsor Castle*, London 1949

POPHAM, WILDE, AND POUNCEY 1953
Arthur E. Popham, Johannes Wilde, and Philip Pouncey, *Italian Drawings in the Department of Prints and Drawings in the British Museum*, vol. 2: *Michelangelo and His Studio*, London 1953

POPP 1927
Anny Popp, "Giovanni da Bologna: Design for a Fountain," *Old Master Drawings*, vol. 2, 1927, p. 23

PROCACCI 1965
Ugo Procacci, *La Casa Buonarroti a Firenze*, Milan 1965

RADCLIFFE 1988
Anthony Radcliffe, review of Pope-Hennessy 1985, *The Burlington Magazine*, vol. 139, 1988, pp. 929–32

RAGGHIANTI 1938
Carlo Ragghianti, "Su un 'corpus photographicum' di disegni," *Critica d'Arte*, vol. 3, 1938, pp. XXV–XXX

RAGGHIANTI COLLOBI 1974
Licia Ragghianti Collobi, *Il libro de' disegni del Vasari*, 2 vols., Florence 1974

RAGIONIERI 1987
Giovanna Ragionieri, *Casa Buonarroti*, Florence 1987

RAGIONIERI 2000
Pina Ragionieri, ed., *I bozzetti michelangioleschi della Casa Buonarroti*, Florence 2000

RAGIONIERI 2005
Pina Ragionieri, ed., *Vittoria Colonna e Michelangelo*, exh. cat., Casa Buonarroti, Florence, 2005

RAGIONIERI 2009
Pina Ragionoeri, ed., *Michelangelo Public and Private: Drawings for the Sistine Chapel and Other Treasures from the Casa Buonarotti*, exh. cat., Seattle Art Museum, 2009

RAMADE 1990
Patrick Ramade, ed., *Disegno: Les dessins italiens du Musée de Rennes*, exh. cat., Musée de Rennes, 1990

RANDOLPH 2002
Adrian W.B. Randolph, *Engaging Symbols: Gender, Politics, and Public Art in Fifteenth-century Florence*, New Haven and London 2002

REBECCHINI 2012
G. Rebecchini, "Giulio Romano e la produzione di argenti per Ferrante ed Ercole Gonzaga," *Prospettiva*, vol. 146, 2012, pp. 32–43

REINLE 1994
Adolf Reinle, *Italienische und deutsche Architekturzeichnungen, 16. und 17. Jahrhundert: Die Plansammlungen von Hans Heinrich Stadler (1603–1660), Johann Ardüser (1585–1665), und ihre gebauten Gegenstücke*, Basel 1994

REITLINGER 1921
Henry Reitlinger, *Victoria and Albert Museum: A Selection of Drawings by Old Masters in the Museum Collection with a Catalogue and Notes*, London 1921

RENNES 1859
Catalogue du Musée de Peinture, Sculpture et Dessins de la ville de Rennes, Rennes 1859

RENNES 1863
Catalogue du Musée de Peinture, Sculpture et Dessins de la ville de Rennes, Rennes 1863

RICHTER 2010
Elinor M. Richter, "Jacopo della Quercia," in *Grove Dictionary of Art Online* (www.oxfordartonline.com/subscriber/article/grove/art/T043135?q=Jacopo+della+Quercia&search=quick&pos=2&_start=1#firsthit), 1996, updated and revised in 2010

RIEBESELL 1995
Cristina Riebesell, "La Cassetta Farnese," in Lucia Fornari Schianchi, ed., *I Farnese: Arte e collezionismo: Studi*, Milan 1995, pp. 58–69

RIEBESELL 2003
Cristina Riebesell, "L'arredo architettonico del Palazzo Farnese di Roma: Vignola e Guglielmo della Porta," in Christoph Luitpold Frommel, Maurizio Ricci, and Richard J. Tuttle, eds., *Vignola e i Farnese: Atti del Convegno Internazionale di Studi*, Milan 2003, pp. 35–59

RIEBESELL 2008
Cristina Riebesell, "Guglielmo della Portas Projekte für die Ausstattung von Neu-Sankt-Peter," in Georg Satzinger and Sebastian Schütze, eds., *Sankt Peter in Rom, 1506–2006: Beiträge der internationalen Tagung vom 22.–25. Februar 2006 in Bonn*, Munich 2008, pp. 195–216

ROBERTS 1988
Jane Roberts, *A Dictionary of Michelangelo's Watermarks*, Milan 1988

ROBERTSON 1992
Clare Robertson, *"Il gran cardinale": Alessandro Farnese, Patron of the Arts*, New Haven and London 1992

ROBERTSON 2004
Clare Robertson, "New documents for the tomb of Paul III," *Römisches Jahrbuch für Kunstgeschichte*, vol. 34, 2001–2 (2004), pp. 201–20

ROBINSON 1870
John Charles Robinson, *A Critical Account of the Drawings by Michael Angelo and Raffaello in the University Galleries, Oxford*, Oxford 1870

ROGGENKAMP 1996
Bernd Roggenkamp, *Die Töchter des Disegno: Zur Kanonisierung der drei bildenden Künste durch Giorgio Vasari*, Münster 1996

ROHLMANN AND THIELEMANN 2000
Michael Rohlmann and Andreas Thielemann, eds., *Akten des Michelangelo-Kolloquiums veranst. vom Kunsthistorischen Institut der Universität zu Köln im Italienischen Kulturinstitut Köln*, Munich and Berlin 2000

RÖLL 2012
Johannes Röll, "Ein Beitrag zum Grabmonument des Giovanni Antonio Lomellino in Sant'Agostino in Rom," in Renata Novak Klemenčič and Janez Höfler, eds., *Historia artis magistra: amicorum discipulorumque munuscula Johanni Höfler septuagenario dicata*, Ljubljani 2012, pp. 275–80

ROSAND 2002
David Rosand, *Drawing Acts: Studies in Graphic Expression and Representation*, Cambridge, Mass., 2002

ROUILLÉ 1553
Guillaume Rouillé, *Prontuario delle medaglie de' più illustri, & fulgenti huomini & donne*, Lyons 1553

RUBIN AND WRIGHT 1999
Patricia Lee Rubin and Alison Wright, *Renaissance Florence: The Art of the 1470s*, exh. cat., National Gallery, London, 1999

RUCELLAI 1960
Giovanni Rucellai, *Giovanni Rucellai ed il suo Zibaldone*, vol. 1: *"Il Zibaldone Quaresimale,"* ed. Alessandro Perosa, London 1960

RUFFINI 2011
Marco Ruffini, *Art Without an Author: Vasari's Lives and Michelangelo's Death*, New York 2011

RUSCHI 2007
Pietro Ruschi, ed., *Michelangelo – architetto a San Lorenzo: quattro problemi aperti*, Florence 2007

RUSCHI 2012
Pietro Ruschi, "Anamnesi come progetto: I disegni di Michelangelo per Porta Pia," in Nova and Maurer 2012, pp. 230–45

SANTI AND STRINATI 2005
Bruno Santi and Claudio Strinati, eds., *Siena e Roma: Raffaello, Caravaggio e i protagonisti di un legame antico*, exh. cat., Santa Maria della Scala and Palazzo Squarcialupi, Siena, 2005

SANUDO 1879–1903
Marino Sanudo, *I Diarii (1496–1533)*, ed. Rinaldo Fulin et al., 58 vols., Venice 1879–1903

SCAGLIA 1982
Giustina Scaglia, "Leonardo's Non-inverted Writing and Verrocchio's Measured Drawing of a Horse," *Art Bulletin*, vol. 64, 1982, pp. 32–44

SCALINI 1995
Mario Scalini, *Benvenuto Cellini*, Florence 1995

SCHER 1994
Stephen K. Scher, ed., *The Currency of Fame: Portrait Medals of the Renaissance*, exh. cat., Frick Collection, New York, and National Gallery of Art, Washington, D.C.; New York 1994

SCHMIDT 1996
Eike Schmidt, "Die Überlieferung von Michelangelos verlorenem Samson-Modell," *Mitteilungen des Kunsthistorischen Institutes in Florenz*, vol. 40, 1996, pp. 78–147

SCHOLTEN 1999
Frits Scholten, ed., *Adriaen de Vries, 1556–1626: Imperial Sculptor*, exh. cat., Rijksmuseum, Amsterdam; Nationalmuseum, Stockholm; J. Paul Getty Museum, Los Angeles; Zwolle 1999

SCHOLTEN 2003
Frits Scholten, ed., *Willem van Tetrode, Sculptor (c. 1525–1580) – Guglielmo Fiammingo scultore*, exh. cat., Rijksmuseum, Amsterdam, and Frick Collection, New York; Zwolle 2003

SCHOLTEN 2007–8
Frits Scholten, "Johan Gregor van der Schardt and the Moment of Self-Portraiture in Sculpture," *Simiolus: Netherlands Quarterly for the History of Art*, vol. 33, 2007–8, pp. 195–220

SCHOTTMÜLLER 1928
Frida Schottmüller, "Landini, Taddeo," in Thieme-Becker 1907–50, vol. 22, Leipzig 1928, p. 297

SCHUBRING 1880
Julius Schubring, "The Royal Academy. – Winter Exhibition, The Athenaeum," *Journal of Englsih and Foreign Literature, Science, the Fine Arts, Music and the Drama*, no. 2727, Saturday, January 31, 1880, pp. 158–60

SCHULZE ALTCAPPENBERG 2007
Hein-Thomas Schulze Altcappenberg, "Disegno/ Ich zeichne. Zur Grossen Ansicht von Florenz, zum Bild des Zeichners," in Schulze Altcappenberg and Thimann 2007, pp. 7–14

SCHULZE ALTCAPPENBERG AND THIMANN 2007
Hein-Thomas Schulze Altcappenberg and Michael Thimann, eds., *Disegno: Der Zeichner im Bild der Frühen Neuzeit*, exh. cat., Kupferstichkabinett Staatliche Museen, Berlin; Munich 2007

SCHWEIKHART 1998
Gunter Schweikhart, ed., *Autobiografie und Selbstportrait in der Renaissance*, Cologne 1998

SCHWEIKHART 2001
Gunter Schweikhart, "Künstler als Gelehrte: Selbstdarstellungen in der Malerei des 16. Jahrhunderts" (1990), in Gunter Schweikhart, *Die Kunst der Renaissance. Ausgewählte Schriften*, ed. Ulrich Rehm und Andreas Tönnesmann, Cologne 2001, pp. 229–38

SCIOLLA 1991
Gianni Carlo Sciolla, ed., *Da Leonardo a Rembrandt, disegni della Biblioteca reale di Torino: Nuove ricerche in margine alla mostra: Atti del Convegno Internazionale di Studi*, Turin 1991

SEIDEL ET AL. 2010
Max Seidel et al., eds., *Da Jacopo della Quercia a Donatello: Le arti a Siena nel primo Rinascimento*, exh. cat., Santa Maria della Scala, Siena; Milan 2010

SELBSTBILDNISSE UND KÜNSTLERPORTRÄTS 1980
Selbstbildnisse und Künstlerporträts von Lucas van Leyden bis Anton Raphael Mengs, exh. cat., Anton Ulrich-Museum, Braunschweig, 1980

SERIE DEGLI UOMINI 1769–76
Serie degli uomini i più illustri nella pittura, scultura, architettura, con i loro elogi, e ritratti incise in rame, cominciando dalla sua prima restaurazione fino ai tempi presenti, 12 vols., Florence 1769–76

SERLIO 1584
Sebastiano Serlio, *Tutte le opere d'architettura*, Venice 1584

SEVERIN 1992
Ingrid Severin, *Baumeister und Architekten: Studien zur Darstellung eines Berufsstandes in Portrait und Bildnis*, Berlin 1992

SEYMOUR 1968
Charles Seymour, Jr., "'Fatto di sua mano': Another Look at the Fonte Gaia Drawing Fragments in London and New York," in Peter Tigler and Antje Middeldorf Kosegarten, eds., *Festschrift Ulrich Middeldorf*, 2 vols., Berlin 1968, vol. 1, pp. 93–105

SEYMOUR 1971
Charles Seymour, Jr., *The Sculpture of Verrocchio*, Greenwich, Conn., 1971

SEYMOUR 1973
Charles Seymour, Jr., *Jacopo della Quercia: Sculptor*, New Haven and London 1973

SHEARMAN 1960
John Shearman, "Rosso, Pontormo, Bandinelli and Others at SS. Annunziata," *The Burlington Magazine*, vol. 102, 1960, pp. 152–56

SHEARMAN 1965
John Shearman, "Titian's Portrait of Giulio Romano," *The Burlington Magazine*, vol. 107, 1965, pp. 172–76

SIEBENHÜNER 1962
Herbert Siebenhüner, "Umrisse zur Geschichte des Ausstattung von Sankt Peter in Rom von Paul III. bis Paul V.," in Karl Oettinger and Mohammed H. Rassem, eds., *Festschrift für Hans Sedlmayr*, , Munich 1962, pp. 229–320

SIRÉN 1928
Osvald Sirén, *Léonard de Vinci: L'artiste et l'homme: Edition entièrement refondue et mis à jour*, 3 vols., Paris and Brussels 1928

SONNABEND 2009
Martin Sonnabend, *Michelangelo Zeichnungen und Zuschreibungen: Drawings and Attributions Städel Museum*, exh. cat., Städel Museum, Frankfurt am Main, 2009

SØRENSEN 1999
Bodil Sørensen, *Gamle mestertegninger fra Sophus Larpents samling*, exh. cat., Nasjionalgalleriet, Oslo, 1999

SPENCER 1973
John Spencer, "Il progetto per il cavallo di bronzo per Francesco Sforza," *Arte Lombarda*, vol. 38–39, 1973, pp. 23–35

SPINELLI 1992
Riccardo Spinelli, "Giovanni Antonio Dosio e il progetto della Cappella Niccolini in Santa Croce a Firenze: quaranta lettere inedite," *Rivista d'Arte*, vol. 8, 1992, pp. 199–296

STEDMAN SHEARD 1978
Wendy Stedman Sheard, "'Asa Adorna': The Prehistory of the Vendramin Tomb," *Jahrbuch der Berliner Museen*, vol. 20, 1978, pp. 117–56

STEDMAN SHEARD 1992
Wendy Stedman Sheard, "Verrocchio's Medici Tomb and the Language of Materials, with a Postscript on his Legacy in Venice," in Steven Bule, Alan Phipps Darr, and Fiorella Superbi Giofreddi, eds., *Verrocchio and Late Quattrocento Italian Sculpture*, Florence 1992 pp. 63–90

STIMATO 2008
Gerarda Stimato, *Autoritratti letterari nella Firenze di Cosimo I: Bandinelli, Vasari, Cellini e Pontormo*, Bologna 2008

STOCK 1984
Julien Stock, ed., *Il valore dei disegni antichi: L'analisi critica, storica ed economica*, Turin: Umberto Allemandi, 1984

STONE 1981
Richard Stone, "Antico and the Development of Bronze Casting in Italy at the end of the Quattrocento," *Metropolitan Museum Journal*, vol. 16, 1981, pp. 87–116

STRASSER 2010
Nathalie Strasser, *Dessins Italiens de la Renaissance au Siècle des Lumières, Collections Jean Bonna*, Geneva, 2010

STREHLKE 2004
Carl Brandon Strehlke, ed., *Pontormo, Bronzino, and the Medici: The Transformation of the Renaissance Portrait in Florence*, exh. cat., Philadelphia Museum of Art, 2004

STRONG 1900
Sandford Arthur Strong, *Reproductions in Facsimile of Drawings by Old Masters in the Collection of the Earl of Pembroke and Montgomery at Wilton House*, London 1900

STRUNCK 2000
Christina Strunck, "Eine radikale Programmänderung im Palazzo Vecchio: Wie Michelangelos Sieger auf Giambologna und Vasari wirkte," in Rohlmann and Thielemann 2000, pp. 265–97

SUIDA 1929
Wilhelm Suida, *Leonardo und sein Kreis*, Munich 1929

SUPINO 1901
Igino Benvenuto Supino, *L'arte di Benvenuto Cellini con nuovi documenti sull'oreficeria fiorentina del secolo XVI*, Florence 1901

SYMMES 1998A
Marilyn Simmes, ed., *Fountains: Splash and Spectacles. Water and Design from the Renaissance to the Present*, exh. cat., Cooper-Hewitt National Design Museum, New York; London 1998

SYMMES 1998B
Marilyn Simmes, "Fountains: Designing the Rise and Fall of Water," *Drawing – The International Review published by The Drawing Society*, vol. 20, 1998, pp. 1–6

SYMONDS 1889
John Addington Symonds, *The Life of Benvenuto Cellini Written by Himself*, London 1889

SYSON AND GORDON 2001
Luke Syson and Dillian Gordon, *Pisanello: Painter to the Renaissance Court*, exh. cat., National Gallery, London, 2001

SYSON AND THORNTON 2001
Luke Syson and Dora Thornton, *Objects of Virtue: Art in Renaissance Italy*, London 2001

SZABÓ 1983
George Szabó, *Masterpieces of Italian Drawing in the Robert Lehman Collection, The Metropolitan Museum of Art*, New York 1983

TAYLOR 2007
Valerie Taylor, 'Art and the Table in Sixteenth-century Mantua: Feeding the Demand for Innovative Design,' in Michelle O'Malley, ed., *The Material Renaissance*, Manchester 2007, pp. 174–96

THIEME-BECKER 1907–50
Ulrich Thieme and Felix Becker, eds., *Allgemeines Lexikon der Bildenden Künstler von der Antike bis zur Gegenwart*, 37 vols., Leipzig 1907–50

THODE 1902–13
Henry Thode, *Michelangiolo und das Ende der Renaissance*, 6 vols., Berlin 1902–13, including vol. 4, *Michelangelo: Kritische Untersuchungen über seine Werke* (1908), and vol. 6, *Michelangelo: Kritische Untersuchungen über seine Werke; Verzeichniss der Zeichnungen, Kartons und Modelle* (1913)

THOMAS 2005
Ben Thomas, "The Academy of Baccio Bandinelli," *Print Quarterly*, vol. 22, March 2005, pp. 3–14

THORNTON 1991
Peter Thornton, *The Italian Renaissance Interior 1400–1600*, New York 1991

THORNTON AND WARREN 1998
Dora Thornton and Jeremy Warren, "The British Museum's Michelangelo Acquisitions and the Casa Buonarroti," *Journal of the History of Collections*, vol. 10, no. 1, 1998, pp. 9–29

TRACHTENBERG 1997
Marvin Trachtenberg, *Dominion of the Eye: Urbanism, Art, and Power in Early Modern Florence*, Cambridge 1997

TRNEK 2004
Renate Trnek, *Selbstbild: Der Künstler und sein Bildnis*, exh. cat., Gemäldegalerie der Akademie der bildenen Künste, Vienna, 2004

TROTTEIN 2004
Gwendolyn Trottein, "Cellini as Iconographer," in Margaret A. Gallucci and Paolo L. Rossi, eds., *Benvenuto Cellini: Sculptor, Goldsmith, Writer*, Cambridge and London 2004, pp. 123–47

TROTTEIN 2009
Gwendolyn Trottein, "Drawing Comparisons: Cellini's 'Perseus Liberating Andromeda' and the Paragone Debate," *RACAR: revue d'art canadienne / Canadian Art Review*, vol. 34, 2009, pp. 55–73

TURNER 1986
Nicholas Turner, *Florentine Drawings of the Sixteenth Century*, London 1986

TUTTLE, forthcoming
Richard J. Tuttle, *The Neptune Fountain in Bologna: Bronze, Marble, and Water in the Making of a Papal City*, Turnhout, forthcoming

TUYLL VAN SEROOSKERKEN 2008
Carel van Tuyll van Serooskerken, *Baccio Bandinelli: Catalogo della mostra*, exh. cat., Musée du Louvre, Paris; Milan 2008

UTZ 1971
Hildegard Utz, "The Labors of Hercules and other Works by Vincenzo de' Rossi," *Art Bulletin*, vol. 53, 1971, pp. 346–66

VALENTINER 1933
Wilhelm Reinhold Valentiner, "Verrocchio's Lost Candlestick," *The Burlington Magazine*, vol. 62, 1933, pp. 228–32; reprinted in Valentiner 1950, pp. 97–112

VALENTINER 1950
Wilhelm Reinhold Valentiner, *Studies of Italian Renaissance Sculpture*, London 1950

VARCHI 1960
Benedetto Varchi, "Due lezzioni" (1549), in Barocchi 1960–62, vol. 1 (1960), pp. 3–91

VARCHI AND BORGHINI 1998
Benedetto Varchi and Vincenzo Borghini, *Pittura e scultura nel Cinquecento*, ed. Paola Barocchi, Livorno 1998

VARNI 1879
Santo Varni, *Ricordi di alcuni fonditori in bronzo*, Genoa 1879

VASARI 1960
Giorgio Vasari, *Vasari on Technique. Being the Introduction to the Three Arts of Design, Architecture, Sculpture and Painting*, trans. Louisa S. Maclehose, New York 1960

VASARI-BELLOSI AND ROSSI 1986
Giorgio Vasari, *Le vite de' piú eccelenti architetti, pittori, et scultori italiani, da Cimabue insino a' tempi nostri*, ed. Luciano Bellosi and Aldo Rossi, Turin 1986

VASARI-BETTARINI 1966–87
Giorgio Vasari, *Le vite de' più eccellenti pittori, scultori, e architettori, nelle redazioni del 1550 e 1568*, ed. Rosanna Bettarini, annotated by Paola Barocchi, 6 vols., Florence 1966–87

VASARI-DE VERE 1912–15
Giorgio Vasari, *Lives of the Most Eminent Painters, Sculptors and Architects*, trans. Gaston du C. de Vere, 10 vols., London 1912–15

VASARI-DE VERE 1996
Giorgio Vasari, *Lives of the Painters, Sculptors, and Architects*, trans. Gaston du C. de Vere, repr., New York 1996

VASARI-MILANESI 1878–85
Giorgio Vasari, *Le vite de più eccellenti pittori, scultori ed architettori scritte da Giorgio Vasari, pittore Aretino, con nuove annotazioni e commenti di Gaetano Milanesi*, ed. Gaetano Milanesi, 11 vols., Florence 1878–85

VASARI-MILANESI 1906
Giorgio Vasari, *Le vite de' più eccellenti pittori, scultori ed architettori*, ed. Gaetano Milanesi, repr., 9 vols., Florence 1906

VASARI-DELLA PERGOLA, GRASSI AND PREVITALI 1964
Giorgio Vasari, *Le vite de' più eccellenti pittori, scultori e architettori*, ed. Paola della Pergola, Luigi Grassi, and Giovanni Previtali, commentary by Detlef Heikamp, Milan 1964

VENTURI 1901
Adolfo Venturi, *Storia dell'arte italiana*, 11 vols., Milan 1901

VENTURI 1967
Adolfo Venturi, *Storia dell'arte italiana: La scultura del Cinquecento*, repr., Milan 1967

VERTOVA 1976
Luisa Vertova, ed., *Maestri toscani del Quattro e del primo Cinquecento: Finiguerra, Pollaiolo, Verrocchio, Ghirlandaio, Lorenzo di Credi, Francesco di Simone Ferrucci, Francesco di Giorgio, Leonardo,* Florence 1976

VIATTE 2011
Françoise Viatte, with Marc Bormand and Vincent Dieulevin, *Inventaire général des dessins italiens: Baccio Bandinelli: Dessins, sculptures, peintures* (Musée du Louvre. Cabinet des dessins), Paris 2011

VICKERS 1986
Nancy J. Vickers, "The Mistress in the Masterpiece," in Nancy K. Miller, ed., *The Poetics of Gender*, New York 1986, pp. 42–62

VITZHUM 1963
Walter Vitzhum, "Disegni di Alessandro Algardi," *Bollettino d'arte*, vol. 48, 1963, pp. 75–98

VÖGE 1896
Wilhelm Vöge, *Raffael und Donatello: ein Beitrag zur Entwicklungsgeschichte der italienischen Kunst*, Strassburg 1896

VOLK-KNÜTTEL 2010
Brigitte Volk-Knüttel, *Peter Candid (um 1548–1628), Gemälde – Zeichnungen – Druckgraphik*, Berlin 2010

VOSSILLA 1997
Francesco Vossilla, "Baccio Bandinelli e Benvenuto Cellini tra il 1540 ed il 1560: disputa su Firenze e su Roma," *Mitteilungen des Kunsthistorisches Insitutes in Florenz*, vol. 41, 1997, pp. 254–313

VOSSILLA 2002
Francesco Vossilla, "La Tomba di Baccio Bandinelli alla Santissima Annunziata di Firenze," in *Praemium Virtutis. Grabmonumente und Begräbniszeremonien im Zeichen des Humanismus*, ed. Joachim Poeschke, Thomas Weigel, and Britta Kusch-Arnhold, Munster 2002, pp. 191–210

VOSSILLA 2010–12
Francesco Vossilla, "'Questa opera addunque tolse a lui la morte,' Baccio Bandinelli e il primo progetto di una fontana per Piazza della Signoria," *Mitteilungen des Kunsthistorischen Institutes in Florenz*, vol. 54, 2010–12, pp. 59–114

WAAGEN 1854–57
Gustav Friedrich Waagen, *Treasures of Art in Great Britain: Being an account of the chief collections of paintings, drawings, sculptures, illuminated mss., etc etc.*, 4 vols., London 1854–57

WALDMAN 2001
Louis A. Waldman, "Bandinelli and the opera di Santa Maria del Fiore," in Margaret Haines, ed., *Santa Maria del Fiore: The Cathedral and its Sculpture*, Fiesole 2001, pp. 221–56

WALDMAN 2004
Louis A. Waldman, ed., *Baccio Bandinelli and Art at the Medici Court: A Corpus of Early Modern Sources*, Philadelphia 2004

WALDMAN 2008
Louis A. Waldman, "A Drawing by Tribolo for Montorsoli's Lost Hercules and Antaeus at Castello," *Bulletin du Musée Hongrois des beaux-arts*, vol. 105, 2006 (2008), pp. 93–100, 259–63

WALKER 1991
S. Walker, 'A Pax by Guglielmo della Porta,' *The Metropolitan Museum Journal*, vol. 26, 1991, pp. 167–76

WALLACE 1994
William Wallace, *Michelangelo at San Lorenzo*, New York 1994

WARD 1978
Roger Ward, "A Catalogue of the Drawings by Baccio Bandinelli in the British Museum," M.A. Report, Courtauld Institute of Art, University of London, 1978

WARD 1981
Roger Ward, "Some Late Drawings by Baccio Bandinelli," *Master Drawings*, vol. 19, Spring 1981, pp. 3–14, 61–77

WARD 1982A
Roger Ward, "Baccio Bandinelli as a Draughtsman," Ph.D. diss., Courtauld Institute of Art, University of London, 1982

WARD 1982B
Roger Ward, "Observations on the Red Chalk Figure Studies of Baccio Bandinelli: Two Examples at Melbourne," *Art Bulletin of Victoria*, vol. 23, 1982, pp. 19–37

WARD 1988
Roger Ward, *Baccio Bandinelli, 1493–1560: Drawings from British Collections*, exh. cat., Fitzwilliam Museum, Cambridge, 1988

WARD 1993
Roger Ward, "New Drawings by Bandinelli and Cellini," *Master Drawings*, vol. 31, 1993, pp. 395–99

WARD 2014
Roger Ward, "I disegni di Bandinelli: alcune aggiunte al corpus," in Heikamp and Paolozzi Strozzi 2014, pp. 333–47

WARD-JACKSON 1979
Philip Ward-Jackson, *Italian Drawings*, vol. 1: *XIVth–XVIth Century* (Victoria and Albert Museum Catalogues), London 1979

WARDLE 2010
Marianne Eileen Wardle, "Naked and Unashamed: A Study of the Aphrodite Anadyomene in the Greco-Roman World", Ph.D. diss., Duke University, 2010

WARDROPPER 2012
Ian Wardropper, "Sketching on Paper and in Clay: Bernini's Use of Preparatory Drawings and Models," in Dickerson, Sigel, and Wardropper 2012, pp. 25–45

WARNKE 1985
Martin Warnke, *Hofkünstler: Zur Vorgeschichte des modernen Künstlers*, Cologne 1985

WARREN 2006
Jeremy Warren, "'A little ould man called John Bollognia … not inferior much to Michell Angelo.' Giambologna in Inghilterra e in America," in Paolozzi Strozzi and Zikos 2006, pp. 126–41

WASSERMAN 2003
Jack Wasserman, *Michelangelo's Florence Pietà*, Princeton and Oxford 2003

WAZBINSKI 1987
Zygmunt Waźbiński, *L'Accademia medicea del disegno a Firenze nel Cinquecento: Idea e instituzione*, 2 vols., Florence 1987

WEEKS 1999
Christopher Weeks, "The Restoration of Desiderio da Settignano's Tomb of Carlo Marsuppini in S. Croce, Florence," *The Burlington Magazine*, vol. 141, 1999, pp. 732–38

WEIL-GARRIS 1974
Kathleen Weil-Garris, *Leonardo and Central Italian Art, 1515–1550*, New York 1974

WEIL-GARRIS 1977
Kathleen Weil-Garris, *The Santa Casa di Loreto: Problems in Cinquecento Sculpture*, 2 vols., New York and London 1977

WEIL-GARRIS 1981
Kathleen Weil-Garris, "Bandinelli and Michelangelo: A Problem of Artistic Identity," in *Art the Ape of Nature: Studies in Honor of H.W. Janson*, ed. Moshe Barasch and Lucy Freeman Sandler, New York 1981, pp. 223–51

WEIL-GARRIS BRANDT 1983
Kathleen Weil-Garris Brandt, "On Pedestals: Michelangelo's *David*, Bandinelli's *Hercules and Cacus* and the Sculpture of the Piazza della Signoria," *Römisches Jahrbuch für Kunstgeschichte*, vol. 20, 1983, pp. 377–415

WEIL-GARRIS BRANDT 1997
Kathleen Weil-Garris Brandt et al., eds., *Giovinezza di Michelangelo*, exh. cat., Palazzo Vecchio, Florence, 1999

WEINBERGER 1967
Martin Weinberger, *Michelangelo, the Sculptor*, 2 vols., London 1967

WENGRAF 2014
Patricia Wengraf, ed., *Renaissance and Baroque Bronzes from the Hill Collection*, exh. cat., Frick Collection, New York; London 2014

WESTON-LEWIS 1998
Aidan Weston-Lewis, ed., *Effigies & Ecstasies: Roman Baroque Sculpture in the Age of Bernini*, exh. cat., National Gallery of Scotland, Edinburgh, 1998

WESTON-LEWIS 2000
Aidan Weston-Lewis, ed., *"A Poet in Paradise": Lord Lindsay and Christian Art*, exh. cat., National Gallery of Scotland, Edinburgh, 2000

WHITAKER 1998
Lucy Whitaker, "Maso Finiguerra and early Florentine Printmaking," in Stuart Currie, ed., *Drawing 1400–1600, Invention and Innovation*, Aldershot 1998, pp. 45–71

WHITAKER 2012
Lucy Whitaker, "The Repetition of Motifs in the Work of Maso Finiguerra, Antonio Pollaiuolo and their collaborators," in *From Pattern to Nature in Italian Renaissance Drawing: Pisanello to Leonardo*, ed. Michael W. Kwakkelstein and Lorenza Melli, Florence 2012, pp. 152–73

WIEMERS 2000
Michael Wiemers, "'Und wo bleibt meine Zeichnung?' Zur Werkgenese im bildhauerische Œuvre des Michelangelo-Rivalen Baccio Bandinelli," in Rohlmann and Thielemann 2000, pp. 235–67

WILDE 1953
Johannes Wilde, *Italian Drawings in the Department of Prints and Drawings in the British Museum: Michelangelo and His Studio*, London 1953

WILDE 1978
Johannes Wilde, *Michelangelo: Six Lectures*, ed. Michael Hirst and John Shearman, Oxford 1978

WILLIAMS 1997
Robert Williams, *Art, Theory and Culture in Sixteenth-Century Italy*, Cambridge 1997

WINNER 1968
Matthias Winner, "Federskizzen von Benvenuto Cellini," *Zeitschrift fur Kunstgeschichte*, vol. 31, 1968, pp. 293–304

WITTKOWER 1966
Rudolf Wittkower, *Gian Lorenzo Bernini. The Sculptor of the Roman Baroque*, 2nd ed., London 1966

WITTKOWER 1977
Rudolf Wittkower, *Sculpture: Process and Principles*, London 1977

WÖLFFLIN 1946
Heinrich Wölfflin, "Ein Künstler über Kunst," in *Kleine Schriften*, ed. Joseph Gantner, Basel 1946, p. 88

WOHL 1986
Helmut Wohl, "The Eye of Vasari," *Mitteilungen des Kunsthistorisches Institutes in Florenz*, vol. 30, 1986, pp. 537–68

WOLF 2003
Gerhard Wolf, "Der Splitter im Auge: 'Cellini' zwischen Narziss und Medusa," in Nova and Schreuers 2003, pp. 315–36

WOLFF 2008
Martha Wolff, *Northern European and Spanish Paintings before 1600 in the Art Institute of Chicago*, New Haven and London 2008

WOLK-SIMON 1992
Linda Wolk-Simon, "Fame, *Paragone*, and the Cartoon: The Case of Perino del Vaga," *Master Drawings*, vol. 30, 1992, pp. 61–82

WOODS-MARSDEN 1998
Joanna Woods-Marsden, *Renaissance Self-Portraiture: The Visual Construction of Identity and the Social Status of the Artist*, New Haven and London 1998

WRIGHT 1994
Alison Wright, "Antonio Pollaiuolo, 'Maestro di disegno,'" in Elizabeth Cropper, ed., *Florentine Drawing at the Time of Lorenzo the Magnificent*, Bologna 1994, pp. 131–46

WRIGHT 2005
Alison Wright, *The Pollaiuolo Brothers: The Arts of Florence and Rome*, New Haven and London 2005

WRIGHT 2010
Alison Wright, *Nameless: Anonymous Drawings of 15th and 16th century Italy from the Bristish Museum, The Courtauld Gallery, National Galleries of Scotland*, exh. cat., Moray Art Centre, Findhorn, 2010

WUNDER 1959
Richard Wunder, *Five Centuries of Drawing*, New York 1959

ZANCHETTIN 2012
Vitale Zanchettin, "Michelangelo e il disegno per la costruzione in pietra: Ragioni e metodi nella rappresentazione ortogonale," in Nova and Maurer 2012, pp. 101–17

ZERI 1948
Federico Zeri, "Salviati e Jacopino del Conte," *Proporzioni*, vol. 2, 1948, pp. 180–83

ZIKOS 2002
Dimitrios Zikos, "Giambologna's Land, House, and Workshops in Florence," *Mitteilungen des Kunsthistorischen Instituts in Florenz*, vol. 46, 2002, pp. 357–408

ZIKOS 2006
Dimitrios Zikos, "Die edlen Formen der Maniera: Praxis und Ideal im bildhauerischen Schaffen Giambolognas," in *Giambologna: Triumph des Körpers*, exh. cat., ed. Wilfried Seipel, Kunsthistorisches Museum, Vienna; Milan 2006, pp. 34–69

ZIKOS 2008
Dimitrios Zikos, "Die Ausbildung von Adriaen de Vries zum Bronzeplastiker in Florenz (ca. 1581–1586)," in *Neue Beiträge zu Adriaen de Vries: Vorträge des Adriaen de Vries Symposiums vom 16. bis 18. April 2008*, ed. Sigmund Adelmann and Dorothea Diemer, Bielefeld 2008, pp. 179–93

ZIMMER 1988
Jürgen Zimmer, *Joseph Heintz der Ältere: Zeichnungen und Dokumente*, Munich and Berlin 1988

ZÖLLNER, THONES, AND PÖPPER 2007
Frank Zöllner, with Christof Thoenes and Thomas Pöpper, *Michelangelo 1475–1564, das vollständige Werk*, Cologne, 2007

ZUCCARO 1961
Federico Zuccaro, *Scritti d'arte di Federico Zuccaro*, ed. Detlef Heikamp, Florence 1961

ZUPKO 1961
Ronald Edward Zupko, *Italian Weights and Measures from the Middle Ages to the Nineteenth Century*, Philadelphia 1981

Selected Index

Photographic Credits

Albertina, Vienna: fig. 6
Alinari, Florence: fig. 61
Alinari / Art Resource, NY: figs. 49, 58, 71
Alinari / Art Resource, NY. Photo: Serge Domingie: fig. 2
Art Resource, NY. Photo: Erich Lessing: fig. 7, cat. 33
Ashmolean Museum, University of Oxford: fig. 8, cats. 9, 17, 41
Associazione Culturale MetaMorfosi: figs. 27, 30, 35, cat. 12, 15
Casa Buonarroti, Florence: cat. 16
© The Cleveland Museum of Art: fig. 19
Collection Trust / © Her Majesty Queen Elizabeth II 2014: fig. 20
Cooper-Hewitt, National Design Museum, Smithsonian Institution / Art Resource, NY: cat. 39
By Courtesy of the Trustees of Sir John Soane's Museum. Photo: Ardon Bar Hama: fig. 29
Courtesy National Gallery of Art, Washington: fig. 66, cats. 22, 24, 26, 46
© DeA Picture Library / Art Resource, NY: fig. 43
© Devonshire Collection, Chatsworth. Reproduced by permission of Chatsworth Settlement Trustees: figs. 1, 69
Digital image courtesy of the Getty›s Open Content Program: fig. 26, cat. 27
Galerie Hans, Hamburg: fig. 50
The Governing Body of Christ Church, Oxford: fig. 3, cat. 18
Isabella Stewart Gardner Museum, Boston: fig. 68, cats. 23, 28
Kunsthistorisches Museum, Vienna: figs. 23, 59
Los Angeles County Museum of Art, www.lacma.org: fig. 65
Martin-von-Wagner-Museum der Universität, Würzburg: fig. 55
Image copyright © Metropolitan Museum of Art. Image source: Art Resource, NY: fig. 45, cats. 1, 6, 7, 8, 11, 34, 35, 37
Metropolitan Museum of Art, Bequest of George Blumenthal, 1941, www.metmuseum.org: fig. 14
Metropolitan Museum of Art, Purchase, Charles and Jessie Price Gift, 2012, www.metmuseum.org: fig. 9
Ministero per i Beni e le Attività culturali, Florence: figs. 28, 37, cats. 4, 31, 42
© Muzeum Narodowe, Gdansk: fig. 15
The Philadelphia Museum of Art / Art Resource, NY: fig. 57
Photograph © 2014 Museum of Fine Arts, Boston: cat. 38
Photography © The Art Institute of Chicago: figs. 54, 73
The Pierpont Morgan Library, New York: cats. 25, 36
© RMN-Grand Palais / Art Resource, NY: cats. 3, 32
© RMN-Grand Palais / Art Resource, NY. Photo: Gérard Blot: fig. 40
© RMN-Grand Palais / Art Resource, NY. Photo: Hervé Lewandowski: fig. 62
© RMN-Grand Palais / Art Resource, NY. Photo: Michele Bellot: fig. 13
© RMN-Grand Palais / Art Resource, NY. Photo: René-Gabriel Ojéda: fig. 16
© RMN-Grand Palais / Art Resource, NY. Photo: Thierry Le Mage: figs. 5, 11, 17, 41, 48, cat. 32
Scala / Art Resource, NY: figs. 32, 33, 51, 70, 74
Scala / Ministero per i Beni e le Attività culturali / Art Resource, NY: cats. 19, 20
Scala / White Images / Art Resource, NY: fig. 56
Scottish National Gallery: cat. 45
Soprintendenza Speciale Per Il Polo Museale Fiorentino: fig. 18
Staatliche Graphische Sammlung, Munich: fig. 60
Staatliche Museen zu Berlin - Preußischer Kulturbesitz, Skulpturensammlung und Museum für Byzantinische Kunst. Photo: Antje Voigt: fig. 44
© Stiftung Museum Kunstpalast - Horst Kolberg – ARTOTHEK: fig. 10
© The Trustees of the British Museum. All rights reserved: figs. 21, 24, 39, 46, 47, 67, cats. 10, 13, 14, 40
Victoria and Albert Museum, London: figs. 4, 22, 38, cats. 2, 5, 29, 30, 43, 44, 47
Vienna, Kupferstichkabinett der Akademie der bildenden Künste: fig. 12